Law and Religion

CRITICAL AMERICA

General Editors: Richard Delgado and Jean Stefancic

White by Law:
The Legal Construction of Race
Ian F. Haney López

Cultivating Intelligence:
Power, Law, and the Politics of Teaching
Louise Harmon and Deborah W. Post

Privilege Revealed:
How Invisible Preference Undermines America
Stephanie M. Wildman
with Margalynne Armstrong, Adrienne D. Davis, and Trina Grillo

Does the Law Morally Bind the Poor?
or What Good's the Constitution When You Can't Afford a Loaf of Bread?
R. George Wright

Hybrid:
Bisexuals, Multiracials, and Other Misfits under American Law
Ruth Colker

Critical Race Feminism: A Reader
Edited by Adrien Katherine Wing

Immigrants Out!
The New Nativism and the Anti-Immigrant Impulse in the United States
Edited by Juan F. Perea

Taxing America
Edited by Karen B. Brown and Mary Louise Fellows

Notes of a Racial Caste Baby:
Color Blindness and the End of Affirmative Action
Bryan K. Fair

Please Don't Wish Me a Merry Christmas:
A Critical History of the Separation of Church and State
Stephen M. Feldman

To Be an American:
Cultural Pluralism and the Rhetoric of Assimilation
Bill Ong Hing

Negrophobia and Reasonable Racism:
The Hidden Costs of Being Black in America
Jody David Armour

Black and Brown in America:
The Case for Cooperation
Bill Piatt

Black Rage Confronts the Law
Paul Harris

Selling Words:
Free Speech in a Commercial Culture
R. George Wright

The Color of Crime:
Racial Hoaxes, White Fear, Black Protectionism, Police Harassment, and Other Macroaggressions
Katheryn K. Russell

The Smart Culture:
Society, Intelligence, and Law
Robert L. Hayman, Jr.

Was Blind, But Now I See:
White Race Consciousness and the Law
Barbara J. Flagg

The Gender Line:
Men, Women, and the Law
Nancy Levit

Heretics in the Temple:
Americans Who Reject the Nation's Legal Faith
David Ray Papke

The Empire Strikes Back:
Outsiders and the Struggle over Legal Education
Arthur Austin

Interracial Justice:
Conflict and Reconciliation in Post-Civil Rights America
Eric K. Yamamoto

Black Men on Race, Gender, and Sexuality:
A Critical Reader
Edited by Devon Carbado

When Sorry Isn't Enough:
The Controversy over Apologies and Reparations for Human Injustice
Edited by Roy L. Brooks

Disoriented: Asian Americans, Law, and the Nation State
Robert S. Chang

Rape and the Culture of the Courtroom
Andrew E. Taslitz

The Passions of Law
Edited by Susan A. Bandes

Global Critical Race Feminism:
An International Reader
Edited by Adrien Katherine Wing

Law and Religion:
A Critical Anthology
Edited by Stephen M. Feldman

Law and Religion

A Critical Anthology

EDITED BY

Stephen M. Feldman

New York University Press

NEW YORK AND LONDON

NEW YORK UNIVERSITY PRESS
New York and London

Library of Congress Cataloging-in-Publication Data
Law and religion : a critical anthology / edited by Stephen M. Feldman.
p. cm. — (Critical America)
Includes bibliographical references and index.
ISBN 0-8147-2679-8 (paper : acid-free paper) —
ISBN 0-8147-2678-X (cloth : acid-free paper)
1. Church and state—United States. 2. Law and religion—United States. 3. Law and religion. I. Feldman, Stephen M., 1955– II. Series.
KF4865 .L39 1999
342.73'0852—dc21 00-008899

New York University Press books are printed on acid-free paper, and their binding materials are chosen for strength and durability.

Manufactured in the United States of America
10 9 8 7 6 5 4 3 2 1

To Laura

Contents

Acknowledgments

As friends warned me beforehand, this collection of essays took more time than initially expected. Still, the final product was worth the effort. I especially thank the contributors; literally, they made this volume possible. I also thank Richard Delgado and Niko Pfund, the editor in chief of New York University Press, for their continued support of my work in the law and religion area.

Some of the chapters have been published previously in whole or part: chapter 2, DePaul Law Review; chapter 3, Harvard University Center for the Study of World Religions; chapter 5, San Diego Law Review; chapter 6, First Things; chapter 7, Hastings Law Journal; chapter 8, DePaul Law Review; chapter 9, San Diego Law Review; chapter 11, Texas Law Review, University of Chicago Law Review, University of Chicago Press; chapter 14, New York University Press; chapter 16, Northeastern University Press; chapter 17, Journal of Law and Religion; chapter 18, Georgetown University Press; chapter 19, Routledge; chapter 20, Columbia Law Review.

Critical Questions in Law and Religion
An Introduction

Stephen M. Feldman

The relationship between law and religion in America has become increasingly controversial since World War II. The Supreme Court's growing solicitude for free exercise and establishment clause claims partially explains this development. Before the 1940s, the Court did not even recognize the religion clauses as applying against the state governments. After the war, though, the Court periodically—albeit not consistently—has found that governmental actions contravene the first amendment. For instance, in one of the most contentious such decisions, *Engel v. Vitale*, decided in 1962, the Court held that the daily recitation of a supposedly nondenominational prayer in the public schools violated the establishment clause. *Engel* provoked a "savage controversy," with widespread ridicule of the Court, which, according to many, "had betrayed the American way of life." A *Wall Street Journal* editorial lamented the likely implications of the Court's decision: "Poor kids, if they can't even sing Christmas carols." *Engel* led to a spurt of proposals to add a Christian amendment to the Constitution; indeed, the 1964 platform of the Republican Party called for such an amendment.[1]

Even with the failure of such constitutional amendments, one should not assume that the Court provides the definitive final word on such intertwined legal and religious matters. Generally, individuals do not reflexively accept the Court's position on a salient public issue. Unsurprisingly, then, the *New York Times* reported in 1994 that despite *Engel* and its progeny, "prayer is increasingly a part of school activities from early-morning moments of silence to lunchtime prayer sessions to pre-football-game prayers for both players and fans. . . . [P]articularly in the South, religious clubs, prayer groups and pro-prayer students and community groups are making religion and prayer part of the school day." In fact, the *Times* added, a school superintendent in a town near Austin, Texas, was removed from office after issuing a directive that prohibited prayers at football games and other school events.[2]

Apart from the large number of postwar Supreme Court cases expressly dealing with the religion clauses, another Court decision further fueled the debates over the relationship between law and religion. *Roe v. Wade*, decided in 1973, held that antiabortion laws violated the due process clause of the fourteenth amendment. *Roe* sparked a long-running (and still-going) political dispute that swirled law and religion inextricably together: for many Americans, the legality or constitutionality of abortion cannot be divorced from religious practices or beliefs.[3]

Many Americans, moreover, are preoccupied with law and politics while also being overtly religious. These dual commitments have magnified the importance of both the abortion conflict, in particular, and the relation between law and religion, in general. Law and politics have practically become an American entertainment industry—witness the long television run of the O.J. Simpson trial and the seemingly endless media coverage of President Clinton's legal and political difficulties, leading to his impeachment. Meanwhile, America remains more religious than any other Western industrialized nation. A 1997 Gallup Poll found that 90 percent of Americans pray, 96 percent believe in God, 63 percent give grace or give thanks to God aloud, and 42 percent attended organized religious services the previous week. With regard to the dominant American religion, Christianity, recent studies suggest that "nine persons in ten believe Jesus Christ actually lived, seven in ten believe he was truly God, and six in ten think one must believe in the divinity of Christ to be a Christian. [Studies also document] consistently high levels of belief in life after death, heaven, and Christ's presence in heaven." Perhaps unexpectedly, statistics suggest that the educated are even more religious than the uneducated.[4] Hence, given Americans' simultaneous commitments to law and politics, on the one hand, and religion, on the other hand, abortion has remained in the center of public contention for more than two decades. Being tossed about in this cauldron of boiling rhetoric, the boundaries between law, religion, and politics have blurred—and this blurring effect has spread far beyond the abortion dispute.

Partly for that reason, Supreme Court doctrine regarding the religion clauses has itself swirled into a remarkably confused mess, as many commentators have noted. In the establishment clause area, from 1971 until the mid-1980s, the Court ordinarily applied a three-pronged test, initially articulated in *Lemon v. Kurtzman*: "First, the statute must have a secular legislative purpose; second, its principal or primary effect must be one that neither advances nor inhibits religion; finally, the statute must not foster 'an excessive government entanglement with religion.'"[5]

Over the past fifteen years or so, while the Court has never rejected the *Lemon* test, different justices have introduced and applied alternative criteria. In *Lynch v. Donnelly*, decided in 1984, a majority of justices applied the *Lemon* test to uphold the public display of a crèche as part of a larger Christmas exhibition. Yet, because of dissatisfaction with the *Lemon* test, Justice Sandra O'Connor wrote an influential concurrence that advocated the adoption of an endorsement test, consisting of two prongs: first, does the state action create excessive governmental entanglement with religion, and second, does the state action amount to governmental endorsement or disapproval of religion.[6]

Over the next several years, the Court continued to apply the *Lemon* test to resolve most establishment clause issues, but simultaneously, the endorsement test gathered enough support to appear likely to emerge eventually as the predominant standard. In *County of Allegheny v. American Civil Liberties Union*, decided in 1989, the Court faced constitutional challenges to two different governmental displays of religious symbols, one including a crèche and one including a Chanukah menorah. Apparently, a majority of justices could not agree on any one test or standard for determining the constitutionality of these displays, so the majority opinion articulated both the *Lemon* and the endorsement tests, suggesting that the latter refined the former.[7] Meanwhile, a plurality opinion in the same case not only fully accepted the endorsement test but also argued that a majority of justices previously had accepted the test, though never in one majority opinion.[8] Finally, Justice Anthony Kennedy, concurring and dissenting, advocated that the Court adopt yet a different approach to establishment clause issues. Kennedy's coercion test had two parts: "government may not coerce anyone to support or participate in any religion or its exercise; and it may not, in the guise of avoiding hostility or callous indifference, give direct benefits to religion in such a degree that it in fact 'establishes a [state] religion or religious faith, or tends to do so.'"[9] In a subsequent case, the Court applied Kennedy's coercion test without rejecting either of the other tests.[10]

In the area of free exercise cases, the Court in 1963 adopted a compelling state interest (or strict scrutiny) test that would remain, at least nominally, as the presumptive standard in free exercise actions for almost three decades. According to this test, as articulated in *Sherbert v. Verner*, a state ordinarily could justify a burden on an individual's free exercise of religion only by showing that the state action was necessary to achieve a compelling state interest. While this judicial standard seemed rigorous and favorable to free exercise claimants, the Court actually held that a governmental action contravened the free exercise clause in only three cases from 1973 until 1990. In all other cases during that time, the Court upheld the governmental actions. For example, in *United States v. Lee*, the Court applied strict scrutiny but nonetheless concluded that the free exercise clause did not require the federal government to exempt an Old Order Amish employer from collecting and paying Social Security taxes.[11]

In 1990, *Employment Division, Department of Human Resources v. Smith* expressly and substantially changed the standard for evaluating free exercise claims. The Court abandoned the strict scrutiny test for free exercise challenges to laws of general applicability, except for cases, like *Sherbert*, that involved the denial of unemployment compensation. Apart from that narrow situation, though, the Court suggested that the "political process" would effectively determine the scope of free exercise rights. Amazingly, then, the *Smith* Court moved from the previous doctrine of presumptively applying strict scrutiny in free exercise cases—at least supposedly showing almost no deference to the political process—to a doctrine without any meaningful judicial scrutiny of challenged governmental actions, a standard showing remarkable deference to the legislative process. In most cases after *Smith*, then, religion should not receive any special judicial protection. Nonetheless, reacting directly against the *Smith* decision, Congress attempted to reinstate the compelling state interest test by enacting the Religious Freedom Restoration Act of 1993 (RFRA), which the Court in *City of Boerne v. Flores* promptly struck down as beyond congressional power. While *City of Boerne* did not specifically include a free exercise claim, the Court's reluctance to defer to Congress seemed oddly in tension with the *Smith* Court's extraordinary respect for the legislative process.[12]

*

The critical essays in this book enter the broad controversy over law and religion from a variety of interrelated perspectives: jurisprudential, religious, sociological, cultural, historical, and philosophical. These are *critical* essays in two senses. First, they contribute important viewpoints on a significant public issue, the relation between law and religion. Second, many of the essays call into question the most settled assumptions of the law and religion debates. Even wide-ranging controversies typically have parameters or assumptions that most participants—including even strongly opposed disputants—take for granted or tacitly accept. This is as true of the law and religion controversy as any other. Yet many of these essays seek to challenge or at least to disturb those very assumptions.

The book is divided into five parts: (I) general perspectives on law, religion, and politics; (II) religion and the public square; (III) religion and Supreme Court doctrine; (IV) outsider views of the separation of church and state; and (V) religion and liberal political theory. The division of the essays into the sundry parts of the book, though, should not be understood to suggest that essays in different parts are unrelated. Many of the essays, even those in different parts, have overlapping themes—so that many essays could have fit into more than one part. Even so, the essays in each part present an array of perspectives on a relatively coherent issue in the law and religion debates.

Part I, "General Perspectives on Law, Religion, and Politics," begins with Steven D. Smith, "Religious Freedom in America: Three Stories," which articulates three competing narratives about law and religion in America. The standard or separationist story, as Smith tells it, is accepted by most legal scholars and Supreme Court justices. Before the American constitutional framing, according to the standard story, almost everybody assumed that church and state needed to be unified or joined to maintain social order and stability. Thomas Jefferson, James Madison, and the framers boldly rejected this long-accepted assumption, and religious freedom and equality have prospered in America ever since. The second or "palace coup" story repudiates the idea that Americans radically broke with the past. Rather, this second story emphasizes continuity: all societies or political communities always have some accepted orthodoxy, and thus in American society, we have not rejected orthodoxy but have replaced one orthodoxy with another. The third or "Tower of Babel" story ties the religion clauses to the Enlightenment. Smith suggests that the Enlightenment quest for human autonomy and reason engendered the religion clauses as a supposed escape from "tradition, authority, and revealed religion." Yet the first amendment has not actually promoted autonomy and reason, as desired, but has instead led to the muddled amalgam of doctrines and theories that currently surround the establishment and free exercise clauses.

With these competing narratives providing a background, Martin E. Marty's essay, "The Widening Gyres of Religion and Law," offers an overview of law and religion as social institutions. Marty emphasizes the overlaps or commonalities between the two institutions: both law and religion, he explains, seek generally to provide order, meaning, and rule in human lives. Yet, at the turn from the twentieth to the twenty-first century, because of the apparently expanding spheres or gyres of each institution, as well as serious disturbances within each, both law and religion seem to be in crises. The two institutions repeatedly clash with each other, producing confusion and even anarchy.

Winnifred Fallers Sullivan's essay, "A New Discourse and Practice," based on her book, *Paying the Words Extra: Religious Discourse in the Supreme Court of the United States*, explores the cultural meaning of religion, particularly in relation to law. Sullivan focuses on the various opinions from the Supreme Court case *Lynch v. Donnelly*, which, as already discussed, upheld the public display of a crèche as part of a larger Christmas exhibition. Sullivan reads the different opinions as *Rashomon*-like views of the first amendment religion clauses: each opinion reveals more about its author and his or her communal discourse than about the meaning of a crèche. Moving beyond the *Lynch* opinions, Sullivan emphasizes the incredible diversity of American religion; far more conceptions of religion exist in America than those represented in the *Lynch* opinions. Indeed, Sullivan suggests that the lived experiences of religion in late-twentieth-century America render the separation of church and state, as understood by the constitutional framers' generation, to be impossible.

Marci A. Hamilton's historical essay, "The Reverend John Witherspoon and the Constitutional Convention," follows Sullivan's initial and brief turn to the framers. While many commentators today assume that the first amendment religion clauses demand a complete separation between religious and governmental affairs—remember that Steven D. Smith calls this the separationist story—Hamilton argues instead that history reveals that religion played an important role in the framing of the Constitution itself. More specifically, Hamilton demonstrates that the Reverend John Witherspoon, a Presbyterian theologian, strongly contributed to the framers' approach to reforming the government of the United States. Witherspoon advocated a republican form of governance—a representative as opposed to a direct democracy—in both church and governmental (state and national) affairs.

Part II, "Religion and the Public Square," opens with Robert Audi, "The Place of Religious Argument in a Free and Democratic Society." Audi begins with a philosophical discussion of what constitutes a religious argument, and then, moving beyond that important point, he introduces one of the central law and religion controversies from the past two decades: To what extent is it appropriate to rely upon religious arguments or motivations in the political sphere or in the so-called public square? For instance, can a citizen, on the one hand, rely upon religious rationales to support a restrictive law, such as a prohibition on abortion? Or must a citizen, on the other hand, banish all considerations of religion when advocating or supporting restrictive laws? Audi provides one response to this crucial issue based on his recognition that, for many citizens, religion is extremely important. He argues that one's moral and political propositions can be partially supported by religious convictions but must also be justified and motivated by secular concepts. Religion, in other words, can play a role in the public square but cannot stand alone.

Richard John Neuhaus's essay, "A New Order of Religious Freedom," presents a very different position regarding the appropriate role of religion in politics and law. Reiterating some of the basic themes from his well-known book *The Naked Public Square*, Neuhaus passionately articulates a series of arguments advocating that religion should play an unencumbered role in public life. Hence, according to Neuhaus, all citizens should have an equal right to express their opinions in the public square, whether those opinions are religious or secular. Citizens should not be urged to reformulate their religious opinions in secular terms. Neuhaus maintains that the American people are "incorrigibly religious"; only "secularized elites" such as John Dewey and John Rawls have argued to remove religion from the public square.

William P. Marshall, in "The Other Side of Religion," argues to the contrary. The nature of religion itself, according to Marshall, justifies restricting its role in the public square. More specifically, Marshall concludes that carefully circumscribed special constraints should be imposed on religion in public decision making exactly because of the "inestimable value" of religion for "human freedom and existence." Marshall draws from literature and social science to argue that religion should be constrained not because it is epistemologically inferior but, rather, because it typically claims infallibility and universality. As such, religion tends toward the dogmatic and authoritarian. Religion, then, might effectively relieve people of the fearful burden of personal and cosmic responsibility and freedom, yet religious views simultaneously—and for the same reason—might hinder the open discussion needed in the public square. Dogmatism and authoritarianism might be functionally useful for religious purposes but are not conducive to democratic deliberation.

Michael J. Perry's carefully argued essay, "Liberal Democracy and Religious Morality," draws from his book *Religion in Politics: Constitutional and Moral Perspectives*. Perry develops three main points. First, religious believers not only can but should assert their religious views in the public square. Perry stresses that such religious views, no less so than other moral and political views, should be tested in the realm of public debate. Yet, and this is the second point, when publicly debating coercive political choices, religious believers (and Perry explicitly includes himself in this category) should be wary of relying on religious arguments unless the believer can also articulate persuasive secular reasons for the same position. But, and this is the third point, there is an important exception to the second point because one particular moral premise is inherently religious and cannot be justified by secular means—namely, that all humans are sacred. In the United States or any other liberal democracy, Perry maintains, this fundamental premise should be accepted in public debate, regardless of its religious basis.

John H. Garvey's "The Pope's Submarine" concludes the part on religion in the public square by approaching the issue from the distinct perspective of a Roman Catholic politician. Garvey largely reacts against a fear of the metaphorical pope's submarine—a fear that the Catholic church will exercise undue influence over public affairs in the United States because elected governmental officials who are Catholic will unflinchingly follow church doctrine. Garvey argues that such fear is largely ungrounded for a variety of reasons, including the nature of Catholicism itself. In fact, he suggests that a Catholic politician may be faced with insurmountable difficulties that counsel recusal from certain official decisions and actions only if the politician is insufficiently devout.

The essays in part III, "Religion and Supreme Court Doctrine," revolve around the question of whether religion should be favored or privileged. Should religion be given special protection under the first amendment, and should the government treat religion with unusual solicitude? According to Scott C. Idleman, "Why the State Must Subordinate Religion," the Court often has claimed to apply some type of balancing test in free exercise cases (such as the compelling state interest test), but the results appear to be distorted. The Court, that is, appears to underenforce the free exercise norm. Idleman explains that this underenforcement arises from the implicit application of an underlying principle—a principle that is not religious at all but, rather, revolves around state sovereignty and superiority. More precisely, the state (or government) must subordinate religion to preserve the supremacy of civil law and government and to maintain the state's hold on the citizenry's allegiance. Idleman, in short, argues that an underlying principle supports the Court's free exercise decisions but that the principle aims at protecting state sovereignty rather than religion.

Christopher Eisgruber and Lawrence Sager's essay, "Equal Regard," agrees with Idleman's assertion that an underlying principle animates free exercise cases. Eisgruber and Sager, though, argue contrary to both Idleman and the Court's *Smith* decision, discussed above, by asserting that religion should receive special protection. According to Eisgruber and Sager, religious practices may not be uniquely valuable, yet they are distinctly vulnerable to discrimination. For this reason, the authors argue, the courts should treat religious liberty not as a privilege in the manner of free speech but as something in need of special protection. Minority religious believers should be protected just as racial minorities are safeguarded under the equal protection clause. Hence, Eisgruber and Sager conclude, the protection of religious liberty is a specific instance of a broader principle of "equal regard." Equal regard "demands that the interests and concerns of every member of the political community should be treated equally, that no person or group should be treated as unworthy or otherwise subordinated to an inferior status."

In "The Incommensurability of Religion," Abner S. Greene elegantly argues against the Court's recent movement toward treating religion on equal or neutral terms with all other forms of belief. First, related to the issue of religion in the public square, Greene maintains that the establishment clause should be interpreted to prohibit laws that are enacted expressly for the purpose of promoting religious values. Such religiously justified laws would improperly exclude nonbelievers from participating in the public dialogue leading to the law's enactment. While citizens and legislators, according to Greene (arguing similarly to Audi), can form their political positions based on their religious beliefs, they must nonetheless offer secular reasons in the public deliberations about a potential law. Second, for exactly this reason—that laws should not be enacted expressly for the purpose of promoting religious values—Greene argues that the free exercise clause should be understood to exempt religious believers from generally applicable laws. Since the establishment clause specifically hampers the participation of religious believers in the democratic process, the free exercise clause should compensate for this disablement by providing such believers with special protection from generally applicable laws.

Mark V. Tushnet, in "Questioning the Value of Accommodating Religion," turns our attention toward whether the government should treat religion with unusual solicitude. He first synthesizes or at least tries to make sense of the Court's various decisions regarding the governmental accommodation of religion, including cases of mandatory and permissible accommodation. He then criticizes judicial and legislative accommodations of religion: while governmental accommodation ordinarily is understood to bolster religion, Tushnet argues, such accommodation instead weakens or threatens religion. For instance, when the government chooses to accommodate certain religions and not others—and the Court upholds the governmental choice—the government effectively deprecates the unaccommodated religions. More important, the possibility of accommodation might induce religious believers to change their practices for the very purpose of securing governmental accommodation.

Part IV, "Outsider Views of the Separation of Church and State," explores the relations between law and religion from the perspectives of religious outgroups and minorities. My essay, "A Christian America and the Separation of Church and State," draws upon arguments that I developed in my book, *Please Don't Wish Me a Merry Christmas: A Critical History of the Separation of Church and State*, which I wrote from the standpoint of an American Jew. Religion clause cases often seem to turn on the Court's understanding of key concepts such as religion, private conduct, secular action, and governmental neutrality. For example, the Court might hold that a certain governmental action does not violate the establishment clause because the action was secular or neutral. The justices on the Court, though, typically understand these concepts consistently with the dominant religious culture—namely, Christianity (particularly Protestantism). The justices therefore not only conceive of religion mainly in Protestant terms but also tend to understand private, secular, and neutral conduct from a distinctly Christian perspective. The separation of church and state, I conclude, largely manifests and reinforces Christian (especially Protestant) imperialism in American society.

Mark A. Graber's essay, "Jewish Voices and Religious Freedom: A Jewish Critique of Critical Jewish Thinking," argues that there is an emerging "critical Jewish studies movement." He writes in support of this movement but nonetheless offers important cautionary suggestions. Critical Jewish studies, as identified by Graber, are of two types. First, some critical Jewish scholars aim to speak in the voice of Jewish law: What does Judaism, that is, have to say about secular issues? Graber stresses that these scholars should recognize the plurality of Jewish voices rather than assuming or suggesting that there is a single voice of Judaism. Second, other critical Jewish scholars aim to speak in the voice of Jewish experience: How does Jewish experience, in other words, illuminate our understanding of the separation of church and state? Graber emphasizes that these scholars must avoid overgeneralizing and equating slights and inconveniences with more serious oppressions.

Frank S. Ravitch's essay, "A Crack in the Wall: Pluralism, Prayer, and Pain in the Public Schools," is adapted from his book, *School Prayer and Discrimination: The Civil Rights of Religious Minorities and Dissenters*. He examines, from a general outsider viewpoint, the problems created by religious practices in public schools. Specifically, Ravitch argues that discrimination and harassment of those who object to or protest against such religious practices should be analyzed as an issue distinct from whether a constitutional violation has occurred. Such discrimination and harassment, Ravitch observes, can occur regardless of whether the Constitution has been contravened. Moreover, discrimination and harassment that is inflicted by non-governmental actors, as is often the case, would ordinarily not be actionable as a constitutional tort or violation (because under the state action doctrine, in general, governmental conduct is needed to trigger constitutional protections).

The essays in part V, "Religion and Liberal Political Theory," examine the problematic role of religion within liberalism. Liberal political theory, as advocated by the likes of Ronald Dworkin and John Rawls, demands that government remain neutral between competing normative visions of the good—including (especially) diverse religious viewpoints. Yet, in today's pluralistic America, with so many different religions, such normative neutrality seems difficult, if not impossible. Daniel O. Conkle's essay, "Secular Fundamentalism, Religious Fundamentalism, and the Search for Truth in Contemporary America," explains the concepts of religious and secular fundamentalism. Fundamentalisms, whether in the religious or secular sphere, depend on faith, shield themselves from incompatible truth claims, and effectively isolate themselves from considering other systems of thought. Fundamentalisms view their designated sources of truth as absolute, plain, and unchangeable. Thus, insofar as political liberalism excludes all religious arguments from public dialogue about truth and the good, Conkle argues, liberalism is a form of secular fundamentalism. While acknowledging that religious fundamentalism cannot be accepted, Conkle nonetheless maintains that other types of religious arguments are open to competing truth claims and therefore should not be excluded from a dialogic and multilingual search for truth.

Ronald F. Thiemann, "The Constitutional Tradition: A Perplexing Legacy," is drawn from various parts of his book *Religion in Public Life: A Dilemma for Democracy*. Thiemann argues that the current understanding of the relation between religion and government in liberal political theory revolves around concepts such as neutrality, church, state, and separation. These concepts, Thiemann maintains, are outmoded manifestations of a dilemma central to American religious and governmental history: on the one hand, America has accepted legal disestablishment; on the other hand, Christianity has culturally and symbolically dominated America. Thiemann thus argues to reconceive the relation between religion and government by emphasizing aspects of a revised political liberalism, namely, freedom, equality, and toleration.

In a similar vein, Anthony E. Cook seeks to revitalize liberalism, particularly a progressive liberalism, but he turns explicitly to religion to do so. More specifically, Cook's essay, "Toward a Normative Framework of a Love-Based Community," adapted from his book, *The Least of These: Race, Law, and Religion in American Culture*, argues that Martin Luther King, Jr.'s Christian conception of love can invigorate the liberal notion of community. Instead of primarily fearing others and enforcing a social order out of self-interest, we should strive to engender King's "Beloved Community," where we would love even the most socially marginalized individuals and groups. Most important, according to Cook, a love-based conception of community "requires a set of overlapping duties orienting us toward a constructive communion with others."

While Thiemann and Cook attempt to modify and improve liberalism, Stanley Fish is not so kind. His essay, "Mission Impossible: Settling the Just Bounds between Church and State," written in Fish's inimitable style, attacks the broad project of liberal political theory by arguing that the irreconcilable normative views of different religions force liberalism into two positions. First, liberal political theory must banish religion to a private sphere so that religious conceptions of the good do not determine governmental stances. Second, the government must tolerate all religious views in the private sphere so as not to assume a normative stance regarding the validity of competing religious views. Ultimately, though, according to Fish, the self-assigned task of liberal political theory is impossible. The government inevitably must take stances on normative issues, and in so doing, it must abandon neutrality and at least implicitly accept distinct religious visions—which nonetheless are then redesignated and supposedly justified as neutral, reasonable, commonsensible, or the like.

Linda Lacey builds on Fish's broad critique of liberal political theory in her essay, "Liberal Thought and Religion in Custody and Visitation Cases," which shows how liberalism fails in a specific legal context, child custody and visitation cases. Liberalism acts as if a child's upbringing by divorced parents with different religions not only is possible but is a good: according to liberal theory, as Lacey describes it, "if one religion is good, then two are even better." But some religions, Lacey argues, are not compatible with others. Indeed, some religions insist that they provide the only true religious path—that other religious choices will lead to hell or damnation or something of the sort. As a religious and cultural matter, a child cannot, for instance, be raised simultaneously as a Fundamentalist Christian and an Orthodox Jew. Thus, insofar as liberalism demands a display of tolerance, equality, and neutrality toward religion, liberal methodology sometimes just cannot work in these family law situations.

Larry Catá Backer's essay, "There Can Be Only One: Law, Religion, Grammar, and Social Organization in the United States," elaborates a cultural critique of liberalism. Backer, in effect, attacks the liberal notion that law and religion can successfully accommodate each other so long as each is kept in its respective and independent realm. At the nation's founding, Backer explains, religion or, more precisely, Christianity, was the foundational source of cultural order. As America developed after World War II, though, law became the foundation, with religion supporting and filtering through the law. Most important, then, according to Backer, law and religion are alternative and distinctive cultural foundations; the privileging of one over the other radically affects the ordering of American society. Yet either law or religion must dominate the other—one and only one can be foundational at any particular time.

In conclusion, the main themes explored in the various parts or sections of this volume closely intertwine with one another. The proper role of religion in the public square (discussed in part II), for instance, can be understood as one manifestation of the larger issue of religion in liberal political theory (discussed in part V). If traditional liberal political theory demands the government to remain neutral among rival conceptions of the good so that citizens can freely deliberate and openly decide on the community's public values and goals, must citizens therefore refrain from relying on their perhaps arational (or even irrational) religiously based ideas of the good in such political dialogue? And how well do competing judicial doctrines in establishment and free exercise cases (discussed in part III) actualize political liberalism in constitutional jurisprudence? Indeed, just as some of the essays in part V doubt the possibility of theoretically achieving the governmental neutrality posited by political liberalism, the outsider views articulated in part IV question the ostensible neutrality of specific judicial doctrines, as well as the equality supposedly promoted by the broad concept of the separation of church and state.

Finally, the essays in this book present a multitude of perspectives on these major issues, central to the relationship between law and religion. Taken all together, the essays certainly do not lead the reader to definitive conclusions. And that, perhaps, is the point. No matter how strongly we advance our legal and political theories and religious convictions, others argue theirs just as vigorously (or so it seems, at least). This precise dilemma, of course, drives many theorists to embrace liberalism, with its claimed neutrality among competing and irreconcilable positions. Yet, again, at least some of the essays in part V seriously question the viability of the liberal solution. Somehow, though, we still must confront the paradoxes engendered by a religiously diverse American society and a constitutional order that includes the establishment and free exercise clauses.

NOTES

1. Engel v. Vitale, 370 U.S. 421 (1962); *Engel v. Vitale*, The New Republic, July 9, 1962, *reprinted in* Religious Liberty in the Supreme Court 142 (Terry Eastland ed. 1993) [hereinafter Eastland] ("savage"); Naomi W. Cohen, Jews in Christian America: The Pursuit of Religious Equality 171 (1992) ("had betrayed"); *In the Name of Freedom*, Wall Street Journal, June 27, 1962, *reprinted in* Eastland, *supra*, at 138. *But cf. Prayer is Personal*, N.Y. Times, June 27, 1962, *reprinted in* Eastland, *supra*, at 137 (supporting decision despite critical public reaction).

2. Peter Applebome, *Prayer in Public Schools? It's Nothing New for Many*, N.Y. Times, Nov. 22, 1994, at A1, A13. For a discussion of social science evidence regarding public responses to Supreme Court decisions, see Timothy R. Johnson & Andrew D. Martin, *The Public's Conditional Response to Supreme Court Decisions*, 92 Am. Pol. Sci. Rev. 299 (1998).

3. Roe v. Wade, 410 U.S. 113 (1973).

4. Robert Wuthnow, The Restructuring of American Religion 300 (1988); David Whitman, *More Moral*, The New Republic, February 22, 1999, at 18 (reporting Gallup Poll results); *see* Winthrop S. Hudson & John Corrigan, Religion in America 390–91, 408–14 (5th ed. 1992); Martin E. Marty, Protestantism in the United States: Righteous Empire 250–58 (2d ed. 1986). On the religiosity of educated Americans, see Steven D. Smith, *The Rise and Fall of Religious Freedom in Constitutional Discourse*, 140 U. Pa. L. Rev. 149, 174–75 (1991) (citing Unsecular America 142 (Richard J. Neuhaus ed., 1986) (appendix at 142, tbl. 20)).

5. 403 U.S. 602, 612–13 (1971) (quoting Walz v. Tax Commission, 397 U.S. 664, 674 (1970)).

6. 465 U.S. 668, 687–88 (O'Connor, J., concurring).

7. 492 U.S. 573, 592–94 (1989).

8. The plurality argued that the four dissenters in *Lynch* actually had accepted the endorsement test, as articulated in O'Connor's *Lynch* concurrence. *See County of Allegheny*, 492 U.S. at 595–97 (plurality).

9. *Id.* at 659 (Kennedy, J., concurring and dissenting) (quoting *Lynch*, 465 U.S. at 678).

10. Lee v. Weisman, 505 U.S. 577 (1992).

11. Sherbert v. Verner, 374 U.S. 398 (1963); United States v. Lee, 455 U.S. 252 (1982). The three cases vindicating free exercise claims between 1973 and 1990 were the following: Frazee v. Illinois Department of Employment Security, 489 U.S. 829 (1989) (holding unconstitutional the denial of unemployment benefits to a Christian who refused to work on Sundays but did not belong to established church or sect); Hobbie v. Unemployment Appeals Commission of Florida, 480 U.S. 136 (1987) (holding unconstitutional the denial of unemployment benefits to a convert to Seventh-Day Adventism); Thomas v. Review Board of the Indiana Employment Security Division, 450 U.S. 707 (1981) (holding unconstitutional the denial of unemployment benefits to a Jehovah's Witness who refused to continue to work in a munitions factory because of his religious objections to war).

12. Employment Division, Dept. of Human Resources v. Smith, 494 U.S. 872, 890 (1990); Religious Freedom Restoration Act of 1993, Pub. L. 103–141, Nov. 16, 1993, 107 Stat. 1488 (codified at 42 U.S.C. §§ 2000bb to 2000bb-4 (1994)) (reinstating the compelling state interest test for laws of general applicability infringing free exercise rights); City of Boerne v. Flores, 117 S.Ct. 2157 (1997) (striking down act).

Part I

General Perspectives on Law, Religion, and Politics

Chapter 1

Religious Freedom in America

Three Stories

Steven D. Smith

It is a common theme in recent legal literature that stories are a central part of law. Some legal scholars talk *about* the importance of stories,[1] while others (especially feminist theorists and critical race theorists) have begun actually *telling* stories—their own stories, or stories that they create, or sometimes a mixture of both.[2] Although controversial, this turn to storytelling may seem attractive to some in part because it brings a kind of humanity back into a discipline that often seems stifling or stodgily formalistic. On the other hand, stories are not *necessarily* liberating. If the law adopts a dominant narrative and excludes or subordinates others, it can become oppressive. So narrative scholarship emphasizes the importance of hearing other stories that may have been suppressed in the dominant culture.[3]

Legal discourse dealing with the First Amendment's religion clauses typically focuses not so much on stories as on drier matter: propositions, principles, doctrines. But I suspect that legal discussions are driven and shaped to a significant extent by background stories that inform our selection and use of the propositions and principles we explicitly emphasize. And as in other areas of law, our discussions can become rigid and uncomprehending, and the law that results from these discussions can become oppressive, if we hear only one dominant story and refuse to listen to others.[4] So what I want to do in this brief essay is describe three different stories—"metanarratives,"[5] perhaps—about law and religion in America.

The first, or what we might call the "standard story" or the "separationist story," should be familiar; it dominates discussion in the courts and the law schools, and it unites citizens and scholars—and Supreme Court justices—who might seem to be in fierce disagreement. But it is not the only story we can tell. A second story might be described as a "palace coup" story, and a third could be called the "Tower of Babel" story. These narratives are less familiar, especially in legal culture, and I'm not really prepared to tell them with any authority. All I'll try to do is suggest that these other stories exist and give a brief, unofficial sketch of how they might be told.

The Standard Story

According to the dominant story, the American founders achieved religious freedom by undertaking a radical and risky departure from all past political understandings and arrangements. The heroes in this story are bold political visionaries like Thomas Jefferson and James Madison, and their heroic imagination consisted in daring to challenge the nearly universal wisdom that insisted that a unity of government and religion is essential to a stable political community. One scholar has described the received wisdom in this way:

> For more than fourteen hundred years . . . it was a universal assumption that the stability of the social order and the safety of the state demanded the religious solidarity of all the people in one church. Every responsible thinker, every ecclesiastic, every ruler and statesman who gave the matter any attention, held to this as an axiom. There was no political or social philosophy which did not build upon this assumption. . . . *[A]ll*, with no exception other than certain disreputable and "subversive" heretics, believed firmly that religious solidarity in the one recognized church was essential to social and political stability.[6]

In the face of this received wisdom, Americans like Jefferson and Madison dared to imagine a radically different possibility—that political stability might be maintained, and progress and freedom promoted, by *separating* government from religion—and they dared to act upon this radical vision.

The crucial chapter in this story tells about the enactment of Jefferson's Statute for Religious Freedom, which ended officially supported and subsidized religion in the state of Virginia. Martin Marty expresses the epic significance of Jefferson's statute in the standard story: "For those who like to speak of an 'Age of Constantine' that began in the fourth century, there is reason to regard the Virginia act as the key moment of the end of that age and the beginning of a new age."[7] In the same spirit, W. E. Garrison maintained that the constitutional establishment of religious freedom in America was one of the "two most profound revolutions which have occurred in the entire history of the church."[8]

In defying the received wisdom, Americans like Jefferson could only view their venture as a radical and dangerous experiment. Separation of church and state was a big gamble, but the gamble has paid off handsomely. The state *has* survived and flourished—indeed, it has flourished beyond anything that Jefferson contemplated or desired—and religion has prospered as well, much more so here than in most European countries where the church continued to claim the support of the state.[9] So the standard story is a story of triumph unforeseeable by conventional wisdom—it is sort of a "Rocky" story—and like Rocky it seems over time to have vanquished almost all competitors, at least within legal culture.

The Supreme Court endorsed the standard story in the famous *Everson* case by narrating the colonial experience as a plot that culminated in the Virginia events, and then by peremptorily transporting the Virginia statute into the Constitution (without deigning to notice the annoying little historical facts that made this transposition utterly implausible as a matter of mere history).[10] Today liberal theorists like Ronald Dworkin, Bruce Ackerman, and John Rawls embellish and extend the standard story by separating government not only from religion but from judgments about "the good" or "the good life." A similar strain is apparent in Justice Jackson's oft-quoted language from the second flag salute case: "If there is any fixed star in our constitutional constellation, it is that no official, high or petty, can prescribe what shall be orthodox in politics, nationalism, religion, or other matters of opinion."[11]

The almost hypnotic power of the standard story is evident, I think, in the fact that even justices and constitutional scholars who disagree fiercely on many specific matters of religious freedom all seem to accept the basic plot line. Modern debates are often divided between people who claim the title of "separationists" and critics who are often grouped together under the label of "accommodationists." But all of these contenders typically agree, it seems, on the one hand that government must be separate from religion and, on the other hand that *some* degree of interaction between religion and government is inevitable and desirable. Thus, even so-called accommodationists typically insist that government cannot actually *establish* religion or even assist it except in scrupulously nonpreferential ways.[12] And even the most rigorous separationist justices in *Everson* conceded that the state should provide churches with police and fire protection.[13]

So these disputes, heated though they often become, are essentially about *degrees* of permissible interaction. In other words, the familiar disagreements occur *within* the standard story. If I might overstate the point slightly for emphasis, from a detached perspective it is as if different storytellers and critics were arguing about whether the bears that Goldilocks met up with were black bears or brown bears, or whether the soup she stole from little bear was vegetable beef or chicken noodle.

But if everyone within *legal* culture seems to accept the broad outlines of the standard story, we might begin to wonder whether that might not be the only story there is. Listening beyond the walls of the law school or the courtroom, though, we can at least dimly hear other stories that might be, and sometimes are, told.

The "Palace Coup" Story

So let me move on to what we might call, a bit awkwardly, the "palace coup" story. While the standard story depicts American religious freedom as a radical break with the past, this second narrative would emphasize continuity. As a prelude to this story, consider again the famous language from Justice Jackson: "If there is any *fixed star*"—the phrase is a telling one—"in our constitutional constellation, it is that no official, high or petty, can prescribe what shall be orthodox." Considered one way, the statement sounds wonderfully open-minded and tolerant: This is a country in which there will be *no official orthodoxy*. Heard another way, though, the statement becomes wonderfully paradoxical. After all, isn't the statement itself a proclamation of an official orthodoxy—a sort of "no orthodoxy" orthodoxy? If this way of considering the statement seems perverse, keep in mind that the statement has been invoked by judges in numerous cases, as in *Barnette* itself, to condemn and stamp out decisions and policies that a variety of nonjudicial institutions believed to be desirable or in the public interest but that somehow ran afoul of the "no orthodoxy" orthodoxy.

We might generalize from this observation and wonder whether it isn't inevitable that *every* political community will, of necessity, have an orthodoxy of some kind—a body of ideas and values and commitments that are thought to define the character and purposes of the community. And it might be that every political community will also have institutions designed to *inculcate* these ideas and values and commitments in citizens, especially the young, so that they can function within and maintain the community. Without such a body of ideas and values and commitments, after all, how would the community be able to make collective decisions? And how would people be able to distinguish between good citizenship and unacceptable or disloyal actions and attitudes? In fact, doesn't the very notion of *community* imply that people have something in common that unites them beyond the accident of inhabiting a common geographical space?

Imagine for a moment that these suppositions are right. Then the continuities linking our governments with past governments may come to seem more basic than the discontinuities. The unity of government and religion that the standard story ascribes to earlier governments would merely be one manifestation of the fact that political communities will always have—and will seek to maintain—an orthodoxy. Our own governments will not—indeed, *could not*—differ from earlier governments in *this* respect. Instead, differences between political communities will turn not on *whether* they have an orthodoxy—they *will*—but, rather, on the *content* of the various orthodoxies and on the particular institutions maintained for the purpose of inculcating the orthodoxies.

Of course, these features will probably not be static, even within a given political community. So we might label the orthodoxy at one point in history "religion," or perhaps "Christianity," while at other points we might call it something different (or, for tactical reasons, we might avoid giving it a name at all, on the supposition that what is not named will not be perceived to exist). And at one point the institutions devoted to inculcating the orthodoxy might be called "churches," while at another point they might be called "schools."[14]

But as the second story tells it, nothing very fundamental of a structural nature has changed. In its general features, the edifice of government remains pretty much as it was; only the particular faces and costumes of its officials are different. The palace is still there; the old palace dignitaries have merely been replaced by new ones. So people like Jefferson and Madison—and the modern Supreme Court—cannot be seen as fighting against the past to free Americans from government-maintained orthodoxy. Instead, they were, and are, fighting with their own contemporaries over what the shape and content of that orthodoxy will be. And "separation" is merely a somewhat misleading title for a story narrating a changing of the official guard.

Of course, like any good narrator, tellers of these different stories will emphasize details and features that support the particular story they want to relate, and will omit to notice other details that might undermine their preferred narrative. Tellers of the standard story will depict preconstitutional orthodoxies as monolithic and static. Blanket terms like "religion" or "Christianity" or "theocracy" serve this flattening purpose nicely—and also serve rhetorically to permit devotees of the standard story to portray opponents in a way that banishes them to the other side of what appears in that story as the pivotal Jeffersonian divide.[15] By contrast, modern orthodoxies will be depicted as pluralistic and dynamic (and, of course, will not be referred to as "orthodoxies" at all).

Conversely, a teller of the second story might emphasize that what separationist storytellers lump under the label of "Christianity" was in reality an ever-changing, highly pluralistic body of ideas and practices that was influenced by a huge array of classical and more modern traditions and philosophies—and that always (even before its fragmentation became visible with the Protestant Reformation) left large numbers of vital questions to the realm of ongoing debate and disagreement.[16] Similarly, the second storyteller might flatten and unify modern notions and practices under something like Sorokin's term "sensate culture"[17] or, to use the terms currently in vogue among people attracted to one version of the "palace coup" story, "secular humanism" or just "secularism"[18]—terms, incidentally, that seem perfectly respectable even in academic circles so long as they are not used by the wrong people for the wrong reasons.

Although the "palace coup" story is not often heard in legal culture, in other disciplines like sociology or anthropology it should seem ordinary enough.[19] More important, in one version or another this second story is quite familiar and even compelling, I think, in some neighborhoods of the general culture. In the nineteenth century, for instance, faced with a public school system that Protestants described (no doubt with complete sincerity) as "nonsectarian," American Catholics seem to have understood the force of the second story.[20] Today, I suspect that evangelicals and Native Americans can easily appreciate that story's virtues.[21]

To be sure, judges and legal scholars in the grip of the standard story seem to find complaints from these quarters almost incomprehensible. But clinging to the standard story is not necessarily a way of avoiding *that* problem. Indeed, the one thing that virtually all students of the religion clauses seem to agree on is that the current constitutional discourse of religious freedom—a discourse grounded in the standard story—is itself often incoherent and incomprehensible. Indeed, at times it almost seems as if an acknowledgment of such incoherence has become a mandatory gesture in law review articles on the subject. This observation leads into still a third story about religious freedom in America, or what I'm calling the Tower of Babel story.

The Tower of Babel Story

The story of the Tower of Babel,[22] you may recall, tells how some years after the great flood, Noah's descendants decided to build a tower that would reach to heaven. Perhaps, not trusting God's promise, they were afraid of being flooded again and wanted a place that would be above water level. Josephus suggests that the tower builders thought they might reach heaven and overthrow God, and Josephus makes clear that the construction project was inspired by human pride or—to translate into more modern, less moralistic terms—by an aspiration to realize human autonomy.[23] But as the story goes, this aspiration remained unfulfilled. Like many a modern large-scale construction project, the building couldn't be completed as scheduled. Quite the reverse, in fact. Human language became so confounded that in the end the builders couldn't even communicate intelligibly with one another.

The story of the American Constitution, and particularly of the religion clauses, might be viewed as a modern version of the Tower of Babel story.[24] The Constitution is often described as a product of the Enlightenment commitment to "reason"—it represented the American project to establish, as Henry Steele Commager puts it, *The Empire of Reason*[25]—and the religion clauses are often seen as the clearest manifestation within the Constitution of this Enlightenment commitment.[26] Moreover, "reason" in modern discourse usually conveys in essence a determination to realize human autonomy by throwing off the weight of tradition, authority, and revealed religion. In his book *Reason and Culture* Ernest Gellner advocates something that he sometimes calls "Cartesian rationalism," which he describes in this way:

> One of the central themes, perhaps indeed the central obsession, of Cartesian rationalism is the aspiration for autonomy. There is the overwhelming desire for a kind of self-creation, for bringing forth a self and a world not simply taken over from an unexamined, accidental, contingent inheritance. Rationalism is the philosophy of the New Broom. Man makes himself, and he does so *rationally*.[27]

So the religion clauses can be—and often are—viewed as potent expressions of a more general modern commitment to achieving a degree of autonomy unprecedented in human history. This autonomy would be exercised in accordance with a faculty called "reason." And the culmination of this project, we now see, is the modern constitutional discourse of religious freedom—a discourse celebrated for its incoherence even within the field of constitutional law (which itself is not exactly distinguished for precision of thought). The comparison is difficult to avoid; I am hardly the first critic to use the term "Babel" to describe modern religion clause jurisprudence.[28]

This ending to the story is not necessarily a tragic one. Scholars like William Marshall and Phillip Johnson have occasionally suggested (although they put the point more diplomatically than I will) that religious freedom has benefited in this country precisely from the fact that our legal ways of *talking about* religious freedom are so confused.[29] If they are right, then those of us who write books and law review articles about religious freedom deserve some credit, I think; it is doubtful that the salutary and exuberant incoherence that flourishes today would be nearly as developed as it is without our help.

Standing amidst the Stories

I've described very briefly three quite different stories that might be told, and that sometimes *are* told, about religious freedom in America. I haven't tried to flesh out the stories or to explore their implications. Still, you might at this point expect that I would at least say something about an obvious question: Which of the stories is *true*? But the answer to that question, I think, is that in a sense all of the stories are true, and in a sense none of them is true. All of the stories, in other words, capture some aspects of our history, overlook or distort other aspects, and supply elements and connecting transitions that are necessary to complete the story but are not in any strong sense "factual." So our decision to highlight one story over the others cannot be determined solely by anything so mundane as historical evidence. Aesthetics, politics, and religious or other commitments will all contribute in different contexts to make one story more appealing than the others.

So, then, what is the point of calling attention to alternative stories when we already have a perfectly good one in place? Part of the answer lies in a familiar point I noticed at the outset of this essay : A dominant story can become oppressive. That is true, I think, of the standard story of religious freedom in America—even though (or perhaps especially because) the story holds itself out as one about overcoming oppression.

But part of the answer also rests on the (admittedly debatable) Socratic notion that self-understanding, including collective self-understanding, is a good thing. The standard story reflects a part of what we are—but only a part. The full tale of religious freedom in America, it turns out, is actually much richer, and much more interesting, than we have usually supposed.

NOTES

A version of this essay was given as a public lecture inaugurating the Byron R. White Professorship at the University of Colorado. Although I have modified the text for this essay (mostly by deleting private jokes and adding supporting footnotes), I have also tried to retain the oral presentation quality of the lecture.

1. See, e.g., Kathryn Abrams, Hearing the Call of Stories, 79 Cal. L. Rev. 971 (1991).

2. See, e.g., Richard Delgado, The Rodrigo Chronicles (1995); Derrick A. Bell, And We Are Not Saved (1987).

3. See Richard Delgado, Storytelling for Oppositionists and Others: A Plea for Narrative, 87 Mich. L. Rev. 2411 (1989).

4. For one study depicting conventional religion clause discourse as the product of a "dominant story" and offering an alternative perspective, see Stephen M. Feldman, Please Don't Wish Me a Merry Christmas: A Critical History of the Separation of Church and State (1997).

5. Our understanding of religious freedom is also influenced by countless smaller or more contained stories—some personal or private, others public. As a private instance, a colleague once told me about how as a schoolchild he had been beaten up by classmates because he did not belong to the regionally dominant religion; this remembered incident had powerfully shaped his entire way of thinking about church-state relations. As a more public example, I suspect that nearly all educated Americans have been exposed at some time or another (on television or in the theater or even, as students have told me, in high school biology classes) to the "Inherit the Wind" story, and many or most people probably believe—mistakenly—that this story is an accurate, "only-the-names-changed" rendition of what actually happened at

the historical "monkey trial" involving Clarence Darrow and Williams Jennings Bryan. Cf. Edward J. Larson, Summer of the Gods (1997). This story may well have had a powerful influence on the attitudes and beliefs of educated Americans, including Supreme Court justices, regarding evolution and creationism. *See* Edwards v. Aguillard, 482 U.S. 578 (1987); Epperson v. Arkansas, 393 U.S. 97 (1968). My sense, based on conversations with colleagues and students, at least, is that many educated Americans know very little about the actual strength of evidence and arguments for and against Darwinist theories; what they *do* "know"—quite likely under the influence of stories like "Inherit the Wind"—is that "enlightened" people are on the side of evolution and that doubters of Darwinism are narrow-minded, parochial, and just not very bright—like the townspeople and Bryan character in "Inherit the Wind." Cf. Phillip E. Johnson, Reason in the Balance (1995).

6. Sidney Mead, The Lively Experiment 60 (1963) (quoting W. E. Garrison).

7. Martin E. Marty, The Virginia Statute Two Hundred Years Later, in The Virginia Statute for Religious Freedom: Its Evolution and Consequences in American History 1, 2 (Merrill D. Peterson & Robert C. Vaughn eds., 1988).

8. Quoted in Mead, *supra* note 6 at 59–60.

9. It is a familiar and plausible view that religion has flourished in this country, by contrast to Europe, precisely because of religious disestablishment. See Jose Casanova, Public Religions in the Modern World 28–29 (1994).

10. Everson v. Board of Educ., 330 U.S. 1 (1947). For criticism of *Everson*'s history, see, e.g., Steven D. Smith, Foreordained Failure: The Quest for a Constitutional Principle of Religious Freedom 17–50 (1995); Robert Cord, Separation of Church and State: Historical Fact and Current Fiction (1988) (first published 1982); Gerard V. Bradley, Church-State Relations in America (1987); Mark DeWolfe Howe, The Garden and the Wilderness (1965).

11. West Virginia State Board of Educ. v. Barnette, 319 U.S. 624, 642 (1943).

12. See, e.g., Wallace v. Jaffree, 472 U.S. 38, 91–113 (1984) (Rehnquist, J., dissenting).

13. 330 U.S. at 60–61 (Rutledge, J., dissenting).

14. Cf. Brown v. Board of Educ., 347 U.S. 483, 493 (1954):

> Compulsory school attendance laws and the great expenditures for education both demonstrate our recognition of the importance of education to our democratic society. . . . It is the very foundation of good citizenship. Today it is a principal instrument in awakening the child to cultural values, in preparing him for later professional training, and in helping him to adjust normally to his environment.

15. For example, this sort of rhetorical "casting out" is evident in virtually every issue of *Church and State*, a journal published by Americans United for the Separation of Church and State.

16. See, e.g., Alister McGrath, The Intellectual Origins of the European Reformation 14 (1987) (describing the "unprecedented expansion in theological speculation in the universities and religious houses of western Europe" in the late Middle Ages and "the astonishing diversity of the late fourteenth and fifteenth centuries").

17. Pitirim A. Sorokin, The Crisis of Our Age: The Social and Cultural Outlook 86–102 (1941).

18. For a helpful discussion of these concepts and cultural developments, see James Davison Hunter, Religious Freedom and the Challenge of Modern Pluralism, in Articles of Faith, Articles of Peace 54, 63–71 (James Davison Hunter & Os Guinness eds. 1990).

19. In these disciplines, that is, the Durkheimian supposition that all societies have at their core, or express themselves in, a religion of some kind is perfectly familiar. For a helpful discussion, see Winnifred Fallers Sullivan, Paying the Words Extra 24–34 (1994).

20. For an overview of the conflict, see Kurt T. Lash, The Second Adoption of the Establishment Clause: The Rise of the Nonestablishment Principle, 27 Az. St. L.J. 1085, 1118—31 (1995).

21. See, e.g., Mozert v. Hawkins Cty. Board of Educ., 827 F.2d 1058 (6th Cir. 1987), *cert. denied*, 484 U.S. 1066 (1988); Bowen v. Roy, 476 U.S. 693 (1986).

22. The most familiar version of the story is in Genesis 11:1–9.

23. Josephus, The Jewish Antiquities, Bk. I, 109–18, in IV Josephus 53–57 (H. St. J. Thackeray trans. 1930).

24. I have elaborated on this suggestion regarding the Constitution as a whole in Steven D. Smith, The Constitution and the Pride of Reason 143–51 (1998).

25. Henry Steele Commager, The Empire of Reason (1977).

26. See, e.g., Suzanna Sherry, Enlightening the Religion Clauses, 7 J. Contemp. Legal Issues 473 (1996).

27. Ernest Gellner, Reason and Culture 157 (1992).

28. See, e.g., David L. Gregory & Charles J. Russo, Let Us Pray (But Not "Them"!): The Troubled Jurisprudence of Religious Liberty, 65 St. John's L. Rev. 273, 295 (1991).

29. William P. Marshall, Unprecedential Analysis and Original Intent, 27 Wm. & Mary L. Rev. 925, 928–29 ((1986); Phillip E. Johnson, Concepts and Compromise in First Amendment Doctrine, 72 Cal. L. Rev. 817 (1984).

Chapter 2

The Widening Gyres of Religion and Law

Martin E. Marty

> Turning and turning in the widening gyre
> The falcon cannot hear the falconer;
> Things fall apart; the centre cannot hold;
> Mere anarchy is loosed upon the world.
> —William Butler Yeats, "The Second Coming"

I. The Vision of Widening Gyres and the End-of-the-Century Scene

The main trends of twentieth-century life have seldom been better represented in English-language poetry than they were in William Butler Yeats's "The Second Coming."[1] Early in the century Yeats saw and foresaw a world of lawlessness, violence, and incoherence. As so often, the poet used a vocabulary of his own. It now demands explanatory footnoting for collegians who first encounter it in the classroom and even for most lovers of poetry, however familiar they may be with the sort of language in its reaches.

Specifically, teachers and expositors are often asked: "What's a gyre?" In the present instance, one might add another question: "Why introduce poetry and a poetic metaphor in an essay on the relation of two elements in human experience, law and religion?" The subject is sufficiently complex even without the employment of an obscure image. Why clutter the pages of law reviews with such?

The second question first: Experts in law and religion may see their subjects with sufficient clarity that they can canonize the main themes of each and define them in legal and religious dictionaries. But most people do not experience them so neatly. Thus very few people who are seen as religious speak of their response to the sacred, to signals of transcendence, or to ritual dimensions of their ways of life as "religion" at all. They simply believe, and practice. Similarly, "law" can mean The Law, as represented in American colloquial talk about the traffic policeman, constitutional life, or what goes on in law school. "Law" can also refer to philosophical discourse on Natural Law and theological talk about divine law.

Given such sprawls, such protean usages and understandings of the two terms, we might choose the Yeatsian image of the gyre to bring to some coherence an aspect of a world that otherwise seems so chaotic. The metaphor of the gyre can help those who ponder it to approach the issue of why religion and law, with all their complementarity and collisions, have grown so complex in our time. Before detailing that issue, however, we take up the first question in a slightly more sustained way; a four-line verse does not do justice to the reality. The image of the gyre works memorably to evoke our main themes. So: "What's a gyre?"

The gyre, one of Yeats's commentators, A. G. Stock, suggests, was the poet's "true symbol for all experience."[2] He liked to speak of "those whirling, interlocking gyres, 'each one living the other's death, dying the other's life.'"[3] They help him elaborate on his own idiosyncratic but by no means irrelevant reduction of the death of civilization in what he foresaw as three phases. They were "mere anarchy," which would be followed by "the blood-dimmed tide," and, finally, they depicted a scene in which "the ceremony of innocence is drowned."[4]

In Yeats's doomsday poem, the image of the trained bird of prey reverting to its wild state served to evoke the understanding of a world turned back to violence. The falcon should be able to hear the falconer, just as it should be able to have clarity and perspective. A falcon can see a handkerchief 5,000 feet away and can zoom toward it at speeds ranging from 100 to 275 miles per hour.

Falconers teach falcons to fly in disciplined orbits. But Yeats sees them breaking out of the spheres or gyres and, in effect, losing the plot of their flight. For us, the falcon-gyre images speak well to many elements in the late-twentieth-century American cultural scene. It is our burden and at the same time gladly accepted assignment to address but two of them, religion and law. We can notice: that which happens to the orbits and spheres of law and religion, and that which happens to those who would like to see disciplining and definition among them, will turn out to be fateful in the lives of the majority of the human race who see the "widening gyres" intersecting. They then turn out to be ever more confusing.

For our effort to frame the discussion of the expansive and hard to define spheres of law and religion, we need one more look at the evocative "The Second Coming." Yeats concludes his observation of the figurative falcon with no vision of a progressive outcome. Such envisionings were still common when he wrote. Instead he foretold an apocalyptic end. In other words, not sharing the view common in the West early in this century, a vision of a world giving birth to progress, peace, civility, and order, Yeats at the end of the poem asked, with his eye on the future: "What rough beast . . . [s]louches to Bethlehem to be born?"[5]

Eight decades and more after he wrote, the poet would not have to make any apologies for having written as he did. Things keep turning out as he knew they would. "Rough beasts" have been born again and again. Yeats would not have to work hard to attract a public that would observe with him that even those two forces that normally lead to restraint, religion and law, contribute more often to ever more mere anarchy. Many of the leaders and exemplars in both spheres also match what came into the poet's field of perception. He saw apathy confronting fanaticism: "The best lack all conviction, while the worst [a]re full of passionate intensity."[6]

And so it is.

In the quoted part of the poem Yeats concluded with a half line: "The centre cannot hold." When dealing with religion and law in a pluralistic society, the kind of human society that will preoccupy us, it is important for us to note that there is not and was never a simply agreed-upon center around the globe or in any of its regions. Thus novelist Thomas Mann often spoke with empirical matter-of-factness in the face of would-be synthesizers. They were prophets who foretold that there would eventually be a gathering of the separate forces, a centering and synthesis among the world's legal systems ("The World Court") and the religions. People like Mann have instead contended that the world has many centers. There is no single organon, encyclopedia, summa, canon, legal code, or synthesis available to and accepted by all the people and all the peoples. Ours turned out to be a century when science propounded "the indeterminacy principle" and "chaos theory." Indeterminacy and chaos rule religion and law when they interact.

On such a spiritual landscape, however, one is naturally moved to ask: Why should religion and law not be "indeterminate" spheres? Why, when their gyres collide or coincide, should they not contribute to "chaos"? In the postmodern period—Yeats seems to have foreseen it—even the individual self is uncertain about identity. No single symbol system unites the arts or makes them intelligible within the culture. Each visit to a gallery forces one to confront a disarray in the form of a display of pastiches, montages, assemblages, and collages. Each act of attendance in a concert hall where music of this century is played calls one to hear dissonances and atonal experiment that sound chaotic.

On such a cultural scene, religion and law could hardly be expected to serve as restraints against "mere anarchy." Instead, they seem to promote it. As the publics respond to their surrounding worlds, whether while recognizing religious ambiguities and bewilderments or when its members give voice to disgust with law and government, it evidences some of this "anarchy." This decentered and decentering scene demands attention.

II. The Affirmation of Law from within Religion, and Vice Versa

The stance of the observer will color something of what is said about religion and law alike. This observer begins without nostalgia but with an awareness that in the past it was often somewhat easier to restrict and define the gyres of law and religion. In earlier America, for instance, after the founders worked to separate church and state and allow for tax exemption of church properties, there did not appear to be many reasons to encounter controversies and collisions over the two spheres. It is our more complex age that has evoked so much discontent.

I have to begin by expressing appreciations of both gyres. Many academics stand outside the spheres of religion, viewing them as irrelevant, obsolete, and waning. But a more careful look will show that the vast majority of humans in all cultures wrestle with whatever it has been to which religion points. For most of them, the gyre of religion represents attempts by humans to hold things together conceptually and to aid them in the practice and walk of life. They want to find a center that holds. They would like to participate in an integrating order. In the pursuits that observers call religion, people aspire to deal with the ultimate, the whole, the unum, the All. They are alert to evocations of awe and wonder. Their sense of the sacred leads most of them to build community and undertake various sorts of mission. Therefore religion, when vital, is never easily contained within a defined and disciplined sphere. Religion is never self-contained, never unconnected. It always stands the potential of being "widened."

Some elements of religion, it is true, can be captured in the neat alphabetized categories of denominations as they are listed under "Churches" (between "Chiropractors" and "Cigars") in the Yellow Pages of the phone books. But in reality, the world is full of charismatic, enthusiastic, imaginative, adventurous, grasping people and phenomena.

Now, in turn face all that confusion about religion with the expanding gyre of law. Through law also people aspire to order life, to provide "-archy," to promote rule instead of anarchy. As part of government, law is imposed on all people. It is inescapable, and it works effectively, even as it "widens"; law is designed to produce regularity, order, restraint. It is true that there may be "world citizens" who in their own minds want to transcend national government and its law. But there is no place for them to hide. At another extreme, anarchists reject all law. But government of some sort and national boundaries of varying natures do encompass all humans, whether they like it or not. On second thought and despite their unease and disgruntlement, most people, having seen the jungle of lawlessness in moments and places where law breaks down, prefer law to nonlaw and seek protection in many laws, not few.

For all the reasons implied in those paragraphs, all religiously believing and practicing citizens relate to two sets of gyres, cycles, circles, or spheres that overlap and intersect. Disturbance in either affects the other. Disturbances in both can lead to disruptions, to "mere anarchy" being loosed upon the world. As the century ends, there is a widespread and easily documented sense that this disruption is threatening civilizations in many polities. Citizens in the United States regularly charge that law is too expansive, even as it remains too often ineffective. Religion does not capture imaginations in ways that can lead either to restraint in support of law or to alternative disciplines where and when law breaks down.

Most of what follows will imply problems that the leaders in religious and legal circles have with each other, or confusions that they experience themselves when they try to read the signs of the times. It is well to bring to mind the fact that most religions, at least those in our culture, have quite consistently included and affirmed legal elements of their own. They have canon law of their own and they comment on law in the civil order. They thereupon have regularly sought and offered theological legitimation and support for the civil law that surrounds the religious bodies. Thus in the heritage of the Hebrew Scriptures, Jews live within a web of sacred law. In the New Testament world of Christians, "the powers that be are ordained of God."[7]

To begin to make sense of the relations of law and religion, it is appropriate to quote Harold Berman, the first of the DePaul Annual Lecturers, speaking in 1983. He talked of integrating law and religion:

> Law is not only a body of rules; it is people legislating, adjudicating, administering, negotiating—it is a living process of allocating rights and duties and thereby resolving conflicts and creating channels of cooperation. Religion is not only a set of doctrines and exercises; it is people manifesting a collective concern for the ultimate meaning and purpose of life—it is a shared intuition of and commitment to transcendent values. Law helps to give society the structure, the gestalt, it needs to maintain inner cohesion; law fights against anarchy. Religion helps to give society the faith it needs to face the future; religion fights against decadence. These are two dimensions of social relations—as well as of human nature—which are in tension with each other: law through its stability limits the future; religion through its sense of the holy challenges all existing social structures. Yet each is also a dimension of the other. . . . Where they are divorced from each other, law tends to degenerate into legalism and religion into religiosity.[8]

Enthusiastic as he may be about the two, Berman for years has been alerting us to profound problems. The West is experiencing

> an integrity crisis, . . . a deeper loss of confidence in fundamental religious and legal values and beliefs, a decline in belief in and commitment to any kind of transcendent reality that gives life meaning, and a decline of belief in and commitment to any structures and processes that provide social order and justice. Torn by doubt concerning the reality and validity of those values that sustained us in the past, we come face to face with the prospect of death itself.[9]

So one can affirm law and religion, as Berman does, and then find special reasons to fear that "the centre cannot hold."

III. The Subordinating or Contracting of the Gyres or Sphere

Thoughtful people who have tried to deal with the crisis often build on time-honored strategies. If there is danger that the two spheres might collide as they expand, logic suggests that citizens and believers should entertain the idea of subordinating one gyre to the other. In such a strategy, one pictures the falconer who has trained two falcons to fly in concentric spheres, the outer one defining the inner one.

A. Strategies of Subordination

How do and how should law and religion interrelate? Back when the center held or where it still to some extent holds in some of its modes, religions subordinated and subordinate law by appeal to a "higher law." Or religious leaders may promote support of the idea of law's being appropriated by conscience in the inner self. At the opposite extreme, more frequently and successfully in the past than now—but think of Iran and its kind as counterexamples in our time—religions have imposed patterns of ecclesiastical dominance in the form of theocracies, hierocracies, or clerocracies.

Free societies such as true republics do allow for the inner spiritual transcendence of law—how could they not? But they reject the patterns of religious dominance that were characteristic of prerepublican or antirepublican times and situations. That is, they allow for opinions about and appeals to "higher law," but they do exact penalties when people follow and act upon such appeals. Martin Luther King, Jr., typically was caught between such honoring of higher law and such exactions and penalties when he had to disobey ordinary laws.

In authoritarian atheistic societies the state tries to repress religion but ordinarily fails. Religion, despite efforts to put it down by law, survives and prospers. This was evident in the greatest twentieth-century example, the Soviet Union and its aftermath. In most of the world, religions are expanding in numbers and complexity. We who live in what I call "the spiritual ice belt" that extends from west of Poland through Western Europe, the British Isles, Canada, and the northern United States to Japan, may not always experience or notice this expansion with all of its intensities. But no view of the global situation can overlook the burgeoning of religious movements, and the affective response to these, whatever "the law" thinks of them. They can spell more confusion and clash ahead.

In the free societies, most republics, it has to be noted that in the formal senses—though not necessarily the moral, intellectual, or spiritual ones—a constitutional society allows for the law to subordinate religion or religious institutions. Thus the conservative legal scholar Walter Berns notices and effectively argues:

> The origin of free government in the modern sense coincides with and can only coincide with, the solution of the religious problem, and the solution of the religious problem consists in the subordination of religion. . . . One can say that the natural rights philosophers spent so much time on the religious question in order to make it possible for the politicians who followed them to ignore it.[10]

In such cases, the sweep of law is by definition coercive. It is in practice protean but not limitless. The gyre of law is widening; we speak of the growth of law. In the formal sense it is law, not religion, that "constitutes," orders, organizes, and puts boundaries around life, including the life of the spirit. But this can be true only in the formal sense. Meanwhile, most accounts of modernity agree, "the center did not hold." The spheres are no longer concentric; there are two separate spheres. As law's gyre widens, if religion's also does, there is a prospect of further and greater confusion and clash.

B. Strategies of Contraction or Constriction of Gyres

If one realm cannot satisfyingly subordinate the other, citizens can still make efforts to improve their understanding by carefully defining the two spheres. But it is precisely this that is done with most difficulty in late modern and postmodern times. In Yeats's terms, there are situations in which still "the falcon can hear the falconer" but cannot thereupon accept the signals. The grounds for these signals have become unacceptable.

To move from metaphor: because of free religion's boundlessness, there is a temptation for legal boundary setters to try to constrict it. In the United States, the First Amendment to the Constitution, through its "Free Exercise" clause, intends to proscribe such a strategy. But in many twentieth-century polities, be they Nazi, fascist, communist or Maoist, leadership set out to constrict, penalize, or abolish religion in all its traditional modes, but without success. Meanwhile, neither establishing nor prohibiting religion, a "free exercise" society neither encourages nor discourages religion in the formal sense.

On the other hand, the "falcon can hear the falconer" in polities in which a single integral religion dominates. On occasion, religions still "fight back" against what they see to be secularizing forces and attempt to constrict and contract the sphere of law. Of course, individuals at any time can restrict law within the blurred bounds of their own perception. They may do this through what turn out to be personally satisfying but civilly unrecognized theological definitions and actions. In the spirit of figures like Henry David Thoreau, others may favor personal or communal gestures of defiance of conventional law. Or, so far as possible, others may simply ignore law for the sake of their own spiritual freedom. Still further, sometimes through legal or revolutionary activity, as in some fundamentalist Islamic activities that are typified by the Iranian revolution, believers set out to reestablish the dominance of religion.

The American constitutional pattern naturally interests us most. In setting forth the First Amendment's two clauses about religion, the founders and the courts that have interpreted and applied their workings have rejected such strategies. Thomas Jefferson conceived of this resolution as taking the form of the erecting of a "wall of separation between church and state." More accurate and more appropriate, in respect to the gyre imagery and the actual legal situation, is James Madison's conception, expressed in one of his letters. Note how he introduces the concept of collisions between the gyres, a concept that will remain with us for the rest of the way:

> It may not be easy, in every possible case, to trace the line of separation between the rights of religion and the Civil authority with such distinctness as to avoid collisions & doubts on unessential points. The tendency to a usurpation on one side or the other, or to a corrupting coalition or alliance between them, will be best guarded against by an entire abstinance [*sic*] of the Government from interference in any way whatever, beyond the necessity of preserving public order, & protecting each sect against trespasses on its legal rights by others.[11]

Madison was giving expression to an ideal. But in our story of late-twentieth-century life when we speak of "widening gyres," it seems clear that the "collisions" of which he spoke are ever more frequent and disruptive.

IV. The Resort to History: When, It Was Believed That "the Falcon Could Hear the Falconer" and There Was Coherence

What I have said so far implies that once upon a time the falcon could hear the falconer, that there was then more coherence and centering, less falling apart and anarchy than there is now. To gain perspective, we can look at three spheres in the recent and longer pasts alike.

First, though it is not our present subject, on the world scene there have been aspirations toward establishing global empires or, more humanely in our own recent past, world courts and with them the world rule of law. Efforts like the United Nations Declaration on Human Rights in 1948 demonstrate such moves. But the mid-twentieth-century organizations like the United Nations, while surviving and on occasion exerting some effective influence, are just as often seen as agents of confusion, generating their own "widening gyres." Witness the difficulties experienced by those who seek to promote intelligible discourse in recent United Nations–sponsored conferences on the environment, population and development, and the rights of women. There is general concurrence in respect to the notion that today the pluralist world would not be capable of writing and agreeing upon a new "declaration of human rights." Religions such as militant Islam and resurgent "tribalisms" are among the forces that resist efforts at finding consensus based on concepts of law that the religious leaders regard as alien and profane. The gyres have widened, but coherence is not apparent.

Second, on the ecclesiastical scene, "the falcon could hear the falconer." It is often presumed, at least by the more nostalgic souls, that at certain moments—e.g., for the West, in medieval Christendom or, for America, in certain colonial situations of religious establishment, there was coherence because the legal sphere was coextensive with the religious. Such ordering is not possible now, thanks to the "separation" of spheres or the drawing of a "line of distinction" in a republic, and specifically in the United States.

Third, in the American past, after legal disestablishment of religion (ending finally in Massachusetts in 1833) there developed, for a time, a pattern of informal covenanting and legal aspiration by the dominant Protestant churches who would—and did, in a way—"run America." The common-school textbook tradition stressed religious homogeneity. While the gyres of religion and law could at least seem to be contracted or restricted, one set of people were privileged to tell the story in ways that favored their own special status. There were in that past some rare Supreme Court rulings that even spoke of Americans as "a Christian people."[12] But the law never underscored this Protestant establishment as much as did the ethos. Thus the American founder John Jay, though he had Dutch and French Huguenot ancestors, in Federalist No. 2, argued that Americans were "a people descended from the same ancestors, speaking the same language, professing the same religion, attached to the same principles of government. . . . Similar sentiments have hitherto prevailed among all orders and denominations of men among us. To all general purposes we have uniformly been one people."[13]

One pictures trying to sell such a white-male New English Protestant concept for the basis of a consensus juris in today's "multiculturalist" America. In truth, John Jay's observations and contentions were not accurate or fair even back when Jay wrote.

It is clear that the global scene, the ecclesiastical past, and the colonial American situation offer no credible models for interpreting the widening gyres of religion and law today—except to underscore the widening and the "things fall apart" theme from Yeats.

V. The Two "Widening Gyres"

So the gyres widened and widen. We must examine the current American situation. The eighteenth-century framers of constitutionalism gave little evidence that they foresaw a widening gyre for religion as we have experienced it for two centuries. They made clear during three decades of argument, centering around 1787, that they did understand religion's potential for defining and "binding" a people, just as it had the potential for unsettling them and being disruptive of their civil life. Many of the founders, partisans of the Enlightenment and no friends of "revealed religion" or "priestcraft," seemed to picture that particularized religions (as opposed to Natural Law or Natural Reason or Nature's God outlooks) would not expand and that they might even wither. Religious awakeners and revivalists may have had other ideas, but at the birth of the Republic, there seemed to be a sense that religion and law both had boundaries and knew their spheres.

Instead of what legal and religious leaders foresaw, we have seen an inevitable enlargement and widening of both spheres. One thinks, for example, of the need for growth in legislation of a sort that necessarily involved religious interests. It was these religious interests that have reacted most vehemently to the legal consequences of technologies through which birth control and abortion possibilities changed, along with legal policies in respect to marriage, sexual expression, and the like. Here was more inevitable "widening."

Around the world this widening trend remains especially visible in the public role of religion as evidenced in the aspirations of Islamic, Jewish, Christian, Buddhist, Hindu, Sikh fundamentalist militancies. It is similarly evident both in religious ethnonationalist and tribal movements on the right and theologies of liberation and world transformation on the left. Here as elsewhere, the gyre of religion widens, as the daily news stories prove.

Of course, as already suggested in the reference to the consequences of medical technology, the gyre of law also widens in an ever more complex society. We can leave to others a detailed accounting of this, while simply noting that the growth of law must have many bearings on religion. I resist temptations at this point to indulge in comment in the form of a "supply-side" analysis in the growth of the numbers of lawyers. In the present context, one must be content to say that if one wanted to dwell on statistics, one would have to deal with the clerical contributions to the "widening gyre" because the number of clergy also grows. Our agenda does not call us to dwell on the subject, rich in consequences for "widening" though it may be.

VI. The Contribution of Pluralism

In American society, the one that remains our focus, the fundamental agent contributing to the widening gyres and "collisions" is realized pluralism in a free society. Given its potential for creating "mere anarchy," it is no wonder that the late Jesuit theologian John Courtney Murray pronounced that "religious pluralism is against the will of God."[14] He said this even as he averred that such pluralism was the "human condition" and would never "marvelously cease to trouble the City."[15] While not all religious thinkers and not even all Catholic theorists, go so far as Murray, he did alert them and all of us to consider how religious pluralism is itself "inherently disintegrative of all consensus and community."[16]

Pluralism, it has to be recognized, cannot be overcome in a free society. The Soviet experience from 1917 to 1989 and post-Soviet experience since then reveals that religion cannot even be successfully suppressed in an unfree one. Indeed, the sudden implosion of Soviet Communism along with its Marxist and Leninist ideology, left a philosophical and spiritual desert, a barren landscape to be filled, with, among other things, insurgent religion(s).

It is futile for anyone to yearn for the end of pluralism so there can be some measure of coherence. In the eyes and practices of the religious public, pluralism cannot be overcome because so many of them conceive their faith to be based on specific and differing divine revelations to them. The contradictory magisteria of religious bodies; the contribution differing religions make to the consensus juris in any pluralist republic; the rhetoric and enterprise of competitive religious leaders; and the free and spontaneous conversions and consents of citizens as believers, all militate against uniformity and conformity, whether these be coerced or voluntary. Today, instead, resort to religion grows, especially as other frameworks for life (e.g., communist ideology, pure eighteenth-century Enlightenment rationalism) appear exhausted. Hence, again, the "widening gyre of religion."

There have been many efforts within pluralist societies to restrain the religious gyres. In the modern period, religion was supposed to have been restricted to private life. But the religious have always, and especially recently, broken the covenant: Catholic, Jewish, mainstream, and African-American Protestants, Mormons, Muslims, other "others," and, now most dynamically, latter-day evangelicalism/fundamentalism/conservatism are taking boundary-crossing public action. Some of these moves to the public style, especially on the Christian Right, were born as a "politics of resentment" by people who were or who felt themselves to have been demeaned, overlooked, or inhibited. But their revenging movements quickly became expressive of a politics of "will to power." In such cases, the agents of the religions in question collide with others who aspire to the same kinds of power. Hence anarchy, if not always of a "mere" sort, is loosed upon the world, in the recent past from within the United States.

Around the world, religions set out to reclaim regimes entirely. This is the case in Shi'ite fundamentalist Islam, the Jewish Gush Emunim, or American Christian reconstructionism or theonomy. More modestly than do the theonomists, other evangelical forces in the United States set out to claim a significant element in politics through the use of coalition and caucus strategies. Because these religions represent rival claims, their expressiveness adds to the "widening gyre" vision and threatens the "falling apart" of the social fabric. Law also sees the development of a widening gyre and contributes to religious and legal pluralism. By definition, law sets boundaries and is capable of self-limitation, but it is expansive and expanding as well. Law today seldom appeals to divine revelation, except as in Islamic resort to shari'a, the sacred body of law. What we might call the legal magisterium is defined in republican cases by a single society-wide constitution. Any consensus juris is arrived at through experiment and pragmatic—and hence, ever more complex—resolution. The professors, writers, and schools of law also gain clout through the use of competitive forms of rhetoric and enterprise. The gyre widens, again for often good and usually natural reasons.

NOTES

1. William Butler Yeats, The Second Coming, in A. G. Stock, W. B. Yeats: His Poetry and Thought 186–87 (1964). For comment—relevant to the present context—on this widely published poem in general anthologies and in collections of Yeats's work, see id.

2. Id. at 130.

3. Id.

4. Id. at 186.

5. Id. at 187.

6. Id. at 186.

7. Romans 13.

8. Harold Berman, The Interaction of Law and Religion 24–25 (1974).

9. Id. at 23.

10. Walter Berns, The First Amendment and the Future of American Democracy 26 (1985).

11. Letter from James Madison to the Rev. Jasper Adams, in Church and State in American History 77–78 (John F. Wilson ed., 1965).

12. United States v. Macintosh, 283 U.S. 605, 625 (1930).

13. The Federalist No. 2, at 5 (John Jay) (Max Beloff ed., 2d ed. 1987).

14. John C. Murray, S.J., We Hold These Truths: Catholic Reflections on the American Proposition 23 (1960).

15. Id.

16. Id. at 73.

Chapter 3

A New Discourse and Practice

Winnifred Fallers Sullivan

> "When *I* use a word," Humpty Dumpty said, in rather a scornful tone, "it means just what I choose it to mean—neither more nor less."
>
> "The question is," said Alice, "whether you *can* make words mean so many different things."
>
> "The question is," said Humpty Dumpty, "which is to be master—that's all."
>
> Alice was too much puzzled to say anything; so after a minute Humpty Dumpty began again. "They've a temper, some of them—particularly verbs: they're the proudest—adjectives you can do anything with, but not verbs—however, *I* can manage the whole lot of them! Impenetrability! That's what *I* say!"
>
> "Would you tell me please," said Alice, "what that means?"
>
> "Now you talk like a reasonable child," said Humpty Dumpty, looking very much pleased. "I meant by 'impenetrability' that we've had enough of that subject, and it would be just as well if you'd mention what you mean to do next, as I suppose you don't mean to stop here all the rest of your life."
>
> "That's a great deal to make one word mean," Alice said in a thoughtful tone.
>
> "When I make a word do a lot of work like that," said Humpty Dumpty, "I always pay it extra."
>
> "Oh!" said Alice.
>
> —Lewis Carroll, *Through the Looking-Glass*, in *The Complete Illustrated Lewis Carroll* (1991)

In 1984, Warren Burger, then Chief Justice of the United States, writing for the majority in *Lynch v. Donnelly*,[1] declared that display of a crèche, at public expense, as a part of a public Christmas display, was not an unconstitutional establishment of religion. The decision rested, in part, on the argument that a crèche is not a religious symbol in the context of a civic Christmas display, and was being displayed in order to effect a purely secular purpose. In 1977 the Supreme Court of Japan declared that a Shinto grounds-purification ceremony, *Jichinsai*, was not a religious ceremony, and, therefore, could be constitutionally sponsored by a public body.[2] In 1988 the Japanese Court held that deification of the dead is not a religious act when performed to honor military casualties.[3]

In each of these cases, the language that the courts use to talk about religion seems to stretch the words close to the breaking point. They seem to be deliberately using words in paradoxical and contradictory ways. What can be more religious than display of a representation of the incarnation of a deity, a ritual of consecration, or an apotheosis? Like Alice, in response to the pronouncements of Humpty Dumpty, the reader suspects that there is something devious and high-handed in making words "mean so many different things."

Why *are* these courts turning traditional categories on their heads? Are these justices simply flexing their power by arbitrarily changing the meaning of words? Are they, as Humpty Dumpty coyly suggests, simply "masters" of the words? The two courts, the American and the Japanese, as well as Humpty Dumpty, can, in my view, more helpfully be seen as creatively rethinking legal and cultural categories, rather than as abusing them. Declaring these events to be secular may be the only alternative the courts see to the insistent tunnel vision of the orthodox separation of church and state, on the one hand, or a naive "accommodation"—a restoration of establishment—on the other.

The refusal by courts to use the conventional political discourse of disestablishment, examples of which could be multiplied many times over, challenges students of religion and of law to see the courts as creative, though often clumsy, constructors of a new cultural language, "opening space for cultural futures,"[4] in James Clifford's words, and to take a closer look at the subtle and slippery interplay between so-called religious and secular symbols and institutions.

In 1951, a Japanese film entitled *Rashomon*, directed by Akira Kurosawa, won the prize for best film at the Cannes Film Festival. The film tells the story of a rape and murder from the viewpoints of the three participants—a samurai, his wife, and a bandit—and from those of three bystanders. Each of the six gives a different version of the events. According to the bandit's story, he killed the husband in a duel over the wife. In the wife's story, she killed her husband because he despised her after the rape. The husband's story, related through a medium, is that he killed himself in grief over his wife's betrayal. A woodcutter, a priest, and a police agent recount their encounters with these principals. The viewer sees each version enacted. Through the testimony of the six witnesses, every detail of each of the versions is called into question. The viewer is left at the end of the picture unable to resolve the multiple stories into one.[5]

The ending of *Rashomon* sends the viewer back to the stories of the witnesses. In attempting to piece together the facts and sort out the true story, the viewer realizes that the film is about the witnesses rather than about what happened, that the truth is in the telling rather than in establishing objective reality. *Rashomon* is not a murder mystery to which there is a solution. It is a film that explores the motives of its protagonists and the subjective nature of reality. Confusion arises if the viewer seeks an answer to the wrong question.

Rashomon-fashion, the reader of the United States Supreme Court's 1984 *Lynch* decision also moves from opinion to opinion as if encountering a completely new story. The decision in *Lynch* was 5–4. There are four opinions: a majority opinion, a concurring opinion and two dissents. (Justice Blackmun's dissent, a footnote really to Justice Brennan's dissent in which he joined, is less than a page. I will not discuss it here.) Like the viewer of *Rashomon*, the reader is persuaded, in turn, by each new version but, finally, is left confused about what happened and why we care.

In the first take, Chief Justice Burger, speaking for the majority, convinces the reader that display of the crèche is a harmless bit of post-Christian cultural tinsel celebrating our common heritage, "a neutral harbinger of the holiday season."[6] Religion as divisive and exclusive is, on this reading, a part of the prehistory of America, not of its present. A concern for the dangers of enforced religious conformity or for the protection of religious freedom is regarded as misplaced, un-American, "overscrupulous," in the words of the Japanese Supreme Court. The reader—worried initially perhaps by the effect of Christmas displays on nonbelievers—is slightly embarrassed by her oversensitivity.

Moving on to Justice O'Connor's concurring opinion, the reader's concern for minority rights is revived. O'Connor says that it is not cultural Christianity but a faith in the Constitution, in political equality, that undergirds a great and free country. The crèche, whatever its meaning, and religion, whatever its kind, are not a proper part of the public conversation. In a very real sense they are irrelevant. What is relevant is how the government treats its citizens. Morality and the sacred are in the law, not in the religion.

The reader is finally left dazed by Justice Brennan's urgent and intense dissent. Once again, she shifts gears. Now the crèche appears a glowing epiphany. It is a *mysterium tremendum*,[7] an encapsulation of the Incarnation, an object of sectarian devotion displayed with sensitive propriety only in the privacy of our homes and churches. The reader is startled to be reminded that religious awe is a part of Christmas—that, for some, the crèche embodies an entire cosmology. There life is given meaning.

A cynical and superficial reading of *Rashomon* might be that Kurosawa intended to relativize truth in a nihilistic fashion. But the film can also be seen as putting into question the need to reconcile the stories. It is not that there is no truth but that it is not found by reducing the six stories to one. The witnesses, on this reading, are an inescapable part of their testimony. Each reveals himself or herself, as well as what happened.

In coming to the last two opinions in *Lynch*, the dissents, we realize that in this set of opinions we learn more about the authors and the communal discourses of which they form a part than about the nature of the crèche. We, too, realize that that was what the first two were also about. And properly so. Our constitutional task is to give meaning to the words of the First Amendment, not to give meaning to the crèche.

The Supreme Court opinions in *Lynch* offer three typical American ways to talk about religion. They are not the only ones. The judges below and the witnesses at the trial offered others. Chief Justice Burger's opinion for the majority represents one American way of talking about religion, religion as celebratory, irenic, and passive, religion with no difference—no power. It is a religion that has made its peace with law and with modern culture. Justice O'Connor's opinion represents another: Law has superseded particular religious traditions as the unifying, motivating, and explanatory force for Americans. The Constitution is its creed. Explicitly religious voices are muffled. Finally, Justice Brennan speaks from within a "dissenting" American religious tradition, seeking to hold on to the intensity of its sacramentalism while insisting on the possibility of a common public life, a secular common life. There are overlaps in these discourses. Taken together, they subvert and nuance one another, like the witnesses in *Rashomon*.

But can they provide a basis for interpretation of the First Amendment? Is the logical result of the reading of the *Lynch* opinions in these chapters that the First Amendment has become unworkable? Is religion too unreliable a category? Especially in a postmodern world? Like truth in *Rashomon*? If *anything* can be religion and if *nothing* is exclusively so, then how can the Court decide when the government is establishing it?

Modernity

Disestablishment, the separation of church and state, is a part of modernity. Like modernity, it is a product, among other events, of the Reformation and of the Thirty Years War, of what Stephen Toulmin[8] calls the Counter-Renaissance. Its historical articulation must be seen in the context of the rationalist dogmatism of the seventeenth and eighteenth centuries, the emergence of the sovereign and secular nation-state, and the distinctively modern individualist piety.

Modernity was, according to Toulmin, beginning with Descartes, a retreat from the broad and tolerant humanism of sixteenth-century Europe, the Europe of Montaigne and Shakespeare. Economic depression, disease, and war taught seventeenth-century theorists to distrust the practical philosophy of Renaissance humanism and caused them to seek, in its place, timeless universal dogmas that would transcend the violence and messiness of particular cultural situations.

Analogously, Toulmin argues that the harsh realities of the first half of the twentieth century, and the accompanying breakdown of the nation-state, are now teaching the West to mistrust the rational cosmopolis. Toulmin sees a postmodern return, at least in Europe, to a new humanism, a more tolerant, more Renaissance, view of the finitude of human beings and of their capacities.

Whereas Toulmin speaks of all Western culture as a unity, the United States is quite distinct in this respect because of its history. Its sovereign existence has been defined exclusively within and by modernity, as Toulmin understands it, so that, while rationalism plagues its institutions and culture in analogous ways, it has no Renaissance to remember or to return to. It may make more sense in the American context to see the needed postmodern correction as coming from and in sympathy with the subversive and insistent voices of the suppressed communities of America—of Native Americans, of African-Americans, of Catholics, of women, of Jews, of fundamentalists and evangelicals—challenging the rationalism and individualism of mainstream American Protestant culture.

The present confusion in the interpretation of the First Amendment provides a nice test of Toulmin's historical thesis. In Toulmin's sense the Religion Clauses were a very modern solution to a very modern problem. The hardening of doctrinal differences and the resulting intersectarian violence in the Reformation led to the need for disestablishment. Whereas religious persecution was not a modern invention, the idea that the solution was a secular public space and private religious practice is peculiarly modern and is most fully realized in the American context. The First Amendment, as understood by Jefferson and Madison, proposes a theoretically clean and apparently practical solution to the violence of the seventeenth century.

And it has worked remarkably well. Religious freedom and disestablishment are hallmarks of a country in which religion seems to flourish. Yet the stifling effect of modernity's quest for certainty and universality, marvelously evoked by Toulmin, is here, too. An increasingly heavy price of the First Amendment, of modern disestablishment, and of its underlying philosophy has been the "establishment" of an excessively narrow understanding of religion and a sometimes strained ghettoization of religion from the rest of life.

American religion is changing, and we are changing the way we understand our own religious history. Religion seems to be bursting out all over—and all across the United States—in complicated ways: fundamentalisms, new age, neopagans, Muslims, voodoo, millennialists, and others. Like the decorative flourishes of post-Miesian architecture, these religious phenomena are hard to fit into modern rational theories and institutions. These realities demand that we change how we understand the First Amendment.

In response to the changing climate of postmodern religion, the academic legal community has gone into high gear in the past five or ten years in an effort to solve the problem of the First Amendment. A great deal of serious thought has gone into reconstructing the history of the First Amendment and into attempting to propose rules of constitutional interpretation that will provide a more consistent basis for the Court's decisions in this area. Underlying and undercutting most of these proposals, however, is a religious anthropology—an understanding of the religiousness of human beings—that is rarely acknowledged and is by no means universal. The dominant discourse about religion represented in the opinions of the Court and in the academic legal literature is, even in its variety, narrowly culturally bound and needs to be expanded and made more self-critical if it is humanistically and accurately to represent American religion.

Interpreting the First Amendment

One difficulty with the present interpretation of the First Amendment is that the two clauses, the Free Exercise and the Establishment clauses, get in each other's way. The outcome of a case and the way in which religion is understood in that case can depend on whether it is framed as a Free Exercise or an Establishment clause case. All religion cases raise both issues. For example, while *Lynch* is framed as an Establishment clause case, there are Free Exercise issues raised both by removing religious symbols from public spaces and by limiting such displays to only one religious tradition. Similarly, while *Employment Division v. Smith*[9]—the peyote case—was framed as a Free Exercise case, selective exemptions to state law for members of particular religious groups raise Establishment clause issues.

One strategy for avoiding the problem of the independence of the two clauses creating conflicting precedents is to read them together into one principle and then to enforce that principle. On the whole, the principle that has been said to unite the two clauses and to be the central goal of the First Amendment is the promotion of religious freedom in a context of government neutrality. A number of serious efforts have been made to fix the meaning of neutrality and to develop methods of testing neutrality on the part of the government.[10]

Michael McConnell and Richard Posner have proposed that economic cost-benefit analysis is the best way of maximizing religious free choice and of testing the neutrality of government regulation of religion.[11] As an example, a religious exemption from laws prohibiting the sale and consumption of alcohol would be economically rational based on a balancing of the marginal impact on the religious group of no exemption and the marginal impact on the government of an exemption. McConnell and Posner disclaim any intention to articulate the "meaning" of the First Amendment. Economic analysis, they suggest, cannot decide what the First Amendment means. It can only help you sort out the hidden costs and benefits of regulating religion. Among general conclusions they reach about the economic effect of the Court's First Amendment decisions are that "[t]he courts may . . . have played a role in the precipitous decline of the mainline Protestant churches in recent decades," and that "the courts may well have increased the demand for religion by increasing the amount of religious 'product variety.'"[12]

McConnell and Posner explicitly assume that the goal of the First Amendment is a free market in religion—the deregulation of religion so as to maximize free choice. This approach risks reducing religion to an economic good and implies that economic analysis is independent of value-laden questions about the anthropology of the human person. The model for human religion they use is a very American one, one that owes its definition to the Enlightenment and to the history of evangelical Protestantism. It is one in which religion is defined as private, as a matter of individual free choice, and is worth protecting only insofar as it has utilitarian value. Although there is strong historical support for this reading of the First Amendment and for this understanding of religion as being a common one in the late eighteenth century, it is a reading with a seriously inadequate religious anthropology for late-twentieth-century Americans.

The apparent rationality and neutrality of the economic approach is, in McConnell's case, as well as in that of others, used to support the promotion of religion as a public good. It conceals a particular understanding of what religion is. It also assumes that the language that is used about religion is unimportant. All you have to do is to decide on the regulatory goal and the application of economic analysis will determine results in particular cases.

But language does matter. How the courts talk about religion is critical because the texture of the public discourse about religion creates a culture about religion. Peoples' lives are given meaning in the spaces created by words. Moreover, religion should not be viewed as either good or bad but as human. Human beings create religion. That should be acknowledged. It is not the role of the government to reify or endorse any particular version.

In his own article summarizing his view of the First Amendment for a bicentennial symposium on the Bill of Rights at the University of Chicago Law School, McConnell acknowledges that neutrality makes sense only if you know what you are being neutral about, if you know the baseline against which you are measuring neutrality. For McConnell, that baseline is also a battle line. McConnell sees the current debate about the First Amendment as boiling down to those who are for and those (the secular humanists) who are against religion: between those who, like him, believe that the Constitution mandates what he calls a pluralist approach and those who believe the Constitution mandates a secular common culture. McConnell sees "a gulf between a largely secularized professional and academic elite and most ordinary citizens, for whom religion commonly remains a central aspect of life."[13] McConnell is concerned that "[*a*]*uthentic* religion must be shoved to the margins of public life"(emphasis added).[14] McConnell summarizes his views as follows:

> The religious freedom cases under the First Amendment have been distorted by the false choice between secularism and majoritarianism, neither of which faithfully reflects the pluralistic philosophy of the Religion Clauses. Instead, the Free Exercise and Establishment Clauses should protect against government-induced uniformity in matters of religion. In the modern welfare-regulatory state, this means that the state must not favor religion over nonreligion, nonreligion over religion, or one religion over another in distributing financial resources; that the state must create exceptions to laws of general applicability when these laws threaten the religious convictions or practices of religious institutions or individuals; that the state should eschew both religious favoritism and secular bias in its own participation in the formation of public culture. This interpretation will tolerate a more prominent place for religion in the public sphere, but will simultaneously guarantee religious freedom for faiths both large and small.[15]

McConnell's represents what might be called a sophisticated proreligion stance, complete with a coopting of multiculturalism and a reading back of that contemporary political position into the eighteenth century.

If religion does not have a constitutionally privileged status, a position strongly represented by Justice Black, Philip Kurland, Justice O'Connor, and others, we will have more martyrs, and sacraments will have to take their chances in the legislatures along with everything else. Sacraments may, in fact, fare better there than in the courts. For example, the religious use of peyote is specifically exempt under the federal narcotics laws and under most state narcotics laws, as was the sacramental use of wine during Prohibition from regulations controlling the sale and consumption of alcohol.[16] The Supreme Court has found no constitutional protection for the religious consumption of peyote, and would, presumably, after *Smith*, find no such protection for the sacramental consumption of alcohol.

If, from a statist perspective, a certain kind of religion is useful to provide ceremony, to perform charitable works, and to provide Sunday schools where citizens learn to be good citizens, then, the argument runs, religion should be privileged. It is doing something for the state that would take a tremendous, perhaps impossible, effort for the state to reproduce. Or if, from a political perspective, the religions provide a location of autonomy for public-spirited criticism of the government, religion should be privileged. If, on the other hand, as many theorists would have it, religion is now seen as a free-floating cultural resource mobilized by fragmented alliances of politically like-minded individuals to express ethnic and political solidarity, perhaps it should not.[17]

Should religion be privileged? Is religion threatened? That is what is currently seen as being at stake in considering the interpretation of the First Amendment. Let us take one step back from that question.

I am inclined to agree with McConnell, although I will not make that argument here, that the First Amendment was not intended to establish nor should it be read as establishing a Deweyan secular faith.[18] A Madisonian pluralism is probably closer to what was intended and to what is currently appropriate. But, more is needed. Secularization is not the problem, or even the situation, as a growing number of sociologists acknowledge. It is not true that the country is divided between a secular elite and a religious proletariat, although these two may, on occasion, speak different languages. Michael McConnell and many other academic lawyers are indulging in inflated rhetoric on this issue by pointing fingers at the unregenerate on the Court and in the universities and by setting up this conversation as one between those who are for and those who are against religion, a classic Calvinist division between the saved and the damned.

It is not that McConnell and the others who advocate a proreligion stand are intentionally exclusive. On the contrary, they are sincerely committed to pluralism. They want to include all "authentic"[19] religious impulses. But, like the Buddhism discovered by avid Romantic researchers, the diverse American religions they celebrate all look a lot like evangelical Protestantism. A radical reorientation is necessary in order to see other peoples' religion as they see it and not to make of it what you will—particularly when you are offering to share public space with it. Virtually everyone in this debate is working with a model of religion that is historically and culturally bound in ways that are rarely fully acknowledged.

How then should the Court talk about religion? Can it find a way to articulate the rich complexity of American religious experience, mind and body, within the framework of the words of the First Amendment? The frustration of the *Lynch* decision, as Brennan observed, is that it manages to offend everyone who cares at all, "believers and non-believers alike." To the "believer," religion seems by these opinions to be trivialized, marginalized, or privatized. To the "non-believer," the opinions appear to be giving an irrational prominence to religion. Is there a way to be tolerant and humanistic about religion?

Talking and Acting about Religion

Paul Giles, in his study of American Catholic art and literature,[20] portrays the culture of the American Catholic community as a kind of subversive in-house critic of the dominant Protestant culture. Whereas the Protestant culture stresses individualism, a pastoral ideal, and an active pioneer quest, Catholic culture is skeptical about the autonomy of the individual, is largely urban and tends toward a passive impotence. In an explicitly religious context, Protestantism stresses individual belief, free choice, and freedom of conscience, while Catholicism stresses a tradition that incorporates the individual and downplays the individual's attitude toward his faith. Giles concludes that "one of the contributions of Catholicism within American culture may be to problematize the idea of what is considered natural. . . . The culture of Catholicism deconstructs the more celebrated American ideologies (Protestant, pastoral, and so on) to reveal them as provisional systems."[21] The existence of other American religious cultures, including an American Catholic culture, thus calls into question the dominant culture's understanding of religion. For the First Amendment, this means that religion in its "natural" state, the religion we are to be neutral about, cannot be limited to any one voice or way of being. It cannot be seen as only private, individual, voluntary, and a matter of conscience.

Ironically, I think, for many Protestants and for some Catholics, another contribution Giles sees Catholicism historically as making is a faith in pluralism: "[W]ithin the American Catholic idiom skepticism is the antithesis of dogmatism, not the antithesis of belief. . . . This illumination of heterogeneity subverts all rigid linear conceptions of rationality and hierarchy; instead, the variety of "Grace" is positioned as a challenge to the institution of human reason."[22] The ancestors of American Catholicism, Giles argues, in this "ontological burlesque," are Erasmus and Montaigne, not the neo-scholastics. This Catholic sensibility suggests a different kind of neutrality and a different kind of pluralism. Rather than leaving everyone alone out of a restrained Protestant respect for individual autonomy, this pluralism and this neutrality is attempted in the Joycean spirit of "Here comes everybody."[23] The in-house critique by American Catholicisms suggested by Giles could be done from the viewpoint of the many dissenting traditions of American religion, African-American, Jewish, Asian, Native American, among others. All such critiques can be seen as subversive of mainstream American cultural assumptions.[24]

What would a religiously sophisticated opinion in *Lynch* look like? It would begin by acknowledging the crèche and its accompaniment as a complex, ambiguous, and multivalent location for Pawtucket piety, a location combining shifting sacred and secular elements. The genius of the American Christmas and of its symbolism, Caplow and his coauthors argue in *All Faithful People*, is in its ability to draw together religious and secular themes that reinforce each other, particularly in the symbol of the family.[25]

Such a reading would acknowledge the diversity both within the Christian community and among religious traditions. And it would acknowledge the inherent ambivalence of religious symbols, challenging the positive utilitarian reading given by the majority in *Lynch* and many others. Even Christmas has its menacing aspect.

It is not accidental that the crèche occupies the central position in the display. It is intended to dominate. Scholars of religion have spent much time analyzing the political and ideological significance of the center in religious symbolism.[26] It should not be surprising that plaintiff Donnelly said that his reaction to the display was one of "fear."

Such a reading would not need to be an academic monograph. It *would* need to give attention to and bring to articulation strong voices in the American legal and religious traditions, voices that understand religion to be a social as well as an individual matter, to be historically and culturally given, to be material and to be embodied, and to be potentially dangerous.

In his book-length essay on the First Amendment,[27] William Lee Miller, after a biting satirical reduction of the Court's establishment clause cases, concludes that the Court's difficulty arises out of its equation of religion and race as discriminatory categories. He says:

> "Creed" and "religion" are not unchangeable givens of a human being's biological makeup or accident of birth, or unalterable past ("previous condition of servitude"), but entail—however theoretically in demographic fact—mind, and will, and choice. Religious belief is not part of the ineluctable externals of a human being's existence, but part of the substance to which he or she has an inner, changing, substantive relationship, and which, individually and communally, provides the frame to guide and shape conduct and define the great issues of living. A human being can become a heretic, a convert, or a backslider, even though in fact most do not. A believer can become an unbeliever; those who come to scoff can stay to pray; Saul of Tarsus and Martin Luther and Roger Williams and Ignatius Loyola and John Henry Newman can alter their beliefs. The young Edmund Wilson—if we may reverse and perhaps descend a little—reading a sentence of Shaw's while riding on the train back to school from Philadelphia, can feel the whole weight of his ancestral Presbyterianism lifted from his shoulders before he reaches Norristown. Religion is culture not nature; belief not biology; mind and spirit not ethnicity.[28]

It is not the Court's business, Miller argues, to get involved in "cultural politics." The Court should stay out of the competition "to articulate truth and win men's souls."

But people do not so easily divide into nature and culture.[29] And culture is not as much a matter of "mind, and will, and choice" as Miller would like. The examples he gives, looked at from an historical perspective, seem much less dramatic to us than they did to those individuals or to their communities. In many important ways Saul of Tarsus was still a hellenized Jew and Martin Luther, a Catholic monk. Roger Williams is part of the Puritan story as well as the Baptist. Newman is an Anglican hero as well as a Roman Catholic one. Even Edmund Wilson remained a Presbyterian in important ways. It does not diminish the importance of the conversions they made to say that religion is not simply a matter of individual conscience and of free choice.

The intractability of the Court's discourse on religion arises not from its failure to stay out of cultural politics. In that it has no choice. It arises from its anthropology. Religion is a given to a greater extent than Miller acknowledges. Brennan's attitude toward the crèche is not merely a decorative flourish to his freely chosen religious belief. It, and other material embodiments of the sacred, are an inescapable cultural location for his religion. Miller's understanding of religion, like that of many Protestants, is profoundly affected by American evangelical piety, a piety that locates religion in the individual mind and heart, and that sees conversion, rather than Christian nurture, as the model for making new Christians.

The religious traditions that religious studies has struggled to understand have challenged it to come to grips with a more material and varied spirituality. The traditions challenge Americans to move from religion viewed as a matter of mind and will and free choice to a view of individuals and of human culture inescapably and creatively various in a religiousness that, like other human cultural productions, involves both cultural givens and creative reinterpretation. Looking at how the religious categories play themselves out in the American political discourse can also highlight the political nature of academic discourse, the tension between the ideologies of academic and political discourses, and the problematic relationship between religious studies and Christianity.

Law and Religion

Understanding the relationship of law and religion is central to understanding American religion. As many have observed, legal structures, institutional and linguistic, have played a key role in shaping American religion. Religious structures, in turn, have played a foundational role in shaping American law and identity. This close interconnection, sometimes harmonious, often in tension, between religion and law can be seen in contexts throughout American history and across religious traditions. A high level of self-consciousness about the need to reconcile the two is also present in many of these contexts, although there are also locations in which the mutually constitutive roles of law and religion require critical retrieval.

At the same time, however, while acknowledging the tremendous influence each has had in shaping the other in this country and in the Western tradition generally, the two are caught in opposition. It is an opposition that might be traced in the Western conversation from Paul's preoccupation with the opposition of faith and law, through the reformers' concerns with faith and works. Perhaps one of the reasons it is difficult to achieve a felicitous reading of the First Amendment is that the tension is merely preserved, not transcended by it. The problem is not solved. It is acknowledged. In a sense the First Amendment embodies a tension that cannot be resolved. Religion has a special relationship to law.

The public celebration of Christmas in the United States presents a nice problem for interpreters of the First Amendment. As an event, as a cultural location for meaning, it displays a tantalizing blend of sacred and secular, public and private, religion and politics, while revealing a kaleidoscope of glimpses of the history of religion and law in the West. Any one reading seems to dissolve before one's eyes. Christmas is many things to many people. The history of the public celebration of Christmas also shows how our sensibilities have changed. Our increased uneasiness about the messages that public symbols and public events convey further destabilizes the meaning.

At the risk of being presumptuous, I submit the following introduction to a proposed opinion in the *Lynch* case—as a trial balloon. Let us start to forge a new language about religion that honors both the commitment of the First Amendment and the lived experience of American religious history.

Proposed Opinion in *Lynch v. Donnelly*

I

The parties to this action ask this Court to draw a line between the religious and the secular in order to determine the constitutionality of a part of a city's Christmas display. The City of Pawtucket, Rhode Island, erected, among other symbols of the season, a "crèche"—a diorama with life-sized figures depicting a scene immediately following the birth of Jesus of Nazareth, the founding figure of Christianity—in a public park, as a part of a civic Christmas holiday celebration. It is the nature of this crèche as a public symbol that is at issue in this case.

This Court has always been extremely reluctant to draw such lines, believing that the First Amendment religion clauses require the government to refrain from entering into theological discussions or trying to define the permissible contours of religious belief and practice. The First Amendment, however, of course, also can make sense only if the word "religion," as it appears in it, has some comprehensible referent. Whatever our reluctance, it is inescapably the difficult task of this Court to define the meaning of that word. That task is not one that can be done in a single case. It is a task that requires the careful building up of understanding and it is one that must acknowledge that such definitions—definitions of whole categories of human culture—are social products that change over time. Religion has a history that extends over the length and breadth of human history. Its definition has challenged scholars for centuries. This Court can only begin by considering this case. But it does so conscious of a host of witnesses from a rich human history.

Petitioners—the mayor and other officials of the City of Pawtucket—argue in their brief that Christmas in the United States has become a national folk festival, that Christmas as a religious holiday has been superseded by a secular celebration:

> Government celebration of Christmas is a secular activity. The American Christmas is a national folk festival which derives from the Christian celebration of the nativity. Although the nativity theme has not disappeared from the contemporary observance, it has been heavily overshadowed by the secular components of the national festival. Most of the modern secularity in Christmas is traceable, one way or another, to religious roots. But the contemporary festival is a vast conglomeration of folk customs and symbols, feasting and fraternizing, music, literature and art. The religious origins in the holiday have evolved into a secular humanism and the nativity scene has evolved into a major element of the artistic component of the national festival.
>
> The City's Christmas observance in this case is completely typical of the American folk festival. It is heavily secular in tone and content. The crèche is one symbol among the Santas and reindeer, Old English figurines, snowmen, cartoon-character cut-outs, trees, lights, bells, candles and stars. There are Christmas carols, parties, free candy and carousel rides. The entire observance is a mélange of the familiar trappings of the American Christmas season.[30]

The crèche, petitioners argue, has become secularized along with the rest of Christmas, and is, therefore, a perfectly proper part of a secular city celebration.

In its Amicus Brief supporting the petitioners' brief, the solicitor general, on behalf of the United States government, argues the opposite. The solicitor general argues that Christmas and the crèche are indeed religious but that the First Amendment permits government sponsorship of such religious symbols:

> The United States, like the City of Pawtucket and countless other state and local governments, has long participated in the celebration of the Christmas season. Congress has declared Christmas to be a national holiday, and the United States has in past years sponsored Christmas pageants that included nativity scenes. Since the days of the Pilgrims, we have devoted, as a Nation, one day every year to giving thanks to God. More broadly, the federal government has, from the earliest days of the Republic to the present, felt free to acknowledge and recognize that religion is a part of our heritage and should continue to be an element in our public life and public occasions. The United States has a deep and abiding interest in maintaining this long-standing tradition.[31]

The solicitor general seems eager to affirm the country's faith and eager not to cede what it sees as the ancient and, to its mind, constitutional, right of the state—to engage in its priestly function.

Respondents offer a third view of Pawtucket's Christmas display. They argue that, of the many objects displayed, only the crèche is religious and that it is only the presence of the crèche that gives a religious taint to what is otherwise a secular display:

> Pawtucket's crèche depicts the miraculous birth of Jesus to Joseph and the Virgin Mary in a manger in Bethlehem. It symbolically re-enacts a central event in Christian religious belief. . . . Pawtucket has placed the imprimatur of the government on a "plainly religious" belief in flat disregard of the Establishment Clause.[32]

If the crèche is removed, they argue, Pawtucket's display will be cleansed and secular—and therefore constitutional.

The District Court and the majority opinion in the Court of Appeals for the First Circuit agree with respondents. The crèche is religious but the Christmas holiday, as a government-sponsored public celebration, is secular. Judge Bownes of the First Circuit, sums up this position:

> Today's American Christmas is a result of the mixing of diverse folk customs and religious beliefs in the melting pot of the New World. Christmas has roots that are embedded in the Christian religion; its roots also extend to folk customs and pagan rites that predate the birth of Christ.
>
> The crèche, however, is tied firmly to the Christian religion; it tells the story of the birth of Christ, the Son of God. Unlike today's Christmas holiday, the crèche is not the result of the combination of folk culture and tradition. The crèche is purely a Christian religious symbol.[33]

Judge Campbell, in dissent, disagrees. Christmas cannot be divided up into sacred and secular:

> [E]ither Christmas itself, because of its inextricably intertwined religious roots, cannot constitutionally be a national holiday, in which case displays of this type here in issue would also be unconstitutional; or else Christmas is constitutional, in which case all its relevant symbols, including those depicting the nativity, are likewise constitutional, *so long as displayed for the purpose of announcing the holiday. . . .*
>
> The fact is, Christmas, with its clear religious as well as its secular roots, has become an ingrained part of our culture. Were one today to seek to make a national holiday out of such a church festival, constitutional objections might well prevail. But Christmas is water over the dam. And so, I would argue, are *all* its established symbols, including carols and crèches. To retain the holiday but outlaw these ancient symbols seems to me an empty even boorish gesture. If crèches are to be outlawed, so too should stars and carols. And, surely, the name itself—Christmas, deriving from "Christ" and "mass"—should be the first to go if the Constitution requires the eradication of any and all religious connotations![34] (Emphasis in original)

This Court is asked to choose among these positions.

Is Christmas a religious holiday? Is a crèche always or only sometimes a religious symbol? Does the presence of a crèche make Christmas more religious? How can the Court answer these questions? What does the First Amendment have to say about Christmas? The answer to these questions cannot be found in a reconstruction of eighteenth-century Christmas celebrations. Both Christmas and government have changed too much since then. Deciding this case demands that the Court pay attention to the role of religion and of government in America today. Is the public display of a crèche at Christmas by a city government at the end of the twentieth century the establishment of religion, religion as it is meant by the establishment clause of the First Amendment?

Religion is not a natural category. It has no universal meaning. Indeed, in many languages there is no word for "religion." Religion is a socially and historically constructed category. This has at least two consequences. On the one hand, the historical meaning of "religion" in the First Amendment must be seen to be a changing and culturally specific one. On the other, constructing a meaning for American religion under the First Amendment must be seen as a civic task for all Americans at the end of the twentieth century. We have a responsibility to take account of the depth and diversity of American religiousness, a diversity that is symbolized only on a very small scale by the diversity among the parties to the Court, and the judges below. We must take account and invest ourselves in it so that the concern for American religion that the Constitution demands is focused on American religion as it exists, rich and varied as it is and as it is constantly changing and being re-created. It must also be a concern that takes its cue from the Fourteenth Amendment mandate that government treat all Americans equally.

Americans face this task of attending to the meaning of religion in public life at a time when the assumptions underlying the secular state are coming into question all over the world. In India, citizenship is being remolded as Indians concerned to preserve an ancient cultural identity insist that to be Indian is, in some sense, also to be Hindu—to be part of the tradition of the Vedas. In eastern Europe communities formerly part of communist countries are searching for ways to assert their precious historical location through a self-definition in religious terms. In Africa socialist ideologies, indigenous religious traditions, and various Islams and Christianities compete to define what it is to be African. In each case the assumption that the law can and should be secular and that religion can and should be private is being questioned.

The historical study of religion teaches us that religion is of many types. Religion can be priestly or prophetic. It can celebrate the center or remain on the periphery. It can be about god or gods. Or not. It can be coextensive with culture or set itself up as separate or as in opposition. It can be about saving the individual soul or about preserving the community. It can be more about what you do or more about what you believe. It includes myth, ritual, prayer, philosophy, sacrifice, and so on. American religion is all of these.

II

While honoring the significance of religion to Americans, both today and in the past, the First Amendment, as applied to the states through the Fourteenth Amendment, requires that the government not "establish" religion. Has the City of Pawtucket done so in erecting a crèche as a part of a civic holiday display? Has it endorsed religion in general or a particular religious faith?

Like most vital symbols, the Pawtucket crèche means different things to different people at different times. Understanding must begin with acknowledging that the crèche cannot be labeled either religious or secular. It is clearly both. As is Christmas. It is also important to acknowledge that to be a folk festival or a folk symbol is not necessarily to be nonreligious. The opposition of religion to folk traditions is an inheritance of the Reformation and smacks of anti-Catholicism.

The three solutions offered by the briefs seem inadequate to the Court. Petitioners argue for the permissibility of Pawtucket's activities by eliminating the distinctions between religion and nonreligion. The First Amendment will not permit such a solution. The First Amendment insists that religion is different.

The United States argues that it is the government's role to thank God and to participate in religious celebrations. This is an ancient role of the state. The recitation of the many historical examples of government endorsement of religious expression seems rather, to us, an example of government's failure to withstand public pressure to give a privileged place to a certain kind of dominant Protestant Christianity rather than as evidence of the consitutionality of such activity.

Respondents' insistence on the unique religiousness of the crèche, like that of the district court, also seems myopic. It leaves little room for multiple religious and secular responses to what is a very common cultural symbol in the context of a multifaceted cultural and religious event.

When the government undertakes to represent the community, and to celebrate for it, when it fulfills its priestly role, it must be scrupulously careful not to do so in a way that defines persons out of the community because of their religion. The crèche is not more or less religious than the reindeer or the star. But, for more of the observers of the display, display of the crèche is seen as endorsement of an embodiment of an exclusive version of the human story. The set of cultural meanings it evokes is located in the tradition of a very specific community. The religious meaning of the rest of the display, as well as of the holiday as a whole, is more diffuse and open to a range of interpretations.

Disestablishment means that government must strive to remain secular. To be secular within the meaning of the First Amendment means to resist all efforts to narrow its meaning or to confine the meaning of religion to the interpretation of a particular tradition. It also means that secular ideologies, such as law, may not be established either.

> Put positively, disestablishment means that the courts, and all government, must see religion as powerful, universal, and varied—a human cultural creation that cannot be confined to a particular religious philosophy or practice. It is the obligation of government to resist any religious expression that reifies a particular interpretation of what religion is. . . .

The First Amendment requires the Supreme Court to talk about religion. It also mandates disestablishment. Disestablishment requires the deconstruction of religion, of any particular religion, while it also requires the acknowledgment of religion as a universal, diverse, and powerful human creation. The First Amendment asks of all of us that we constantly reimagine the relationship of religion and law in this country.

A new discourse about the relationship of law and government must begin with a law that is secular because religion is disestablished. A public conversation about religion requires attention to the variety and complexity of human religiousness. The solution here identified with Justices Black and O'Connor is unconstitutional to the extent that it establishes law as religion. No particular construction of what religion is may be established, as Justice Brennan does in *Lynch*. And, finally, the power and distinctiveness of human religiousness must be acknowledged and honored, as the majority opinion in *Lynch* fails to do. Somehow, by giving our attention to what we mean by religion, we must acknowlege the religiousness of Americans without establishing it.

Attention has been called in a number of different contexts to the problematic nature of writing—of texts—of reducing life to words. Johannes Fabian has carefully shown the ways in which anthropologists, through various stylistic habits of their writing, distance themselves from the lives of the people they write about.[35] Michel Foucault has made us all painfully conscious of the insidious combination of power and limitation in our language.[36]

Religion and law, although largely concerned, particularly in the Western context, with the production and study of texts, share an inescapable materialism. Each has real effects on the material circumstances of peoples' lives. For many Christians, the Incarnation is more than an idea expressed in words. It transformed the world and continues to transform peoples' lives. It has implications that are acted on and it colors perception of the material world. A crèche displayed is not simply the illustration of a text. Law, too, is embodied not just in statute books and case reports but in the people whose lives it shapes and distorts. The violence and the power of religion and of law are evident in the physical shape of human existence. The possibilities for peace and understanding are there embodied also.

Johannes Fabian, Charles Long, and Lawrence Sullivan have all called for a form of praxis as a way of overcoming the distances and distortions caused by the texts of cultural studies: texts interpreting other peoples' lives.[37] Fabian calls for the dialectic of "communicative praxis."[38] Long calls for "exchange."[39] Sullivan calls for "the end of the text."[40] In different ways each seeks to turn attention from the words to the ways words are used to enslave, but each also seeks to transcend the enslaving power of words in a shared community.

In interpreting the words of the Constitution respecting religion, the United States Supreme Court has an opportunity to acknowledge the material circumstances and embodiedness of religion and of law. It has an opportunity to act about religion in a way that embraces religious actors—to create a practical discourse about human religiousness.

Centering on a close examination of the written opinions in one American case concerned with the appropriate relationship between law and religion, *Lynch v. Donnelly*, I have here offered a reading of those opinions as revealing a paradox of postmodern industrial society: religious disestablishment, the separation of church and state, while it remains essential to pluralistic civil society, is, as conceived in the language and culture of the Constitution makers, impossible.[41] Government cannot be purged of religion, though it is not through want of trying.

Although each of the opinions in *Lynch* contains important perceptions about the relationship of law and religion in American society, each is also handicapped by a discourse about religion, created largely in the context of the Enlightenment and of mainstream American Protestantism, that is inadequate to give an account of the religiousness of Americans. The inadequacy of that discourse about religion, in turn, hobbles the development of a shared public discourse about the meaning of the First Amendment religion clauses.

Can we, by giving attention to the circumstances and variety of the lives of Americans, as religious people with a profound commitment to the rule of law, generate a richer discourse and practice about religion in American public life? Can we take Humpty Dumpty's advice, and, through this commitment, in effect, "pay the words extra"?

NOTES

This essay is a reworking (for clarity—not for updating) of the final chapter of my book *Paying the Words Extra: Religious Discourse in the Supreme Court of the United States* (Cambridge: Harvard University Center for the Study of World Religions, 1994). The book, through a close reading of the opinions in *Lynch v. Donnelly* (465 U.S. 668 [1983]) and a comparison of those opinions with the opinions of the Japanese Supreme Court in the Nakaya case (Showa 63 [1988] June 1. Showa 63 refers to the 63d year of the reign of Emperor Hirohito. All Japanese government documents are dated by reign year.) argues that the confusion in the American Court's First Amendment jurisprudence is caused in part by the inadequacy of its language about religion.

I would like to thank Alexandra Brown and Margaret Fallers for their repeated and helpful rereadings of this essay.

1. 465 U.S. 668 (1983).
2. Showa 52 [1977] July 13.
3. Showa 63 [1988] June 1.
4. James Clifford, *The Predicament of Culture* (Cambridge: Harvard University Press, 1988), 15.
5. A transcript of the film and reprints of contemporary reviews may be found in Donald Richie, ed., *Rashomon* (New Brunswick: Rutgers University Press, 1987).

6. 465 U.S. at 727. These words characterizing the majority opinion are from Justice Blackmun's dissenting opinion.

7. Rudolf Otto, *The Idea of the Holy*, 2d ed., trans. John W. Harvey (Oxford: Oxford University Press, 1950), 12.

8. Stephen Toulmin, *Cosmopolis: The Hidden Agenda of Modernity* (Chicago: University of Chicago Press, 1990).

9. 494 U.S. 872 (191).

10. See, for example, Philip B. Kurland, *Religion and the Law: Of Church and State and the Supreme Court* (Chicago: Aldine, 1961); and Douglas Laycock, "Formal, Substantive, and Disaggregated Neutrality," *DePaul Law Review* 39 (1990): 993.

11. Michael W. McConnell and Richard A. Posner, "An Economic Approach to Issues of Religious Freedom," *University of Chicago Law Review* 56 (Winter 1989): 1–60.

12. Ibid., 59.

13. Michael W. McConnell, "Religious Freedom at a Crossroads," *University of Chicago Law Review* (Winter 1992): 115, 126.

14. Ibid., 127. See, also, Stephen Carter, *The Culture of Disbelief: How American Law and Politics Trivialize Religious Devotion* (New York: Basic Books, 1993), for a lengthy and impassioned argument of this position.

15. McConnell, "Religious Freedom at a Crossroads," 194.

16. 21 C.F.R. sec. 130.31 (1989), National Prohibition Act, Title II, sec. 3, 41 Stat. 308.

17. N. J. Demerath, III, and Rhys Williams, "Secularization in a Community Context: Tensions of Religion and Politics in a New England City," *Journal for the Scientific Study of Religion* 31 (December 1992): 189–206.

18. For the view that the Constitution established a Deweyan common faith, see Kathleen M. Sullivan, "Religion and Liberal Democracy," *University of Chicago Law Review* 59 (Winter 1992): 195–223.

19. McConnell, "Religious Freedom at a Crossroads," 127.

20. Paul Giles, *American Catholic Arts and Fictions: Culture, Ideology, Aesthetics* (Cambridge: Cambridge University Press, 1992).

21. Ibid., 526, 531.

22. Ibid., 508.

23. Ibid., 506.

24. Another related strategy is the widespread effort in American church history in the past twenty years to retrieve the other traditions that make up American religion, to problematize the canon of American religious history. See, for example, Catherine L. Albanese, *America, Religions, and Religion* (Belmont, Calif.: Wadsworth, 1981); Albert Raboteau, *Slave Religion: The "Invisible Institution" in the Antebellum South* (Oxford: Oxford University Press, 1980); and the myriad efforts to make a space for the others of American religion, including Native American religious traditions.

25. Theodore Caplow et al., *All Faithful People: Change and Continuity in Middletown's Religion* (Minneapolis: University of Minnesota Press, 1983), 192. See, also, Adam Kuper, "The English Christmas and the Family: Time Out and Alternative Realities," in Daniel Miller, ed., *Unwrapping Christmas* (Oxford: Clarendon Press, 1993).

26. See, for example, Jonathan Z. Smith, *Map Is Not Territory: Studies in the History of Religions* (Leiden: E. J. Brill, 1978).

27. William Lee Miller, *The First Liberty: Religion and the American Republic* (New York: Paragon House, 1985).

28. Ibid., 320.

29. Clifford Geertz, "The Growth of Culture and the Evolution of Mind," in *The Interpretation of Cultures* (New York: Basic Books, 1973).

30. Petitioners' Brief at 8.

31. Brief for the United States at 1–2.

32. Respondents' Brief at 21–22.

33. 691 F. 2d at 1037.

34. Ibid. at 1038.

35. Johannes Fabian, *Time and the Other: How Anthropology Makes Its Object* (New York: Columbia University Press, 1983). See, also, Clifford Geertz, *Works and Lives: The Anthropologist as Author* (Stanford: Stanford University Press, 1988).

36. Michel Foucault, *The Order of Things: An Archaeology of the Human Sciences* (New York: Vintage Books, 1970).

37. Fabian, *Time and the Other*; Charles H. Long, "The University, the Liberal Arts, and the Teaching and Study of Religion," and Lawrence E. Sullivan, "'Seeking an End to the Primary Text' or 'Putting an End to the Text as Primary,'" in Frank E. Reynolds and Sheryl L. Burkhalter, eds., *Beyond the Classics? Essays in Religious Studies and Liberal Education* (Atlanta: Scholars Press, 1990).

38. Fabian, *Time and the Other*, 71.

39. Long, "The University, the Liberal Arts and the Teaching and Study of Religion," 37.

40. Sullivan, "'Seeking an End to the Primary Test,'" 44.

41. This point has often been made by cultural critics of modernity. For example, in his new introduction to *Tokugawa Religion: The Cultural Roots of Modern Japan*, rev. ed. (New York: Free Press, 1985), Robert Bellah criticizes his own earlier work, which saw religion as a means on the road to modernity and calls for a consideration of "religion as religion." The "other" of modernity, religion, has returned to the center for postmodern thinkers of many stripes.

Chapter 4

The Reverend John Witherspoon and the Constitutional Convention

Marci A. Hamilton

> Cousin America has run off with a Presbyterian parson and that was the end of it.
>
> —Horace Walpole

The connections between theology and the constitutional Framers' choices have been left surprisingly untouched. Some legal scholars have asked what theological theories might explain the religion clauses, but too few have looked to the theological underpinnings of the Constitution's other requirements.[1] There are times when one is tempted to wonder whether the Establishment Clause's rule against favoring particular religions has so permeated the legal scholars' mind-set that we have lost the ability to draw the connections between the great theologians and our scheme of government. Or perhaps the omission of theological education in the universities is to blame. Whatever the cause, it is a striking omission.

There has been no lack of inquiry into the philosophical sources of the Constitution. John Locke, Thomas Hobbes, and Montesquieu, to name just a few, have been the subject of extended analysis. Of course, the *Federalist Papers*, the pro-Constitution propaganda that was written by Alexander Hamilton, John Jay, and James Madison, have been thumbed to death.

At the same time that constitutional scholars have focused on nonsectarian sources to explain the Constitution's structure, a small cadre of Presbyterian Church historians has been making the claim that the Presbyterian Church structure influenced the Framers' structural decisions. In fact, there are strong parallels between the Presbyterian Church structure and the governmental scheme finally chosen by the constitutional Framers.[2] Some have gone as far as to claim that the Presbyterian tradition forms the archetype for the American constitutional structure.[3] Others have rejected the claim that Presbyterian precepts were the sole cause of the representative scheme chosen in the Constitution.[4] On any of these accounts, "whatever may be said of the similarities and the differences between the two constitutions, both were the result of those ideas of representative popular government of which [the Presbyterian] Synod was the outstanding illustration and the most influential advocate throughout the colonial period."[5] There is much to be learned about the Constitution's structuring of representative democracy by examining Presbyterian Church polity theory and structure.[6]

This essay argues that at least one Presbyterian theologian at the time of the framing played a key role in shaping how the Framers approached the task of reforming the United States government. Of particular interest is their choice of republicanism, rule by elected representatives, over direct democracy, rule by the people. That Presbyterian is the Reverend John Witherspoon, president of the College of New Jersey (later to become Princeton University) and mentor to James Madison.[7]

The Reverend John Witherspoon and Early American Political Development

The Reverend John Witherspoon was a widely respected Calvinist theologian who was persuaded to leave a prominent position in Scotland to head the College of New Jersey. Witherspoon brought a Calvinist sensibility to politics and played an influential role in America's history from the Revolution through the crafting of the Constitution. An ordained Presbyterian minister and president of the College of New Jersey, Witherspoon also served in the Continental Congress, where he signed the Declaration of Independence, and later in the New Jersey state legislature as well as New Jersey's ratifying convention for the Constitution.[8] He was an "amalgamation of the older power of Calvinistic religion and the newer political spirit. Other clergymen may have been as active as he in fostering the spiritual temper of the Revolutionary Days; but he was the only clergyman in America to cap that activity by serving the country in the Continental Congress, and by aiding it to shape its new national individuality."[9]

Even his enemies conceded his importance to the American cause. One British officer wrote: "An account of the present face of things in America would be very defective indeed if no mention was made of this political firebrand, who perhaps had not a less share in the Revolution than Washington himself. He poisons the minds of his young students and through them the Continent."[10] Witherspoon's contribution certainly did not end with the Revolution. He foresaw the political revolution that would displace the Articles of Confederation with the Constitution, saying that America was headed toward a "revolt against Congress and the formation of a new government."[11]

Witherspoon and his Calvinist principles also had their influence on the Constitutional Convention in two important ways. First, he was the mentor to James Madison (as well as other Framers), who declared that Witherspoon had prescribed to him "a strong dose of Calvinism."[12] The lessons learned at the College of New Jersey certainly were not limited to secular topics; the curriculum included mandatory daily chapel attendance, for example.[13] Second, at the same time that the convention was being held in Philadelphia, the Presbyterian Church was crafting its new constitution, also in Philadelphia. The two products are quite similar in their choice of governing structure. Witherspoon was the chair of the committee appointed to revise the Presbyterian constitution. Hence, his contribution to the atmospherics contributing to the convention's product deserves close scrutiny.

Witherspoon's Theories on Polity Organization

For Witherspoon, the Reformation stood as a visible backdrop to America's rejection of British rule and its establishment of a new form of government. The Reformation was remembered as a crusade to return the corrupted Christian church to its purer roots. Likewise, the Revolution was cast as a response to tyranny that was intended to return the people of the states to a truer path. In a sermon delivered at Princeton on May 17, 1776, Witherspoon made this analogy between the birth of America and the Reformation:

> [A]t the time of the Reformation when religion began to revive, nothing contributed more to facilitate its reception and increase its progress than the violence of its persecutors. Their cruelty and the patience of the sufferers naturally disposed men to examine and weigh the cause to which they adhered with so much constancy and resolution. At the same time also, when they were persecuted in one city, they fled to another and carried the discoveries of Popish fraud to every part of the world. It was by some of those who were persecuted in Germany that the light of the Reformation was brought so early into Britain.
>
> . . . . [T]he violent persecution which many eminent Christians met with in England from their brethren, who called themselves Protestants, drove them in great numbers to a distant part of the world where the light of the gospel and true religion were unknown.[14]

Later in the sermon, Witherspoon echoed this Reformation theme of the weak but courageous battling against powerful tyrants, invoking the biblical story of David, whom he described as a "stripling with his sling and his stone," and Goliath, "the champion armed in a most formidable manner."[15] Like the Reformation, "the cause in which America is now in arms is the cause of justice, of liberty, and of human nature."[16] In this way, he framed the Revolution as a holy war, one the faithful could not forgo without imperiling their salvation. The task that remained after the war was the reconstruction of a viable government. Witherspoon's lectures focused on how to construct a government that would best serve the cause of liberty.

Witherspoon lectured his students on the different types of government under the heading of "moral philosophy." By moral philosophy, he did not mean a philosophy necessarily divorced from religious principles. Rather, he stated that the rules of moral philosophy, which are the product of reason, do not necessarily contradict or displace religion but rather the true rules are "coincident with the word of God."[17] He criticized the Hutchinsonians for believing that all knowledge comes from revelation. The scripture does not "teach us every thing."[18] Reason, rather, is a God-given ability for divining moral philosophy. Revealing a bias toward Calvinist systematic theology, he divided moral philosophy into ethics and politics, and assigned jurisprudence to the politics branch.[19]

Witherspoon believed that the "end of the union should be the protection of liberty."[20] He identified four qualities of a good government: "(1.) Wisdom to plan proper measures for the public good. (2.) Fidelity to have nothing but the public interest in view. (3.) Secrecy, expedition, and dispatch in carrying measures into execution. And, (4.) Unity and concord, or that one branch of the government may not impede, or be a hindrance to another."[21] In short, wisdom, fidelity to the public interest, efficiency, and community. According to Witherspoon, no one simple form of government was capable of achieving all, but the government that did achieve all four ends would ensure "liberty."

In a section entitled "of the different forms of government," Witherspoon described the different building blocks of government. He divided the most basic forms of government into three categories: monarchy, aristocracy, and democracy. Witherspoon did not believe that nations must or did choose only one form or the other but, rather, that these "simple forms" could be combined "in equal or in different proportions."[22] His evenhanded analysis of the different basic forms of government invited the listener to experiment with the forms and, also, to analyze any form of government as a complex in the context of understanding that certain qualities make a government good.

The presumption that governments were complex forms of basic building blocks paved the way for the Framers, who were charged with the job of "fixing" the Articles of Confederation. By laying out the building blocks and identifying the qualities of good governments, he laid the groundwork for the Framers' overt experimentation with various building blocks at the convention. Witherspoon thus gave his students intellectual tools that would permit them to analyze past governments and the model they built in the course of the convention, but he also gave them guidance on the end to be achieved.

Each form—by itself—had its strengths and its weaknesses. Witherspoon defined monarchy as that system where the "supreme power is vested in one person."[23] He ranked monarchy high in terms of efficiency but criticized it for offering no guarantee of "wisdom or goodness."[24] It was "another name for tyranny, where the arbitrary will of one capricious man disposes of the lives and properties of all ranks."[25] Aristocracy, or the employ of persons of the "first rank" to govern, exceeded the other two forms for wisdom but completely failed to ensure fidelity to the people's interest or unity.[26] It "always ma[de] vassals of the inferior ranks."[27] Democracy was better than either monarchy or aristocracy in ensuring fidelity to the public good, but it failed to secure wisdom, community, and utterly failed in efficiency.[28] "Pure democracy," or direct rule by the people, could not last for long, because it was "subject to caprice and the madness of popular rage."[29] Moreover, the people tended to trust their leaders with "such power" that they could make the people serve their whims.[30] In short, "none of the simple forms [of government] are favourable to [liberty]."[31] He thus led his listeners to the conclusion that every form of good government "must be complex."[32]

Witherspoon offered a threefold prescription for crafting good governments, each of which was followed at the convention. First, it should be assumed that all rulers, including the people if they were rulers, would be tempted to abuse their powers.[33]

From his earliest sermons, he emphasized the "preliminary truth" that all men are sinners and "liable to the stroke of [God's] justice."[34] What is the "history of past ages," he asked, "but the history of human guilt?"[35] His was not solely a pessimistic view, however. He was neither a Hobbesian or an early Camus. Rather, he expressed the Calvinist view that virtuous rulers could appear, but that one should expect all to be tempted to forsake virtue for power. Thus, any form of government *could* produce virtue and happiness or tyranny.[36]

Second, liberty (his synonym—like John Calvin's—for good government) was achievable if the various elements of government were balanced so that one element would check another.[37] In other words, no one part of the government should be permitted to hold overweening power but, rather, should have just enough to carry out its duties in the interest of the public good and no more. He thought there should be an overarching balance to the entire scheme.

Balance implies movement and change on either side of the fulcrum. Change is an essential thesis in the Calvinist construct. A constitution (whether for a government or a church) cannot be eternal. It is, after all, drafted by imperfect humans. A constitution, rather, has its "old age and its period."[38] Thus, constitutions inevitably will undergo change. They may differ in longevity, but none can provide the final answer to how man shall be governed. Reflecting this precept, the Presbyterian constitution self-consciously refers to the church as "reformed, always reforming,"[39] just as the Constitution contains within itself the means of its own alteration through ratification.

Third, these mutually balanced elements must be interdependent to some degree so that they would not whirl away on their own orbits.[40] Power must be divided and distributed evenly throughout, but one had to guard against each center of power separating completely from the others. There must be some necessity binding the mutually independent forces together.

This mix—distrust combined with hope, balance, and interdependence—was Witherspoon's prescription for civil liberty. All of the forms of government could produce virtue and happiness, but only this mix of elements could ensure liberty. And why was liberty so precious? Because it alone "put in motion all the human powers." It was the "nurse of riches, literature, and heroism."[41]

Witherspoon not only named for his students the building blocks of government and suggested how they ought to be combined to produce good government, he also prescribed a pragmatic approach to the problem of crafting a new government. He rejected the notion that one ought to "reason downward from metaphysical principles."[42] Rather, he believed it was "safer" to reason by "trac[ing] facts upwards."[43] Thus, the man who would formulate good government would do best to take into account the facts in front of him, to take seriously the lessons taught by the past. By pointing the direction away from Platonic forms or from crystalline metaphysical concepts, he drove the inquiry away from idealism and toward pragmatic solutions to experienced problems. The forms of government were not to be vapid structures to be brought together by dilettantes with no reference to political realities. To the contrary, all of one's reason—both practical and theoretical—was to be brought to bear on the problem posed. The convention debates reflect this attitude to an interesting degree. While the Framers were fond of referring to governmental structures from history, they did not limit their debates to the construction of a merely metaphysically sound structure. Rather, they borrowed from the experiences in the post-Revolutionary era to reject rule by the people and from the experiences of the English mixed government. Throughout, they assumed any entity in the society could abuse its power.

While Witherspoon was instructing his students on the Calvinist principles that should drive polity formation from his perspective, there was a lively debate between Presbyterians and Congregationalists regarding the proper church structure. Among others, one Presbyterian minister "poured pages of inky contempt on Congregational democracy," arguing against its "localism, independence, [and] individualism."[44] Just as John Calvin had, the colonial Presbyterians disdained anarchy almost as much as tyranny. Moreover, they saw direct parallels between the structural necessities of church and civil government. Representative government—as opposed to the direct democracy of the Congregationalists—was necessary in both spheres in order to avoid anarchy and even licentiousness:

> Man's depraved apostate Condition renders Government needful. Needful both in the State and the Church. In the former without Government Anarchy wou'd soon take place with all its wild and dire Effects and Men wou'd be like the Fishes of the Sea where the greater devour the less. Nor is Govern[ment] in the Church less needful than in the State and this for the same Reason.[45]

Witherspoon "spoke and worked for representative democracy in church and state [and] believed the state was to be governed by its elected representatives according to the general welfare of the whole people and not by a direct democracy in which the whole body of citizens gather as a kind of 'town meeting' to make effective their general will."[46] While direct democracy was unacceptable to Presbyterians,[47] equally so was a bishopric order. The Presbyterian representative system mediates between unfettered, tyrannical rule and anarchical democracy. The American Presbyterian Church's constitution reflects the preference for representation over direct democracy and for responsible leaders: "Presbyters [representatives within the church] are not simply to reflect the will of the people, but rather to seek together to find and represent the will of Christ. Decisions shall be reached in governing bodies by vote, following opportunity for discussion, and a majority shall govern."[48] In short, representatives are called to a higher vision than the will of the people.

Presbyterian representatives, though, are not delegated unlimited power. Rather, their power derives from the people of the churches and they have "no power but that intrusted to them under the laws."[49]

Witherspoon was chosen as the chair of the committee to frame the Presbyterian constitution. Some have asserted that "in framing the constitution of the Church his opinions were all but dominant."[50] This may be a bit hyperbolic, for it appears that he did not even attend all of the meetings discussing the framing. There is little question, though, that his vision of the proper polity was borne out by the constitution drafted, that he was a highly respected member of the committee, and therefore that he likely had significant influence on the product even though not physically present at every committee meeting.

In the Presbyterian system he helped to construct, the congregation elects a group of laymen to be "ruling elders." Along with the minister, they form the "session."[51] Several sessions are then combined into a ruling body labeled the "presbytery," which makes governing decisions. For most decisions, the presbyteries govern, though appeal can be taken to the "synod" or the "general assembly," both of which are composed of elected representatives from the presbyteries, the main difference being that the general assembly comprises representatives from all of the presbyteries in the system, and the synods are regional.[52] In this way, the scheme echoes the state/federal divide being contemplated at the federal Constitutional Convention.

As did the federal constitutional scheme being crafted at the same time, the Presbyterians rejected direct democracy in their constitution. The people's role was one of participation through election of their representatives rather than lawmaking. The Presbyterian scheme is premised on a belief in the "right of the Christian laity to participate, through its chosen representatives, in the government of the church."[53] Thus, "authority [is] vested, not in individuals, such as bishops, but in representative [entities called presbyters]."[54]

For the Presbyterian, the people's representatives are the people's trustees and answer to a higher call than the collective voice of the people. Once elected, the presbyters are not subject to a people's right to instruct or limited by the views of the majority of electors: "Presbyters are not simply to reflect the will of the people, but rather to seek together to find and represent the will of Christ."[55]

Witherspoon thought these principles of representation properly applied to the American government as well. In a statement that applies as readily to the Presbyterian Church he helped construct as to the federal Constitution, he stated that there is a "double duty—that of the people who choose their rulers, and that of the representatives to whom is entrusted the exercise of this delegated authority."[56]

Calvinist theory has never limited itself solely to organization of the church structure. It is the mark of Calvinist, and especially Presbyterian, theory that it has political application. The colonial era was the high point for the spread of the precepts of American Presbyterianism through church as well as secular government. "Nothing in colonial life was alien to the pioneers of this Church. No part of human life fell outside the reign of God and the responsibility of the Church."[57] Thus, Witherspoon served in positions of honor in the state and federal governments as readily as he served as the leader of American Presbyterianism and president of its most influential college.

The era of the framing of both constitutions was propititious for the Presbyterian-style structure to achieve prominence over the Congregationalist town meeting–style democracy. In response to the British monarchy, many of the states had stripped the executive of any real power and placed all of the government's political power in the branch closest to the people, the legislative branch. If there were ever to be a moment in history favoring rule by the people it would have been in the heady days following the Revolution. Without a significant check on their exercise of power, however, the state legislatures had degenerated into cabals rather than deliberative lawmaking bodies.[58] Thus, direct democracy seemed less attractive than it might have earlier, and Witherspoon's message of distrust, limiting power, and balance found fertile ground.

Presbyterian Precepts at the Constitutional Convention

There was a decided Presbyterian presence at the Constitutional Convention. Both numbers and the prominence of some Presbyterian members show the likelihood of this influence on the choices made. Six of the Framers were Presbyterian, with Hugh Williamson of North Carolina a Presbyterian minister.[59] Ten, two of whom were Presbyterian, were educated at the states' preeminent Presbyterian college, the College of New Jersey.[60] Four others appear to have had some meaningful contact with Presbyterianism.[61] Of those Framers who attended the College of New Jersey, five studied under the Reverend John Witherspoon while he was president of the College, including James Madison and William Churchill Houston, who became a professor at the college.[62] The themes of his lectures resonate in the convention debates.

At the Constitutional Convention, James Madison summarized the states' experience under a system dominated by the legislature:

> Experience had proved a tendency in our governments to throw all power into the legislative vortex. The Executives of the States are in general little more than Cyphers; the legislatures omnipotent. If no effectual check be devised for restraining the instability & encroachments of the latter, a revolution of some kind or other would be inevitable.[63]

The state constitutions, however, had swung the pendulum too far toward the legislature. The post-Revolutionary state constitutions had set in place governmental schemes that proved legislatures were difficult to control. "The legislature will continually seek to aggrandize & perpetuate themselves; and will seize those critical moments produced by war, invasion or convulsion for that purpose."[64] The legislature was characterized as home to "intrigue and cabal" and "corruption."[65] In sum, the legislature—unchecked by other institutions—was likely to become mired in petty politics and the pursuit of power at the expense of the polity.

The Framers, thus, felt duty bound to construct a system that generated a better balance of power between branches than the states had achieved.[66] The legislature, as the branch closest to the people, would remain the seat of lawmaking, but the executive would be vested with significant powers.[67] The two branches would check each other and thus render the balance necessary to forestall tyranny.

If direct democracy ever had a chance of being enshrined in the United States Constitution, that chance was lost when the post-Revolution state legislatures abused their powers and sank into a morass of politics. Democracy had its golden moment immediately following the Revolution.[68] In the glow of the Revolution's defiance to monarchical authority, the only justification for turning to the legislature, rather than the people themselves, was that direct democracy was impracticable.[69] Had the legislatures proved reliable, the next logical step could have been endorsement of direct democracy to the extent practically feasible.

Yet, the Framers came to the convention persuaded that direct democracy could not work. They feared the "excesses of democracy."[70] Indeed, they brought to the convention utter disrespect for the people, whom they characterized as "blind," uninformed, and ignorant.[71] For obvious reasons, the *Federalist Papers*, which were propaganda aimed at persuading the people to ratify the Constitution, did not repeat the vitriol heaped on the people at the convention.[72] Despite the *Federalist Papers'* relative silence on the point, the debates at the convention strongly suggest that the Constitution rests on the presupposition that the people are not fit to rule by themselves.

The Framers assailed democracy as the ruination of the confederation.[73] Far from being persuaded by the post-Revolutionary experience that democracy was a viable political structure, they came armed with the understanding that democracy must be mediated. Moreover, it must be mediated not only by a legislature but also by an executive with true power. They rejected direct democracy not only for the federal government but also for the states.[74]

The Framers perceived themselves to be architects of a reformed government that corrected the errors of the past. They intended to improve upon the democratic schemes of antiquity and England.[75] Both monarchy and direct democracy (town meeting–style democracy) were rejected as unacceptable and unworkable, respectively.[76] Instead, they settled upon a scheme of legislative and executive representation complemented by a judiciary that would decide particular cases and controversies.

The three structural options—monarchy, direct democracy, and representation—are echoed in post-Reformation church structures: (1) the episcopal structure, or government by bishops; (2) the congregationalist structure, or government by the masses; and (3) the presbyterian structure, or government by duly elected representatives.[77] All three were evident in the states, each with their own particular strongholds, and each was well represented at the Constitutional Convention.[78]

In the wake of the Revolution, only a very few of the Framers favored monarchy in any form.[79]

The Framers also rejected direct democracy, or rule by the people. The Constitution places no lawmaking power in the hands of the people. Even though the town meeting–style of democracy was plainly visible to the Framers in the New England colonies and in Congregationalist churches, as well as in the Greek system of democracy referred to more than once during the convention, the Framers rejected such a system. While the Ninth and Tenth Amendments eventually stated that the people get the Constitution's "leftovers," the powers and rights not mentioned in the Constitution, the Constitution plainly structured the process of lawmaking to filter the people's views.

It was a Presbyterian-style representative system the Framers settled upon, and for all the same reasons the Presbyterians themselves had alighted on representation: the infeasibility of direct democracy, a fear of anarchy, an interest in accountability, a belief in balancing society's powers, and perhaps most important, the fundamental belief that all grants of power carry with them the temptation to abuse. Even the people cannot be trusted. The Constitution echoes Witherspoon's prescriptions by employing practical political insights and a Calvinist-inspired republican form of government to construct the Constitution's representation scheme.

Conclusion

An examination of Witherspoon's work brings new light to the attitudes and approaches brought to the convention and to the Constitution itself. The Constitution's representative structure appears to have been influenced by the Reverend John Witherspoon and the Presbyterian concepts he delivered through his teaching and through his lengthy and distinguished public service. As a result, when the Framers sat down to the task of reforming the Articles of Confederation, many, including the most influential, seem to have looked through the lens of reformed theology.

Theology, on this account, informed not only the constitutional relationship between church and state but also the constitutional relationship between the people and their rulers. So much for the theories that would seat theology and theologians on the sidelines of legal history and constitutional scholarship.

NOTES

1. Some of the best work to date can be found in John Witte's exploration of the Puritan contribution to constitutionalism. *See, e.g.*, John Witte, Jr., *How to Govern a City on a Hill: The Early Puritan Contribution to American Constitutionalism*, 39 EMORY L.J. 41 (1990).

2. RANDALL BALMER & JOHN R. FITZMIER, THE PRESBYTERIANS 39 (1993) [hereinafter BALMER & FITZMIER].

3. *Id. See* FREDERICK W. LOETSCHER, ADDRESS ON THE 200TH ANNIVERSARY OF THE ADOPTING ACT 9–10 (1814) [hereinafter LOETSCHER].

4. *See* generally LEONARD TRINTERUD, THE FORMING OF AN AMERICAN TRADITION: A RE-EXAMINATION OF COLONIAL PRESBYTERIANISM (1949).

5. LOETSCHER, *supra* note 3, at 10; *see also* ROBERT MCAFEE BROWN, THE PRESBYTERIANS 7 (1966) [hereinafter BROWN] ("Presbyterians, then, represent that family within Protestant Christendom that owes its distinctive emphases to the Calvinist wing of the Reformation, and whose form of government (or 'polity') is based on the representative rule of elders or 'presbyters.'").

6. 3 THE COMPLETE WORKS OF REV. THOMAS SMYTH: THE TRUE ORIGIN AND SOURCE OF THE MECKLENBURG AND NATIONAL DECLARATION OF INDEPENDENCE 35 (J. Wm. Flinn ed., R. L. Bryan Co. 1908) (1847) [hereinafter WORKS OF REV. THOMAS SMYTH] (stating that the Presbyterian "system of polity" was being devised "at a time when the general principles of government . . . [were] more thoroughly and anxiously discussed than at any other period since the settlement of this country. It was during this time when the sages of America were employed in framing the Federal constitution. . . . And the men who drew up this plan of government for the church, were, many of them at least, men deeply versed in civil and ecclesiastical history; and who had borne no inconsiderable part in the eventful period which preceded. Perhaps this may in some measure account for the striking similarity which occurs in the fundamental principles of [the Presbyterian] polity, and the form of government adopted by the United States of America.").

7. Though the focus of this essay is on Witherspoon, I do not mean to give the impression that he was the only Presbyterian educator who could have played or did play an important role through the Revolution to the framing of the Constitution. Francis Allison, who taught at New London Academy and the College of Philadelphia, also played a significant role as a Presbyterian teacher of moral philosophy to those who "shaped the destinies of eighteenth century American resistance to British authority and the new American nation which was born thereof." *See* James L. McAllister, Jr., *Francis Allison and John Witherspoon: Political Philosophers and Revolutionaries*, 54 J. PRESBY. HIST. 33, 55 (1976) [hereinafter McAllister, *Francis Allison and John Witherspoon*].

8. VARNUM L. COLLINS, 2 PRESIDENT WITHERSPOON: A BIOGRAPHY 3, 165 (1925) [hereinafter WITHERSPOON BIOGRAPHY].

9. *Id.* at 183.

10. *Id.* at 133.

11. *Id.* at 133–34.

12. THE SELECTED WRITINGS OF JOHN WITHERSPOON 34 (Thomas Miller ed. 1990) [hereinafter SELECTED WRITINGS]. On issues of religious liberty, Madison was also influenced by other Presbyterian clerics. See BERNARD BAILYN, THE IDEOLOGICAL ORIGINS OF THE AMERICAN REVOLUTION 260 (1967) (stating that the Virginia Declaration of Rights was written by James Madison, who was "confessedly influenced by the claims of Presbyterians and the 'persecuted Baptists' as well as by enlightenment ideals.").

13. *Id.* at 131, 138, 148.

14. *Id.* at 135–36.

15. *Id.* at 139.

16. *Id.* at 140.

17. *Id.* at 10; *see also id.* at 11 ("scripture is perfectly agreeable to sound philosophy").

18. *Id.* at 11.

19. *Id.* at 12.

20. *Id.* at 189, 191.

21. *Id.* at 99.

22. *Id.* at 98.

23. *Id.* at 97.

24. *Id.* at 99.

25. *Id.* at 100.

26. *Id.*

27. *Id.*

28. *Id.*

29. *Id.* at 101.

30. *Id.* at 100, 101.

31. *Id.* at 100.

32. *Id.* at 101.

33. *Id.* at 101, 104.

34. 2 THE WORKS OF JOHN WITHERSPOON 9, 11 (Edinburgh 1804) [hereinafter 2 WORKS OF JOHN WITHERSPOON]; *see also* 3 THE WORKS OF JOHN WITHERSPOON 88 (Edinburgh 1804) (referring to the "strength of corruption within us").

35. 2 WORKS OF JOHN WITHERSPOON, *supra* note 34, at 18; *see id.* at 21 (stating that the "great transactions of the world [have turned on] ambition, cruelty, injustice, oppression, and raging lust and impurity").

36. SELECTED WRITINGS, *supra* note 12, at 106.

37. *Id.* at 101.

38. WITHERSPOON BIOGRAPHY, *supra* note 8, at 9.

39. FRANK A. BEATTIE, COMPANION TO THE CONSTITUTION OF THE PRESBYTERIAN CHURCH (U.S.A.): POLITY FOR THE LOCAL CHURCH 4 (1996).

40. SELECTED WRITINGS, *supra* note 12, at 101.

41. *Id.* at 106.

42. *Id.* at 150.

43. *Id.*

44. Leonard J. Kramer, *Presbyterians Approach the American Revolution*, 31 J. PRESBY. HIST. SOC'Y 71, 72 (1953).

45. *Id.* at 72.

46. McAllister, *Francis Allison and John Witherspoon, supra* note 7, at 52.

47. WORKS OF REV. THOMAS SMYTH, *supra* note 6, at 43–44 (stating that Presbyterian representative structure checks the "unreflecting passions and revolutionary spirit of the multitude" and the "deluge of fierce and anarchical democracy" and in that way is "distinguished from pure democracies").

48. THE CONSTITUTION OF THE PRESBYTERIAN CHURCH (USA), PART II, BOOK OF ORDER (The Office of the General Assembly) [hereinafter CONSTITUTION OF THE PRESBYTERIAN CHURCH]. *See also* WORKS OF REV. THOMAS SMYTH, *supra* note 6, at 438 ("principles of republicanism in contrast with democracy, on the one hand, and an aristocratic sovereignty, on the other . . . are clearly and prominently presented in the system of doctrine and government adopted by the Presbyterian Church").

49. WORKS OF REV. THOMAS SMYTH, *supra* note 6, at 46.

50. WITHERSPOON BIOGRAPHY, *supra* note 8, at 162. *But see* TRINTERUD, *supra* note 4, at 292–93 (arguing that Witherspoon's "record on the committee" was insufficient to prove his dominance).

51. BROWN, *supra* note 5, at 8–9; BALMER & FITZMIER, *supra* note 2, at 15–16.

52. BALMER & FITZMIER, *supra* note 2, at 15–16.

53. LOETSCHER, *supra* note 3, at 9; see also WILLIAM HENRY ROBERTS, THE PRESBYTERIAN SYSTEM 35 (1895) [hereinafter ROBERTS] ("the people of Christ are entitled to participation in the government of the Church").

54. ROBERTS, *supra* note 53, at 35.

55. CONSTITUTION OF THE PRESBYTERIAN CHURCH, *supra* note 48, at G-4.0301; 3.d (Principles of Presbyterian Government).

56. WITHERSPOON BIOGRAPHY, *supra* note 8, at 128.

57. TRINTERUD, *supra* note 4, at 308.

58. *See* GORDON WOOD, THE CREATION OF THE AMERICAN REPUBLIC 1776–1787, 403–13 (1998); *see also* Howard Miller, *The Grammar of Liberty: Presbyterians and the First American Constitutions*, 54 J. PRESBY. HIST. 142, 161 (1976) (stating that "some Presbyterians feared that in the state constitutions the democratic thrust of the American Revolution had somehow got out of hand").

59. William Churchill Houston (NJ); William Livingston (NJ); James McHenry (MD); Hugh Williamson (NC); William Paterson (NJ); and James Wilson (PA). Gunning Bedford (DE) also may have been Presbyterian. James Wilson later converted to Anglicanism.

60. Gunning Bedford (DE); David Brearly (NJ); William R. Davie (NC); Jonathan Dayton (NJ); Oliver Ellsworth (CT); William Churchill Houston (NJ); James Madison (VA); Alexander Martin (NC); Luther Martin (MD); and William Paterson (NJ). George Clymer (PA) lived in Princeton in anticipation of sending his children there, but apparently did not attend himself.

61. Jared Ingersoll, Jr. (PA) (buried in Presbyterian cemetery); John Dickinson (DE) (buried in Presbyterian cemetery); Alexander Hamilton (NY) (educated as a child by Presbyterian missionaries, though later rejected by College of New Jersey [Princeton]); and George Washington (VA) (reportedly attended Presbyterian services in Virginia).

62. David Brearly (NJ); William R. Davie (NC); Jonathan Dayton (NJ); William Churchill Houston (NJ); James Madison (VA).

63. JAMES MADISON, NOTES OF DEBATES IN THE FEDERAL CONVENTION OF 1787 312 (Adrienne Koch ed., Ohio Univ. Press 1966) (statement of James Madison); *see also id.* at 34–35 (statement of Pierce Butler) (stating opposition to granting Congress significant power until Randolph Plan suggested dividing its power between two houses).

64. *Id.* at 322 (statement of Gouverneur Morris); *id.* at 324 (statement of Gouverneur Morris) (expressing fear that executive could be "the tool of a faction, of some leading demagogue in the Legislature").

65. *Id.* at 308 (statement of Gouverneur Morris); *id.* at 307 (statement of James Wilson).

66. *See* Marci A. Hamilton, *The Paradox of Calvinist Distrust and Hope at the Constitutional Convention, in* CHRISTIAN PERSPECTIVES ON LEGAL THOUGHT (Angela Carmella et al. eds., forthcoming) (discussing principle of balance in Constitution).

67. U.S. CONST. arts. I, II; *see also* MADISON, *supra* note 63.

68. "Governments are instituted among Men, deriving their just Powers from the Consent of the Governed, that whenever any Form of Government becomes destructive of these Ends, it is the Right of the People to alter or to abolish it, and to institute new Government, laying its Foundation on such Principles, and organizing its Powers in such Form, as to them shall seem most likely to effect their Safety and Happiness." THE DECLARATION OF INDEPENDENCE (U.S. 1776).

69. *See* MADISON, *supra* note 63, at 41 (statement of Pierce Butler).

70. *Id.* at 39 (statement of Elbridge Gerry).

71. *Id.* at 368 (statement of Elbridge Gerry).

72. *See* THE FEDERALIST.

73. *See* MADISON, *supra* note 63, at 74 (statement of James Wilson) ("Representation is made necessary only because it is impossible for the people to act collectively."); *id.* at 75–77 (statement of James Madison); *id.* at 83–84 (statement of James Madison) (discussing the evils of direct democracy).

74. *See* U.S. CONST. art. IV, § 4.

75. *See, e.g.*, MORTIMER SELLERS, AMERICAN REPUBLICANISM: ROMAN IDEOLOGY IN THE UNITED STATES CONSTITUTION (1994).

76. See *Presbyterians and the American Revolution*, 54 J. PRESBY. HIST. 1, 52 (James H. Smylie ed., 1976).

77. *See* BROWN, *supra* note 5, at 5–6.

78. *See, e.g.*, WILLIAM WARREN SWEET, RELIGION IN THE DEVELOPMENT OF AMERICAN CULTURE 1765–1840, 85 (1952) (stating that 19 of the framers were Episcopalians, 8 Congregationalists, 7 Presbyterians, 2 Roman Catholics, 2 Quakers, 1 Methodist, and 1 Dutch Reformed).

79. MADISON, *supra* note 63, at 84–85 (statement of John Dickinson).

Part II

Religion and the Public Square

Chapter 5

The Place of Religious Argument in a Free and Democratic Society

Robert Audi

Introduction

We are living in a period of increasing secularity in the industrialized world and increasing sectarianism in much of the less industrialized world. In the West, however, and particularly in the United States, secularization is by no means welcomed by all, and is feared and resented by many who consider themselves religious. In the United States, at least, the tradition of separation of church and state has contributed to secularization. But even a strong separationist tradition is neither necessary nor sufficient for secularization except in certain matters of law and public policy. Many aspects of society can be largely unaffected by separation of church and state. The domains of law and public policy are, of course, large areas of human life, and any major secularization in those domains is bound to have wider effects. Still, it is easy to exaggerate how much a reasonable separation of church and state must secularize a society that practices it. The degree of secularization of a society may be less a matter of its operative principles of separation than of the personal inclinations and the historical and cultural traditions of its people.

This essay presents a theory of how, from the point of view of normative sociopolitical philosophy, religious arguments may be properly used in a free and democratic society in a way that neither masks their religious character nor undermines a desirable separation. This task requires an account of what constitutes a religious argument. It also requires a basic catalogue of the uses religious arguments may have and attention to the main contexts in which they play a socially and politically significant role. In the course of clarifying the nature and proper role of religious arguments, I will articulate two general principles of separation of church and state and illustrate how a society that abides by them can realize religious as well as secular ideals.[1] My primary focus, however, will not be the most common preoccupation of church-state discussions, the relation of the state to religious institutions. Rather, my focus will be on the sociopolitical role of religious arguments and the explicit use of, or tacit reliance on, religious considerations as grounds for laws or public policies. These arguments may occur in a variety of contexts, and they can be as important in the conduct of individuals acting outside governmental or religious institutions as they are in the official work of the church or the state.

I. The Concept of a Religious Argument

What is a religious, as opposed to a secular, argument? Frequent references to religious arguments suggest that the notion of a religious argument is well understood. However, apart from the examples people commonly have in mind—such as arguing from one of the Ten Commandments as a premise to a conclusion about how people should behave—the notion of a religious argument is frequently misunderstood. The question of what constitutes a religious argument turns out to be particularly difficult when we realize that an argument can be religious in a way that is important for church-state issues even when it does not explicitly appeal to any religious notion or doctrine.[2] There are several criteria for a religious argument, each of them providing a condition that is sufficient (but not necessary) for an argument's being religious.

A. The Content Criterion

First, there is a content criterion: on this standard, an argument with essentially religious content (as opposed to, say, merely quoted religious statements) is religious. Paradigmatically, this is theistic content such as a reference to a divine command. There are also other cases, such as appeals to scripture, or to a religious leader, as a guide in human life. Full clarification of the concept of religious content would require nothing less than an analysis of the notion of a religion. For our purposes, it is sufficient to think in terms of theistic, especially monotheistic, religions like Christianity, Judaism, and Islam, which are highly representative of the challenges faced by a liberal democracy seeking to give proper weight, in civil and political life, to religious considerations.

We should also construe the relevant kind of religious content as substantive, for example, as expressing divine commands. We are not concerned with noncommittal or accidental religious content, as where a speaker refers, without endorsement, to someone else's statement of a religious doctrine.[3] A more difficult case, which does concern us, is one in which legislators or other public officials argue for a position on the ground that the vast majority of their constituents, for deep religious reasons, favor it. There are at least two subcases here: one in which the reference to the religious convictions of constituents is simply added information, perhaps to indicate the depth of the people's convictions, and the other, in which the constituents' being religious is given justificatory weight in the argument. In the latter but not the former case religious content is essential to the legislator's argument. Nonetheless, the latter is only a second-order religious argument; roughly, one in which a positive evaluation of a set of religious reasons, but no religious reason itself, is given a justificatory role.

In the former case, where religious reasons are simply taken as evidence of deep conviction, a church-state issue arises in a way that might lead some people to call the argument religious. Granting that one's constituents' favoring of something for religious reasons is not itself a religious as opposed to sociological fact, giving it weight as deeply felt because of those reasons raises questions about the appropriate role of religious considerations in a liberal democracy. Would one, for example, take political, or ethical, or aesthetic reasons as seriously? If not, would that be justifiable solely on sociopsychological grounds concerning what does or does not indicate depth of conviction? This essay is designed to help us in dealing with such issues in whatever kind of argument they may arise. Contentually religious arguments are the primary kind that people think of as religious and may be the sort that most often raise church-state issues. They are not, however, the only kind of religious argument. We must certainly consider others if we are to develop an adequate theory of the relation between religious considerations, for example, and the sociopolitical domain.

B. The Epistemic Criterion

The second criterion of religious argument is the epistemic criterion. By this standard, an argument is religious not because of what it says but, roughly speaking, because of how it must be justified. Specifically, I propose to call an argument epistemically religious provided that (a) its premises, or (b) its conclusion, or (c) both, or (d) its premises warranting its conclusion cannot be known, or at least justifiably accepted, apart from reliance on religious considerations, for example, scripture or revelation.

Most epistemically religious arguments will also be theistic in content, but not all arguments with theistic or religious content need be epistemically religious. Consider, for instance, a poor argument for a sound, purely moral conclusion, say, that one should try to render aid to neighbors in dire need. Let the premise be an approving attribution of a moral view to the Bible, for example, the statement that according to Moses, God prohibited bearing false witness against one's neighbors. This attribution is not a statement of a moral view or otherwise evidentially sufficient for the conclusion, which is on a different though related topic—rendering aid to neighbors in need. Thus, this argument would not meet the proposed epistemic criterion. Specifically, the argument meets none of the basic conditions of the criterion. First, its premise, being only an attribution of a moral view and not itself a moral statement, does not warrant its conclusion, which is a moral statement. Second, the premise cannot be, even on a religious basis, known or justifiedly believed to warrant it[4] (so on this score there is no knowledge of justification to be had). Third, the truth of the premise can be known on textual as opposed to religious grounds. Finally, the conclusion itself could, on the nonskeptical assumptions I am making, also be known or justifiably believed on secular moral grounds.

A major reason for the importance of singling out epistemically religious arguments is that it seems possible for an argument to be epistemically religious without having any religious content. It is hard to find uncontroversial examples, but even a controversial one will bring out the nature of an epistemically religious argument. Consider a version of the notorious genetic argument for the personhood of the zygote: because all the normal human genetic information is present in the zygote and will normally result in a clear case of a person at the end of a natural process (pregnancy), the zygote itself is a person. Now it might be contended that if this conclusion can be known or justifiably believed through these premises, it is on a religious basis (e.g., on the basis of grounds for the belief that God ensouls members of the human species at conception). A plausible counter to construing the genetic argument as epistemically religious is the contention that there may be a purely metaphysical argument for ensoulment or personhood at this stage. It is not clear, however, that any such metaphysical arguments are sound or have even been widely taken to be sound.[5]

A related source of examples derives from natural law. Consider the argument that since the natural end of intercourse is procreation, and contraception thwarts that end, contraception is wrong. It is not evident that these premises can be known or justifiably believed apart from theistic grounds. But even supposing that they can be, given a statistical or other naturalistic standard of what is natural, the premises arguably cannot warrant the conclusion except on assumptions that patterns in the natural order reveal divine intentions regarding how human life should be conducted. Unless thwarting the natural end of an act is contrary to divine intention, why should it be morally important? It is this sort of dependency on religious considerations that seems to many to underlie the typical natural law arguments for moral conclusions and hence to undermine their ostensibly naturalistic, or at least nontheistic, character.

C. The Motivational Criterion

Third, there is a motivational criterion, according to which an argument, as presented in a context, is religious provided an essential part of the person's motivation for presenting it is to accomplish a religious purpose (for example, to elicit obedience to God's will or to fulfill a religious obligation to one's church). There may be more than one such purpose, and the purposes may be causally or evidentially independent, as where each derives from respect for an independent religious authority or source such as text and religious experience. This is a different kind of criterion from the first two. To understand the difference, notice that "argument" has two main uses. First, the term may designate a linguistic process, roughly the offering of one or more propositions as reasons for another proposition. Second, the term may refer to an abstract product of such a process, roughly the essential content put forward in arguing. The motivational criterion is an illocutionary[6] one, a criterion for an argument as linguistically presented not a propositional criterion, one applicable to an argument construed as an abstract structure of propositions. A propositional criterion applies no matter who presents the argument; an illocutionary criterion is proponent-relative and contextual. Thus, strictly speaking, the motivational criterion applies primarily to reasoning processes and only derivatively to arguments as the abstract structures realized in those processes. But since arguments do their chief work when so realized, it is appropriate to treat the motivational criterion as applicable to them.

The content of a motivationally religious argument need not be religious. Perhaps the genetic argument is an example of this. Certain natural law arguments might also illustrate the point. And if some of them, at least, need not be epistemically religious, they could exemplify arguments that are motivationally religious, but neither contentually nor epistemically so.

D. The Historical Criterion

Fourth, there is a historical criterion. It is illocutionary, like the motivational standard, but looser. The idea is roughly this: an argument, as used on a particular occasion, is religious in the historical sense provided that, as used on that occasion, it genetically traces, explicitly or implicitly, by some mainly cognitive chain, such as a chain of beliefs, to one or more arguments that are religious in one of the above senses, or to one or more propositions that are either religious in content or epistemically dependent on a proposition that is religious in content. Consider the argument that because taking an innocent human life is wrong, suicide is wrong. Here we have an argument that seems to many to be persuasive in its own right. Yet, there is no question that on many occasions of its use the argument traces to, and derives some of its persuasive power from, religious ideas such as the idea that God gives life, and only God should take it away, at least apart from self-defense and punishment.

There are, as this example about the permissibility of suicide suggests, at least two interesting subcases of historically religious arguments. First, there are those that are persuasively autonomous, in the sense that their persuasive power does not depend on their historically religious character. Second, there are those that are persuasively dependent, in that some of their persuasive power derives, whether evidentially or otherwise, from one or more religious sources to which they are traceable. Since persuasive power may depend on the audience, an argument can be persuasive in one case and not another, or persuasively autonomous with one audience and persuasively dependent with another. Consider the argument that monogamous marriage should be the only legally permissible kind because the only normal marital relation is between females and males. This normative assumption might, in turn, be partly based, evidentially, or historically, or in both ways, on the idea that only parents, or potential parents, or at least people who can identify in a certain way with parents, of the same child or children, should marry. Either idea might be historically religious, tracing to religious injunctions about marriage as divinely ordained for men and women from the Garden of Eden onward. The latter idea, however, might be partly based on some religious view and partly founded on a supposed moral obligation of parents to rear their children and a supposed right of children to be reared by both of their parents. An argument can thus have a mixed lineage: deriving, evidentially, or historically, or in both ways, from both a religious and a moral basis.

Two further points are in order and are readily understood in relation to the apparent historical dependence of the innocent-life, antisuicide argument or the life-as-a-divine-gift argument. First, I take an argument or proposition to be implicit in the background of another argument, on an occasion of the presentation of the latter, when the first argument or proposition is not articulated, but the latter argument as presented is based on at least one of the premises of the former as a ground, or would at least be taken to be so based by a reasonable interpreter in the context. Second, the genetic line need not go through the speaker's mind. It is enough if the argument as presented has a history that meets the condition of traceability to religious considerations. The relevant causal chain, moreover, can branch. A single argument offered on one occasion can trace back historically, as it can motivationally, to two or more sources that are causally or evidentially independent, or independent in both ways.

The notion of a historically religious argument is of interest largely because, in some cases, we cannot account for the plausibility of an argument without so conceiving it. It convinces, as it were, by its pedigree or its associations rather than by its evidential merits. For example, whether the aforementioned marriage argument has any persuasive force apart from its religious historical connections is debatable. Note, however, that even if it has none apart from those connections, its conclusion could still be supported by any number of powerful considerations. Yet, it is neither epistemically religious nor necessarily motivationally religious. To say, then, that an argument is historically religious is not, even from a secular point of view, to imply an epistemic criticism of its conclusion. Of the four kinds of religious arguments, it is only those that are epistemically religious that depend on religious considerations for the justification of some essential element in them.

II. Roles of Religious Arguments

Religious arguments can play an indefinite number of roles. Some of these roles are perfectly compatible, such as expressing oneself and guiding someone else. There is no hope of providing an exhaustive list, but some of the roles most important for an account of the question of the appropriate uses of religious arguments in a liberal democracy should be noted.

One role of religious arguments is expressive, not merely in the minimal sense of putting something forth but in the sense of "self-revelatory": to set out one's perspective on an issue, to articulate one's feelings on a major event, to get something off one's chest, and the like. This point has a major implication. A society that protects free expression must protect the freedom to express one's religious views, even in contexts in which there are good reasons to offer a secular case for those views, as in certain public forums. Thus, any constraints we establish as reasonable for religious arguments must operate within these freedoms. The constraints will apply to the appropriate discretion in exercising our freedoms, rather than restrict our right to do so.[7]

A second, closely related role of religious arguments is communicative, to get across to someone else one's deepest feelings or to show someone else where one is "coming from." This kind of communicative argumentation may also be expressive, and must be so in the wide sense of expressing something. Here, however, the aim of argument is not mainly to articulate one's own position but to change the understanding of someone else. There will be times when one cannot convey one's special sense of an issue or one's distinctive approach to a topic without using religious arguments, at least implicitly. Even if I do not expect a religious argument to persuade you, I may want to offer it as an indication of how deeply I feel and of the sources of my views. Far from necessarily seeming dogmatic or insular, this practice might suggest some common ground between us, religious or secular.

Still another role of religious argument is persuasive, above all, to get people to agree with our view, or follow our prescriptions, or identify with us. Persuasion may often be best when one is communicative and self-revelatory, but it need not have either of those characteristics. There are at least two major cases. The first is persuading people who accept one's general religious view. The second is persuading those who are either nonreligious or religiously different from oneself. Often, in the second case, some arguments with religious conclusions are needed first by way of partial conversion. But persuasion may be achievable simply through getting the addressee to acknowledge the importance of one's conclusion if only because it is religious. In the former case, redirection is usually the main strategy (for instance showing others how a shared religious premise has led to resisting a conclusion). In the latter, one must create enough common ground to support the conclusion.

A fourth role of religious argument is evidential, to offer supporting reasons for a view or course of action. It may be that only religious people will accept the reasons in question as good, but that is not the point. It would be quite wrong to omit this purpose of using religious argument. It is an important underpinning for many instances of religious argumentation by conscientious people. That they regard their arguments as good is important for how those arguments should be received, even by those who reject them.

Fifth, religious arguments may play an important heuristic role. For instance, by raising the question what God would command, or what the Gospels or the Psalms imply, religious arguments may stimulate the discovery of new truths. The value of this approach should not be underestimated. The appeal to God's intellect or will as a standard of knowledge or value can open up hypotheses and clarify assumptions that might otherwise be lost. And the great religious texts are inexhaustible sources of ideas, standards, and practical wisdom. To exclude their study from public education is neither good academic policy nor required by a reasonable separation of church and state.

All five roles can be played by religious arguments in sociopolitical contexts. Here we encounter a host of questions about what, from the point of view of both normative political philosophy and the ethics of citizenship, their appropriate uses are. Those questions are the main topic of part III.

III. The Proper Roles of Religious Arguments in Ethics and Politics

Liberal democracies are free societies and are above all committed to preserving freedom, especially in religion. There are many conceptions of liberal democracy. At one end of the spectrum, perhaps unoccupied by any major historical figure in the liberal tradition, are minimalist, procedural conceptions. These simply provide for a framework in which democracy can operate, and they impose no constraints whatever on the social goals appropriate to a free and democratic society.[8] At the other end are rich substantive conceptions that also incorporate such goals as respect for persons and social flourishing, a notion that itself can be substantively developed to a greater or lesser degree. Although a detailed conception cannot be presented here, this essay proceeds on the hypothesis that a major basis for determining how much substance is permissible is what might be called a fidelity to essential premises constraint: a liberal political theory should build into its vision of a just society enough substance to fulfill the theory's essential underlying ideals.

If the fidelity constraint is assumed, it seems reasonable for a liberal society to build into its structure as much in the way of substantive promotion of the good as is implied in the essential premises underlying the liberal political theory by which it lives. These are not necessarily premises actually appealed to by proponents but, rather, those that must be common to all the sets of grounds sufficient to justify the sociopolitical vision. The relevant premises are defined, then, as those minimally required for justification, not those historically used for the purpose. Normally, these two categories substantially overlap, and if they did not, the fidelity to premises idea would be less interesting. But the historical inspiration for a liberal democracy could in principle lack justificatory force, and the minimally justifying grounds could, in some historical circumstances, lack persuasive power.

To illustrate the fidelity to premises idea, suppose that justification of a liberal political theory as a basis for governing a society requires at least ideals of democracy, in a sense implying one vote for each person; autonomy, in the sense of self-determination; respect for persons, implying at least equal treatment before the law and a legal system nurturing self-respect; and material well-being. In that case, proponents of the liberal theory in question might reasonably require that a society take positive steps to protect and nurture these ideals.

Although such an approach would warrant something at least close to the five ideas of the good that John Rawls finds in justice as fairness,[9] the purpose of this essay does not require endorsing any specific list of goods as essential aims in a liberal democracy. It is easy to go too far here. Someone might, for example, require religious observances by all citizens. Notice also that if a liberal society chooses to justify its liberal theory solely on certain pragmatic grounds, such as maximizing preference satisfaction within a framework of social and political liberties, it may have to use a thinner notion of the good. If, however, a morally inspired liberal political theory is justified, a richer notion of the good might be objectively warranted, such as one that emphasizes enhancing freedom and capacity for actualization of one's human capacities. But this society, being unable to countenance the grounds of that theory, would not be justified, in practice, in building in that richer notion.

Even within a fidelity to essential premises conception of liberalism, there is an important distinction between grounds appropriate for a liberal society in justifying promotion of the goods it may endorse and grounds appropriate to justifying coercion. Here again I appeal to a general principle as a constraint. It seems to me that once autonomy is taken sufficiently seriously—as it will be not only by liberal political theorists but also by any sound moral theory—the way is open to view the justification of coercion in a framework that gives high priority to respect for the self-determination of persons. For purposes of sociopolitical philosophy, it may be fruitful to work from a surrogacy conception of justified coercion, especially in cases of governmental coercion. According to this view, coercing a person, S, for reason R, to perform an action, A, in circumstances C is fully justified if and only if at least the following three conditions hold in C: (a) S morally ought to A in C, for example, to abstain from stealing from others (perhaps someone has a right, in the circumstances, against S that S A—certainly a feature of most cases in which a liberal democracy can reasonably coerce its citizens); (b) if fully rational and adequately informed about the situation, S would see that (a) holds and would, for reason R (say, from a sense of how theft creates mistrust and chaos, or for some essentially related reason), perform A, or at least tend to A;[10] (c) A is both an "important" kind of action (as opposed to breaking a casual promise to meet for lunch at the usual place) and one that may be reasonably believed to affect someone else (and perhaps not of a highly personal kind at all).[11] Thus, it is permissible, on grounds of the general welfare, to coerce people to pay taxes only if they ought to do so in the circumstances, and would (if fully rational and adequately informed) be appropriately motivated by seeing that they ought to do so. By contrast, it is not permissible to coerce someone to give up, say, smoking, unless it significantly affects others. (It is not self-evident that each citizen has a right that other citizens pay their taxes, but this is at least arguable.)

As these examples suggest, the greater the coercion needing to be justified (say, in terms of how much liberty it undermines), the more important the behavior in question must be; and parentalism, for normal adults, is ruled out. According to this view, then, we may coerce people to do only what they would autonomously do if appropriately informed and fully rational.[12] This view explains why justified coercion is not resented by agents when they adequately understand its rationale, why some coercion is consonant with liberal democratic ideals of autonomy, and why the kind that is can be supported by citizens independently of what they happen to approve of politically, religiously, or, to a large extent, even morally.

If the perspective on liberal democracy I have sketched is correct, then it is easy to understand why in such a society the use of secular reason must in general be the main basis of sociopolitical decision. Indeed, if there is secular reason that is esoteric in a sense implying that a normal rational person lacks access to it, then a stronger requirement is needed; one might thus speak of public reason, as Rawls and others do. This seems to apply especially to decisions that result in coercion, whether through law or even through restrictive social policies not backed by legal sanctions. If I am coerced on grounds that cannot motivate me, as a rational informed person, to do the thing in question, I cannot come to identify with the deed and will tend to resent having to do it. Even if the deed should be my obligation, still, where only esoteric knowledge—say, through revelation that only the initiated experience—can show that it is, I will tend to resent the coercion. And it is part of the underlying rationale of liberalism that we should not have to feel this kind of resentment—that we give up autonomy only where, no matter what our specific preferences or particular worldview, we can be expected, given adequate rationality and sufficient information, to see that we would have so acted on our own.

One might think that the importance of secular reasons is derivative from that of public reasons. But this is not so. For one thing, a liberal democracy must make special efforts to prevent religious domination of one group by another. There are, in turn, at least two reasons for this. One is that the authority structure common in many religions can make a desire to dominate other groups natural and can provide a rationale for it. (What could be more important or beneficial to others than saving their souls?) Another reason is that the dictates of a religion often extend to the religious as well as the secular conduct of persons, so that if domination occurs, it undermines even religious freedom. (To save people's souls they must not only cease performing evil deeds but worship appropriately.) Religious freedom is a kind quite properly given high priority by a liberal democracy. And, if religious considerations threaten it more than nonpublic influences in general, additional reasons exist for a liberal democracy to constrain the role of those considerations.

Another ground for denying that the importance of specifically secular reason is not derivative from that of public reason is connected with the authority that religious principles, directives, and traditions are commonly felt to have. Where religious convictions are a basis of a disagreement, it is, other things being equal, less likely that the disputants can achieve resolution or even peacefully agree to disagree. If God's will is felt to be clear, there may seem to be only one way to view the issue. This can apply as much to prima facie nonreligious problems such as physical health care as it does to specifically religious practices. Granted, a nonreligious source of conviction can also be felt to be infallible, and it may also be nonpublic. But not every nonpublic source of views and preferences poses the authority problem, or the special threat to religious freedom, that can arise from certain kinds of unconstrained religious convictions. Particularly when people believe that extreme measures, such as bravely fighting a holy war, carry an eternal reward, they tend to be ready to take them. Being ready to die, they may find it much easier to kill.

So far, I have been imagining coercion by laws or institutional policies. But in my view, the same sorts of considerations imply that individual as well as institutional conduct—the more common domain of discussions of religion and politics—should be constrained in a related way. More specifically, I believe that just as we separate church and state institutionally, we should, in certain aspects of our thinking and public conduct, separate religion from law and public policy matters, especially when it comes to passing restrictive laws. This separation in turn implies the need for motivational as well as rationale principles. If, for example, some group has religious reasons for favoring circumcision, they should not argue for a legal requirement of it without having evidentially adequate secular reasons for such a law. Nor should they offer secular reasons that are not evidentially convincing to them or, for that reason or any other, cognitively motivating, such as statistics about cervical cancer in women married to men who are not circumcised. To do this would be to allow these reasons to serve as—or even to use them as—secular rationalizations that cloak the underlying religious motivation for seeking the legislation.

In earlier work I have articulated two principles to express these constraints upon conscience. First, the principle of secular rationale says that one has a prima facie obligation not to advocate or support any law or public policy that restricts human conduct unless one has, and is willing to offer, adequate secular reason for this advocacy or support.[13] A secular reason is roughly one whose normative force does not evidentially depend on the existence of God or on theological considerations, or on the pronouncements of a person or institution qua religious authority.[14] The second, the principle of secular motivation, adds the idea that one also has a prima facie obligation to abstain from such advocacy or support unless one is sufficiently motivated by adequate secular reason.[15] This implies that some secular reason is motivationally sufficient, roughly in the sense that one would act on it even if, other things remaining equal, other reasons were eliminated.[16]

Since an argument can be epistemically, motivationally, or historically religious without being religious in content, one might fail to live up to at least the second of these principles even in offering arguments that on their face are neither religious nor fail to provide an adequate secular reason for their conclusion. It might be argued, for example, that some people, in presenting a genetic argument for the personhood of the zygote, are not sufficiently motivated by the secular considerations cited in their argument and would not find the argument convincing apart from underlying religious beliefs.

Application of the principle of secular motivation can be complicated because it may be difficult to tell whether a reason for doing or believing something is in fact motivating. This difficulty is especially likely to occur before the relevant event or long afterward. But what the motivation principle (beyond the rationale principle) requires of conscientious citizens contemplating support of restrictive laws or policies is at most this: (a) an attempt to formulate all the significant reasons for each major option—itself often a very useful exercise; (b) where one or more reasons is or are religious, consideration of the motivational weight of each reason taken by itself as well as in the context of the others (if none is religious, the principle does not imply any need to go any further into motivation); and (c) an attempt to ascertain, by considering hypothetical situations and motivational or cognitive impulses or tendencies, whether each reason is motivationally sufficient. I should ask myself, for example, whether I would believe something if I did not accept a certain premise and whether a given reason taken by itself seems persuasive, in the sense of providing a sense of surety. At least one secular reason should emerge as such.

In short, my principles imply that one should ask of one's reasons certain evidential, historical, and hypothetical questions. One is entitled to use practical wisdom in deciding how much effort is reasonable to expend in a given case. Here as elsewhere in applying a standard, one can be conscientious but mistaken. For instance, I might be wrong, but not unreasonably so, in believing a reason to be secular. I might then be subject to no criticism, or at least none deriving from the rationale or motivation principles as opposed to purely evidential ones. An interesting case here would be one's being mistaken in just this way, but so disposed that if one did not believe, of what is in fact a religious reason, that it is secular, one would not be moved by it. This is a kind of second-order conformity to the motivation principle simultaneously with first-order failure to abide by it, and the former adherence would help to excuse the latter deviation.

Fortunately, if the motivation principle is widely accepted, and perhaps even if it is not, and one is in good communication with people who disagree on the issue at hand, one will likely get substantial help from them. Whenever religious reasons seem motivationally too strong, people who disagree should be expected to help one probe. Others may think of revealing questions about us that we ourselves overlook, or observe words or deeds that tell us something we did not realize about our own thinking or motivation.[17]

It could turn out that most people are not usually good at forming reasonable judgments regarding what reasons they have, much less which, if any, are motivating.[18] If this is how it does turn out, the effort to find out may be all the more needed; if I cannot tell what my reasons are, I should probably wonder whether I have any worthy of the name, and I am likely to make better decisions if I try to find some good reasons. If I cannot accurately tell which reasons motivate me and how much they do so, I cannot adequately understand myself or reasonably predict my own behavior.

The problem of ascertaining and weighing motivating reasons is not peculiar to my view. In assigning moral praise or responsibility, for instance, we need to know not just what was done but for what reasons it was done. Acting in accordance with duty, but for a selfish reason, earns one no moral praise. In any case, if there are any important questions, such as the abortion issue, in which people can identify their main reasons and can form reasonable judgments regarding which reasons are motivating, that gives the principle of secular motivation an important job to do. Surely there are some such issues.

It is important to emphasize two points about the proposed principles. First, the principle of secular motivation provides that one may also have religious reasons and be motivated by them. Second, my use of such separationist principles by no means presupposes that religious reasons cannot be evidentially adequate. My principles also allow that religious reasons may be motivationally sufficient (though not motivationally necessary, since secular reasons could not then be motivationally sufficient—they would be unable to produce belief or action without the cooperation of religious elements). The principles even allow a person to judge the religious reasons to be more important than the secular ones, or be more strongly motivated by them, or both. The rationale and motivation principles do not rule out a major role for religious considerations, even in public political advocacy. They simply provide a measure of protection against their domination in contexts in which they should be constrained.

While my principles do not imply that religious reasons are never evidentially adequate, their evidential adequacy is not a presupposition of liberal democracy.[19] Neither is their evidential inadequacy. Indeed, it may be that the absence of both presuppositions is a negative foundation of liberal democracy. It would be inappropriate for a liberal theory to contain either epistemological claim. This point need not be a positive plank in even a fully articulated democratic constitution, but it is an important strand in much liberal democratic theory.[20]

Neither of my principles precludes just pointing out to people how their religious commitments imply some conclusion that one is pressing. Telling me that I have an antecedent religious ground for agreeing with you is not arguing from that ground, and it can be done without implying that the ground is evidentially cogent. It is a persuasive, not an evidential, use of an appeal to a reason. We might call it leveraging by reasons; it is using other people's reasons to move them, as opposed to offering our own. In leveraging, one need not imply that the cited ground is sufficient to give any warrant to the conclusion. But, if one believes it is not, one is probably being manipulative rather than respectfully persuasive, since one is inviting, or exploiting, weak reasoning. I believe, however, a sufficient secular basis for using this strategy is necessary. Even then, its use can invite unwarranted appeal to religious considerations, since it may tacitly endorse their unrestricted appropriateness to laws or public policy conclusions.

Despite these restrictions, religious arguments can, in certain ways, be quite properly used in all the roles I have mentioned—expressive, communicative, persuasive, evidential, and heuristic—whether in public policy contexts or others. My thesis is that their use should be constrained, not that they should be eliminated. The implicit secularization is restricted and may be quite circumscribed. Indeed, it is quite appropriate to a secular ethic to endorse a principle that religion should be taken seriously because doing so is an aspect of one's integrity as a person. This is in part because ideals and commitments should be taken seriously; doing so is important to being a mature and integrated person, and it might be considered to be implicit in the duty of self-improvement as understood by such moral philosophers as Kant and W. D. Ross. It is also in part true because morality proscribes hypocrisy, and it is hypocritical to profess a religion and pay mere lip service to it.

If secular ethics may encourage taking one's religion seriously, what about government's role in this respect? Since government should not prefer the religious as such, law and public policy may not differentially encourage religious practice. But they may encourage living up to one's ideals within the constraints of mutual respect and of separation of church and state. This allows, however, that governments may require or even encourage employers to grant leaves for self-development. Governments may even encourage employers and schools to set aside time to pursue ideals, say by declaring a holiday for reflection and stock taking. This kind of attitude might in effect lead to respect for religious holidays in a way that gives visible governmental concern for the religious. But that outcome is neither inevitable nor necessarily objectionable, and the aim of the policy need not be specifically religious.

The goals of governmental policy and the kinds of reasons appropriate to laws and sociopolitical policy are the main focus of separation of church and state. It is not reasonable to prohibit policies that are properly motivated, even if they foreseeably favor the religious or the nonreligious. However, there are special cases here, such as a vast effect that would significantly reduce the freedom of nonreligious minorities.[21] An example of a policy that might be secularly motivated but affect the freedom of nonreligious minorities would be the mandatory observance of the Sabbath by closing government offices, where this is done for the convenience of a majority religious group though not because it is religious but because it represents a majority. The required placement of condom machines in all public restrooms, even if motivated by public health concerns, might affect the freedom of religious minorities (who object to public exposure of such things). Perhaps requiring all normal adults to donate blood in wartime or epidemic would be an example favoring the nonreligious and some of the religious over religious minorities who strongly oppose the practice. Each of these cases is different from the others, and they all come in variant forms too numerous to discuss here. With any such cases, a point may come at which secularly motivated legislation can have a religiously significant effect that makes the legislation objectionable on reasonable grounds of separation. But there is no simple criterion of ascertaining that point.

IV. Religious Arguments and Moral Principles

The restricted role I suggest for religious arguments is compatible with the idea that there can be religious knowledge in ethical and sociopolitical matters. I think, however, that liberal democracy is or at least should be committed to the conceptual and epistemic autonomy of ethics (in the broad sense in which ethics encompasses normative political philosophy). This commitment does not imply affirming the ontic independence of ethics; it is above all a commitment to the possibility of knowledge or at least justified moral beliefs or attitudes and is neutral with respect to the possibility that such beliefs can be true apart from God's existence (an ontological matter). Just as one might understand a poem and know its aesthetic merits without knowing who its author is (or even that it has one), one might understand and know the truth or at least justification of a moral principle without knowing who its author is, or even whether it has one. If I believe that God necessarily exists, and is indeed the ultimate ground of moral truths and a kind of condition for the existence of anything, I can still embrace liberal democracy and defend the full sociopolitical rights of atheists. But I doubt that I could readily endorse all this if I thought there was no nontheistic route even to moral justification.

For reasons already given, it seems that liberal democracy is also committed to the possibility of justifying, on a secular moral basis, any coercion necessary for maintaining civil life, even where the conduct subject to coercion is defended by a religious justification, as with some religiously rationalized persecutions of religious minorities. Here secular coercion may have a justification that, in a liberal democracy, overrides a sincere and articulate religious rationale for allowing the proscribed conduct. This sociopolitical ascendency of secular argument in justifying coercion does not, however, imply a commitment to its being epistemically better than all religious argument. Agreeing on the principles—and referees—of a game does not entail believing that, from a higher point of view, there can be no better game or superior referees.[22] But at least as long as we consent to play the game, we are obligated to abide by its rules.[23]

Teachers of ethics, and indeed teachers in general, should presuppose the epistemic autonomy of ethics, even if in a noncognitivist version.[24] It is a further question whether specific moral principles, such as the principle that people should be allowed a high degree of free expression, must be presupposed by liberal democracy and teachers. I believe that some of them must be, if only because they reflect underlying premises of such a system, and the very name "liberal democracy" suggests the same conclusion. But it is arguable that only a pragmatic assumption to this effect is presupposed. The issue is whether liberal democracy must be in a sense morally constituted, as opposed to being grounded simply in instrumental considerations concerning the preference of the founding parties or the current citizens. I am not certain that it must be morally constituted, but I do feel sure that, even from the point of view of nonmoral values, it is best that a liberal democracy be morally constituted.

Everything I have said here is intended to be compatible with the existence of a religious grounding of ethics, and even of a religious grounding of moral knowledge—there can be epistemic overdetermination here. That is, there can be two routes that, from the point of view of knowledge and justification, are independent ways to reach moral principles. Moreover, on the assumption of at least a broadly Western theism, we can say this much: God would surely provide a route to moral truth along rational secular paths—as I think Aquinas, for one, believed God has done. Given how the world is—for instance, with so much evil that even many theists are tempted by the atheistic conclusion that such a realm could not have been created by God—it would seem cruel for God to do otherwise. Religious doubt, and certainly rejection of theism, would have to be accompanied, in reasonably reflective people, by moral nihilism, which would only compound the problem in ways there is no good reason to think God would wish to allow.[25]

Indeed, on the assumption that God is omniscient and omnibenevolent—all-knowing and all-good—any cogent argument, including an utterly nonreligious one, for a moral principle is in effect a good argument for God's knowing that conclusion, and hence for urging or requiring conformity to it. How could God, conceived as omniscient and omnibenevolent, not require or at least wish our conformity to a true moral principle? I should think, moreover, that in some cases good secular arguments for moral principles may be better reasons to believe those principles divinely enjoined than theological arguments for the principles, based on scripture or tradition; for the latter arguments seem more subject than the former to extraneous cultural influences, more vulnerable to misinterpretation of texts or their sheer corruption across time and translation, and more liable to bias stemming from political or other nonreligious aims. This turns one traditional view of the relation between ethics and religion on its head; it may be better to try to understand God through ethics than ethics through theology.

These considerations from philosophical theology suggest a positive approach. Ideally, the religious should try to achieve theo-ethical equilibrium, a rational integration between, on one side, religious deliverances and insights and, on the other, considerations drawn from secular thought and discussion. A seemingly moral conclusion that goes against scripture or well-established religious tradition should be scrutinized for error; a religious demand that appears to abridge moral rights should be studied for misinterpretation, errors of translation, or distortion of religious experience. Given the conception of God as omniscient, omnipotent, and omnibenevolent, the possibility of such equlibrium should surely be expected. A mature, conscientious theist who cannot reach it should be loath to stake too much on the unintegrated proposition.

It is possible that a person believes, on authority or revelation, that God commands a certain kind of action, yet has no understanding of why it should be divinely commanded or otherwise obligatory.[26] This might hold for persons of little education, particularly on matters where the available arguments, if there are any, are difficult to grasp. My principles do not deny such a person a right to act, even publicly, in favor of the commanded conduct. But they also suggest an obligation to seek secular grounds for that conduct if it promotes any law of policy restricting freedom. On the other hand, if religious authorities are the source of the person's belief, we may certainly ask that the relevant people should themselves try to provide a readily intelligible secular rationale if they are promoting laws or public policies that restrict liberty. This may be what they would reasonably wish regarding their counterparts who promote practices incompatible with their own. The kind of commitment to secular reason that I propose may constrain the use of some religious arguments, but it can protect people against coercion or pressure brought by conflicting religious arguments from others.

If I have been right about the possibility, and indeed, the desirability, of a theoethical equilibrium for religious people who are citizens in a liberal democracy, then separation of church and state may seem far less of a detriment to the sociocultural influence of religion, or at least of traditional monotheistic religion, in proportion as the moral requirements of religion are properly understood in the light of the divine attributes. Not only should traditional theists expect there to be secular routes to moral truth, these same paths should also be secular routes to divine truth.[27]

V. Rights, Ideals, and the Range of Oughts

My position as applied to individual conduct is above all one that lays out what we ought to do in something like an ideal case. It describes an aspect of civic virtue, not a limitation of civil (or other) rights. I have not meant to suggest that, for example, there is no right to base one's vote on a religious ground. But surely we can do better than guide our civic conduct merely within the constraints imposed by our rights. If ethics directs us merely to live within our rights, it gives us too minimal a guide for daily life.

One important way in which my position is highly consonant with theistic religion, and in particular with the Hebraic-Christian tradition, is its insistence that morality speaks to the heart and mind, not just to the hand and mouth; our thoughts, attitudes, and feelings can be morally criticizable or praiseworthy, as well as our words and deeds. And our deeds, however well they can be rationalized by the reasons we can offer for them, bespeak the reasons that motivate them. We are judged more by the reasons for which we act than by the reasons for which we could have acted. Loving one's neighbors as oneself implies appropriate motives as well as good deeds, and it is far more than extending them their rights of civic courtesy.

I must reiterate that in addition to expressing mainly ideals of citizenship as opposed to rights of citizens in a liberal democracy, the domain of application of my principles is primarily contexts of political advocacy and of public policy decision.

The principles are addressed especially to citizens as voters and supporters of laws and public policy, to legislators in their official capacities, to judges in making and justifying decisions, and to administrators, especially government officials, laying down and interpreting policies. But the principles apply differently in different contexts. They apply less, for instance, in the classroom than in the statehouse, and less in private discussion than in corporate boardrooms.

There are, to be sure, various models of democracy, and some are highly permissive. I have been thinking of a liberal democracy, not just any system in which the people govern themselves. I am indeed particularly thinking of a constitutional democracy. My claim is that a substantially weaker separation of church and state than I have defended is not fully consonant with the ideals of liberal democracy, at least as it is best understood. I think that sound ethics itself dictates that, out of respect for others as free and dignified individuals, we should always have and be sufficiently motivated by adequate secular reasons for our positions on those matters of law or public policy in which our decisions might significantly restrict human freedom. If you are fully rational and I cannot convince you of my view by arguments framed in the concepts we share as rational beings, then even if mine is the majority view I should not coerce you. Perhaps the political system under which we live embodies a legal right for the majority to do so, for certain ranges of conduct; perhaps there is even a moral right to do so, given our mutual understanding of majority rule. But the principles I am suggesting still make a plausible claim on our allegiance. They require partial secularization of our advocacy, argumentation, and decisions, in certain contexts and for certain purposes. But they do not restrict our ultimate freedom of expression, and they leave us at liberty to fulfill our cherished religious ideals in all the ways compatible with a system in which those with differing ideals are equally free to pursue theirs.

NOTES

This essay has benefited much from my discussions of the issues at the University of San Diego School of Law Conference on the Place of Religious Argument in a Liberal Democracy. For comments (written, oral, or both) and helpful discussions, I thank Larry Alexander, Theodore Blumoff, Charles Larmore, Michael Perry, Philip Quinn, Donald Scheid, and, especially, Kent Greenawalt.

1. The principles I shall generally presuppose are those stated in Robert Audi, The Separation of Church and State and the Obligations of Citizenship, 18 Phil. & Pub. Aff. 259 (1989) (hereinafter Audi, Separation). For critical discussion of that article, see Paul J. Weithman, The Separation of Church and State: Some Questions for Professor Audi, 20 Phil. & Pub. Aff. 52 (1991). For my response to Professor Weithman, see Robert Audi, Religious Commitment and Secular Reason: A Reply to Professor Weithman, 20 Phil. & Pub. Aff. 66 (1991). Also highly relevant to this essay is Kent Greenawalt, Religious Convictions and Political Choice (Oxford University Press ed., 1988). I have discussed the theory of that book in Religion and the Ethics of Political Participation, 100 Ethics 386 (1990), and Professor Greenawalt has replied to me and others in Religious Convictions and Political Choice: Some Further Thoughts, 39 DePaul L. Rev. 4 (1990).

2. I follow the common and useful practice of using "church" generically to apply to any religious institution.

3. A sociological argument may be religious in content in the sense of having premises attributing religious beliefs to people; here the attribution itself carries no religious commitment, and so it is not relevant to the notion we need here.

4. If the premise does not warrant the conclusion, it cannot be known through that premise. Presumably, in this example religious considerations also could not justify attributing a warranting relation, but that is not quite self-evident. Still, it would not be expected in a case like this, where the premise is largely irrelevant to the conclusion.

5. Here is a different example. Imagine an island society's discovering an inscription on the beach that reads: "Circumcise!" Someone might argue that this writing cannot be an accident. Hence, we should (prima facie) practice circumcision. Now arguably this conclusion cannot be known or justifiedly believed on ethical or medical grounds (at least for an adequately hygienic society). If it can be, it would likely be on grounds of just the sort of authority that only a deity could have. One might reply that the argument is enthymematic and has a suppressed religious premise, in which case it is religious in content, but to insist on that seems to me to import the likeliest defense of the argument into its content. The only obvious presupposition of this sort is something like this: We ought (prima facie) to heed a directive nonaccidentally found in nature.

6. "Illocutionary" means, roughly, "in producing a locution."

7. This point underlies my emphasis on setting forth prima facie normative principles rather than restricting rights. See Audi, Separation, supra note 1.

8. For one kind of minimalist view—a neutrality conception—see Charles E. Larmore, Patterns of Moral Complexity (Cambridge University Press ed., 1987). I, too, embrace a neutrality condition but one less strong than his.

9. These are "(1) the idea of goodness as rationality, (2) the idea of primary goods, (3) the idea of permissible comprehensive conceptions of the good, (4) the idea of political virtues, and (5) the idea of the good of a well-ordered (political) society." See John Rawls, The Priority of Right and Ideas of the Good, 17 Phil. & Pub. Aff. 251 (1988). For related discussions, see Thomas Nagel, Equality and Partiality (Oxford University Press ed., 1991); Michael J. Perry, Morality, Politics, and Law: A Bicentennial Essay (New York: Oxford University Press, 1988); Richard E. Flathman's essays in Toward a Liberalism (Cornell University Press ed., 1989); Richard W. Miller, Moral Differences (Princeton University Press ed., 1992). Perry is a critic of liberalism; Flathman a defender of it. For wide-ranging studies of Perry's views quite relevant to this essay, see Theodore Y. Blumoff, Disdain for the Lessons of History: Comments on Love and Power, 20 Cap. U. L. Rev. 159 (1991), and Edward B. Foley, Tillich and Camus, Talking Politics, 92 Colum. L. Rev. 954 (1992) (reviewing Michael J. Perry, Love and Power: The Role of Religion and Morality in American Politics (1991)).

10. The reason must be essentially related because otherwise the agent's hypothetical attitude will not be sufficiently connected with the coercive reason to warrant the coercion. A typical case would be this: where R is the state's reason, for example to protect other citizens, the related reason would be, say, to fulfill my duty not to harm others. Roughly, if the agent's reason is not R, it is something like a first-person version of R. It should also be noted that this approach does not imply that all moral obligation is discernible by reflection of this kind. It does seem appropriate, however, that the obligations grounding state rights of coercion should be discernible by such reflection. This is one reason to think that such obligations correspond to rights of citizens.

11. I assume here that a fully rational person with certain information about others has

certain altruistic desires. If rationality is understood more narrowly, my formulation must be revised (unless we may assume, as I do not, that motivation to do something is entailed simply by a realization that it is one's moral obligation). The basic idea could, however, be largely preserved. I make a case for such desires in The Architecture of Reason, 62 Proc. & Addresses Am. Phil. Ass'n 227 (Supp. 1988).

12. This is so, at least, on the plausible assumption that fully rational persons can see their moral obligations. A further qualification is this: If purely rational considerations would convince a fully rational person to do certain religious deeds, such as worship God and follow certain religious principles, then they are not an appropriate basis of coercion. This is one reason the condition stated here is only necessary. Similar restrictions would apply to other possible domains in which a liberal society protects one's freedom to decline even what reason requires. Morality, I take it, is not such a domain, and some of its principles are essential to fully justifying liberalism.

13. See Audi, Separation, supra note 1, at 279–80.

14. An interesting question, put to me by Kent Greenawalt, is whether reasons presupposing atheism are ruled out as religious in the broad sense that they directly concern religion. I have not construed such reasons as religious, though the wording of my principles may allow including them, and certainly doing so may be appropriate to the overall spirit of my position. But these reasons are at least not religiously neutral and on that ground may be objectionable in certain ways in a liberal democracy. This allows, but does not entail, that there may be special church-state reasons to restrict their use. However, the two principles proposed here are not intended to exclude them.

15. Audi, Separation, supra note 1, at 284–86.

16. Two points are important. First, it may be common that this reason would in fact be sufficient only in the context of other elements, such as a general interest in civic duty, but it may still be sufficient as a specific reason for the conduct in question. Second, the person's believing the reason sufficient is neither necessary nor sufficient for its being so, but a justified false belief that it is so would have some excusatory force.

17. Weithman has questioned how feasible it is to try to follow the principle of secular rationale. See Weithman, supra note 1. See also Lawrence B. Solum, Faith and Justice, 39 DePaul L. Rev. 1083, 1089–92 (1990). Also relevant is Paul J. Weithman, Liberalism and the Privatization of Religion: Three Theological Objections Considered, 22 J. Religious Ethics (spring 1994). The above is only the beginning of a reply to such worries.

18. One might think that a person must have some motivating reason for a belief or action. But this is not so, if we distinguish reasons from causes or, more subtly, reasons for which one believes or acts from mere (explanatory) reasons that one does. Wishful thinking is a nonrational source of beliefs, and actions not performed intentionally need not be done for a reason.

19. The Declaration of Independence is one famous document supporting liberal democracy that seems to imply otherwise, but I am not certain that it must be so read, nor do I take it to be as authoritative on this matter as the work of John Stuart Mill.

20. An interesting problem arises here. Suppose one can have an objectively good secular argument for (a) God's existence and (b) His commanding our A-ing. One might then claim to have an (ultimately) secular reason for our A-ing. But notice that I characterize a secular reason as one whose justificatory force does not evidentially depend on God's existence or on theological considerations. So this argument would not qualify as providing a secular reason; it would evidentially depend on God's authority. Someone might protest that it does provide a secular route to moral knowledge, and that is all separation of church and state should

demand. But although the route is open to any rational person, it may be questioned whether it is truly secular, since God is encountered (at least intellectually) on the way. Even apart from this, I think we need epistemically secular reasons for, and not merely epistemically secular routes to, the relevant conclusions. For (1) not all rational persons can be expected to take this route, even though it is open to them all if it is indeed objectively good. In any case, (2) one would still not have (unless through having other arguments) a sufficient (purely) secular reason for one's belief or act, and thus would be speaking, or acting (for example, voting), in a primarily religious way. And (3) in practice, people of other religious persuasions would be uncomfortable. Even if they followed the same route in their arguments, they would not like having to travel through someone else's theology. That brings us to the question of the truth of the supposition: even if there are, from purely naturalistic premises, objectively justifiable arguments for God's existence, the arguments for his specific commands, especially in areas in which there is moral disagreement, are far from generally justificatory or purely naturalistic. Granted, one's having what one reasonably, even if wrongly, takes to be good secular arguments for (a) and (b) is somewhat excusing (though that term is misleading because I do not deny a right to vote religiously). But the best ideal is still not met. Now, is the best ideal one that is simply a sociopolitical ideal reasonable in a liberal democracy, or is it a moral ideal? The contrast may be artificial. If there is a sufficient moral case for liberal democracy, the best ideal can be argued to be moral. If not, it may not be moral, but there are principles about how to treat others in matters of coercion that are independent of liberal democracy and that support the rationale and motivation principles. Hence, there can be an independent moral case for them.

21. This paragraph has benefited from correspondence on the topic with Richard Arneson.

22. These among other points in this essay bear on the case made by Professor Larry Alexander to the effect that liberalism tends to assume that the epistemic credentials of religious claims are inferior to those of scientific claims. See Larry Alexander, Liberalism, Religion, and the Unity of Epistemology, 30 San Diego L. Rev. 763, 764 (1993).

23. I do not take consent to play to entail having consented to play, and the analogy to the consent of the governed is intended. I am not even implying "tacit consent" if that entails some act of consent, as opposed to having certain dispositions and behaving in certain ways.

24. In this case one would speak of, for example, justified moral attitudes rather than of moral knowledge or warranted moral belief. One might even be a skeptic and think that ethics is autonomous in a sense. Ethics has arguments independent of theology; they simply are not good enough, and hence there is no moral knowledge (or, for a stronger skeptic, even moral justification).

25. It might be objected that the same should hold for the evils themselves, or at least moral evils constituted by wrongdoing, that there must be a secular route to their elimination. Even if there is some plausibility to this conclusion, notice that it apparently presupposes that there is a secular route to moral principles. Otherwise free agents would not be overcoming evil or responsibly abstaining from it but, at best, luckily avoiding its commission.

26. This possibility was put to me by Kent Greenawalt.

27. Of course, on one traditional theistic outlook there is a sense in which every contingent truth is divine, since God is at least responsible for the truth of all contingent propositions, by virtue of knowingly realizing the possible world in which they hold. But we may still distinguish—and must do so to understand the problem of evil—between those truths God willingly ordains and those he merely permits, for example, those describing evils that are necessary for a greater good.

Chapter 6

A New Order of Religious Freedom

Richard John Neuhaus

More than he wanted to be remembered for having been president, Mr. Jefferson wanted to be remembered as the author of the Virginia "Bill for Establishing Religious Freedom." In the text of the bill he underscored this line: "The opinions of men are not the object of civil government, nor under its jurisdiction." In a republic of free citizens, every opinion, every prejudice, every aspiration, every moral discernment has access to the public square in which we deliberate the ordering of our life together.

"The opinions of men are not the object of civil government, nor under its jurisdiction." And yet civil government is ordered by, and derives its legitimacy from, the opinions of the citizenry. Precisely here do we discover the novelty of the American experiment, the unique contribution of what the Founders called this *novus ordo seclorum*, a new order for the ages. Never before in human history had any government denied itself jurisdiction over that on which it entirely depends, the opinion of its people.

That was the point forcefully made by Lincoln in his dispute with Judge Douglas over slavery. Douglas stubbornly held to the *Dred Scott* decision as the law of the land. Lincoln had the deeper insight into how this republic was designed to work. "In this age, and this country," Lincoln said, "public sentiment is every thing. With it, nothing can fail; against it, nothing can succeed. Whoever moulds public sentiment, goes deeper than he who enacts statutes, or pronounces judicial decisions. He makes possible the inforcement of these, else impossible."

The question of religion's access to the public square is not first of all a question of First Amendment law. It is first of all a question of understanding the theory and practice of democratic governance. Citizens are the bearers of opinion, including opinion shaped by or espousing religious belief, and citizens have equal access to the public square. In this representative democracy, the state is forbidden to determine which convictions and moral judgments may be proposed for public deliberation. Through a constitutionally ordered process, the people will deliberate and the people will decide.

In a democracy that is free and robust, an opinion is no more disqualified for being "religious" than for being atheistic, or psychoanalytic, or Marxist, or just plain dumb. There is no legal or constitutional question about the admission of religion to the public square; there is only a question about the free and equal participation of citizens in our public business. Religion is not a reified "thing" that threatens to intrude upon our common life. Religion in public is but the public opinion of those citizens who are religious.

As with individual citizens, so also with the associations that citizens form to advance their opinions. Religious institutions may understand themselves to be brought into being by God, but for the purposes of this democratic polity they are free associations of citizens. As such, they are guaranteed the same access to the public square as are the citizens who compose them. It matters not at all that their purpose is to advance religion, any more than it matters that other associations would advance the interests of business or labor or radical feminism or animal rights or whatever.

For purposes of democratic theory and practice, it matters not at all whether these religious associations are large or small, whether they reflect the views of a majority or minority, whether we think their opinions bizarre or enlightened. What opinions these associations seek to advance in order to influence our common life is entirely and without remainder the business of citizens who freely adhere to such associations. It is none of the business of the state. Religious associations, like other associations, give corporate expression to the opinions of people and, as Mr. Jefferson said, "The opinions of men are not the object of civil government, nor under its jurisdiction."

It is to be feared that those who interpret "the separation of church and state" to mean the separation of religion from public life do not understand the theory and practice of democratic governance. Ours is not a secular form of government, if by "secular" is meant indifference or hostility to opinions that are thought to be religious in nature. The civil government is as secular as are the people from whom it derives its democratic legitimacy. No more, no less. Indeed a case can be made—and I believe it to be a convincing case—that the very founding principle that removes opinion from the jurisdiction of the state is itself religious in both historical origin and continuing foundation. Put differently, the foundation of religious freedom is itself religious.

"We hold these truths," the Founders declared. And when these truths about the "unalienable rights" with which men are "endowed by their Creator" are no longer firmly held by the American people and robustly advanced in the public square, this experiment will have come to an end. In that unhappy case, this experiment will have turned out to be not a *novus ordo seclorum* but a temporary respite from humanity's penchant for tyranny. Yet in this the second century of the experiment, secularized elites in our universities and our courts became embarrassed by the inescapably religious nature of this nation's founding and fortune.

These secularized elites have devoted their energies to explaining why the Founders did not hold the truths that they said they held. They have attempted to strip the public square of religious opinion that does not accord with their opinion. They have labored assiduously to lay foundations other than those laid in the beginning. From John Dewey to John Rawls, and with many lesser imitators in between, they have tried to construct philosophical foundations for this experiment in freedom, only to discover that their efforts are rejected by a people who stubbornly persist in saying with the Founders, "We hold these truths." A theory of democracy that is neither understood nor accepted by the democracy for which it is contrived is a theory of democracy both misbegotten and stillborn. Two hundred years ago, and even more so today, the American people, from whom democratic legitimacy is derived, are incorrigibly religious. This America continues to be, in the telling phrase of Chesterton, "a nation with the soul of a church."

And yet there are those who persist in the claim that "the separation of church and state" means the separation of religion from public life. They raise the alarm about "church-state conflicts" that are nothing of the sort. There are conflicts, to be sure, but they are the conflicts of a robust republic in which free citizens freely contend in the public square. The extreme separationists will tolerate in public, they may even assiduously protect, the expression of marginal religious opinion, of opinion that is not likely to influence our common life. But they take alarm at the voice of the majority. In that voice it is the people that they hear; it is the people that they fear; it is democracy that they fear.

Mr. Jefferson did not say that the civil government has no jurisdiction over opinion except when it is religious opinion. He did not say that the civil government has no jurisdiction over opinion except when it is expressed through associations called churches or synagogues. He did not say that the civil government has no jurisdiction over opinion except when it is majority opinion. He said, "The opinions of men are not the object of civil government, nor under its jurisdiction."

Many worry about the dangers of raw majoritarianism, and well we all should worry. The Founders worried about it, and that is why they devised a constitutional order for representative governance, and for the protection of minority opinion and behavior. But, without the allegiance of the majority to that constitutional order, such protections are only, in the words of James Madison, "parchment barriers" to tyranny. As Lincoln observed, without the support of public sentiment, statutes and judicial decisions—including those intended to protect citizens who dissent from public sentiment—cannot be enforced.

In our day, minorities seeking refuge in the protections of the Constitution frequently do so in a manner that pits the Constitution against the American people. That is understandable, but it is a potentially fatal mistake. We must never forget the preamble and irreplaceable premise of the Constitution: "We the people . . . do ordain and establish this Constitution for the United States of America." That is to say, the Constitution and all its protections depend upon the sentiment of "we the people." Majority rule is far from being the only principle of democratic governance, but it is a necessary principle. In the Constitution, the majority imposes upon itself a self-denying ordinance; it promises not to do what it otherwise could do, namely, ride roughshod over the dissenting minorities.

Why, we might ask, does the majority continue to impose such a limitation upon itself? A number of answers suggest themselves. One reason is that most Americans recognize, however inarticulately, a sovereignty higher than the sovereignty of "we the people." They believe there is absolute truth but they are not sure that they understand it absolutely; they are, therefore, disinclined to force it upon those who disagree. It is not chiefly a secular but a religious restraint that prevents biblical believers from coercing others in matters of conscience. For example, we do not kill one another over our disagreements about the will of God because we believe that it is the will of God that we should not kill one another over our disagreements about the will of God. Christians and Jews did not always believe that but, with very few exceptions, we in this country have come to believe it. It is among the truths that we hold.

Then too, protecting those who differ is in the self-interest of all. On most controverted issues in our public life, there is no stable majority, only ever-shifting convergences and divergences. Non-Christians, and Jews in particular, sometimes see an ominous majoritarian threat in the fact that nearly 88 percent of the American people claim to be Christian. As a matter of practical fact, however, that great majority is sharply divided along myriad lines when it comes to how civil government should be rightly ordered. Furthermore, a growing number of Christians, perhaps most Christians, have a religiously grounded understanding of the respect that is owed living Judaism. Those Christians who argue that "Christian America" should be reconstructed in conformity with a revealed biblical blueprint for civil government are few and marginal, and are likely to remain so.

Father John Courtney Murray observed that, while in theory politics should be unified with revealed truth, "it seems that pluralism is written into the script of history." Some of us would go further and suggest that it is God who has done the writing. Pluralism is our continuing condition and our moral imperative until the End Time, when our disagreements will be resolved in the coming of the Kingdom. The protection against raw majoritarianism, then, depends upon this constitutional order. But this constitutional order depends, in turn, upon the continuing ratification of the majority, who are "we the people." Among the truths these people hold is the truth that it is necessary to protect those who do not hold those truths.

It is a remarkable circumstance, this American circumstance. It is also fragile. We may wish that Lincoln was wrong when he observed that "in this age, and this country, public sentiment is every thing." But he was right, and in the conflict over slavery he was to see public sentiment turn against the constitutional order and nearly bring it to irretrievable ruin. We are dangerously deceived if we think that Lincoln's observation about our radical dependence upon public sentiment is one whit less true today.

The question before us, then, is not the access of religion to the public square. The question is the access, indeed the full and unencumbered participation, of men and women, of citizens, who bring their opinions, sentiments, convictions, prejudices, visions, and communal traditions of moral discernment to bear on our public deliberation of how we ought to order our life together in this experiment that aspires toward representative democracy. It is of course an aspiration always imperfectly realized.

I noted at the start that the question before us is not first of all a question of First Amendment law. It is a question, first of all, of understanding the origins, the constituting truths, and the continuing foundations of this republic. That having been said, the question before us is also and very importantly a question of the First Amendment, and of the first liberty of that First Amendment.

The first thing to be said about that first liberty is that liberty is the end, the goal, and the entire rationale of what the First Amendment says about religion. This means that there is no conflict, no tension, no required "balancing" between free exercise and no-establishment. There are not two religion clauses. There is but one religion clause. The stipulation is that "Congress shall make no law," and the rest of the clause consists of participial modifiers explaining what kind of law Congress shall not make. This may seem like a small grammatical point, but it has far-reaching jurisprudential significance.

The no-establishment part of the religion clause is entirely and without remainder in the service of free exercise. Free exercise is the end; no-establishment is a necessary means to that end. No-establishment simply makes no sense on its own. Why on earth should we need a no-establishment provision? The answer is that no-establishment is required to protect the rights of those who might dissent from whatever religion is established. In other words, no-establishment is required for free exercise. It is, one may suggest, more than a nice play on words that Mr. Jefferson's bill of 1779 was called the "Bill for Establishing Religious Freedom." The purpose of the non-establishment of religion is to establish religious freedom. It follows that any interpretation of no-establishment that hinders free exercise is a misinterpretation of no-establishment.

In recent history, especially in the past four decades, the priority of free exercise has been dangerously obscured. Indeed, one must go further. The two parts of the religion clause have been quite thoroughly inverted. One gets the distinct impression from some constitutional scholars and, all too often, from the courts that no-establishment is the end to which free exercise is something of a nuisance. To take but one prominent example, Laurence Tribe writes in his widely used *American Constitutional Law* that there is a "zone which the free exercise clause carves out of the establishment clause for permissible accommodation of religious interests. This carved-out area might be characterized as the zone of permissible accommodation."

There we have the inversion clearly and succinctly stated. Professor Tribe allows—almost reluctantly, it seems—that, within carefully prescribed limits, the means that is no-establishment might permissibly accommodate the end that is free exercise. This is astonishing, and it is the more astonishing that it no longer astonishes, for Professor Tribe is hardly alone. Scholars and judges have in these few decades become accustomed to having the religion clause turned on its head.

Once we forget that no-establishment is a means and instrument in support of free exercise, it is a short step to talking about the supposed conflict or tension between the two provisions. And from there it is a short step to the claim that the two parts of the religion clause are "pitted against each other" and must somehow be "balanced." And from there it is but another short step to the idea that the no-establishment provision protects "secular liberty" and the free exercise provision protects "religious liberty." When the religion clause is construed according to this curious inversion, it is no surprise that religious liberty comes out the loser. Any impingement of religion upon public life is taken to violate the "secular liberty" of the nonreligious. Thus has no-establishment become the master of the free exercise that it was designed to serve.

We need not speculate about the practical consequences of this curious inversion of the religion clause. The consequences are plainly to be seen all around us. In the name of no-establishment, wherever government advances religion must retreat. And government does inexorably expand its sway over the entire social order. In education, social services, and other dimensions of public life, it is claimed that, for the sake of the nonestablishment of religion, Americans must surrender the free exercise of religion. Those who insist upon the exercise of religious freedom in education, for example, must forgo the government support that is available to those who do not so insist. Thus is religious freedom penalized in the name of a First Amendment that was designed to protect religious freedom. Thus has the constitutionally privileged status of religion been turned into a disability. Thus has insistence upon the free exercise of religion been turned into a disqualifying handicap in our public life.

The argument that public policy should not discriminate against citizens who are religious is said to be an instance of special pleading by those who have an interest in religion. That seems very odd in a society where more than 90 percent of its citizens claim to be religious. It is more than odd, it is nothing less than grotesque, that we have become accustomed to the doctrine that public policy should not benefit religion. What is this "religion" that must not be benefited? It is the individually and communally expressed opinion of a free people. To say that government should not be responsive to religion is to say that government should not be responsive to the opinion of the people. Again, the argument of extreme separationism is, in effect, an argument against democratic governance.

Once more, Mr. Jefferson: "The opinions of men are not the object of civil government, nor under its jurisdiction." The state of current First Amendment jurisprudence is such that the opinions of men and women, when they are religious, have been placed under the jurisdiction of the government. According to the inverted construal of the religion clause, wherever the writ of government runs the voice of religion must be silenced or stifled—and the writ of government runs almost everywhere. No-establishment, the servant of the free exercise of religion, has become the enemy of the free exercise of religion.

To contend for the free exercise of religion is to contend for the perpetuation of a nation "so conceived and so dedicated." It is to contend for the hope "that this nation, under God, shall have a new birth of freedom; and that government of the people, by the people, for the people, shall not perish from the earth." Despite the perverse jurisprudence of recent decades, most Americans still say with the Founders, "We hold these truths." And, with the Founders, they understand those truths to be religious both in their origin and in their continuing power. Remove that foundation and we remove the deepest obligation binding the American people to this constitutional order.

The argument here is not for an unbridled freedom for people to do whatever they will, so long as they do it in the name of religion. That way lies anarchy and the undoing of religious freedom in the name of religious freedom. There are of necessity limits on behavior, as distinct from opinion. But the constitutionally privileged and preferred status of religious freedom is such that, when free exercise is invoked, we must respond with the most diligent caution. The invocation of free exercise is an appeal to a higher sovereignty. The entire constitutional order of limited government is premised upon an acknowledgment of such higher sovereignty.

Sometimes—reluctantly, and in cases of supreme and overriding public necessity—the claim to free exercise protection for certain actions must be denied. Where such lines should be drawn is a matter of both constitutional law and democratic deliberation. It is a matter that engages the religiously grounded moral discernments of the public, without whose support such decisions cannot be democratically implemented. In other words, in this age and this country, the limits on the free exercise of religion must themselves be legitimated religiously.

A morally compelling reason must be given for refusing to allow people to do what is morally compelling. Those who seriously invoke the free exercise of religion claim to be fulfilling a solemn duty. As Madison, Jefferson, and others of the Founders understood, religious freedom is a matter less of rights than of duties. More precisely, it is a matter of rights derived from duties. Denying a person or community the right to act upon such duty can be justified only by appeal to a yet more compelling duty. Those so denied will, of course, usually not find the reason for the denial compelling. Because they may turn out to be right about the duty in question, and because, even if they are wrong, religion bears witness to that which transcends the political order, such denials should be both rare and painfully reluctant.

We have in this past half century drifted far from the constituting vision of this *novus ordo seclorum*. The free exercise of religion is the irreplaceable cornerstone of that order. In his famed Memorial and Remonstrance, James Madison wrote: "It is the duty of every man to render to the Creator such homage, and such only, as he believes to be acceptable to Him. This duty is precedent, both in order of time and in degree of obligation, to the claims of Civil Society."

The great problem today is not the threat that religion poses to public life, but the threat that the state, presuming to embody public life, poses to religion. The entire order of freedom, including all the other freedoms specified in the Bill of Rights, is premised upon what Madison calls the precedent duty that is religion. When the American people can no longer publicly express their obligations to the Creator, it is to be feared that they will no longer acknowledge their obligations to one another—nor to the Constitution in which the obligations of freedom are enshrined. The free exercise of religion is not about mere "access." The free exercise of religion is about the survival of an experiment in which civil government has no jurisdiction over the expression of the higher loyalties on which that government depends.

Debates over the niceties of First Amendment law must and will continue. We should not forget, however, that our real subject is the constituting vision of a constitutional order that, if we have the wit and the nerve for it, may yet turn out to be a new order for the ages.

Chapter 7

The Other Side of Religion

William P. Marshall

Introduction

Religion and religious freedom hold a special place in the American experience and in American constitutional law.[1] The search for religious freedom played a paramount role in the settling of the colonies and in the founding of the nation. Religious tradition is deeply embedded in our cultural heritage.[2] Americans are among the most religious people in the world,[3] and religion holds an incalculable importance in their lives.[4] Religion forges community bonds, provides moral direction, and shapes individual self-identity.[5] Most important, religion addresses the central concerns of human existence: the search for meaning, understanding, and truth.[6]

Religion's special status in American life has not, however, entitled it only to special deference. There has been one area where religion has been subject to special constraints. That area is "the public square"[7]—the metaphorical location that hosts the process of public political decision making. In this arena, both formal and informal structures inhibit religion's participation.

The Establishment Clause of the First Amendment is the formal constraint. It limits the extent to which religion may be benefited or endorsed by government action, even though other beliefs or ideas are subject to no comparable limitations.[8] The informal constraint is the general perception that religion and religious conviction are purely private matters that have no role or place in the nation's political process.[9] While the informal constraint has no legal effect (and indeed there is no question that those advocating religious beliefs have a complete right to freely enter into the political debate under the First Amendment's Speech Clause),[10] it has been used as a rhetorical objection to question the propriety of religious involvement in matters of public controversy.[11]

There has been much debate over whether the special constraints upon religion's role in the public square are justified. The breadth of this debate, however, has been narrow. Those arguing in favor of a greater role for religion in the public square tend to emphasize only the beneficial function of religion in society. Those on the other side rely primarily upon the contention that religious beliefs are epistemologically unsuited to the political process. Neither side, however, has investigated whether there is something about the nature of religion itself that justifies the special constraints placed upon it.[12] This essay is an effort to introduce that issue into the debate. Part I provides the necessary background. It briefly outlines the current attack on the special constraints placed upon religion and explains why the efforts to defend those constraints on epistemological grounds are not persuasive. Parts II and III examine the aspects of religion that potentially support a special constraint upon its role in the public square. Part II proceeds from literature. It recounts the story of Dostoevsky's Grand Inquisitor to illustrate how the needs of humanity can lead to the creation of a church, which in order to make people happy, denies freedom and invites intolerance and persecution. Part III parallels the analysis in Part II from the perspective of social science. It examines the psychological and sociological forces inherent in religious experience that can lead to intolerance and persecution. Part IV draws upon the understanding of religion set forth in parts II and III in order to address whether the special constraints placed upon religion's participation in the public square are warranted.

The essay concludes that imposing carefully circumscribed special constraints upon religion's role in public decision making is defensible despite, or perhaps because of, religion's inestimable value to human freedom and existence.

I. Background

The legitimacy of imposing special constraints upon religion's involvement in public decision making has been forcefully attacked on a number of counts. It has been argued that restricting the role of religion in political decision making (1) is artificial if not impossible; (2) undercuts society's ability to make informed moral and political judgments; and (3) sets forth an inappropriate dichotomy that forces religion and religious values to be "privatized" or "marginalized" in a manner that demeans religion's role in the life of the individual as well as in society at large.[13]

The response to this attack has rested primarily on epistemological grounds. It has been contended that because religious principles are based on faith rather than reason, they are not commonly accessible to the polity and, therefore, cannot serve as a basis for political decision making.[14] According to this view, religion is an epistemologically inferior belief system from which to construct norms of public behavior and morality.

For a number of reasons, this argument is not persuasive. First, it is descriptively inaccurate. Just as not all nonreligious postulates and mores depend on reason, not all religious principles derive from faith.[15] Second, the epistemology of the reason versus religion dichotomy is not sound. Reason may be subject to the same sort of epistemological attack as faith.[16] The belief that reason inspires moral or political truths is just that—a belief.[17] The acceptance of reason, in short, depends upon the acceptance of assertions as to the epistemological superiority of reason that are ultimately unverifiable.[18] Third, even if faith can be epistemologically distinguished from reason, the conclusion that mores produced by rational discourse are superior to those derived by faith seems arbitrary at best. Dialogue and accessibility do not assure beneficial results.[19] Finally, the epistemological attach on religion suggests a hierarchy of beliefs that is inconsistent with First Amendment Speech Clause jurisprudence, which posits that all ideas are equal.[20]

Ultimately the epistemological attack on religion does not support special constraints upon religion's role in political decision making.[21] If such constraints are justified, they must stem from another source. In the following sections, that source will be identified. Specifically, this essay asserts that the primary argument in favor of limiting religion's role in the public square stems from the manner in which religion and its followers may, at times, interact. It is the potential, and sometimes actual, dynamic of religion and not its epistemology that is problematic.

This thesis, however, has been recounted previously by story and it is to that story I now turn.

II. The Grand Inquisitor

The Grand Inquisitor is a story within a story—a "poem" told by one fictional brother to another in Dostoevsky's *Brothers Karamazov*.[22] Ivan, the story's narrator, believes he is an atheist. Alyosha, the listener, is a monk. The story describes Jesus' visit to Seville during the Spanish Inquisition. Ivan introduces the tale as follows:

> My story is laid in Spain, in Seville, at the worst time in the Inquisition, when fires were lighted every day to the glory of God, and in the splendid *auto da fé* the wicked heretics were burnt.
>
> . . . In His infinite mercy he came once more among men in that human shape in which He walked among men for three years fifteen centuries ago. He came down to the "hot pavement" of the southern town in which on the day before almost a hundred heretics had, *ad majorem gloriam Dei,* been burnt by the cardinal, the Grand Inquisitor, in a magnificent *auto da fé,* in the presence of the king, the court, the knights, the cardinals, the most charming ladies of the court, and the whole population of Seville.[23]

The people recognized Jesus in Ivan's story. They are drawn to him; they feel his compassion. They see him perform wondrous works: He cures an old man from blindness and raises a small child from death.[24]

These events are witnessed by the Grand Inquisitor, "an old man, almost ninety, tall and erect, with a withered face and sunken eyes from which a light like a fiery spark gleams."[25] The Grand Inquisitor's response is quick and startling. He orders Jesus' arrest:

> He knits his thick gray brows and his eyes gleam with a sinister fire. He holds out his finger and bids the guards take Him. And such is his power, so completely are the people cowed into submission and trembling obedience to him, that the crowd immediately makes way for the guards, and in the midst of the tomblike silence that has suddenly fallen they lay hands on Him and lead Him away.[26]

The people, who only a moment before had lavished their adoration on Jesus, now turn to the Grand Inquisitor: "The crowd instantly as one man bows down to the earth before the old inquisitor. He blesses the people in silence and passes on."[27]

Jesus is imprisoned in "the ancient palace of the Holy Inquisition."[28] After night has fallen, he is visited in his cell by the Grand Inquisitor. The Grand Inquisitor speaks:

> "Is it You? You?" but receiving no answer, he adds at once, "Don't answer, be silent. Indeed, what can You say? I know too well what You would say. And You have no right to add anything to what You had said of old. Why, then, have You come to hinder us? For You have come to hinder us, and You know that. But do You know what will happen tomorrow? I do not know who You are and I don't care to know whether it is You or only a semblance of Him, but tomorrow I will condemn You and burn You at the stake as the worst of heretics. And the very people who today kissed Your feet, tomorrow at the faintest sign from me will rush to heap up the embers of Your fire. Do You know that? Yes, maybe You know it," he added with earnest reflection, never for a moment taking his eyes off the Prisoner.[29]

What follows is a remarkable dialogue, although perhaps soliloquy is a better term, for Jesus does not speak. The only words are those of the Grand Inquisitor. He addresses Jesus in anger, chastising him, blaming him for humanity's suffering, charging him of "acting as though You did not love them at all."[30]

A. The Terrible Gift of Freedom

The Grand Inquisitor accuses Jesus of causing unbearable unhappiness by offering humanity the "terrible" gift of freedom.

> You wanted man's free love. You wanted him to follow You freely, enticed and captured by You. In place of the rigid ancient law, man was hereafter to decide for himself with a free heart what is good and what is evil, having only Your image before him as his guide.[31]

According to the Grand Inquisitor, humanity does not want freedom but desires only happiness and salved conscience. Freedom, the old man claims, is merely torment: "Did you forget that man prefers peace, and even death, to freedom of choice in the knowledge of good and evil? Nothing is more seductive for man than his freedom of conscience, but at the same time nothing is a greater torture."[32] The Grand Inquisitor's love of humanity and his need to save it from suffering lead him to decry Jesus' terrible gift and to predict that the people will reject the freedom that Jesus has offered: "They will cry aloud at last that the truth is not in You, for they could not have been left in greater confusion and suffering than You have caused, laying upon them so many cares and unanswerable problems."[33]

The Grand Inquisitor proclaims that exorcising freedom from Jesus' vision has been the task of the church for fifteen hundred years. He vaunts that the church has completed this mission in the name of Jesus himself.[34] As Ivan explains in an aside to Alyosha, "[The Grand Inquisitor] claims it as a merit for himself and his like that at last they have vanquished freedom and have done so to make men happy."[35] This explains why Jesus must be imprisoned. The Grand Inquisitor's task has been to save humanity from Jesus' offer of freedom.[36] Jesus' return can only serve to interfere with the old man's work.

B. Miracle, Mystery, and Authority

Equally significant to the Grand Inquisitor's renouncement of Jesus' religion of freedom is what he and his church have given humanity in its stead. The religion of the Grand Inquisitor is based not upon the individual's exercise of freedom but upon powers of miracle, mystery, and authority—powers that have the ability to "capture the conscience" of humanity.[37]

According to the Grand Inquisitor, Jesus was offered these powers when "the wise and mighty spirit in the wilderness" presented Him with the three great temptations.[38] Jesus, however, refused because he knew that his acceptance would prevent humanity from choosing him freely. The Grand Inquisitor scolds Jesus for this decision. He argues that if Jesus had yielded to the temptations, he would have saved humanity from its unbearable unhappiness.

It has then fallen on the church to use the powers that Jesus refused: "We have corrected Your work and have founded it up *miracle, mystery and authority*."[39] And humanity responded: "[M]en rejoiced that they were again led like a flock, and that the terrible gift that had brought them such suffering, was, at last, lifted from their hearts."[40]

This explains a more subtle question in Ivan's story: why the crowd does not resist when Jesus is arrested, and why it bows only to the Grand Inquisitor even as its "Savior" is led away in chains. It is the church, and not Jesus, that has mastered the power to satisfy humanity's conscience and make humanity happy. It is the church, and not Jesus, that holds humanity's allegiance.

C. The Competing Visions of Jesus and the Grand Inquisitor

Ivan's story presents two differing visions of religion and religious belief. The religion that Jesus offers is predicated upon freedom: the choice between good and evil is to be made with a free heart. But this freedom has its costs. It denies certainty; it creates anguish and suffering. The religion of the Grand Inquisitor, on the other hand, is based upon "miracle, mystery and authority."[41] Its concern is with humanity's cry for happiness. Like the religion of Jesus, however, it too exacts a terrible cost—it absolves humanity of its freedom.

It is tempting to view the Grand Inquisitor as representing the malevolent religious leader and Jesus as depicting the good.[42] The comparison, however, is more complex. The Grand Inquisitor's motivation is his love for humanity.[43] He wants humanity to be happy. He is willing to suffer the burden of humanity's conscience in order to lessen the anxiety of those weaker than himself. Jesus, on the other hand, while ostensibly appealing to humanity's higher nature, is willing to sacrifice humanity's happiness for an abstract goal that is beyond the reach of most individuals.[44] Only the very strong can meet Jesus' demands. It is left to the Grand Inquisitor and his church to care for the vast majority of people who are unable to live with the anguish and uncertainty that Jesus' way requires.

Neither the religious vision of Jesus nor the Grand Inquisitor are then necessarily good or bad. With both there is selflessness and higher purpose; with both there is serious cost. What does provoke a normative response, however, are the background fires of the Inquisition and the reaction of the crowd that submissively allows Jesus to be taken away. Dostoevsky's point is clear; the religion of the Grand Inquisitor leads to intolerance and persecution. Why it does so, however, is explained not so much in what *The Grand Inquisitor* tells us about religion but rather in what it reveals about humanity.[45]

D. The Grand Inquisitor and the Danger of Religion

Why does humanity respond to miracle, mystery, and authority? In Dostoevsky's tale, it is because of a troubling relationship between humanity's fear of its own freedom and its need for spiritual and moral solace. Humanity's greatest desire is to abandon its freedom and the responsibility of its own conscience: "I tell you that man is tormented by no greater anxiety than to find someone to whom he can hand over quickly that gift of freedom with which the unhappy creature is born."[46] But humanity also needs assurance that it has relinquished its freedom to the right place. Religion's powers of miracle, mystery, and authority serve as confirmation to the individual that she has acted correctly.

Humanity as described by Dostoevsky is thus not aspiritual. Rather, it has everlasting spiritual cravings.[47] It needs someone to worship, certainty as to the truth of its beliefs, and universal unity in its beliefs.[48] Nor is humanity amoral. It needs its conscience to be salved. Indeed, it is humanity's passionate need to be morally and spiritually right that makes its freedom so painful.

It is here that Dostoevsky's story reveals the aspect of religion that necessitates a special caution. Religion and humanity have a potentially dangerous symbiotic relationship. Humanity needs religion to alleviate its spiritual and moral anxiety. Humanity wants to be led, to be told that it is right, and to be relieved of the burden of its own conscience. In order to respond to these needs and anxieties, religion must proclaim its infallibility and universality. It must be dogmatic and authoritarian; if it were to express self-doubt, it would no longer possess the claim to certainty that makes it attractive.

For similar reasons, religion must also attack the validity of other beliefs. If those seeking religion need to feel certainty, then the presence of conflicting beliefs can only interfere with that desire. As the Grand Inquisitor explains:

> [Humanity is] concerned not only to find what one or the other can worship, but to find something that all would believe in and worship; what is essential is that all may be *together* in it. This craving for *community* of worship is the chief misery of every man individually and of all humanity from the beginning of time. For the sake of common worship they've slain each other with the sword. They have set up gods and challenged one another, "Put away your gods and come and worship ours, or we will kill you and your gods!"[49]

This passage, describing as it does, the genesis of religious persecution and intolerance is quite disturbing. But what is most troubling is that the persecution and intolerance could not be ascribed to the malevolence of religious leaders. The Grand Inquisitor's motivation, after all, was his love for humanity and his desire to save humanity from unhappiness. He did not act for personal wealth or gain. He was not personally evil or cruel.[50]

Yet, this realization only makes religion's dogmatism and intolerance more frightening because it cannot be explained as merely the abuse of power by misguided individuals. The point of Dostoevsky's story is that the Inquisition was not for the benefit of the church; it was for the people.

III. Religion and the Nature of Humanity

Dostoevsky's story is, of course, a caricature. Not all religions nor all religious beliefs fit the model of the church of the Grand Inquisitor. Indeed, the Jesus character in the story is an eloquent testament to religion's decidedly nonauthoritarian and nonpersecutory side, the side of religion that focuses on humanity's quest for truth and meaning. Moreover, even for those who choose not to follow the highly individualized faith of Dostoevsky's Jesus, religion is not always authoritarian or intolerant. The religion of the Grand Inquisitor is not the only alternative to the religion of Dostoevsky's Jesus.

The Grand Inquisitor also does not fully explore why humanity seeks a religious outlet. The need for religion cannot be explained solely as humanity's attempt to avoid the exercise of freedom and the responsibility of individual conscience. To many, religious affiliation and belief is a measure of altruism or humility; to others, it is part of community; and to some, it just is.

Finally, although *The Grand Inquisitor* may be seen as a call for the separation of church and state—indeed that is arguably the lesson of Jesus' rejection of authority[51]—the role of religion in the political sphere cannot be viewed as entirely negative. Religious communities may serve as intermediate groups that protect against totalitarian regimes.[52] Religious values also provide moral foundations for political choices.[53]

Nevertheless, the church of the Grand Inquisitor is not purely fictional. Rather, substantial social science literature indicates that Dostoevsky's story accurately captures what may be termed the "dark side" of religion and religious belief—the side of religion that is inherently intolerant and persecutory.[54] It is this dark side of religion that has surfaced throughout the course of history and continues to play a prominent role in contemporary world politics. It is this dark side of religion that was well known to the constitutional Framers, including Thomas Jefferson, who wrote: "I have never permitted myself to mediate a specific creed. These formulas have been the bane and ruin of the Christian church, which, through so many ages, made of Christendom a slaughterhouse and at this day divides it into castes of inextinguishable hatred to one another."[55] It is this dark side of religion that supports the special constraints placed upon its role in the political process.

A. The Dark Side of Religious Belief: Human Response to the Tremendum

The human spirit is driven to understand its role in the cosmos. This drive is, in part, an aspect of humanity's desire for knowledge. Because humanity instinctively resists the idea that human existence is random or incomprehensible,[56] it searches for meaning and order amidst chaos.[57] Indeed, as sociologist Peter Berger has indicated, in times of crises, humanity's need for meaning may become "even stronger than the need for happiness."[58]

Humanity's search for understanding is also based on fear. Humanity is plagued by existential anxiety. The knowledge of one's mortality heightens an already intractable need to comprehend the purpose of life. People are afraid that their lives may be no more than meaningless, insignificant accidents or, at the other extreme, fearful that they exist according to a divine yet incomprehensible plan fraught with eternal consequence.

The meaning that people seek contrasts with the chaos of existence. The universe yields no answers. The person who, devoid of religious belief, attempts to reconcile herself to this empty universe confronts a terrifying abyss beyond which lies only death and meaninglessness. The source of the existential fear that grips humanity as a result of this encounter has been referred to as the "tremendum."[59] To some theorists, this encounter is an inevitable part of existence.[60] To others, the encounter occurs only when existing social structures break down and force the individual to confront the universal void.[61] In either case, the tremendum manifests itself as chaos.[62]

B. Religion as a Response to the Tremendum

Religion and religious belief may be explained, at least in part, as a protection against the tremendum.[63] But the relationship is complex.[64] On the one hand, the believer is concerned with the existential problems raised by the tremendum. On the other hand, the believer seeks religion to shield herself from the tremendum [65] because facing it directly, without the protection of any religious belief, is so disturbing.[66]

Religion protects the believer from the tremendum through doctrine [67] and ritual.[68] These devices work to create what James Breech has termed a "holding mode" of consciousness that functions by allowing the believer to anchor herself to what she sees as a stable and comprehensible God.[69] By substituting doctrine and ritual for a naked encounter with the tremendum, she is able to construct a sense of order and security that effectively hides the tremendum.[70] The religious belief system, in essence, provides a psychological defense against overwhelming feelings of insignificance and chaos.[71]

That the believer needs to shield herself from the tremendum in this manner is often reflected in the structure of organized religion.[72] Insulating the believer from the terror of God, for example, is a common religious pattern. Organized religion often places one intermediary or several layers of intermediaries between God and the believer. The first layer often takes the form of the prophet, who is often described as a descendant, an incarnation, or a representative of God. The prophet and the worshipper may be divided by yet another layer of divinity—the priest, who serves as the interpreter of God's message.

Doctrine and ritual, which may work with a priest or independently, are also critical components in insulating the believer from the tremendum. In the initial stages of any religion, religious doctrine begins as a way of providing insight into the terror of God. The doctrine unfolds from the disciples' explanation of the words of the prophet, who has purportedly confronted the tremendum directly.[73]

As religious doctrine develops, its role in the religion and in the adherent's belief system becomes more pervasive. This is partially due to the natural maturing process of any organization, but it is also due to the inherent power of the doctrine. The more rigid and expansive the doctrine, the more the believer is shielded from the tremendum. Eventually, because of the strength of its appeal, doctrine replaces God as the center of the religious experience.[74]

A similar process occurs with respect to ritual. Ritual is initially created to memorialize the prophet's insight and enthusiasm.[75] As the religion matures, the ritual becomes more rigid and central to the religious experience. Eventually, people forget how the ritual connects them to the divine. Ritual ceases to be a vehicle for experiencing God and instead becomes an end in itself. At this point, the meaning of the ritual is lost and the rites become merely comforting obligations.[76]

As described thus far, the believer's devotion to religion, while interesting, is not problematic. This devotion becomes problematic when the believer is faced with competing beliefs or ideas that are inconsistent with her belief structure. Because fear is a primary motivation for the adoption of a belief structure, the believer may be upset by any suggestion that her adopted belief system is fallible. The attack on an individual's beliefs does no less than threaten to plunge her world into chaos and expose her to the pain and terror of an uncertain universe.

As a result, the believer's response may be to overcompensate by clinging passionately to her religious structure. This means, at the least, that she is unlikely to be open to discussing competing belief systems. As Breech explains, the "holding mode" of consciousness requires closing oneself off to new insight.[77] In more extreme circumstances, believers may respond with religious persecution.[78] Because the forces that assault a believer's religious structure are so fundamentally upsetting, believers may see these forces as threatening evils that must be eliminated. The prophet that rises to challenge established doctrine and ritual may be branded a heretic. Those who ascribe to other belief systems may be classified as infidels who need to be purged or converted in the name of God. As Eliade wrote:

> Since "our [the believer's] world" is a cosmos, any attack from without threatens to turn it into chaos. And as "our world" was founded by imitating the paradigmatic work of the gods, the cosmogony, so the enemies who attack it are assimilated to the enemies of the gods, the demons. . . . "Our" enemies belong to the powers of chaos.[79]

IV. Are Special Constraints Advisable? Lessons from a Privatized Culture

The previous sections establish that religion has its dark side. This dark side, moreover, has the potential to be a powerfully destructive political force. It may, for example, harm the process of political decision making. A believer who sees those who oppose or question her beliefs as aligned with the "powers of chaos" is likely to treat the public square as a battleground rather than as a forum for debate. Religion, if unleashed as a political force, may also lead to a particularly acrimonious divisiveness among different religions. Those religions that are accused of representing the powers of chaos are likely to react with similar vehemence in denouncing their attackers. Finally, and most problematically, religion's participation in the political process can produce dangerous results: Fervent beliefs fueled by suppressed fear are easily transformed into movements of intolerance, repression, hate, and persecution. There are, in short, substantial reasons for exercising caution with respect to religious involvement in the public square.[80]

Yet, if religion poses the threats to the political process suggested above, then why have these threats not materialized in the United States history?[81] Undoubtedly, one reason is demographics. The religious diversity and pluralism of the United States make appeals to religious intolerance politically inexpedient. As Professor Gedicks has argued, a politician seeking to command a majority cannot seek the support of only one religious group.[82]

But it may also be that the special constraints upon religious participation in the public square have been effective. The Establishment Clause and the cultural tendency to view religious involvement in politics with suspicion (what has been referred to in this essay as the informal constraint upon religion) may have served to minimize religious strife, intolerance, and divisiveness.[83]

This is not to deny that religion has been an important political force from time to time in American history.[84] But religion has been carefully solicitous of the notion that there is an appropriate boundary between church and state.[85] Indeed, the commitment to limiting the role of religion in politics is so strong that even those who argue that religion has been improperly excluded from the public square seem to concede that religion's involvement in the political sphere must be approached cautiously.[86]

It has been suggested that this argument claims too much and that the tradition of separation in American culture has meant only the "institutional" separation of church and state and not a full "secularized politics."[87] According to this view, while institutional separation may have helped to create a nondivisive religious climate, secular politics is too recent a phenomenon to have been a contributing factor.[88] It is difficult to see, however, how acknowledging the benefits of the institutional separation of church and state does not cede the greater point that special constraints upon religion are justifiable. Recognizing the merits of this separation certainly admits that the injection of religion into politics can be problematic. More broadly, it necessarily supports special constraints on the way religious ideas are presented in the public square. After all, where does the improper participation of institutional religion end and the advocacy of that religion's specific beliefs begin?[89] The answer, of course, is that there is no clear line. Therefore, those wishing to avoid charges of improperly bringing religion into the public square must be careful in the way they characterize their political goals. Particular positions cannot be presented as institutionally required or as theologically right. Instead, they must appeal to more general political or social interests. The advocacy of positions, in short, must be accomplished without the passion or vehemence of religious imperative.

In the end, then, the only question in dispute is when should religion's participation in the public square be limited? Should religion be invited to fully participate in the public square unless special circumstances dictate otherwise? Or should religion's undiluted participation in the public square be seen as normally inappropriate?[90]

In deciding this question, one additional factor should be considered—the possible effect of special constraints on the religious believer. The argument thus far has stressed the external aspect of the special constraints upon religion—the control of religious intolerance from without. There is, however, a beneficial internal effect as well.

The notion that religion should be "privatized" may quiet religious fervor. If religion is seen as private and not universal, there is less imperative to conquer the religious beliefs of others. Instead of viewing the religious beliefs of others as a challenge to an individual's belief structure, the individual who accepts privatization sees others' beliefs as routine and nonthreatening.[91] The only threat occurs when others violate the privatization norm by seeking to use the public square for their own religious purpose.[92]

A second consideration stems from an understanding of intolerance. In *Abrams v. United States*,[93] Justice Holmes argued that a logical result of deep conviction is intolerance.[94] As Dean Bollinger has added, failing to attempt to silence what one believes to be false might be seen as a sign of weak conviction.[95] If this is so, then based upon the psychology underlying religious belief, the believer's motivation to silence threatening views should be particularly strong. As we have seen, the fear of uncertainty leads some individuals to seek to impose their beliefs with a sense of fervency.[96] To the zealous adherent, intolerance and persecution become, in a sense, the measure of her commitment to her religious beliefs.

If, however, external limitations dictate that imposing one's beliefs upon others is not a viable political option, the believer would not feel that she is exhibiting weakness of conviction in declining to take political action to further her political goals. In this manner, the principle that politics is generally off-limits to religion may have the salutary effect of diluting the urge to be intolerant. On the other hand, if the cultural norm suggests that religion and politics should not occupy separate spheres, the believer may feel she must test her commitment by seeking to politically vindicate her beliefs or by urging her religious leaders to do so. In this latter instance, the public square becomes a religious free-for-all.

Hopefully, the lesson is clear. Religious adherents are unlikely to exercise self-restraint in entering the public square if the prevailing social norm is that it is acceptable to forgo such self-restraint. The dynamic of intolerance suggests that the erection of a presumptive barrier against religious participation in the public square is defensible.

Conclusion

Special constraints upon religion in the public square are warranted. They are warranted, however, not because of any epistemological second-class status of religious ideas but because of the way in which religion and humanity potentially interact. Religion is one of the most important forces in society. It provides immeasurable benefits to both humanity and the individual. But religion cannot be greeted in the public square solely with celebration; it must also be greeted with caution.

NOTES

1. *See* Michael E. Smith, *The Special Place of Religion in the Constitution,* 1983 *Sup. Ct. Rev.* 83, 83–84.

2. *See* Mark DeWolfe Howe, *The Garden in the Wilderness: Religion and Government in American Constitutional History* 11–12 (1965).

3. A. James Reichley, *Religion in American Public Life 2* (1985).

4. Justice Douglas captured the pervasive importance of religion in the United States when he wrote: "We are a religious people whose institutions presuppose a Supreme Being." *Zorach v. Clauson,* 343 U.S. 306, 313 (1952).

5. *See* Daniel O. Conkle, *Toward a General Theory of the Establishment Clause,* 82 Nw. U. L. Rev. 1115, 1164–66 (1988).

6. *See, e.g.,* Thomas Jefferson, *A Bill for Establishing Religious Freedom,* in *The Complete Jefferson* 946, 946–47 (Saul K. Padover ed., 1943). The bill is codified at *Va. Code Ann.* § 57-1 (Michie 1986). In the bill, Jefferson offered a search-for-truth rationale as supporting the exercise of religion and the prohibition on the government's establishment of religion. *Id.*

The relationship of religious freedom to the search for truth is further explored in William P. Marshall, *In Defense of Truth as a First Amendment Justification,* 30 Ga. L. Rev. 1 (1995), and William P. Marshall, *Truth and the Religion Clauses,* 43 DePaul U. L. Rev. 243 (1994).

7. *See* Richard J. Neuhaus, *The Naked Public Square* 10, 26 (1984).

8. *See, e.g., Lee v. Weisman,* 112 S. Ct. 2649, 2657–58 (1992).

9. The line between the formal and informal constraints upon religion is obviously not clear-cut. Occasionally religion's participation in public decision making, if too obviously successful, may raise formal Establishment Clause concerns. Government actions whose purpose is deemed to be religious are unconstitutional under current Establishment Clause standards. *E.g., Wallace v. Jaffree,* 472 U.S. 38, 55–56, 61 (1985).

10. *E.g., Cox v. New Hampshire,* 312 U.S. 569, 578 (1941) (holding that a state law requiring a special license to march in a parade was constitutional because it was not aimed at any restraint of freedom of speech or religion); *Cantwell v. Connecticut,* 310 U.S. 296, 303–4 (1940) (holding unconstitutional a law conditioning the solicitation of money for religious causes upon a state determination as to what is a religious cause); *see* Douglas Laycock, *Towards a General Theory of the Religion Clauses: The Case of Church Labor Relations and the Right to Church Autonomy,* 81 Colum. L. Rev. 1373, 1393 (1981); *cf. McDaniel v. Paty,* 435 U.S. 618, 626, 628–29 (1978) (Free Exercise Clause protects right of clergyman to run for public office).

11. This rhetorical objection is ably described and criticized in Frederick M. Gedicks, *Public Life and Hostility to Religion,* 78 Va. L. Rev. 671 (1992) (hereinafter Gedicks, *Public Life*).

12. In *Lee v. Weisman,* the Court came closest to discussing this issue when it alluded to the "history that was and is the inspiration for the Establishment Clause, the lesson that in the hands of government what might begin as a tolerant expression of religious views may end in a policy to indoctrinate and coerce." 112 S. Ct. at 2658. The Court did not explain, however, what might cause this phenomenon. *Id.*

13. *E.g.*, Gerard V. Bradley, *The Enduring Revolution: Law and Theology in the Secular State,* 39 Emory L.J. 217, 247–51 (1990); Stephen L. Carter, *Evolution, Creationism, and Treating Religion as a Hobby,* 1987 Duke L.J. 977, 985–86, 992–93; Gedicks, *Public Life, supra* note 11, at 678–81, 685–86; Richard S. Meyers, *The Supreme Court and the Privatization of Religion,* 41 Cath. U. L. Rev. *19,* 56–57, 72 (1992); Steven D. Smith, *Separation and the "Secular": Reconstructing the Disestablishment Decision,* 67 Tex. L. Rev. 955, 999–1007 (1989); *see also* Michael J. Perry, *Morality, Politics, and Law* 57–73 (1988) (concluding "that the relation between morality and politics envisioned by liberal political philosophy is impossible to achieve").

14. There is a lack of unanimous opinion as to the degree to which religion should be excluded. *Compare* Bruce A. Ackerman, *Social Justice in the Liberal State* 345–48 (1980) (asserting that "all of us [should] accept the discipline of dialogue and restrain the temptation to destroy those whom we cannot convince") *with* Kent Greenawalt, *Religious Convictions and Political Choice* 49–84 (1988) (explaining that in political decision making there are times "when religious convictions appropriately come into play and when they do not"). *But see* Neuhaus, *supra* note 7, at 248–64 (defending the value of religion in the public debate); Stephen L. Carter, *The Religiously Devout Judge,* 64 Notre Dame L. Rev. 932, 937, 943–44 (1989) (same).

15. St. Anselm is responsible for the most famous attempt to prove rationally the existence of God. *See St. Anselm's Proslogion* (M. J. Charlesworth trans., 1965). Thomas Aquinas had slightly different views on religion and faith. He believed that reason was a prerequisite for faith. *See* 1 Thomas Aquinas, *Summa Theologica* 19–27 (Fathers of the English Dominican Province trans., 1920). For a more contemporary discussion on the relationship between rationality and religion, see Meyers, *supra* note 13, at 70–73.

16. *See* Duncan B. Forrester, *Beliefs, Values and Policies 5* (1989); Frederick M. Gedicks, *The Religious, the Secular, and the Antithetical,* 20 Cap. U. L. Rev. 113, 139 (1991) (hereinafter Gedicks, *The Religious*); *see also* Myers, *supra* note 13, at 72 and n.306 (pointing out that "rationality" can begin with diametrically opposed premises).

17. *See* Michael J. Perry, *Comment on "The Limits of Rationality and the Place of Religious Conviction: Protecting Animals and the Environment,"* 27 Wm. & Mary L. Rev. 1067, 1068 (1986) ("The liberal attempt to disqualify religious judgments or beliefs is an attempt to privilege a particular conception or range of conceptions of rationality, and thus liberalism is not at all as 'neutral' or 'impartial' as it aspires and advertises itself to be."); *see also* Sanford Levinson, *The Confederation of Religious Faith and Civil Religion: Catholics Becoming Justices,* 39 DePaul L. Rev. 1047, 1077 n.90 (1990) (questioning distinctions between religious and secular morality in philosophical discourse).

18. *See* Frederick M. Gedicks and Roger Hendrix, *Choosing the Dream: The Future of Religion in American Public Life* 115–31 (1991) ("In postmodern thought, the Enlightenment project is a failure, having only succeeded in replacing worship of God with worship of science."); David Hume, *An Enquiry Concerning Human Understanding* 24–41 (1949) (1748) (scientific knowledge is only a prediction of the future because it is based on past experience; knowledge derived from experience does not absolutely determine what will happen in the future); Gedicks, *The Religious, supra* note 16, at 137 (arguing that postmodern rejection of objective truth refutes the "empirical argument for keeping religious discourse out of public life"); Smith, *supra* note 13, at 1010–11 (both secular and religious belief "may exhibit or lack generality, coherence, and regularity").

19. Smith, *supra* note 13, at 1008 n.290 (observing that there is "delicious irony" in the argument that religious values are inaccessible to the general community, and then goes on to replace these religious values with political theories that are accessible only to academics).

20. *See, e.g., Police Dept. v. Moseley*, 408 U.S. 92, 95 (1975) (holding that an ordinance is unconstitutional because it impermissibly distinguishes between labor picketing and other peaceful picketing); Kenneth L. Karst, *Equality as a Central Principle in the First Amendment,* 43 U. Chi. L. Rev. 20, 23–26 (1975)(stating that the realization of the goals of the First Amendment requires equality of expression). For this reason, I have suggested elsewhere that religion is not entitled to special protection under the Free Exercise Clause. *See* William P. Marshall, *In Defense of Smith and Free Exercise Revisionism, 58 U. Chi. L. Rev.* 308, 320 (1991); William P. Marshall, *The Case Against the Constitutionally Compelled Free Exercise Exemption,* 40 *Case W. Res. L. Rev.* 357, 388–89 (1990).

21. *See* Gedicks, *The Religious, supra* note 16, at 139 (arguing that secularism's exclusion of religion from public life should not and cannot persist).

22. Fyodor Dostoevsky, *Notes from the Underground and the Grand Inquisitor* at vii (Ralph E. Matlaw trans., 1960).

23. *Id.* at 121.

24. *Id.* at 122.

25. *Id.*

26. *Id.* at 123.

27. *Id.*

28. *Id.*

29. *Id.*

30. *Id.* at 126–29.

31. *Id.*

32. *Id.*

33. *Id.*

34. *Id.* at 124.

35. *Id.* at 125.

36. *Id.* at 123; *id.* at 132 (The Grand Inquisitor asks Jesus, "Why . . . have You come now to hinder us?").

37. "There are three powers, only three powers that can conquer and capture the conscience of these impotent rebels [humanity] forever, for their own happiness—those forces are miracle, mystery and authority." *Id.* at 129–30.

38. *Id.* at 126, 130–31. The three temptations were turning stones into bread, casting himself down from the pinnacle of the temple, and reigning over all the kingdoms of earth. The biblical accounts of the temptations are found in Matthew 4:1–11, Mark 1:12–13, and Luke 4:1–13.

39. *Id.* at 132.

40. *Id.*

41. *Id.* (emphasis omitted).

42. Dostoevsky's own view is ambiguous. At the end of the story, Jesus kisses the Grand Inquisitor and the Grand Inquisitor, rather than sentencing Jesus to death, merely sends him away. *See id.* at 139; *see also* Geir Kjetsaa, *Fyodor Dostoevsky, A Writer's Life* 341–42 (Siri Hustvedt and Daniel McDuff trans., 1987) (discussing critics' views of whether Dostoevsky was "on the side of" the Grand Inquisitor or Jesus). *But see* Ellis Sandoz, *Political Apocalypse* 246–47 (1971) (arguing that identifying Dostoevsky with the Inquisitor is untenable).

43. At the close of the story, Ivan reminds his brother that the Grand Inquisitor faced the temptations of the desert. "But yet all his life he loved humanity, and suddenly his eyes were opened, and he saw that it is no great moral blessing to attain the perfection of the will. . . ." Dostoevsky, *supra* note 22, at 137.

44. *Id.* at 131–32.

45. According to Professor Kjetsaa, "[t]he story of the Grand Inquisitor has demonstrated that it is not a question of what man wishes to be but what man is and is capable of being." Kjetsaa, *supra* note 42, at 342.

46. Dostoevsky, *supra* note 22, at 128–29.

47. *Id.* at 128.

48. *Id.* at 132–33.

49. *Id.* at 128.

50. Importantly, this explanation of the Grand Inquisitor's motivations comes not from the Grand Inquisitor himself but from Ivan, the story's narrator. *Id.* at 137–38. The fact that this depiction comes from Ivan suggests that the depiction of the Grand Inquisitor as selfless rather than malevolent is what Dostoevsky intended.

51. Sandoz, *supra* note 42, at 159–66.

52. *See* Martin E. Marty, *Religion and Republic* 51 (1987); Fredrick M. Gedicks, *Toward a Constitutional Jurisprudence of Religious Group Rights,* 1989 Wis. L. Rev. 99, 115–16; Michael W. McConnell, *Accommodation of Religion,* 1985 Sup. Ct. Rev. 1, 18. *But see* Hank Johnston and Jozef Figa, *The Church and Political Opposition: Comparative Perspectives on Mobilization Against Authoritarian Regimes,* 27 *J. for* Sci. Stud. Religion 32, 42–43 (1988) ("the ecclesiastical hierarchy tends to exert a moderating influence on church involvement in activities [in opposition to the state]").

53. Neuhaus, *supra* note 7, at 20–22; Kent Greenawalt, *Religious Convictions and Lawmaking,* 84 Mich. L. Rev. 352, 378–80 (1985).

54. *See infra* part II.A; Jonathan K. Van Pattern, *In the End Is the Beginning: An Inquiry into the Meaning of the Religion Clause,* 27 St. Louis U. L.J. 1, 47 (1983)(citing Dostoevsky's *The Brothers Karamazov*); *cf.* Frederick Gedicks and Roger Hendrix, *Democracy, Autonomy, and Values: Some Thoughts on Religion and Law in Modern America,* 60 S. Cal. L. Rev. 1579, 1590 (1987) (mentioning the "dark side" of religion).

55. *15 The Writings of Thomas Jefferson* 374 (A. Bergh ed., 1903) (letter to Reverend Thomas Whittemore).

56. *See* Peter L. Berger, *The Sacred Canopy* 56 (1967) ("Man cannot accept aloneness and he cannot accept meaninglessness.").

57. *See* Robert Wuthnow, *Meaning and Moral Order* 25–26 (1987) (arguing that the threat of chaos or "meaninglessness" shaped the social theories of both Weber and Durkheim: "With some form of alienation or estrangement being identified as the fundamental problem facing human existence, the highest calling of scholarship in the classical tradition became that of finding ways to reunite subject and object.").

58. Berger, *supra* note 56, at 58.

59. Rudolf Otto called the fear produced by a religious encounter *"mysterium tremendum."* Rudolf Otto, *The Idea of the Holy* 12–23 (John W. Harvey trans., 2d ed. 1950).

60. According to some theorists, chaos is the genesis of religious belief; believers create religion in order to hide the chaos of existence. Erwin R. Goodenough, *The Psychology of Religious Experiences* 8–14 (1965); Otto, *supra* note 59, at 14–15.

61. Durkheim and Eliade hold a more intricate view of the relationship between chaos and religious belief. To them, unlike Otto, chaos does not serve as the genesis of religious belief. Rather, the threat of chaos works to entrench the believer in preexisting religious structures. The greater the threat that chaos poses, the more intricate the religious structure. *See generally* Emile Durkheim, *The Elementary Forms of the Religious Life* 21–33 (J. Swain trans., 1965) (discussing the effects of the threat of chaos on belief systems); Mircea Eliade, *The Sa-*

cred and Profane 31, 47–50 (Willard R. Trask trans., 1959) (discussing the development of religious and magical "defenses" to threats to order).

62. The tremendum also represents the possibility of God or, more accurately, the fear induced by the realization that one's existence is insignificant in relation to an omnipotent God beyond human understanding. For example, the Old Testament passage in which Abraham perceives himself as no more than "dust and ashes" in the face of God is cited by Otto to support the idea that confrontation with the Holy makes people recognize their own insignificance. Otto, *supra* note 59, at 9. Annie Dillard has stated this idea in more colloquial terms:

> The churches are children playing on the floor with their chemistry sets, mixing up a batch of TNT to kill a Sunday morning. It is madness to wear ladies' straw hats and velvet hats to church; we should all be wearing crash helmets. Ushers should issue life preservers and signal flares; they should lash us to our pews. For the sleeping god may wake someday and take offense, or the waking god may draw us to where we can never return.

Annie Dillard, *Teaching a Stone to Talk: Expeditions and Encounters* 40–41 (1982).

63. *See* Otto, *supra* note 59, at 14 ("It is this feeling [mysterium tremendum] which, emerging in the mind of primeval man, forms the starting-point for the entire religious development in history."); *see also* Goodenough, *supra* note 60, at 1–29; Bronislaw Malinowski, *Magic, Science and Religion, in Science, Religion, and Reality* 1, 32 (J. Needham ed., 1925) (using the fishing practices of the Trobriand Islanders as an example of ritual that orders the terror of existence: "It is most significant that in the Lagoon fishing, where man can rely completely upon his knowledge and skill, magic does not exist, while in the open-sea fishing, full of danger and uncertainty, there is extensive magical ritual to secure safety and good results.").

64. The paradox of religion is that it allows the believer to avoid the tremendum by ostensibly confronting it. Goodenough, *supra* note 60, at 1–29.

65. An exception to this approach is taken by Dostoevsky's Jesus, who asks the individual to deal with the tremendum by embracing it. Dostoevsky, *supra* note 22, at 126–34; *see also* T. S. Eliot, *East Coker, in The Complete Poems and Plays* 123, 126 (1971) ("I said to my soul, be still, and let the dark come upon you / Which shall be the darkness of God.").

66. The terrifying experience of confronting God is a consistent religious theme. Throughout the history of religions, there are few accounts of believers directly encountering the sacred. Even when the deity is revealed to the faithful, they never directly see God because this vision is so horrifying. In Greek mythology, for example, when Zeus descended to earth he would always disguise himself. *See* Edith Hamilton, *Mythology* 41, 79, 298 (1969). In the Old Testament, God does not speak to Moses or Job directly but does so out of a burning bush or a whirlwind. *See* Exodus 3:2; Job 38:1. In the New Testament, God comes in human form to save humanity. In the Koran, the angel Gabriel first visits the prophet Mohammed in a dream. *The Koran Interpreted* I:40 (Arthur J. Arberry trans., 1955).

67. The broad definition for doctrine includes virtually all aspects of religious teaching and explanation, including parables and symbols as well as specific tenets.

68. *See* Victor R. Turner, *The Ritual Process: Structure and Anti-Structure* 195–99 (1969); Max Gluckman, *Les Rites de Passage, in Essays on The Ritual of Social Relations* 1, 1–52 (Max Gluckman ed., 1962).

69. James Breech, *The Silence of Jesus* 46 (1983).

70. *See* Durkheim, *supra* note 61, at 21–33; Eliade, *supra* note 61, at 64–65; Goodenough, *supra* note 60, at 7.

71. *See, e.g.,* Berger, *supra* note 56, at 53–80 (analyzing the ways divergent groups have built belief structures to address their anxieties, needs, and problems).

72. *Cf.* Dean M. Kelly, *Why Conservative Churches Are Growing* 83 (new and updated ed. 1977).

73. The prophet is generally a person who has rejected established doctrine as vestigial or corrupt. *See generally* Max Weber, *The Sociology of Religion* 46–59 (Ephraim Fischoff trans., 1963) (discussing religion's doctrinal development).

74. Religious doctrine is seen as valid for only a discrete amount of time. When a religious practice begins to lose meaning, the natural response is to shore up its structure. Eventually, however, new belief systems rise to challenge the old. *See* Berger, *supra* note 56, at 29–52.

A classic example of this phenomenon is Martin Luther's split with the Catholic Church. Luther believed that Catholic doctrine had become tired and corrupt and had replaced Jesus as the object of devotion. Accordingly, he sought to reinfuse God into Christianity. Otto, *supra* note 59, at 94–108.

75. Victor W. Turner, *Passages, Margins, and Poverty: Religious Symbols of Communities, in High Points of Anthropology* 510, 514 (Paul Bohannon and Mark Glazer eds., 2d ed. 1988) ("This primal impetus [the enthusiasm of the prophet] . . . soon attains its apogee and loses its impetus; as Weber says, '*charisma* becomes routinized,' and the spontaneous forms of communitas are converted into institutionalized structure, or become routinized, often as ritual.").

76. Robert K. Merton, *Social Theory and Social Structure* 150–51 (enlarged ed. 1968).

77. *See* Breech, *supra* note 69, at 43–50.

78. Wuthnow, *supra* note 57, at 119–44 ("Any deviation from conventional expectations or any ambiguity in the face of novel circumstances creates uncertainties not only for the immediate actors in the situation but also for the larger society. Public rituals such as witch trials provide a means of coping with uncertainty.").

79. Eliade, *supra* note 61, at 47–48. Whether these enemies come from inside or outside the religious tradition, they threaten the established religious order. Wuthnow notes that heretics can come from inside the tradition. "Catholics did not round up Protestants and accuse them of heresy, nor Protestants, Catholics. Each group found subversives within its own camp, not traitors who were explicitly allied with the enemy, but weak souls endangering the solidarity of the total community by practicing sorcery." Wuthnow, *supra* note 57, at 117.

80. Of course, religion is not the only source of doctrinal rigidity and persecution of dissent. The secular ideologies of communism and fascism, for example, have shown that religion does not have a monopoly on either the strength of its ideological hold or the generation of ideological persecution. Therefore, the constraints applied to religious participation in the public square might also be applicable to secular "nondialogic" beliefs. *Cf.* Daniel O. Conkle, *Religious Purpose, Inerrancy, and the Establishment Clause,* 67 Ind. L. Rev. 1 (1991) (arguing for exclusion of nondialogic religious beliefs from political decision making).

On the other hand, religion's unique relationship to one of humanity's deepest fears suggests that it possesses an inherent volatility that secular ideologies do not. Moreover, the argument that there are special concerns posed by religion's involvement in politics is buttressed, rather than weakened, by the realization that nationalism may also pose the risk of intolerance and persecution. Nationalism arguably approaches religion in its ability to maintain a fervent hold on its adherents. Therefore, keeping religion out of the political sphere assures that these powerful forces do not combine and increase their dangers.

81. The short answer is that the history of religion in the United States is not unblemished. American religion readily established that it was not immune to the forces of intolerance and xenophobia in both the anti-Mormon movement of the nineteenth century and the anti-Catholic movement in the late nineteenth and twentieth centuries. Douglas Laycock, *The*

Remnants of Free Exercise, 1990 Sup. Ct. Rev. 1, 61–63. For a brief history of the Catholic struggle in the United States, *see Lemon v. Kurtzman*, 403 U.S. 602, 628–30 (1971) (Douglas, J., concurring). For an example of a particularly harsh anti-Mormon decision, *see Davis v. Beason*, 133 U.S. 333, 346–47 (1889) (upholding a restriction denying the right to vote to those having a religious belief in polygamy).

82. Gedicks, *The Religious, supra* note 16, at 121–22 ("A politician who needed votes from a theologically diverse electorate could succeed only if he used a language that appealed to all without offending any.").

83. *But see id.* at 139 (contending that the use of American history is a "curious" argument for secularized politics because secularism is recent).

84. Examples of instances in which religion has had a profound effect include the antislavery movement, the civil rights movement, the temperance movement, and the abortion movement (both pro-choice and anti-choice).

85. Robert Wuthnow has concluded:

> What both sides [evangelicals and liberals] recognized, of course, was that the symbolic boundary between morality and politics was crucial. If the boundary was blurred, and if the category of morality was allowed to spill over into the public domain, then evangelicals had a right to take action and to do so with moral conviction. If the boundary was clear and impermeable, keeping morality in the private domain, then evangelicals were merely meddling in matters that had better be left to those who knew more about politics.

Robert Wuthnow, *The Restructuring of American Religion* 211 (1988).

86. *See, e.g.*, Arlin M. Adams and Charles J. Emmerich, *A Heritage of Religious Liberty*, 137 U. Pa. L. Rev. 1559, 1666–69 (1989) (discussing the limits of the religion clauses); Gedicks, *The Religious, supra* note 16, at 144 (acknowledging "risk" involved in including religious ideas in public debate).

87. Adams and Emmerich, *supra* note 86, at 1615–25; Gedicks, *The Religious, supra* note 16, at 116–19, 139; Smith, *supra* note 13, at 962–71.

88. *See* Gedicks, *The Religious, supra* note 16, at 139; Smith *supra* note 13, at 971–79.

89. It is particularly problematic to make this determination today when the advocacy of any view is so expensive that it often requires major institutional support.

90. As noted previously, religion and those espousing religious beliefs have a clear First Amendment right to participate in the political process. *See supra* note 10 and accompanying text. The question is whether this participation can be subject to rhetorical objection.

91. In a sense, the "belief" in toleration becomes internalized as a part of the adherent's religious belief structure. Interestingly, Locke advocated that religious toleration be extended only to those religions that adopted toleration as one of the tenets of their faith. John Locke, *A Letter Concerning Toleration, in 6 The Works of John Locke* 1 (London 1823); *see also* Michael W. McConnell, *The Origins and Historical Understanding of Free Exercise of Religion*, 103 Harv. L. Rev. 1410, 1514–15 (1990).

92. Indeed, this is yet another reason that the breakdown of the privatization norm is so dangerous. Even those religious groups that would normally be unlikely to enter into the political debate might choose to do so if they saw other religious groups actively utilizing the political processes in order to gain governmental imprimatur for their religion and their religious beliefs. *See* Geoffrey R. Stone, *In Opposition to the School Prayer Amendment*, 50 U. Chi. L. Rev. 823, 839–41 (1983) (suggesting that battles like those between religious groups who contested the content of England's *The Book of Common Prayer* would accompany an American attempt to draft a sectarian school prayer).

93. 250 U.S. 616 (1919).

94. *Id.* at 630 (Holmes, J., dissenting) ("If you have no doubt of your premises or your power and want a certain result with all your heart you naturally express your wishes in law and sweep away all opposition.").

95. Lee C. Bollinger, *The Tolerant Society* 61–63 (1986).

96. Believers may feel motivated to impose their beliefs on others because they fear appearing uncertain about their beliefs. *Id.* at 61–64.

Chapter 8

Liberal Democracy and Religious Morality

Michael J. Perry

> It would truly be a sad thing if the religious and moral convictions upon which the American experiment was founded could now somehow be considered a danger to free society, such that those who would bring these convictions to bear upon your nation's public life would be denied a voice in debating and resolving issues of public policy. The original separation of church and state in the United States was certainly not an effort to ban all religious conviction from the public sphere, a kind of banishment of God from civil society. Indeed, the vast majority of Americans, regardless of their religious persuasion, are convinced that religious conviction and religiously informed moral argument have a vital role in public life.
>
> —Pope John Paul II[1]

The political community we call the United States of America is, whatever else it is, a democracy.[2] The United States is, moreover, a liberal democracy: a democracy committed—in the case of the United States, *constitutionally* committed—to certain basic human freedoms, understood both as constitutive of "genuine democracy"[3] and as limits on the laws a political majority may enact, the policies it may pursue, the actions it may take.[4] I have discussed one such freedom elsewhere: freedom of religion, which in the United States is, famously, a constitutional freedom.[5]

The general question I want to address here is this: In a liberal democracy, like the United States, what role is it proper for religion to play in politics? More precisely: What role is it proper for *religious arguments about the morality of human conduct* to play in politics? More precisely still: First, is it proper for religious believers to present such arguments *in public political debate*; second, is it proper for religious believers to rely on such arguments *as a basis of political choice*?

Two phrases appear throughout my discussion: "religious arguments" and "political choices." The political choices with which I am concerned in this essay are those that ban or otherwise disfavor one or another sort of human conduct based on the view that the conduct is immoral.[6] A law banning abortion is a prime example of the kind of political choice I have in mind; a legislature's refusal to grant legal status to same-sex unions is another. The religious arguments with which I am concerned here are arguments that one or another sort of human conduct, like abortion or homosexual sexual conduct, is immoral. By a "religious" argument, I mean an argument that relies on, *inter alia*, a religious belief: an argument that presupposes the truth of a religious belief and includes that belief as one of its essential premises. A "religious" belief is, for present purposes, either the belief that God exists—"God" in the sense of a transcendent reality that is the source, the ground, and the end of everything else—or a belief about the nature, the activity, or the will of God.[7] This definition of a "religious" argument covers, for example, the claim that the Bible is God's revealed word, and the claim that when speaking *ex cathedra* on matters of faith or morals the pope speaks infallibly. Both claims are based on a belief about the activity of God.

I. Religious Arguments in Public Political Debate

Let's turn first to this question: Is it proper for religious believers to present, in public political debate—in public debate about what political choices to make—religiously based arguments about the morality of human conduct? I want to begin by disaggregating the question into two distinct but related inquiries, the first of which concerns the politics of the United States, the second, the politics of any liberal democracy, including the United States. First, as a matter of American constitutional law, *may* religious believers present religiously based moral arguments in public political debate? Second, as a matter not of constitutional law but only of what we may call, for want of a better term, political morality, *should* religious believers present such arguments in public political debate; that is, is it proper, as a matter of (non-constitutional) political morality, for them to do so?

I have addressed the former question elsewhere. The question is not difficult, and the answer I have given is not controversial: Neither citizens nor even legislators or other governmental policy makers would violate the constitutional requirement that government not "establish" religion were they to present religiously based moral arguments arguments in public political debate. (Hereafter, when I say policy makers, I mean governmental policy makers, like the president of the United States or the governor of a state.)[8] Indeed, although government would almost certainly violate the constitutional requirement that it not "abridge the freedom of speech" were it to ban or otherwise restrain political speech because of the content of the speech, government would violate, in addition, the constitutional requirement that it not "prohibit the free exercise of religion" were it to ban or otherwise restrain political speech because the content of the speech was religious.[9]

However, that citizens and even legislators and other policy makers *may*, as a matter of constitutional law, present religious arguments about the morality of human conduct in public political debate—that they are constitutionally free to present such arguments in public political debate—does not entail that as a matter of political morality they *should* do so. Is it proper for them to do so?[10] I have addressed that question at length elsewhere;[11] here I will be brief.

Imagine that it is proposed to make, or to maintain, a political choice banning or otherwise disfavoring a particular sort of human conduct—for example, the political choice not to grant legal recognition to same-sex unions. Imagine, too, that a widely accepted religious argument supports the claim that the conduct is immoral—for example, the argument that God reveals in the Bible that each and every instance of homosexual sexual conduct is immoral. It is inevitable, in the United States, that some citizens and legislators (and other policy makers) will support the political choice at least partly on the basis of the religious argument. It is also inevitable that some citizens and legislators, because they accept the religious argument, will take more seriously than they otherwise would, and perhaps accept, a secular argument that supports the political choice—for example, the argument that homosexuality, like alcoholism, is a pathology that ought not to be indulged, or the argument that granting legal recognition to same-sex unions would threaten the institution of heterosexual marriage and other "traditional family values." Because of the role that religiously based moral arguments inevitably play in the political process, then, it is important that such arguments, *no less than secular moral arguments*, be presented in public political debate—*so that they can be tested there.*[12]

All of this is obvious; at least, all of this seems obvious to me. Nonetheless, some persons want to keep religiously based moral arguments out of public political debate as much as possible. For example, American philosopher Richard Rorty has written approvingly of "privatizing religion—keeping it out of . . . 'the public square,' making it seem bad taste to bring religion into discussions of public policy."[13]

One reason for wanting to "privatize" religion is that religious debates about controversial political issues can be quite divisive.[14] But American history does not suggest that religious debates about controversial issues—racial discrimination, for example, or war—are invariably more divisive than secular debates about those or other issues.[15] Some issues are so controversial that debate about them is inevitably divisive without regard to whether the debate is partly religious or, instead, only secular. To be sure, religious discourse in public—whether in public political debate or in other parts of our public culture—is sometimes quite sectarian and therefore divisive. But religiously based moral discourse is not necessarily more sectarian than secular moral discourse. It can be much less sectarian. After all, certain basic moral premises common to the Jewish and Christian traditions, in conjunction with the supporting religious premises, still constitute the fundamental moral horizon of most Americans—much more so than do Kantian (or neo-Kantian) premises, or Millian premises, or Nietzschean premises, and so forth.[16]

Another reason for wanting to keep religiously based moral arguments out of public political debate focuses on the inability of some persons to gain a critical distance on their religious beliefs—the kind of critical distance essential to truly deliberative debate. But in the United States and in other liberal democracies, many persons *are* able to gain a critical distance on their religious beliefs;[17] they are certainly as able to do so as they and others are able to gain a critical distance on other fundamental beliefs.[18] Undeniably, some religious believers are unable to gain much if any critical distance on their fundamental religious beliefs. As so much in the twentieth century attests, however, one need not be a religious believer to adhere to one's fundamental beliefs with closed-minded or even fanatical tenacity.

Although no one who has lived through recent American history should believe that religious contributions to the public discussion of controversial moral issues are invariably deliberative rather than dogmatic, there is no reason to believe that religious contributions are never deliberative. Religious discourse about the difficult moral issues that engage and divide us citizens of liberal democratic societies is not necessarily more monologic (or otherwise problematic) than resolutely secular discourse about those issues. Because of the religious illiteracy—and, alas, even prejudice—rampant among many nonreligious intellectuals, we probably need reminding that, at its best, religious discourse in public culture is not less dialogic—not less open-minded, not less deliberative—than is, at its best, secular discourse in public culture. (Nor, at its worst, is religious discourse more monologic—more closed-minded and dogmatic—than is, at its worst, secular discourse.) David Hollenbach's work has developed this important point:

> Much discussion of the public role of religion in recent political thought presupposes that religion is more likely to fan the flames of discord than contribute to social concord. This is certainly true of some forms of religious belief, but hardly of all. Many religious communities recognize that their traditions are dynamic and that their understandings of God are not identical with the reality of God. Such communities have in the past and can in the future engage in the religious equivalent of intellectual solidarity, often called ecumenical or interreligious dialogue.[19]

A central feature of Hollenbach's work is his argument, which I accept, that the proper role of "public" religious discourse in a society as religiously pluralistic as the United States is a role to be played, in the main, much more in public culture—in particular, "in those components of civil society that are the primary bearers of cultural meaning and value—universities, religious communities, the world of the arts, and serious journalism"—than in public debate specifically about political issues.[20] He writes: "[T]he domains of government and policy-formation are not generally the appropriate ones in which to argue controverted theological and philosophical issues."[21] But, as Hollenbach goes on to acknowledge, "it is nevertheless neither possible nor desirable to construct an airtight barrier between politics and culture."[22]

There is, then, this additional reason for not opposing the presentation of religiously based moral arguments in public political debate: In a society as overwhelmingly religious as the United States,[23] we do present and discuss—and we should present and discuss—religiously based moral arguments in our public culture.[24] Rather than try to do the impossible—maintain a wall of separation ("an airtight barrier") between the religiously based moral discourse that inevitably and properly takes place in public culture ("universities, religious communities, the world of the arts, and serious journalism") on the one side and the discourse that takes place in public political debate ("the domains of government and policy-formation") on the other side—we should simply welcome the presentation of religiously based moral arguments in *all* areas of our public culture, *including* public debate specifically about contested political choices. Indeed, we should not merely welcome but *encourage* the presentation of such arguments in public political debate—so that we can test them there.

But we can and should do more than test religiously based moral arguments in public political debate. We should also, in the course of testing such arguments, let ourselves be tested by them. In a political community that aspires to be not merely democratic but *deliberatively* democratic, there is surely virtue in allowing ourselves to be tested by arguments with which we, at the outset, disagree. About ten years ago, in my book *Morality, Politics, and Law*, I wrote:

> If one can participate in politics and law—if one can use or resist power—only as a partisan of particular moral/religious convictions about the human, and if politics is and must be in part about the credibility of such convictions, then we who want to participate, whether as theorists or activists or both, must examine our own convictions self-critically. We must be willing to let our convictions be tested in ecumenical dialogue with others who do not share them. We must let ourselves be tested, in ecumenical dialogue, by convictions we do not share. We must, in short, resist the temptations of infallibilism.[25]

Again, Richard Rorty thinks that it makes sense to "privatiz[e] religion—[to] keep[] it out of . . . 'the public square,' making it seem bad taste to bring religion into discussions of public policy." Rorty should think again. Not only are the reasons for wanting to privatize religion weak, there is, as I have explained, a strong countervailing case for wanting to "public-ize" religion, not privatize it. We should make it seem bad taste to sneer when people bring their religious convictions to bear in public discussions of controversial political issues, like homosexuality and abortion. It is not *that* religious convictions are brought to bear in public political debate that should worry us but *how* they are sometimes brought to bear (for example, dogmatically). But we should be no less worried about how fundamental secular convictions are sometimes brought to bear in public political debate. We should encourage the presentation of religiously based moral arguments in the public square for all the reasons I have given here:

- We cannot maintain an airtight separation between religiously based moral argument in public culture, which is not merely unproblematic but important, and such argument in public political debate.
- Religiously based moral argument is not necessarily more sectarian or divisive than secular moral argument.
- Religiously based moral argument is not necessarily less deliberative than secular moral argument.
- Given the influential role that religiously based moral argument inevitably plays in our politics, it is important that we test such argument in public political debate.
- Moreover, if our political culture is to be truly and fully deliberative, it is important that we let ourselves be tested by religiously based moral argument; it is important, at least, that we not exclude such argument from public political debate and thereby diminish the possibility that we will be tested by it.

II. Religious Aguments as a Basis of Political Choice

Now, let's turn to a different but related inquiry: Is it proper for religious believers to rely on religious arguments as a basis of political choice? (Again, by religious arguments, I mean religiously based moral arguments: religious arguments about the morality of human conduct.) I want to disaggregate this inquiry, too, into two distinct questions, the first of which concerns the politics of the United States: As a matter of American constitutional law, may religious arguments serve as a basis of political choice? I have addressed this question elsewhere. Here I want only to report my answer, not defend it. In my judgment, the constitutional requirement that goverment not "establish" religion means that no political choice outlawing or otherwise disfavoring one or another sort of human conduct believed to be immoral may be made *unless a plausible secular argument or rationale supports the claim that the conduct is immoral.*[26] (There is an important exception to this rule, as I will explain in subsection B of this section.) That there be a plausible secular rationale is not a very consequential requirement, as a real-world matter, because there are few if any significant political controversies where there is not a plausible secular rationale for a political choice outlawing or otherwise disfavoring human conduct believed on religious grounds to be immoral.

The second question concerns the politics not just of the United States but of any liberal democracy: As a matter not of constitutional law but only of political morality—or perhaps I should say, as a matter of nonconstitutional political morality—is it proper for religious believers to rely on religious arguments as a basis of political choice? Whether or not I am right about the question of constitutional law—and, so, even if I am not—the question of political morality remains. One possible answer to the political-moral question is that neither citizens nor, especially, legislators or other policy makers should rely on a religious argument in making a political choice (that is, a political choice outlawing or otherwise disfavoring human conduct) *unless, in their view, a secular rationale supports the choice—a secular rationale that they themselves find persuasive.*[27] A more restrictive answer is that neither citizens nor legislators or other policy makers should rely on a religious argument in making a political choice *even if, in their view, a secular rationale supports the choice.* A more permissive answer is that citizens and even legislators and other policy makers may rely on a religious argument in making a political choice *even if, in their view, no secular rationale supports the choice.*

My answer to the political-moral question is different from—it is more complicated than—any of the three answers I just listed.

A. False Starts

Why might one be inclined to conclude that government—in particular, legislators and other policy makers, acting collectively—should not rely on religious arguments in making political choices about the morality of human conduct (even if, in their view, a secular rationale supports the choice; or, at least, unless a secular rationale supports the choice)? Two reasons come to mind, one of which is moral in character, the other of which is practical. (Although the moral reason might be directed specifically at religiously based moral arguments, it is typically directed at moral arguments without regard to whether they are religious or secular.) According to the moral reason, for government, in making a political choice (or, at least, a coercive political choice), to rely on a moral argument that some persons subject to the choice reasonably reject is for government to deny to those persons the respect that is their due as human beings—or, as Rawls has put it, as "free and equal" persons.[28] Variations on this claim appear frequently in essays presenting "liberal" political-philosophical views. For example, Stephen Macedo has recently written that "[t]he liberal claim is that it is wrong to seek to coerce people on grounds that they cannot share without converting to one's faith."[29]

This moral position is deeply problematic. The following comment by William Galston, though it somewhat misconceives the position, goes to the heart of the matter:

> [Charles] Larmore (and Ronald Dworkin before him) may well be right that the norm of equal respect for persons is close to the core of contemporary liberalism. But while the (general) concept of equal respect may be relatively uncontroversial, the (specific) conception surely is not. To treat an individual as person rather than object is to offer him an explanation. Fine; but *what kind* of explanation? Larmore seems to suggest that a properly respectful explanation must appeal to beliefs already held by one's interlocutors; hence the need for neutral dialogue. This seems arbitrary and implausible. I would suggest, rather, that we show others respect when we offer them, as explanation, what we take to be our best reasons for acting as we do.[30]

Let me offer two friendly amendments to Galston's comment. First, it is never to show respect for a human being for one person to offer to another—for example, for a Nazi to offer to a Jew—a reason to the effect that "you are not truly or fully human," even if the Nazi sincerely takes that to be his best reason for acting as he does. Second, Larmore's position, which Galston somewhat misconceives, is that political "justification must appeal, not simply to the beliefs that the other happens to have, but to the beliefs he has on the assumption (perhaps counterfactual) that he affirms the norm of equal respect."[31]

Nonetheless, it remains altogether obscure why we do not give to others the respect that is their due as human beings "when we offer them, as explanation, what we take to be our best reasons for acting as we do" (so long as our reasons do not assert, presuppose, or entail the inferior humanity of those to whom the explanation is offered). According to Robert Audi, "If you are fully rational and I cannot convince you of my view by arguments framed in the concepts we share as rational beings, then even if mine is the majority view I should not coerce you."[32] But *why*? As Gerald Dworkin has observed, "There is a gap between a premise which requires the state to show equal concern and respect for all its citizens and a conclusion which rules out as legitimate grounds for coercion the fact that a majority believes that conduct is immoral, wicked, or wrong. That gap has yet to be closed."[33]

According to a second, practical reason for wanting government to forgo reliance on religiously based moral arguments, the social costs of government relying on such arguments in making political choices (or, at least, coercive political choices)—costs mainly in the form of increased social instability—are too high. It is implausible to believe that in the context of a liberal democratic society like the United States, governmental reliance on religiously based moral arguments in making political choices (even coercive ones) is *invariably* destabilizing—or that it is invariably *more* destabilizing than governmental reliance on controversial secular moral arguments. Some imaginable instances of political reliance on a religiously based moral argument might, with other factors, precipitate social instability. However, "[c]onditions in modern democracies may be so far from the conditions that gave rise to the religious wars of the sixteenth century that we no longer need worry about religious divisiveness as a source of substantial social conflict."[34] John Courtney Murray warned against "project[ing] into the future of the Republic the nightmares, real or fancied, of the past."[35] As Murray's comment suggests, a rapprochement between religion and politics forged in the crucible of a time or a place very different from our own is not necessarily the best arrangement for our time and place. "[W]hat principles of restraint, if any, are appropriate may depend on time and place, on a sense of the present makeup of a society, of its history, and of its likely evolution."[36]

In my view, neither of the two reasons just examined—neither the moral reason nor the practical reason—bears the weight of the proposition that government should not rely solely on religious arguments in making political choices (much less the proposition that it should not rely even partly on such arguments). More generally, nothing in the morality or ethics of liberal democracy—at least, nothing I can discern—requires religious believers, in making political choices, to forgo sole reliance on religious arguments just in virtue of the fact that the arguments are religious. I agree with Nicholas Wolterstorff and others, like Douglas Laycock and Michael McConnell, that liberal-democratic morality, properly understood, requires no such thing.[37] (I therefore disagree with John Rawls and others, like Robert Audi, on this important point, as I have explained elsewhere.)[38] Listen to Wolterstorff:

> [T]he ethic of the citizen in a liberal democracy imposes no restrictions on the reasons people offer in their discussion of political issues in the public square, and likewise imposes none of the reasons they have for their political decisions and actions. If the position adopted, and the manner in which it is acted upon, are compatible with the concept of liberal democracy, and if the discussion concerning the issue is conducted with civility, then citizens are free to offer and act on whatever reasons they find compelling. I regard it as an important implication of the concept of liberal democracy that citizens should have this freedom—that in this regard they should be allowed to act as they see fit. Liberal democracy implies, as I see it, that there should be no censorship in this regard.[39]

B. Religious Arguments about Human Worth

Liberal-democratic morality does not require religious believers, in making political choices, to forgo sole reliance on religious arguments *just because the arguments are religious.* Moreover, there is, as I now explain, one very important kind of religious argument—one very important kind of religiously based moral argument—that not only is not inappropriate in a liberal democracy but is, to the contrary, especially appropriate.

Religious arguments about the morality of human conduct typically address one or both of two fundamental moral issues. First: Are all human beings sacred (or "inviolable"),[40] or only some; does the well-being of every human being merit our respect and concern, or the well-being only of some human beings? (There is a related question, but it is really just a variation on the question about the sacredness *vel non* of all human beings: Who is a human being; that is, what members of the species Homo sapiens are truly, fully human? Women? Nonwhites? Jews?)[41] Second: What are the requirements of human well-being; what is friendly to human well-being, and what is hostile to it; what is good for human beings, and what is bad?[42] There are, correspondingly, two basic kinds of religious argument about the morality of human conduct: religious arguments about who among all human beings are sacred, and religious arguments about the requirements of human well-being. I now want to explain why religious argument of the first sort—religious argument about who among all human beings are sacred, which I will call simply "religious arguments about human worth"—is especially appropriate in a liberal democracy like the United States.

The only claim about human worth on which government in the United States constitutionally may rely is that all human beings (or, at least, all born human beings), and not just some (for example, white persons, men, Christians), are truly, fully human and, as such, are sacred.[43] Moreover, the only claim about human worth consistent with the international law of human rights is that each and every human being is inviolable or sacred.[44] Claims to the effect that all human beings are sacred are quite common in the United States, where the most influential religious traditions teach that all human beings are children of God and sisters and brothers to one another. (As Hilary Putnam has noted, the moral image central to what Putnam calls the Jerusalem-based religions "stresse[s] equality and also fraternity, as in the metaphor of the whole human race as One Family, of all women and men as sisters and brothers.")[45] The opening passage of a statement, in 1995, by the Catholic bishops of Florida, on the controversial political issue of welfare reform, is illustrative: "The founding document of our nation says that all are endowed by their Creator with inalienable rights, including the right to life, liberty, and the pursuit of happiness. And as Jesus has told us: 'Amen, I say to you, whatever you did for the least of these brothers and sisters of mine you did for me.'"[46] Moreover, claims that all human beings are sacred are quite common not just in the United States, but throughout the world. Indeed, the first part of the idea of human rights—an idea that has emerged in international law since the end of World War II and that is embraced by many persons throughout the world who are not religious believers as well as by many who are—is that each and every human being is sacred.[47]

The proposition that all human beings are sacred is, for many persons, a religiously based tenet.[48] However, many persons who are not religious believers embrace the proposition as a fundamental principle of morality. The proposition is an axiom of many secular moralities as well as a fundamental principle, in one or another version, of many religious moralities. The widespread secular embrace of the idea of human rights is conclusive evidence of that fact. As Ronald Dworkin has written: "We almost all accept . . . that human life in all its forms is *sacred*. . . . For some of us, this is a matter of religious faith; for others, of secular but deep philosophical belief."[49] Indeed, the proposition that every human being is sacred is axiomatic for so many secular moralities that many secular moral philosophers have come to speak of "the moral point of view" as that view according to which "every person [has] some sort of equal status."[50] Bernard Williams has noted that "it is often thought that no concern is truly moral unless it is marked by this universality. For morality, the ethical constituency is always the same: the universal constituency. An allegiance to a smaller group, the loyalties to family or country, would have to be justified from the outside inward, by an argument that explained how it was a good thing that people should have allegiances that were less than universal."[51]

I reported earlier in this essay that, in my judgment, the "nonestablishment" norm of the United States Constitution forbids government to rely on a religious argument in making a political choice outlawing or otherwise disfavoring human conduct believed immoral unless a plausible secular rationale supports the choice. That report was not entirely accurate; let me now amend it. I have elsewhere called attention to the possibility that there is no plausible or even intelligible secular argument that every human being is sacred—that the only intelligible arguments to that effect are religious in character.[52] (That an argument is intelligible does not mean that it is persuasive or even plausible.) Let us assume, for the sake of argument, that no plausible secular argument supports the claim that every human being is sacred. It would be silly to insist that because no plausible secular argument supports the claim that every human being is sacred, the nonestablishment norm forbids government, in making a political choice, to rely on the claim that every human being is sacred. After all, the proposition that all human beings (nonwhite as well as white, women as well as men, and so on) are truly, fully human and, as such, are sacred is a fundamental part of the Constitution itself—in particular, of the Fourteenth Amendment. In a review of my book *Religion in Politics*, Kurt Lash has written: "[Perry] never explains why *this* religious belief [that is, that every human being is sacred], but not others, *constitutionally* may be imposed on nonbelievers."[53] I hope the explanation is now clear: The proposition that every human being is sacred is a fundamental part of the Fourteenth Amendment to the Constitution of the United States. The Constitution not only does not forbid government, in making political choices, to rely on the proposition, it forbids government to rely on the contrary proposition that some persons are not sacred.

Similarly, it would be silly to insist that (apart from what the Constitution might or might not forbid), citizens, legislators, and other policy makers should therefore forgo reliance on the claim that every human being is sacred unless in their judgment a persuasive (to them) secular argument supports the claim. Whether or not a persuasive secular argument supports the claim—and, so, even if none does—the proposition that all human beings are sacred is a fundamental constituent of the moral culture of the United States. It is a fundamental moral conviction of us Americans that, in the words of our Declaration of Independence, all human beings "are created equal, and endowed by their Creator with certain unalienable rights." Therefore, we must conclude that, in making a political choice outlawing or otherwise disfavoring human conduct believed immoral, government may, under the nonestablishment norm, and legislators and others may, as a nonconstitutional matter, rely on the claim that every human being is sacred *whether or not any persuasive or even plausible secular argument supports the claim about the true and full humanity and sacredness of every human being.* This conclusion should trouble few if any persons who are committed to liberal democracy, however, even if they are religious nonbelievers, because the proposition that each and every human being is sacred is not only embedded, in one form or another, in many different religious traditions,[54] it is also axiomatic for most persons, including most nonbelievers, who are committed to liberal democracy as the morally best form of government and, more broadly, to the idea of human rights. Any argument, including any religious argument, that only *some* human beings are sacred (inviolable and so on) is contrary both to liberal democracy and to the idea of human rights.

> [P]erhaps the litmus test of whether the reader is in any sense a liberal or not is Gladstone's foreign-policy speeches. In [one such speech,] taken from the late 1870s, around the time of the Midlothian campaign, [Gladstone] reminded his listeners that "the sanctity of life in the hill villages of Afghanistan among the winter snows, is as inviolable in the eye of almighty God as can be your own . . . that the law of mutual love is not limited by the shores of this island, is not limited by the boundaries of Christian civilization; that it passes over the whole surface of the earth, and embraces the meanest along with the greatest in its unmeasured scope." By all means smile at the oratory. But anyone who sneers at the underlying message is not a liberal in any sense of that word worth preserving.[55]

C. Religious Arguments about Human Well-Being

Recall that there are two basic kinds of religious argument about the morality of human conduct: religious arguments about who among all human beings are sacred and religious arguments about the requirements of human well-being. I have just explained why religious argument of the first sort is especially appropriate in a liberal democracy like the United States. What about religious argument of the second sort? Again, liberal-democratic morality does not require religious believers, in making political choices, to forgo sole reliance on religious arguments—including religious arguments about the requirements of human well-being—*just because the arguments are religious.* But we should not stop there. After all, religious believers might have one or more reasons to forgo sole reliance on religious arguments, or some religious arguments, other than a reason rooted in liberal-democratic morality. Many religious believers *do* have such a reason—an *internal* reason, *a reason rooted in their own theological understanding*—to accept the following claim:

- In making a political choice, legislators and other policy makers and even ordinary citizens should forgo reliance on a religious argument about human well-being—at least, they should be exceedingly wary about relying on such a religious argument—*unless an independent secular argument that they themselves accept, that they themselves find persuasive, reaches the same conclusion about the requirements of human well-being as the religious argument.*

As I am about to explain, for most religious believers in the United States, at least, and probably for most religious believers in other liberal democracies, especially liberal democracies that are religiously pluralistic, the persuasiveness or soundness of any religious argument about human well-being depends, or should depend, partly on there being at least one persuasive secular argument (that is, one secular argument that *they themselves* find persuasive) that reaches the same conclusion about the requirements of human well-being as the religious argument. (Some theologically conservative Christians—in particular, "fundamentalist" Christians and some "evangelical" Christians—will disagree. I address such Christians in the next section of this essay.) A qualification is necessary here. Imagine a religious argument according to which perfect human well-being consists, at least in part, in union with God and therefore requires, among other things, prayer or other spiritual practice conducive to achieving such union. By definition, no "secular" argument can reach such a conclusion about the nature or requirements of human well-being.[56] But, as I have explained elsewhere, no government committed to the ideal of nonestablishment will take any action based on the view that a practice or practices are, as *religious* practice—as practice embedded in and expressive of one or more religious beliefs—truer or more efficacious spiritually or otherwise better than one or more other religious or nonreligious practices or than no religious practice at all.[57] The United States is constitutionally committed to the ideal of nonestablishment. (Moreover, no government committed to freedom of religion, as a liberal democracy is, will coerce its citizens to engage in any religious practices.) Nonetheless, to be as precise as possible, I should say: The persuasiveness of any religious argument about human well-being—any religious argument, that is, on which a government committed *not* to discriminate in favor of religious practice would be prepared to rely—should depend in part on there being at least one sound secular argument that reaches the same conclusion as the religious argument. At least, no religious argument about human well-being should be deemed sufficiently strong to ground a political choice, least of all a coercive political choice, unless a persuasive secular argument reaches the same conclusion about the requirements of human well-being.

Why should the persuasiveness of every religious argument about human well-being (on which a government committed not to discriminate in favor of religious practice would be prepared to rely) depend partly on there being at least one sound secular route to the religious argument's conclusion about the requirements of human well-being? A "religious" argument about human well-being—like a religious argument about anything—is, as I said earlier, an argument that relies on (among the other things it relies on) a religious belief: an argument that presupposes the truth of a religious belief and includes that belief as one of its essential premises. (Again, a "religious" belief is, for present purposes, either the belief that God exists—"God" in the sense of a transcendent reality that is the source, the ground, and the end of everything else—or a belief about the nature, the activity, or the will of God.) The paradigmatic religious argument about human well-being relies principally on a claim about what God has revealed. Such an argument might be made by someone who believes that we human beings are too fallen (too broken, too corrupt) to achieve much insight into our own nature and that the safest inferences about human nature, about the requirements of human well-being, are based on God's revelation. However, religious believers—even religious believers within the same religious tradition—do not always agree with one another about what God has revealed. Moveover, many religious believers understand that human beings are quite capable not only of making honest mistakes but even of deceiving themselves about what God has revealed—including what God might have revealed about the requirements of human well-being.[58]

Therefore, and as many religious believers understand, an argument about human well-being—about what is truly good for (all or some) human beings, or about what is truly bad for them—that is grounded on a claim about what God has revealed is highly suspect if there is no secular route to the religious argument's conclusion about the requirements of human well-being. So long as no persuasive secular argument supports the conclusion about the requirements of human well-being reached by a religious argument of the kind in question, the religious argument is problematic. (This is not to say either that the existence of a persuasive secular argument entails the persuasiveness of the religious argument or that the nonexistence of a persuasive secular argument entails that the religious argument is incorrect.) Indeed, in the absence of any persuasive secular argument, the religious argument is of doubtful soundness for anyone who believes, as do most Christians, for example, that no fundamental truth about the basic requirements of human well-being is unavailable to any (rational) human being—that every such truth, even if available only to some human beings by the grace of "supernatural" revelation, is nonetheless available "in principle" to every human being by virtue of so-called "natural" reason.[59] The Roman Catholic religious-moral tradition has long embraced that position:[60]

> Aquinas remained . . . convinced that morality is essentially rational conduct, and as such it must be accessible, at least in principle, to human reason and wisdom. . . . In the teaching of Aquinas, the purpose of revelation, so far as morality is concerned, appears to be essentially remedial, not absolutely necessary for man. . . . [T]he Christian revelation contains in its moral teaching no substantial element over and above what is accessible to human reason without revelation. . . . Revelation as such has nothing in matters of moral behaviour to add to the best of human thinking.[61]

Aquinas's enormous influence on the Christian religious-moral tradition extends far beyond just Catholic Christianity. Christians generally, and not just Catholics, would "want to argue (at least, many of them would) that the Christian revelation does not require us to interpret the nature of man in ways for which there is otherwise no warrant but rather affords a deeper understanding of man as he essentially is."[62]

No religious argument about human well-being—indeed, no religiously based moral argument of any kind—is a persuasive basis of political choice for religious nonbelievers. But even for religious believers—in particular, for religious believers, whether Christian or not, who accept what has been the dominant Christian understanding of the relation between "revelation" and "reason"—any religious argument about human well-being should be a highly suspect basis of political choice if no persuasive secular argument reaches the same conclusion about the requirements of human well-being as the religious argument. Given the demonstrated, ubiquitous human propensity to be mistaken and even to deceive oneself about what God has revealed, the absence of a persuasive secular argument in support of a claim about the requirements of human well-being fairly supports a presumption that the claim is probably false, that it is probably the defective yield of that demonstrated human propensity. At least, it fairly supports a presumption that the claim is an inappropriate ground of political choice, especially coercive political choice.

A religious community might try to insulate itself from such a presumption by means of one or more doctrines about its own privileged and perhaps even infallible insight into God's revelation, including God's revelation about the requirements of human well-being. But any such doctrine is destined to seem to outsiders to the community—and, depending on the degree of historical self-awareness among the members of the community, even to some insiders, and perhaps to many of them—as little more than a prideful and self-serving stratagem. In any event, no such doctrine can be politically effective in a society as religiously pluralistic as the United States. Indeed, no religious community that fails to honor the ideal of self-critical rationality can play a meaningful role in the politics of a religiously pluralistic democracy like the United States.[63] As Richard John Neuhaus has warned: "So long as Christian teaching claims to be a privileged form of discourse that is exempt from the scrutiny of critical reason, it will understandably be denied a place in discussions that are authentically public."[64] Listen, too, to J. Bryan Hehir, who, as the principal drafter of the U.S. Catholic bishops' 1983 letter on nuclear deterrence,[65] has some experience in the matter:

> [R]eligiously based insights, values and arguments at some point must be rendered persuasive to the wider civil public. There is legitimacy to proposing a sectarian argument within the confines of a religious community, but it does violence to the fabric of pluralism to expect acceptance of such an argument in the wider public arena. When a religious moral claim will affect the wider public, it should be proposed in a fashion which that public can evaluate, accept or reject on its own terms. The [point] . . . is not to banish religious insight and argument from public life[, but only to] establish[] a test for the religious communities to meet: to probe our commitments deeply and broadly enough that we can translate their best insights to others.[66]

The drafters of *The Williamsburg Charter*, a group that included many prominent religious believers, have articulated a similar contention: "Arguments for public policy should be more than private convictions shouted out loud. For persuasion to be principled, private convictions should be translated into publicly accessible claims. Such public claims should be made publicly accessible . . . because they must engage those who do not share the same private convictions."[67] Richard Neuhaus, who was instrumental in the drafting of *The Williamsburg Charter*, has cautioned that "publicly assertive religious forces will have to learn that the remedy for the naked public square is not naked religion in public. They will have to develop a mediating language by which ultimate truths can be related to the penultimate and prepenultimate questions of political and legal contest."[68]

Again, any religious community that would play a meaningful role in the politics of a religiously pluralistic democracy like the United States must honor the ideal of self-critical rationality. Insisting on a persuasive secular argument in support of a claim about human well-being is obviously one important way for the members of a religious community to honor the ideal of self-critical rationality; it is one important way for them to conform their practice to the ideal. Moreover, it is one important way—and, indeed, a relatively ecumenical way—for the citizens of a religiously pluralistic democracy, including citizens who are religious believers, to test the various statements about what God has revealed, including statements about God's revealed will, that are sometimes articulated in public political debate—for example, statements that certain biblical passages "'prove' that heterosexuality is God's exclusive intention for human sexuality and that homosexuality is an abomination before God."[69]

I have just indicated why, in making political choices about the morality of human conduct, legislators, other policy makers, and even ordinary citizens should not rely on—at least, they should be exceedingly wary about relying on—a religious argument about human well-being if, in their view, no secular argument that is persuasive to them reaches the same conclusion about the requirements of human well-being. Should we go further and conclude that legislators and others should not rely on a religious argument about human well-being even if, in their view, a persuasive secular argument *does* reach the same conclusion? Should legislators and others rely *only* on the persuasive secular argument? Our historical experience teaches us to be deeply skeptical about government—about politics, about the politically powerful—acting as an arbiter of *religious* truth.[70] Politics is not a domain conducive to the discernment of theological truth; it is, however, a domain extremely vulnerable to the manipulative exploitation of theological controversy. (Theologically conservative Christians should know this as well as anyone else.) Nonetheless, it seems unrealistic to insist that legislators and others support a political choice about the morality of human well-being only on the basis of a secular argument they find persuasive if they also find persuasive a religious argument that supports the choice. How could such a legislator be sure that she was relying *only* on the secular argument, putting no weight whatsoever on the religious argument? She could ask whether she would support the choice even if the religious argument were absent, solely on the basis of the secular argument. However, trying to ferret out the truth by means of such counterfactual speculation is perilous at best and would probably be, as often as not, self-deceiving and self-serving.[71]

More fundamentally, the relevant question for a legislator (or other policy maker or citizen) is *not* whether she would find persuasive a secular argument about human well-being if she did not already find persuasive a religious argument that reaches the same conclusion as the secular argument. To ask herself that question would be for the legislator to ask herself whether she would find the secular argument persuasive if she were someone other than the person she is, someone without the particular religious beliefs she has. Such a counterfactual inquiry is not only often hopelessly difficult but, more important, beside the point: The proper question is not whether *someone else* would find the secular argument persuasive but whether, on reflection, *she* finds it persuasive. The question she should ask herself is whether, in addition to the religious argument she accepts, she finds persuasive a secular argument that reaches the same conclusion about the requirements of human well-being. True, one might be more inclined to find persuasive a secular argument if one already accepts a religious argument that reaches the same conclusion. But there's nothing to be done about that.

That a legislator or other policy maker or citizen cannot reach a judgment about the soundness of the relevant secular argument or arguments on her own is not disabling, because she can seek the help of those whose judgment she respects and trusts; she can, in the end, rely on their judgment. After all, relying on the judgment of those we respect and trust is one quite ordinary way we decide whether to accept propositions that for one reason or another we are not competent or otherwise in a position to evaluate by ourselves. The judgment of others we respect and trust is typically a fundamental criterion of the persuasiveness of such propositions. This is true with respect to propositions about, say, subatomic reality or the performance of the stock market. It is no less true with respect to propositions about the requirements of human well-being.[72]

The principle of self-restraint I am recommending here is quite modest if and to the extent it would not be difficult for a religious believer to locate an independent, corroborating secular argument about the requirements of human well-being that she could accept as sound. Indeed, if one believes that it would rarely if ever be difficult for a religious believer to locate such an argument, one might wonder whether my principle of self-restraint isn't modest to the point of being inconsequential and scarcely worth defending. Moreover, one might wonder why it should matter if some policy makers were to make a political choice about the morality of human conduct solely on the basis of a religious argument about human well-being, if it is extremely unlikely that in a country like the United States, any such political choice would be established (or maintained) as law or public policy unless supported by a widely accepted secular argument about the requirements of human well-being?

My response to such thoughts relies on the value of maintaining a pervasively and vigorously "ecumenical" politics.[73] (I have written at length, in *Love and Power*, in support of an ecumenical politics.)[74] Consider the ecumenical function of the practice I am recommending here; consider the ecumenical political culture such a practice can help to cultivate. For citizens and, especially, their elected representatives to decline to make a political choice about the morality of human conduct unless a persuasive secular argument supports the choice, *and, concomitantly, for them to rely at least partly on a secular argument in public political debate about whether to make the choice,* helps American politics to maintain a relatively ecumenical character rather than a sectarian one. It does so by de-emphasizing one of the most fundamental things that divides us—religion—and in that sense and to that extent is one way of reinforcing, rather than tearing, the bonds of political community.[75] Note, too, that having to present and defend a secular argument in public political debate is at least somewhat constraining. But even if the practice is not, for some, very constraining, secular political arguments, once presented in public political debate, are available for testing there; they are not immune to counterargument. At the end of the day, such an argument may be less credible—and therefore less widely influential—than it was at the beginning. Consider, in that regard, how well secular arguments about the (im)morality of same-sex marriages are faring.

It is difficult to understand why any religious community that honors the ideal of self-critical rationality (as any religious community should) would object to the "ecumenizing" practice I am recommending here, given that, as I said, insisting on a persuasive secular argument in support of a claim about the requirements of human well-being is one important way for a religious community to honor the ideal. It is especially difficult to understand why any religious community that values ecumenical dialogue with those outside the community would object to such a practice, which can only serve to facilitate such dialogue.[76] Only a historically naive religious (or other) tradition would doubt the value of ecumenical dialogue, which is, among other things, a profoundly important project for anyone committed to the ideal of self-critical rationality.

> There is, of course, much to gain by sharpening our understanding in dialogue with those who share a common heritage and common experience with us. . . . Critical understanding of the [religious] tradition and a critical awareness of our own relationship to it, however, is sharpened by contact with those who differ from us. Indeed, for these purposes, the less they are like us, the better.[77]

Defending the moderate style of his participation in public discourse about abortion and other issues implicating what he famously called "the consistent ethic of life," the late Joseph Cardinal Bernardin, archbishop of Chicago, said:

> The substance of the consistent ethic yields a style of teaching it and witnessing to it. The style should . . . not [be] sectarian. . . . [W]e should resist the sectarian tendency to retreat into a closed circle, convinced of our truth and the impossibility of sharing it with others. . . . The style should be persuasive, not preachy. . . . We should be convinced we have much to learn from the world and much to teach it. A confident church will speak its mind, seek as a community to live its convictions, but leave space for others to speak to us, to help us grow from their perspective.[78]

For the sake of clarity, let me restate the basic position I am defending here: In making a political choice about the morality of human conduct, especially a coercive political choice, legislators and other policy makers and even ordinary citizens have good reason to forgo reliance on a religious argument about human well-being unless, in their view, a persuasive secular argument reaches the same conclusion about the requirements of human well-being as the religious argument. Now, someone might conclude that according to this position, the moral insight achieved over time by the various religious traditions, by the various historically extended religious communities, has at most only a marginal place in public political debate about the morality of human conduct. (Consider, in that regard, the statement by Pope John Paul II that I have put at the beginning of this essay—the statement the pope made, in December 1997, in receiving the credentials of Lindy Boggs as ambassador to the Holy See.) But such a conclusion would be mistaken—for four reasons.

1. First, as I emphasized earlier in this essay, there are good reasons not merely for tolerating but for encouraging the airing—and testing—of religiously based moral arguments in public political debate. There is no need to rehearse the point here.

2. Second, unlike religious arguments about human well-being, religious arguments about human worth—in particular, religious arguments that each and every human being is sacred—are not covered by the position I am defending here.

In his review of *Religion in Politics*, Kurt Lash writes that "[Perry's] vision of reasonable religious dialogue seems but a shadow of the impassioned rhetoric that [has] characterized" religious participation in debates about such matters as slavery and abortion.[79] Lash continues:

> [T]o remove, or "civilize," the religious voice whenever it is based on controversial religious assumptions seems to me to remove what is simultaneously most valuable and most dangerous about religious rhetoric. "Dogmatic" religious arguments may, of course, lead to holy wars, crusades, and the burning of heretics. But they may also lead to the abolition of slavery, prod a national conscience into passing civil rights legislation, or shame us into consideration of the poor, the infirm, and the untouchable. In other words, religious rhetoric is capable of radical evil and radical good. For every William Lloyd Garrison there is a John Brown.[80]

Lash's point is misdirected. The fundamental religious argument that the issues Lash mentions all implicate—the issues of slavery, abortion, racial discrimination, the condition of the poor, the infirm, and other marginalized ("untouchable") groups—is the argument that each and every human being is sacred. But it is precisely *that* argument that is *not* covered by the position I am defending here. (It is not covered for the reasons I have presented in section II.B of this essay.) Therefore, it simply misconceives my position to say that "the impassioned religious rhetoric" that has characterized religious participation in debates about such matters as slavery and abortion would be, if my prescription were followed, reduced to a shadow of itself. For example, nothing that Martin Luther King, Jr., said about the fundamental equality of each and every human being in the eyes of the Creator God would be in the least bit problematic according to the position I am defending in this essay.

3. Third, my point is not that in making a political choice about the morality of human conduct, religious believers ought not to rely on a religious argument about human well-being; my point is only that they ought not to do so *unless* a persuasive (to them) secular argument reaches the same conclusion as the religious argument on which they are inclined to rely. In other words, in making a political choice about the morality of human conduct—a political choice that rests on a claim about the requirements of human well-being—religious believers should rely at least partly on a secular argument about the requirements of human well-being. This is not even to say that a believer's principal reliance should always be on the secular argument.

Thus, there could be, under my position, "impassioned religious rhetoric" even about an issue, like the morality of same-sex marriage, that implicates religious beliefs about the requirements of human well-being. My argument, in this essay, is only that in making a policy choice about the morality of human conduct, Christians and other religious believers have *their own* reasons—reasons *internal both to their own religious (theological) tradition and to their own historical experience*—to forgo reliance on a religious argument about human well-being in the absence of an independent, corroborating secular argument. (Again, this is not even to say that a believer's principal reliance should always be on the secular argument.) I amplify this point, about the kind of reasons ("internal" reasons) that Christians and others have, in the next section of this essay.

4. Fourth, the moral insight achieved over time by a religious tradition—the insight into the requirements of human well-being—because it is *the yield of the lived experience of an historically extended human community*, might well have a resonance and indeed an authority that extends far beyond just those who accept the tradition's religious claims. Put another way, many of the most basic claims about human well-being made by one or another religious tradition are often made, and in any event can be made, without invoking any religious claim (that is, any claim about the existence, nature, activity, or will of God). What Catholic moral theologian James Burtchaell has explained about the nature of moral inquiry or discernment in the Catholic religious tradition is true of any religious tradition—though not every religious tradition will accept it as true:

> The Catholic tradition embraces a long effort to uncover the truth about human behavior and experience. Our judgments of good and evil focus on whether a certain course of action will make a human being grow and mature and flourish, or whether it will make a person withered, estranged and indifferent. In making our evaluations, we have little to draw on except our own and our forebears' experience, and whatever wisdom we can wring from our debate with others. . . . Nothing is specifically Christian about this method of making judgments about human experience. That is why it is strange to call any of our moral convictions "religious," let alone sectarian, since they arise from a dialogue that ranges through so many communities and draws from so many sources.[81]

The fourth reason merits elaboration. Many religious believers and nonbelievers alike seem to overlook the overwhelming extent to which both the development of insight into human well-being and the debate that attends such development is, inside religious traditions as much as outside them, nonrevelational and even nontheological. Because the moral insight achieved over time by the various religious traditions is substantially nonrevelational and even nontheological, bringing that insight to bear in a politics in which religious believers' participation is self-restrained in the way I am recommending here (or in a politics restrained by the ideal of nonestablishment) is not the problem some religious believers and nonbelievers imagine it to be. The Jesuit priest and sociologist John Coleman has observed, in a passage that reflects Aquinas's influence: "[M]any elements and aspects of a religious ethic . . . can be presented in public discussion in ways that do not presume assent to them on the specific premises of a faith grounded in revelation. Without being believing Hindus, many Westerners, after all, find in Gandhi's social thought a superior vision of the human than that of ordinary liberal premises."[82] Martin Marty has commented, in much the same spirit, that "religionists who do not invoke the privileged insights of their revelation or magisterium can enhance and qualify rationality with community experience, intuition, attention to symbol, ritual, and narrative."[83]

Indeed, to embrace a religious premise—a biblical premise, for example—about what it means to be human, about how it is good or fitting for human beings to live their lives, and then to rely on the premise in public discourse, is not even *necessarily* to count oneself a participant in the religious tradition that has yielded the premise; it is not even necessarily to count oneself a religious believer. One certainly doesn't have to be Jewish to recognize that the prophetic vision of the Jewish Bible is profound and compelling, any more than one has to be Catholic or Presbyterian or Baptist or even Christian to recognize that the Gospel vision of what it means to be human is profound and compelling. Gandhi was not a Christian, but he recognized the Gospel vision as profound and compelling. As the eminent Catholic theologian David Tracy has emphasized:

> Some interpret the religious classics not as testimonies to a revelation from Ultimate Reality, . . . but as testimonies to possibility itself. As Ernst Bloch's interpretations of all those daydreams and Utopian and eschatological visions that Westerners have ever dared to dream argue, the religious classics can also become for nonbelieving interpreters testimonies to resistance and hope. As Mircea Eliade's interpretations of the power of the archaic religions show, the historian of religions can help create a new humanism which retrieves forgotten classic religious symbols, rituals, and myths.[84]

Tracy continues: "If the work of Bloch and [Walter] Benjamin on the classic texts and symbols of the eschatological religions and the work of Eliade and others on the primal religions were allowed to enter into the contemporary conversation, then the range of possibilities we ordinarily afford ourselves would be exponentially expanded beyond reigning Epicurean, Stoic, and nihilistic visions."[85]

So, there are four main reasons that it is simply not true that according to my position, the moral insight achieved over time by the various religious traditions has at most only a marginal place in public political debate about the morality of human conduct. These reasons include the point I have just been emphasizing: If, as the comments by Burtchaell, Coleman, and Tracy suggest, religious-moral insight can speak with a powerful resonance even to nonbelievers, and thereby play a central role even in a thoroughly secularized politics, then such insight can certainly play a central role in American politics, which is far from being thoroughly secularized.

III. Theologically Conservative Believers

Again, most Christians in the United States today—including Catholics, Lutherans, Episcopalians, Methodists, and "reformed" Christians (for example, Presbyterians)—have no basis in their religious-moral traditions for doubting that any religious argument about the requirements of human well-being is of questionable soundness unless a persuasive secular argument reaches the same conclusion about those requirements as the religious argument. Nor, in particular, do they have a basis in their traditions for doubting that any argument about the requirements of human well-being that is grounded on a claim about what God has revealed is highly suspect if no persuasive secular route reaches the religious argument's conclusion about the requirements of human well-being. Such Christians understand that they do not have to choose between "faith" and "reason"; for them, faith and reason are not in tension, they are not incompatible. To the contrary, faith and reason are, for such Christians, mutually enriching. David Hollenbach explains:

> Faith and understanding go hand in hand in both the Catholic and Calvinist views of the matter. They are not adversarial but reciprocally illuminating. As [David] Tracy puts it, Catholic social thought seeks to correlate arguments drawn from the distinctively religious symbols of Christianity with arguments based on shared public experience. This effort at correlation moves back and forth on a two-way street. It rests on a conviction that the classic symbols of Christianity can uncover meaning in personal and social existence that common sense and uncontroversial science fail to see. So it invites those outside the church to place their self-understanding at risk by what Tracy calls conversation with such "classics."[86]

Hollenbach then adds, following Tracy:

> At the same time, the believer's self-understanding is also placed at risk because it can be challenged to development or even fundamental change by dialogue with the other—whether this be a secular agnostic, a Christian from another tradition, or a Jew, Muslim, or Buddhist.[87]

Predictably, some Christians—in particular, "fundamentalist" Christians and some "evangelical" Christians—will be skeptical that an argument about human well-being that is grounded on a claim about what God has revealed is highly suspect if there is no secular route to, if there is no argument "based on shared public experience" for, the religious argument's conclusion about the requirements of human well-being. For such Christians, faith—including faith in what God has revealed—and reason are often incompatible; in their view, human reason is too corrupted to be trusted. For example, David Smolin, a law professor who identifies himself as an evangelical Christian, has written that

> even our intellectual capacities have been distorted by the effects of sin. The pervasive effects of sin suggest that creation, human nature, and human reason are often unreliable means for knowing the law of God. . . . Thus, scripture and Christian tradition have come to have a priority among the sources of knowledge of God's will. Indeed, these sources of revelation are considered a means of measuring and testing claims made on behalf of reason, nature, or creation, in order to purify these now subsidiary means of the distortive effect of sin.[88]

However, theologically conservative Christians should not overlook that, as the history of Christianity discloses, sin can distort, and indeed has often distorted, "scripture and Christian tradition," not to mention what human beings believe about "scripture and Christian tradition." Given their belief in the "fallenness" of human nature—which is, after all, *their* nature, too—Christians should be especially alert to this dark possibility. Smolin privileges religiously based moral arguments over secular moral arguments, but *both* sorts of arguments are, finally, human arguments. Why, then, doesn't a truly robust sense of "the distortive effect of sin" counsel that religious believers test religious arguments about the morality of human conduct—in particular, religious arguments about human well-being, both those based on scripture and those based on tradition—not only with competing religious arguments about the morality of human conduct but also with secular arguments about the morality of human conduct? (Understandably, a religious believer might want to move in the other direction as well: She might want to test secular arguments about the morality of human conduct with religiously based moral arguments as well as test the latter with the former.)[89]

Few religious believers, after all, will want to argue that secular arguments are rarely if ever to be trusted, for most religious believers rely on secular arguments every day: secular arguments about what food is best to eat, about what the weather is likely to be tomorrow, about what medicine to take to combat an infection, and so on. Theologically conservative Christians—and, indeed, theologically conservative members of other religious traditions as well—would do well to study Mark Noll's powerful, eloquent book, *The Scandal of the Evangelical Mind* (1994). Noll—the McManis Professor of Christian Thought at Wheaton College (Illinois), one of the foremost Christian (Protestant) colleges in the United States—is himself a committed evangelical Christian. Noll comments critically, in one chapter of his book, on the emergence of "creation science" in evangelical Christianity: "[I]f the consensus of modern scientists, who devote their lives to looking at the data of the physical world, is that humans have existed on the planet for a very long time, it is foolish for biblical interpreters to say that 'the Bible teaches' the recent creation of human beings." Noll explains:

> This does not mean that at some future time, the procedures of science may shift in such a way as to alter the contemporary consensus. It means that, for people today to say they are being loyal to the Bible and to demand belief in a recent creation of humanity as a sign of obedience to Scripture is in fact being unfaithful to the Bible, which, in Psalm 19 and elsewhere, calls upon followers of God to listen to the speech that God has caused the natural world to speak. It is the same for the age of the earth and for all other questions regarding the constitution of the human race. Charles Hodges's words from the middle of the nineteenth century are still pertinent: "Nature is as truly a revelation of God as the Bible, and we only interpret the Word of God by the Word of God when we interpret the Bible by science.[90]

Consider, too, the Protestant historian George Marsden's observations:

> Some [historical] knowledge cuts across all theories and paradigms, and it provides all people of good sense a solid reality basis for testing some aspects of theories. So in practice there is a common ground of historical inquiry. When we look at the past, if we do it right, what we find will in large measure correspond to what other historians find.
>
> From a Christian perspective, we may explain this phenomenon simply by observing that God in his grace seems to have created human minds with some ability to experience and know something of the real world, including the past. Furthermore, these structures are substantially common to all normal people so that, despite the notorious theoretical problems of subjectivism and point of view, we can in fact communicate remarkably well and be assured that we are talking about the same things. It may be difficult to explain, except as a matter of faith, what basis we have for reliance on these common abilities; but the fact remains that only philosophers and crackpots can long deny that often they are reliable.[91]

Why should we believe that what Noll says about the proper relation between religious faith and secular inquiry into the origins of human beings is not also true about the proper relation between religious faith and secular inquiry into the conditions of human well-being? Why should we believe that what Marsden says about historical inquiry is not also true about inquiry into the conditions of human well-being? Why should we not say, with Anthony of the Desert, a fourth-century Christian monk: "My book, O philosopher, is the nature of created things, and any time I wish to read the words of God, the book is before me."[92]

Two clarifications are in order at this point. First, and as I have already emphasized, my point is not that in making a political choice about the morality of human conduct, religious believers ought not to rely on a religious argument about human well-being; my point is only that they ought to forgo reliance on such an argument *unless* a persuasive (to them) secular argument reaches the same conclusion about the requirements of human well-being as the religious argument on which they are inclined to rely. In other words, in making a political choice about the morality of human conduct—a political choice that rests on a claim about the requirements of human well-being—religious believers should rely at least partly on a secular argument about those requirements.

Second, the principle of political self-restraint I recommend here does not presuppose that in making political choices about the morality of human conduct, Christians should forget that they are Christians; it does not presuppose that they should "bracket" their Christian identity, that they should act as if they are persons who do not have the religious beliefs that they in fact do have. (I have contended against such "bracketing" elsewhere:

> One's basic moral/religious convictions are (partly) self-constitutive and are therefore a principal ground—indeed, the principal ground—of political deliberation and choice. To "bracket" such convictions is therefore to bracket—to annihilate—essential aspects of one's very self. To participate in politics and law . . . with such convictions bracketed is not to participate as the self one is but as [someone else].")[93]

Rather, it is *because* they are Christians—it is because they are, *as Christians*, painfully aware of the fallenness, the brokenness, of human beings—that they should be extremely wary about making a political choice, least of all a coercive political choice, on the basis of a religious argument about human well-being in the absence of any independent, corroborating secular argument. This is not to suggest that persons other than Christians can't or don't have their own powerful reasons to insist on what Christians call the fallenness or brokenness of human beings.

Thus—and I want to underscore this—my position is not of the sort that Nicholas Wolterstorff has recently criticized; my position is not that the morality or ethics of liberal democracy requires Christians to forgo reliance on a religious argument about human well-being in the absence of an independent, corroborating secular argument.[94]

Again, I agree that liberal-democratic morality, properly understood, requires no such thing. Rather, my position, as I said earlier, is that Christians have *their own* reasons—reasons *internal both to their own religious (theological) tradition and to their own historical experience*—to forgo such reliance in making a policy choice about the morality of human conduct. In that sense, my argument is not that a commitment to liberal democracy somehow entails or otherwise supports the principle of self-restraint that I have recommended here—though, as I have argued elsewhere, the American constitutional ideal of "nonestablishment" does, in my judgment, warrant such a principle. Rather, my argument is that without regard to what a commitment to liberal democracy entails or otherwise supports, Christians—at least, *some* Christians—have their own reasons for embracing the principle of self-restraint recommended here. (Though some others, it must be admitted, have their own reasons for rejecting it.)

It scarcely seems radical, much less unfaithful, to suggest that Christians, too, like other religious believers, must be alert to the possibility that a scripture-based or a tradition-based religious argument about the morality of human conduct—about the requirements of human well-being—no less than a secular argument, is mistaken or worse. (The Christian argument for the permissibility of slavery was worse than mistaken; it was sinful.) Indeed, the theological and experiential reasons that Christians have, as Christians, for embracing the principle of self-restraint that I have recommended here are also reasons that they have, as Christians, for being alert to the dark possibility that one of their religious arguments about the morality of human conduct is mistaken or worse. (I think here of the argument, which I have criticized elsewhere, that all homosexual sexual conduct is immoral, *even homosexual sexual conduct that is embedded in and expressive of a lifelong, monogamous relationship of faithful love—indeed, that is a generative matrix of such a relationship, of such love.*)[95] There is no virtue in adhering to a position uncritically, so that one is unable to discern whether the position is, or might be, mistaken. Again, "[w]e must be willing to let our convictions be tested in ecumenical dialogue with others who do not share them. We must let ourselves be tested, in ecumenical dialogue, by convictions we do not share. We must, in short, resist the temptations of infallibilism."[96] Although some might think that my point here is obvious—even banal—the point is too often neglected in debates about the proper role of religion in politics and, so, bears emphasis.

> At any stage in history all that is available to the Church is its continual meditation on the Word of God in the light of contemporary experience and of the knowledge and insights into reality which it possesses at the time. To be faithful to that set of circumstances . . . is the charge and the challenge which Christ has given to his Church. But if there is a historical shift, through improvement in scholarship or knowledge, or through an entry of society into a significantly different age, then what that same fidelity requires of the Church is that it respond to the historical shift, such that it might be not only mistaken *but also unfaithful* in declining to do so.[97]

IV. A Concluding Comment

I have occasionally been asked about the "voice" that informs my conception of the proper role of religion in politics. I am a Christian[98]—in particular, a Catholic Christian thoroughly imbued with the spirit of the Second Vatican Council (1962–65).[99] But I am a Christian who is extremely wary of the God-talk in which most Christians (and many others) too often and too easily engage; in that sense, my Christianity tends toward the apophatic.[100] Thus, I stand between, on the one side, all religious nonbelievers and, on the other, many Christian and other religious believers—especially theologically conservative believers.

Religious nonbelievers, many of whom (like Richard Rorty) would like to marginalize the role of religious discourse in public political debate, are the principal addressees of my argument that it is not merely permissible but important that religious arguments about the morality of human conduct be presented in public political debate. (This point seems obvious enough in any political community committed—as any genuine liberal democracy is committed—to freedom of expression.) Religious nonbelievers are also the principal addressees of my argument that the premise that all human beings are sacred is an unproblematic basis of political choice in the United States—and, more broadly, in any liberal democracy—*even if, as I have suggested elsewhere, no plausible or even intelligible secular argument supports the premise.*

By contrast, religious believers—in particular, Christians, who, as the twentieth century draws to a close, still constitute the largest group, by far, of religious believers in the United States—are the principal addressees of my argument that in making a political choice about the morality of human conduct, especially a coercive political choice, we believers have good reason to forgo reliance on, at least we have good reason to be exceedingly wary about relying on, a religious argument about human well-being unless, in our view, a persuasive secular argument reaches the same conclusion about the requirements of human well-being as the religious argument. Because theologically conservative Christians are more likely than other Christians to be skeptical about that final aspect of my position—the aspect in which my wariness about God-talk is most engaged—I have spoken especially to them in the preceding section of this essay. I want to underscore that in speaking to such Christians, I have addressed them not imperially, from the outside, as a enlightened religious nonbeliever speaking to benighted religious believers about what the morality of liberal democracy proscribes. Rather, I have sought here to address them fraternally, from the inside, as a religious believer speaking to fellow believers, to fellow Christians, about what our shared religious (theological) tradition and our shared historical experience suggest about the proper role of religion in politics. I hope that in speaking to such Christians, I also speak, if only indirectly, to theologically conservative members of other religious traditions as well.

NOTES

This essay, which served as the basis of the 1998 Annual Lecture of the DePaul University Center for Church/State Studies, was originally published in the *DePaul Law Review*. See Michael J. Perry, "Liberal Democracy and Religious Morality," 48 DePaul L. Rev. 1 (1998). I am grateful to the *DePaul Law Review* for permission to republish the essay (with a few minor revisions) here. (The version of the essay published here contains substantially less footnote material than the version published in the *DePaul Law Review*.) This essay draws on, clarifies, and develops some arguments originally presented in my book *Religion in Politics: Constitutional and Moral Perspectives* (Oxford, 1997). I am grateful to the Oxford University Press for permission to include material from *Religion in Politics* in this essay. For a fuller treatment of some of the issues addressed in this essay, the reader should consult *Religion in Politics*.

For helpful comments on one or another draft of this essay, I am grateful to several friends and colleagues: Robert Audi, Tom Berg, John Coleman SJ, John Deigh, Chris Eberle, Marie Failinger, Margaret Farley, Mayer Freed, David Friedman, Fred Gedicks, Jim Heft, Tim Jackson, Richard Kraut, Gary Leedes, Errol Rohr, Stephen Siegel, Doug Smith, Larry Solum, Dave Van Zandt, Paul Weithman, and Nicholas Wolterstorff. I am especially indebted to Steve Smith and Laura Underkuffler. Thanks in part to the comments that these friends and colleagues have provided, I am acutely aware that this essay is far from finished; it is a work-in-progress.

This essay is dedicated to the memory of a beloved, exceptional young man, son of Fred and Nicea Gedicks, who died in the first semester of his freshman year at Wake Forest University: Alexander Philip Gedicks, 1978–1997.

1. Documentation, "John Paul II on the American Experiment" (Dec. 17, 1997), First Things, April 1998, at 36–37.

2. More precisely, the United States is, in the main, a representative rather than a direct democracy.

3. See Henry J. Steiner & Philip Alston, eds., International Human Rights in Context: Law, Politics, Morals 572 (1996) (commenting on the European Convention on Human Rights):

> [T]he third major impetus towards a Convention [was] the desire to bring the non-Communist countries of Europe together within a common ideological framework and to consolidate their unity in the face of the Communist threat. "Genuine democracy" (to which the Statute of the Council of Europe commits its members) or the "effective political democracy" to which the Preamble of the Convention refers, had to be clearly distinguished from the "people's democracy" which was practiced and promoted by the Soviet Union and its allies.

4. See Amy Gutman, "Democracy, Philosophy, and Justification," in Seyla Benhabib, ed., Democracy and Difference: Contesting the Boundaries of the Political 340 (1996): "Polyarchies, or what we might call nonideal democracies, are characterized, at a minimum, by guarantees of free political speech, press, association, and equal suffrage for all adults, the right of all adults above a certain age to run for political office, the rule of law, and frequent, competitive elections that are procedurally fair."

5. See Michael J. Perry, Religion in Politics: Constitutional and Moral Perspectives, ch. 1 (1997).

6. Cf. Kent Greenawalt, "Legal Enforcement of Morality," 85 J. Crim. L. & Criminology 710, 710 (1995): "[M]uch legal enforcement of morality is uncontroversial and rarely discussed. Disagreement arises only when the law enforces aspects of morality that do not involve protecting others from fairly direct harms. More precisely, people raise questions about legal requirements (1) to perform acts that benefit others, (2) to refrain from acts that cause indirect harm to others, (3) to refrain from acts that cause harm to themselves, (4) to refrain from acts that offend others, and (5) to refrain from acts that others believe are immoral."

7. A belief can be "nonreligious," then, in one of two senses. The belief that God does not exist is nonreligious in the sense of "atheistic." A belief that is about something other than

God's existence or nonexistence, nature, activity, or will is nonreligious in the sense of "secular." In addition to religious arguments, we can imagine both "atheistic" arguments and "secular" arguments. One who is "agnostic" about the existence of God—who neither believes nor disbelieves that God exists—will find only (some) secular arguments persuasive. Cf. Kent Greenawalt, Private Consciences and Public Reasons 63 (1995) ("assum[ing] that a principle of restraint against reliance on religious grounds would also bar reliance on antireligious grounds").

8. I often refer, in this essay, to legislators and other governmental policymakers. What about judges? Are they a special case? See Perry, Religion in Politics, *supra* n. 5, at 102–4.

9. See id. at 32–33. See also Douglas Laycock, "Freedom of Speech That Is Both Religious and Political," 29 U.C. Davis L. Rev. 793, 795–807 (1996).

10. It bears emphasis that the question I am about to address, about the role of religious arguments in public political debate, is about political morality, not political strategy.

> [T]he distinction between principle and prudence should be emphasized. The fundamental question is not whether, as a matter of prudent judgment in a religiously pluralist society, those who hold particular religious views ought to cast their arguments in secular terms. Even an outsider can say that the answer to that question is clearly, "Yes, most of the time," for only such a course is likely to be successful overall.

Mark Tushnet, "The Limits of the Involvement of Religion in the Body Politic," in James E. Wood, Jr., & Derek Davis, eds., The Role of Religion in the Making of Public Policy 191, 213 (1991).

11. See Perry, Religion in Politics, *supra* n. 5, ch. 2.

12. Moreover, it is sometimes fitting that such an argument be tested, in the to-and-fro of public political debate, by a competing religious argument of the same genre—for example, a scripture-based argument. Scripture scholar Luke Timothy Johnson's admonition is relevant here:

> If liberal Christians committed to sexual equality and religious tolerance abandon these texts as useless, they also abandon the field of Christian hermeneutics to those whose fearful and—it must be said—sometimes hate-filled apprehension of Christianity will lead them to exploit and emphasize just those elements of the tradition that have proved harmful to humans. If what Phyllis Trible has perceptively termed "texts of terror" within the Bible are not encountered publicly and engaged intellectually by a hermeneutics that is at once faithful and critical, then they will continue to exercise their potential for harm among those who, without challenge, can claim scriptural authority for their own dark impulses.

Luke Timothy Johnson, "Religious Rights and Christian Texts," in John Witte, Jr., & Johan David van der Vyver, eds., Religious Human Rights in Global Perspective: Religious Perspectives 65, 72–73 (1996).

It is easy to anticipate the reply that public political debate is simply too debased to serve as a context for serious critical discussion of religiously based moral arguments. My response is twofold. First, if public political debate is too debased to serve as a context for serious critical discussion of religiously based moral arguments, then it is too debased to serve as a context for serious critical discussion of secular moral arguments as well—or of much else too. Second, the issue that engages me in this essay is the proper role of religion not in a politics too debased for serious critical discussion of moral arguments but in a politics fit for such discussion.

13. Richard Rorty, "Religion as Conversation-Stopper," 3 Common Knowledge 1, 2 (1994).

14. Cf. McDaniel v. Paty, 435 U.S. 618, 640–41 (1978) (Brennan, J., concurring in judgment).

15. Cf. Michael W. McConnell, "Political and Religious Disestablishment," 1986 BYU L. Rev. 405, 413: "Religious differences in this country have never generated the civil discord experienced in political conflicts over such issues as the Vietnam War, racial segregation, the Red Scare, unionization, or slavery."

16. According to John Coleman, "[T]he tradition of biblical religion is arguably the most powerful and pervasive symbolic resource" for public ethics in the United States today." See John A. Coleman SJ, An American Strategic Theology 192–95 (1982).

17. See Daniel O. Conkle, "Different Religions, Different Politics: Evaluating the Role of Competing Religious Traditions in American Politics and Law," 10 J.L. & Religion 1 (1993–94).

18. David Tracy speaks for many of us religious believers when he writes:

> For believers to be unable to learn from secular feminists on the patriarchal nature of most religions or to be unwilling to be challenged by Feuerbach, Darwin, Marx, Freud, or Nietzsche is to refuse to take seriously the religion's own suspicions on the existence of those fundamental distortions named sin, ignorance, or illusion. The interpretations of believers will, of course, be grounded in some fundamental trust in, and loyalty to, the Ultimate Reality both disclosed and concealed in one's own religious tradition. But fundamental trust, as any experience of friendship can teach, is not immune to either criticism or suspicion. A religious person will ordinarily fashion some hermeneutics of trust, even one of friendship and love, for the religious classics of her or his tradition. But, as any genuine understanding of friendship shows, friendship often demands both critique and suspicion. A belief in a pure and innocent love is one of the less happy inventions of the romantics. A friendship that never includes critique and even, when appropriate, suspicion is a friendship barely removed from the polite and wary communication of strangers. As Buber showed, in every I-Thou encounter, however transient, we encounter some new dimension of reality. But if that encounter is to prove more than transitory, the difficult ways of friendship need a trust powerful enough to risk itself in critique and suspicion. To claim that this may be true of all our other loves but not true of our love for, and trust in, our religious tradition makes very little sense either hermeneutically or religiously.

David Tracy, Plurality and Ambiguity: Hermeneutics, Religion, Hope 84–85, 86, 97–98, 112 (1987).

19. David Hollenbach SJ, "Civil Society: Beyond the Public-Private Dichotomy," 5 The Responsive Community 15, 22 (Winter 1994/95). One of the religious communities to which Hollenbach refers is the Catholic community. See David Hollenbach SJ, "Contexts of the Political Role of Religion: Civil Society and Culture," 30 San Diego L. Rev. 877, 891–96 (1993).

20. See Hollenbach, "Civil Society," *supra* n. 19, at 22.

21. Hollenbach, "Contexts of the Political Role of Religion," *supra* n. 19, at 900. See also Kent Greenawalt, "Religious Convictions and Political Choice: Some Further Thoughts," 39 DePaul L. Rev. 1019, 1034 (1990) (expressing skepticism about "the promise of religious perspectives being transformed in what is primarily political debate").

22. Hollenbach, "Contexts of the Political Role of Religion," *supra* n. 19, at 900.

23. The citizenry of the United States is one of the most religious—perhaps even the most religious—citizenries of the world's advanced industrial democracies. According to recent polling data, "[a]n overwhelming 95% of Americans profess belief in God." Richard N. Ostling, "In So Many Gods We Trust," Time, Jan. 30, 1995, at 72. Moreover, "70% of American adults [are] members of a church or synagogue." Book Note, "Religion and *Roe*: The Politics of Exclusion," 108 Harvard L. Rev. 495, 498 n. 21 (1994) (reviewing Elizabeth Mensch & Alan

Freeman, The Politics of Virtue: Is Abortion Debatable? (1993)). Cf. Andrew Greeley, "The Persistence of Religion," Cross Currents, Spring 1995, at 24.

24. Cf. Paul G. Stern, "A Pluralistic Reading of the First Amendment and Its Relation to Public Discourse," 99 Yale L.J. 925, 934 (1990).

25. Michael J. Perry, Morality, Politics, and Law 183 (1988). See also Jeremy Waldron, "Religious Contributions in Public Deliberation," 30 San Diego L. Rev. 817, 841–42 (1993). Cf. Michael J. Sandel, "Political Liberalism," 107 Harvard L. Rev. 1765, 1794 (1994).

26. See Perry, Religion in Politics, *supra* n. 5, at 33–37.

27. I have suggested that those with the principal policy-making authority and responsibility—in particular, legislators—should ask themselves whether they find a secular rationale persuasive. By contrast, the issue for a court evaluating the constitutionality of the choice under the nonestablishment norm is only whether a plausible secular rationale supports the choice. See id. at 123 n. 97.

28. See John Rawls, Political Liberalism 217 (1993).

29. Stephen Macedo, "Transformative Constitutionalism and the Case of Religion: Defending the Moderate Hegemony of Liberalism," 26 Political Theory 56, 71 (1998).

30. William A. Galston, Liberal Purposes 108–9 (1991).

31. Michael J. Perry, "Religious Morality and Political Choice: Further Thoughts—and Second Thoughts—on *Love and Power*," 30 San Diego L. Rev. 703, 711 n. 23 (1993) (quoting Larmore).

32. Robert Audi, "The Place of Religious Argument in a Free and Democratic Society," 30 San Diego L. Rev. 677, 701 (1993). I wonder what it might mean for one to be "fully rational"—and also what "concepts we share as rational beings."

33. Gerald R. Dworkin, "Equal Respect and the Enforcement of Morality," 7 Social Philosophy & Policy 180, 193 (1990) (criticizing Ronald Dworkin). See also John M. Finnis, Natural Law and Natural Rights 221–22 (1980) (criticizing Ronald Dworkin). I concur in Nicholas Wolterstorff's critique of Audi's position on this point. See Nicholas Wolterstorff, "Audi on Religion, Politics, and Liberal Democracy," in Robert Audi & Nicholas Wolterstorff, Religion in the Public Square 145, 159–61 (1997).

A related argument for disfavoring sole reliance on religious arguments in making political choices about the morality of human conduct is that citizens who do not subscribe to the relevant religious premise or premises will be, or will feel, politically alienated in consequence of such reliance. I have explained elsewhere why, in my judgment, this argument is implausible. See Perry, Religion in Politics, *supra* n. 5, at 50–52. Cf. Steven D. Smith, Foreordained Failure: The Quest for a Constitutional Principle of Religious Freedom 164–65 n. 66 (1995):

> [T]he very concept of "alienation," or symbolic exclusion, is difficult to grasp. How, if at all, does "alienation" differ from "anger," "annoyance," "frustration," or "disappointment" that every person who finds himself in a political minority is likely to feel? "Alienation" might refer to nothing more than an awareness by an individual that she belongs to a religious minority, accompanied by a realization that at least on some issues she is unlikely to be able to prevail in the political process. . . . That awareness may be discomforting. But is it the sort of phenomenon for which constitutional law can provide an efficacious remedy? Constitutional doctrine that stifles the message will not likely alter the reality—or a minority's awareness of that reality.

Smith quotes Mark Tushnet: "[N]onadherents who believe that they are excluded from the political community are merely expressing the disappointment felt by everyone who has lost a fair fight in the arena of politics." Mark V. Tushnet, "The Constitution of Religion," 18 Conn. L. Rev. 701, 712 (1986) (quoted in Smith, this note, at 164–65 n. 66).

34. Lawrence B. Solum, "Faith and Justice," 39 DePaul L. Rev. 1083, 1096 (1990). Solum is stating the argument, not making it. Indeed, Solum is wary of the argument. See id. at 1096–97. Solum cites, as an instance of the argument, Stephen L. Carter, "The Religiously Devout Judge," 64 Notre Dame L. Rev. 932, 939 (1989). For another instance, see Maimon Schwarzschild, "Religion and Public Debate in a Liberal Society: Always Oil and Water or Sometimes More Like Rum and Coca-Cola?" 30 San Diego L. Rev. 903 (1993).

35. John Courtney Murray, We Hold These Truths 23–24 (1960).

36. Kent Greenawalt, Private Consciences and Public Reasons, *supra* n. 7, at 130.

37. Wolterstorff, "Audi on Religion, Politics, and Liberal Democracy," *supra* n. 33, at 147. See also Laycock, "Freedom of Speech That Is Both Religious and Practical," *supra* n. 9; Michael W. McConnell, "Correspondence: Getting Along," First Things, June–July 1996, at 2.

38. See Perry, Religion in Politics, *supra* n. 5, at 54–61.

39. Wolterstorff, "Audi on Religion, Politics, and Liberal Democracy," *supra* n. 33, at 147.

40. In *Life's Dominion*, Dworkin writes:

> Some readers . . . will take particular exception to the term "sacred" because it will suggest to them that the conviction I have in mind is necessarily a theistic one. I shall try to explain why it is not, and how it may be, and commonly is, interpreted in a secular as well as in a conventionally religious way. But "sacred" does have ineliminable religious connotations for many people, and so I will sometimes use "inviolable" instead to mean the same thing, in order to emphasize the availability of that secular interpretation.

Ronald Dworkin, Life's Dominion: An Argument about Abortion, Euthanasia, and Individual Freedom 25 (1993).

41. Cast as the claim that only some persons are human beings, the claim that only some human beings are sacred has been, and remains, quite common. According to Nazi ideology, for example, the Jews were pseudohumans. See Johannes Morsink, "World War Two and the Universal Declaration," 15 Human Rights Q. 357, 363 (1993).

42. The first question is about who has full moral status: Who is sacred (inviolable, etc.)? The second question is about what is good for those with full moral status, or about what is bad for them—about what is friendly to their well-being, or about what is hostile it. Thanks to Laura Underkuffler for suggesting this clarification.

43. See Michael J. Perry, We the People: The Fourteenth Amendment and the Supreme Court, ch. 3 (Oxford University Press, 1999).

44. That every human being (or, at least, every born human being) is sacred or inviolable is represented in the Universal Declaration of Human Rights (Article 2) by this language: "Everyone is entitled to all the rights and freedoms set forth in this Declaration, without distinction of any kind, such as race, colour, sex, language, religion, political or other opinion, national or social origin, property, birth or other status."

45. Hilary Putnam, The Many Faces of Realism 60–61 (1987).

46. Florida Bishops, "Promoting Meaningful Welfare Reform," 24 Origins 609, 611 (1995) (quoting Matthew 25:40).

47. The second part of the idea is that, because every human being is sacred, there are certain things that ought not to be done to any human being and certain other things that ought to be done for every human being. I have discussed the idea of human rights at length elsewhere. See Michael J. Perry, The Idea of Human Rights: Four Inquiries (1998).

48. In the essay "The Spirituality of the Talmud," Ben Zion Bokser and Baruch M. Bokser write: "From this conception of man's place in the universe comes the sense of the supreme sanctity of all human life. 'He who destroys one person has dealt a blow at the entire universe, and he who sustains or saves one person has sustained the whole world.'" Ben Zion Bokser &

Baruch M. Bokser, "Introduction: The Spirituality of the Talmud," in The Talmud: Selected Writings 7 (1989).

49. Ronald Dworkin, "Life is Sacred. That's the Easy Part," New York Times Magazine, May 16, 1993, at 36. (Dworkin has emphasized that in this context the terms "sacred" and "inviolable" are interchangeable. See *supra* n. 40.) I have criticized Dworkin's conception of the "sacred." See Perry, The Idea of Human Rights, *supra* n. 47, at 25–29.

50. James Griffin, Well-Being: Its Meaning, Measurement, and Moral Importance 239 (1987).

51. Bernard Williams, Ethics and the Limits of Philosophy 14(1985).

52. See Perry, The Idea of Human Rights, *supra* n. 47, ch. 1 ("Is the Idea of Human Rights Ineliminably Religious?").

53. Kurt T. Lash, "Civilizing Religion," 65 Geo. Wash. L. Rev. 1100, 1109 (1997).

54. See Dan Cohn-Sherbok, ed., World Religions and Human Liberation (1992); Hans Küng & Jürgen Moltmann, eds., The Ethics of World Religions and Human Rights (1990); Leroy S. Rouner, ed., Human Rights and the World's Religions (1988); Arlene Swidler, ed., Human Rights in Religious Traditions (1982); Robert Traer, Faith in Human Rights: Support in Religious Traditions for a Global Struggle (1991).

55. Samuel Brittan, "Making Common Cause: How Liberals Differ, and What They Ought to Agree On," Times Lit. Supp., Sept. 20, 1996, at 3, 4.

56. William Collinge has said, in correspondence, that

> as a Catholic, I would say that *ultimate* human well-being is sharing in the life of God, participating as somehow befits our status as created beings in the divine Trinity. Talk of grace, "beatific vision," mystical union all points in the same direction. Many adherents of other religions have corresponding beliefs about what is ultimately best. How could there be a secular argument for something like that?

Letter to Michael J. Perry, Sept. 1, 1995.

57. See Perry, Religion in Politics, *supra* n. 5, at 20–21.

58. Charles Curran, the eminent Catholic moral theologian, has raised a helpful question, in correspondence, about my "emphasis on human well-being and human nature. Some people might criticize that [emphasis] as being too anthropocentric and not theocentric enough for a truly Protestant position. . . . The primary question perhaps even in the reformed tradition is what is the will of God and not what is human flourishing or human nature." Letter to Michael J. Perry, Aug. 7, 1995. However, given two assumptions that few Christians would want to deny, the distinction between doing "what God wills or commands us to do" and doing "what fulfills our nature" is quite false. The two assumptions are, first, that human beings have a nature—indeed, a nature fashioned by God—and, second, that it is God's will that human beings act so as to fulfill or perfect their nature. As Bernard Williams as observed, "[Preferred ethical categories] may be said to be given by divine command or revelation; in this form, if it is not combined with a grounding in human nature, the explanation will not lead us anywhere except into what Spinoza called 'the asylum of ignorance.'" Williams, *supra* n. 51, at 96.

59. "In principle", because

> [t]he participation by man in God's eternal law through knowledge . . . can be corrupted and depraved in such a way that the natural knowledge of good is darkened by passions and the habits of sin. For Aquinas, then, not all the conclusions of natural law are universally known, and the more one descends from the general to the particular, the more possible it is for reason to be unduly influenced by the emotions, or by customs, or by fallen nature.

John Mahoney SJ, The Making of Moral Theology: A Study of the Roman Catholic Tradition 105–6 (1987).

60. For an illuminating recounting, see id. at 103–15.

61. Id. at 106, 107, 109. Mahoney then adds: "[B]ut such human thinking is not always or invariably at its best." Id. at 109.

62. Basil Mitchell, "Should Law Be Christian?" Law & Justice, No. 96/97 (1988), at 12, 21. Moreover, as the American philosopher Robert Audi (who identifies himself as a Christian) has explained, "[G]ood secular arguments for moral principles may be *better* reasons to believe those principles to be divinely enjoined than theological arguments for the principles, based on scripture or tradition." This is because the latter—in particular, scripture-based and tradition-based religious arguments—"seem (even) more subject than the former to cultural influences that may distort scripture or tradition or both; more vulnerable to misinterpretation of religious or other texts or to their sheer corruption across time and translation; and more liable to bias stemming from political or other non-religious aims." Robert Audi, "Liberal Democracy and the Place of Religion in Politics," in Audi & Wolterstorff, *supra* n. 33, at 1, 20–21. (Christianity's acceptance of slavery comes to mind here—an acceptance that persisted for most of the two millennia of Christianity. Audi's conclusion: "Granting, then, that theology and religious inspiration can be sources of ethical insight, we can also reverse this traditional idea: one may sometimes be better off trying to understand God through ethics than ethics through theology." Audi, "Liberal Democracy and the Place of Religion in Politics," this n., at 20–21. (One can accept Audi's point and nonetheless believe that there is no intelligible secular argument for the foundational moral proposition that each and every human being is sacred.)

63. On self-critical rationality, see Michael J. Perry, Love and Power: The Role of Religion and Morality in American Politics, ch. 4 (1991).

64. Richard John Neuhaus, "Reason Public and Private: The Pannenberg Project," First Things, March 1992, at 55, 57.

65. See National Conference of Catholic Bishops, Challenge of Peace: God's Promise and Our Response (1983).

66. Bryan Hehir, "Responsibilities and Temptations of Power: A Catholic View," unpublished MS (1988).

67. The Williamsburg Charter: A National Celebration and Reaffirmation of the First Amendment Religious Liberty Clauses 22 (1988).

68. Richard John Neuhaus, "Nihilism Without the Abyss: Law, Rights, and Transcendent Good," 5 J.L. & Religion 53, 62 (1987). In commenting on this passage, Stanley Hauerwas has said that "[r]ather than condemning the Moral Majority, Neuhaus seeks to help them enter the public debate by basing their appeals on principles that are accessible to the public." Stanley Hauerwas, "A Christian Critique of Christian America," in J. Roland Pennock & John W. Chapman, eds., Religion, Morality, and the Law 110, 118 (1988).

69. Jeffrey S. Siker, "Homosexual Christians, the Bible, and Gentile Inclusion," in Jeffrey S. Siker, ed., Homosexuality in the Church 178, 184 (1994). For Siker's criticism of such interpretations, see id. at 184–91.

70. History teaches us to be skeptical as well about government acting as an arbiter of *moral* truth, but there is no way that even a government of very limited powers can avoid making some moral judgments. By contrast, there is simply no need for government to make religious judgments about the requirements of human well-being.

71. Thus, I am skeptical that Robert Audi's requirement of adequate secular motivation

could often be implemented. For a recent critique of Audi's position, see Jeff Jordan, "Religious Reasons and Public Reasons," 11 Public Affairs Q. 245 (1997).

72. Cf. John H. Garvey, "The Pope's Submarine," 30 San Diego L. Rev. 849 (1993).

73. Thanks to Laura Underkuffler for helping me to see this.

74. See Perry, Love and Power, *supra* n. 63, ch. 6.

75. I have discussed the nature of political community, understood as a "community of judgment," elsewhere—and I have explained why political community, thus understood, is a good. See id., ch. 6.

76. I have discussed the value of ecumenical political dialogue elsewhere. See id., ch. 6. See also David Lochhead, The Dialogical Imperative: A Christian Reflection on Interfaith Encounter 79 (1988): "In more biblical terms, the choice between monologue and dialogue is the choice between death and life. If to be human is to live in community with fellow human beings, then to alienate ourselves from community, in monologue, is to cut ourselves off from our own humanity. To choose monologue is to choose death. Dialogue is its own justification."

77. Robin W. Lovin, "Why the Church Needs the World: Faith, Realism, and the Public Life," unpublished MS (1988 Sorenson Lecture, Yale Divinity School).

78. Joseph Cardinal Bernardin, "The Consistent Ethic of Life After *Webster*," 19 Origins 741, 748 (1990).

79. Lash, *supra* n. 53, at 1101.

80. Id. at 1119. In support of his position, Lash quotes Mark Tushnet: "When faced with an issue of transcendent importance—slavery in the nineteenth century, or abortion (for some) in the twentieth—, people can reasonably say, 'Getting the right answer to this question is more important than preserving a stable moral order in which injustice prevails.'" Id. at 1120 (quoting "Mark Tushnet, *The Constitutional Law of Religion Outside the Courts*" (unpublished manuscript on file with author)).

81. James Tunstead Burtchaell, "The Sources of Conscience," 13 Notre Dame Mag. 20, 20–21 (Winter 1984–85). (On our neighbor's always turning out to be the most unlikely person, see Luke 10:29–37 ("Parable of the Good Samaritan").)

82. Coleman, An American Strategic Theology, *supra* n. 16, at 196.

83. Martin E. Marty, "When My Virtue Doesn't Match Your Virtue," 105 Christian Century 1094, 1096 (1988). Marty adds: "Of course, these communities and their spokespersons argue with one another. But so do philosophical rationalists." Id.

84. Tracy, Plurality and Ambiguity, *supra* n. 18, at 88:

85. Id. at 88–89.

86. Hollenbach, "Contexts of the Political Role of Religion," *supra* n. 21, at 894.

87. Id. at 894–95.

88. David M. Smolin, "The Enforcement of Natural Law by the State: A Response to Professor Calhoun," 16 U. Dayton L. Rev. 318, 391–92 (1991).

89. The "asymmetry" that characterizes Robert Audi's position also characterizes mine. See Robert Audi, "Wolterstorff on Religion, Politics, and the Liberal State," in Audi & Wolterstorff, *supra* n. 33, at 121, 123:

> [T]he chief asymmetry in my treatment of secular and religious reasons is in the absence of a counterpart condition regarding religious reasons—one requiring an evidentially adequate and motivationally sufficient religious reason in the same cases. To require this would not only make theological assumptions that are inappropriate to liberalism, but would also require some sort of religious attitude on the part of citizens who

conscientiously take part in the full range of democratic decisions open to them as participants in the business of government.

90. Mark Noll, The Scandal of the Evangelical Mind 207–8 (1994).

91. George Marsden, "Common Sense and the Spiritual Vision of History," in C. T. McIntire and Ronald A. Wells, eds., History and Historical Understanding 55, 59 (1984).

92. Quoted in Thomas Merton, ed., The Wisdom of the Desert 62 (1960).

93. Perry, Morality, Politics, and Law, *supra* n. 25, at 181–82. See also Perry, Love and Power, *supra* n. 63, at 4.

94. See Wolterstorff, "Audi on Religion, Politics, and Liberal Democracy," *supra* n. 33, at 147.

95. See Perry, Religion in Politics, *supra* n. 5, at 82–96.

96. Perry, Morality, Politics, and Law, *supra* n. 25, at 183.

97. Mahoney, *supra* n. 59, at 327 (emphasis added). John Noonan's eloquent plea bears quotation here:

> One cannot predict future changes; one can only follow present light and in that light be morally certain that some obligations will never alter. The great commandments of love of God and of neighbor, the great principles of justice and charity continue to govern all development. God is unchanging, but the demands of the New Testament are different from those of the Old, and while no other revelation supplements the New, it is evident from the case of slavery alone that it has taken time to ascertain what the demands of the New really are. All will be judged by the demands of the day in which they live. It is not within human competence to say with certainty who was or will be saved; all will be judged as they have conscientiously acted. In new conditions, with new insight, an old rule need not be preserved in order to honor a past discipline. . . .
>
> In the Church there can always be fresh appeal to Christ, there is always the possibility of probing new depths of insight. . . . Must we not, then, frankly admit that change is something that plays a role in [Christian] moral teaching?
>
> . . . Yes, if the principle of change is the person of Christ.

John T. Noonan, "Development in Moral Doctrine," 54 Theological Stud. 662, 676–77 (1993).

98. See David Tracy, "Approaching the Christian Understanding of God," in Francis Schüssler Fiorenza & John P. Galvin, eds., Systematic Theology: Roman Catholic Perspectives, vol. 1, 131, 147 (1991): "[According to Christian belief,] God, the holy mystery who is the origin, sustainer, and end of all reality . . . is disclosed to us in Jesus Christ as pure, unbounded love." See also John Dominic Crossan, Jesus: A Revolutionary Biography 20 (1994): "Christian belief is (1) an act of faith (2) in the historical Jesus (3) as the manifestation of God."

99. See David Hollenbach SJ, "Afterword: A Community of Freedom," in R. Bruce Douglass & David Hollenbach SJ, eds., Catholicism and Liberalism: Contributions to American Public Philosophy 323, 337 (1994).

100. On apophatic Christianity, see William C. Placher, The Domestication of Transcendence: How Modern Thinking about God Went Wrong (1996).

Chapter 9

The Pope's Submarine

John H. Garvey

This essay was originally written as part of a symposium convened to discuss the place of religious arguments about public policy in a liberal democracy. We typically look at the problem through the lens of legal theory or political theory. I want to approach it from the opposite direction—to look at how liberal politics might get in the way of a public official's religious obligations, and how the conscientious politician can deal with this dilemma. Religious obligations differ across denominations, so I will confine my observations to the Catholic politician. I focus on Catholics for several reasons. I myself am one, so the issue has some personal interest. And Catholics are the largest denomination in the United States, so the question matters for a lot of people. The Catholic Church also asserts more authority over its members (a stricter obligation on their part to obey) than most American sects do. In addition, the American Catholic bishops in recent years have exercised their teaching authority across a range of publicly salient issues—the economy, nuclear war, abortion, medical care, and so on. These facts, taken together, multiply and intensify the occasions when Catholic politicians are forced to reconcile their religious and political loyalties. Sometimes the drama is compelling enough to capture the attention of the newspapers.

Consider the case of Mario Cuomo. He is the governor of New York and a liberal Democrat. In September 1984, he gave an address at the University of Notre Dame entitled "Religious Belief and Public Morality: A Catholic Governor's Perspective."[1] He began by explaining that he accepted the church's teaching about abortion as the rule for his own life.[2] But as a public official he could not approve a legal prohibition of abortion.[3] Most of New York's citizens were not Catholics, and many of them (indeed many Catholics) disagreed with what the church said. An antiabortion law would be unfair to them, and ineffective in the way Prohibition was.[4] Cuomo added that he also favored Medicaid funding of abortions for the poor.[5]

A month later Archbishop (now Cardinal) John J. O'Connor of New York said that, although he would not urge voters to choose any particular candidate in the upcoming elections, the most important question they faced was the need to "protect the rights of the unborn."[6] O'Connor may have had several politicians in mind. Geraldine Ferraro, another New York Catholic whose views mirrored Cuomo's, was then running for vice president. Two years later O'Connor's vicar general, Bishop Joseph T. O'Keefe, announced that parishes within O'Connor's archdiocese should not provide a platform to speakers "whose public position is contrary to [the] teaching of the Church."[7] O'Keefe said the policy was not aimed at Cuomo, though it would of course apply to him.[8]

The controversy has not subsided. In November 1989, the National Conference of Catholic Bishops passed a resolution declaring that "no Catholic can responsibly take a 'pro-choice' stand when the 'choice' in question" involves abortion.[9] Three months later Bishop Thomas V. Daily, the new head of the Brooklyn Diocese (where Cuomo has lived most of his life), said he would not permit the governor to speak on abortion in any of his diocese's churches.[10] And in June 1990, Cardinal O'Connor warned that Catholic politicians who make public funds available for abortions "are at risk of excommunication."[11]

I want to use this case as a context for thinking about three questions. First, why should Cuomo, as a Catholic, have to pay any heed to the views of the bishops? What are the grounds of the religious authority that the Catholic Church asserts over its members? Second, when and to what extent does Cuomo's religion oblige him to heed his church's teaching? What are the scope and strength of the Catholic Church's teaching authority over its members? Third, if Cuomo did heed his church's teaching out of a sense of religious obligation, would this be illegal, impolitic, or illiberal? Is this kind of religious authority inconsistent with the letter or spirit of the American system of government?

I. The Grounds of Religious Authority

There was a time when people relied upon their religious sense to help them understand the idea of political authority. This is why German kings for centuries claimed the title Holy Roman Emperor. I think the tables are turned today. For most of us political authority is a familiar—even congenial—notion, but it is hard to see why we should take seriously a claim of religious authority. Though the two ideas are not congruent, there is some overlap, and a brief review of the grounds of political authority is a good way to approach the subject of part I.

In what follows I will ask you to suppose that X is a citizen and Y is a political official, a political institution, or the government itself (in a collective sense) in X's society. When we say that Y has authority over X we mean, among other things, that X has an obligation to obey Y in certain matters. I pass over such details as the scope of Y's jurisdiction, the strength of X's obligation (whether it is certain or merely prima facie, absolute or defeasible), and so on. Authority is thus a kind of jural contradictory of freedom: If Y has authority over X, then X lacks freedom to that extent.[12] Why would X be willing to give up her freedom and submit to Y's political authority? Or more briefly, what are the grounds of political authority?

One obvious justification for political authority is that it is the only sensible solution to coordination problems. For many political issues, it matters more that we resolve them than how we resolve them. It is a matter of indifference to me whether I drive on the right or the left side of the road, but I don't want any oncoming traffic on my side. To take a more timely subject, given that I have to pay income taxes, I don't really care whether I pay them on April 15 or July 1, but it is administratively simpler to have everyone pay on the same day. All that we need in these cases is a convention. There are a number of possibilities to which we would agree. The problem is how to signal everyone so that we can act harmoniously and not collide, like Alphonse and Gaston going through a doorway. The obvious solution is to let Y specify the convention and require everyone to observe it.[13]

We can justify the use of authority to solve prisoners' dilemmas on similar grounds. Here the choice among outcomes is not a matter of indifference, but citizens will opt for a mutually harmful outcome unless they are assured that others will cooperate. The provision of public goods (street lights; the army) is an example. If no one enforced the tax laws, the wise course for each X would be to cheat: if others paid, X would get free lighting and defense; if others did not pay, X would be foolish to do so. And if each X reasoned that way, we would have no public goods. The solution that is mutually most satisfactory can be reached only if each X grants Y enough authority to prevent cheating.[14]

Not all political issues, however, are simple problems of coordination. That is a justification for political authority that reaches only some of the things governments do. A second kind of argument holds that authority is justified when it rests on consent. This is a familiar theory to students of American government. The Declaration of Independence asserts that governments derive "their just powers from the consent of the governed." In the Constitution, the people "vest" power in the three branches of government. Statutory law (made by elected officials) is superior to common law (made by judges) because the former are better attuned to the voice of the people.

Consent is also the organizing principle of social contract theory. Locke argues in The Second Treatise that no one can be "subjected to the political power of another without his own consent."[15] Now there are various ways of explaining why consent should be significant, but one very influential one is this: The primary axiom of moral theory (many people say) is that I should pursue my own good in my own way. Political authority appears to be inconsistent with this axiom, because it deprives me of the freedom to act as I wish. But if I authorize the authority to act for me—if I make it my agent—its acts are my own. So there is no loss of autonomy when I consent to authority.

Why, though, would I want an authority to act for me? One strand of social contract theory says I do so for instrumental reasons: I undertake obligations in return for other benefits that, on the whole, outweigh the burden of submission. When I hire a lawyer, I authorize the lawyer to bind me in negotiations, at trial, and so on. This has a cost, but it also amplifies my own power to act. So too with the government. Submission to political authority has a cost but, say Hobbes and Locke, it is the only sure way to preserve my life, liberty, and estate. It might also afford benefits (like culture) that are not possible outside political society.

The other strand of social contract theory, found in Rousseau, takes a noninstrumental view of consent. It holds that there is moral value in shaping my own world, the projects I undertake and the relationships I enter into. Just as the relationship between husband and wife has intrinsic value, so it might be with the relation between citizen and society. Consent is a constituent element in these relationships.[16]

Like the need for coordinated action, consent is not a completely satisfactory foundation for political authority. There are two obvious problems with relying too heavily on it. One is that, except for naturalized citizens, people do not actually consent to the government's authority. The other is that the government's authority is so extensive that even if people did consent, it is hard to see how their consent could be informed and intelligent.

Joseph Raz has recently proposed a third ground for political authority. He suggests that Y's authority depends on a showing that X "is likely better to comply with reasons which apply to him (other than the alleged authoritative directives) if he accepts the directives . . . as authoritatively binding and tries to follow them, rather than by trying to follow the reasons which apply to him directly."[17] Consider this illustration. I have investment objectives that I communicate to my broker: do not do anything risky; aim for long-term growth, not short-term profits; diversify; and so on. These are what Raz would call "reasons which apply to X." Until recently I made my own investments and earned an average of 5 percent annually. Now I let my broker choose for me, and I earn 10 percent. I satisfy my own investment objectives better by giving him authority over my account.

I need to clear up a point about the nature of this authority. Suppose that in 1991 I tried a mixed approach. I considered my broker's advice as an independent and weighty reason bearing on each investment decision. But I also factored in my own hunches and tips and made my own judgments, because sometimes my broker has been wrong and I wanted to correct for those cases. In 1991 I made 7 percent. When I say that he now has authority over my account, I mean that he has preemptive authority—I let him decide even in cases where I think he is wrong.[18]

Raz calls this the "service conception" of authority because the "role and primary normal function [of authorities] is to serve the governed."[19] We often see the service conception at work in administrative law. The Environmental Protection Agency and the courts have the same reasons for wishing to stamp out air pollution—the reasons that moved Congress to pass the Clean Air Act. But in litigation under the act courts can best comply with these higher-order reasons by following the EPA's rules because this is a complicated matter, the EPA knows a lot about science and industry, it has investigated the problem in depth, and it has to make a pattern of interlocking practical judgments. A court should not ignore the EPA's rules just because it thinks they are wrong. Nor should it treat the EPA's opinion as a kind of expert testimony, to be added to the mix of reasons for and against a particular policy. The EPA has authority, binding on the courts, to decide questions like these.[20] But the basis for its authority is that it can best serve the people.

The service conception of authority is not an argument that works at wholesale. It is more or less convincing for different Ys, different Xs, and different subject matters. Some agencies (the SEC, the NLRB) get considerable deference from the courts; others get less. Some rules ("Stay out of the deep water") provide different levels of service to different Xs (this example may actually disserve the interests of good swimmers). And Y's pronouncements on different subject matters may vary in authoritativeness. (Compare the respect the Supreme Court gives to Congress's decisions on free speech and on federalism.)

Let me turn now to the question of religious authority, and particularly the authority of the Catholic Church. Why should individual Catholics heed the instructions of their church in cases where, left to their own devices, they would do otherwise? The first justification I offered for political authority was that it solved coordination problems. Coordination problems naturally arise within the Catholic Church, a large institution, and its authority is a convenient solution. There are no specific religious reasons for celebrating the feast of the Assumption on August 15, but because there are reasons for celebrating the feast at some time within the year, and celebration is a community enterprise, it suits everyone to let the church pick a date.

If we recognize religious authority for reasons like these, however, we run little risk of conflict between church and state. In coordination cases people are interested only in having an issue resolved; they do not care how. This means that the church will have a range of acceptable solutions, and it can accommodate the state's demands without compromising any religious belief. If the Assumption were celebrated on April 15 and this caused many Catholics to miss filing their income tax returns, there would be no reason not to move the feast to another date. (For that matter, the state could change the income tax filing date. This is what it has done in laying out the workweek: people generally have Saturday and Sunday off.)

For this reason, I will pass over the coordinating function as a basis for the authority of the Catholic Church. There is a second argument that looks very much like this one but that is in fact quite different. The best way to understand it is by contrast with the notion of consent. In arguments about political authority, consent lets me square the government's commands with the assumption that I must be allowed to pursue my own good in my own way. This scheme is fundamentally individualist: what makes the government legitimate is that I adopt it as my agent. It serves my purposes by protecting my liberty and property. Or maybe it is one of my purposes—a relationship that I enter into because it has (for me) intrinsic value. The second argument for the Catholic view of church authority begins with a different assumption. It is a mistake to suppose that an individual can carry on a religious enterprise by herself. The smallest religiously significant unit is the church. Consider the metaphors Catholics use for the church: the family (we are all brothers and sisters of Christ, and God is our father), a flock of sheep (the church is a flock, and Jesus is the Good Shepherd), the body (the church's many members are parts of one body, and Jesus is the Head). This way of thinking carries over to Catholic methods of worship. The chief liturgical activity is the mass, a celebration in the form of a meal (communion) that all members of a local church are supposed to attend.[21]

That Catholics (indeed, most Christians) think this way is obvious. The reasons are slightly more complex. One part of the explanation is that the communal way of thinking grows naturally out of the Old Testament. The Jews thought of themselves as God's chosen people who were collectively promised salvation. Christians imagine that God has made good on that promise but extended it to a larger group. The Dogmatic Constitution on the Church approved by Vatican II states, "It has pleased God . . . to make men holy and save them not merely as individuals without any mutual bonds, but by making them into a single people."[22] So the group matters because God's plan of salvation is communal.

The group also matters because Catholics see in the church a preview of the kingdom of God. The relations of members with one another and with God have intrinsic value. I do not want to say that this union makes people happy—that suggests that we value it for the individual emotions it produces. A more accurate way of putting it is that being connected in this way just is good, the way the love of husband and wife just is good (even though it does not always make us happy).

A third reason for the church's communal aspect is that the church is a kind of sacrament: "a sign and an instrument" of "intimate union with God, and of the unity of all mankind."[23] Part of its job is to show the world by example how to love one another and live together in peace. This has to be a collective undertaking.

Suppose that I accept this way of looking at the church and my role in it. In this scheme, authority does not rest on my consent. Contract theorists use consent to harmonize political authority with the axiom that I should pursue my own good in my own way. But the church's communal value comes ahead of its value to me; we start with a different axiom. One reason to support religious authority could be that it promotes unity in the church.

This is not the same as the idea that authority helps us solve coordination problems. It is more like the notion of "family unity" that relatives sometimes appeal to in times of bitterness and division. A law that says "drive on the right" is a sensible signal that helps us all accomplish what we want. Family unity is an independent value that we invoke as a reason for tolerating unfair distributions and unjust treatment.

Catholics argue for papal primacy chiefly on the ground that it promotes unity. It "serves to promote or preserve the oneness of the church by symbolizing unity, and by facilitating communication, mutual assistance or correction, and collaboration in the church's mission."[24] On a smaller scale, "[t]he individual bishop . . . is the visible principle and foundation of unity in his particular church."[25] Primacy is different from infallibility. There is a point to pursuing church unity and recognizing episcopal leadership even if it is sometimes wrong.

Let me turn now to a third justification for religious authority in the Catholic Church. This one has some points in common with Raz's service conception of authority. Raz argued that we could justify Y's authority by showing that X "is likely better to comply with reasons which apply to him" if he follows Y's directives than if he tries to follow the reasons themselves. Is there some reason to think that religious authority renders such a service?

Catholics claim that there is, though in part for reasons that we would not admit in the political realm. They believe that local bishops, and the college of bishops under the leadership of the pope (the bishop of Rome), are guided by God himself in their teaching on matters of faith and morals. This does not mean that they will not make mistakes, though errors should not be frequent. And under certain circumstances the pope himself, or in company with the bishops, can make infallible declarations. These "definitions, of themselves, and not from the consent of the Church, are justly styled irreformable, for they are pronounced with the assistance of the Holy Spirit."[26] I do not want to overstate these beliefs, as often happens both in and outside the church. Catholics do not claim (1) that popes and bishops can give correct direction effortlessly whenever they speak; nor (2) that they can do so over the objections of the church's members; nor even (3) that the magisterium (which means, in the narrow sense, the teaching authority grounded in episcopal office) is the only source of teaching authority within the church. As to (1), Vatican II emphasized that the pope "and the bishops, in view of their office and of the importance of the matter, strive painstakingly and by appropriate means to inquire properly into . . . revelation and to give apt expression to its contents" before offering any direction.[27] As to (2), though the consent of church members is not required to ratify a decree (as the Senate must ratify a treaty), still the church emphasizes that in the case of infallible teachings "the assent of the Church can never be wanting, on account of the activity of that same Holy Spirit, whereby the whole flock of Christ is preserved and progresses in unity of faith."[28] To turn it around, strong dissent is a sign that a teaching has not been infallible. As to (3), though there is no denying the hierarchical structure of the Catholic Church, it is a mistake to suppose that all teaching authority operates from the top down. The church's bishops are not by training or occupation its best informed members on questions of politics, science, social science, or even theology. The laity is expected to make practical, prophetic, and scholarly contributions.[29]

These are issues I will return to in the next section. Having stated them here, I want to stress that they qualify, but do not negate, my main point, which is about the basis for the church's teaching authority. Catholics justify that authority in part by a kind of service conception. Just as I can advance my investment objectives by heeding the advice of my broker, so can I advance the cause of my salvation by heeding the church's advice on matters within its jurisdiction. The helpfulness of the church's advice has a different warrant, but if I accept it the cases are not all that different.

II. The Scope of Religious Authority

In discussing Raz's service conception of authority, I noted that it is a retail, not a wholesale, argument. Its effectiveness varies with the identities of authority and subject, the nature of the issue, and so forth. In this section I want to develop that observation and apply it to religious authority. My ultimate concern is to explain the kind of deference Governor Cuomo (as a practicing Catholic) should give to the church's teaching. But it turns out that we cannot state that explanation in a simple formula. In part II, section A, I will examine the claims of authority that the Catholic Church makes over all its members in their daily lives. In part II, section B, I will look at the special case of public officials.

A. Ordinary Catholics

The authoritativeness of the church's teaching for ordinary Catholics depends in part on who the teacher is. Vatican II states that the highest authority resides in the college of bishops with the pope at their head. In the modern church this is a lot of bishops, and they do not often get together. When they do (in an ecumenical council like Vatican II), they exercise their authority in a particularly "solemn way."[30] Even when not gathered together the bishops can sometimes teach with the same authority, provided "they concur in a single viewpoint as the one which must be held conclusively."[31] The pope can also act alone with an authority equivalent to that of an ecumenical council. He is, Vatican II observes, "the supreme teacher of the universal Church."[32] Each of these actors (ecumenical council, the dispersed college of bishops, the pope) is thought to be capable of acting infallibly, though they seldom do so, and such action depends on other factors.

These are not the only church officials capable of acting authoritatively. Individual bishops have jurisdiction over church members within their territory. Their pronouncements are obligatory (though not infallible) in a sense that I will explore below.[33] Groups of bishops may also gather together on a national or territorial basis to form episcopal conferences, a practice encouraged by Vatican II. The National Conference of Catholic Bishops is a fairly active example. These groups, like their members, can act authoritatively but not infallibly.[34] Then there is a whole host of congregations, commissions, offices, and so on that make up the Vatican bureaucracy and that function in ways not unlike the modern administrative state.

I need not detail the positions of all the various actors within the church hierarchy to make my first point, which is simply that the authoritativeness of church teaching varies with (among other things) the identity of the speaker. It also varies with the speaker's intention. The pope teaches infallibly only when "he proclaims by a definitive act some doctrine of faith or morals."[35] The bishops do so only when "they concur in a single viewpoint as the one which must be held conclusively."[36] The principle is like the clear-statement rule that we sometimes use in interpreting statutes: Y is understood to have acted with infallible authority only when it has made perfectly clear its intention to do so.[37] And the significance of intentions is not confined to the question of infallibility. None of the many documents produced by Vatican II was meant to be definitive in that way. But they bear various titles intended to indicate the degree of authoritativeness attached to each: "dogmatic constitution," "pastoral constitution," "constitution," "decree," "declaration."

The authoritativeness of church teaching thus varies with the speaker's office and intentions. It also varies with the subject matter. The idea is a familiar one to lawyers. The United States Supreme Court is often said to have ultimate authority to interpret the federal constitution, but it has no such authority with regard to state law. We sometimes express this by talking about the scope of its jurisdiction. So it is with the church, whose jurisdiction is limited to matters of "faith or morals."[38] Though it has sometimes pretended otherwise, for example, it has no brief explaining to us the proper form (monarchical, democratic) that civil government ought to take.

Even within the domain of faith and morals, there is a great variety of issues, and the church speaks with more authority on some of them than on others. There are, in the first place, those things said to be revealed in the gospel message (for example, that Jesus is God). Theologians say that these are the primary object of the church's magisterium, things about which it can speak with most authority—at times infallibly. Then there is a range of other matters, more or less closely related to these, to which the church can speak with diminishing degrees of authority (recognition of a church council as ecumenical; canonization of saints; and so on).[39] I do not want to dwell on these details but mention them only to indicate how highly refined and variable is the notion of authority, and because they bear on my main interest, which is the deference due from observant Catholics to the church's instructions on moral questions—abortion in particular. That is a subject on which various authorities within the church have taught with a fairly consistent voice for a long time. The Second Vatican Council condemned the practice in the Pastoral Constitution on the Church in the Modern World.[40] Pope Paul VI repeated this condemnation in his encyclical Humanae Vitae.[41] The National Conference of Catholic Bishops has done the same on numerous occasions.[42] So has the Congregation for the Doctrine of the Faith.[43] Cardinal O'Connor and the bishop of Brooklyn have echoed these positions.[44] What obligations do these teachings impose on Mr. Cuomo?

As a matter of church law, Cuomo's obligations depend in part on whether the teachings of the pope and the council are supposed to be infallible, and that is an uncertain point. Neither the Pastoral Constitution nor the encyclical displays the kind of clear intention that accompanies infallible pronouncements. It may nonetheless be that papal and episcopal opinion on the subject merits that status because it has been so unanimous and so longstanding.[45] I will assume that it does not, for the sake of making a point that can be applied more widely. Here is what Vatican II said about the appropriate response to noninfallible moral teachings:

> Bishops, teaching in communion with the Roman Pontiff, are to be respected by all as witnesses to divine and Catholic truth. In matters of faith and morals, the bishops speak in the name of Christ and *the faithful are to accept their teaching and adhere to it with a religious assent of soul.* This *religious submission of will and of mind* must be shown in a special way to the authentic teaching authority of the Roman Pontiff, even when he is not speaking ex cathedra.[46]

I understand the two italicized phrases to be essentially equivalent, and for simplicity's sake I will focus on the phrase "religious submission of will and of mind." This claims two kinds of authority. One is practical, over how X acts ("submission of will"). The other is epistemic, over how X thinks (submission "of mind"). Political authority, by contrast, is strictly practical. It requires obedience but not agreement. Indeed, the First Amendment protects our freedom to disagree with the law. But the church, because it is concerned with the formation of consciences, pays as much attention to mental states as it does to behavior.

There is a scene in *Peter Pan* where Peter is instructing the Darling children how to fly. The secret is to think lovely thoughts, but that is something he cannot get them to do. Like Peter, the church cannot always get me to think lovely thoughts. Even when I am willing, I may not be able. Suppose that I am a pregnant woman considering whether to have an abortion. I can conform my behavior (submission of will) to church teaching by just refusing to abort. But how can I get myself to think that abortion is wrong (submission of mind) if, notwithstanding what the church tells me, my mind will not go along with that proposition? Learning about morals is like learning geometry. I do not learn geometry by committing propositions to memory. Unless I work out the proofs, I cannot apply them and will not remember them—in a word, I do not understand them. So it is with the proposition that abortion is wrong. This will fit with some of my convictions (how I feel toward the life growing inside me; how I think I should behave toward my father, who is on a respirator) and not with others (what I think about incest, rape, and pregnant teenagers), and I cannot affirm or deny it until I have worked it through.[47]

What, then, does submission of mind mean for this process? It means, in the first place, that I should recheck my proof if I get a different answer than the church did. The church's teaching counts for something if it gives me reason to think that my own convictions may be wrong. Submission of mind might also mean that I should try reasoning backward through my proof, beginning with the authoritative answer. This sometimes works in mathematics, where knowing the answer helps me to figure out the other steps in the problem. And if none of this gets me to the orthodox conclusion, I think I should remain willing to hear new arguments and new evidence, that is, make my judgment interlocutory rather than final.[48] Finally, there will be cases where after long reflection I find the balance of moral reasons uncertain. (Suppose I simply cannot decide whether I think that human life begins at conception.) Here the church's teaching could change the outcome of my thinking because it is an additional piece of evidence—a kind of morally expert testimony that changes the balance of proof.

These observations explain an important difference between epistemic and practical authority. In discussing Raz's service conception, I noted how we give some authorities preemptive effect. My broker has this kind of authority over my account. I do not weigh his advice along with other reasons and sometimes reject it. I follow his direction even when I think it is wrong. Consider another example. A court decision rests on reasons (stated in an opinion); but once the decision becomes final, it is itself a reason for X to act as directed. X cannot impeach the decision by showing that the reasons supporting it are weak; that is what it means for a matter to be *res judicata*. The decision preempts the reasons that led to it.

Epistemic authority, unlike practical authority, cannot have this preemptive effect. It can influence, and in uncertain cases determine, the direction of my thought. But if I think it is wrong, it ipso facto fails.

I now want to say a few words about the submission of will. Suppose I am pregnant and cannot bring myself to think—though I have tried—that abortion would be wrong in my case. (I am in frail health.) Must I nonetheless carry my pregnancy to term? In a word, yes. The church's practical authority is preemptive, like a conscription law whose morality I might dispute. An observant Catholic can and should comply with it notwithstanding her disagreement.

But is this not asking me to behave irrationally, and maybe at times immorally? (Think again about conscription laws.) In general I think not. One kind of justification for it is the service conception of the church's authority. This case is formally like the preemptive authority of my broker: I know that I will get a better return by following his advice than I will by making my own decisions in cases where I think he is wrong. This is true even though he sometimes is wrong, because his error rate is lower than mine. Of course I have different reasons for confidence in the two cases, but that cuts in the church's favor. I think that it has a low error rate because I believe that Jesus is God, and that Jesus remains with the church in various ways (in its sacraments, its scripture, its tradition, and so on)—in a word, for reasons that are fairly fundamental.

The second kind of justification has nothing to do with whether the church is right or wrong in its teaching in this case. It is that in at least some cases orthopraxis, like orthodoxy, is a way of expressing the principle of unity that has an independent religious value in the life of the church. We see parallel examples in the affairs of unions (solidarity), political parties (party loyalty), families ("blood is thicker than water"), armies ("ours is not to reason why"), and nations ("my country right or wrong"). In many of these cases the principle is not a strong one. Indeed, the standard example is a caricature of the individual who gives this principle too much weight when it collides with another moral imperative. But the weight it deserves varies from one case to another depending on the justification for collective action, and church unity may be more important than some other kinds.

I do not want to overstate this point. I have been picturing a case where X thinks that abortion is not immoral and favors that course because it would promote her own medical health. But imagine another case (make it compelling) where X has given her most conscientious attention to the church's epistemic authority, and yet concludes that the course prescribed by the church would be actually immoral. Under these circumstances it is hard to justify giving the church's practical authority preemptive effect. The service conception holds that X can reduce her error rate by obedience in all cases. But it cannot justify immoral action as a means to that end. Nor should we urge immoral action as a way of achieving church unity. In this case I think that X is morally obliged to deviate from the church's teaching, even though the church might impose sanctions on her for doing so.[49]

B. Public Officials

All this talk so far, you might say, is beside the point, because Governor Cuomo concedes his obligation to conform (in mind and will) to the church's teaching in his own life. He quarrels only with the cardinal's assertion that he should make that teaching the law of the state of New York. What state officials must do in their official capacity, he contends, is a matter that is beyond the church's jurisdiction.

Not quite. The church acknowledges (though it has not always) that "Christ [gave it] no proper mission in the political, economic, or social order."[50] But this does not mean everything that strict separationists might hope. The church also rejects "the outmoded notion that 'religion is a purely private affair' or that 'the Church belongs in the sacristy.' Religion is relevant to the life and action of society."[51] In particular, it maintains that it "has the right to pass moral judgments, even on matters touching the political order, whenever basic personal rights or the salvation of souls make such judgments necessary."[52] This of course entails that it should speak out on the issue of abortion, which it sees as involving both "personal rights" (of the fetus) and "salvation" (of those who procure and perform abortions). But there are several reasons that its teachings in this forum might be less authoritative than the model I have discussed above.

To begin with, of course, most citizens of the state are not members of the church.

Over them the church has no authority at all, only such influence as the force of its arguments deserves. Cuomo is not exempt on that account, but it is a fact that bears on his obligations in a second way. It is no less true for Catholics than it is for others that duty is limited by possibility. Compromise is an unpleasant but necessary feature of political life. If the governor finds it impossible to secure enactment of the church's agenda, he can hardly be condemned for doing only what he can.

The need to compromise with nonmembers is not the only limit facing the observant Catholic politician. It is not self-evident that the full resources of the state should be used to enforce moral norms even in cases where a majority of the voters would stand for it. No one argues that Cuomo should work for passage of laws to enforce the moral norms (binding within the church) against contraception and divorce. Consider the observation of Thomas Aquinas regarding the limits of law:

> Laws when they are passed should take account of the condition of the men who will be subject to them; for, as Isidore says: the law should be "possible both with regard to nature and with regard to the custom of the country." But capacity to act derives from habit, or interior disposition: not everything that is possible to a virtuous man is equally possible to one who lacks the habit of virtue. . . .
>
> Now human law is enacted on behalf of the mass of men, the majority of whom are far from perfect in virtue. For this reason human law does not prohibit every vice from which virtuous men abstain; but only the graver vices from which the majority can abstain; and particularly those vices which are damaging of others, and which, if they were not prohibited, would make it impossible for human society to endure: as murder, theft, and suchlike, which are prohibited by human law.[53]

The principal point here is that the moral law is a command of perfection that would land us all in jail were the state to enforce it to the letter. That would have disastrous implications for the corrections budget. And it might mean that none of us would show up for work on Monday. There is also a subsidiary point that Aquinas overlooks, but that we who are more familiar with federal forms of government can more easily appreciate. There are any number of institutional problems connected with efforts by one legal authority to assimilate the regulatory law of another. It would be hard for the secular legal system to be sure that it correctly understood the corpus of Catholic moral rules. The borrowed norms might clash with existing New York law in ways too numerous to anticipate. The borrowed offenses might involve elements (for example, questions about a sinner's mental state) that the existing secular law system (adversary procedure, rules of discovery, evidence, methods of trial and review) was incompetent to prove. (Remember that in the Catholic Church penitents confess their sins.) The burden of enforcing a supplementary set of norms might overload a justice system designed to do other work. And so on.

All of the reasons I have given so far are jurisdictional (the problem of nonmembers) or prudential (the need for compromise; the danger of pursuing perfection; the costs of assimilation). They do not go to the merits. By that I mean that they are consistent with saying that the church rules would be best if we could have them. But that is not necessarily so. Consider the rules about economic due process. Although the Supreme Court asserts authority over constitutional questions, it gives great leeway to other branches on matters of business regulation.[54] One common justification is that it knows little about business and economics, and the legislature (or the agency), so long as it stays within wide limits, is more likely to reach the right answer. Conservative Catholics make precisely the same point about the Catholic bishops' efforts in the economic realm.[55] Though they say they are in complete agreement with the bishops' ultimate aims, they argue that we can get there faster by concentrating on production rather than (as the bishops naively do) distribution. I do not necessarily endorse this conclusion, but the method of argument is perfectly sensible. Moral questions arise in contexts that church authorities will know little about, and in such cases other people might get to the right answer first.

The church's authority over observant Catholic public officials is, then, qualified in a number of important ways. Let us consider what this might mean for the question of abortion. I should rather say questions, because there are many, and the answers differ. Consider first the precise issue for which *Roe v. Wade*[56] is taken to stand: whether abortion is a fundamental human right protected by the Due Process Clause. That is a fairly abstract ethical proposition, unmixed with the kinds of contingencies that lead bishops astray. It is also obviously inconsistent with the church's teaching that abortion is an "unspeakable crime."[57] If we confine our attention to the simple question whether to recognize the right, there are few prudential reasons that would move one in sympathy with the church's position to do so.[58] It is difficult for me to see how Cuomo, if he accepts the church's teaching about abortion, could agree with the Supreme Court's decision in *Roe*. But this is also an issue that he has no influence over. It can be determined only by the Supreme Court or by a constitutional amendment.

On the other hand, accepting the church's teaching would not, I think, commit Cuomo to the proposition that New York should make procuring or performing an abortion a criminal offense. This is an issue, unlike the last, where enforcing the church's position would control the behavior of nonmembers. That is not inherently improper; Cuomo routinely enforces the position of the Democratic Party against nonmembers. But it would lead non-Catholics to vote against him, and to undo any successes he had along this line. I am not convinced that Cuomo is morally obliged to pursue pyrrhic victories.

Quite apart from its effect on nonmembers, a criminal abortion law might entail very high enforcement costs. Proponents of abortion usually cite the example of Prohibition. The offense there is trivial but the point is not. If we had a high rate of illegal abortions and prosecuted violations vigorously, we could put a lot of young women and doctors in jail. If doctors complied (I assume they would) and women continued to abort, they would run a new set of health risks. If juries balked at convicting (and they often would), we would encourage disrespect for the law and waste enforcement resources that we could employ elsewhere with more success (drunk drivers and drug dealers also kill people).

This is not to say that antiabortion laws are, absolutely speaking, a bad idea—only that the government cannot successfully get too far out ahead of public opinion. I hasten to add that that has not been Cuomo's problem. I suspect that the people of New York are, if anything, more willing than he to accept some limitation on abortion rights.[59] If that is so, the governor could find common ground with church nonmembers for doing something about the problem. And a law that had popular support would not entail the enforcement costs I have hypothesized. In short, I see no prudential reason that Cuomo can cite for declining to stand with at least one foot on his principles.[60]

The third abortion question involved in Cuomo's case is the issue of government funding, which he supports. On this issue it is harder for the observant Catholic official to depart from the church's teaching. It is not just a matter of declining for prudential reasons to enforce the moral law. Funding abortions actually promotes (what Cuomo concedes is) evil. And taxing church members to raise the funds implicates them too. Cuomo argues that it is unjust to withhold funds because doing so leaves poor women worse off than rich ones.[61] But if he is concerned about equalizing standards of living, this is hardly the place to start.

I want to conclude this section with a few observations about the enforcement of church authority. Suppose that the governor publicly contradicts some authoritative teaching of the church, or like Cuomo, affirms that he will obey in his personal life but takes an inconsistent political position. What sanctions are (from the church's point of view) proper?

Under canon law, one who procures an abortion is subject to automatic excommunication.[62] This means that she is unable to receive the sacraments, to participate in certain ways at mass and other public worship, and to hold any church office or perform any official ecclesiastical function.[63] The excommunication becomes effective without any trial, though this cannot happen inadvertently. The offender must know in advance not only about the gravity of the offense but also about the church's punishment.[64]

But that is not the offense that Catholic politicians are typically concerned with. Cuomo, for example, has rejected abortion as a possibility in his own life.[65] His offense (if it is one) has been to support the actions of women who want to have abortions, by a course of official conduct (failure to promote regulation; approval of Medicaid funding) and public statements (his speech at Notre Dame).[66] I have suggested that some, at least, of these activities are inconsistent with the church's teaching on abortion, which Catholics are expected to heed. Canon 752 of the Code of Canon Law codifies the obligation to heed church teaching and "to avoid whatever is not in harmony with that teaching."[67] Canon 1371 deals with sanctions for violation of these obligations:

The following are to be punished with a just penalty:

> 1. [A] person who teaches a doctrine condemned by the Roman Pontiff or by an ecumenical council or who pertinaciously rejects the doctrine mentioned in can. 752.[68]

What counts as a "just penalty" can vary. The local bishop seems to have considerable discretion, and the code encourages him to proceed cautiously.[69] Cardinal O'Connor suggested that excommunication was a possibility, but no American bishop has tried it. Bishop Maher in San Diego withheld communion (a less severe sanction) from Lucy Killea, a state senator who advocated abortion rights.[70] O'Connor's vicar and Bishop Daily of Brooklyn have barred Cuomo from speaking at parish churches.

These sanctions are intended to be coercive in the way that civil contempt is coercive: they aim at reformation of the offender's conduct.[71] But they are effective only against religious believers. If I had no interest in participating in the religious life of the Catholic community, excommunication would not concern me. (It would be like being thrown out of the Book of the Month Club.) And once I was willing to sever my religious ties, the church would have no independent source of leverage. It does not, for example, have control over its members' financial assets.

III. Religious Authority and the Liberal Constitution

I now want to consider two situations that a Catholic politician like Cuomo might find himself in if he heeded religious authority in his public life. I want to observe in each case whether our liberal principles and our Constitution permit him to comply with the requirements of his faith. In Case One, Cuomo heeds and is persuaded by the church's epistemic authority and wants to act accordingly. In Case Two, Cuomo is unconvinced by the Church's teaching but willing to submit to its practical authority. Case One does not present any problems for the observant politician; Case Two does.

Suppose first, then, that Cuomo believes that abortion is evil because human life begins at conception. This conviction is consistent with Catholic Church teaching, and Cuomo reached it in part because of the church's persuasion and example. But it is like a proposition in geometry that Cuomo has worked out for himself: the teacher helped him to get it, but now he can kick away the props and get it himself. Or consider another simile: The alcoholic in the back row at the A.A. meeting does not go home and tell his wife that the speaker said that anyone with his drinking behavior is a drunk. He says that his eyes were finally opened and now, with the speaker's help, he sees what everyone else but himself had long seen but he could not bear to see. The man says this as something he owes to a wise and helpful mentor, but now it is something he is vouching for himself.[72]

The politician who holds this conviction in this way will not think that *Roe v. Wade*[73] was right in saying that abortion is a fundamental right. Nor will he favor public funding of abortion (though he may have doubts about criminal penalties). Is there a problem with taking these positions on questions of public policy when the belief that underlies them had its origin in an exercise of religious authority?

No. In the first place, what else would we have Cuomo do? This is not a case where he can centrifuge his beliefs and separate the religious element. We sometimes ask juries to do that when hearsay evidence slips in. But here religious teaching is not a piece of evidence. It is a way of looking at the world that Cuomo has appropriated. He can no more set it aside than he can set aside his idea of color or shape in looking at a picture. We cannot ask him to act without reliance on his religious convictions, because he probably has no idea what he would do in that case. It would be like asking him how he would decide if he were someone else.

If we were determined to avoid any religious influence on politics, we might then ask Cuomo to recuse himself from any decision involving abortion. But as Kent

Greenawalt has pointed out, it is not clear why a liberal society would want to exclude all religious influence in a case like this.[74] The question about the moral worth of the fetus is not one that anyone can answer on the basis of shared premises and publicly accessible reasons.[75] So everyone who thinks about the question (and it is unavoidable in making abortion policy) will have to rely on some "private" or "personal" grounds.[76] Only a society actually hostile to religion would want to treat it worse than other kinds of "personal" reasons.[77]

Liberal principles, then, should not prevent Cuomo from acting on his religious belief about the morality of abortion. It would be both impossible and unfair to do so. As a matter of constitutional law, I think the case for Cuomo is even stronger, in large part because our Constitution does not rest entirely on liberal principles. The only conceivable constitutional objection would be that the Establishment Clause forbade public officials to act on beliefs that had religious origins. But this has the rules exactly backward. I would argue not only that the Establishment Clause permits such action but that the Free Exercise Clause positively encourages it.

That assertion requires a longer defense than I can make without changing the focus of this essay, so I will content myself with a sketch. I begin with the assumption that freedom of religion is a special form of protection for religious believers. From the Constitution's point of view, religious activity (ritual acts, the acquisition and propagation of religious knowledge, observance of moral obligations) is a good thing. The Free Exercise Clause encourages us to engage in it. There are several limits to our enthusiasm for such activity, but they do not stem from doubts about its worth. One is that we should not coerce people to perform ceremonies they do not believe in (prayer, worship, declarations of belief) because it is futile, or even counterproductive from a religious point of view, to do so.[78] Another is that the best way for society to grasp religious truth is to allow free inquiry for everyone—atheists and agnostics as well as believers.[79] A third is that religious compulsion can cause civil strife and leave everyone worse off.[80]

Official action to limit abortions (by outright restrictions or by withholding funds), even if it has its origin in religious conviction, does not transgress these limits. Restrictions may be coercive, but they do not force women to engage in religious activity or affirm a religious belief. Nor do they affect in any way the dissenter's ability to complain. And while they may cause contention, that alone is not enough for an Establishment Clause violation. (Some people were moved by religious principle to vote for the 1964 Civil Rights Act, and it caused contention.) This is an argument that relies on the lessons of history. And if history is to be our guide, the kind of contention we should fear results from a division along identifiably religious lines (Puritan/Baptist, Catholic/Protestant, Christian/Jew, Muslim/Baha'i) over indisputably religious questions.

Let me turn now to Case Two, which I view as more difficult. Suppose that Cuomo has listened attentively to the church's teaching on abortion and has tried to come around to that point of view in his own mind, but he just does not get it. (He thinks that the fetus very early in pregnancy is like the very old person in a persistent vegetative state: we are not obliged to keep either one alive at great personal cost.) But as an observant Catholic, he is aware that the church asks its members to conform their conduct to its teaching (submission of will) even if they do not agree (submission of mind). It asserts practical as well as epistemic authority.

Suppose too that Cuomo is willing to comply with the church's practical authority, for several reasons. One justification for the authority of the Catholic Church, as I explained in part I, is that it promotes unity within the church. Orthopraxy is a way of keeping faith with the religious community, and that might be important enough to Cuomo for him to act against his better judgment.

Cuomo might also be willing to conform his own behavior to the church's teaching because of something like the service conception of authority. He is unable in his own mind to distinguish some cases of abortion and termination of life support. To that extent he does not agree with the church's teaching. But his experience and his religious beliefs about God's guidance of his church tell him that the church has a lower error rate than he does. In doing as the church requires, he trusts, though he is by no means convinced, that he will be doing the right thing.

Suppose further that in this case Cuomo is willing to obey church teaching not just in his personal life (he would not urge his wife to have an abortion) but also in his public life (he follows the "Catholic line" in his political positions). As I explained in part II, the church's teaching authority in this area is qualified in numerous ways. But there are some points (like abortion funding) about which it is quite clear, and here Cuomo heeds what the church has to say. Is there anything illiberal or unconstitutional in obedience to authority under these circumstances?

Unlike Case One, here it is possible for Cuomo to separate his religious from his secular convictions. Cuomo actually believes that there is nothing wrong with abortion under some circumstances. If you asked him, he would tell you that. The reason he votes against abortion funding and publicly opposes *Roe v. Wade*[81] is that he feels obligated to follow his church's teaching. In asking Cuomo to set aside his religious beliefs, then, we would not be asking him to do the impossible. Would we be asking something that was unfair or otherwise improper?

Notice a second difference between this case and the last one. In Case One, Cuomo could justify his public actions (for example, a veto of abortion funding) in terms of harms, benefits, and reasons that all citizens should recognize. He would say that abortion takes innocent life, which society should protect. And he would argue that our concept of rights cannot embrace actions so intrinsically evil. It is true that he came to believe these things by a specifically Catholic route, but other people have reached the same conclusions by other roads (some religious, some not), and there is nothing sectarian about saving lives.

In Case Two, it is harder for Cuomo to point to a public benefit that justifies his actions. One reason he follows the "Catholic line" is that orthopraxy promotes church unity, and that is good for a variety of religious reasons. But there is no reason that non-Catholic citizens should care about the unity of Cuomo's church. If Cuomo vetoes abortion funding or approves abortion restrictions solely for that reason, he puts the interest of his church ahead of the public interest. That is troubling, both morally and constitutionally. As a moral matter, Cuomo is bound both by oath and by promise to represent all the citizens of New York and to uphold the Constitution. As a constitutional matter, the case I have so far put is one where he takes official action for the sole purpose of promoting the religious aims of his church. That is certainly inconsistent with the *Lemon* rule against religious purposes.[82] It is also an invitation to civil strife along religious lines in the classical form: Cuomo's action appeals just to Catholics, rests only on religious reasons, and imposes the costs on nonmembers.

What makes me most uncomfortable about this case, I think, is that it confirms the stereotype of Catholics as citizens with divided loyalties. Cuomo's sole reason for acting is that his church has directed him to—and by "his church" I mean here the bishops and the pope. Locke said he would not extend toleration to churches whose members "pass into the allegiance and service of another prince."[83] His sentiments are still in fashion. Twentieth-century Americans have been willing to "imagine the papal submarine ready to land the First Lord of its Admiralty in Chesapeake Bay when the White House is properly occupied."[84] Part of my effort in this essay has been to show that this dilemma will rarely arise because (i) church authority is binding in varying degrees; (ii) politicians need not always implement church teaching; (iii) people may quite properly act on religious beliefs in cases like Case One; and of course (iv) the Catholic Church, unlike other sovereigns, has no control over unwilling members. But the dilemma for the observant Catholic in Case Two is real. The solution is not, as Justice Brennan once suggested, to set aside his religious beliefs.[85] It is to recuse himself, if that is possible, or resign if it is not.

So far in discussing Case Two, I have supposed that Cuomo is willing to heed the church's practical authority only for the sake of church unity. But suppose he also justified obedience by reference to the service conception of authority. He might believe that the church was a better judge of moral questions (as my broker is a better judge of investments), and though he himself could not see the wrongness of abortion he might "take the Church's word for it." Is there a problem with this kind of reliance on authority?

Here too, as in my first version of Case Two, Cuomo will have no difficulty separating his religious from his secular convictions. As far as he can tell, there is nothing wrong with abortion under some circumstances. He acts on the contrary assumption only because the church says otherwise and he trusts its judgment. Unlike Case One, we would not be asking Cuomo to do the impossible in setting aside his religious beliefs.

But unlike my first version of Case Two, Cuomo here can honestly justify his public actions on grounds that all citizens should recognize. He would argue that abortion is bad because it takes innocent life, which society should protect. It is true that he has only a tenuous grip on that proposition. He holds it the way I hold the special theory of relativity: I really do believe that mass increases with velocity, and that time slows down, but I have to say it does not make sense to me. Still, he does hold it, and it is a perfectly appropriate basis for making public policy.

Should it matter that Cuomo's belief in the immorality of abortion derives wholly from religious premises (the church teaches it, and God inspires the church's teaching)? This is a difficult question, but I think not. It is permissible for a public official to hold an activity immoral simply because our tradition teaches that it is. And such beliefs can be identical in form and substance to Cuomo's belief about abortion. In form because we apply to tradition the service conception of authority: we think it is likely to be right even if we cannot see the point. In substance because the tradition itself can be plainly religious. (Consider the tradition against sodomy, which the Court upheld in *Bowers v. Hardwick*.[86]) The point is that most of us, not just Catholics, see nothing wrong with relying on authority to decide moral questions. And if that is so, there is no reason to disqualify religious authorities.

NOTES

I would like to thank Walter Bado, Gerard V. Bradley, James T. Burtchaell, David Little, Thomas L. Shaffer, Richard G. Wilkins, and the symposium participants for reading this essay with unusual care and making a host of thoughtful suggestions, some of which I have been wise enough to heed.

1. Mario M. Cuomo, Religious Belief and Public Morality: A Catholic Governor's Perspective, Address at the University of Notre Dame (Sept. 13, 1984), in 1 Notre Dame J.L. Ethics & Pub. Pol'y 13 (1984).

2. Mr. Cuomo stated: "As a Catholic, I accept the Church's teaching authority. . . . I accept the Bishops' position that abortion is to be avoided. As Catholics, my wife and I were enjoined never to use abortion to destroy the life we created, and we never have. We thought Church doctrine was clear on this, and, more than that, both of us felt it in full agreement with what our hearts and our consciences told us." Id. at 21.

3. Id. at 24.

4. Id. at 25.

5. Id. at 25–26.

6. Kenneth A. Briggs, Fight Abortion, O'Connor Urges Public Officials, N.Y. Times, Oct. 16, 1984, at A1.

7. Nat Hentoff, John Cardinal O'Connor: At the Storm Center of a Changing American Catholic Church 139 (1988).

8. Id. at 138–54.

9. Peter Steinfels, Cardinal Accepts Discord on Abortion, N.Y. Times, Mar. 21, 1990, at A24.

10. Ari L. Goldman, New Brooklyn Bishop to Bar Cuomo Over Abortion, N.Y. Times, Feb. 21, 1990, at A1.

11. Ari L. Goldman, O'Connor Warns Politicians Risk Excommunication Over Abortion, N.Y. Times, June 15, 1990, at A1.

12. There are those who dispute the idea that authority entails a duty to obey. See Rolf Sartorius, Political Authority and Political Obligation, 67 Va. L. Rev. 3 (1981); Robert Ladeson, In Defense of a Hobbesian Conception of Law, 9 Phil. & Pub. Aff. 139 (1980). I am persuaded otherwise for the reasons detailed in Joseph Raz, The Morality of Freedom 23–37 (1986). On the notion of jural contradictories, see R. W. M. Dias, Jurisprudence 33–65 (3d ed. 1976).

13. See the discussion in Raz, supra note 12, at 30, 49. A broader though related argument is made in Yves Simon, Nature and Functions of Authority (1940). Simon contends that authority would be necessary even in a community of intelligent adults acting with perfect goodwill. Its essential function would be "to assure the unity of action of a united multitude." Id. at 17. But he has in mind, apart from coordination problems, cases of persistent disagreement in matters of practical reason.

14. See the discussion in Edna Ullmann-Margalit, The Emergence of Norms 18–73 (1977).

15. John Locke, The Second Treatise of Government § 95 (Thomas P. Peardon ed., 1952). See also Thomas Hobbes, Leviathan 112 (Michael Oakeshott ed., 1962).

16. Joseph Raz, Government by Consent, in Authority Revisited: XXIX Nomos 76 (J. Roland Pennock & John W. Chapman eds., 1987); Raz, supra note 12, at 80–94.

17. Raz, supra note 12, at 53 (emphasis omitted).

18. Id. at 57–62.

19. Id. at 56.

20. Chevron, Inc. v. Natural Resources Defense Council, 467 U.S. 837 (1984). Chevron also relies heavily on the idea of consent. The EPA derives its authority in part, the Court argues, from the elected branches. Congress has delegated power to it, and the president influences its policy determinations.

21. Dogmatic Constitution on the Church (Lumen Gentium), in The Documents of Vatican II §§ 1–8 (Walter M. Abbott ed. & Joseph Gallagher trans. ed., 1966) (hereinafter Lumen Gentium). In discussing various documents promulgated by the Second Vatican Council, I refer to the section numbers used in the documents rather than to the page numbers in Abbott's compilation.

22. Id. § 9. Cf. Jeremiah 31:31–34 ("I will be their God, and they shall be my people.").

23. Lumen Gentium, supra note 21, § 1.

24. Papal Primacy and the Universal Church, Lutherans and Catholics in Dialogue V, at 12 n.4 (Paul Empie & T. Austin Murphy eds., 1974).

25. Lumen Gentium, supra note 21, § 23.

26. Id. § 25; Carlo Cardinal Colombo, Obedience to the Ordinary Magisterium, in Obedience and the Church 75, 78–82 (1968).

27. Lumen Gentium, supra note 21, § 25.

28. Id.

29. Id. §§ 30–38; Pastoral Constitution on the Church in the Modern World (Gaudium et Spes), in The Documents of Vatican II, at 199 (Walter M. Abbott ed. & Joseph Gallagher trans. ed., 1966) (hereinafter Gaudium et Spes); Avery Dulles, The Survival of Dogma 97–98 (1971).

30. Lumen Gentium, supra note 21, § 22.

31. Id. § 25.

32. Id. It is a little puzzling to see plenary authority lodged thus in two institutions. It is as though lawmaking authority were given to parliament (with the prime minister at its head) and also to the prime minister acting alone. The best explanation for the arrangement is this. The standard method for making really important pronouncements is an ecumenical council. Sometimes popes act on their own, as Pius IX did in 1854 (in proclaiming the dogma of the Immaculate Conception) and Pius XII did in 1950 (in proclaiming the dogma of the Assumption). When they do so, they are exercising the authority of the college of bishops. The pope does not need authorization or consent to act in this manner, but it is practically impossible for him to act without extensive consultation. See Karl Rahner, On the Relationship between the Pope and the College of Bishops, 10 Theological Investigations 50–70 (1973); Francis A. Sullivan, Magisterium: Teaching Authority in the Catholic Church 100–106 (1983).

33. Lumen Gentium, supra note 21, §§ 23, 25.

34. 1983 Code c.753; Decree on the Bishops' Pastoral Office in the Church (Christus Dominus), in The Documents of Vatican II §§ 36–38 (Walter M. Abbott ed. & Joseph Gallagher trans. ed., 1966); Jan Schotte, A Vatican Synthesis, 12 Origins 691, 692 (1983); James Hickey, The Bishop as Teacher, 12 Origins 142, 142 (1982).

35. Lumen Gentium, supra note 21, § 25.

36. Id.; 1 Commentary on the Documents of Vatican II, at 210 (Herbert Vorgrimler ed., 1967).

37. Will v. Michigan Dept. of State Police, 491 U.S. 58 (1989); Pennhurst State Sch. & Hosp. v. Halderman, 451 U.S. 1 (1981); Kent v. Dulles, 357 U.S. 116 (1958).

38. Lumen Gentium, supra note 21, § 25.

39. Sullivan, supra note 32, at 129–36.

40. Gaudium et Spes, supra note 29, §§ 51, 27.

41. Pope Paul VI, Humanae Vitae § 14 (July 29, 1968).

42. National Conference of Catholic Bishops, Documentation on the Right to Life and Abortion (1974); Quest for Justice: A Compendium of Statements of the United States Bishops on the Political and Social Order 1966–1980 (J. Brian Benestad & Francis J. Butler eds., 1982).

43. Sacred Congregation for the Doctrine of the Faith, Declaration on Procured Abortion, in Vatican Council II: More Postconciliar Documents 441 (Austin Flannery ed., 1982).

44. Hentoff, supra note 7, at 113, 250–51, 256–57, 259–60; Goldman, supra note 10. See also James T. Burtchaell, The Giving and Taking of Life 51–68 (1989).

45. Lumen Gentium, supra note 21, § 25. See James L. Heft, Dissent in the Church, Dimensions, Nov. 1986, at 2, 3; William E. May, Catholic Moral Teaching and the Limits of Dissent, in Vatican Authority and American Catholic Dissent 87, 91–94 (William E. May ed., 1987). There are, of course, those who say otherwise. See, e.g., Charles E. Curran, Toward an American Catholic Moral Theology 46 (1987).

46. Lumen Gentium, supra note 21, § 25 (emphasis added). Canon 752 of the Code of Canon Law uses almost the same language. See 1983 Code c.752.

47. See Elizabeth Anscombe, Authority in Morals, in Problems of Authority 179 (John M. Todd ed., 1962).

48. Sullivan, supra note 32, at 153–73; Joseph A. Komonchak, Ordinary Papal Magisterium and Religious Assent, in Readings in Moral Theology No. 3: The Magisterium and Morality 67 (Charles E. Curran & Richard A. McCormick eds., 1982).

49. Cf. 18 Thomas Aquinas, Summa Theologica: Principles of Morality 59–65 (Thomas Gilby, trans., Black Friars 1966) (Question 19, Article 5).

50. Gaudium et Spes, supra note 29, § 42; see also Declaration on Religious Freedom (Dignitatis Humanae) in The Documents of Vatican II, at 675 (Walter M. Abbott ed. & Joseph Gallagher trans. ed., 1966) (hereinafter Dignitatis Humanae).

51. Dignitatis Humanae, supra note 50, § 4 n.11.

52. Gaudium et Spes, supra note 29, § 76.

53. Thomas Aquinas, Summa Theologica: The Powers of Human Law, in Aquinas: Selected Political Writings 133, 133–35 (A. P. D'Entreves ed. & J. G. Dawson trans., 7th ed. 1978) (citation omitted) (Question 96, Article 2).

54. Think about judicial review of price controls, or of public utility rates. See FPC v. Hope Nat'l Gas Co., 320 U.S. 591 (1944); Nebbia v. New York, 291 U.S. 502 (1934).

55. National Conference of Catholic Bishops, Economic Justice for All: Pastoral Letter on Catholic Social Teaching and the U.S. Economy (1986).

56. 410 U.S. 113 (1973).

57. Gaudium et Spes, supra note 29, § 51.

58. Now that *Roe* has been decided, stare decisis is a reason for leaving it in place. See Planned Parenthood of Southeastern Pa. v. Casey, 112 S. Ct. 2791, 2808–16 (1992). I cannot think of another.

59. I do not have figures on New York itself. However, only about 20 percent of Americans support abortion on demand (about the same fraction that favors a total prohibition). Burtchaell, supra note 44, at 273–74. Mary Ann Glendon has shown that the American constitutional rules enforcing that regime are more permissive than those of any other nation (Glendon studies twenty other nations) in Europe and North America. Mary A. Glendon, Abortion and Divorce in Western Law: American Failures, European Challenges 145–57 (1987).

60. I have been assuming, in discussing this second issue, that the constitutional regime would permit abortion regulation if the voters wanted it. Ours does not, as a general matter, though there are some modest possibilities available after Planned Parenthood, 112 S. Ct. 2791.

61. Cuomo, supra note 1, at 25–26.

62. 1983 Code of Canon Law c.1398.

63. Id. c.1331, § 1.

64. 2 Sacramentum Mundi: An Encyclopedia of Theology 176 (Adolf Darlap ed., 1968) (hereinafter 2 Sacramentum Mundi).

65. See supra note 2.

66. See supra notes 3–5 and accompanying text.

67. Canon 752 states: "A religious respect of intellect and will . . . is to be paid to the teaching which the Supreme Pontiff or the college of bishops enunciate on faith or morals when they exercise the authentic magisterium . . . ; therefore the Christian faithful are to take care to avoid whatever is not in harmony with that teaching. 1983 Code c.752." There is some disagreement, which I am not competent to arbitrate, about the proper interpretation of the Latin phrase "*religiosum . . . intellectus et voluntatis obsequium*" used in both Lumen Gentium § 25 and canon 752. The English version of Lumen Gentium translates it as "religious submission of will and of mind." The English version of canon 752 translates it as "religious respect of intellect and will." I follow the former usage for reasons explained in Sullivan, supra note 32, at 158–60.

68. 1983 Code c.1371.

69. See id. c.1341.

70. Russell Chandler, Bishops Facing a Dilemma on Pro-Choice Politicians, L.A. Times, Nov. 22, 1989, at A1.

71. 2 Sacramentum Mundi, supra note 64, at 174–75.

72. Burtchaell, supra note 44, at 265.

73. 410 U.S. 113 (1973).

74. Kent Greenawalt, Religious Convictions and Political Choice 144–72 (1988).

75. Id.

76. Id.

77. Id.

78. In Milton's phrase, to force a ritual performance is "to compell hypocrisie not to advance religion." 7 John Milton, A Treatise of Civil Power in Ecclesiastical Causes, in Complete Prose Works of John Milton 238, 256 (Yale, 1980).

79. We think of this as an argument for free speech, but Milton, to whom we most often attribute it, was actually making a theological claim. 2 John Milton, Areopagitica, in Complete Prose Works of John Milton 480, 551 (Yale, 1959) ("this is the golden rule in Theology").

80. McGowan v. Maryland, 366 U.S. 420, 464 (1961) (Frankfurter, J., concurring).

81. 410 U.S. 113 (1973).

82. Lemon v. Kurtzman, 403 U.S. 602, 612–613 (1971).

83. John Locke, Epistola de Tolerantia [A Letter on Toleration] 133 (Raymond Klibansky & J. W. Gough trans. eds., 1968).

84. Burtchaell, supra note 44, at 260.

85. See Sanford Levinson, The Confrontation of Religious Faith and Civil Religion: Catholics Becoming Justices, 39 DePaul L. Rev. 1047, 1062–64 (1990) (discussing Brennan's remarks).

86. 478 U.S. 186, 190–96 (1986).

Part III

Religion and Supreme Court Doctrine

Chapter 10

Why the State Must Subordinate Religion

Scott C. Idleman

The First Amendment Free Exercise Clause, as Justice Black would have reminded us, is written in absolute terms. "Congress shall make *no law* . . . prohibiting the free exercise [of religion]."[1] In turn, one might surmise that courts would accord it an absolutist reading, particularly given the relative clarity of the clause's language, the primacy normally accorded to clear textual mandates of the Constitution, and the fact that its companion provision—the Establishment Clause—is itself interpreted in precisely this manner.[2] Such has not been the case, however. When defining the protection accorded to religiously based conduct, the judiciary has never adopted an absolutist interpretation, even in cases of intentional prohibition.[3] Rather, the conventional model for judicial analysis has entailed a less determinate balancing of competing interests, in which the value of free exercise is essentially conceptualized in relative, even instrumental, terms.

This essay will argue that, at bottom, this judicial resistance to a strong reading of the Free Exercise Clause has little to do with text or tradition as such but, rather, with sovereignty. In particular, the state *must* subordinate religion in order to preserve its jurisdictional supremacy and to maintain its grasp on the allegiance of the citizenry. Under this view, the balancing tests thus serve not only as a doctrinal apparatus within which religious liberty claims are formally resolved but ultimately and more importantly as a protective apparatus by which the government's sovereign character is effectively preserved. The outer boundaries of permissible free exercise, in other words, are fundamentally defined not by the articulated competing interests themselves but by the state's need to limit the citizenry's observance of laws other than its own.

Initially, a sovereignty-based reading of the judiciary's free exercise interpretations may seem a rather abstract perspective on religious freedom, far removed from the resolution of any particular dispute. But it is clearly of more than theoretical significance. Not only does it explain the resistance to an absolutist interpretation, it suggests that such an interpretation will never be embraced. Even where a rigorous nonabsolutist approach (such as strict scrutiny) is employed in the protection of religious freedom, a sovereignty-based reading further suggests that such an approach will never yield the results that it does in other contexts—a differential that has frequently been noted, often criticized, but rarely explained. Finally, to the extent that interference with the sovereignty of civil government truly marks the outer bounds of protected free exercise, it may provide a new standard, whether or not acknowledged by courts, for predicting outcomes in certain free exercise cases—and, when combined with the conventional model, at the very least provides a more complete picture of free exercise analysis.[4]

I. Conventional Free Exercise Doctrine and Its Inadequacy

A. The Conventional Model

Before critiquing and then departing from the conventional model of free exercise analysis, its basic structure and elements must first be considered. Under the Free Exercise Clause, the government may act unconstitutionally in several ways: by discriminating on the basis of religious status, by prohibiting religious belief, by requiring a particular religious belief or practice, or by prohibiting or otherwise regulating religious conduct. While the first three are forbidden absolutely, especially where the government action is intentional,[5] claims alleging the restriction of religious *conduct* are not so absolutely protected but instead are ultimately subjected to a balancing inquiry.[6]

In order to reach this inquiry, a plaintiff asserting a conduct-based free exercise claim must establish five prima facie elements. First, the government action must constitute a "law" within the meaning of the First Amendment.[7] Second, the claimant's conduct must stem from beliefs that are "religious" within the meaning of that amendment.[8] Third, these beliefs must be sincerely held by the claimant.[9] Fourth, the practice must have a constitutionally cognizable relation to the claimant's religion; that is, it must implicate a "central practice" or "core tenet" of the religion,[10] or must otherwise be mandated, or at least motivated, by the claimant's religious beliefs.[11] Finally, and perhaps alternatively, the practice or one's religious life as a whole must be burdened or substantially burdened by the government conduct in question.[12]

Once these five elements are satisfied, the challenged government action will be subjected to one of two levels of scrutiny. Under current doctrine, strict scrutiny obtains if the government action is not neutral or not generally applicable,[13] or if the free exercise claim is asserted in tandem with another constitutional right.[14] In such instances, the evidentiary burden shifts to the government to demonstrate that its action "advance[s] 'interests of the highest order' and . . . [is] narrowly tailored in pursuit of those interests."[15] In all other cases, rational basis scrutiny applies, and the evidentiary burden remains with the claimant to demonstrate that the action is not rationally related to a legitimate government interest.[16]

Regardless of which level of scrutiny is invoked, the fundamental nature of the inquiry concerns whether the government interest and the manner of its implementation outweigh the claimant's interest in religious liberty. Balancing, in other words, pervades the resolution of conduct-based free exercise cases despite the absolutist phrasing of the First Amendment. Prior to the assessment of any given dispute, of course, at least some of the elements—such as the scope of "religion"—will necessarily have been categorically delineated, and this process may itself entail a kind of absolutism. But the essential nature of conventional free exercise analysis involves the balancing of interests, principally that of religious liberty in relation to one or more governmental objectives.

Later in the essay it will be argued that this balancing process is in many respects inadequate and incomplete, and that free exercise analysis at some level is actually driven by a judicially enforced but unarticulated interest in preserving the supremacy of the state. Before proceeding to these arguments, however, it is important to examine the government interests that the judiciary formally recognizes as sufficient to override an asserted interest in the free exercise of religion. For convenience, these government interests can be divided into three categories: police power interests, administrative interests, and judicial interests.

The most familiar category encompasses the state's so-called police power,[17] and includes matters relating to public health, welfare, safety, and morals.[18] Although these matters are not intrinsically governmental as such but, rather, public or societal, their furtherance by force of law reflects a contractual view of the state that recognizes the existence of "manifold restraints to which every person is necessarily subject for the common good."[19] Within rational basis scrutiny, police power interests virtually always are, and by definition should be, legitimate.[20] Presumably this is why the Supreme Court could state, rather matter-of-factly, that providing nothing more than rational basis scrutiny would essentially "leav[e] accommodation [of religious practices] to the political process."[21] As for strict scrutiny, here too the government's police power interests are often (though not always) deemed sufficient—"compelling" in the language of strict scrutiny[22]—despite the supposed rigor of the test.[23]

A second category of government interests concerns the administration of government itself—"the legitimate conduct by government of its own affairs."[24] These include matters such as cost or effectiveness and, like police power interests, have been recognized as legitimate in a variety of settings.[25] Unlike police power interests, however, they are less frequently deemed compelling.[26] And for good reason. As Professor Douglas Laycock has remarked, "There is no government bureaucrat in America who doesn't believe that his program serves a compelling interest in every application,"[27] and the necessary prevalence of administrative interests would empty the term "compelling" of virtually all meaning were it regularly to be so broadly construed.

A third and final category of government interests can be labeled judicial interests. Because the power of final constitutional review in the United States has been vested in (or at least assumed by) the judicial branch of government,[28] constitutional interpretations are necessarily shaped by the institutional values and interests of the bench. Constitutional interpretation, in other words, is ultimately informed not only by text, tradition, original intent or understanding, and a host of other sources and canons but also by the peculiar considerations of judicial decision making.[29] Such considerations include a sensitivity to the allocation of scarce judicial resources and to docket management;[30] to the limited but important role of courts in the political-constitutional scheme;[31] and to various judicial traditions such as the concept of justiciability and doctrine of stare decisis.[32] While these interests pervade constitutional decision making, they rarely if ever serve explicitly as government interests in the balancing of conduct-based free exercise claims. (Courts themselves, after all, are seldom the target of a free exercise challenge, and, even where they are, the challenged judicial action normally does not implicate these particular judicial interests.) Instead they tend to surface at the stage of formulating, as opposed to applying, the analytical doctrines. In *Smith*, for example, the Court clearly expressed its concern that the adoption of the *Sherbert-Yoder* test across the board would place courts in a constitutionally untenable position.[33] Nonetheless, there is no particular reason to think that such interests do not also play a role, at some level, in the actual application of free exercise doctrines.

B. The Inadequacy of the Conventional Model

Although the conventional model of free exercise analysis is obviously workable insofar as it can be applied by judges to produce results in particular cases, it is nevertheless inadequate insofar as its relationship to the text of the Free Exercise Clause is strained, its formal doctrines do not capture the reality of judicial application, and it is not explicitly grounded in a coherent theory of religious liberty. These inadequacies are noted and will be explored here because their number and magnitude signal the operation of unarticulated norms, the most important of which, it shall be argued, is the preservation of the supremacy of civil law and thus the sovereignty of civil government.

This section will address four such anomalies within current free exercise doctrine. First, there is simply the avoidance of an absolutist interpretation, despite the interpretive dissonance that such avoidance—in the absence of persuasive justification—generates. Second, within the conventional analytical framework, certain elements are inexplicably distorted in a manner that can severely diminish the likelihood that particular free exercise claims will prevail. Third, and relatedly, a good case can be made that the substantial burden requirement was devised and is employed precisely because it allows courts to discard troublesome free exercise claims that otherwise appear colorable under the terms of the conventional model. Finally, and more generally, there is the rather stark fact that the Supreme Court has never set forth a theory or principle of conduct-based free exercise, despite ample opportunity and warrant to do so.

Although each anomaly may be independently explicable—and some explanations are considered—what this essay shall argue is that collectively they can more easily be explained, and perhaps best explained, by reference to a governmental concern about the maintenance and furtherance of its own sovereignty in relation to religion.

1. THE UNEXPLAINED AVOIDANCE OF AN ABSOLUTIST INTERPRETATION

The first indication that unarticulated norms are afoot involves the judiciary's reluctance to interpret the clause in an absolutist manner, as its text would appear to command. More specifically, there is a reluctance to justify in logically persuasive terms why such an interpretation should not be adopted. What typically appears in judicial opinion is either total silence, an appeal to historical practice or understanding, or an outright declaration that an absolutist interpretation would simply be intolerable. Silence, of course, is hardly a justification, though it is arguably probative of the lack of an articulable rationale. Likewise, appeals to historical practice or original understanding may lend formal legal backing to a contemporary interpretation, and may even explain genealogically the roots of a nonabsolutist interpretation, but such appeals merely beg the question of present-day justification.

As for the notion that an absolutist interpretation would prove unacceptable, here too there is ultimately a failure of adequate justification. Several norms of unacceptability are invoked. There is, for example, the generic notion that an absolution interpretation is simply not "in the nature of things"[34]—leaving the reader to nod concurringly on whatever basis he or she finds agreeable. Alternatively, there is the outright appeal to hyperbole: an absolutist interpretation, it is proposed, would literally bring the operations of civil government, indeed civil society, to a screeching halt.[35] Or, there is the curious notion that the judicial extension of absolute protection from religious belief to religious conduct "might leave government powerless to vindicate compelling state interests"[36]—a line of reasoning that appears to overlook the fact that the medium of judicial review, employing strict scrutiny, is precisely where the government *can* vindicate its interests if truly compelling.

The lack of any real substance to these appeals, resting as they do upon the anticipated intuitive or commonsensical assent of readers, is strong circumstantial evidence that the courts are adverting to a deeper but unarticulated normative calculus in their decision making. Of course, intuition and common sense do enjoy a distinguished place in constitutional interpretation, and to deprive judges of recourse to them would do violence to the role of judgment in judicial decision making. As Chief Justice Marshall observed, "It is essential to just construction, that many words which import something excessive, should be understood in a more mitigated sense—in that sense which common usage justifies."[37] But mitigating the sense of a phrase and justifying that mitigation are different undertakings, and the permissibility of the former does not by any means excuse a neglect of the latter.

One theory periodically asserted by judges is that an absolutist reading of the Free Exercise Clause would overrun or cancel out the Establishment Clause.[38] As described by one judge: "[T]here is an inherent tension between the two clauses. If the Free Exercise Clause were interpreted as an absolute mandate, it would subsume the Establishment Clause. Paradoxically, making 'Free Exercise' an absolute mandate would . . . effectively destroy 'freedom of religion' as we know it."[39] But this argument is problematic for several reasons. For one thing, it overlooks the fact that the Free Exercise Clause's companion provision, the Establishment Clause, does operate in a categorical, absolutist fashion,[40] and yet courts have somehow managed to shield the former from the latter's absolutist interpretation. For another thing, it uncritically accepts that there is, or must be, a tension between the two clauses, when in fact such a tension is largely an outgrowth of the judiciary's expansive Establishment Clause jurisprudence. And even if such a tension is unavoidable, it does not explain why a substantially emasculated Establishment Clause (necessary to accommodate a stronger reading of the Free Exercise Clause) would be so devastating from a constitutional standpoint.

In the alternative, it has been suggested that "[i]f the Free Exercise Clause protected all religious activity, it would not be possible to maintain a civil, pluralistic society."[41] According to this judge:

> [I]t is easy to see how the absolute protection of religious activity would quickly lead to an establishment of religion. If a school principal's religious beliefs commanded him or her to "save" others and taught him or her that other religions were false, he or she might consider it his or her religious duty to "establish" his or her religion in that particular school. And, if the Free Exercise Clause were an absolute, the principal would have a constitutional right to press his or her religious views on students through official school channels.[42]

Although this appears to be a strong argument, it too is not without difficulties. It assumes, for example, that the government ought to be operating schools at all, or that the Establishment Clause was intended to apply to state and local governments. But the validity of these premises is not universally shared, and each has taken hold largely by the passage of time. More fundamentally, it assumes that the principal's in-school activities must be deemed the free exercise of religion, or must be protected to the same degree as his out-of-school activities, when in fact the Free Exercise Clause could be categorically interpreted to provide absolute protection only for activities undertaken in a private capacity or setting. The flaw in this judge's analysis, in other words, is that of bootstrapping: he rejects an absolutist reading largely because it is incongruent with a legal regime in which such a reading has already been rejected.

Finally, there is the more compelling (but not often articulated) proposition that one's free exercise cannot be permitted to cause measurable harm to another, and an absolutist interpretation would undermine this limitation. As the Court has remarked, religious "[c]onduct remains subject to regulation for the protection of society."[43] But unless one adopts an extremely broad notion of harm, including harm to oneself, even this principle does not explain the total or across-the-board rejection of an absolutist interpretation. At most, it points toward a rather rigorous level of constitutional scrutiny, with full protection except in those rare cases, such as religiously motivated homicide or battery, where such harm is clearly demonstrated.

2. THE DISTORTION OF THE BALANCING ANALYSIS

Not only do courts fail to justify adequately the use of balancing in lieu of an absolutist reading, they also tend to distort (without justification) the resulting balancing process in favor of the government, thus further suggesting reliance on one or more deeper yet unarticulated principles. When strict scrutiny is employed in free exercise cases, for example, the range of government interests that qualify as "compelling" is generally much broader than in other constitutional contexts, such as free speech or equal protection, where strict scrutiny is also employed.[44] The compelling interest test, in other words, is watered down in such a way that substantially decreases the likelihood than free exercise claimants might prevail. Moreover, when analyzing the degree to which the government's interest is compelling, courts often (though certainly not always) examine the importance of the government program in its entirety or in the abstract, rather than examining the relative importance of the particular element of the program from which an individualized exemption is sought.[45]

Last, and regardless of what level of scrutiny is invoked, courts also tend to adopt an "objective" analytical disposition that explicitly downplays the potential free exercise injury, thus keeping the balance from tilting too far in the claimant's favor. As the Supreme Court has remarked in regard to claims implicating government administration, "Whatever may be the exact line between unconstitutional prohibitions on the free exercise of religion and the legitimate conduct by government of its own affairs, the location of the line cannot depend on measuring the effects of a governmental action on a religious objector's spiritual development."[46] Other than a concern about the range of lawsuits that might be brought,[47] however, there is offered no explanation for rejecting a posture that is more neutral, let alone skewed toward the perspectives of claimants.[48]

The first two of these progovernment distortions are especially ironic, given that strict scrutiny is supposed to entail a presumption that the government has acted unconstitutionally, thus absolving the judiciary of its normal obligation to uphold a government enactment by any reasonable means. More fundamentally, they are all significant insofar as they reveal that judges must not consider the balancing process adequate, on its own terms, to protect some larger but unarticulated interest. Rather, there is apparently a perceived need to skew the process—to transcend the inherent limits of the asserted government interest and to ignore the potential potency of the free exercise interest—so that, in the end, the former simply will not prevail against the latter.

3. THE USE OF THE BURDEN REQUIREMENT

Of course, before even arriving at this balancing analysis, claimants must first demonstrate that the government has "burdened" or "substantially burdened" their free exercise to a constitutional significant degree. This seems reasonable enough, but as it turns out the burden requirement often serves as a "gatekeeper doctrine[], which function[s] to increase the likelihood of failure at the prima facie stage, and thereby to reduce the number of claims that must be afforded the searching inquiry demanded by the free exercise clause."[49] It is true, of course, that the judiciary must implement some type of adverse treatment requirement, if only to give meaning to the element "prohibit" as found in the Free Exercise Clause.[50] It is also true that other constitutional provisions, too, have threshold requirements for the demonstration of a prima facie case—for example, that there is a racial classification, or that speech is involved, or that one's liberty or property has been deprived. The substantial burden requirement, however, stands out in terms of its indeterminacy and, thus, its judicial manipulability.[51]

These characteristics are significant precisely because they are the product of judicial choice. When devising doctrines and selecting terms, including those used as threshold requirements, courts often have a full range of options from which to choose, and their choice will reflect not only the congruence of the doctrine and its terms with the provision being interpreted but also the degree of judicial discretion that will be retained. In turn, courts generally devise indeterminate and manipulable threshold requirements when they desire to retain significant discretion over which claims will, and will not, proceed. And underlying this perceived need for discretion is likely a sense that the subsequent analysis—here, some form of balancing test—will produce outcomes that are inconsistent either with the purpose of the constitutional provision or with larger principles of constitutional governance.

The selection and use of the burden requirement, then, are likely not coincidental but instead reflect a desire to advance certain objectives or protect certain interests that are not sufficiently advanced or protected by the larger doctrinal framework, particularly the balancing process. As Professor Ira Lupu observes:

> [Free exercise] claims are often deeply troubling. First and foremost, they typically require exemption from or cessation of some government policy that the political branches have ratified and that has legitimate, secular justification. Behind every free exercise claim is a spectral march; grant this one, a voice whispers to each judge, and you will be confronted with an endless chain of exemption demands from religious deviants of every stripe. . . .
>
> The structure of free exercise claims has developed in response to this pressure and its accompanying fears. . . . Indeed, the struggle over the scope of the burden concept can be understood only in relation to this overall structure. To the extent that free exercise claims create discomfort, pressure mounts to find techniques and doctrines for rejecting such claims without seeming unreasonable or unsympathetic to values of religious liberty. When the burden concept is compared to the inquiries into sincerity, religiosity, and state interest frequently demanded by current free exercise norms, one can readily understand the attraction of courts to a restrictive doctrine at the threshold of claims.[52]

4. THE AVOIDANCE OF A THEORY OF RELIGIOUS FREEDOM

One final dimension of the conventional model that strongly implies the operation of unarticulated norms is the Court's steadfast failure to articulate a meaningful theory or set of principles underlying the Free Exercise Clause and, in turn, animating the Court's interpretation of it. Although from time to time the Court purports to explain the purpose of the clause, generally such explanations are either circular or unilluminating.[53] Indeed, neither the Court's most protective free exercise cases nor its least protective cases ever meaningfully explains why, from the perspective of religious liberty itself, the level of protection recognized is appropriate.

Given the obvious necessity of this undertaking, especially within a legal system that prizes reason and definition, the Court's failure could imply a number of possibilities. First, the articulation of a theory or principle of religious liberty may simply not be possible because the religion clauses by design or circumstance possess no such theory or principle.[54] Yet, even assuming that this thesis is correct, it does not absolve the Court from the obligation to articulate the theoretical grounds under which it is necessarily deciding cases, however fabricated or incoherent they may be. The Court is, after all, resolving disputes, and therefore its members, individually or collectively, must be operating on *some* theoretical principle that is susceptible to formulation and articulation.

Alternatively, the articulation of a theory of religious liberty may simply not be institutionally prudent to the extent that the theory articulated would not be sufficiently defensible in terms of traditional constitutional reasoning or consonance with the views of the people. Professor Frederick Gedicks, for example, argues that "secular individualism" is the Court's reigning theoretical commitment within its jurisprudence of the religion clauses.[55] If fully articulated, however, such a theory would be wide open to allegations of judicial activism in the manner of *Lochner v. New York*,[56] and the justices are necessarily sensitive to the criticism that their constitutional interpretations may reflect nothing more than some fashionable elitist philosophy.[57]

Or perhaps the nonarticulation of a theory of religious liberty reflects an avoidance not of theorizing itself but of the possibility that any such theory might yield claims whose premises or resolutions would be inconsistent with other interests or norms that the judiciary is attempting to advance or protect. One such interest, and the one that shall provide the focus for the remainder of the essay, is that of protecting the supremacy of the state vis-à-vis claims of competing sovereignty. It is to that possibility that the essay now turns.

II. Religion and the Sovereignty of Civil Government

The foregoing analysis indicates that there are disjunctions or analytical shortfalls not only between the text of the Free Exercise Clause and the conventional model of free exercise analysis but also between that model and the actual judicial analysis of religious freedom cases. Initially, it might be tempting to conclude that these shortfalls are simply a product of inevitable indeterminacy—a necessary residuum of play in the constitutional joints, if you will—and that there is no meaningful pattern to the case law beyond the doctrines applied, let alone a grand theory of religious freedom operating *sub silentio*. The magnitude and nature of the disjunctions suggest otherwise, however.

The remainder of the essay will argue that these shortfalls may be explained, partly if not largely, by an implicit understanding (judicially enforced) that religious free exercise must often be subordinated to preserve the supremacy of civil law and government. That an absolutist reading is rejected, that the balancing analysis is skewed, that the burden requirement functions as a gatekeeper, and that the judiciary refuses to expound the principle of religious liberty—these are not, in other words, coincidences. Rather, they constitute an awkward but effective means of cabining religion in an effort to maintain the primacy of the state and its legal apparatus.

This argument will be developed in three stages. Section A will briefly examine the concept of sovereignty, particularly its traditional and contemporary importance to American government. Section B will explain why religious adherence poses a special threat to the sovereignty of civil government. Section C will then contend that this threat, and the judiciary's response to it, can substantially account for the underenforcement of the Free Exercise Clause and for many of the textual, doctrinal, and conceptual distortions that have marked that this underenforcement.

A. The Interest in Sovereignty

In legal circles, both domestic and international, the most revered status is that of sovereign. This status either implies or guarantees a variety of rather useful powers or characteristics, including a jurisdictional realm over which is exercised ultimate, often exclusive authority,[58] and general autonomy or immunity from the jurisdictional authority of other sovereigns.[59] Sovereignty and its attendant powers thus tend to be jealously guarded by their possessors, lest they might find their own sovereignty functionally if not formally diminished. As the Supreme Court has remarked: "Any restriction upon [the jurisdiction of the nation], deriving validity from an external source, would imply a diminution of its sovereignty to the extent of the restriction, and an investment of that sovereignty to the same extent in that power which could impose such restriction."[60]

Not surprisingly, the American legal system has generally been resistant to, or at best ambivalent toward, the establishment of quasi-sovereign enclaves within its territorial jurisdiction.[61] The allegiance of a people to a geopolitical entity, after all, is typically seen not only as a requirement of good citizenship but also as a legitimate claim of the entity as a function of its sovereign status.[62] In turn, the sovereign may advance this claim by proscribing, whether outright or by disincentive, various forms of allegiance to other sovereign or quasi-sovereign entities.[63] Federal law, for example, requires that would-be citizens, among other things, "renounce and abjure absolutely and entirely all allegiance and fidelity to any foreign prince, potentate, state, or sovereignty of whom or which the applicant was before a subject or citizen."[64]

From a functional perspective, there exist several forms of extra-allegiance that can undermine one's fidelity to the state. The classical form is lateral, whereby one pledges or retains allegiance to another sovereign political entity. This kind of extra-allegiance is proscribed by the mechanism of citizenship (either its loss or its nonattainment) and, in extreme cases, by the criminalization of treason.[65] Extra-allegiance may also be internal, whereby one's self-absorption and civic apathy are so acute that one effectively becomes, for all intents and purposes, a dysfunctional or noncitizen. Although this condition by itself cannot be punished, should it manifest itself in, say, a disregard for law by the commission of a felony, one may then be legally disenfranchised.[66] Finally, extra-allegiance may be vertical, whereby one pledges allegiance to a transcendent being or body of principles that very well could conflict with the demands of the state. It is the thesis of this essay that such vertical extra-allegiance, which undergirds many free exercise claims, is effectively dealt with by the judiciary's underenforcement of the Free Exercise Clause.

Before turning to the relationship between religion and sovereignty, it is instructive to examine the American legal system's treatment of other attempted claims of sovereign or quasi-sovereign status within its domain. Such claims include assertions of Indian tribal sovereignty vis-à-vis state government, assertions of state sovereignty vis-à-vis the federal government, and assertions of citizen group sovereignty vis-à-vis both federal and state government. First, although the federal courts have generally held that Indian tribes possess limited, vestigial attributes of sovereignty,[67] tribes remain "subject to ultimate federal control"[68] and retain only those attributes that do not conflict with or undermine the sovereignty of the federal government.[69] Tribal sovereignty, in other words, is not truly recognized as true sovereignty, especially since it "exists only at the sufferance of Congress and is subject to complete defeasance."[70] Likewise, although the states retain or possess a fair measure of autonomy or immunity from federal action,[71] "the sovereignty of the States is limited by the Constitution itself"[72] and the Supreme Court, with some recent exceptions, has been reluctant to circumscribe in any meaningful way Congress's power in relation to the states.[73] As Chief Justice John Marshall explained, a state "cannot be viewed as a single, unconnected, sovereign power, on whose legislature no other restrictions are imposed than may be found in its own constitution. She is a part of a large empire; she is a member of the American union; and that union has a constitution the supremacy of which all acknowledge, and which imposes limits to the legislatures of the several states, which none claim a right to pass."[74] Finally, the government has consistently denied the capacity of citizens to assume forms of immunity or authority—legal or military, for example—that would be inconsistent with its own exclusive possession of such authority.[75] In the words of the Supreme Court, "The right voluntarily to associate together as a military company or organization, or to drill or parade with arms, . . . cannot be claimed as a right independent of law. Under our political system they are subject to the regulation and control of the state and federal governments, acting in due regard to their respective prerogatives and powers."[76]

B. Religious Allegiance as a Threat to Sovereignty

Given this antipathy toward various forms of competitive sovereignty and the extra-allegiance they foster, it would be surprising indeed if government were not to perceive religion—and if judges were not to perceive free exercise claims—with anything but a jaundiced eye. For it is arguably the case that no form of extra-allegiance, other than lateral allegiance to another geopolitical sovereign, is more problematic for the state than religious adherence.[77] Three common characteristics of religion render it so. First, religious faith and beliefs by definition involve the core of individual and social identity and, at least for the devout, cannot easily be suppressed or dislodged. Second, religion typically generates or transmits normative commitments or obligations that periodically conflict with certain duties imposed by the state[78] but that "generally are not seen as matters of individual choice and evaluation" and "are, instead, understood to be externally imposed upon the faithful."[79] Third and finally, religion quite often claims some degree of transcendent ultimacy or supremacy vis-à-vis temporal institutions, including civil government.[80] When all three characteristics converge, the potential for conflict is obvious, especially where the state itself proves unyielding in its demands.[81]

In such instances, religion essentially poses the threat of a competing sovereign, manifest by the allegiance of its adherents to superior and normatively binding claims.[82] As Sanford Levinson has observed:

> [R]eligion . . . makes obvious claims of sovereignty as against other social institutions. A staple of political theory following the development of the notion of political sovereignty by Bodin is that there cannot be two sovereigns within a polity. By definition sovereignty is an exclusive status. Yet anyone who takes (at least Western) religion seriously poses an alternative sovereign against the claims of the State, however much the claims are dissipated by doctrines like the Talmudic injunction to follow the local law or by Christian doctrines about God and Caesar.[83]

In turn, "[t]heistic religion necessarily implies a limit on the authority of the state because sincere religious faith refuses to recognize the government's sovereignty as ultimate. Theism posits another sovereignty—a God or gods—that is above, beyond, and before the state."[84]

When one considers the Free Exercise Clause's interpretation, the potential significance of this model of competing sovereigns is obvious. If religious adherence by its nature involves vertical extra-allegiance to a transcendent authority, then every free exercise case is at some level a clash of sovereigns and a challenge to the supremacy of the state. Many, in fact, have argued that the clause rests in part on a recognition of this unique conflict of allegiance potentially faced by those who take seriously their religious obligations.[85] If this essay's thesis is accurate, however, one would expect to encounter in the jurisprudence of free exercise *not* solicitude for such citizens and their beliefs but some measure of apprehension—and ultimately some form of subordination. How this subordination is achieved will provide the focus for the remainder of the essay.

C. The Explanatory Force of a Sovereignty-Based Reading

Describing the relationship between religion and government in terms of sovereignty might be nothing more than just another interesting perspective were it not for two interrelated circumstances: first, the failure of existing doctrines to account for the actual interpretation and implementation of the Free Exercise Clause, and second, the substantial ability of a sovereignty-based reading of free exercise jurisprudence to fill this role. The former circumstance has already been documented; the latter will provide the focus here.

Consider once again the anomalies mapped out in part I: the avoidance of an absolutist interpretation, the distortion of the balancing analysis, the use of the burden requirement as a gatekeeper, and the judicial lack of a theory of religious freedom. If one's goal is the maximum feasible protection of religious liberty, or even something less ambitious, it would be difficult to account for each and every such anomaly. As demonstrated, too many factors and outcomes would simply have too be ignored. If one's goal, however, is understood as the preservation of the supremacy of civil government against claims of a higher and competing authority, the utility and overarching logic of these phenomena become much more apparent, to the point perhaps that they no longer appear analogous.

Most obviously, neither an absolutist interpretation nor even a strong balancing analysis is consistent with a conception of civil government that is exclusive in its sovereignty. Absent intentional discrimination against its citizens (which is a violation of the charter of its powers), no true sovereign would need to justify its general lawmaking authority by having to demonstrate that its ends are compelling and its means are necessary before a citizen must obey its laws. To countenance this would be to place the citizen's religious allegiance above his civic allegiance, and to cede the sovereignty of the state to the sovereignty of God or conscience. In order to prevent this, therefore, courts have rejected an absolutist reading, have more recently rejected a strong balancing analysis, and—particularly before rejecting a strong balancing analysis—have employed the burden requirement as a means of avoiding a confrontation between religion and the state. Even the judicial unwillingness to articulate a theory of religious freedom is consistent with a concern about state sovereignty. For any *meaningful* theory of religious freedom—and courts, whether for historical or contemporary reasons, would be compelled to theorize about free exercise in meaningful terms—would necessarily support and invite claims that would be inconsistent with the supremacy of the state, either in their premises or their desired outcomes.[86]

Other aspects of free exercise jurisprudence are also congruent with a sovereignty-based approach. Two such phenomena, one conceptual and the other empirical, deserve particular mention. First, the judiciary has gone to great lengths to avoid conceptualizing free exercise in terms of the competing sovereignty of religion and the state, let alone conceptualizing the state as the inferior of the two, despite the fact that the clause's principal drafter, James Madison, appeared to conceptualize the relationship in precisely those terms.[87] Rather, the judiciary has essentially characterized the religious practitioner as a kind of intruder or squatter and the state as extant and proprietary. Even the terms used by the courts, such as "claimant" or "accommodation," lend "rhetorical support to the idea that it is the government, and not the citizen, that is somehow being burdened by the other's demands."[88] More generally, the judiciary has conceptualized religion as a thoroughly private matter, not only in the sense that it is nongovernmental but in the sense that its practice or observance need not be public and that its exclusion from the public sphere, whether as a matter of nonestablishment or otherwise, is entirely appropriate.[89]

Second—and fully consistent with the phenomena of doctrinal distortion and conceptual marginalization—there is the simple empirical fact that most religious liberty claims do not prevail,[90] despite the ultimate importance of religious obligations to individuals and communities. Assuming that many such claims are not in fact foreclosed by formal doctrine when fairly interpreted, this track record can mean one of two things: either the judiciary does not understand this ultimate importance or the judiciary understands it only too well.

The first possibility is that the general failure of free exercise claims reflects nothing more than an inability of judges, steeped as they often are in the ways of the world, to take seriously the claims of the religiously devout.[91] Such inability may reflect either their own diminished religious devoutness or their heightened commitment to empirical, rationalist modes of knowledge and discourse which—in the view of some—do not include religious belief.[92] In either case, the underprotection of religious liberty may be simply a judicial personnel issue, unless one believes that judges as a sociopolitical class will inevitably consist of persons who disproportionately devalue religious adherence.

The other possibility is that judges *do* take seriously the claims of the religious devout and, in turn, that they understand quite well what those claims signify vis-à-vis the authority of civil government (including their own authority). If this is so, then the underprotection of religious liberty is not a judicial personnel issue as such but, rather, one of inherent institutional obligation. Judges, by their nature, must protect and reinforce the sovereignty of civil government, even if it means that otherwise legitimate claims of religious free exercise, as well as doctrinal and theoretical integrity, will be sacrificed. The judiciary, in other words, is the ultimate guardian of civil supremacy and, through its reasoning and holdings, the ultimate apologist of the state.[93] "Courts, at least the courts of the state, are characteristically 'jurispathic'"[94]—as they declare law and the authoritative legal tradition, they must essentially kill off the competing alternatives.[95] Consider Chief Justice John Marshall's defense to the proposition that the United States did not properly possess title to certain Indian lands. "Conquest," said Marshall, "gives a title which the Courts of the conqueror cannot deny, whatever the private and speculative opinions of individuals may be, respecting the original justice of the claim which has been successfully asserted."[96] That is to say, the proposition simply could not be embraced legally because it would have ultimately called into question the validity and supremacy of the federal government, including the Court.

So it is, and also must be, with regard to religious claims. To embrace the proposition that the secular law does not reach, and indeed may be subordinate to, the dictates of religious faith is to cast doubt upon the sovereignty of the government and, in turn, its ability to maintain order and stability and to uphold the rule of law.[97] And the infusion of doubt into the authority of their own government is something that judges simply cannot countenance, regardless of what sacrifices might be incurred by free exercise claimants,[98] of any doctrinal incoherence that might result,[99] and of the judges' preexisting political or philosophical dispositions.[100]

To be sure, this principle has at times been expressed by the Court, most notably in *Reynolds v. United States*,[101] which was essentially the Court's first significant interpretation of the Free Exercise Clause, and in *Employment Division v. Smith*,[102] which is the Court's most recent significant exposition of the clause's meaning and scope. In *Reynolds*, faced with a challenge to a territorial criminalization of plural marriage, the Court asked: "[A]s a law of the organization of society under the exclusive dominion of the United States, it is provided that plural marriages shall not be allowed. Can a man excuse his practices to the contrary because of his religious belief? To permit this would be to make the professed doctrines of religious belief superior to the law of the land, and in effect to permit every citizen to become a law unto himself. Government could exist only in name under such circumstances."[103] Likewise in *Smith* the Court, drawing in part upon *Reynolds*, explained that

> [t]he government's ability to enforce generally applicable prohibitions of socially harmful conduct, like its ability to carry out other aspects of public policy, "cannot depend on measuring the effects of a governmental action on a religious objector's spiritual development." To make an individual's obligation to obey such a law contingent upon the law's coincidence with his religious beliefs, except where the State's interest is "compelling"—permitting him, by virtue of his beliefs, "to become a law unto himself,"—contradicts both constitutional tradition and common sense.[104]

More generally, a sovereignty-based reading of the Court's First Amendment jurisprudence also helps to explain why the Court, today at least, rejects mandatory accommodations (whereby the Free Exercise Clause is read to mandate governmental accommodation of claimants' religious practices) but permits discretionary accommodation (whereby governments may, in their discretion, provide such accommodation without violating the Establishment Clause). The doctrine of mandatory accommodation conceptually elevates religious liberty above the state, except where the state's fundamental organic purposes, as expressed by compelling interests, cannot otherwise be achieved. As argued by one pair of commentators in their critique of the Religious Freedom Restoration Act (RFRA),[105] to embrace a doctrine of large-scale, mandatory accommodation (as did RFRA) is to embrace "the idea that religiously motivated persons and groups are to a considerable degree sovereigns among us—that they enjoy the license to disregard legal restraints and burdens that other Americans must respect."[106] The doctrine of discretionary accommodation, by comparison, conceptually places religion subordinate to, and at the mercy of, the state. Whereas mandatory accommodation constitutionalizes the idea that a certain fraction of sovereignty has been withheld from the state, or ceded by the state, discretionary accommodation implies full sovereignty followed by voluntary dispensations of legislative grace.

At the same time, a sovereignty-based reading of the Court's religion jurisprudence also helps to explain why the Court, here under the Establishment Clause, is willing to countenance certain governmental appropriations of religious symbolism[107] but views the sharing of governmental power with religious institutions or individuals as impermissible entanglement.[108] Under the former arrangement, the state is merely augmenting its legitimacy without either diminishing its own actual power or elevating the status or authority of religion; indeed, the state crosses the line when its conduct primarily advances religion[109] or appears to endorse the religious symbolism that it appropriates.[110] Under the latter arrangement, by contrast, the state is both partially ceding its power and vesting religious bodies with some measure of sovereign authority, providing, in the Court's words, "a significant symbolic benefit to religion in the minds of some by reason of the power conferred."[111] And, if preservation of civil sovereignty is the concern, this it may not do.

There is, in summary, significant explanatory force to a sovereignty-based reading of the Court's constitutional jurisprudence of religion and government, and in particular its interpretation and implementation of the Free Exercise Clause. While such a reading does not explain all variations in the application of the clause—claimants do, for example, periodically prevail against the state[112]—it does serve to round out the incomplete picture portrayed by official doctrine.

Conclusion

The maxim *imperium in imperio* invokes the traditional view that two sovereigns cannot rule the same territory. Today, of course, jurisdiction is no longer conceptualized in such Newtonian terms; it can be concurrent or partial, not simply exclusive and exhaustive.[113] But the maxim's relevance to the dynamics between religion and government remains undiminished. Unable to be confined to the realm of unmanifested belief, religion necessarily generates acts of conscience that periodically conflict with the civil law and, given the nature of religious adherence, challenge the state's jurisdictional supremacy.

This essay has argued that the de facto American solution to this conflict, implemented through the process of judicial review, is to subordinate religion by underenforcing the Free Exercise Clause, at times complemented by corollary doctrines of the Establishment Clause. Religion is not subordinated in the sense that it is deliberately oppressed. But it is domesticated, and never is it accorded a degree of sovereignty that renders it truly competitive with, let alone superior to, the state.

NOTES

1. U.S. CONST. amend. I. Although the First Amendment textually binds only Congress, its strictures have been interpreted as binding all branches of government, including, by Fourteenth Amendment incorporation, those of the states as well. *See* Lynch v. Uhlenhopp, 78 N.W.2d 491, 500 (Iowa 1956).

2. *See, e.g.*, Church of Scientology Flag Serv. Org., Inc. v. City of Clearwater, 2 F.3d 1514, 1539 (11th Cir. 1993), *cert. denied*, 513 U.S. 807 (1994).

3. *See, e.g.*, Church of the Lukumi Babalu Aye, Inc. v. City of Hialeah, 508 U.S. 520, 533 (1993) (providing that a law whose "object . . . is to infringe upon or restrict practices because of their religious motivation" may still be valid if "it is justified by a compelling interest and is narrowly tailored to advance that interest").

4. If correct, this thesis raises a number of questions that will not be addressed in the essay. For example, is this arrangement inevitable, particularly within a regime of regulatory government? Is it congruent with the original conception or an original understanding of the First Amendment? Should it be acknowledged more forthrightly in the process of interpreting and implementing the First Amendment? If so, what form should that acknowledgment take?

5. Respectively, see Employment Div. v. Smith, 494 U.S. 872, 877 (1990) (citations omitted) ("The government may not . . . impose special disabilities on the basis of religious views or religious status."); *City of Hialeah*, 508 U.S. at 533 ("[A] law targeting religious beliefs as such is never permissible."); and Braunfeld v. Brown, 366 U.S. 599, 603 (1961) ("[C]ompulsion by law of the acceptance of any creed or the practice of any form of worship is strictly forbidden.").

6. *See* Bowen v. Roy, 476 U.S. 693, 699 (1986) ("Our cases have long recognized a distinction between the freedom of individual belief, which is absolute, and the freedom of individual conduct, which is not absolute."); Bob Jones Univ. v. United States, 461 U.S. 574, 603 (1983) ("On occasion this Court has found certain governmental interests so compelling as to allow even regulations prohibiting religiously based conduct."); United States v. Rasheed, 663 F.2d 843, 847 (9th Cir. 1981) ("What one does with one's faith . . . may not necessarily enjoy the same absolute protection. The First Amendment protects religiously grounded conduct, but such conduct is subject, in some situations, to the police power of the government."), *cert. denied*, 454 U.S. 1157 (1982).

7. *Cf.* Zwerling v. Reagan, 576 F. Supp. 1373, 1376–78 (C.D. Cal. 1983).

8. Thomas v. Review Bd. of Ind. Employment Sec. Div., 450 U.S. 707, 713 (1981).

9. *See, e.g.*, Mosier v. Maynard, 937 F.2d 1521, 1523, 1526–27 (10th Cir. 1991); Philbrook v. Ansonia Bd. of Educ., 757 F.2d 476, 481 (2d Cir. 1985), *aff'd*, 479 U.S. 60 (1986). However, they "need not be acceptable, logical, consistent, or comprehensible to others," Thomas v. Review Bd. of Ind. Employment Sec. Div., 450 U.S. 707, 714 (1981); consistent with the beliefs of fellow adherents to the same religion, see Hernandez v. Commissioner, 490 U.S. 680, 699 (1989); Lyng v. Northwest Indian Cemetery Protective Ass'n, 485 U.S. 439, 457–58 (1988); *Thomas*, 450 U.S. at 715–16; or held by the claimant for any particular length of time, see Hobbie v. Unemployment Appeals Comm'n of Fla., 480 U.S. 136, 144 (1987).

10. *See, e.g.*, *Hernandez*, 490 U.S. at 699; Forest Hills Early Learning Ctr., Inc. v. Lukhard, 728 F.2d 230, 240 (4th Cir. 1984).

11. *See, e.g.*, Chalifoux v. New Caney Indep. Sch. Dist., 976 F. Supp. 659, 670 (S.D. Tex. 1997).

12. *See, e.g.*, *Hernandez*, 490 U.S. at 699. These last two requirements may simply be variations of each other. *See* Employment Div. v. Smith, 494 U.S. 872, 887 n.4 (1990).

13. *See City of Hialeah*, 508 U.S. at 531, 542; *Smith*, 494 U.S. at 877–80. A law is not neutral if its "object . . . is to infringe upon or restrict practices because of their religious motivation." *City of Hialeah*, 508 U.S. at 533. General applicability concerns whether or not the law itself provides for exceptions or exemptions, a standard that is complicated by the fact that many laws are in some sense not generally applicable because they target one class of persons or activities, but not others. *See id.* at 542 (noting that "[a]ll laws are selective to some extent").

14. *See Smith*, 494 U.S. at 881–82.

15. *City of Hialeah*, 508 U.S. at 546 (quoting McDaniel v. Paty, 435 U.S. 618, 628 (1978) (plurality opinion)) (internal quotation marks omitted); *see also* Sherbert v. Verner, 374 U.S. 398, 407 (1963).

16. *Smith* does not expressly impose a rationality requirement as such, but it is implicit in the requirement that the government action must be "consistent with the Federal Constitution." *Smith*, 494 U.S. at 876.

17. *See, e.g.*, Prince v. Commonwealth of Mass., 321 U.S. 158, 165–75 (1944); Jacobson v. Commonwealth of Mass., 197 U.S. 11, 24–25 (1905).

18. *See, e.g.*, Crowley v. Christensen, 137 U. S. 86, 89 (1890).

19. *Jacobson*, 197 U.S. at 26; *see also* United States v. Lee, 455 U.S. 252, 259 (1982); *Crowley*, 137 U. S. at 89–90; Minor v. Happersett, 88 U.S. (21 Wall.) 162, 165–66 (1875). Even the federal government, which does not possess full-scale regulatory police powers as such, nevertheless is permitted to regulate for the general good in the exercise of its limited enumerated powers. Under the Commerce Clause, for example, Congress prohibits racial discrimination in the workplace and in places of public accommodation—see 42 U.S.C. §§ 2000a and 2000e-2, respectively—and it is well understood that Congress's goal is not the smooth

flow of interstate commerce per se but, rather, the eradication of racial discrimination itself. Moreover, certain federal operations, such as the military and prisons, are clearly undertaken for public safety and welfare and accorded a level of judicial deference equal to, if not greater than, the deference normally accorded to exercises of state police power. *See* O'Lone v. Estate of Shabazz, 482 U.S. 342 (1987) (prisons); Goldman v. Weinberger, 475 U.S. 503, 507 (1986) (military).

20. *See* Wisconsin v. Yoder, 406 U.S. 205, 220 (1972); *see also Smith*, 494 U.S. at 885 (recognizing "[t]he government's ability to enforce generally applicable prohibitions of socially harmful conduct"); *Braunfeld*, 366 U.S. at 607; Cantwell v. Connecticut, 310 U.S. 296, 304 (1940).

21. *Smith*, 494 U.S. at 890.

22. *See* Scott C. Idleman, *The Religious Freedom Restoration Act: Pushing the Limits of Legislative Power*, 73 TEX. L. REV. 247, 275 & n.132 (1994). Such interests have included the eradication of racial discrimination in education, see Bob Jones Univ. v. United States, 461 U.S. 574, 604 (1983), and of marital discrimination in housing, see McCready v. Hoffius, 586 N.W.2d 723, 729 (Mich. 1998) (applying compelling interest requirement under MICH. CONST. art. I, § 4); the enforcement of controlled substances laws, see Idleman, this note, at 276 & nn.140–41; the prevention of fraud and other crimes, see Scott v. Rosenberg, 702 F.2d 1263, 1273–75 (9th Cir. 1983), *cert. denied*, 465 U.S. 1078 (1984); the maintenance and regulation of the armed forces, see Gillette v. United States, 401 U.S. 437, 462 (1971); the management of natural resources, see Idleman, this note, at 278 n.157; and the prohibition of nonmonogamous marriages, see Potter v. Murray City, 760 F.2d 1065, 1070 (10th Cir. 1985), *cert. denied*, 474 U.S. 849 (1985). The Court has held, however, that "[w]here government restricts only conduct protected by the First Amendment and fails to enact feasible measures to restrict other conduct producing substantial harm or alleged harm of the same sort, the interest given in justification of the restriction is not compelling." *City of Hialeah*, 508 U.S. at 546–47.

23. The facility with which courts find compelling interests, notwithstanding their presumed rarity, stems partly from the fact that the process of discerning compelling interests itself remains ill defined. *See* Idleman, *supra* note 22, at 274–75 & n.130.

24. Lyng v. Northwest Indian Cemetery Protective Ass'n, 485 U.S. 439, 451 (1988).

25. For example, they have been recognized in the implementation of welfare programs, see Bowen v. Roy, 476 U.S. 693, 699, 700, 707–08 (1986) (food stamps and AFDC); the administration of the tax system, see Jimmy Swaggart Ministries v. Board of Equalization of Cal., 493 U.S. 378, 391 (1990); the use of public lands, see *Lyng*, 485 U.S. at 453; the prevention of fraud against the government, see *Bowen*, 476 U.S. at 709; and the general enforcement of laws, see *Braunfeld*, 366 U.S. at 608.

26. *See* Hernandez v. Commissioner, 490 U.S. 680, 699–700 (1989) (administration of tax system); United States v. Lee, 455 U.S. 252, 258–59 (1982) (social security).

27. Douglas Laycock, *Free Exercise and the Religious Freedom Restoration Act*, 62 FORDHAM L. REV. 883, 901 (1994).

28. *See* City of Boerne v. Flores, 117 S. Ct. 2157, 2171 (1997); Powell v. McCormack, 395 U.S. 486, 549 (1969); Baker v. Carr, 369 U.S. 186, 211 (1962).

29. *See generally* Jon O. Newman, *Between Legal Realism and Neutral Principles: The Legitimacy of Institutional Values*, 72 CAL. L. REV. 200, 208–14 (1984).

30. *See, e.g.*, Illinois v. Milwaukee, 406 U.S. 91, 93–94 (1972) (original jurisdiction); National Iranian Oil Co. v. Mapco Int'l, Inc., 983 F.2d 485, 490 (3d Cir. 1992) (linking prudential mootness to judicial economy); Natural Resources Defense Council, Inc. v. United States Envtl. Protection Agency, 859 F.2d 156, 166 (D.C. Cir. 1988) (linking prudential ripeness to judicial economy).

31. *See, e.g.*, McCulloch v. Maryland, 17 U.S. (4 Wheat.) 316, 423 (1819).

32. *See, e.g.*, Planned Parenthood of S.E. Pa. v. Casey, 505 U.S. 833, 854–61 (1992).

33. *See Smith*, 494 U.S. at 886–87 & n.4, 890; *see also Lyng*, 485 U.S. at 457–58; *Gillette*, 401 U.S. at 449–58.

34. Cantwell v. Connecticut, 310 U.S. 296, 303–4 (1940).

35. *See, e.g.*, *Lyng*, 485 U.S. at 452 ("[G]overnment simply could not operate if it were required to satisfy every citizen's religious needs and desires."); *see also Smith*, 494 U.S. at 888 (declaring, in regard to the idea of mandatory exemptions for religious claimants from generally applicable laws, that "[a]ny society adopting such a system would be courting anarchy"); Ira C. Lupu, *Where Rights Begin: The Problem of Burdens on the Free Exercise of Religion*, 102 Harv. L. Rev. 933, 947 (1989) (describing the fear that "[b]ehind every free exercise claim is a spectral march; grant this one, a voice whispers to each judge, and you will be confronted with an endless chain of exemption demands from religious deviants of every stripe").

36. McDaniel v. Paty, 435 U.S. 618, 627 n.7 (1978) (plurality opinion).

37. *McCulloch*, 17 U.S. (4 Wheat.) at 414.

38. *See, e.g.*, United States v. Woodley, 751 F.2d 1008, 1020–21 & n.6 (9th Cir. 1985) (Norris, J., dissenting).

39. Chandler v. James, 958 F. Supp. 1550, 1555 (M.D. Ala. 1997) (citations omitted), *aff'd in part and vacated in part on other grounds*, 180 F.3d 1254 (11th Cir. 1999).

40. *See supra* note 2. The Establishment Clause, moreover, is not the only constitutional provision that so operates. The Fifth Amendment Takings Clause—which mandates just compensation where a taking of property has occurred—also operates in an absolute fashion.

41. *Chandler*, 958 F. Supp. at 1555.

42. *Id.* at 1555–56 (footnote omitted).

43. *Cantwell*, 310 U.S. at 304.

44. See Marci A. Hamilton, *The Belief/Conduct Paradigm in the Supreme Court's Free Exercise Jurisprudence: A Theological Account of the Failure to Protect Religious Conduct*, 54 Ohio St. L.J. 713, 751–54 (1993); Idleman, *supra* note 22, at 279 & n.159.

45. *See, e.g.*, United States v. Lee, 455 U.S. 252 (1982) (citing "the broad public interest in maintaining a sound tax system"); United States v. Little, 638 F. Supp. 337, 339 (D. Mont. 1986) (citing the "government's interest in protecting and preserving our national forests for this and future generations").

46. *Lyng*, 485 U.S. at 451; *see also* Bowen v. Roy, 476 U.S. 693, 700–701 n.6 (1986) (remarking that in "the adjudication of a constitutional claim, the Constitution, rather than an individual's religion, must supply the frame of reference"); Barbara Bezdek, *Religious Outlaws: Narratives of Legality and the Politics of Citizen Interpretation*, 62 Tenn. L. Rev. 899, 987 n.432 (1995) (stating that "courts have . . . leaned toward statist/objective evaluation of free exercise claims, and the result has almost uniformly been denial of the claim").

47. *See Lyng*, 485 U.S. at 452.

48. This distortion is not limited to free exercise adjudication. As one author notes, "Most of our legal discussions of church and state view the issues involved from the position of the state. Perhaps inevitably these discussions tend to assume state sovereignty and to see churches among other competing internal groups." Carol Weisbrod, *Family, Church and State: An Essay on Constitutionalism and Religious Authority*, 26 J. Fam. L. 741, 769 (1987–88).

49. Lupu, *supra* note 35, at 935.

50. *See Lyng*, 485 U.S. at 451.

51. *Cf.* Lupu, *supra* note 35, at 965–66 (noting its "pervasive uncertainty of scope, with its concomitant invitation to unprincipled, result-oriented application" and remarking that,

while "[t]his problem . . . is hardly unique to this corner of constitutional law . . . the danger to constitutional values is particularly acute here because the threat encompasses the regime of religious liberty and equality").

52. *Id.* at 947–48 (footnotes omitted).

53. In 1990, for example, the Court reiterated that "[t]he Free Exercise Clause . . . 'withdraws from legislative power, state and federal, the exertion of any restraint on the free exercise of religion. Its purpose is to secure religious liberty in the individual by prohibiting any invasions thereof by civil authority.'" Jimmy Swaggart Ministries v. Board of Equalization of Cal., 493 U.S. 378, 384 (1990) (quoting Abington Sch. Dist. v. Schempp, 374 U.S. 203, 222–23 (1963)). But this declaration merely defers the question of *why* such liberty should be protected and, in turn, does not explain when a "restraint" or "invasion[]" is impermissible.

54. *See* Steven D. Smith, Foreordained Failure: The Quest for a Constitutional Principle of Religious Freedom (1995).

55. *See* Frederick Mark Gedicks, The Rhetoric of Church and State: A Critical Analysis of Religion Clause Jurisprudence (1995); Frederick Mark Gedicks, *The Improbability of Religion Clause Theory*, 27 Seton Hall L. Rev. 1233 (1997).

56. 198 U.S. 45 (1905).

57. *See* Cass R. Sunstein, Lochner's *Legacy*, 87 Colum. L. Rev. 873, 873 (1987).

58. This is the traditional conception of sovereignty. *See, e.g.*, Preston King, *Sovereignty*, in The Blackwell Encyclopaedia of Political Thought 492–93 (David Miller ed., 1987); Stephen D. Krasner, *Pervasive Not Perverse: Semi-Sovereigns as the Global Norm*, 30 Cornell Int'l L.J. 651, 654 (1997); Jack N. Rakove, *Making a Hash of Sovereignty, Part I*, 2 Green Bag 2d 35, 36 (1998). For judicial pronouncements on this and related aspects of sovereignty, see Late Corp. of the Church of Jesus Christ of Latter-Day Saints v. United States, 136 U.S. 1, 44–46 (1890); McCulloch v. Maryland, 17 U.S. (4 Wheat.) 316, 409–10 (1819).

59. *See* Krasner, *supra* note 58, at 655 ("International legal sovereignty is a ticket of admission. . . . Recognition provides the acts of a state with protection from legal attacks in the judicial systems of other states.").

60. The Schooner Exch. v. McFaddon, 11 U.S. (7 Cranch) 116, 136 (1812).

61. *See* Mark D. Rosen, *The Outer Limits of Community Self-Governance in Residential Associations, Municipalities, and Indian Country: A Liberal Theory*, 84 Va. L. Rev. 1053, 1057–60, 1088–89 (1998).

62. *Cf., e.g.*, Hamilton v. Regents of Univ. of Cal., 293 U.S. 245, 262–63 (1934).

63. *See* Sanford Levinson, *Constituting Communities Through Words That Bind: Reflections on Loyalty Oaths*, 84 Mich. L. Rev. 1440, 1449–56 (1986) (discussing the history of loyalty oaths and the current conditions and oath required of applicants for U.S. citizenship).

64. 8 U.S.C. § 1448(a)(2), *quoted in* Levinson, *supra* note 63, at 1453; *see also* 8 C.F.R. § 337.1(a).

65. *See, e.g.*, 8 U.S.C. § 1481(a) (providing for loss of nationality upon allegiance to a foreign state, renunciation of nationality, or commission of treason or related crimes); 18 U.S.C. § 2381 (criminalizing treason, punishable by death).

66. *See* Richardson v. Ramirez, 418 U.S. 24, 41–56 (1974) (upholding state disenfranchisement of convicted felons who complete their sentences and paroles); Note, *The Disenfranchisement of Ex-Felons: Citizenship, Criminality, and "The Purity of the Ballot Box,"* 102 Harv. L. Rev. 1300, 1301 (1989) (noting that "[f]ifteen American states disenfranchise exfelons for life").

67. *See* United States v. Wheeler, 435 U.S. 313, 323 (1978). What tribes retain is the power of "internal self-government," *id.* at 322, which in the absence of federal preemption "includes

the right to prescribe laws applicable to tribe members and to enforce those laws by criminal sanctions," *id.*, as well as "the power to determine tribe membership; to regulate domestic relations among tribe members; and to prescribe rules for the inheritance of property." *Id.* at 322 n.18 (citations omitted).

68. *Id.* at 322.

69. *See* Washington v. Confederated Tribes of Colville Indian Reservation, 447 U.S. 134, 153–54 (1980).

70. *Wheeler*, 435 U.S. at 323.

71. *See, e.g.*, U.S. Const. amends. X, XI; Printz v. United States, 117 S. Ct. 2365 (1997); Seminole Tribe of Fla. v. Florida, 517 U.S. 44 (1996); New York v. United States, 505 U.S. 144 (1992).

72. Garcia v. San Antonio Metropolitan Transit Auth., 469 U.S. 528, 548 (1985). Examples include the limitations of article I, § 10, *see* Barron v. City of Baltimore, 32 U.S. (7 Pet.) 243, 248–49 (1833), as well as the expanded power of Congress in the enforcement clauses of the Reconstruction Amendments. *See Ex parte* Commonwealth of Va., 100 U.S. (10 Otto) 339, 345 (1880).

73. *See, e.g.*, *Garcia*, 469 U.S. at 546–57 (abrogating virtually all doctrinal limits on Congress's power to regulate states).

74. Fletcher v. Peck, 10 U.S. (6 Cranch) 87, 136 (1810).

75. Regarding efforts to assert legal authority, see Jeremiah W. Nixon & Edward R. Ardini, Jr., *Combatting Common Law Courts*, Crim. Just., Spring 1998, at 12; United States v. Greenstreet, 912 F. Supp. 224, 228–29 (N.D. Tex. 1996). Regarding efforts to assert military authority, see Presser v. Illinois, 116 U.S. 252, 267 (1886); Vietnamese Fishermen's Assoc. v. Knights of the Ku Klux Klan, 543 F. Supp. 198, 209 (S.D. Tex. 1982); Application of Cassidy, 51 N.Y.S.2d 202, 205 (N.Y. App. Div. 1944) (per curiam), *aff'd*, 73 N.E.2d 41 (N.Y. 1947).

76. *Presser*, 116 U.S. at 267.

77. *Cf.* Gillette v. United States, 401 U.S. 437, 464 n.2 (1971) (Douglas, J., dissenting).

78. *See, e.g.*, Paul M. Landskroener, Note, *Not the Smallest Grain of Incense: Free Exercise and Conscientious Objection to Draft Registration*, 25 Val. U. L. Rev. 455, 476–77 (1991) (enumerating various religious arguments against participation in war that could give rise to a claim of conscientious objection).

79. Stanley Ingber, *Religion or Ideology: A Needed Clarification of the Religion Clauses*, 41 Stan. L. Rev. 233, 282 (1989) (footnote omitted).

80. *See, e.g.*, United States v. Macintosh, 283 U.S. 605, 633–34 (1931) (Hughes, C.J., dissenting); Stephen L. Carter, *Introduction to Faith and the Law Symposium*, 27 Tex. Tech. L. Rev. 925, 928 (1996).

81. *See, e.g.*, Ira C. Lupu, *Models of Church-State Interaction and the Strategy of the Religion Clauses*, 42 DePaul L. Rev. 223, 230 (1992).

82. *See, e.g.*, Stephen L. Carter, *The Supreme Court, 1992 Term—Comment: The Resurrection of Religious Freedom?* 107 Harv. L. Rev. 118, 138 (1992); Steven M. Tipton, *Republic and Liberal State: The Place of Religion in an Ambiguous Polity*, 39 Emory L.J. 191, 197 (1990); Weisbrod, *supra* note 48, at 745.

83. Levinson, *supra* note 63, at 1467 (footnote omitted).

84. Carl H. Esbeck, *A Restatement of the Supreme Court's Law of Religious Freedom: Coherence, Conflict, or Chaos?* 70 Notre Dame L. Rev. 581, 637 (1995) (footnote omitted).

85. *See, e.g.*, Church of the Lukumi Babalu Aye, Inc. v. City of Hialeah, 508 U.S. 520, 575–76 (1993) (Souter, J., concurring); Timothy L. Hall, *Religion, Equality, and Difference*, 65 Temp. L. Rev. 1, 9, 32 (1992).

86. *See* Garrett Epps, *What We Talk About When We Talk About Free Exercise*, 30 Ariz. St. L.J. 563, 567 (1998) ("Lurking beneath the surface of many appellate opinions is the fear that a well-defined free exercise right, recognized by the courts as applicable by individuals against the government, might prove to be a fatal loophole in the social contract.").

87. *See, e.g.*, W. Cole Durham, Jr., *Religious Liberty and the Call of Conscience*, 42 DePaul L. Rev. 71, 82 (1992) ("Madison's picture portrays religious liberty as a matter of interacting sovereigns—the Creator as the ultimate source of conscientious obligation, the individual as the vessel of conscience, and civil society as an artificial construct whose very existence is conditioned and bounded by preexisting obligations set up by the other two sources of sovereignty.... Exemptions for conscientious conduct are not bestowed as a matter of grace by the state.... They are simply reserved spheres of free conduct built into the original structure of the social compact."); Michael W. McConnell, *Free Exercise Revisionism and the* Smith *Decision*, 57 U. Chi. L. Rev. 1109, 1151–52 (1990) (summarizing Madison's writings); E. Gregory Wallace, *When Government Speaks Religiously*, 21 Fla. St. U. L. Rev. 1183, 1240 (1994) (discussing Madison's view, remarking that "[p]erhaps the most striking recognition of God's sovereignty over the political order came from James Madison, whose argument for religious liberty rested primarily on the ground that religion represents irresistible obligations to a higher Being who is beyond the jurisdiction of the state").

88. Scott C. Idleman, *The Sacred, the Profane, and the Instrumental: Valuing Religion in the Culture of Disbelief*, 142 U. Pa. L. Rev. 1313, 1371 n.203 (1994) (reviewing Stephen L. Carter, The Culture of Disbelief: How American Law and Politics Trivialize Religious Devotion (1993)); *see also* Henry J. Hyde, *Contemporary Challenges to Catholic Lawyers*, 38 Cath. Law. 75, 80 (1998) (decrying the Supreme Court's marginalizing view of free exercise as "something merely to be accommodated, if possible"); Douglas Laycock, *Summary and Synthesis: The Crisis in Religious Liberty*, 60 Geo. Wash. L. Rev. 841, 846 (1992) (remarking that the term "accommodation" "implies that government is going out of its way to do religion a favor").

89. *See* Gedicks, *supra* note 55, at 1242, 1244 (arguing that "secular individualism has largely captured religion clause doctrine" and that "[s]ecular individualist discourse assumes that, although individuals may choose to be religious in private life, there is no public role for religion beyond the effect of private choice"); Idleman, *supra* note 88, at 1328–29.

90. *See* Douglas W. Kmiec, *The Original Understanding of the Free Exercise Clause and Religious Diversity*, 59 UMKC L. Rev. 591, 596 (1991) (noting in terms of Supreme Court cases that "[e]xcept for the unemployment compensation cases and the cases allowing Amish parents to keep their children out of public school after eighth grade, claims for religious exemptions were largely unsuccessful") (footnote omitted); Ira C. Lupu, *The Failure of RFRA*, 20 U. Ark. Little Rock L.J. 575, 585 (1998) (concluding that the Religious Freedom Restoration Act, which statutorily reinstated strict scrutiny after *Smith*, "failed to produce any substantial improvement in the legal atmosphere surrounding religious liberty in the United States"); James E. Ryan, Note, Smith *and the Religious Freedom Restoration Act: An Iconoclastic Assessment*, 78 Va. L. Rev. 1407, 1412 (1992) (concluding that "the decisions in the United States courts of appeals over the ten years preceding *Smith* reveal[s] that, despite the apparent protection afforded claimants by the language of the compelling interest test, courts overwhelmingly sided with the government when applying that test").

91. *See, e.g.*, Carter, *supra* note 80, at 929 (arguing, in regard to the question of how conflicts between religious dictates and civil law should be resolved, that "secular law has lately preferred to pretend that the question does not exist—or rather, that the answer is obvious. Of course one's first allegiance is to the secular sovereign; of course the laws of that secular sovereign trump any religious principles with which they come into contact; of course rea-

sonable religious people understand this hierarchy and abide by it. Anybody who believes anything else, we dismiss as a fanatic."); Idleman, *supra* note 22, at 255–57 & nn.31–38 (discussing elite discomfort with religious devoutness).

92. *Cf.* Frederick Mark Gedicks, *Toward a Constitutional Jurisprudence of Religious Group Rights*, 1989 Wis. L. Rev. 99, 141 (noting that judges operate within "a culture that generally values rationalism over the nonrational ways of knowing, understanding, and living that characterize much of religious life"); Paul Horwitz, *The Sources and Limits of Freedom of Religion in a Liberal Democracy: Section 2(a) and Beyond*, 54 U. Tor. L. Rev. 1, 5 (1996) ("To the degree that the state bases its decisions on a rational, liberal framework, the qualities that make religion unique and valuable—its allegiance to the irrational and the supernatural—will cause religious goals to be subordinated to state goals.") (footnote omitted). An example of this judicial obstuseness may be found in Romer v. Evans, 517 U.S. 620 (1996). By its own account, the *Romer* majority was unable to interpret the Colorado citizenry's preclusion of particularized legal protection for homosexuals and bisexuals as "anything but animus toward the class that it affects," *id.* at 632, while in fact such preclusion could plausibily have been viewed as "rather a modest attempt by seemingly tolerant Coloradans to preserve traditional sexual mores against the efforts of a politically powerful minority to revise those mores through use of the laws." *Id.* at 636 (Scalia, J., dissenting).

93. *See, e.g.*, Ferriter v. Tyler, 48 Vt. 444, 469 (1876) (interpreting the religious freedom provision of the Vermont Constitution, see Vt. Const. ch. 1, art. 3, and remarking that the court must "deal with the subject as jurists, regarding the constitution and the laws, and what is done under them, with reference to principles and reasons that appertain to the subject in its legal elements, qualities, and aspects, and not as religionists, not as sectaries, not as those who regard something besides the government as of ultimate supremacy in the affairs of men on earth, but as those who regard the government created by the constitution, and the laws made under the authority and within the scope of the constitution, as the ultimate sovereignty in this state, and as equally obligatory and effectual upon all"); J. Thomas Sullivan, *Requiem for RFRA: A Philosophical and Political Response*, 20 U. Ark. Little Rock L.J. 795, 798 (1998) (commenting that "judges are the instruments of secular institutions, committed to furthering an agenda central to secularly-determined values—*i.e.*, commitment to the 'rule of law,' as opposed to the 'rule of God'").

94. Robert M. Cover, *The Supreme Court, 1982 Term—Foreword: Nomos and Narrative*, 97 Harv. L. Rev. 4, 40 (1983).

95. *See id.* at 53 ("[J]udges characteristically do not create law, but kill it. Theirs is the jurispathic office. Confronting the luxuriant growth of a hundred legal traditions, they assert that this one is law and destroy or try to destroy the rest.").

96. Johnson v. M'Intosh, 21 U.S. (8 Wheat.) 543, 588 (1823).

97. *See, e.g.*, Note, *Religious Exemptions Under the Free Exercise Clause: A Model of Competing Authorities*, 90 Yale L.J. 350, 356 (1980) (arguing that religion-based exemptions are vulnerable, among other things, to the objection that they "contradict the rule of law").

98. *See* United States v. Lee, 455 U.S. 252, 259 (1982) ("To maintain an organized society that guarantees religious freedom to a great variety of faiths requires that some religious practices yield to the common good. Religious beliefs can be accommodated, but there is a point at which accommodation would 'radically restrict the operating latitude of the legislature.'") (quoting Braunfeld v. Brown, 366 U.S. 599, 606 (1961)).

99. *See* Hamilton, *supra* note 44, at 725 (critiquing the belief-conduct distinction in free exercise jurisprudence but noting that "the Court views itself as responsible for ensuring the stability of the larger social order, and the belief/conduct paradigm serves that role" and that

"the rhetoric of the paradigm—which speaks in terms of absolute protection and governmental needs—serves to paper over otherwise difficult and intractable problems of the inevitable clash between religion and society").

100. *See* Sullivan, *supra* note 93, at 798 ("Typically, elected and appointed judges share a common perspective in which the preservation of order is central to their administration. This perspective often predominates over their philosophical and political views, so that liberals and conservatives alike tend to share a common belief in the need for social stability reflected in orderly governmental process.").

101. 98 U.S. (8 Otto) 145 (1878).

102. 494 U.S. 872 (1990).

103. *Reynolds*, 98 U.S. (8 Otto) at 166–67; *cf. also* Long v. State, 137 N.E. 49, 50 (Ind. 1922).

104. *Smith*, 494 U.S. at 885 (quoting Lyng v. Northwest Indian Cemetery Protective Ass'n, 485 U.S. 439, 451 (1988), and *Reynolds*, 98 U.S., at 167, respectively).

105. 42 U.S.C. §§ 2000bb to 20004.

106. Christopher L. Eisgruber & Lawrence G. Sager, *Congressional Power and Religious Liberty After* City of Boerne v. Flores, 1997 Sup. Ct. Rev. 76, 136.

107. *See, e.g.*, Lynch v. Donnelly, 465 U.S. 668, 685 (1984) (upholding a municipality's inclusion of a creche in its Christmas display); *see also* County of Allegheny v. ACLU, Greater Pittsburgh Chapter, 492 U.S. 573 (1989) (upholding one religious display and invalidating another).

108. *See, e.g.*, Larkin v. Grendel's Den, Inc., 459 U.S. 116, 123, 127 (1982) (invalidating a Massachusetts statute that "delegat[ed] a governmental power to religious institutions," "substitut[ing] the unilateral and absolute power of a church for the reasoned decisionmaking of a public legislative body acting on evidence and guided by standards, on issues with significant economic and political implications" and thereby "enmesh[ing] the churches in the processes of government"); *see also* Board of Educ. of Kiryas Joel Village Sch. Dist. v. Grumet, 512 U.S. 687, 696 (1994) (invalidating a New York statute creating a school district essentially for a religious community largely because it "depart[ed] from th[e] constitutional command [of neutrality] by delegating the State's discretionary authority over public schools to a group defined by its character as a religious community"); *cf.* State of Oregon v. City of Rajneeshpuram, 598 F. Supp. 1208 (D. Or. 1984); State v. Celmer, 404 A.2d 1 (N.J. 1979), *cert. denied*, 444 U.S. 951 (1979). Significantly, the *Grumet* Court noted that New York, by empowering the religious community to exercise governmental authority over education, had "delegate[d] a power this Court has said 'ranks at the very apex of the function of a State.'" *Grumet*, 512 U.S. at 709–10 (quoting Wisconsin v. Yoder, 406 U.S. 205, 213 (1972)).

109. *See Lynch*, 465 U.S. at 679.

110. *See* Capital Sq. Review & Advisory Bd. v. Pinette, 515 U.S. 753, 763–69 (1995); *County of Allegheny*, 492 U.S. at 597; Elewski v. City of Syracuse, 123 F.3d 51, 53–54 (2d Cir. 1997), *cert. denied*, 118 S. Ct. 1186 (1998).

111. *Larkin*, 459 U.S. at 125–26.

112. *See, e.g.*, Hobbie v. Unemployment Appeals Comm'n of Fla., 480 U.S. 136 (1987); Thomas v. Review Bd. of the Ind. Employment Sec. Div., 450 U.S. 707 (1981); Wisconsin v. Yoder, 406 U.S. 205 (1972); Sherbert v. Verner, 374 U.S. 398 (1963). It is perhaps not coincidental, however, that the Court, in at least two of these cases, took pains to note that the claimants were otherwise upstanding citizens who posed no threat to the existing political or economic order. *See Yoder*, 406 U.S. at 222 & n.11 (commenting that "the Amish community has been a highly successful social unit within our society"; that "[i]ts members are produc-

tive and very law-abiding members of society"; and that "[t]he record in this case establishes without contradiction that the Green County Amish had never been known to commit crimes, that none had been known to receive public assistance, and that none were unemployed"); *Sherbert*, 374 U.S. at 410 (commenting that "[t]his is not a case in which an employee's religious convictions serve to make him a nonproductive member of society").

113. *See McCulloch*, 17 U.S. (4 Wheat.) at 410 ("In America, the powers of sovereignty are divided between the government of the Union, and those of the states. They are each sovereign, with respect to the objects committed to it, and neither sovereign, with respect to the objects committed to the other."); Akhil Reed Amar, *Of Sovereignty and Federalism*, 96 Yale L.J. 1425, 1439–66 (1987) (discussing the reallocation of sovereignty under the U.S. Constitution).

Chapter 11

Equal Regard

Christopher L. Eisgruber and Lawrence G. Sager

I. Introduction: The Problematic Status of Religious Liberty

In *Employment Division, Department of Human Resources of Oregon v. Smith*, the Supreme Court held that members of the Native American Church were not constitutionally entitled to ingest peyote as part of their religion's sacrament in the face of an Oregon law outlawing the use of peyote.[1] Many aspects of the *Smith* decision have been sharply criticized, but none so much as the general view of religious exemptions announced by Justice Scalia's opinion for the Court. Justice Scalia distinguished freedom of religious belief from behavior driven by religious belief, and further distinguished laws directed at religion from general laws that merely collide with behavior driven by religious belief. That work done, Justice Scalia had a simple and flat response to the constitutional claimants in *Smith*: religious believers have no constitutional license to disregard otherwise valid general laws that conflict with the dictates of their religion.[2]

Smith sharply divided the Court on the question of extant doctrine as to the constitutional status of religious exemptions. Four of the justices—Justice O'Connor, who concurred in the outcome only, and the three dissenters—were outraged at what they saw as the Court's startling departure from precedent. In their view, it had become settled doctrine that only governmental interests of "the highest order" could justify a state's interference with religiously driven behavior.[3] Justice Scalia and his colleagues in the majority saw matters very differently; for them, the idea that religious motivation could exempt one from the reach of an otherwise valid general law was wholly novel and out of step with constitutional law and the rule of law generally.[4]

Actually, neither of these characterizations of constitutional law ante-*Smith* was fair. Doctrine governing religious exemptions was in a shambles. In a small but durable line of cases involving the entitlement to unemployment benefits of persons whose religious scruples prevented them from working under certain conditions (*Sherbert v. Verner*[5] and its progeny), the Court had consistently held that the state could put people to a choice between their consciences and material disadvantage only if its reasons for doing so were markedly weighty. But only in one other case had the Court actually appeared to act on that principle: in *Wisconsin v. Yoder*,[6] it held that Wisconsin's stake in requiring all children to pursue a recognized program of education until the age of sixteen was not sufficient to justify the state's interference with the religiously motivated commitment of the Amish to integrate children into their working society at the age of fourteen. Everywhere else there were strong indications that the Court could not live with the broad dictum of *Sherbert*.

In the Court's recent cases, the *Sherbert* line and *Yoder* emerge as exceptions rather than the rule. In some cases since *Yoder* and outside the unemployment benefits area, the Court has paid lip service to the *Sherbert* rule, but in each of these cases it has found the compelling state interest test of *Sherbert* satisfied.[7] While in other constitutional areas the compelling state interest test is fairly characterized as "'strict' in theory and fatal in fact,"[8] in the religion cases the test is strict in theory but notably feeble in fact. Furthermore, even before *Smith*, the Court had begun to find reasons for rejecting the *Sherbert* formulation altogether in particular exemption contexts.[9]

A candid assessment of the corpus of case law confronting the Court in *Smith* would have emphasized disarray, not order. And *Smith* itself, *unhappily*, did nothing to improve the situation. Neither the majority nor the dissenting positions in *Smith* offered a view of the exemption problem that can at once explain the distinct status of religion in our constitutional tradition, offer a workable and attractive approach to the exemption issue, and make more or less good sense out of the scattered pattern of precedent.

What is needed is a fresh start. At the root of the exemptions controversy is a fundamental mistake about the constitutional concern with religious liberty: judges and commentators have commonly assumed that it is the unique value of religious practices that occasionally entitles them to constitutional attention. We need to abandon that idea. What properly motivates constitutional solicitude for religious practices is their distinct vulnerability to discrimination, not their distinct value; what is called for, in turn, is protection against discrimination, not privilege against legitimate governmental concerns. When we have replaced value with vulnerability, and the paradigm of privilege with that of protection, then it will be possible both to make sense of our constitutional past in this area and to chart an appealing constitutional future.

That is the project of this essay.[10] We hope to demonstrate that the privilege view of religious liberty is normatively unjustified and unattractive in its practical implications, while the protection view is both justified and attractive in its consequences.

II. Two Modalities of Constitutional Justice

A. Privilege and Protection

The vigorous pursuit of political justice in modern constitutional law has two great paradigms: the right of free expression and the right of African-Americans to equal protection. These two traditions have dominated our modern constitutional sensibility, and discourse about the propriety of vigorous judicial intervention on behalf of other values often proceeds by way of comparison to them. There is a structural difference between these two pillars of constitutional justice, and understanding that difference illuminates the claim that religion makes on our constitutional judgments.

We have in mind the difference between the Constitution's privileging persons or practices and the Constitution's protecting such persons or practices. Speech is a practice that is privileged in our constitutional tradition, indeed privileged to a high degree. The state is often barred from restricting speech because of its content, even when there is reason to suppose that important concerns would be advanced if the speech in question were suppressed. In contrast, African-Americans are not privileged but, rather, protected. Constitutional law struggles to abolish caste and its residue, to secure for African-Americans treatment as full and equal citizens of our national community.

In our constitutional tradition, a claimant who locates her behavior within the core of protected speech activity acquires the privilege of immunity from the reach of governmental authority, even under circumstances that would otherwise offer strong grounds for the exercise of that authority against her. She may act in a fashion that increases the likelihood that injuries to the property or persons of others may take place; she may act in a fashion that is itself injurious to others; she may even and especially act in a fashion that is injurious to the national interest as it is currently conceived. Her behavior is privileged, as against other behavior that shares these abstract features, and as against the interests of those persons who may be injured by that behavior.

A claimant who argues for exemption from the reach of state authority on grounds of racial equality stands in a different posture. She is insisting on parity, not advantage: she demands that the state behave in a fashion fully consistent with her status as an equal citizen, as opposed to treating her as a member of a subordinate class who by virtue of that membership does not enjoy the same concern and respect. She invokes the Constitution against subordination. She is asking for something that is in principle the due of every member of our political community. Her racial status is constitutionally distinct in the sense that it marks her as vulnerable to injustice, to treatment as other than an equal; her claim is for protection from that injustice.

Speech and racial equality are thus both treated distinctly and favorably by virtue of their inclusion in the agenda of judicial enforcement of the Constitution, and other claims of political justice—most prominently those diverse claims we lump into the broad category of "economic rights"—are excluded. But only speech is privileged by the substance of the norms upon which the constitutional judiciary draws when it acts. Put another way, privilege and protection refer not to the fact of constitutional (or judicial) priority but to the grounds for such priority. A claim for constitutional privilege requires a showing of virtue or precedence; a claim for constitutional protection requires a showing of vulnerability or victimization. The distinction between privilege and protection is therefore ultimately a distinction in constitutional objective. From the recognition of victimization, and of vulnerability to future victimization, flows the constitutional objective of protection; from the recognition of virtue or precedence flows the constitutional objective of privilege.

The distinction between privilege and protection in constitutional justice cannot always be read from the surface of the rules employed by courts to protect constitutional principles: the compelling state interest test, for example, figures in both speech and racial equality doctrine. But beneath the facial rules of constitutional law, at the level of constitutional justice, the justification for distinct constitutional treatment and the appropriate scope of that treatment are different if the claim is one of privilege or one of protection.

In our constitutional jurisprudence there is no privileging of persons; indeed, opposing caste or subordination is one of the most robust projects of modern constitutional law. One might think that the converse is also true: because protection flows from a concern about vulnerability or victimization, it might seem that only persons or groups, rather than activities, may be the object of constitutional protection. But as religion itself vividly illustrates, persons and groups can be vulnerable to victimization by virtue of their shared commitments and practices. The bitter divisions of humanity along religious lines, and the global persecution of religious minorities throughout most of recorded history, make the victims of religious intolerance the ultimate and tragic exemplars of vulnerability.

Nevertheless, most modern commentary has proceeded on the assumption that the constitutional status of religious exemptions rises or falls on the degree to which religious practices are constitutionally privileged—privileged in the way, for example, that speech is privileged. If religiously motivated people are to be exempt from the application of laws that they would otherwise be required to obey, it is assumed, this must be because religion is esteemed by the Constitution in a way that most other human commitments, however intense or laudable, are not.

B. Equal Regard: Protecting Religion

We advocate an approach to the question of religious liberty founded on protection rather than privilege. Protection can explain and justify the distinct status of religion in our constitutional tradition, offer a workable and attractive approach to religious exemptions, and make sense out of the patchwork of precedent regarding religious exemptions.

History provides ample evidence that religious distinctions inspire the worst sorts of political oppression. Post-Reformation religious strife and the religious persecution from which many colonial settlers fled come immediately to our minds. But we should not imagine that we need to look that far; within the memory of many adults, anti-Catholicism and anti-Semitism were rampant in many parts of the United States. The sad history of religious intolerance and the unfortunate sociological truths upon which it rests invite and demand the constitutional protection of minority religious beliefs.

To execute this constitutional project, we recommend the principle of "equal regard." In our view, equal regard is a general requirement of a politically just society. It demands that the interests and concerns of every member of the political community should be treated equally, that no person or group should be treated as unworthy or otherwise subordinated to an inferior status. It has special shape and vigor as a constitutional principle in the area of religious liberty because of the cultural entailments of religion. Religious commandments are not necessarily founded on or limited by reasons accessible to nonbelievers; often they are understood to depend on fiat or covenant and to implicate forces or beings beyond human challenge or comprehension. Religion is often the hub of tightly knit communities whose habits, rituals, and values are deeply alien to outsiders. At best, this is likely to produce a chronic interfaith "tone deafness," in which the persons of one faith do not easily empathize with the concerns of persons in other faiths. At worst, it may produce hostility, even murderous hatred, among different religious groups.

Moreover, the dynamic of religious vulnerability extends even beyond these widely varying forms of antagonism. From the perspective of some faiths, it is desirable to convert nonbelievers rather than injure them. Such messianic faiths may have the welfare of the nonbelievers genuinely and fully in mind as they zealously seek converts to the true faith; they may even have the welfare of the nonbelievers fully in mind as they seek to shape the legal regime to discourage or prevent the nonbelievers from pursuing their own beliefs. Even when conversion is not their aim, dominant faiths (or clusters of faiths) that ought in principle to recognize the value and concerns of others may nevertheless use political power to favor themselves. For example, Christians might seek to benefit their faith by prescribing prayers in public schools or by shutting down businesses on Sundays. Proponents might regard these partisan favors as rewards for the virtuous or as inducements to nonbelievers—or simply as nondiscriminatory benefits available to all wise enough to recognize the propriety of the Christian way of life.

Understood as an especially compelling instance of the requirements of equal regard, the Constitution's evocations of religious liberty insist that one's status as a member of our political community ought not to depend in any way upon one's religious beliefs. Accordingly, the Constitution's commitment to religious liberty comprehends at least three more specific principles, each related to the general idea of equal regard. First, the government is obliged to treat the deep religious commitments of members of minority religious faiths with the same regard as it treats the deep commitments of other members of the society. Second, government policy must be justified by public reason, by secular reasons recognizable by—and in principle, endorsable by—any person committed to living in a pluralist society governed by the precepts of equal regard. Third, government must not act so as to divide the community along lines of religious affiliation; that is, government must not encourage members of our political community to devalue their fellow citizens on the grounds of religious belief or to lose the sense of plural-belief-but-equal-citizenship upon which equal regard depends.

III. The Case for Equal Regard

A. How the Constitution Secures Religious Liberty

The case for equal regard has two components. First, equal regard enables judges to fashion an attractive, robust constitutional jurisprudence of religious liberty. It therefore accords with the intuition, which most Americans share, that religious conduct is an important focus of constitutional solicitude. Second, equal regard achieves these objectives without showing any special favoritism to religion. It thereby respects a second, equally important intuition about religious liberty: namely, that government ought to be impartial with regard to differences in religious belief and affiliation.

1. UNCONTROVERTED ELEMENTS OF (RELIGIOUS) LIBERTY

In our constitutional culture, this much seems common ground: Persons are entitled to their religious beliefs and cannot on account of those beliefs be punished or deprived of benefits otherwise their due; further, important aspects of religious practice—for example, the choice by a religious group of its compensated spiritual leaders—are largely beyond the reach of the collective authority of the state. Some people believe that the only way to explain these bedrock constitutional convictions is by privileging religion, so that religious commitments would enjoy a special constitutional entitlement to flourish unimpaired by public interests and policies.[11] But that belief rests upon a chronic misreading of the convictions in question. The best explanation for each of these attractive limits on state authority does not involve privileging religion. We can see this if we consider each in turn a little more closely.

Consider first the observation that persons are, in a deep sense, entitled to hold their particular religious beliefs. No one may be punished for her religious beliefs; or made to affirm other beliefs; or denied the opportunity to discuss and publish her beliefs; or prevented from associating with others to reflect upon, celebrate, and consummate their beliefs in (otherwise benign) ceremonies of affirmation or worship. All this is true and sits high in the pantheon of constitutional truths, but none of it is distinct to religious belief. We have in our constitutional tradition a strong freedom of belief, famously invoked by Justice Jackson in *West Virginia State Board of Education v. Barnette*:

> If there is any fixed star in our constitutional constellation, it is that no official, high or petty, can prescribe what shall be orthodox in politics, nationalism, religion, or other matters of opinion or force citizens to confess by word or act their faith therein.[12]

Our freedom of belief extends to political, aesthetic, and moral matters, to matters that are areligious and antireligious. It is certainly true, for example, that belief in an orthodox deity cannot be made a condition of public office; but neither can belief in the virtues of religion generally, or belief in the falsity of religion, or belief in the virtues of maintaining an open mind to religion, or belief that religion is worth worrying about, or belief in the justness of capital punishment or the redistribution of wealth, or belief in the comparative genius of Van Gogh and Giorgione, or belief in the likelihood that the Higgs Particle actually exists and will help us unravel the secrets of the universe. These beliefs are privileged not on analogy to religious beliefs, or on the view that they occupy the same role in the lives of the persons who hold them as do religious beliefs, but on the simple and sufficient ground that they are beliefs, and that our political community deeply respects the capacity of its members to arrive at and champion their individual understandings of the world.

Consider next the observation that important religious practices have a distinct status in our understanding of constitutional justice, as illustrated, for example, by the widely held view that it would be constitutionally inappropriate to apply Title VII prohibitions of race and sex discrimination to the employment of religious leaders such as priests, pastors, or rabbis.[13] Here, the story is a little more complex but ends in much the same way as did our observations about freedom of belief. We have in our constitutional tradition—in clear spirit, and if not in clear letter, only because the occasions to spell the point out have not often arisen—an important, morally indispensable sense of the private and the public. Thus, the state can tell us whom we must accommodate at our lunch counters but not at our dinner tables. The question is not one of "state action" but of state authority, and it does not turn on an obtuse, clunky view that private and public can be mechanically or sweepingly distinguished. But the distinction exists, and it may ultimately be the most important source of liberty there is. The state cannot insist that we ignore the race or religion of potential marital partners, or prescribe how our spouses and we divide up our household responsibilities, but it can and must protect marital partners from the abuse of their spouses. The quality of public and private is nuanced to domain and demand.

Often, private behavior takes place in private places and in private ways: classically, in the home, with relationships born of love, respect, and duty, not contract and compensation. Public behavior finds its most common venues in more widely accessible spaces. One form of public behavior is largely economic; it centers on the office, factory, hotel, or restaurant, and its most common mode is the commercial transaction, the exchange of goods or services for money. Another form is political; it transpires most frequently in assembly halls, streets, and newspapers, and its common modes include the vote and the argument.

Often, but not always. Organized religious activity projects distinctly private behavior into public space and involves distinctly private relationships that are bound by contract and compensated by dollars. Religious leaders are moral advisors, confidants, friends, and spiritual guides. The state cannot prescribe a nondiscriminatory protocol for a group's choice of the person who is to bear this private responsibility to its members any more than the state could prescribe such a protocol for the selection of a psychiatrist, or of a neighbor in whom to confide one's hopes and concerns. The aspects of religious practice that are uncontroversially secure from the reach of some state commands are so secure because they are private in general and recognizable ways, not because they are religious.

There are, of course, aspects of all these relationships—priest/parishioner, psychiatrist/patient, friend/friend—that are appropriately vulnerable to state regulation. A religious group may be restrained from making a child its leader under circumstances threatening to the child's well-being, or enslaving or otherwise coercing the service of its adult religious guide, or beating or starving her in the name of ecstatic insight.

2. THE SHERBERT QUARTET

As we have just seen, the Constitution secures religious liberty partly through general privileges that are in no way special to religion. These doctrines—such as the doctrines protecting speech (whether religious or not) and private conduct (whether religious or not)—operate within the constitutional modality we call *privilege*, but they do not privilege *religion*. Such doctrines arise from grounds that are independent of the ideal of equal regard. Nevertheless, they are entirely consistent with that ideal since they neither favor nor disfavor religion in general, or any particular religious sect.

The controversial aspect of religious exemptions begins at precisely the point where the general shield of private behavior leaves off. In the present state of constitutional law, for example, persons are not entitled to consume banned drugs like peyote alone in the privacy of their homes, or with good friends who join them in a search for enlightenment through altered states of consciousness. Should religious believers enjoy a unique, constitutionally protected exemption from restrictions upon these practices? Likewise, under current constitutional doctrine, willing partners are not entitled to enter into polygamous or polyandrous marriages. Does the Constitution demand that an exception be made for the benefit of persons who wish to enter into such marriages for religious reasons? It is with respect to these cases that the ideal of equal regard makes one of its most distinctive and helpful contributions to the protection of religious liberty.

Judges and commentators often assume that cases of this kind present an all-or-nothing choice: either we must privilege religion by comparison to other, equally serious personal commitments, or else we must abandon any hope of protecting religious practice from burdens imposed by generally applicable laws. In fact, however, this choice is a false one: it ignores a normatively attractive, practically workable middle ground defined by the ideal of equal regard. As an illustration, consider the *Sherbert* quartet: *Sherbert v. Verner* and the short but durable line of unemployment benefits cases that follow its lead. These cases are widely perceived as supporting the privileging view of religious freedom. In each of them, the Court held that a religiously motivated person was constitutionally entitled to retain her eligibility for state unemployment insurance, notwithstanding her observation of the Sabbath[14] or scrupled refusal to work in the manufacture of armaments.[15] *Sherbert* was the first case to assert that laws interfering with religiously motivated conduct must be analyzed under the compelling state interest test.[16] While that promise is largely unfulfilled in other contexts, *Sherbert* itself has never been directly questioned by the Court and enjoys widespread support in critical commentary. On the privileging account, *Sherbert* is taken at its most literal and expansive word: most of us, most of the time, must take laws as we find them, but when we act in response to the dictates of our religion, the laws must yield to us unless they are crucial to very important state interests.

In *Smith*, justices on both sides of the exemption issue seemed to agree—at least tacitly—that *Sherbert* must be understood as privileging religion in this way. The four justices who resisted the majority approach to religious exemptions rested their case squarely on *Sherbert*;[17] and Justice Scalia, writing for the majority, struggled unconvincingly to confine a privileging view of *Sherbert* to the unique circumstances of the unemployment insurance cases.[18] Commentators on the exemption problem largely replicate the binary structure of disagreement among the justices in *Smith*: either *Sherbert* is right and religiously motivated conduct prevails against all but the most compelling of state interests, or *Sherbert* is wrong and religiously motivated conduct is not so privileged, bringing serious constitutional scrutiny to an effective close.

Neglected by all these commentators is an understanding of *Sherbert* that honors the ideal of equal regard—an understanding that hinges on the protection of minority religious believers rather than the privileging of religiously motivated conduct. Government need not sympathize with religious interests to accommodate them. That much is clear from our attitude toward physical disabilities: we certainly do not consider disabilities beneficial to society, but we believe it wrong to hold the disabled responsible for their condition and believe that the government should do something to make their lives easier. Likewise, even those who consider religiousness a matter for regret might nevertheless support accommodation because it makes religious individuals happier. Of course, the existence of individual interests in accommodation does not by itself generate a constitutional claim. What transforms religious accommodation from a mere policy concern to a constitutional issue is the vulnerability of religion to prejudice and persecution.

Reconceived pursuant to this insight, the *Sherbert* quartet ceases to be an anomaly in the jurisprudence of religious freedom and the Constitution more generally, and stands as precedent for a more reasonable and nuanced view of the exemptions issue. In *Sherbert* itself, South Carolina's violation of norms sounding in protection was transparent, and was an explicit and important element in the Court's opinion. Ms. Sherbert was a Sabbatarian, whose unavailability for work on Saturdays was treated by the state as making her ineligible for the receipt of unemployment benefits. But South Carolina had a Sunday-closing law, so that mainstream religious believers were not put to the painful choice between fidelity to the commands of their religion and eligibility for important state benefits in hard times. Writing for the Court, Justice Brennan emphasized this disparity in circumstance.[19]

The choice of Sunday as a uniform day of rest is itself constitutionally provocative, but we are concerned now with a different point. South Carolina's election of Sunday, placed side by side with its refusal to accommodate the needs of Sherbert and other Sabbatarians to decline Saturday employment, gives one overwhelming reasons to suppose that the state has disadvantaged a vulnerable group.

Thomas v. Review Board of the Indiana Employment Security Division[20] is less obviously a case of religious discrimination; it too, however, is best understood in this way. Thomas was a Jehovah's Witness who worked in a foundry of a large munitions company. When he was transferred from the foundry to a department that manufactured turrets for tanks, his religious scruples made it impossible for him to continue, and he resigned. Indiana refused to pay him unemployment benefits, on the ground that he had resigned his job without good cause. Unlike *Sherbert*, *Thomas* presented no facial disparity in the treatment of mainstream and minority religious beliefs. But like all the unemployment benefits cases, *Thomas* involved a state administrative hearing and an individuated judgment that Thomas's religious scruples did not constitute "good cause" for his resignation. Here there is good reason to suppose that Thomas's nonmainstream religious reason for quitting his job was inappropriately devalued as against other nonreligious and religious reasons. It is hard to imagine, for example, that Thomas would have been refused benefits had he resigned because of a serious allergy to the metal used in tank turrets; yet Thomas did have a serious allergy, a moral allergy to the job he was being asked to perform. It is also hard to imagine that if Thomas had been an orthodox Jew who was transferred to the pork-tasting division of the large company where he worked that Indiana would have found a lack of good cause in his refusal to continue. A state that puts in place a discretionary process to assess reasons for quitting work, and then turns a deaf ear to adherence to religious commandments as good cause, opens itself to the conclusion that it is not giving equal regard to the deep religious commitments of nonmainstream religious believers.

To those who have become accustomed to the idea that *Sherbert* carves out a preferred place for religion, our reinterpretation of these cases may be surprising.[21] The argument is not unprecedented, however. Indeed, important elements of it have figured prominently in the opinions of some Supreme Court justices. In *United States v. Lee*, Justice Stevens observed that treating a "religious objection to the new job requirements as though it were tantamount to a physical impairment that made it impossible for the employee to continue to work under the changed circumstances could be viewed as a protection against unequal treatment rather than a grant of favored treatment for the members of the religious sect."[22] And in *Bowen v. Roy*, Chief Justice Burger's plurality opinion distinguished *Sherbert* and *Thomas* on the ground that where a state has "created a mechanism for individualized exemptions[,] . . . its refusal to extend an exemption to an instance of religious hardship suggests a discriminatory intent."[23]

Seen through the lens of equal regard, *Sherbert* no longer sits uncomfortably with the idea of equal citizenship and uniform laws: South Carolina's insensitivity to the deep commitments of Saturday observers in the face of abiding concern for mainstream observers of the Sunday sabbath was a classic instance of a failure of equal regard. *Smith* was, on this account, half right: The Court was right to reject the notion—inspired by the mistaken idea that religion is constitutionally privileged—that religious believers are entitled to carve out their own microenvironments of law, but wrong not to consider the live possibility that Oregon was treating the religious needs of the members of the Native American Church with lower regard than it showed to the special needs of other citizens, including mainstream religious believers.[24]

If the exemption issue has seemed more obdurate to an agreeable solution than other parts of the constitutional canon, the explanation does not lie in the impossibility of arriving at a satisfactory understanding of religious liberty but, rather, in the faulty terms in which the question has been framed. Those who have argued that religious believers are constitutionally entitled to a broad range of exemptions from otherwise valid general laws have typically supposed that religion is constitutionally privileged; those who have resisted have found the resulting prospect of a political community in which each religious believer is entitled to her own microenvironment of law normatively indefensible and practically unlivable. This made the exemption issue a problem with two unattractive, all-or-nothing solutions.

When we recognize that *protection*, and not *privilege*, is the normative core of the Constitution's special solicitude for religious liberty, the exemption problem becomes tractable. Minority religious believers are entitled to have their deep religious commitments treated with the same regard as the comparable commitments of mainstream religious believers and the deep secular concerns of other members of the particular community. Legislatures can make otherwise valid general laws more or less absolute as their democratic judgment dictates; but to the extent that variance from these laws is or would be permitted to accommodate the discrete and opposing interests of some members of the political community, equal regard insists that the same accommodation be made for the deep interests of minority religious believers. This offers both a convincing account of our constitutional past and a template for a workable and powerful jurisprudence of religious exemptions.

B. The Constitutional Commitment to Impartiality

1. PARTISANSHIP

Our account of the *Sherbert* quartet has a second advantage. Not only does equal regard provide a workable and highly protective standard against which to assess religious liberty claims, it also successfully explains the result in cases like *Thornton v. Caldor, Inc.*,[25] a case that, if viewed from the standpoint of privilege, seems out of harmony with the *Sherbert* quartet. Connecticut passed a law requiring all employers to permit their religious employees to take their day of worship off from work. Caldor, Inc., which had refused to let Thornton off work on Sundays, challenged the constitutionality of Connecticut's accommodation. The Court sided with Caldor. If the *Sherbert* quartet were about privileging religion, this result might seem hard to fathom. Connecticut may have singled out a religious observance for favorable treatment when compared to secular practices, but that legislative preference seems unobjectionable from a constitutional perspective if the Constitution itself privileges religion. When we change perspective from privilege to protection, the picture rapidly clears. Connecticut's statute, unlike the Court's rule in *Sherbert* and *Thomas*, does single out religious believers for a distinct accommodation. Many people have "good cause" for taking particular days off; only religious believers are protected against dismissal. The *Sherbert* quartet is thus consistent with the Establishment Clause theory successfully pursued by Caldor.

Juxtaposing *Sherbert* and *Caldor* in this way highlights a deep constitutional norm, one that is at the core of Establishment Clause jurisprudence. Constitutional justice requires that we live under arrangements that are justifiable in impartial terms. It is impossible to defend the privileging view of religious liberty in any way consistent with this requirement of impartiality; as a result, every theory that supposes religion to be constitutionally privileged will run afoul of basic norms associated with the Establishment Clause.

To see the problem, begin by considering how religious believers might attempt to justify a constitutional privilege for their commitments. Here is one especially blunt strategy. "Our God's commands," they might say, "are the highest commands; we must answer to them in priority to the mundane commands of the State." This is straightforward enough, and might be a good reason for privileging religion in a monistic society of shared religious belief. Note, though, that the constitution would privilege only one religion—"our religion"—not religion generally. "Our God" speaks to (the hypothetical) "us" with binding normative authority, and nothing more need be said. Our God's authority does not give us a reason for privileging anyone else's religious commitments. As a result, there is nothing in this line of speculation that resonates with the themes of diversity and tolerance that are integral to the American constitutional tradition of religious liberty.

Suppose, therefore, that we remake the religious believer's claim so that it displays a reciprocal spirit more suitable to a plural society. The claim might go this way: "God's commands are the highest commands. We should recognize that there are other religious groups who believe that their 'God' is the true God, and who take themselves to be bound to the word of their 'God' as we are in fact bound to God's."[26] In a society that was deeply plural as among divergent religious beliefs but nonetheless remarkably monistic in the view that there was a god—or the normative equivalent, from whom or which binding precepts emanated—this would be a basis for the constitutional privileging of religion, perhaps. But we are not such a society; there are many persons in our society who are not religious at all, and many others who are not religious in the pertinent sense—that is, who do not understand their lives to be ordered such that their highest commitments are to a set of religious commandments.

In a nation with many groups, many values, and many views of the commitments by which a good life is shaped, the shared understanding among some groups that they are each bound by the commandments of a (different) god they believe deserves/demands obeisance is unacceptably sectarian as a basis for the constitutional privileging of religion. Their claim, as a union of groups within a broader, pluralistic society is no different in principle than is the sectarian claim of the religious believer we first considered, who reasoned, wholly from within his own religious tradition, that his God was the true, supreme god, and thus the state must permit each believer in the true God to subordinate the state's commands to those of God. As against the artist for whom art is the highest command of life, the activist to whom the pursuit of racial justice is all, or any of us who happen not to be members of the union of the deeply religious, the members of the union have no reason to offer, from within their own beliefs, for the privileging of their commitments that the rest of us lack with regard to our deep commitments.

There are, however, two arguments for the constitutional privileging of religion that do not suffer from this sectarian defect. The first appeals to persons within our political community to recognize—from the outside, in effect—the anguished state of the religious believer who is under state fiat to behave in a way that flatly contradicts the demands of her religion. The second suggests that organized religion enables our society to maintain an important place for the moral, non-self-regarding aspects of life.

The best version of this first nonsectarian argument for privileging religion emphasizes mortal conscience rather than eternal consequences. It encourages us to see that the religious believer is in the grip of conscience—a motivation that is at once powerful and laudable—and to regard that circumstance as grounds for excusing her from obedience to laws that force her to choose between her conscience and her well-being at the hands of the state. Yet, again, religious conscience is just one of many very strong motivations in human life. There is no particular reason to suppose that it is likely to matter more in the run of religious lives generally than will other very powerful forces in the lives of both the nonreligious and the religious.

The second nonsectarian argument for the constitutional privileging of religion appeals to our desire as a society to remain alive to the moral, non-self-regarding aspects of life, and sees organized religion as a taproot of this vital aspect of human flourishing. But while religion sponsors the highest forms of community, compassion, love, and sacrifice, one need only look around the world or probe our own history to recognize that it also sponsors discord, hate, intolerance, and violence. Religion is enormously varied in the demands it places on the faithful. Religious faith or belief need not be founded in reason, guided by reason, or governed in any way by the reasonable. Religious commandments can be understood as inspired by beneficent forces that are beyond human comprehension or verification, or by the result of the spite, play, accident, or caprice of entities or forces that do not necessarily hold human welfare paramount. The only limitations are those of the human imagination or the range of divine circumstance (depending on whether one looks from within or without religious beliefs): the bounds of the former are very broad indeed, and the logic of the latter implies the absence of any bounds whatsoever. We mention all this because, while the commitment to forces outside and above ourselves seems an attractive human capacity and impulse, the substance of the commitment matters, and there is no warranty on the laudability of religious commitments.

We must remember that the claim for the laudability of religious commitment is offered as a reason for exempting behavior that defies otherwise valid general laws. This simple fact is prejudicial to abstract arguments for the virtues of religious conscience. If we believe in a given case that the polity's decision to enact a law was sound, the claim that a conscientious defiance of this same law is virtuous requires some moral gymnastics. There are situations in which our own ambivalence or distaste toward the necessary makes it possible to hold these two views simultaneously. The draft is a good example. We go to war with great moral unease. At best, the intentional killing of soldiers and civilians seems justified rather than just. In such a case, we can sensibly believe that the conscientious dissenter is a morally attractive figure, epitomizing the moral regret that we ourselves feel and hope not to lose, even as we conscript thousands and calculate how to destroy our enemy. But this is a special case, and we would be mistaken to extrapolate from it to a general view about religious conscience.

Religions, of course, are by no means the only sources of moral reflection and impulse; nor are moral reflection and impulse the only forms of elevated human activity. These are not small quibbles to be worked out empirically. They go very much to the heart of the objection to privileging religion. A plural democratic society like ours must develop constitutional principles that recognize that a citizen's ability to contribute to the regime does not depend upon membership in any particular religion, or, indeed, upon religiosity at all. To hold otherwise would simply be another way to insist upon the truth of a particular religion, or to deny the truth of secular ethics. Of course, it might be true, as a contingent empirical matter, that religious faith correlates well with civic virtue, even if there is no theoretically necessary relationship between the two. But that sort of contingent empirical connection between religious belief and constitutional objectives is not an appropriate ground for privileging religion.

Once we have agreed that society must respect the virtue of individuals without regard to their religious beliefs, the claim that religion so breeds virtue that it is constitutionally privileged becomes indefensibly partisan among conflicting views of what is valuable in life and how that which is valuable is best realized. We use the term *partisan* here, rather than *sectarian* as before, because there is a difference between the argument that God's commands are prior to those of the state and the arguments we are considering now. The nonsectarian arguments are available to a person from outside religious belief, unlike the sectarian claim for obeisance. But they are nevertheless inconsistent with our constitutional tradition, which contemplates a modern, pluralistic society, whose members find their identities, shape their values, and live the most valuable moments of their lives in a grand diversity of relationships, affiliations, activities, and passions that share a constitutional presumption of legitimacy.

2. NEUTRALITY

Justifications for privileging religion turn out to be impermissibly sectarian or partisan. In an effort to save their theory, proponents of a privileging view sometimes claim that impartiality is impossible to achieve. They point out that no constitutional arrangement will be *neutral* among religions. They say that any set of institutions and doctrines will inevitably favor some set of theological positions at the expense of others, and hence it is unfair to criticize the privileging of religion on the ground that it favors religious commitments at the expense of others. This argument is mistaken; as we shall see, it capitalizes upon a crucial ambiguity in the slippery concept of neutrality.

Is equal regard "neutral" among religions? In one respect, the answer is no. Not all religions will fare equally well under a constitutional regime of equal regard. The point is made most easily by reference to the problem of school financing. Suppose that government is choosing among three possible stances with respect to educational subsidies: (1) the government will finance only state-run secular schools; (2) the government will grant parents vouchers, which they may use to purchase education at the school of their choice; and (3) the government will not finance education at all. Suppose further that the choice among these policies should be made on secular grounds. Government will not be able to choose among the three policies without favoring some views over others; in particular, state-run secular schools, which dominate American practice today, are more favorable to secular views than a voucher plan would be. Nor is this example unique. Once the basic point is appreciated, it becomes apparent that many government choices—the availability of public spaces for group activity, family law, the scope of property rights, the tax structure, and the size of local government units, to name only a few—will influence the extent to which various religious and secular beliefs flourish. Equal regard does not protect minority religions against this blunt reality.

But this does not disable equal regard as an account of religious liberty. Conventional references to "neutrality" obscure the distinction between two different ideas. The first, attractive idea is that government must not favor some individuals over others on the basis of their religious viewpoint. This idea is firmly rooted in the constitutional requirement of impartiality, and it is implemented by the ideal of equal regard. The second, unworkable idea is that government must create a regime equally hospitable to all belief systems. This idea is normatively unattractive and is utterly impossible to implement.

A secular analogy may help to clarify the distinction. We believe that the government must respect the principle of viewpoint neutrality when it regulates speech. For example, we believe the government may not prohibit racist speech or deny racist speakers access to public fora. But it does not follow that the government must be indifferent to the spread of racist ideas. The government not only may but (in our view) must combat racism by passing antidiscrimination laws and by constituting the public school curriculum in a way that is consistent with egalitarian principles and inconsistent with racism. These polices will make the regime less hospitable to racist ideas. But they do not disfavor or penalize the speaker who expresses such ideas.

The idea of neutrality has similar scope, and similar limits, in the realm of religious freedom. We believe that the government can, and should, be neutral among religions in the sense that it ought never to make the legal obligations and opportunities of its citizens dependent upon their religious affiliation (or the lack thereof). So, for example, the government may neither require that its officials swear religious oaths nor prohibit ministers from holding office, nor may it single out the ritual slaughter of animals for special regulation.[27] The government can, and should, also be neutral among religions in the sense that it ought not to endorse particular faiths or religion in general or secularism in general.[28] Finally, the government can, and should, be neutral among beliefs when it is called upon to weigh the interests of individuals.

Yet, the government cannot be neutral among beliefs in the sense of being equally hospitable to all belief systems. It is true that the government's selection of school financing schemes will inevitably influence the development of religious belief one way or another, and, indeed, the same point could be made about virtually every decision that government must make. Indeed, the composition of religious belief in the United States will depend heavily on constitutional principles and social policies not explicitly concerned with religious freedom. So, for example, legal protection for sexual equality will erode support for religions that favor clearly defined gender roles. The free flow of commerce will generate material temptations that will lure adherents away from ascetic religions and may dilute the intensity of religious faith in general. Freedom of the press will undermine allegiance to religions that endorse censorship or require the uniformity of opinion. National citizenship will fragment religions that depend upon the maintenance of homogenous, localized communities.

The Constitution will, of course, protect the right of Americans to affiliate themselves with religions that are inegalitarian, ascetic, censorial, and insular. But it would be remarkable to believe that the laws will have no influence upon the development of social mores, or that religious faith will evolve without regard to social mores. Any conception of constitutional justice, and indeed any conception of religious liberty, will invoke values that some religion rejects—not all religions, after all, embrace the ideal of religious liberty. The relevant question, however, is not whether equal regard (or, more generally, the ideal of religious liberty) asserts a theoretically contestable value but whether it is part of the most attractive account of political justice in a religiously plural society and whether it is properly assignable to the Constitution. Precisely because our society is religiously plural, no theory of religious liberty will be acceptable unless it includes a basic respect for the equal status of persons of widely differing faiths and philosophies.

3. EXEMPTIONS OR FAVORS?

We have been pursuing some very abstract arguments, but these theoretical points find blunt and vivid embodiments in case law. If the Free Exercise Clause were understood as ensuring that religious commitments enjoyed a position of special constitutional privilege, then Free Exercise rights would inevitably collide with equality principles—within and without the domain of religious liberty—essential to our notion of constitutional government. We have already noticed this point once, when we compared *Sherbert* to *Caldor*. The point is equally well illustrated by the recent case of *City of Boerne v. Flores*.[29] *Flores* arose as a statutory claim under the Religious Freedom Restoration Act (RFRA). RFRA was passed by Congress in response to *Smith*; it sought to restore the "compelling interest test" that the Supreme Court rejected in *Smith*, and it rested upon the privileging view that we have been criticizing. In *Flores*, the Supreme Court held that RFRA was unconstitutional because it exceeded Congress's authority under Section 5 of the Fourteenth Amendment. We have defended that conclusion elsewhere, but for present purposes we wish to focus on a more limited feature of the case: namely, the way in which it illustrates the collision between doctrines of religious privilege and basic constitutional antifavoritism principles.

Flores arose out of a zoning dispute in a small town not far from San Antonio. St. Peter's Catholic Church was located in the downtown historic district in Boerne, Texas. The church's membership was swelling, and the church wanted to expand. The church invoked RFRA to claim an exemption from the restrictions imposed upon buildings located in the historic district. Absent such an exemption from the ordinance, St. Peter's Catholic Church will either have to sell its building and buy or build a larger structure to house its swelling congregation, or split its congregation in two and buy or build a smaller church for the newly created congregation. These options may be quite expensive or inconvenient to the church, and perhaps to its parishioners as well, who may have additional travel burdens. On the other hand, the church is not claiming that St. Peter's rests on uniquely sacred ground or that it operates under a divine command not to relocate elsewhere. Indeed, under other quite plausible conditions—if, for example, St. Peter's occupied a lot too small to permit construction of a larger building—it is clear that the church would have moved or divided.

So, if either RFRA or the Free Exercise Clause were to exempt St. Peter's from the burdens imposed by Boerne's zoning scheme, it would have to do so on the ground that churches should be presumed exempt from financially burdensome—and possibly inconvenient—regulations. The logical scope of this claim is breathtaking. Suppose a church owns wetlands property. It could make a great deal of money by building homes on the property and renting them. Should it be exempt from environmental statutes prohibiting development? Suppose a church owns property in a residential neighborhood. It could make money by opening a restaurant in the neighborhood. Should it be exempt from statutes prohibiting a commercial use? A church could make more money if it were also exempt from the minimum wage law. Is it entitled to the exemption? Or, more sympathetically, but not conceptually at odds, suppose a church wanted to open a soup kitchen to feed the poor; is it constitutionally entitled to locate the kitchen anywhere it wants? And if so, can a church that must slaughter animals locate its slaughterhouse anywhere it wants?

Flores and the possibilities of fiscal favoritism it raises expose the normative incongruity of the idea that religious activity should be constitutionally privileged. Virtually everybody agrees that the Constitution prohibits the government from singling out churches for special subsidies. That portion of Establishment Clause jurisprudence is uncontroversial. Some commentators (and we are among them) believe that, at least until recently, the Supreme Court has been too reluctant to permit the government to include religious institutions, including religious schools, among the beneficiaries of neutrally defined, nonsectarian subsidies. But almost nobody believes that government may choose to subsidize religious institutions exclusively. We do not see any way to reconcile this uncontroversial axiom with the claim that churches should enjoy exemption from financially burdensome regulations.

There is, in short, no sound reason to distinguish subsidies from exemptions that alleviate purely financial burdens (and thereby provide a financial benefit). If it is impermissible to prefer religion in one setting, it cannot be mandatory to prefer it in the other. Embarrassed by this problem, defenders of RFRA have sometimes suggested that mere financial burdens or inconveniences should be excluded from the reach of the rights they recommend. Proposals of this kind smack of expedience; they arbitrarily truncate the principle of religious privilege to which RFRA and its defenders profess allegiance. In any event, these convenient limiting suggestions do not solve the basic problem but merely hide it. Their effect is to shift the location of the line between those cases where we would radically favor religious believers and organizations by relieving them and them alone of the legal burdens that the rest of us must bear, on the one side, and those cases where we prohibit subsidies precisely because they favor religion on the other side. The suggestions preserve the line, however, and the result is still genuinely anomalous. In, the end, it does not matter whether financial-burden cases like *Flores* fall on the mandated exemption or prohibited subsidy side of the line: those who ask us to view religious liberty through the lens of privilege still have to explain how it is that a strong favoritism and a strong antifavoritism principle can live side by side in a coherent regime of constitutional liberty.

IV. Failed Arguments from Text and History

It is impossible to articulate a satisfactory normative foundation for the view that religion enjoys special constituitonal privilege. Any such argument will be impermissibly sectarian or partisan, and, as a direct result of that defect, it will collide head-on with firmly established and widely admired antifavoritism principles. Perhaps for that reason, proponents of a privileging view often abandon normative argument entirely and seek refuge in the claim that blunt textual or historical facts require us to distinguish burdens upon religion from even the most serious impositions upon secular well-being. This argument assumes that the Constitution's meaning is historically located, recoverable, and articulate to the question of religious privilege. But neither the Constitution's text nor its history enables us to choose between privileging and protecting accounts of religious liberty.

Take the text first. The Free Exercise Clause provides, "Congress shall make no law . . . prohibiting the Free Exercise [of religion]." So the obvious question: Which laws prohibit the free exercise of religion? Put another way: From what must religion be free in order to be freely exercised? Consider the following interpretations: (1) "The exercise of religion is free so long as it is free from deliberate political persecution"; (2) "The exercise of religion is free so long as it is free from burdens greater than those government places upon other, comparable activities"; (3) "The exercise of religion is free only if it is free from all burdens except those justified by a state interest of the highest order"; and (4) "The exercise of religion is free only if it is free from any cost at all."

The first of these interpretations corresponds to the most narrow reading of the Supreme Court's doctrine in *Smith*; the second reflects our own position; the third was embodied in RFRA; and the fourth expresses a more absolute privilege for religion. Whatever might be said about the merits of these positions, one cannot choose among them by staring at the words of the Free Exercise Clause. It is legitimate to question what religion must be free from in order to be freely exercised—nobody believes that it must be free from every hindrance, as the fourth interpretation would suggest—and one cannot answer that question by repeating the words "free exercise" and "law."

Moreover, even if we imagined, for the sake of argument, that the Religion Clauses of the First Amendment should be read to privilege religion, we still would have to account for the subsequent impact of the Equal Protection Clause, which might have equalized (among other things) religion and nonreligion, and thereby deprived religion of any special constitutional respect it had enjoyed before Reconstruction. From a purely textual standpoint, this argument seems especially important with respect to cases involving state law, since the Free Exercise Clause does not mention the states, and the Fourteenth Amendment does not mention religion.

Historical evidence is equally indeterminate. Probably the most richly documented attempt to justify a constitutional privilege for religious conduct on the basis of historical evidence is Michael McConnell's; his failure illustrates why history cannot dispose of the questions that concern us. McConnell's extensive research into the origins of the Free Exercise Clause contrasts Thomas Jefferson's views with James Madison's. According to McConnell, Jefferson took an "'Enlightenment-Deist-rationalist' stance toward religious freedom" and "never once showed concern for those who wish to practice an active faith." For Jefferson, "liberty of conscience meant largely freedom from sectarian religion, rather than freedom to practice religion in whatever form one chooses."[30]

McConnell argues that Madison was more sympathetic to the demands of religious practice. Madison never displayed Jefferson's "disdain . . . for the more intense manifestations of religious spirit." According to McConnell, Madison's "more affirmative stance toward religion" led him to "advocate . . . a jurisdictional division between religion and government based on the demands of religion rather than solely on the interests of society."[31]

McConnell believes that "[n]o other figure played so large a role in the enactment of the Religion Clauses as Jefferson and Madison." McConnell then presents a historical argument purporting to show that "Madison, with his more generous vision of religious liberty, more faithfully reflected the popular understanding of the free exercise provision that was to emerge both in state constitutions and the Bill of Rights."[32] Even if we suspend doubts about this claim, and even if we ignore complications introduced by the Fourteenth Amendment, McConnell's history does not resolve the crucial questions about the meaning of the Free Exercise Clause. The modalities of protection and privilege are equally able to respect "intense manifestations of religious spirit." Conceptions of religious liberty derived from these contrasting aspects of constitutional justice differ not about whether to respect religious needs but about whether those religious needs should be treated with greater solicitude than other very serious needs—such as a handicapped person's need for special accommodations, or a single parent's need to spend time with her children.

So McConnell gains no ground when he recommends that we repudiate the "disdain" for religion that he ascribes (rightly or wrongly) to Thomas Jefferson. McConnell's opposition between "freedom from sectarian religion" and "freedom to practice religion in whatever form one chooses" is largely irrelevant to today's debates about religious liberty. The crucial question is not about whether to endorse "the freedom to practice religion" but about what that principle entails. On this point, McConnell's history is useless.

V. The Prospects for a Constitutional Jurisprudence of Equal Regard

There is in train a revisionary spirit in the Supreme Court's treatment of religious liberty. Though far from settled or fully matured, there are many features of the Court's recent jurisprudence that are sympathetic to the equal-regard account of religious liberty. In *City of Boerne v. Flores*, six justices affirmed the rejection by the Court in *Smith* of the proposition that persons motivated by their deep religious beliefs enjoy a presumptive constitutional right to disregard otherwise valid laws of general application. One of those, Justice Stevens, would have gone further and held that the attempt to confer such a sweeping right was itself violative of the Establishment Clause. *Flores*, in this respect, is consistent with a general tendency in both Establishment Clause and Free Exercise Clause cases: The Court has increasingly emphasized that government's fundamental obligation is to treat all deep personal commitments equally, regardless of whether those commitments are secular or religious, mainstream or unusual.

The *Smith* Court's reformulation of *Sherbert* is an instance of this. So too are decisions in which the Court has relaxed restrictions it had previously imposed upon the government's freedom to include religious institutions among the beneficiaries of neutrally defined, nonpreferential subsidy programs[33]—and even found constitutional reasons to insist that a state-run college fund student religious activities along with comparable secular ones.[34] In effect, the Court is departing on the one side from its nominal commitment to exceptional privilege and departing on the other side from its wavering commitment to special disability, and converging toward a view that normalizes religion and sees equal regard as the essence of religious liberty.

Indeed, less than two weeks before it decided *Flores*, the Court handed down its decision in *Agostini v. Felton*,[35] overruling a twelve-year-old restriction upon the means the states could use to facilitate remedial education for disadvantaged students in parochial schools. *Agostini* was a literal rerun of *Aguilar v. Felton*.[36] In *Aguilar*, a five-justice majority of the Court held that New York violated the Establishment Clause when it sent remedial teachers paid with federal funds into parochial school classrooms (as well as classrooms in public schools and nonreligious private schools). The *Aguilar* majority relied on the controversial "*Lemon* test," pursuant to which a governmental act ran afoul of the Establishment Clause if it had a religious purpose, had the effect of advancing religion, or entangled the government with religion.[37] New York's attempt to avoid the advancement of religion by monitoring the activities of the federally funded teachers was held to violate the entanglement prong of *Lemon*.[38]

In *Agostini*, the Court revisited exactly the same facts. Justice O'Connor, writing for the Court in *Agostini*, advanced both a broad and a narrow rationale for overruling *Aguilar*. The broad claim was a straightforward application of equal regard: Justice O'Connor suggested that the aid program in *Aguilar* avoided Establishment Clause problems because it benefited religious institutions solely as the result of private choices rather than because of a public decision to do so. New York's program aided religious schools only to the extent that parents chose to send their disadvantaged children to such schools. The New York program did not provide parents with any special incentive to send their children to religious rather secular schools. Therefore, Justice O'Connor said, the program neither advanced nor endorsed religion.[39] Justice O'Connor's opinion went on, however, to highlight an additional feature of

New York's program with narrower implications: it did not contribute any dollars directly to the coffers of a religious school or organization. New York sent teachers, not money, and the teachers taught subjects that were "supplemental to the regular curricula"—and so did not necessarily "'relieve sectarian schools of costs they would otherwise have borne.'"[40]

Agostini is thus an ambiguous precedent, but it nevertheless seems clear that equality norms are exerting a powerful pull upon the justices. To be sure, the overlap between the majorities in the egalitarian Establishment Clause cases, such as *Agostini*, and the egalitarian Free Exercise Clause cases, *Smith* and *Flores*, is not perfect. Justice Stevens joined the majorities in *Smith* and *Flores* but dissented in *Agostini*; Justice O'Connor did the opposite. Justice Ginsburg, who was not on the Court when *Smith* was decided, joined the majority in *Flores* but dissented in *Agostini*.

Nevertheless, there is a solid four-vote coalition—consisting of Rehnquist, Kennedy, Scalia, and Thomas—driving both the *Smith-Flores* and *Agostini* lines of cases. Other justices on the Court have also endorsed the equality principles that, in our view, undergird the shifting face of the Court's doctrine. Indeed, the positions of Stevens and O'Connor are ironic because the two justices have been among the most vocal proponents of equality norms in religious liberty cases.[41] Any effort to construct a "view of the Court" when disparate majorities prevail by one- or two-vote margins is uncertain, but the Court's consistent emphasis upon equal treatment is unmistakable—and, we think, eminently sound.

Pursuant to this emphasis on equal treatment, religious minorities and religious practice continue to receive special judicial solicitude. Statutes that single out religious practice for special burdens are subjected to even harsher scrutiny than statutes that target communicative activity receive under the Free Speech Clause. Indeed, while any law specifically targeting ritual practice would receive strict scrutiny under *Lukumi Babalu Aye*, some laws singling out communicative behavior—such as, for example, time, place, and manner regulations—receive less demanding scrutiny.[42] In that respect, the post-*Smith* Court actually gives Free Exercise claims better treatment than it gives Free Speech claims.

Religious discrimination is, moreover, no less suspect than racial discrimination. Indeed, federal courts after *Smith* appear more willing to look for disparate impact discrimination under the Free Exercise Clause than they are in race discrimination cases under the Equal Protection Clause.[43] Consider: in *Keeler v. Mayor and City Council of Cumberland*, a federal district court exempted a church from a local landmarking ordinance, claiming that the ordinance was constitutionally defective because it contained exemptions for financial hardship but not religious hardship;[44] in *Rader v. Johnston*, a federal district court found evidence of discrimination when the University of Nebraska granted various freshmen the privilege of living off campus but denied permission to a religious student who wished to live in a Christian residence;[45] in *Fraternal Order of Police v. City of Newark*, the United States Court of Appeals for the Third Circuit said that if the Newark police department permitted officers to wear beards to avoid skin rashes, then it must also permit officers to wear beards to satisfy religious obligations.[46]

VI. Conclusion

One of the most striking notions in all of constitutional discourse is the idea that religiously motivated persons and groups are to a considerable degree sovereigns among us—that they enjoy the license to disregard legal restraints and burdens that other Americans must respect. Were this claim to succeed, it might be the case that religiously motivated parents were constitutionally entitled to educate their children at home, but that other parents were not; that religiously motivated landlords were entitled to discriminate among tenants on grounds of race, gender, or sexual orientation, but other landlords were not; that religiously motivated persons of the same sex could marry, but that others could not; or that churches or other religious organizations were free to disregard the historic preservation or zoning restrictions that bind everyone else in their communities.

If it is possible at all to find a respectable pedigree for this idea, it may trace to the seductive if enigmatic idea that the Constitution erects a "wall of separation" between church and state.[47] Over the past half century, that metaphor has associated itself with the idea that religion was special in some way that made it constitutionally privileged. The goal of separation suggested to some that religion ought to flourish or decline unimpaired by government policies or political values—hence the judiciary ought to enable religious actors to practice their faiths unconstrained even by democratically enacted laws that everybody else must obey. The idea of separation also exerted a powerful, countervailing pull on the Supreme Court's Establishment Clause jurisprudence, where the separation metaphor invited skepticism about any program that sent government aid to churches or, especially, religious schools: religion ought to grow or shrink uninfluenced by government largesse and political power.

Separation has always existed in uneasy tension with another powerful vision of religious liberty, one based upon the equality of persons and the idea that minority interests ought to be protected from disrespectful or hostile treatment. From the standpoint of equality, neither the Court's dogmatic opposition to aid for religious interests nor its occasional willingness to privilege believers with special exemptions made any sense. Why should the law privilege religious believers with exemptions unavailable for comparably serious secular commitments? The Supreme Court acknowledged the force of this point in various ways. For example, in *Caldor* and other cases,[48] the Court either modified or struck down laws giving special privileges to religious believers. But the Court's most impressive, if tacit, acknowledgment of the equality principle was its toothless application of *Sherbert*'s compelling state interest. In one case after another, the justices found ways to duck the test and deny exemptions to claimants who sought to cash in on *Sherbert*'s expansive promise.

Conversely, from the standpoint of equality, it was hard to see why churches should not be eligible for government benefits on the same terms as comparable secular enterprises, including, for example, private schools and secular charities. In *Everson v. Ewing Township Bd. of Education*,[49] at the very outset of the Court's Establishment Clause jurisprudence, Justice Black noted that it would be unfair to deny churches and religious schools the benefit of publicly funded police and fire protection; no opponent of public aid for religious education has ever been dogmatic enough to contest that point. Black's concession effectively foreshadowed the unhappy career of the *Lemon* test, in which the Court struggled to distinguish between invalid policies that "advanced religion" and permissible policies that merely made religious institutions incidental beneficiaries of subsidies aimed at some secular goal (such as police protection, fire safety, or cheap transportation).

Since 1990, the Supreme Court's religious liberty jurisprudence has undergone a fundamental change. The unstable mix of separation and equality has given way to a jurisprudence emphatically centered upon equality. The transition is manifest in the demise of separation's two doctrinal avatars, the *Lemon* and *Sherbert* tests. *Lemon* has passed quietly, ignored rather than overruled in cases like *Agostini*. *Sherbert*'s compelling state interest standard, in contrast, met an operatic end, dying loudly and at great length in *Smith* and *Flores*.

These developments have been widely noticed. Several scholars have called attention to the developing unity between the Court's Free Exercise and Establishment Clause jurisprudence; some have recognized that equality is beginning to achieve doctrinal primacy over separation. Most of these treatments have, however, assumed that the separation metaphor captured an attractive, or at least coherent, model for some portions of the Court's jurisprudence. That is a mistake, and a bad one. In this essay, we have insisted upon two points. First, the Constitution's Free Exercise and Establishment Clauses are conceptually integrated. The Supreme Court's cases under the two clauses are converging upon a single principle neither because of methodological whim nor because of political choice but, rather, because the two lines of cases raise the same issues. Second, the model of special constitutional privilege for a religion is both normatively indefensible and practically unworkable. If the Court is ever to achieve a coherent doctrine in this troubled field, it has to reject that model and the doctrinal tests—*Lemon* and *Sherbert*—and the metaphors—like "separation"—that go with it.

NOTES

1. 494 U.S. 872, 890 (1990).
2. Id. at 877–80.
3. Id. at 892 (O'Connor concurring); id. at 907–8 (Blackmun dissenting).
4. Id. at 879.
5. 374 U.S. 398 (1963).
6. 406 U.S. 205 (1972).
7. See *Bob Jones University v. United States*, 461 U.S. 574, 604 (1983) (government interest in eradicating discrimination in education); *United States v. Lee*, 455 U.S. 252, 260 (1982) (government interest in preserving a sound tax system); *Johnson v. Robison*, 415 U.S. 361, 385–86 (1974) (government interest in raising and supporting armies). In other cases, the Court has rejected Free Exercise claims on the ground that the challenged practice imposed no actual burden upon the religious convictions of the claimants. See, for example, *Lyng v. Northwest Indian Cemetery Protection Ass'n*, 485 U.S. 439, 448–49 (1988) (building road over

sacred area did not burden religious belief); *Bowen v. Roy*, 476 U.S. 693, 700 (1986) (requiring disclosure of a social security number for welfare benefits did not burden religious beliefs); *Alamo Foundation v. Secretary of Labor*, 471 U.S. 290, 304–5 (1985) (imposing a minimum wage requirement does not burden religious believers who refuse, for religious reasons, to accept wages).

8. The phrase belongs to Gerald Gunther, *The Supreme Court, 1971 Term—Foreword: In Search of Evolving Doctrine on a Changing Court: A Model for a Newer Equal Protection*, 86 Harv. L. Rev. 1, 8 (1972).

9. See, for example, *O'Lone v. Estate of Shabazz*, 482 U.S. 342 (1987) (compelling interest analysis not applicable to prison regulations); *Bowen*, 476 U.S. at 708 (Burger plurality) (when a challenged statute merely regulates the availability of government benefits, neutral and uniform rules that burden religious beliefs are constitutional so long as they are a reasonable means to promote a legitimate government interest); *Goldman v. Weinberger*, 475 U.S. 503, 506–7 (1986) (compelling interest analysis not applicable to military regulations).

10. This essay borrows generously from several of our earlier efforts to address this problem: Christopher L. Eisgruber and Lawrence G. Sager, *The Vulnerability of Conscience: The Constitutional Basis for Protecting Religious Conduct*, 61 U. Chi. L. Rev. 1245 (1994); Christopher L. Eisgruber and Lawrence G. Sager, *Unthinking Religious Freedom*, 74 Tex. L. Rev. 577 (1996); and Christopher L. Eisgruber and Lawrence G. Sager, *Congressional Power and Religious Liberty After* City of Boerne v. Flores, 1997 S. Ct. Rev. 79.

11. The resulting principle of "unimpaired flourishing" is both demanding and difficult to limit in any principled fashion. For discussion, see Eisgruber and Sager, *The Vulnerability of Conscience*, 61 U. Chi. L. Rev. at 1254–60.

12. 319 U.S. 624, 642 (1943).

13. Title VII explicitly exempts religious organizations from the statutory provisions prohibiting discrimination in employment on the basis of religion. See 42 U.S.C. § 2000e-1 (1988). See also *Corporation of Presiding Bishop v. Amos*, 483 U.S. 327 (1987) (upholding the constitutionality of this exemption). Courts have implied additional exceptions for the benefit of churches. See, e.g, *McClure v. Salvation Army*, 460 F. 2d 553 (5th Cir 1972) (implied statutory exemption permits religious organizations to discriminate on the basis of sex in some circumstances).

14. Id. at 410.

15. *Thomas v. Review Board of the Indiana Employment Security Division*, 450 U.S. 707, 709 (1981).

16. 374 U.S. at 406–7.

17. Smith, 394 U.S. at 893–95 (O'Connor concurring); id. at 908–9 (Blackmun dissenting).

18. Id. at 883–84.

19. *Sherbert*, 374 U.S. at 406. By saying that the Sunday exception "compound(s)" South Carolina's constitutional delict, Justice Brennan suggests that a constitutional problem would exist even absent the statute's express favoritism. We believe that this transparent favoritism strengthens the underlying constitutional claim, but—as our analysis of *Thomas* makes clear—we agree that it is not essential to *Sherbert*'s constitutional argument.

20. 450 U.S. 707 (1981).

21. Our analysis is easily extended to the two remaining cases in the *Sherbert* quartet, *Hobbie v. Unemployment Appeals Commission*,480 U.S. 136 (1987), and *Frazee v. Illinois Department of Employment Security*, 489 U.S. 829 (1989).

22. 455 U.S. 252, 263–64 n. 3 (1982) (Stevens concurring). In *Hobbie*, Justice Stevens concurred on the ground that Florida had regarded "religious claims less favorably than other

claims" so that Court intervention was "necessary to protect religious observers against unequal treatment." 480 U.S. at 148, quoting *Bowen v. Roy*, 476 U.S. 693, 707 n. 17 (1986) (Stevens, concurring in part and concurring in the result).

23. 476 U.S. at 708.

24. For example, Oregon, like many states, made exceptions to its alcohol laws to accommodate the sacramental use of wine.

25. 472 U.S. 703 (1985).

26. Michael McConnell takes a position of this kind when he recommends as a constitutional principle the proposition that "[e]ven the mighty democratic will of the people is, in principle, subordinate to the commands of God, as heard and understood in the individual conscience." Michael W. McConnell, *The Origins and Historical Understanding of Free Exercise of Religion*, 103 Harv. L. Rev. 1409, 1516 (1990).

27. See U.S. Const. art. VI, cl. 3 ("[B]ut no religious Test shall ever be required as a Qualification to any Office or public Trust under the United States"); *Torcaso v. Watkins*, 367 U.S. 488 (1961) (state officials cannot be required to swear a religious oath); *McDaniel v. Paty*, 435 U.S. 618 (1978) (ministers cannot be excluded from public office); *Church of Lukumi Babalu Aye v. City of Hialeah*, 113 S. Ct. 2217, 2232–34 (1993) (cities cannot selectively prohibit the ritual slaughter of animals).

28. See *Larson v. Valente*, 456 U.S. 228 (1982) (state may not favor some religions over others); *Lee v. Weisman*, 505 U.S. 577, 599 (1992) (nonsectarian prayer at a school-sponsored graduation ceremony impermissibly favors religion over nonreligion).

29. 117 S. Ct. 2157 (1997).

30. McConnell, 103 Harv. L. Rev. at 1452–53.

31. Id. at 1452.

32. Id. at 1455.

33. See, e.g., *Witters v. Washington Dept. of Services for the Blind*, 474 U.S. 481 (1986) (upholding a state program that permitted college students pursuing religious training to share in an aid program subsidizing vocational education for all blind students); *Bowen v. Kendrick*, 487 U.S. 589 (1988) (upholding a program that allowed religious institutions to share in federal funding available to support pregnancy counseling); *Zobrest v. Catalina Footbills School Dist.*, 509 U.S. 1 (1993) (upholding the constitutionality of a program in which public funds were used to supply a sign-language interpreter for a deaf student attending Catholic school).

34. *Rosenberger v. Rector and Visitors of the University of Virginia*, 515 U.S. 819 (1995).

35. 117 S. Ct. 1997 (1997).

36. 473 U.S. 402 (1985).

37. *Lemon v. Kurtzman*, 403 U.S. 602, 612–13 (1971).

38. 473 U.S. at 409.

39. 117 S. Ct. at 2011–12.

40. Id. at 2013 (quoting *Zobrest*, 509 U.S. at 12).

41. See, e.g., *Kiryas Joel*, 512 U.S. at 715 (O'Connor concurring) (an "emphasis on equal treatment is, I think, an eminently sound approach"); *Lee*, 455 U.S. at 263 n. 2 (Stevens concurring) ("The risk that governmental approval of some [religious claims] and disapproval of others will be perceived as favoring one religion over another is an important risk the Establishment Clause was designed to preclude.").

42. See generally Geoffrey R. Stone, *Content-Neutral Restrictions*, 54 U. Chi. L. Rev. 46 (1987).

43. In *Washington v. Davis*, 426 U.S. 229 (1976), the Court construed the Equal Protection Clause to reach only intentional discrimination.

44. 940 F. Supp 879 (D. Md. 1996). The Keeler court found that Cumberland's historic preservation statute was not a "law of general application," and so was subject to strict scrutiny, even after *Smith*. Id. at 885.

45. 924 F. Supp. 1540 (D. Neb. 1996). The court found both that the university's policy did not amount to a rule of general application and that the university had applied the rule in a discriminatory fashion.

46. No. 97-5542 (CA3 March 3, 1999) (1999 LEXIS 3338).

47. Thomas Jefferson used the "wall of separation" metaphor in his January 1, 1802, letter to the Danbury Baptist Association, and it appears in both the Court's first Free Exercise case, *Reynolds v. United States*, 98 U.S. 145, 164 (1878), and the Court's first Establishment Clause case, *Everson v. Bd. of Education*, 330 U.S. 1, 16 (1947). In *Reynolds*, of course, the Court used the idea of "separation" to argue against religious privilege rather than for it.

48. E.g., *Texas Monthly v. Bullock*, 489 U.S. 1 (1989) (finding unconstitutional a Texas law that exempted religious publications from a sales tax applicable to other publications).

49. 330 U.S. 1.

Chapter 12

The Incommensurability of Religion

Abner S. Greene

The central question for scholars of the Constitution's religion clauses is this: Is religion special? Does the Constitution require, or permit, or forbid government to treat religious belief as distinctive? The trend in the academy and on the Court is toward denying the distinctiveness of religious belief. Both the Establishment Clause and the Free Exercise Clause are being gutted; a certain type of equality claim has moved to the forefront. In this essay, I will first describe the movement from the treatment of religion as distinctive (during the Warren and Burger Courts) to the subsuming of religion with other forms of belief (during the Rehnquist Court). I will then describe the connection between the Court's more general equality jurisprudence and this development in cases and scholarship involving the religion clauses. Finally, I will state the type of argument that I believe is needed to ward off this attack on the distinctiveness of religion, and then offer one version of such an argument.

The Warren and Burger Courts: Religion as Distinctive

Without much grounding other than the First Amendment text, the Warren and Burger Courts issued fairly broad readings of both the Establishment and Free Exercise Clauses. The Establishment Clause cases involved the use of religious argument in the lawmaking process, the channeling of public funds to religious schools, and prayer in public schools. In Epperson v. Arkansas,[1] the Court struck down a state law forbidding the teaching of evolution in public schools. Such a law does not on its face promote any particular religion. But the Court, relying on the clear legislative history, invalidated the law as the product of religious fundamentalist fervor. Laws are often the product of strong lobbying by ideologically invested groups; the Court was certainly not suggesting that all such laws were invalid. Rather, because the First Amendment forbids the establishment of religion—and does not speak to the establishment of anything else—the Court stated a rule about laws based in predominantly religious arguments. It has since applied the *Epperson* principle three times—twice during the Burger Court and once in the first term of the Rehnquist Court—to invalidate laws that, while not religious on their face, were seen to be the product of predominantly religious arguments.[2]

In Lemon v. Kurtzman,[3] the Court struck down state laws funding teachers in religious primary and secondary schools. Even though the funding was for secular courses only, the Court was concerned with the risk that such funds could be used for religious ends and with the problem of government supervision to ensure against such a risk. No similar injunction was issued against the funding of secular schools. After *Lemon*, the Warren and Burger Courts policed the public funding of religious schools carefully, sometimes upholding such funding, sometimes striking it down.[4]

The school prayer cases round out the Warren Court's treatment of the Establishment Clause. In two landmark rulings of the early 1960s, the Court invalidated the practice of teacher-led prayer in public schools.[5] Again, the Establishment Clause text enabled the Court to reason that such prayer tended toward the establishment of religion. Again, the Court had nothing to say about teacher-led recitation of nonreligious speech, such as the pledge of allegiance.[6]

Just as the Establishment Clause cases singled out religion for distinctive treatment, so did the Warren and Burger Courts' Free Exercise Clause cases. The key Warren Court case was Sherbert v. Verner,[7] in which the Court insisted that a woman fired for refusing to work on her Sabbath be given unemployment compensation, even though the state board had ruled that her refusal to work did not fall within the state law's accepted reasons for voluntary refusal. Whether *Sherbert* is properly thought of as a case involving an exemption from general law is a hard question; there are strong arguments that it is not, that instead it is an example of the Court's policing a type of active discrimination against religion.[8] In any event, *Sherbert*'s dicta clearly stated that the government must have a compelling reason for applying law in a way that burdened religious belief, and *Sherbert* was directly followed once during the Burger Court and once during the first term of the Rehnquist Court.[9] A more straightforward example of an exemption for religious belief came in the key Burger Court Free Exercise holding, Wisconsin v. Yoder.[10] Wisconsin required all children to attend school—either public or private, secular or religious—until the age of sixteen. Amish families objected that their fourteen- and fifteen-year-old children needed to be at home and working on the farm, to help protect the Amish religious culture. The Court agreed, and explicitly stated that a similar exemption would not have been granted for nonreligious believers.

Thus, at the end of the Warren and Burger Courts, the distinctiveness of religion was clearly established in the Court's jurisprudence. Without elaborating any particular theory for such treatment, the Court was mostly content to rely on the First Amendment's text and the Court's own developing precedent, to hold that sometimes religion must be specially disfavored (*Epperson*; *Lemon*; the school prayer cases), while sometimes it must be specially favored (*Sherbert*, perhaps; *Yoder*).

The Rehnquist Court: Religion Subsumed

Perhaps because of the paucity of justification for the Warren and Burger Courts' treatment of religion as distinctive, the Rehnquist Court has, piece by piece, begun dismantling the edifice, pursuant to an equally-not-well-justified view of neutrality, or equality. In the Establishment Clause arena, the Court cut back on the *Lemon* line of cases in Agostini v. Felton.[11] There, the Court overruled a prior case that had relied on *Lemon*, Aguilar v. Felton,[12] and permitted a New York program funding the salaries of public school teachers to teach remedial education classes in religious schools. The Court has not, yet, permitted the funding of the salaries of religious school teachers who teach secular courses in religious schools (nor of those who teach religious courses in those schools). And it has overruled neither *Epperson* nor the school prayer cases.[13] But in Rosenberger v. University of Virginia,[14] it held that a public university may fund a student religious publication if it is also funding other, nonreligious student publications.[15]

In both *Agostini* and *Rosenberger*, the Court relied heavily on a conception of neutrality. So long as the government's funding programs were sufficiently broad—covering both the religious and the secular—they cannot be deemed to establish religion. So long as religion is treated just like everything else, in other words, it is not being favored and thus there is no Establishment Clause prohibition.

The Court relied on the same conception of neutrality to backpedal from its Free Exercise Clause holdings. In Employment Division v. Smith,[16] the Court held that the Constitution requires no exemptions for religious believers from generally applicable law. It upheld a state's power to apply its controlled substance laws to religious ingestion of peyote, an hallucinogenic drug. To grant such an exemption would be to give religion special treatment, said the Court, and it deemed this unwarranted. Rather, religious believers must suffer under adverse laws just as secularists do. *Smith* makes sense under one view of political obligation: Why should anyone have a constitutional right to be exempt from general legislation? If one has the opportunity to speak, use the press, petition for redress of grievances, and vote, then one must suffer the consequences of legislative loss just as one reaps the benefits of legislative gain. The channels of protest are open; receiving a judicial exemption would seem to be a second bite at the apple. Only if one were in fact cut off, somehow, from full participation in the legislative process, should one have a legitimacy claim, and a possible exemption.

The Court's refusal to grant exemptions in *Smith*, I believe, paves the way for an overruling of *Epperson* and its progeny, for *Epperson* depends on a view that religious justifications must be specially disfavored in the legislative process, and *Smith* depends on the assumption that such justifications have been given full play in such a process. I will discuss the connection between these two conceptions—disfavoring religious justifications and then granting religious exemptions—in detail below.

The Domination of the Equality Model

The Warren and Burger Courts, relying on not much more than the First Amendment text, treated religion as distinctive. The Rehnquist Court, relying on not much more than a very broad view of neutrality, or equality, has undercut some key Warren and Burger Court rulings and is poised to do even greater damage. Is there more to be said for the Rehnquist Court's view?

I believe there is, and various scholars have begun to make the arguments.[17] Underlying all of them—often implicitly—is the Equal Protection Clause. We have seen an extraordinary expansion of equality jurisprudence in the past fifty years. Beginning with Brown v. Board of Education,[18] the Court has time and again invalidated legislation as violating a principle of equality. Not only are racial minorities protected but so are women, illegitimate children, illegal aliens, and now, perhaps, gay men and lesbians.[19] And the principle is not one of antisubordination, despite the cogent arguments of many. Rather, the Court has adopted a seemingly capacious and formal antidiscrimination principle: for various categories (e.g., race, sex), government may neither grant special favor nor impose special burdens.

This broad conception of equality has been incorporated into the religion clause scholarship, and can best explain the Rehnquist Court's doctrinal shiftings. Singling out religion for special disadvantage—as one might argue is the case in *Epperson*, *Lemon*, and the school prayer cases—violates this broad conception of equality, for why should religious arguments be given any less weight than secular ones, or religious schools be any less worthy of funding that secular ones? Would this not involve a kind of active disadvantaging of religion, of playing favorites on behalf of the secular? Similarly, would not granting exemptions for religious belief but not for secular belief involve a different but equally unjustified playing of favorites? Perhaps religion is like race or sex—perhaps it must be treated according to a particular conception of equality, one that relies not on an antisubordination principle,[20] but rather on the naming of the category in question (here, "religion"), and then the conclusion that no special favoring or disfavoring may occur.

This is not an outlandish position. The Equal Protection Clause has arguably been the most important source of rights in the past fifty years, and subsuming religion under it in the way suggested above has a certain doctrinal neatness to it. It also carries a deeper message: the source of one's beliefs should not be a reason for special governmental favoring or disfavoring. That sounds good, neat, American. But is it correct?

In the remainder of this essay, I will set forward first a précis of the type of argument I believe necessary to defeat the subsuming of religion into the broad conception of equality, and then lay out a particular version of the argument. In short, it involves first recognizing religious belief as epistemologically distinct from secular belief (either actually or as perceived), and then adopting a special disfavoring and consequent favoring of religion that flows from this recognition.

An Epistemological Defense of Religion's Distinctiveness

If one were a strict textualist, one could argue: The First Amendment singles out religion for two clauses all its own; one appears to require disfavoring, the other, favoring. This move is insufficient; what type of favoring and disfavoring the text requires remains to be seen, and one must thus rely on either history or theory or something else beyond the text. So whether textualist or not, the argument for religious distinctiveness needs more.

If one could show that religion must be specially disfavored in the lawmaking process, then one would lay the groundwork for religious exemptions, for if religious justifications were blocked from a full role in the lawmaking process, then binding the makers of such arguments to the output of that process would raise serious legitimacy problems. One solution would be to restore full participation; another would be to award exemptions. This second solution—that exemptions follow logically from gag rules—has a few obstacles but makes much intuitive sense. The predicate—that religious justifications must be specially disfavored in the lawmaking process—is much harder,[21] and relies ultimately, I believe, on acceptance of an epistemological uniqueness of religious belief, or at least on a perceived epistemological uniqueness. First I will lay out the argument for disfavoring religious justifications in the lawmaking process; then I will turn to the remedy, exemptions.[22]

Why Religious Justifications for Law Should Be Disfavored

Basing law on an express reference to an extrahuman source of value should matter for Establishment Clause analysis because such reference effectively excludes those who don't share the relevant religious faith from meaningful participation in the political process. Consider a law based on the maxim "you should love your neighbor as you love yourself"—a law enacting some form of Good Samaritan obligation, say. The legislature's reliance on that maxim might be based on express reference to facts about human behavior and conclusions reached about the causes and effects of such behavior. In that case, the law would not be based on a source of value beyond human experience. Although it might be hard or impossible to "prove" these conclusions and to "show" why they should lead to a particular law, at least the door is left open for dissenters to seek to alter the law based on arguments accessible to all involved. In this sense, reference to human experience can be seen as the common denominator for political debate. Suppose, on the other hand, that the Good Samaritan law were based expressly on the ground that God (or, more generally, any source of value beyond human experience) commands us to love our neighbors as ourselves.[23] To be sure, dissenters may argue with the religious believers about whether they have properly construed the commandments of their faith. At some point in this discussion, the believers may advert to the ultimate source of their beliefs, their faith in God. If the dissenters are people who do not share this faith, they are by definition excluded from access to the relevant source of authority, God (unless they see the light and share the faith).

In other words, although secular as well as religious beliefs might not be provable, there is nonetheless a significant difference between expressly grounding law in premises accessible to citizens as citizens, on the one hand, and only to those with a particular religious faith, on the other hand. It might be hard to show that some person or group should be considered "trustworthy,"[24] for example, but we still go about doing so by breaking down the meaning of that term and amassing evidence based on human experience, which we have in common as citizens. Even nonrational secular premises, although perhaps not strictly provable, at least operate through reference inward rather than outward. Basing law expressly on religious faith, on the other hand, involves pointing toward a source of value that people can share not as United States citizens but only as citizens in the kingdom of the same God. When religious believers enact laws for the express purpose of advancing the values believed to be commanded by their religion, they exclude nonbelievers from meaningful participation in political discourse and from meaningful access to the source of normative authority predicating law.[25] They force their "reference out" on others, disempowering nonbelievers. For this reason, it is proper to insist that law be grounded expressly in sources of value accessible to citizens as citizens, not merely to those citizens who happen to share a faith in a separate, extrahuman source of authority.[26]

Some scholars have suggested that a law should withstand Establishment Clause challenge if a plausible secular purpose can be articulated on its behalf.[27] Thus, laws requiring prayer in public school would be held to violate the Establishment Clause because their only plausible purpose is religious,[28] while laws banning abortion would never violate that clause—regardless of the reasons actually advanced in support of the laws. The argument that a law with a plausible secular purpose should be upheld is often packaged with the argument that individual citizens must be able to rely on their religious values in forming political views.[29] People taking this position stress that so long as a law has a plausible secular purpose, it can be accepted even by those who don't share the relevant religious faith, while the religious believers can still rely in the political process on the religious values that they hold most dear.

I believe this argument to be an important mistake. I have no quarrel with citizens and legislators relying on their religious beliefs when they form political positions or when they decide how to vote (for laws or for representatives). The problem arises when a law appears to have been passed because of a sectarian religious concern.[30] Even those who argue for sustaining legislation with a plausible secular purpose would agree that a religious sect (I use the term broadly) may not require all citizens to engage in a religious practice that is specific to that sect. A Jewish majority in a town, for instance, cannot require that all citizens light Sabbath candles on Friday night. In my view, it is just as problematic for adherents to a religious faith to forbid abortions, say, if they make clear in the relevant political fora that their reason for enacting the ban is their belief that God condemns abortion.[31] A nonbeliever is effectively denied participation in the political process because the nonbeliever has no access (without taking the religious leap of faith) to the extrahuman source of value undergirding the argumentation of the believers. For the same reason, however, I see no problem if the religious believers are willing to translate their religious source of value into secular terms, because then the nonbeliever perceives that she can participate in the debate.[32]

Imagine, for example, legislators arguing for the banning of abortions "because they're immoral." If pressed in debate, assume that the legislators explain that they (a) have observed human suffering, (b) distinguish human beings from animals because of the language abilities of the former, (c) are concerned about slippery slopes, and (d) resolve close questions in favor of preserving life. That sort of response is quite different from the response of legislators who say, "We believe in Christ as Lord, and His scriptures say that life is sacred, and therefore abortion is wrong."

Nonbelievers can have a dialogue with the former legislators based on sharable observations and conclusions about human experience; with the latter legislators, a nonbeliever might reasonably feel muted by the reference to the legislators' God and the claim of authority based in an extrahuman power.

Requiring that laws have an express secular purpose rather than merely a plausible one might transform the legislative process in a way consistent with the dictates of the Establishment Clause.[33] In some cases, the same laws will be passed that otherwise would have been passed, but pursuant to secular rather than religious justification.[34] In other cases, the unavailability of a strong secular justification will mean that a law will not be passed. This transformation of the legislative process will eliminate the Establishment Clause injury of excluding nonbelievers from meaningful participation in the political process. That we see so many laws passed on the basis of secular justification, when religious justifications no doubt are stronger in the souls and minds of many legislators, is testament not to the fact that the Establishment Clause proscription on enacting faith into law will have little real-world effect but, rather, to the fact that it is already having such an effect.

Let me explain why I have not suggested forbidding laws based on an underlying religious purpose as well as those based on an expressly religious purpose. One can imagine four different situations: (1) a law is religious on its face; (2) a law not facially religious is enacted for an expressly religious purpose; (3) a law not facially religious is enacted for an expressly secular purpose that appears to be a pretext for the real purpose, which is religious; and (4) a law not facially religious is enacted for an expressly secular purpose that does not appear pretextual, but the real underlying purpose is religious. The first three types of law should be invalid under the Establishment Clause because they foreclose meaningful political participation by nonbelievers. All three laws are, in the terminology I am using in this essay, "expressly" religious. But if religious believers can translate their "true" religious reasons successfully enough to make it appear to nonbelievers that the secular reasons are the real ones, then from the nonbelievers' perspective, their political participation is meaningful. One might argue that to be consistent, I should condemn even type (4) laws in principle and then acknowledge that the judiciary can't enforce this condemnation because the true reasons behind the laws will be inaccessible to it. But my Establishment Clause argument does not condemn type (4) laws. It turns not on the underlying reasons for laws but, rather, on the reasons that are apparent in the political process. Invalidating type (3) laws will cover all instances in which believers think they have successfully masked their true reasons but have not. If a religious reason can be successfully translated into a secular one—if a nonbeliever sees the secular argument as one made in good faith, and finds the ensuing debate meaningful—then the concern with exclusion from political participation is eliminated.

Many laws will be expressly based not on a single religious or secular purpose but on an intertwined set of purposes, some religious and some secular. This is inevitable in a society in which most citizens claim to be religious. Merely showing that a law was expressly based in part on religious faith cannot be sufficient to invalidate that law if we accept the fact that many people are religious and reach conclusions about many issues from religious premises. But accepting the presence of expressly religious purposes for law does not require accepting laws that are dominantly based on express references to religious faith. There is a point at which the mere acknowledgment of the religious values held by many citizens slips into the establishment of those values as the basis of law. That is the line that a legislature may not cross. Thus, I would put the test this way: For a law to be upheld against an Establishment Clause challenge, the law's dominant express purpose must be secular, and any expressly religious purpose for the law must be no more than ancillary and not itself dominant.[35]

The Court has followed this test, though without stating it clearly and certainly without explaining which characteristics of "religion" forbid religious values from being enacted into law. In Epperson v. Arkansas,[36] which struck down an Arkansas law forbidding the teaching of evolution in public school, the Court examined the historical context of the law's enactment and concluded, "It is clear that fundamentalist sectarian conviction was and is the law's reason for existence."[37] In Stone v. Graham,[38] the Court summarily invalidated a Kentucky law requiring the posting of the Ten Commandments on the wall of each public classroom. The legislature had required a notation on each posting that stated, "The secular application of the Ten Commandments is clearly seen in its adoption as the fundamental legal code of Western Civilization and the Common Law of the United States."[39] The Court dismissed this notation as pretextual, concluding that the "pre-eminent purpose for [the law] is plainly religious in nature."[40] Likewise, in Wallace v. Jaffree,[41] the Court struck down an Alabama law authorizing a period of silence for "meditation or voluntary prayer" because it "had no secular purpose;"[42] as in *Epperson*, the Court supported this conclusion with references to the context of the law's enactment, and in particular to the legislative history. Finally, in Edwards v. Aguillard,[43] the Court invalidated a Louisiana statute forbidding the teaching of evolution in public school unless accompanied by the teaching of "creation science." Again after examining the history of the law's enactment, the Court dismissed the proffered secular justification of promoting "academic freedom" as pretextual, concluding that the legislature's "preeminent" purpose was religious.[44]

The epistemological argument for barring legislation based in dominant, expressly religious justification comes in two versions. The first, offered above, refers to the religious nonbelievers' perception of exclusion, of their lack of access to the extrahuman source of value animating expressly religious argumentation. The second focuses not on the religious nonbelievers but on the religious believers. For example, consider two citizens, a believer in the economic theories of Milton Friedman and a believer in the divinity of Jesus Christ. Put aside the questions of what follows from being a Friedmanite, and of what follows from being a Christian. Instead, focus on the question of the accessibility of the belief that Friedmanism is true or that Christianity is true. A Friedmanite might try to convince me that Friedmanism is true, and would rely on evidence about markets and so on to do so. A Christian might also rely on human experience to convince me of the truth of Christianity. For most religious Christians, however, belief in the truth of Christianity depends on an additional source of authority. Indeed, I would have thought this difference important to religious Christians. For most religious people, religious faith is indeed different in kind from other beliefs. Faith in the divinity of Jesus Christ, for example, is not ordinarily considered on par with faith in the belief that Roger Maris hit sixty-one home runs, or that George Washington was our first president.[45] One who believes these facts would rely on tracings back to people who saw and recorded history. Most Christians wouldn't trace their faith back in this sense but, rather, would accept Christ's divinity based more on what we call a "leap of faith." Granted this leap might include biblical passages, teachings of wise people, views held by respected persons in the community, and so on, but for most religious people the leap toward theistic belief is distinct in kind from other beliefs.[46]

Another way of putting this is that religion often self-consciously revels in the unsensible, whereas science and other sources from which people make arguments at least purport to rely solely on the observable, on what we share as humans.[47] So even if science (both natural and social) is based—as religion is—in an important way on faith (nondeducible premises), the critical difference is that by its own terms, science points to the human and natural world for the source of value, whereas religion, by its own terms, points not only to the human and natural world but also outward to an extrahuman realm. Even if religion relies in part on human experience and reason, it relies as well on something else, namely, an extrahuman source of authority.[48]

In sum, although it is surely correct to suggest that the nonreligious can debate religious arguments, to point out that secular as well as religious beliefs are based in an important sense on faith, and to observe that religious as well as secular belief is based in human reason and experience, this position overlooks the precise way in which religion is distinctive. In the lawmaking process, reference to religion includes reliance on a type of authority—extrahuman—to which only some citizens have access. To enact law based expressly on such an exclusive source of authority denies the nonbeliever any real ability to apprehend or affirm the source of value under which she is being told to live. Moreover, from the point of view of many religious people, religious faith occupies a distinctive place in their lives, and it would surely come as little surprise that express reliance on such faith in political argumentation would be specially disempowering to religious nonbelievers.[49]

The Case for a Free Exercise Clause Offset

In the lawmaking process, we are free to make political, moral, and philosophical arguments to support our positions. But the central point of the Establishment Clause argument made above is that the lawmaking process in a nontheistic government should not be dominated by appeals to religious faith. In fact, one principal feature that distinguishes a country like ours from theocracies is the preclusion of law based expressly on religion. Religious belief goes a step beyond standard measures of justification for law: It involves a leap of faith to an extrahuman source of value. One can try to persuade others to take the same leap (by evangelizing and proselytizing, say), but the ultimate leap that religious argument calls for is different from what political, moral, or philosophical argument demands. Because of this difference, the latter should be part of public political justification; the former should not, or at least should not be permitted to dominate the process.

Enter the Free Exercise Clause. Lawmaking is a "contractual" process in the sense that if the political, moral, or philosophical arguments that we favor fail to attract enough support, we are bound by the resulting law even if it violates our political, moral, or philosophical sensibilities. Part of losing—of being the minority on an issue—is having to obey the law or to suffer the consequences. But precisely because we should exclude religious faith from being the dominant, express basis for law, an appeal to religious faith as the ground for a constitutional right of conscientious objection does not violate the "contractual" premise of obedience once one loses. The person basing a claim of conscience on religious faith hasn't lost the "faith argument" in the lawmaking process; if the participants adhered to constitutional strictures, that argument was restricted in the role it was allowed to play in that process.

Sometimes the position that religious faith should be kept out of law is understood to forbid all legislative exemptions for religion.[50] On this view, we separate religion from civil government by denying it recognition as the basis either for law or for exemptions from law. This position secures a sort of facial or formal "neutrality." But if we preclude religious faith from being the dominant, express purpose behind law, then exemptions are required to compensate religious people for the obstacle that this disability poses to their participation in the democratic process. Just as we grant special judicial protection to discrete and insular minorities who are effectively excluded from political power,[51] and just as we enhance judicial scrutiny when legislation blocks the channels of political change,[52] so should we recognize the need for religious exemptions from laws created by a process that is closed in an important way to religious people.

Thus, the Free Exercise Clause can be seen as providing a political counterweight to the Establishment Clause. If the latter should be read to prevent religious faith from being the dominant, express justification for law, then the former should be construed to make religious faith a ground for avoiding the obligations of law. In other words, a religious person can justifiably say, "You're keeping my religion out of your politics, now keep your politics out of my religion."

It is easy to see how a religious minority might be burdened by an otherwise valid law: Because the incidental, unintended effects of the law do not burden the majority, members of the majority are less likely to tailor the law to prevent such incidental burdens on the minority. But one might suggest that we sufficiently compensate minority religions for any Establishment Clause burden by giving legislatures the discretion—not the obligation—to enact toleration-based exemptions. If we exclude religious faith from grounding law, the argument would go, then we offset this burden by permitting the burdened group to argue for an accommodation of its religious practice.

The ability to argue for a toleration-based exemption is insufficient compensation for the Establishment Clause burden because members of the minority religion still are prevented from urging more general legislation to advance their beliefs. Consider a state in which marijuana use is a crime. A decriminalization law could be based on the desirability of tolerating a religious group whose faith compels such use. But it could not be based expressly on the idea that the faith of that religion is true and that therefore marijuana use should not be criminal.[53] This exclusion removes some arrows from the religious group's quiver; religious faith as such has been disabled as an express source of law. The disability is sufficiently substantial that if marijuana use is not decriminalized, the fact that the members of the religion may still ask for an exemption from the criminal law isn't sufficient to compensate for the burden of not being able to urge the truth of their faith itself as a reason to decriminalize the drug. There are situations in which a general repeal of the law might be the religious group's only shot, because a more limited exemption would not pass.

The facts of *Smith* and of this hypothetical case, however, suggest another objection. Are we really disabling the members of the minority religion by excluding religious faith from grounding law? If there was no chance that the minority could have enacted its faith into law, isn't the disability ephemeral?

It is true that many cases about Free Exercise Clause exemptions involve minority religions that would have been hard pressed to garner majority support for enacting their faith into law. But the Establishment Clause argument advanced here still excludes certain values from grounding law, and in particular it prohibits a minority religion from seeking to persuade the majority that it should enact a law because the minority faith is the true one. Furthermore, legislation often passes even if backed by less than "the majority"; smaller groups often capture the legislature for particular programs, and the arguments of such small groups—although insufficient to carry the day alone—might in some cases be enough to tip the legislative balance. If we are forbidding religious faith from playing even this incremental role, then the proper compensation is to construe the Free Exercise Clause as requiring exemptions from laws that burden religion.

So far my examples have focused on minority religions. But suppose that a member of a religious majority in the relevant jurisdiction claims a Free Exercise Clause exemption from an otherwise valid law. Here, it is easy to see how the Establishment Clause disability might have harmed members of the majority religion by shifting the way in which favored legislation could be enacted. But one might wonder how it is possible that a law could have the incidental effect of burdening the majority. Wouldn't the majority have prevented the enactment of such a law, or secured the law's repeal?

Again, this view of the legislative process is too simple. Many laws might impose on religious practice burdens not initially recognized as such or simply unanticipated; furthermore, legislation might be passed by a small faction capturing the legislature. For a variety of reasons, members of the majority religion might have insufficient legislative capital to alter such laws, which might be seen as producing good results apart from the burden on religious practice. Arguing that majority religions would never enact law that burdens their faith, like arguing that minority religions could never enact their faith into law, takes too simple a view of a process that often results in laws enacted because of a strong push by a small group and in laws with unintended effects that prove hard to undo because of the laws' concomitant benefits.

Let me offer some more specific examples of how the offset might work. (Note at the outset that under *Smith*, Free Exercise Clause exemptions would not be required in any of the following situations.) First, consider Epperson v. Arkansas,[54] in which the Court invalidated a law forbidding the teaching of evolution in public schools. There wasn't much of a secular argument for banning such teaching;[55] the obvious purpose and clear history of the law was to advance the religious faith of those who believed in creationism rather than evolution. By striking the law down, the Court sent a signal that law cannot be grounded in express or otherwise obvious religious purposes. But what if the parents who supported the law sincerely claimed that their religious faith prohibited their children from being taught evolution in the science portion of their public school classes? Under my calculus, they should be entitled to a Free Exercise Clause right (at least prima facie)[56] to remove their children from class during the portions of instruction that violate their religious principles. This prima facie exemption would arise precisely because parents are not allowed to rely on their religious faith to dictate the curriculum of the public schools.[57]

Next, assume a world without Roe v. Wade[58] and Planned Parenthood v. Casey,[59] and imagine a state with a Catholic majority. Under the view of the Establishment Clause advanced above, the legislature may not ban abortion if the dominant, express purpose is to reflect a Catholic view of when life begins. Suppose that abortion remains legal. Now assume that there is a general law compelling doctors to treat indigent patients for all legal medical procedures. Catholic doctors whose religious faith condemns abortion should be exempt from having to perform abortions under this law because their faith has been removed from the realm of arguments that may be advanced to outlaw abortion.

Now assume that a state has a law against polygamy, and that under the Establishment Clause it is improper to repeal the law for the dominant, express purpose of advancing a religious faith that requires polygamy (although it would be permissible to repeal it out of toleration for that faith). Because the Establishment Clause has altered the political rules in a way that forecloses one route to removing the legislative burden on that faith, a religious practitioner of polygamy should receive a prima facie right to exemption from the law.

Finally, assume that a state makes workers who are fired for good cause ineligible for unemployment compensation. Under my view of the Establishment Clause, a law requiring employers to give employees the Sabbath off cannot be passed for the dominant, express purpose of advancing a particular religious faith or faiths.[60] As a result, a person who is fired for refusing to work on her Sabbath should be entitled to a prima facie exemption from the eligibility requirement.[61]

The standard argument for Free Exercise Clause exemptions has nothing to do with offsetting an Establishment Clause burden. Rather, the argument is that because members of a majority religion are likely to protect their own religious practices when writing laws but to ignore (not necessarily intentionally) the harm that otherwise valid laws cause minority religions, the Free Exercise Clause should be read to protect minority religions against this flaw in the political process.[62]

I have two responses to this argument. First, the Court has rejected precisely this approach to protecting minority interests in the race area. Although the white majority often passes laws that cause unintended disproportionate harm to blacks, the Court has held that the Equal Protection Clause requires a showing of discriminatory intent and does not forbid unintended disparate impact.[63] This is not the place to discuss the virtues and vices of this rule. But so long as the rule is on the books, adopting a different rule for religion requires an argument that religion is different from race in such a way that disparate impact should be policed. By showing how religion is special for Establishment Clause purposes, the argument that I advance in this essay explains why the Free Exercise Clause should be read to require exemptions from unintended harm without relying on the mere existence of disparate impact.

Second, and more important, it is unclear why religion deserves special exemptions from otherwise valid law unless religion must bear an accompanying burden under the Establishment Clause. What makes religion special—its reference to an extrahuman source of value—does not of itself argue for exemptions. That one person's imperative comes from an extrahuman source of value doesn't distinguish her from a person whose imperative comes from intrahuman experience, if both are able to urge those values as grounds for law. The "reference out" that makes religion special becomes relevant to the Free Exercise Clause calculus only if one sees it as a reason to disable religion under the Establishment Clause.

And now, a clarification. I have argued that when we exclude religious values from being enacted into law, we should require a compensating exemption from laws that conflict with those values. This does not mean that we should require an exemption from an otherwise valid law that conflicts with racist values (for example) because we have forbidden laws passed with an expressly racist purpose. The only kind of value that we should protect from legal obligation because we have excluded it from grounding such obligation is a value that we otherwise seek to foster when held privately. In contrast to racist values, we exclude religious values from grounding law not because we consider the values bad in and of themselves but because we consider religious values to be both (a) good things to hold and (b) permissible as the ground of private decision making but not of law. In this way, the religion clauses can be seen as establishing the prototypical public/private line: We exclude religious values from grounding law while including them in the development of the private self.[64] I do not mean to suggest that religious values cannot be public; they simply cannot be public in the sense that they provide the dominant, express purpose behind law.

Uncommon Ground

The argument I have made differs from that of many liberal theorists, who seek to overcome the problem of political conflict among citizens who hold radically different comprehensive views of the good by relying on broad, abstract principles about which we can supposedly all agree, if we would only be reasonable. That is, I agree with critics such as Stanley Fish who argue that the following moves cannot place liberalism on a higher, common ground:[65]

1. "Common ground is sometimes found in a very high level of generality ('be good,' 'don't be cruel') that floats above the situations that provoke disagreements."
2. "Others find common ground in a (claimed) universal distaste for certain views, which, once identified, allow one to arrive at more widely acceptable views by a process of subtraction."
3. "Still others find common ground in a set of procedural rules, akin to traffic lights or the rule of driving on the right side of the road, with no substantive content whatever, while substantive matters are left to be debated in the spaces provided by the private associations of home, church, social club, etc."
4. "Finally, common ground is often identified with whatever distribution of goods and powers a majority has ratified (or at least not rebelled against)."

As Fish brilliantly points out, each of these moves masks substantive commitments to contested views of the good, thus depriving liberalism of a higher, common ground. My argument for a political balance of the religion clauses is not an attempt at seeking higher, common ground. Rather, it acknowledges that we are mired in uncommon ground—in fundamental differences of opinion about the good that will not go away and that we wish to respect. By refusing to accept laws backed by dominant, expressly religious justification,[66] but by granting prima facie exemptions to those burdened in their religious practice by law, we can be clear-eyed about the impossibility of finding higher, common ground, while meeting the demands of legitimacy. Sovereignty must be seen as permeable rather than as unitary. Government must be run according to secular justifications, but religious people and religious communities must be permitted to live by their own law, at least as a prima facie matter.[67]

NOTES

This essay continues work begun in the following articles: The Political Balance of the Religion Clauses, 102 Yale L.J. 1611 (1993); Uncommon Ground—A Review of *Political Liberalism* by John Rawls and *Life's Dominion* by Ronald Dworkin, 62 Geo. Wash. L. Rev. 646 (1994); Is Religion Special? A Rejoinder to Scott Idleman, 1994 U. Ill. L. Rev. 535; *Kiryas Joel* and Two Mistakes about Equality, 96 Colum. L. Rev. 1 (1996); The Irreducible Constitution, 7 San Diego J. Contemporary Legal Issues 293 (1996).

1. 393 U.S. 97 (1968).

2. See Stone v. Graham, 449 U.S. 39 (1980) (*per curiam*); Wallace v. Jaffree, 472 U.S. 38 (1985); Edwards v. Aguillard, 482 U.S. 578 (1987).

3. 403 U.S. 602 (1971).

4. See Committee for Public Educ. and Religious Liberty v. Nyquist, 413 U.S. 756 (1973) (invalidating funding); Meek v. Pittenger, 421 U.S. 349 (1975) (invalidating funding); Wolman v. Walter, 433 U.S. 229 (1977) (invalidating funding, in part, upholding funding, in part); Committee for Public Educ. and Religious Liberty v. Regan, 444 U.S. 646 (1980) (upholding funding); Mueller v. Allen, 463 U.S. 388 (1983) (upholding funding); Aguilar v. Felton, 473

U.S. 402 (1985) (invalidating funding); Grand Rapids School Dist. v. Ball, 473 U.S. 373 (1985) (invalidating funding); Witters v. Washington Dept. of Services for the Blind, 474 U.S. 481 (1986) (upholding funding).

5. Engel v. Vitale, 370 U.S. 421 (1962); Abington Township School Dist. v. Schempp, 374 U.S. 203 (1963).

6. See Abner S. Greene, The Pledge of Allegiance Problem, 64 Fordham L. Rev. 451 (1995).

7. 374 U.S. 398 (1963).

8. See Christopher L. Eisgruber and Lawrence G. Sager, The Vulnerability of Conscience: The Constitutional Basis for Protecting Religious Conduct, 61 U. Chi. L. Rev. 1245, 1277–82 (1994).

9. See also Thomas v. Review Bd., 450 U.S. 707 (1981); Hobbie v. Unemployment Appeals Comm'n, 480 U.S. 136 (1987).

10. 406 U.S. 205 (1972).

11. 521 U.S. 203 (1997). See also Zobrest v. Catalina Foothills School Dist., 509 U.S. 1 (1993).

12. 473 U.S. 402 (1985). The *Agostini* Court also overruled, in part, Grand Rapids School Dist. v. Ball, 473 U.S. 373 (1985).

13. The Court extended its school prayer holdings to the setting of a middle school commencement, invalidating a school-sponsored prayer in Lee v. Weisman, 505 U.S. 577 (1992).

14. 515 U.S. 819 (1995).

15. The Court first held that the Free Speech Clause required the university to fund religious publications if it was funding other, nonreligious publications. It then held that the Establishment Clause did not forbid such funding.

16. 494 U.S. 872 (1990).

17. See Larry Alexander, Liberalism, Religion, and the Unity of Epistemology, 30 San Diego L. Rev. 763 (1993); Stephen L. Carter, The Culture of Disbelief (1993); Jesse H. Choper, Securing Religious Liberty: Principles for Judicial Interpretation of the Religion Clauses 97–159 (1995); Eisgruber and Sager, *supra* note 9; Frederick Mark Gedicks, The Rhetoric of Church and State: A Critical Analysis of Religion Clause Jurisprudence 37, 45 (1995); Scott C. Idleman, Ideology as Interpretation: A Reply to Professor Greene's Theory of the Religion Clauses, 1994 U. Ill. L. Rev. 337; William P. Marshall, In Defense of Smith and Free Exercise Revisionism, 58 U. Chi. L. Rev. 308 (1991); Michael McConnell, The Selective Funding Problem: Abortion and Religious Schools, 104 Harv. L. Rev. 989 (1991). But see John H. Garvey, What Are Freedoms For? 42–57 (1996) (argument for the distinctiveness of religion from a believer's viewpoint).

18. 347 U.S. 483 (1954).

19. See Romer v. Evans, 517 U.S. 620 (1996) (invalidating Colorado amendment forbidding localities from extending antidiscrimination provisions to gays and lesbians; not holding that sexual orientation is subject to strict scrutiny but applying a hearty version of rational basis scrutiny, nonetheless).

20. Such a principle might have upheld affirmative action for race and required exemptions for religion, while forbidding the use of majority power to advance a favored religion or race.

21. See Christopher L. Eisgruber and Lawrence G. Sager, Congressional Power and Religious Liberty After City of Boerne v. Flores, 1997 Sup. Ct. Rev. 79, 121 (describing my argument as having the "shape of a sensible and compelling normative claim for privileging religiously motivated conduct," and expecting that defenders of religious exemptions "will repair to some version of [my] claim with increasing frequency," but maintaining that the predicate

"depends upon a view of the Establishment Clause which radically handicaps religious speech and religious participation in politics").

22. The discussion that follows represents primarily substantial edited excerpts from my article The Political Balance of the Religion Clauses, 102 Yale L.J. 1611 (1993), which are reprinted here by permission of the Yale Law Journal Company and Fred B. Rothman & Company.

23. See Luke 10:25–37.

24. Cf. Kent Greenawalt, Religious Convictions and Political Choice 63 (1988); David A. J. Richards, Toleration and the Constitution 76 (1986)

25. See Kent Greenawalt, *supra* note 24, at 216–17; see also Kent Greenawalt, Religious Convictions and Political Choice: Some Further Thoughts, 39 DePaul L. Rev. 1019, 1031 (1990) (hereinafter Greenawalt, *Further Thoughts*) ("There is . . . no interpersonal way in which the weight of personal experience is to be assessed. If a law were based largely on religious beliefs that were mainly confirmed by personal experiences, those who had not shared in the experience might understand why the law had been adopted, but to them, there would be no reasoned basis on which they would be able to conclude that the law was sound."); *id.* at 1035 ("If political argument were comprised largely of debate about the meaning of particular biblical passages, those who did not believe in the same kind of authoritativeness for biblical passages would be bound to feel excluded."); Kent Greenawalt, Private Consciences and Public Reasons 157 (1995) (hereinafter K. Greenawalt, *Private Consciences*).

26. Cf. Frederick Schauer, May Officials Think Religiously? 27 Wm. & Mary L. Rev. 1075, 1077 (1986) ("Perhaps implicit in the idea of a liberal democracy . . . is an obligation of . . . an official to rely on reasons not that necessarily are held by all of the people, but that could be held by all of the people. Religious argument, to the extent that it intrinsically appeals to and includes those who share common religious presuppositions while simultaneously excluding those who do not subscribe to certain religious tenets, may very well fail this test. Religious argument may ultimately require addressees of the argument either to disagree or to give up their religious faith, in a way that secular argument in the realm of the nonrational does not. Religious decisionmaking by an official, therefore, may be of a different order than other forms of choosing between courses of action, even on nonrational grounds, and for that reason religious decisionmaking may be inconsistent with the obligations of an official in a liberal democracy.").

27. The reasons advanced for this test vary considerably. Thus, while Steven Smith urges the test as part of an argument to permit religiously backed law, see Steven D. Smith, Separation and the "Secular": Reconstructing the Disestablishment Decision, 67 Tex. L. Rev. 955, 1004–5 (1989), Kathleen Sullivan—who builds a case against religiously backed law—urges the test to avoid the perils of inquiry into legislative motivation, see Kathleen Sullivan, Religion and Liberal Democracy, 59 U. Chi. L. Rev. 195, 197 n. 9. See also Michael J. Perry, Religion in Politics: Constitutional and Moral Perspectives 34–37 (1997).

28. The argument that the purpose of these laws is for calming down the students seems pretextual, since a general moment of silence could suffice for that. See Wallace v. Jaffree, 472 U.S. 38 (1985).

29. See, e.g., Mark Tushnet, The Limits of the Involvement of Religion in the Body Politic, in The Role of Religion in the Making of Public Policy 195, 203 (James E. Wood, Jr. & Derek Davis, eds., 1991).

30. See Greenawalt, *Further Thoughts*, *supra* note 25, at 1022 (arguing that legislators can rely on religious sources in forming their judgments, but that "[c]ivility and respect for minorities counsel that public advocacy be conducted in the nonreligious language of shared premises and modes of reasoning").

31. Cf. Webster v. Reproductive Health Servs., 492 U.S. 490, 565–72 (1989) (Stevens, J., concurring in part and dissenting in part); John Paul Stevens, The Bill of Rights: A Century of Progress, 59 U. Chi. L. Rev. 13, 30–33 (1992). In discussing Roe v. Wade, 410 U.S. 113 (1973), Laurence Tribe once suggested that the Establishment Clause should be read to invalidate legislation when "the involvement of religious groups in the political process surrounding a subject of governmental control is convincingly traceable, as it is in the case of abortion, to an intrinsic aspect of the subject itself in the intellectual and social history of the period." Laurence H. Tribe, The Supreme Court, 1972 Term—Foreword: Toward a Model of Roles in the Due Process of Life and Law, 87 Harv. L. Rev. 1, 25 (1973) (footnote omitted). Tribe has since changed his mind, stating that his prior view "appears to give too little weight to the value of allowing religious groups freely to express their convictions in the political process, underestimates the power of moral convictions unattached to religious beliefs on this issue, and makes the unrealistic assumption that a constitutional ruling could somehow disentangle religion from future public debate on the question." Laurence H. Tribe, American Constitutional Law 1350 (2d ed. 1988) (footnotes omitted); see also *id.* at 1211 (criticizing strict secular-purpose requirement).

32. Michael McConnell has made a strong argument that the "no endorsement of religion" test now fashionable among some on the Court is not a workable Establishment Clause test. See Michael W. McConnell, Religious Freedom at a Crossroads, 59 U. Chi. L. Rev. 115, 147–57 (1992). But to the extent that the test is helpful, it is because "endorsement of religion" is precisely what happens when a legislative majority relies expressly on its religious faith to ground law. Conversely, one might argue that certain laws are legitimate, even though originally based on enacting faith into law, because now most people understand the law's dominant purpose to be secular. In these cases, the original religious purpose becomes embedded, as it were, in the long-standing practice, and the secular purpose rises to dominance. See Mark V. Tushnet, Reflections on the Role of Purpose in the Jurisprudence of the Religion Clauses, 27 Wm. & Mary L. Rev. 997, 1004 (1986). This is how one can justify McGowan v. Maryland, 366 U.S. 420 (1961), in which the Court upheld laws requiring businesses to be closed on Sunday. Central to upholding state action in this category is that the practice at issue be generally perceived today as secular rather than religious. So although Michael McConnell might be correct to state that the pretty lights on Michigan Avenue in Chicago have religious significance, that "most of us do not recognize the symbolism" is the more important observation. See McConnell at 189.

33. Cf. John H. Mansfield, The Religion Clauses of the First Amendment and the Philosophy of the Constitution, 72 Cal. L. Rev. 847, 894–95 (1984).

34. This is similar to the administrative law doctrine requiring remand to an agency if it relied upon an improper reason but permitting the agency to reach the same substantive result on different grounds. See SEC v. Chenery Corp., 318 U.S. 80 (1943).

35. For other formulations, see Edwards v. Aguillard, 482 U.S. 578, 590–91 (1987) (finding legislation invalid if backed by "preeminent religious purpose"); *id.* at 599 (Powell, J., concurring) (observing that "religious purpose must predominate" for legislation to be invalid).

36. 393 U.S. 97 (1968).

37. *Id.* at 107–08.

38. 449 U.S. 39 (1980) (*per curiam*).

39. *Id.* at 41.

40. *Id.*

41. 472 U.S. 38 (1985).

42. *Id.* at 56.

43. 482 U.S. 578 (1987).

44. *Id.* at 590–91.

45. For a discussion of this example and a rejection of the position I take, see Alexander, *supra* note 17, at 769 (1993). For a response to Alexander focusing on the unique character of religious revelation, see K. Greenawalt, *Private Consciences, supra* note 26, at 46–50; Kent Greenawalt, Grounds for Political Judgment: The Status of Personal Experience and the Autonomy and Generality of Principles of Restraint, 30 San Diego L. Rev. 647, 656–60 (1993).

46. Perhaps we should ideally distinguish between, on the one hand, religious faith based in revelation and other sorts of "personal" experiences and, on the other hand, religious faith based in evidence that can be assessed by others, in the way that evidence is ordinarily assessed. But it is hard to disentangle faith based on "leaps" and faith based on sharable evidential tracings. Furthermore, for many people, both nonbelievers and believers, religious faith connotes a leap from hard evidence. Cf. K. Greenawalt, *Private Consciences, supra* note 25, at 102.

47. I do not mean to say, as Scott Idleman suggests (see Scott C. Idleman, Ideology as Interpretation: A Reply to Professor Greene's Theory of the Religion Clauses, 1994 U. Ill. L. Rev. 337, 348), that religion is never based in some way on human experience. What matters to the accessibility discussion is the singular way in which religious arguments depart from intrahuman experience and claim a relationship with an extrahuman source of value.

48. The previous two paragraphs represent material edited from my article Is Religion Special? A Rejoinder to Scott Idleman, 1994 U. Ill. L. Rev. 535, 540.

49. But see M. Perry, *supra* note 27, at 51.

50. See Philip B. Kurland, Of Church and State and the Supreme Court, 29 U. Chi. L. Rev. 1, 7 (1961); William P. Marshall, In Defense of *Smith* and Free Exercise Revisionism, 58 U. Chi. L. Rev. 308, 326 (1991); William P. Marshall, The Case Against the Constitutionally Compelled Free Exercise Exemption, 7 J. L. & Religion 363, 397 (1989). But see Douglas Laycock, The Remnants of Free Exercise, 1990 Sup. Ct. Rev. 11, 13.

51. See United States v. Carolene Prods. Co., 304 U.S. 144, 152 n. 4 (1938).

52. For an extensive elaboration on these themes, see John Hart Ely, Democracy and Distrust (1980).

53. Although there might be no plaintiff with standing sufficient to challenge such a law, I am assuming that legislators will act pursuant to proper constitutional norms and that the Establishment Clause argument made above is a proper constitutional norm.

54. 393 U.S. 97 (1968).

55. But see Justice Black's concurrence, arguing that the state might have banned the teaching of evolution to remove a controversial subject from the schools. *Id.* at 112.

56. Here and in the examples that follow, the right to exemption is only prima facie and might be outweighed by other interests. I do not address how the balance between governmental and individual interests should be struck.

57. Cf. Mozert v. Hawkins County Pub. Schools, 647 F.Supp. 1194 (E.D.Tenn.1986), rev'd and remanded, 827 F.2d 1058 (6th Cir.1987), cert. denied, 484 U.S. 1066 (1988).

58. 410 U.S. 113 (1973).

59. 505 U.S. 833 (1992).

60. Cf. Thornton v. Caldor, Inc., 472 U.S. 703 (1985).

61. Cf. Hobbie v. Unemployment Appeals Comm'n, 480 U.S. 136 (1987); Thomas v. Review Bd., 450 U.S. 707 (1981); Sherbert v. Verner, 374 U.S. 398 (1963).

62. See Douglas Laycock, Formal, Substantive, and Disaggregated Neutrality Toward Religion, 39 DePaul L. Rev. 993, 1014 (1990); Michael W. McConnell, Free Exercise Revisionism

and the *Smith* Decision, 57 U. Chi. L. Rev. 1109, 1130–36 (1990); Stephen Pepper, A Brief for the Free Exercise Clause, 7 J. L. & Religion 323, 353 (1989); Sullivan, *supra* note 28, at 216.

63. See Washington v. Davis, 426 U.S. 229 (1976).

64. John Garvey has argued that religion is somewhat like insanity, for in both cases we exempt someone from legal obligations because of the inaccessibility to others of the agent's reasons for action and because of the special compulsion felt by the agent in acting contrary to law. See John H. Garvey, Free Exercise and the Values of Religious Liberty, 18 Conn. L. Rev. 779, 798–801 (1986). We exempt the insane from legal obligation, however, not because we wish to protect their private values but, rather, in spite of the fact that we wish their private values (i.e., their insanity) would go away.

65. See Stanley Fish, Mission Impossible: Settling the Just Bounds Between Church and State, 97 Colum. L. Rev. 2255, 2262–63 (1997).

66. Fish does not support this position, agreeing instead with Larry Alexander and others when he writes, "Epistemology-wise . . ., the vocabularies and premises of science, religion, liberal humanism, communitarianism, etc., are on a par, each one an orthodoxy to itself." *Id.* at 2307.

67. Parts of this paragraph were drawn from my article Uncommon Ground—A Review of *Political Liberalism* by John Rawls and *Life's Dominion* by Ronald Dworkin, 62 Geo. Wash. L. Rev. 646, 673 (1994).

Chapter 13

Questioning the Value of Accommodating Religion

Mark V. Tushnet

Sometimes legal scholars make major contributions by showing us how to look at familiar problems differently. Michael McConnell's great article on accommodation of religion is such a contribution.[1] McConnell explained how an apparently disparate group of problems actually presented the courts with a single analytic question: Whether the legislation at issue was a constitutionally permissible form of accommodating the needs of religious believers and the demands of the regulatory state. It is a measure of McConnell's achievement that he wrote just after the Court grappled with *Thornton v. Caldor, Inc.*[2] There the justices were puzzled about the analytic framework in which to place the problem posed by a statute that required employers to give the Sabbath off to any employee. Chief Justice Burger saw that *Thornton* presented a novel issue, but his grasp on the problem was sufficiently unsure that he could not persuade his colleagues that the issue's novelty justified a distinctive analytic approach.[3] Today, in contrast, we can easily see that *Thornton* is a standard accommodation-of-religion case.

McConnell's initial analysis did not, however, clearly distinguish among several variants of the accommodation problem.[4] McConnell stressed the importance of the constitutionally *mandatory* accommodation.[5] The problem of mandatory accommodation arises when the state enacts a general regulation that adversely affects the practices of some religious believers. The believers argue that the regulation impairs the free exercise of their religion, and that the Constitution therefore *requires* that they be given an exemption from compliance with the regulation.[6]

A second version of mandatory accommodation has recently emerged. The problem is easier to see in the context of state programs granting assistance to a range of groups, but it occurs in the regulatory context as well. *Rosenberger v. Board of Rectors of the University of Virginia* involved a program at a state university in which student fees were distributed to support a range of student activities, from which religious publications were excluded.[7] The Supreme Court held that this exclusion violated the free speech provision of the First Amendment because it denied a benefit to religious groups on the basis of the viewpoints—religious—they held. A similar problem would arise were a state to enact a program authorizing parents to use public funds, in the form of vouchers, to pay tuition at nonpublic schools but refused to allow vouchers for tuition at religiously affiliated schools.

These are problems of equality, and they can arise in connection with regulatory programs as well. No regulatory program is in fact comprehensive in scope; all contain some exemptions. And, once some are exempted from compliance with the regulation, the way is open to develop religious equality arguments supporting the exemption of those with religious beliefs as well. The existence of some exemptions shows that the state's regulatory goals can be served by a less-than-comprehensive program. That allows advocates for religious accommodation to argue that the marginal impairment of the state's regulatory goals occasioned by an accommodation of religion would not be significantly greater than the impairment the state has already chosen to accept through its existing exemptions.

The final variant is the constitutionally *permissible* accommodation of religion. This occurs when the legislature enacts a regulatory program and specifically *exempts* religious believers from its scope, or in some other way grants relief to those with religious beliefs that is not available to those with other beliefs. For example, those who had conscientious religiously based objections to war in any form were exempted from compulsory service in the armed forces while those who had equally conscientious but nonreligious objections to war in any form were not.[8] *Thornton* involved a statute requiring employers to give employees their Sabbath off but did not require them to give an equivalent number of days off to nonreligious employees. Mandatory accommodations raise questions of free exercise and equality. The constitutional question about permissible accommodations is precisely whether they *are* permissible, that is, whether they violate the nonestablishment clause.

The core of the current law of accommodation of religion is fairly easy to identify, although like all bodies of law, as one examines it in detail, lines that seemed clear at first begin to blur. Under the Supreme Court's peyote decision, the Constitution rarely *requires* the government to adjust its general regulatory programs to take account of the programs' impact on religious belief and practice.[9] The government may not devise a regulatory program that purports to be general but is actually targeted on religion alone,[10] but otherwise the government is free to regulate.

The Court did identify some exceptions, which have some generative potential. Sometimes, the Court suggested, regulations that would not violate the free exercise clause itself might nonetheless infringe on some *other* constitutional right. The Court suggested that it would require the government to accommodate these hybrid claims. This exception to the general nonaccommodation rule is somewhat puzzling. If the regulation directly violated the *other* constitutional right, we would not need the free exercise interest as part of the reason for invalidating the regulation. And if the regulation did not violate the free exercise clause standing alone, and did not violate the other constitutional right standing alone, it is not obvious how two invalid constitutional claims somehow combine to make one valid one. But if the "hybrid claims" exception is taken seriously, it has real potential to undermine the general nonaccommodation rule. In virtually every case a careful litigant can identify another constitutional claim that rides along with the free exercise one: most obviously, free speech claims, but occasionally substantive due process claims as well. For example, one case widely held up as demonstrating why the peyote decision was wrong allowed the government to override a religiously based objection to an autopsy for which there were no apparent medical or investigative reasons.[11] After the peyote decision, litigators could make a hybrid claim here, blending the free exercise claim with a substantive due process claim about the right of families to make fundamental decisions for or about their members.

A good example of the problems posed by the idea of hybrid constitutional rights is a decision by the United States Court of Appeals for the Ninth Circuit.[12] An Alaska statute and a city ordinance barred discrimination in housing on the basis of marital status. Enforcement officials threatened to sue landlords who refused to rent an apartment to an unmarried couple because to do so would violate the landlords' religious beliefs. The court of appeals found that the landlords had raised a hybrid claim that combined the free exercise issue with a claim that the regulations infringed on the landlords' right to exclude people from their property, a right protected (in some sense) by the Fourteenth Amendment's guarantee that property not be taken without due process of law. The difficulty is that an antidiscrimination law does not by itself violate a landlord's property rights; otherwise *every* landlord, not just religious ones, could object to antidiscrimination statutes. The court of appeals adopted a peculiar analysis in which the landlords did not have to have a *valid* constitutional claim, whether it be a free exercise or property-based one, to trigger a high level of scrutiny. Instead, the court of appeals said, a hybrid claim could be made out if the landlords could make a "colorable" claim that the antidiscrimination statute violated their property rights, by which it meant that the landlords had to show that they had a "fair probability" of succeeding on the property right claim. This is decidedly odd, because, after all, it is the court of appeals itself that *could* decide not just whether the landlords had a "fair probability" of succeeding but whether they actually *would* succeed. If they succeeded in establishing a violation of their property rights, they would not need to show anything about the free exercise claim. And if they failed to show a violation of their property rights, it is hardly obvious why the fact that they *might have* (but did not) won adds any weight to their religious claim.

Most readers of the peyote decision think the Court was not entirely serious about the exception for hybrid claims, believing that the Court devised the exception so that it would not have to overrule the widely admired *Yoder* decision.[13] And it seems more likely that the justices will revisit the peyote decision and overrule it than that they will try to expand the exceptions embedded in the decision.[14]

These points apply as well to the Court's other exception in the peyote case. Attempting to salvage a line of decisions in which the Court required workers' compensation systems to accommodate their rules to religious beliefs that kept workers out of work, the Court said that the government might have to accommodate religion when it had in place a system for determining, on a case-by-case basis, whether a person ought to be relieved of the otherwise applicable regulatory burden. Again the rationale for this exception is unclear. One possibility is that the government might be found to discriminate against religion if it provided relief to individuals making some kinds of claims but not to those making religiously based ones. Another is that antireligious gerrymandering might be at work if the government refused to allow people to obtain relief by using a procedure already in place for case-by-case decisions. The existence of such a procedure means that using it to grant religious exemptions would not increase the government's administrative costs substantially. It would, however, increase the overall *social* cost of the program by limiting its effective scope, and so it is not clear why the mere existence of a procedure for case-by-case decisions should matter at all.

Again, this exception may in fact have little real content. But it does connect the Court's stated rule against mandatory accommodations to its position on equality-based accommodation claims. Such claims can come in two forms. First, the claimant may point out that the government provides categorical exemptions from regulation, or provides benefits to broad categories of people, but does not include religion as one of the protected or preferred categories. Sometimes, the Court has said, this constitutes unconstitutional discrimination against religion, at least where religion is excluded from the protected or preferred categories because of the religious views that define the category.[15] Second, the claimant may point out that the government is making decisions on a case-by-case basis. Two arguments then become available. First, the claimant may argue that in his or her particular case the government refused the exemption or denied the benefit for impermissible viewpoint-based reasons.[16] Second, and perhaps more interesting, the claimant may argue that the very fact that the government has in place a procedure for case-by-case determinations means that it must provide a categorical exemption for religious belief and practice.

Current constitutional law, then, appears to be hostile to the pure version of mandatory accommodations, albeit with exceptions that have some growth possibility, and to be moderately receptive to the equality-based version of mandatory accommodations. It is similarly moderately receptive to permissible accommodations. Here the doctrinal structure remains unclear, largely because the Court has confronted the question only rarely. The Court's holding in *Thornton* can best be understood on the theory that *broad* legislative accommodations of religion are impermissible. The Court invalidated the requirement that employers make an employee's Sabbath a day off in large part because the requirement failed to take into account the burden the statute placed on employers and other employees. There is some indication, too, that *narrow* legislative accommodations are impermissible. The Court struck down an exemption from sales taxes of religious books, including the Bible,[17] but it upheld the property-tax exemption available to religious institutions as part of a broader category of tax-exempt nonprofit organizations.[18] The distinction appears to be that the property-tax exemption went to churches as part of a sufficiently large group of which they were only a subgroup, while the sales-tax exemption went only to religious publications.

Kiryas Joel v. Grumet may also be a case involving a too-narrow accommodation.[19] Residents of the Village of Kiryas Joel were nearly all members of a Jewish sect, the Satmar Hasidim. For religious reasons, they objected to educating their children in gender-integrated settings. They operated private schools for most of their children but concluded that it would be too expensive to provide special education equivalent to what was available in public schools. After finding efforts to place their children in the existing special education classes at public schools unacceptable, the community persuaded the New York legislature to enact a statute creating a school district for Kiryas Joel. The Supreme Court invalidated this statute. One might try to understand this case too as one involving an excessively narrow accommodation. Narrowness might matter because it is too reminiscent of the sect favoritism that is at the heart of all contemporary understandings of the practices against which the nonestablishment clause is directed. And broad accommodations would be troubling, perhaps, because they might be the way in which a majority religion employed government power to advance its interests, again in contravention to the central idea of the nonestablishment clause.

I doubt, however, that this is satisfactory. There are quite a few narrow legislative accommodations that have never been seriously questioned, although they have rarely come to the courts' attention in postures that make it likely that the courts will think seriously about the constitutional questions involved. Congress has enacted a statute authorizing religious believers to wear headgear that does not conform to the military's general rules, and the statute is written in a way that benefits only Jews who must wear yarmulkes (and perhaps a handful of others).[20] There is an odd provision in the federal tax code using general terms to exempt certain groups from some tax obligations, and the terms are such that the exemption is available to a single denomination.[21] And, finally, there are many statutes exempting from the general criminal statutes the use of peyote in the religious ceremonials of the Native American Church.

How can these statutes be permissible accommodations while the statute in *Kiryas Joel* is not? Justice Scalia's dissent in *Kiryas Joel* identified the reason, I believe, and his argument provides the transition to the critique of accommodations of religion, both mandatory and permissible, that I develop in the remainder of this essay. According to Justice Scalia, the Court's invalidation rested on the majority's sense, which never quite reached direct expression, that the statute resulted from the exercise of "excessive" political power by the denomination's adherents.[22] The accommodations that have gone unquestioned, in contrast, might seem to be benign, even benevolent exercises of the majority's power—or, perhaps more precisely, benevolent decisions by the majority to forgo exercising the power it unquestionably has.

The seeming benevolence of accommodations of religions is precisely what I wish to question here.[23] One central theme runs through the argument that follows: The state's seeming benevolence in awarding accommodations of religion, either through its legislature or its courts, is ultimately not in the interests of religion. This theme can be traced back to Roger Williams, for whom separation of church and state was important not to protect the state from religion, as Thomas Jefferson thought, but to protect religion from the state. Sometimes those taking Williams's position asserted that religion could accept "favoring tributes" from the state, which is in some tension with the view I present in this essay,[24] but I follow Williams's more general perception that even seemingly benign government actions threaten religion.[25]

These threats come in various forms. Some accommodations present only one type of threat; others present several. And not all the threats are always of large significance in particular settings. But in the aggregate, across all accommodations and all settings, the threat to religion posed by accommodations of religion are, I believe, substantial enough to make the value of accommodations of religion highly doubtful from the point of view of religion itself.

1. The problem of strings. Perhaps the most obvious problem is that accommodations do not usually come free. Most have strings attached, sometimes obviously and sometimes less so. An obvious string is an explicit condition on obtaining the accommodation. Consider the argument that legislatures should be allowed to accommodate religious believers' decisions to send their children to religiously affiliated schools by providing public aid in the form of teachers of remedial education. The Supreme Court upheld such an accommodation in 1997.[26] But the remedial assistance was provided according to a set of rules, one of which required that all religious symbols be removed from the classrooms in which the public school teachers conducted the remedial education classes.[27] Other similar accommodationist programs will have other strings; voucher programs, for example, will require that educational programs satisfy state-prescribed curricula, or that teachers satisfy state licensing requirements. These strings will sometimes themselves pose problems for believers, as when the prescribed curriculum in biology requires instruction about the Darwinian theory of human evolution. What is for some an attractive accommodation will be for others an imposition of the state on religious belief.

One might respond that those who find the accommodation unattractive because of the strings attached need not accept its benefits. Sometimes this will be an acceptable response, but not always, because it ignores the less-than-conscious ways in which religious belief can be altered (and religion thereby threatened). Here we can consider the less obvious strings attached to accommodations. These come in the form of the definitions of the activities or beliefs entitled to the accommodation. So, for example, draft exemptions were available to those who had religious grounds for opposing war in any form, but not to those who had equally religious grounds for opposing particular wars. Such accommodations offer subtle inducements to cut one's beliefs to fit the qualifying conditions. Similarly with the more obvious strings. True, one can decline to accept the accommodation if one finds the strings unattractive, but one has to be willing consciously to forgo the benefit. It would hardly be surprising to discover that some people changed their beliefs in ways that made it possible for them to live with the strings.[28]

Not that religion is threatened by change in itself. The selective conscientious objector may be no less religious than the comprehensive objector. And, perhaps more dramatically, the modern Church of Latter-Day Saints is just as religious as the original one, even though the modern one no longer has a commitment to polygamy because it abandoned that commitment at a time when it faced enormous pressures from the United States government. But the manner in which the church changed its commitments is crucial. The church abandoned its commitment to polygamy as a result of a new revelation, which was the means sanctioned by the religion itself for changes in core beliefs. That is, religious change occurred for *religious* reasons, in the manner the religion itself acknowledged as correct, and not for *instrumental* reasons.[29] The threat to religion comes not from change but from change for the wrong reasons. Religion has suffered a severe blow when it, or when a religious person, changes beliefs because, at a level below consciousness, the change is induced by the availability of an accommodation with strings.

2. The problem of religious discrimination in the guise of accommodation. Accommodations may threaten the religions that accept them. They may also threaten other religions. Here the second type of string—the restriction of accommodations to those religions that satisfy state-prescribed criteria—is the more important one. Such criteria draw lines between religions that qualify for accommodations and those that do not. The latter become the unaccommodated, and implicitly deprecated, Other.

We can see this in some of the Supreme Court's most important proaccommodation decisions. Explaining why the Constitution required Wisconsin to accommodate the religiously motivated opposition of the Old Order Amish to formal schooling beyond the age of sixteen, Chief Justice Warren Burger counterposed the Amish to "group[s] claiming to have recently discovered some 'progressive' or more enlightened process for readying children for modern life."[30] But this is to say that adherents of New Age religions making exactly the same claim for accommodation that the Old Order Amish did might not receive it because New Age religions are understood in pejorative terms. And, dissenting from the Court's peyote decision, Justice Harry Blackmun was almost explicit in saying that he would not require an accommodation for the religious use of marijuana by Rastafarians.[31]

One might think that the New Agers or the Rastafarians would have an equality claim for accommodation. And some religions indeed might. It is hardly obvious, for example, why the mere age of the Old Order Amish denomination shows that the government's interests in promoting education are not substantial enough to overcome the religious claims. Chief Justice Burger suggested that it was not age in itself but the long experience the Amish had in producing succeeding generations of people who made valuable contributions to the wider society that explained why the accommodation was consistent with general public values. New Agers might be unable to make *that* showing. But some of them might point out that their religious beliefs place in question the value society today places on the matters that Chief Justice Burger thought important. Denying an accommodation to New Agers because their children will not be corporate executives or even operators of small farms, when the New Age belief may be that corporate existence and farming in capitalist society do not satisfy the spirit's demands, is to discriminate against religion, not in defining the category of those eligible for accommodation but in identifying the reasons for which accommodations may be denied.

Creating an unaccommodated other religion is inevitable in the law of accommodations. The only real question is whether accommodations for some religions can be sustained without deprecating the religious commitments of religions that do not receive accommodations. In part this is a question about rhetoric. I suppose that it is possible in theory for a decision maker to grant an accommodation to some religions but not to others without thinking that the ones receiving the accommodation are somehow better than the others, but I think it unlikely to occur in practice. Chief

Justice Burger's pejorative language is not, I think, an idiosyncrasy or an accident. The reason is that those granting accommodations almost necessarily think of themselves as acting benignly toward religion, and therefore as being generally humane and responsible people. And how, they are likely to think, could such persons act with hostility toward any real religion? Religions outside the scope of the accommodation must be unworthy, for otherwise the decision maker's humane instincts would lead him or her to make them eligible for the accommodation.[32] The law of accommodations, that is, is likely to be systematically discriminatory in a troubling way. Religions that are deviant in some statistical sense may receive accommodations, but only if they are not too far from the mainstream.

3. The problem of self-satisfaction. Focusing on the psychology of the decision maker who grants accommodations suggests another danger. One of the most dramatic facts about the law of mandatory accommodations before the Court cut it back in the peyote decision was how rarely they were given.[33] On the high level of articulated law, the Constitution generously accommodated deviant religious belief by requiring legislatures to exempt religion from the coverage of its statutes. But on the low level of everyday life, the Constitution allowed all sorts of intrusions on religious practice. Such a discrepancy signals that the articulated law is promoting ends other than the protection of religion that it nominally seeks to promote. I believe that the real end served by a law of accommodation is the self-justification of decision makers who in fact do much damage to religion even as they accommodate some religious groups.

For me, Justice Sandra Day O'Connor's opinion in the peyote case is exemplary. She vigorously criticized the Court for abandoning its previous doctrine according to which accommodations were constitutionally required unless the government could show that a regime without exemptions was the most narrowly tailored method of accomplishing compelling government interests. But, she concluded, applying that stringent test would nonetheless show that the state could make the use of peyote in religious ceremonies a crime. The doctrine she invoked allowed her to present herself as a humane person concerned about the religious harms legislatures can unthinkingly inflict on nonmajority religions, while at the same time it allowed her to inflict exactly that harm. And, to some extent, the harm she inflicts is worse than the one inflicted by the state legislature. The legislature, after all, probably really was unthinking. It probably had not had the problem of the use of peyote in religious ceremonies in mind when it enacted its general laws against drug use, and so it probably did not know that its laws would inflict religious harm. Justice O'Connor, in contrast, knew exactly what she was doing.

Governments *will* harm religion. Accommodationist doctrines provide the opportunity for people to overlook that fact. Mandatory accommodations do mean that a government that enacts laws that harm religion without meaning to may do less harm than occurs without mandatory accommodations. But a strict rule against accommodations may produce less actual harm to religion. Without the possibility of accommodating *any* religion, legislatures may be more careful about the laws they do enact. And even when harm does occur, accommodationist doctrines allow decision makers to conceal from themselves the fact that they have done so, and perhaps done so unnecessarily. The antiaccommodationist position ensures that we will see the blood on the hands of governments that harm religion—as they will.

4. The problem of disappointment. The fact that governments will harm religion means that accommodations cause another type of harm to religions that receive them. The harm is disappointment—not while the religions receive them but when they are sought and denied, or when they are withdrawn. No matter how religion-friendly the test is for deciding when to accommodate religion, it will inevitably have some limits. Some religious practices will simply be outside the scope of what any government will regard as the reasonable, and the government will conclude that its interests override the religious interests implicated in other practices even though it regards the practices as reasonable. For U.S. constitutional law, human sacrifice is the obvious example in the former category, and the handling of poisonous snakes may be another. Once again, Justice O'Connor's position in the peyote case exemplifies the latter category. More interesting are the rather routine cases in which government interests in historic preservation are described as sufficiently important as to override a church's interest in altering its building so that it can perform its religious functions more effectively.[34] In such cases the government interest rarely seems that important to outsiders, although people close to the situation are likely to see things differently. Neighbors who get a city to enforce zoning regulations against churches that provide too few parking spaces are likely to feel rather strongly about the disruptions the church's presence imposes on them, even as outsiders see the problems as the ordinary parking problems attendant on modern life.

Of course not all religions will always test the limits of what government will accommodate, and some religions will rarely do so. But at least in theory all religions are potentially at odds with government's demands. Mainline religious groups, for example, played an important role in the sanctuary movement sheltering refugees from Central American political violence in a manner the government contended was a breach of national immigration laws.[35] Having lived in a society whose government accommodated some or many of their beliefs, some religious believers will be disappointed when they discover that the government's willingness to accommodate religion has its limits.

This disappointment, however, may not be a harm *to religion*. Clearly, it may make believers disaffected from government, but that is a harm to government. Failures to accommodate may harm religion indirectly, though, if believers disappointed with the government transfer their disaffection to the religions. People receive normative communications from many institutions, including both their religions and their governments. A governmental refusal to accommodate might be taken by some believers to establish that their religion's practices are not truly valuable. They might then either fall away from the religion, or agitate for changes in the religious practices so that the government would be able to accommodate the new practices. Once again, one cannot quarrel with the fact of religious change, but the mechanism of change is important. Changes induced by a desire to gain government's approval through accommodations are different from changes made in accordance with the religion's own criteria, be they reason or revelation.

I have argued that accommodations may harm religion by inducing change in religious belief for instrumental rather than religious reasons, by unavoidably discriminating among religions, by concealing the harms that government inflicts on religion, and by systematically disappointing those who think the government should accommodate religious belief. These are, in a sense, practical concerns about accommodationist doctrines. There are also what I believe are theological concerns.

The first of these is that the possibility of accommodating religion places religious believers in the position of supplicants to the state. They may approach legislators or executive decision makers to plead the case for a permissible exemption. If that fails they may approach judges pleading for a mandatory accommodation. I find this psychologically distasteful; if one should be on bended knee before someone, it is surely not the state. Further, on some views of the relation among people, the sovereign state, and the Sovereign, people should be supplicants only before the Sovereign of all. In other terms, the possibility of accommodations can lead religious believers to think, erroneously, that the sovereign state has jurisdiction over their religious beliefs and practices. In truth, on this view, the state lacks jurisdiction entirely in this area.

The notion of jurisdiction underlies the second, and more obviously theological, concern about accommodations of religion. The idea that government must or may accommodate religion might be taken as an implicit concession that government and religion operate in the same domain, and that what needs to be done is to carve up that domain in a way that respects the interests of both. But, it might be thought, religion and government operate in entirely different domains, which have no points of contact except insofar as religion and governments both act on and through people. Where the law allows for accommodations of religion, religious people facing governmental pressure on their beliefs and practices may seek to relieve that pressure by seeking an accommodation. But that acknowledges that government has *some* proper role in regulating religious practices. And religion may be harmed by making that concession.

On this view, perhaps religious people can accept accommodations that the government freely offers, but they ought not *seek* accommodations. Unfortunately, the difference between accepting and seeking accommodations is hard to maintain. Consider *Corporation of Presiding Bishop v. Amos*, the Supreme Court's leading case on permissible accommodations of religion.[36] Federal civil rights law makes it illegal to discriminate in employment on the basis of religion, but it contains an exemption that allows religious institutions to discriminate in connection with their core religious activities. In *Amos*, the church owned and operated a nonprofit gymnasium, and it imposed a religious qualification for employment there. One important issue in the case was whether the statutory exemption applied to the nonprofit but not obviously religious activities of churches, such as the gymnasium operation. The Supreme Court held that the exemption did apply to the gymnasium, and was constitutionally permissible.

The question of interest to the present discussion is this: in urging that the statute should be interpreted to cover the gymnasium's operation, was the church accepting a freely offered accommodation or was it seeking one? On one interpretation, the church was saying that Congress had *already* accommodated religion, but on another it was asking the courts, themselves arms of the government, to provide the accommodation.

Amos shows how difficult it is to live practically with a religiously based view that accommodations can be accepted but ought not be sought. And yet that may be precisely the point. Look at the problem first from the government's side. Initially, it adopts a law that has an adverse impact on some religious practices. The government is then faced with a choice when that adverse impact is brought to its attention: it can go on as it has, thereby continuing a regime that oppresses religion in practice, or it can change in light of its own difficulties living as an oppressor. It is not obviously bad to put governments to that choice. Now look at the problem from religion's side. The religion can accept whatever accommodations the government offers. But suppose government does not attempt to accommodate religion. Believers then have their own choices to make. They can reflect on the fact of oppression, from within their religious tradition, and perhaps conclude that the practice causing oppression is not something they are religiously required to continue. I take this to be the story of the abandonment of religious commitment to polygamy by the Church of the Latter Day Saints; under circumstances of oppression, the church's leader had a revelation, the kind of experience that the religion recognized as authoritative, that polygamy should be relinquished. Or they can conclude that the oppressive government is of *this* world but not of *their* world, and move on. I take this to be the story of such denominations as the Mennonites, who historically have maintained their beliefs rigidly and have relocated to other territory when they encountered governments unwilling to offer accommodations.

Despite what initially appear to be attractive features, doctrines requiring or allowing accommodations of religion pose real dangers to religion. Perhaps the law ought to allow the state to offer accommodations of religion. But the threats such accommodations pose are, in my view, so serious that we should be extremely skeptical about any legal doctrines requiring accommodations of religion, and only slightly less skeptical about doctrines allowing them to be offered. In the end, however, the benefits of doctrines of accommodation to nonreligious people are large enough that we can expect them to be a permanent part of the law. So, under the guise of protecting religion by accommodating it, the state may continue to undermine religion.

NOTES

1. Michael McConnell, *Accommodation of Religion*, 1985 S.CT. REV. 1.
2. 472 U.S. 703 (1985).
3. The internal Court deliberations are revealed in the Thurgood Marshall Papers, Manuscript Division, Library of Congress, box 363, file 10. For a brief discussion, see Mark V. Tushnet, Making Constitutional Law: Thurgood Marshall and the Supreme Court, 1961–1991, at 40 (1997).
4. Perhaps immodestly, I believe that my article *The Emerging Doctrine of Accommodation of Religion (Dubitante)*, 76 GEO. L.J. 1691 (1988), was the first to introduce the major necessary refinement.

5. I believe he did so for reasons associated with his role as an important and impressive advocate on behalf of religious groups seeking accommodations of their belief.

6. This formulation does not address the standard for determining *when* an accommodation is mandatory. For example, few advocates of mandatory accommodations contend that they are required even if the burden on religious exercise is insubstantial though real.

7. 515 U.S. 819 (1995).

8. The Supreme Court interpreted *religion* in the draft statutes so broadly that there were few people with nonreligious conscientious objections, particularly because the Court also denied exemption to those with conscientious religious objections to particular wars. *See* United States v. Seeger, 380 U.S. 163 (1965); Welsh v. United States, 398 U.S. 333 (1970); Gillette v. United States, 401 U.S. 437 (1971).

9. Employment Division, Department of Human Resources v. Smith, 494 U.S. 872 (1990).

10. Church of Lukumi Babalu Aye, Inc. v. Hialeah, 518 U.S. 520 (1993).

11. Yang v. Sturner, 750 F. Supp. 558 (D. R.I. 1990), *cited in* City of Boerne v. Flores, 117 S.Ct. 2157, 2177 (1997) (O'Connor, J., dissenting).

12. Thomas v. Anchorage Equal Rights Comm'n, 165 F.3d 692 (9th Cir. 1999).

13. 406 U.S. 205 (1972), discussed critically below.

14. In *City of Boerne v. Flores*, 521 U.S. 507 (1997), for example, four justices indicated their willingness, and in some instances desire, to overrule the peyote decision.

15. Rosenberger, 515 U.S. 819 (1995).

16. National Endowment for the Arts v. Finley, 118 S.Ct. 2168 (1998).

17. Texas Monthly, Inc. v. Bullock, 489 U.S. 1 (1989).

18. Walz v. Tax Commission, 397 U.S. 664 (1970).

19. Board of Education of Kiryas Joel Village School District v. Grumet, 512 U.S. 687 (1994).

20. 45 U.S.C. § 774 ("[A] member of the armed forces may wear an item of religious apparel while wearing the uniform of the member's armed forces [unless] the wearing of the item would interfere with the performance of the member's military duties [or] the item of apparel is not neat and conservative.").

21. 26 U.S.C. § 1402 (g) (exempting from the Social Security self-employment tax people with certain religious objections, provided that the religion to which the person adheres "has been in existence at all times since December 31, 1950").

22. In Justice Scalia's words,

> The Court today finds that the Powers That Be, up in Albany, have conspired to effect an establishment of the Satmar Hasidim. I do not know who would be more surprised at this discovery: the Founders of our Nation or Grand Rebbe Joel Teitelbaum, founder of the Satmar. The Grand Rebbe would be astounded to learn that after escaping brutal persecution and coming to America with the modest hope of religious toleration for their ascetic form of Judaism, the Satmar had become so powerful, so closely allied with Mammon, as to have become an "establishment" of the Empire State.

512 U.S. at 732 (Scalia, J., dissenting).

23. I draw on my previously published work here, which includes *The Rhetoric of Free Exercise Discourse*, 1993 BYU L. REV. 117; *The Underside of Mandatory Accommodations of Religion*, 26 CAP. U. L. REV. 1 (1997); *Will Context-Dependent Balancing Do the Job We Want Done?*, 31 CONN. L. REV. 861 (1999); and Comment, CAL. L. REV. (forthcoming).

24. The term *favoring tributes* comes from MARK DeWOLFE HOWE, THE GARDEN AND THE WILDERNESS 11 (1965) (asserting that "[t]he evangelical tradition of separation endorsed a host of favoring tributes to faith," and associating Roger Williams with that tradi-

tion). The tension might be resolved or lessened by noting that the threat to religion from "favoring tributes" is smaller when they are voluntarily proffered to religion by the government rather than sought by religion. *See* Comment, *supra* note C. Still, drawing the line between accepting and seeking accommodations is quite difficult (for example, does a church accept or seek an accommodation when it argues that a statute already on the books ought to be interpreted to provide it with an accommodation?), and the temptation to seek accommodations is likely to be strong.

25. For a recent overview of Williams's thought, see TIMOTHY HALL, SEPARATING CHURCH AND STATE: ROGER WILLIAMS AND RELIGIOUS LIBERTY (1998). It is perhaps worth noting that similar arguments have arisen in other contexts.

26. Agostini v. Felton, 117 S.Ct. 1997 (1997).

27. This particular requirement might be challenged as an unconstitutional condition on the receipt of public assistance, but I am not confident that such a challenge would succeed, partly because the law of unconstitutional conditions is notoriously uncertain and partly because the Court was so sharply divided on the merits in *Agostini* that modifications in the program might shift it across the line into unconstitutionality.

28. There may be more subtle forms of belief change. The process of thinking about whether to accept a proffered accommodation may change a religious institution, for example by introducing a new source of internal discord or by diverting resources from other religious activities such as pastoral counseling.

29. I do not rule out the possibility that there may be religions in which instrumental reasons count as religious ones, but my sense is that the category has few if any members.

30. 406 U.S. at 235.

31. 494 U.S. at 918 (Blackmun, J., dissenting) (asserting that an accommodation for religious uses of marijuana would "seriously compromis[e] law enforcement efforts").

32. I suspect, though I cannot prove, that underlying the judicial resistance to accommodating Rastafarian beliefs is a sense that the Rastafarians are invoking religion as a facade to conceal their hedonistic desire to get high.

33. For a brief review of the studies, showing success rates between 12 and 23 percent, see *Rhetoric of Free Exercise Discourse*, supra note 23, at 121–22.

34. This was the underlying issue in the Supreme Court's RFRA case, *City of Boerne v. Flores*, 521 U.S. 507 (1997). As with many such cases, the parties ultimately negotiated a resolution that allowed some modification of the building while allowing the city to promote its historic district in a manner the city thought adequate.

35. *See* United States v. Aguilar, 883 F.2d 662 (9th Cir. 1989) (describing activities of the sanctuary movement, including sheltering aliens at Presbyterian and Lutheran churches).

36. 483 U.S. 327 (1987).

Part IV

Outsider Views of the Separation of Church and State

Chapter 14

A Christian America and the Separation of Church and State

Stephen M. Feldman

Most discussions of the establishment and free exercise clauses build upon one dominant or standard story of the separation of church and state. This oft-repeated and commonly accepted story asserts, in part, that the separation of church and state stands as a constitutional principle that equally protects the religious liberty of all Americans, especially religious outgroups. According to a recent Supreme Court opinion, for example, the religion clauses "are recognized as guaranteeing religious liberty and equality to 'the infidel, the atheist, or the adherent of a non-Christian faith such as Islam or Judaism.'"[1]

This essay challenges this dominant story. I argue that the separation of church and state is far more (or far less) than a principle that equally protects the religious liberty of all Americans. Contrary to the dominant story, the separation of church and state looms, to a great extent, as a political and religious development that manifests and reinforces Christian (especially Protestant) imperialism in American society. While the national government never has had an established church and the last state establishment was eliminated more than 150 years ago, the United States nonetheless is more religious than any other western industrialized nation—by far. And the religion of the United States is clearly Christianity. Despite some ebb in the religiosity of Americans during the 1960s and 1970s, recent studies suggest that "nine persons in ten believe Jesus Christ actually lived, seven in ten believe he was truly God, and six in ten think one must believe in the divinity of Christ to be a Christian. [Studies also document] consistently high levels of belief in life after death, heaven, and Christ's presence in heaven."[2] Furthermore, statistics suggest that the educated are more religious than the uneducated: "Among college graduates in this country, only 3% say they do not believe in God, while 77% report that their relationship with God is either 'extremely close' or 'somewhat close.' The percentage of college graduates who believe in life after death (76%) is the same as that for the general population, and the percentage of college graduates who attend church nearly every week (30%) is slightly higher than the national average."[3]

Because most Supreme Court justices are themselves largely embedded in the symbols and structures of American Christian society, they tend to reach decisions that manifest and then reproduce those very symbols and structures. The Court, more often than not, interprets the concept of separation of church and state in a manner that remains consistent with most practices and values of the dominant Christian majority. This phenomenon emerges most obviously in cases where the Court explicitly relies on American history or traditions to throw light on the meaning of the religion clauses. Christian domination is deeply rooted in American history, so any judicial reliance on tradition or history likely will result in the constitutional approval of Christian practices and values. Predictably, then, in *Marsh v. Chambers*, the Court upheld the practice of having a publicly paid chaplain open state legislative sessions with a prayer, even though the same Protestant minister had served as chaplain for sixteen consecutive years. The Court stressed that the use of such publicly paid chaplains was a common tradition in state and federal legislatures throughout American history. In such a case, the Court's reliance on history tends to give a constitutional imprimatur to the preexisting symbols and structures of American society—to the symbols and structures of Christian domination. Indeed, in *Marsh*, the Court stressed that it sought to acknowledge "beliefs widely held among the people of this country"; such beliefs unavoidably manifest Christian values and practices.[4]

The remainder of this essay, though, examines more subtle manifestations of Christian bias and imperialism in Supreme Court opinions. Part I argues that the Court tends to conceive of religion in distinctly Christian (especially Protestant) terms. Part II then explores how the Court's conceptions of private, secular, and neutral conduct also reflect a Christian bias.

What Is Religious?

One popular formulation of the dominant story of the separation of church and state maintains that the Supreme Court decisions of the latter half of the twentieth century fulfilled the American principle of religious liberty. To be sure, during some of the period after World War II, the Court articulated first amendment doctrine that seemed especially protective of religious minorities. For instance, for much of this period, the Court claimed to decide free exercise cases pursuant to a strict scrutiny test: a state could justify a burden on an individual's free exercise of religion only by showing that the state action was necessary to achieve a compelling state interest. Despite such doctrine, though, a study of the holdings in religion clause cases reveals far fewer victories for religious outgroups than the dominant story would lead one to expect.

Probably the most common type of free exercise case is the exemption claim: a member of a religious minority or outgroup seeks an exemption from a generally applicable law that burdens the exercise of her religion. Incredibly, in the Supreme Court, while members of small Christian sects sometimes win and sometimes lose such free exercise claims, non-Christians *never* win. The significance of Christianity to a successful free exercise claim emerged most clearly in *Wisconsin v. Yoder*. The Court there emphasized that Old Order Amish communities were devoted "to a life in harmony with nature and the soil, as exemplified by the simple life of the early Christian era that continued in America during much of our early national life." Thus, the Court seemed especially receptive to the Amish's claim for a free exercise exemption from a state compulsory-education law because they were able to appeal to the justices' romantic nostalgia for a mythological past—for a simple Christian America. This national past—however mythological it might be—was one that most of the justices (as Protestants) could readily understand; its meaning resonated with the religious and cultural horizons of the justices themselves. Thus, whereas members of non-Christian religious minorities have difficulty convincing the Court of the sincerity and meaningfulness of their religious convictions, the *Yoder* Court quoted the New Testament in reasoning that "the traditional way of life of the Amish is not merely a matter of personal preference, but one of deep religious conviction." Because the Amish were Christians, the Court could easily relate their way of life to Christian society and Christian history:

> Whatever their idiosyncrasies as seen by the majority, this record strongly shows that the Amish community has been a highly successful social unit within our society, even if apart from the conventional "mainstream." Its members are productive and very law-abiding members of society; they reject public welfare in any of its usual modern forms. . . . We must not forget that in the Middle Ages important values of the civilization of the Western World were preserved by members of religious orders who isolated themselves from all worldly influences against great obstacles. There can be no assumption that today's majority is "right" and the Amish and others like them are "wrong."[5]

The Court consequently sympathized with the Amish's contentions in *Yoder* far more than it ever seemed to do with non-Christians, whether Jews, Moslems, or otherwise. The *Yoder* Court's receptive attitude contrasts sharply, for instance, with the Court's approach to the free exercise claim of an Orthodox Jewish air force officer in *Goldman v. Weinberger*. In rejecting Goldman's request for a free exercise exemption to allow him to wear his yarmulke (skullcap) despite air force regulations, the Court wrote: "The considered professional judgment of the Air Force is that the traditional outfitting of personnel in standardized uniforms encourages the subordination of personal preferences and identities in favor of the overall group mission." Two points in this passage bear emphasis. First, the Court's stress upon "standardized uniforms" disregards the fact that the *standard* almost always will mirror the values and practices of the dominant majority—namely, Christians. Put bluntly, the United States military is unlikely to require everyone to wear a yarmulke as part of the standard uniform. Second, and most clearly opposed to the *Yoder* Court's receptiveness, the *Goldman* Court characterized the wearing of a yarmulke as a matter of mere *personal preference*. Evidently, the majority of the justices (all of the justices at this time were Christian) were unable to comprehend the significance of the yarmulke. In Orthodox Judaism, the wearing of a yarmulke or other head covering is far from a personal preference; it is a custom going back so many centuries that it has attained the status of a religious law. For many Orthodox Jews, wearing a yarmulke is not a choice but a necessary part of being Jewish; to fail to wear one would amount to a sin. Moreover,

Justice Blackmun's dissent revealed that the Court was informed about the significance of the yarmulke to Orthodox Jews. Apparently, the majority nevertheless could not grasp the meaning of this non-Christian religious practice.[6]

In *Employment Division, Oregon Department of Human Resources v. Smith*, the Court brushed away any semblance of doctrine that had suggested the free exercise clause equally protects the religious freedom of all, including outgroups. If *Smith* has a virtue, then, it lies in the forthright manner in which the majority declared that religious outgroups will not receive judicial protection from most instances of majoritarian overreaching and insensitivity. Quite simply, when the government enacts a law of general applicability, the protection of religious liberty and equality will depend upon the political process. The Court will not attempt to enforce any particular principle of religious freedom and instead will defer to the legislative decision, so long as it is not infected by discriminatory intent. Moreover, the *Smith* Court expressly acknowledged that this judicial approach to free exercise favors the religious majority.[7]

While the *Smith* Court candidly admitted that it would no longer pretend to judicially protect religious outgroups under the free exercise clause, the Court was either less forthright or less aware that its very conception of religion was distinctly Christian. This Christian concept of religion was evident in at least two related ways (both of which have appeared in other cases). First, the Court emphasized a distinction between belief and conduct: the first amendment fully protects religious beliefs but does not similarly protect religiously motivated conduct.[8] This constitutional doctrine mirrors basic Christian, especially Protestant, dogma: that salvation depends largely on faith or belief in the truth of Jesus Christ and not on works or conduct in this world. Hence, from a Protestant standpoint, the potential for uncoerced belief in Christ must be protected in order for salvation to be possible, but the protection of this-worldly conduct is unnecessary because such conduct is largely unrelated to salvation. Indeed, the *Smith* Court closely echoed the sixteenth-century Protestant Reformers Martin Luther and Jean Calvin by emphasizing that while the government cannot be allowed to coerce beliefs, the government must be able to regulate conduct to prevent social chaos, or in the Court's words, to avoid "courting anarchy."[9]

Second, the Court's Christian conception of religion was evident in the justices' assumption that only *individual choices* have religious significance sufficient to require constitutional protection. The Court wrote: "The government's ability to enforce generally applicable prohibitions of socially harmful conduct, like its ability to carry out other aspects of public policy, 'cannot depend on measuring the effects of a governmental action on a religious objector's spiritual development.'"[10] From the Court's standpoint, so long as the government does not coerce religious belief, governmental activity is unlikely to seriously affect an individual's religious well-being. An individual's religious development or salvation—again particularly in the Protestant world view—depends upon freedom of conscience. As freedom of conscience originally was conceived during the Protestant Reformation, particularly by Calvin, it did not entail even the remotest notion of a freedom to choose among a variety of religious paths, whether Christian or non-Christian. Rather, freedom of conscience denoted that the individual must be able to follow the dictates of conscience to the truth of Christ. This Protestant concept of freedom of conscience then expanded in nineteenth-century America to encompass an individual freedom to choose Christian salvation, a freedom to choose to accept Christ. The Supreme Court's conception of religion, it appears, follows from this expanded Protestant conception of freedom of conscience. The Court consistently upholds governmental actions so long as they do not seem to prevent individuals from making religiously significant choices, even though such governmental actions might otherwise burden non-Christian religious practices. For instance, the Court has upheld the constitutionality of governmental activities that impeded the religious use of peyote, in *Smith*, and that damaged lands sacred to Native Americans, in *Lyng v. Northwest Indian Cemetery Protective Association*. From the Court's Christian-biased perspective, these governmental actions supposedly did not interfere with the individual's freedom to make religiously significant choices, and consequently, the governmental actions were deemed constitutionally permissible under the free exercise clause.[11]

In establishment clause cases, too, the centrality of the Protestant conception of freedom of conscience stands paramount. *Lee v. Weisman* might be considered a good case from the perspective of religious minorities: Weisman, a Jew, won the case as the Court held that public schools violate the establishment clause by having clergy deliver invocation and benediction prayers at graduation ceremonies. Indeed, since the *Weisman* Court displayed unusual sensitivity and empathy for the experiences of religious outgroups, the decision unquestionably stands as one of the best of the good cases, enforcing a strong wall of separation between church and state. Yet, even in *Weisman*, the Court's Christian conception of religion was unmistakable as the majority opinion emphasized the importance of freedom of conscience under both the free exercise and establishment clauses: "A state-created orthodoxy puts at grave risk that freedom of belief and conscience which are the sole assurance that religious faith is real, not imposed."[12] Similarly, in another apparently good case, *Wallace v. Jaffree*, holding unconstitutional a statute authorizing a period of silence for "meditation or voluntary prayer," the Court underscored the significance of freedom of conscience to both religion clauses by identifying "the individual's freedom of conscience as the central liberty that unifies the various Clauses in the First Amendment." Then, in a passage dripping with unintended irony, the Court appeared to stress that first amendment protections extend equally to all religions, but in making this argument, the Court unwittingly used Protestant imagery, focusing on individual faith and voluntary choice in religious matters.

> Just as the right to speak and the right to refrain from speaking are complementary components of a broader concept of individual freedom of mind, so also the *individual's freedom to choose* his own creed is the counterpart of his right to refrain from accepting the creed established by the majority. At one time it was thought that this right merely proscribed the preference of one Christian sect over another, but would not require equal respect for the conscience of the infidel, the atheist, or the adherent of a non-Christian faith such as Islam or Judaism. But when the underlying principle has been examined in the crucible of litigation, the Court has unambiguously concluded that the individual *freedom of conscience* protected by the First Amendment embraces the right to select any *religious faith* or none at all. This conclusion derives

> support not only from the interest in respecting the *individual's freedom of conscience*, but also from the conviction that religious beliefs worthy of respect are the product of *free and voluntary choice by the faithful*, and from recognition of the fact that the political interest in forestalling intolerance extends beyond intolerance among Christian sects—or even intolerance among "religions"—to encompass intolerance of the disbeliever and the uncertain.[13]

Ultimately, while the separation of church and state occasionally protects minority or outgroup religions, that protection often dwindles into a limited, hypothetical, or even nonexistent refuge. One implication of the Court's Christian-biased conception of religion is that outgroup religions are more likely to be protected when their practices and tenets resemble those of Christianity. As already discussed, the Court in *Goldman v. Weinberger* refused to protect a Jewish air force officer's wearing of a yarmulke, an Orthodox Jewish practice that does not closely parallel or resemble any Christian custom. Yet, the Court nonetheless has upheld the public display of a Chanukah menorah; because Chanukah usually falls at the same time of the year as Christmas, the lighting of a menorah seems to parallel the display of a Christmas tree, at least from a Christian standpoint. In these cases, then, the Court's perception seemed to turn more on the relation between the disputed Jewish practice and Christian practices than on the significance of the Jewish practice within Judaism itself.[14]

What Is Private, Secular, or Neutral?

Regardless of the Court's conception of religion, the symbols, practices, and beliefs of Christianity can be imposed on members of outgroup religions through the instrumentality of the government so long as legal discourse labels or codes the governmental action as private, secular, or neutral. When, for example, a particular activity is defined or coded as *private*—as separate from government—then the constitutional constraints imposed upon state actors are rendered irrelevant. This distinction between private as opposed to governmental (or public) activity—an aspect of the public/private dichotomy—was crucial in *Capitol Square Review and Advisory Board v. Pinette*, decided in 1995. The Court held that the display of a large Latin (Christian) cross on public property did not violate the establishment clause. The public property, a "state-owned plaza surrounding the Statehouse in Columbus, Ohio," qualified as a traditional public forum because "[f]or over a century the square [had] been used for public speeches, gatherings, and festivals." More important, though, the plurality opinion emphasized that a private actor, the Ku Klux Klan, and not the government had erected the cross: "[P]rivate religious expression receives *preferential* treatment under the Free Exercise Clause. It is no answer to say that the Establishment Clause tempers religious speech. By its terms that Clause applies only to the words and acts of government. It [does not impede] purely private religious speech. . . ." Thus, even when the government must grant a permit to a speaker (as in *Pinette*), the constraints of the establishment clause do not apply; private actors remain free to disseminate their Christian messages on publicly owned property. In fact, quite predictably, after the district court issued an injunction permitting the Klan to erect its cross, the state "then received, and granted, several additional applications to erect crosses on [the public plaza]."[15]

The *Smith* case, when viewed in conjunction with *Pinette*, elucidates the intimate link between the public/private dichotomy and Christian societal domination. In holding that the compelling state interest test should not be used in most instances to adjudicate the constitutionality of laws of general applicability, the *Smith* Court acknowledged that the religious majority occasionally might act through the legislative process to the disadvantage of religious minorities. Nonetheless, to the Court, this possibility was an "unavoidable consequence of democratic government."[16] Thus, while *Pinette* emphasized that the free exercise clause extends preferential treatment to private religious expression, *Smith* declared that the free exercise clause allows the majority, through legislation, to restrict the religious practices of minorities. If these two cases are read together in the context of American society, they suggest that the free exercise clause extends *preferential* treatment to *Christian* religious expression and beliefs. Because the overwhelming majority of Americans are Christian, not only will most private religious expression be Christian (and protected by *Pinette*), but also most legislative actions will reflect or harmonize with Christian beliefs and practices (and be protected by *Smith*).[17]

In a similar vein, when a particular activity is defined or coded as *secular*, the activity supposedly has been removed from the realm of the religious and is therefore legitimated by the principle of separation of church and state. Despite the possibility that a member of a non-Christian outgroup or minority might experience or perceive that very activity as decidedly Christian, the declaration of secularity (by the Supreme Court or some other empowered governmental actor or institution, such as a school board) justifies the activity within the dominant discourse. And quite often, constitutional rhetoric imperialistically ignores religious outgroups and the oppressive consequences of Christian activities and symbols for members of such outgroups; there is, in other words, a denial of experiences and perceptions that differ from the Christian viewpoint. In this manner, constitutional rhetoric effectively neutralizes or normalizes many common forms of Christian societal domination by declaring or coding them to be secular.

For example, in *McGowan v. Maryland* and *Braunfeld v. Brown*, the Supreme Court upheld the constitutionality of Sunday-closing laws in the face of establishment and free exercise clause challenges. The Court claimed to identify the general sentiments of the American people by effacing the differences between Christian Americans and other Americans (the plaintiffs in *Braunfeld*, for instance, were Orthodox Jews).

> [I]t is common knowledge that the first day of the week has come to have special significance as a rest day in this country. *People of all religions and people with no religion* regard Sunday as a time for family activity, for visiting friends and relatives, for late sleeping, for passive and active entertainments, for dining out, and the like. "*Vast masses of our people, in fact, literally millions*, go out into the countryside on fine Sunday afternoons in the Summer. . . ." Sunday is a day apart from all others. The cause is irrelevant;

> *the fact exists.* It would seem unrealistic for enforcement purposes and perhaps detrimental to the general welfare to require a State to choose a common day of rest other than that which *most persons* would select of their own accord.[18]

The Court trivialized the long history of Sunday blue laws, a history that showed that they originated and developed to support Christian beliefs. According to the Court, the governmental choice of Sunday for a day of mandated rest was "of a secular rather than of a religious character."[19] Consequently, the Orthodox Jewish plaintiffs in *Braunfeld* were forced, in effect, to observe the Christian day of rest, Sunday, even though their own Sabbath was Saturday.

Based on similar (though perhaps more outrageous) reasoning, *Lynch v. Donnelly* held that the public display of a crèche does not violate the establishment clause. The Court wrote:

> When viewed in the proper context of *the Christmas Holiday season*, it is apparent that ... there is insufficient evidence to establish that the inclusion of the crèche is a purposeful or surreptitious effort to express some kind of subtle governmental advocacy of a particular religious message. In a pluralistic society a variety of motives and purposes are implicated. The City ... has principally taken note of a *significant historical religious event* long celebrated in the Western World. The crèche in the display depicts the *historical origins* of this *traditional event* long recognized as a *National Holiday*. ... The narrow question is whether there is a secular purpose for Pawtucket's display of the crèche. The display is sponsored by the City to celebrate *the Holiday* and to depict the origins of that Holiday. These are legitimate secular purposes.[20]

This passage illustrates how the Court used legal discourse to neutralize the Christian message of a crèche for purposes of constitutional adjudication. In the Court's terms, Christmas—the Christian holiday celebrating the birth of Jesus Christ—somehow becomes secular. The Court coded (or labeled) Christmas as a traditional and historical event, and the very birth of Jesus himself becomes merely the historical origin of that event. Hence, members of religious outgroups are symbolically absorbed into the Christian mainstream so that they too must enjoy and celebrate "*the*" holiday. The *Lynch* Court, in other words, strikingly denied the potentially divergent views of non-Christian religious outgroups. The Court emphasized that, prior to the *Lynch* lawsuit, nobody had complained about the crèche even though it had been publicly displayed for forty years. To the Court, this silence meant that the crèche had not generated dissension—apparently, everybody happily supported the Christmas display. Yet, in the face of cultural imperialism, outgroup members often figuratively and sometimes literally stop speaking—so that there is nothing to be heard. The Court overlooked the possibility, therefore, that Christian imperialism had produced the silence of religious outgroup members. Silence can bespeak domination, not consensus.[21]

In recent years, the Court's establishment clause doctrine has fallen into disarray, with the justices articulating and relying upon a variety of different doctrinal tests. In some cases, then, the justices have eschewed articulating any definitive doctrine for adjudicating establishment clause issues and instead have stressed a general need for governmental *neutrality* in religious affairs. For example, in *Zobrest v. Catalina*

Foothills School District, the Court held that a public school district can provide a sign-language interpreter for a student in a Roman Catholic high school without contravening the establishment clause. The Court reasoned, in typical language, that "government programs that neutrally provide benefits to a broad class of citizens defined without reference to religion are not readily subject to an Establishment Clause challenge just because sectarian institutions may also receive an attenuated financial benefit."[22]

Yet, just as with the definition of private actions and secular governmental conduct, the Court's conception of and reliance upon governmental neutrality can be infused by a Christian bias. Indeed, the Court's insistence on abstract governmental neutrality can lead to rather bizarre results. In *Board of Education of Kiryas Joel Village School District v. Grumet*, the state of New York statutorily created a special school district following the boundary lines of the Village of Kiryas Joel. All of the residents of the village belonged to a small Jewish sect, the Satmar Hasidim. The Satmars sent most of their children to private religious schools, but these schools were unable to provide adequate facilities for handicapped children. When the Satmars initially sent these children to public schools in neighboring communities, the children suffered "panic, fear, and trauma . . . in leaving their own community and being with people whose ways were so different." New York therefore created the special public school district so that the village could operate a publicly funded school for the handicapped children. The Court held, however, that the state had violated the establishment clause because the statute was not neutral: state assistance of the Satmar Hasidim offended the "principle at the heart of the Establishment Clause, that government should not prefer one religion to another, or religion to irreligion." This reasoning underscores that the Court refuses to recognize differences between the social realities of mainstream Christians and religious outgroups such as the Satmar Hasidim.[23] To the Court, neutrality is the criterion for constitutionality, yet in a Christian-dominated society, such as America, "neutrality" equals Christianity.

The link between neutrality and Christianity becomes even clearer when *Grumet* is compared with *Rosenberger v. Rectors and Visitors of the University of Virginia*, decided in 1995. Once again emphasizing governmental neutrality, the *Rosenberger* Court held that the establishment clause did not prohibit the University of Virginia from funding an explicitly Christian magazine created and run by students. The Christian nature of the magazine was undisputed: it expressly challenged "Christians to live, in word and deed, according to the faith they proclaim and to encourage students to consider what a personal relationship with Jesus Christ means." In dissent, Justice Souter unequivocally characterized the magazine as evangelical proselytization. Nonetheless, the majority reasoned that the governmental action was *neutral* because the university funded other student activities as well as the magazine. In fact, the Court stated that if the university failed to fund the magazine, the university "could undermine the very neutrality the Establishment Clause requires."[24] Thus, by ostensibly enforcing governmental neutrality, the Court—first in *Grumet* and then in *Rosenberger*—reinforced Christian domination. According to the Court, neutrality prohibited New York from creating a public school for the handicapped children of a small and insular Jewish sect, yet neutrality also somehow demanded that Virginia fund a magazine devoted to Christian proselytizing.[25]

Conclusion

We undoubtedly should refrain from overestimating the power of Supreme Court decisions to mold or change American society. The public does not reflexively accept the Supreme Court's positions on salient political issues. So long as this nation remains pervasively Christian, legal discourse—even Supreme Court constitutional discourse on the religion clauses—cannot eradicate Christian domination. Supreme Court decisions, one might say, are not self-executing: decisions holding, for example, that prayers in the public schools are unconstitutional do not necessarily beget the eradication of public school prayers throughout the nation. The *New York Times* reported in 1994 that, despite the Court rulings, "prayer is increasingly a part of school activities from early-morning moments of silence to lunchtime prayer sessions to pre-football-game prayers for both players and fans. [P]articularly in the South, religious clubs, prayer groups and pro-prayer students and community groups are making religion and prayer part of the school day." In fact, the *Times* added, a school superintendent in a town near Austin, Texas, was removed from office after issuing a directive that prohibited prayers at football games and other school events. In short, with Christian domination being so deeply entrenched in the symbols and structures of American society, the Court's ability to seriously reduce such domination is highly questionable (assuming that the Court actually wanted to do so, which it does not).[26]

Even so, the Supreme Court's decisions and opinions do matter. The Court may not control American society, but relative to other societal institutions, the Court remains a powerful contributor to the constant construction and reconstruction of cultural symbols and social structures. It is significant, then, that most justices and commentators alike subscribe to the dominant story of the separation of church and state. According to the dominant story, the religion clauses of the first amendment create a constitutional principle that equally protects the religious liberty of all Americans, especially religious outgroups. And, to be sure, consistent with this dominant story, members of religious outgroups and minorities occasionally emerge from litigation with a victory—a decision, for example, that prohibits the Christian majority from using the instrumentality of the government to impose Christian practices or values. These victories, though, are often less pronounced than they at first appear. Even when upholding the rights of religious minorities, the Court conceptualizes the very notion of religion in distinctively Christian terms. Thus, while judicial victories for religious outgroups are not necessarily Pyrrhic, such victories nonetheless often come with significant costs.

In fact, regardless of the Christian bias embedded in many of the Court's opinions, a simple review of the establishment clause holdings reveals fewer victories than suggested by the dominant story of church and state. Most of the victories have come in cases that challenged either, on the one hand, egregious impositions of religious (usually Christian) practices and values in public schools or, on the other hand, governmental aid to religious schools (overwhelmingly Roman Catholic). In some notable victories, the Court struck down the following governmental actions as violating the establishment clause (this list is not exhaustive): voluntary Bible reading and reciting the Lord's Prayer in the public schools;[27] the daily recitation of a state-created "nondenominational" prayer in the public schools;[28] a released time program with instruction on public school grounds;[29] a statute that prohibited public schools from teaching the theory of evolution;[30] state programs providing financial aid to church-related schools by, for instance, supplementing teacher salaries and paying for instructional materials;[31] a tuition tax scheme providing tax credits and deductions for parents with children in nonpublic schools;[32] a statute that required the posting of the Ten Commandments on public classroom walls;[33] a state law regulating charitable solicitations that favored certain religions over others;[34] a statute authorizing a period of silence for meditation or voluntary prayer in the public schools;[35] a statute that required public school teachers to teach creation science whenever they taught the theory of evolution;[36] the governmental display of a crèche standing alone;[37] and a public school policy to have clergy deliver invocation and benediction prayers at graduation ceremonies.[38]

The decisions enumerated above are significant, but they do not justify the pervasive belief in the dominant story of church and state. Even if these cases represented genuine victories for religious outgroups seeking the strict separation of church and state, then a similar number of cases represented equally significant losses. During the post–World War II era, the Court upheld the following governmental actions as not violating the establishment clause (again, this list is not exhaustive): the governmental reimbursement of transportation costs for children attending either public or Catholic schools;[39] a released time program when religious instruction was not on public school grounds;[40] Sunday-closing laws without exemptions for Jews or others with non-Sunday Sabbaths;[41] a statute lending books to parochial school students;[42] the granting of property tax exemptions to churches;[43] a state university's opening its facilities to registered student groups including an evangelical Christian student group that focused on religious worship and discussion;[44] a statute providing all parents with a tax deduction for certain educational expenses regardless of whether their children attended public or nonpublic schools;[45] having a publicly paid chaplain open state legislative sessions with a prayer;[46] the governmental exhibit of a crèche as part of a larger Christmas display;[47] a statutory exemption of religious organizations for employment discrimination on the basis of religion in connection with secular nonprofit activities;[48] the governmental provision of a sign-language interpreter for a student at a Roman Catholic high school;[49] the display on public property by a private actor of a large Latin (Christian) cross;[50] and the governmental financial support of an explicitly Christian student publication.[51]

One of the most remarkable *losses* for religious outgroups was *Thornton v. Caldor, Inc.*, decided in 1985. In *Thornton*, the Court considered the constitutionality of a Connecticut statute that excused employees from working on their religious Sabbath, whatever day of the week that might be. The statute, without doubt, manifested an unusual degree of legislative sensitivity to religious outgroups: the state legislature recognized that not everybody is a Christian celebrating a Sunday Sabbath, so the state provided non-Sunday Sabbath observers (such as Jews) with benefits similar to those enjoyed for two centuries by most Christians in states with Sunday closing laws. Significantly, as already discussed, the Court previously had upheld the constitutionality of Sunday laws in the face of free exercise and establishment clause challenges. If the dominant story of church and state were accurate—that is, if the separation of church and state truly were a constitutional principle that equally protects the religious freedom of all, including outgroups—then one would expect the Court to uphold this Connecticut statute. After all, the Court already had upheld Sunday laws, and this statute appeared merely to accommodate the religious practices of outgroups. Nonetheless, the Court held that the statute violated the establishment clause. To reach this conclusion, the Court reasoned that the primary effect of the statute was to advance religion.[52] Consequently, despite the professions (or pretensions?) of the dominant story, the Court not only upheld (in previous cases) the constitutionality of Sunday closing laws, thus approving the legal imposition of the traditional Christian Sabbath, but then the *Thornton* Court also struck down a statute designed to accommodate the Sabbaths of religious outgroups, thus denying equal treatment and full religious liberty to certain minorities.

Predictably, the *Thornton* Court's reasoning displayed a distinctly Christian conception of religion. From the Court's perspective, a person's conduct in observing the Sabbath seemed relatively unimportant because (from the Protestant standpoint) it could not affect salvation (which is solely a matter of belief or faith). Furthermore, according to the Court, the religious individual remains free to choose whether or not to observe the Sabbath in the first place. The Court ignored (or was unaware) that for some outgroup religions, such as Judaism, conduct may be as or even more important than belief. And for many Jews, especially the Orthodox, following the Sabbath is far from being a matter of individual choice; rather, it is a central component of the religion. "The Sabbath is more than an institution in Judaism," according to Morris N. Kertzer. "It is *the* institution of the Jewish religion."[53] Considering that the disputed statute was expressly intended to accommodate members of outgroup religions, the justices' failure to seriously heed the views of minorities revealed the incredible tenacity of the Court's Christian bias.

The Court, moreover, does not always show such indifference toward Sabbath observance. If *Thornton* is compared with another case from the 1980s, *Frazee v. Illinois Department of Employment Security*, the Court's indifference (or hostility?) toward religious outgroups (and their Sabbaths) and not toward Sabbath observance in general is underscored. In *Frazee*, the Court held that the state had violated the free exercise clause by denying Frazee unemployment benefits when he refused to work on Sunday because he was Christian. Most telling, in comparison with *Thornton*, the *Frazee* Court reasoned that the claimant's desire to observe Sunday as the Sabbath was not a "purely personal preference," even though he was *not* a member of any particular Christian church or sect.[54] Apparently, for the *Frazee* Court, a bald assertion of Christianity was sufficient to establish the importance of the Sabbath and the legitimacy of the resultant free exercise claim.

In conclusion, I do not mean to suggest that the Supreme Court justices never have been motivated, even in part, by a desire to follow their conception of the separation of church and state as a constitutional principle. Undoubtedly, some justices were so motivated (at least sometimes). Nonetheless, the justices' very conceptions of separation of church and state most often arose from their Christian backgrounds. Indeed, totally apart from the *justices'* respective conceptions or understandings, the historical development of the separation of church and state, especially the idea of freedom of conscience or free exercise, is closely tied to Christian practices and beliefs.[55] The dominant story of church and state, therefore, is woefully simplistic and seriously misleading. A constitutional principle of separation of church and state does *not* equally protect the religious liberty of all, including outgroups, and does *not* determine judicial outcomes in religion clause cases. The true story is far more complex. To be sure, religious outgroups would not necessarily do better without the separation of church and state, which has, in some instances, protected outgroups from oppression. But all in all, the separation of church and state provides far less shelter for religious outgroups than the dominant story would lead one to expect. Ultimately, the dominant story of church and state is revealed to be dominant not only because it is so commonly accepted but also because it is told from the distinct perspective of the dominant Christian majority. And telling the story of religious freedom and equality from the perspective of the dominant religion has produced a tale that is both self-congratulatory and lacking in nuance.

NOTES

1. County of Allegheny v. American Civil Liberties Union, 492 U.S. 573, 590 (1989) (quoting Wallace v. Jaffree, 472 U.S. 38, 52 (1985)). For a more complete discussion of the dominant story of the separation of church and state, *see* Stephen M. Feldman, Please Don't Wish Me a Merry Christmas: A Critical History of the Separation of Church and State 4–5 (1997).

2. Robert Wuthnow, The Restructuring of American Religion 300 (1988); *see* Winthrop S. Hudson & John Corrigan, Religion in America 390–91, 408–14 (5th ed. 1992); Martin E. Marty, Protestantism in the United States: Righteous Empire 250–58 (2d ed. 1986).

3. Steven D. Smith, *The Rise and Fall of Religious Freedom in Constitutional Discourse*, 140 U. Pa. L. Rev. 149, 174–75 (1991) (citing Unsecular America 142 (Richard J. Neuhaus ed., 1986) (appendix at 142, tbl. 20)).

4. *Marsh*, 463 U.S. 783, 792 (1983).

5. Wisconsin v. Yoder, 406 U.S. 205, 210, 216, 222–24 (1972). The Court explicitly stressed the long history of the Amish (as Christians) as significant to the decision: "It cannot be overemphasized that we are not dealing with a way of life and mode of education by a group claiming to have recently discovered some 'progressive' or more enlightened process for rearing children for modern life." *Id.* at 235. The Court also emphasized that "the Amish community has been a highly successful social unit within our society." *Id.* at 222.

I refrain from categorically asserting that non-Christians never win any free exercise cases because a few cases are ambiguous enough to render such a bald assertion at least questionable. Church of the Lukumi Babalu Aye, Inc. v. City of Hialeah, 508 U.S. 520 (1993); Bowen v. Roy, 476 U.S. 693 (1986); Cruz v. Beto, 405 U.S. 319 (1972); Torcaso v. Watkins, 367 U.S. 488 (1961); United States v. Ballard, 322 U.S. 78 (1944). Some of these cases involve religions that may or may not be categorized as Christian, depending on the definition of Christianity. None of the cases, though, can be reasonably categorized as involving the enforcement of a free exercise exemption on an otherwise generally applicable law. For example, in *Cruz v. Beto*, 405 U.S. 319 (1972), a non-Christian seemed to win a free exercise case where the government explicitly and overtly discriminated against the exercise of Buddhism. The Court held that the lower court should not have dismissed Cruz's complaint for failure to state a claim when allegations asserted that Cruz was a Buddhist and "denied a reasonable opportunity of pursuing his faith comparable to the opportunity afforded fellow prisoners who adhere to conventional religious precepts." *Id.* at 322. Even in that case, I refrain from asserting that Cruz, as a non-Christian, outright won the case because of its procedural posture. Since the lower court had dismissed for failure to state a claim without benefit of a trial, the case presented the free exercise violation as a conditional or hypothetical, the validity of which would therefore depend on the further development of facts at trial. Cruz thus might have an opportunity to present evidence at a trial, but after such a trial, he might then win or lose. Moreover, in dissent, Justice Rehnquist even suggested that Cruz, proceeding in forma pauperis, might still have the complaint dismissed as frivolous under 28 U.S.C. § 1915(d). *Id.* at 328 (Rehnquist, J., dissenting). On the importance of Christianity to free exercise claims, see Mark Tushnet, "*Of Church and State and the Supreme Court": Kurland Revisited*, 1989 S. Ct. Rev. 373, 381.

6. 475 U.S. 503, 508 (1986); *see id.* at 525 (Blackmun, J., dissenting); Roy A. Rosenberg, The Concise Guide to Judaism 124–25 (1990) (discussing the importance of a yarmulke). Also, the Amish, it is worth noting, do not always win. *See, e.g.*, United States v. Lee, 455 U.S. 252 (1982).

7. 494 U.S. 872, 890 (1990). After *Smith*, Congress acted to statutorily reinstate the compelling state interest test for laws of general applicability infringing free exercise rights. Religious Freedom Restoration Act of 1993, Pub. L. 103–141, Nov. 16, 1993, 107 Stat. 1488 (codified at 42 U.S.C. §§ 2000bb to 2000bb-4 (1994)). Subsequently, the Court struck down this act as beyond congressional power. City of Boerne v. Flores, 117 S.Ct. 2157 (1997).

8. The Court wrote: "The free exercise of religion means, first and foremost, the right to believe and profess whatever religious doctrine one desires. Thus, the First Amendment obviously excludes all 'governmental regulation of religious beliefs as such.'" *Smith*, 494 U.S. at 877 (quoting Sherbert v. Verner, 374 U.S. 398, 402 (1963)).

9. *Smith*, 494 U.S. at 888; *see* Marci A. Hamilton, *The Belief/Conduct Paradigm in the Supreme Court's Free Exercise Jurisprudence: A Theological Account of the Failure to Protect Religious Conduct*, 54 Ohio St. L.J. 713 (1993). Hamilton notes that many other commentators attempt to downplay the importance of the belief/conduct dichotomy. *See* Hamilton, *supra*, at 721 & n.30. For a discussion of Luther's and Calvin's views on church and state, see Feldman, *supra* note 1, at 54–78.

10. *Smith*, 494 U.S. at 885 (quoting Lyng v. Northwest Indian Cemetery Protective Assn., 485 U.S. 439, 451 (1988)).

11. *Lyng*, 485 U.S. 439 (1988); *see Goldman*, 475 U.S. 503 (1986) (upholding governmental action to prevent Orthodox Jew from wearing yarmulke); Feldman, *supra* note 1, at 54–203 (tracing the development of the idea of freedom of conscience from Reformation through nineteenth-century America); David C. Williams & Susan H. Williams, *Volitionalism and Religious Liberty*, 76 Cornell L. Rev. 769, 811–13, 828–34, 846–47 (1991) (emphasizing the Court's protection of volitionalist religions). While the *Smith* Court stressed the religious significance of individual choice—which is especially important in American Protestantism—it is worth noting that author of the majority opinion (Justice Scalia) and another member of the majority (Justice Kennedy) are Roman Catholic.

12. *Weisman*, 112 S.Ct. 2649, 2658 (1992); *see id.* at 2656 (religious beliefs and choices are within private sphere); *see also id.* at 2657–58 (fuller discussion of free exercise and establishment clauses).

13. 472 U.S. 38, 41–42, 50, 52–54 (1985) (emphasis added in indented quotation).

14. County of Allegheny v. American Civil Liberties Union, 492 U.S. 573 (1989) (upholding display of menorah); Goldman v. Weinberger, 475 U.S. 503 (1986) (not protecting wearing of yarmulke).

15. 115 S.Ct. 2440, 2444–45, 2449 (1995) (emphasis added); *see id.* at 2447–49.

16. Employment Division, Oregon Department of Human Resources v. Smith, 494 U.S. 872, 890 (1990).

17. In O'Connor's *Pinette* concurrence, she at least recognizes the possibility of majority domination: "At some point, for example, a private religious group may so dominate a public forum that a formal policy of equal access is transformed into a demonstration of approval." *Pinette*, 115 S.Ct. at 2454 (O'Connor, J., concurring).

The public/private dichotomy also was supposedly decisive in *Corporation of the Presiding Bishop of the Church of Jesus Christ of Latter-day Saints v. Amos*, 483 U.S. 327 (1987). In *Amos*, the Court upheld a Title VII exemption allowing religious organizations to discriminate in employment on the basis of religion, even though in this instance, the Mormon Church had discriminated in connection with *secular nonprofit activities* as opposed to specifically religious activities. The Court emphasized that the church (a private actor) and not the government had forced the employee to choose whether to change his religious practices or lose his job. *See, e.g., id.* at 337 n.15 (distinguishing *Amos* from *Thornton v. Caldor, Inc.*, 472 U.S. 703 (1985)).

18. McGowan v. Maryland, 366 U.S. 420, 451–52 (1961) (citations omitted; emphasis added); *see* Braunfeld v. Brown, 366 U.S. 599 (1961).

19. *McGowan*, 366 U.S. at 444. In *Braunfeld*, the plurality reasoned that keeping one's business open or closed is merely a secular activity; 366 U.S. at 605. While that assertion may be partly correct, it is certainly not true that keeping one's business open or closed on *Sunday* is secular. Rather, the choice of Sunday obviously reflects the religious preferences of the dominant Christian majority. *See id.* at 614 (Brennan, J., dissenting); Naomi W. Cohen, Jews in Christian America: The Pursuit of Religious Equality 55–56, 61–62 (1992); *cf. McGowan*, 366 U.S. at 431–35 (on the history of the Sunday laws).

20. 465 U.S. 668, 680–81 (1984) (emphasis added).

21. *Id.* at 684–85; *see id.* at 693 (O'Connor, J., concurring). In a subsequent case, *County of Allegheny v. American Civil Liberties Union*, the Court held that the public display of a crèche, standing alone, violated the establishment clause. Although this holding might initially appear to recognize the strong Christian symbolism of Christmas and Christmas displays—including a crèche—the Court nonetheless noted: "The presence of *Santas* or other *Christmas* decorations elsewhere in the county courthouse . . . fail to negate the endorsement effect of the crèche. The record demonstrates clearly that the crèche, with its floral frame, was its own display distinct from any other decorations or exhibitions in the building." 492 U.S. 573, 598–99 n.48 (1989) (emphasis added). Hence, the Court held that a crèche standing alone is religious, but in so doing, the Court legitimated as secular the display of many other Christmas symbols, such as a Santa Claus and a Christmas tree. These are, to be sure, *Christian* symbols; as Winnifred Fallers Sullivan notes, items such as a Santa, a tree, and the like are "the very stuff of ritual and of religious symbolism." Winnifred Fallers Sullivan, Paying the Words Extra: Religious Discourse in the Supreme Court of the United States 53 (1994). In fact, the Court bizarrely suggested that a crèche would be rendered secular if it were displayed *with* such other Christmas decorations.

On the silence of oppressed outgroups, *see* Pierre Bourdieu, Language and Symbolic Power 52 (Gino Raymond & Matthew Adamson trans., 1991) (arguing that dominated speakers can become speechless); James C. Scott, Domination and the Arts of Resistance: Hidden Transcripts 3 (1990) (the greater the domination of a subordinate group, the more likely the subordinated will say, if anything, what the dominant want to hear); Robin West, *Feminism, Critical Social Theory and Law*, 1989 U. Chi. Legal F. 59, 66–78 (arguing that patriarchal power produces silence in women).

22. 113 S.Ct. 2462, 2466 (1993). In *Board of Education of Kiryas Joel Village School District v. Grumet*, 114 S. Ct. 2481, 2491 (1994), the Court emphasized that governmental power "must be exercised in a manner neutral to religion."

23. 114 S.Ct. 2481, 2485, 2491 (1994); *see id.* at 2494. The Court writes: "Here the benefit flows only to a single sect, but aiding this single, small religious group causes no less a constitutional problem than would follow from aiding a sect with more members or religion as a whole." *Id.* at 2492. Jeffrey Rosen argues, however, that the Satmar Hasidim used coercive measures to maintain their own hegemonic position within their small community. *See* Jeffrey Rosen, *Village People*, The New Republic, April 11, 1994, at 11.

24. 115 S.Ct. 2510, 2515, 2525 (1995); *see id.* at 2521–25; *see also id.* at 2535, 2539 (Souter, J., dissenting).

25. In his concurrence in *Grumet*, Justice Kennedy almost seems to understand this outsider viewpoint. He writes:

> The Satmars' way of life, which springs out of their strict religious beliefs, conflicts in many respects with mainstream American culture.... [B]y creating the district, New York did not impose or increase any burden on non-Satmars, compared to the burden it lifted from the Satmars, that might disqualify the District as a genuine accommodation.

114 S.Ct. at 2502 (Kennedy J., concurring). Of course, Kennedy nonetheless concludes that the statute ultimately violates the establishment clause.

26. Peter Applebome, *Prayer in Public Schools? It's Nothing New for Many*, N.Y. Times, Nov. 22, 1994, at A1, A13; *see* Gerald N. Rosenberg, The Hollow Hope: Can Courts Bring About Social Change? (1991) (questioning the power of courts to institute serious social change); Timothy R. Johnson & Andrew D. Martin, *The Public's Conditional Response to Supreme Court Decisions*, 92 Am. Pol. Sci. Rev. 299 (1998) (discussing social science evidence regarding public responses to Supreme Court decisions); Jerry Fink, *School Prayer Bill Praised in Poteau*, Tulsa World, March 17, 1995 (in response to the near-unanimous approval by the Oklahoma House of Representatives of a school prayer bill, a spokesperson for the Poteau Ministerial Alliance said that the bill, if it became law, merely would reaffirm the current practices of the Poteau school district). In 1962, *The New Republic* reported that more than a decade after *McCollum v. Board of Education*, 333 U.S. 203 (1948), held that the Illinois released time program violated the establishment clause, the released time program in Illinois "continued relatively unabated." *Engel v. Vitale*, The New Republic, July 9, 1962, *reprinted in* Religious Liberty in the Supreme Court 142, 143 (Terry Eastland ed. 1993).

27. Abington School District v. Schempp, 374 U.S. 203 (1963).

28. Engel v. Vitale, 370 U.S. 421 (1962).

29. McCollum v. Board of Education, 333 U.S. 203 (1948).

30. Epperson v. Arkansas, 393 U.S. 97 (1968).

31. Lemon v. Kurtzman, 403 U.S. 602 (1971).

32. Committee for Public Education & Religious Liberty v. Nyquist, 413 U.S. 756 (1973).

33. Stone v. Graham, 449 U.S. 39 (1980).

34. Larson v. Valente, 456 U.S. 228 (1982).

35. Wallace v. Jaffree, 472 U.S. 38 (1985).

36. Edwards v. Aguillard, 482 U.S. 578 (1987).

37. County of Allegheny v. American Civil Liberties Union, 492 U.S. 573 (1989).

38. Lee v. Weisman, 112 S.C•t. 2649 (1992).

39. Everson v. Board of Education, 330 U.S. 1 (1947).

40. Zorach v. Clauson, 343 U.S. 306 (1952).

41. Gallagher v. Crown Kosher Super Market of Massachusetts, Inc., 366 U.S. 617 (1961); Two Guys from Harrison-Allentown, Inc. v. McGinley, 366 U.S. 582 (1961); McGowan v. Maryland, 366 U.S. 420 (1961).

42. Board of Education v. Allen, 392 U.S. 236 (1968).

43. Walz v. Tax Commission, 397 U.S. 664 (1970).

44. Widmar v. Vincent, 454 U.S. 263 (1981).

45. Mueller v. Allen, 463 U.S. 388 (1983).

46. Marsh v. Chambers, 463 U.S. 783 (1983).

47. Lynch v. Donnelly, 465 U.S. 668 (1984).

48. Corporation of the Presiding Bishop of the Church of Jesus Christ of Latter-Day Saints v. Amos, 483 U.S. 327 (1987).

49. Zobrest v. Catalina Foothills School District, 113 S.Ct. 2462 (1993).

50. Capitol Square Review and Advisory Board v. Pinette, 115 S.Ct. 2440 (1995).

51. Rosenberger v. Rectors and Visitors of the University of Virginia, 115 S.Ct. 2510 (1995).

52. 472 U.S. 703 (1985); *see id.* at 709–10. The *Thornton* Court thus relied on the second prong of the so-called *Lemon* test, from *Lemon v. Kurtzman*, 403 U.S. 602 (1971). For the cases upholding the constitutionality of Sunday laws, see Gallagher v. Crown Kosher Super Market of Massachusetts, Inc., 366 U.S. 617 (1961) (emphasizing establishment clause claim); Braunfeld v. Brown, 366 U.S. 599 (1961) (emphasizing free exercise claim); Two Guys from Harrison-Allentown, Inc. v. McGinley, 366 U.S. 582 (1961) (emphasizing establishment clause claim); McGowan v. Maryland, 366 U.S. 420 (1961) (emphasizing establishment clause claim).

53. Morris N. Kertzer, What Is a Jew? 151 (1953) (emphasis in original); *see* Rosenberg, *supra* note 26, at 13, 126 (on Jewish Sabbath).

54. 489 U.S. 829, 833 (1989).

55. Feldman, *supra* note 1, at 10–174.

Chapter 15

Jewish Voices and Religious Freedom

A Jewish Critique of Critical Jewish Thinking

Mark A. Graber

The idea of a critical Jewish studies movement may seem a bad joke or a pathetic imitation, of as much enduring value as the "Jewfros" Jewish teenagers from Great Neck, New York, sported during the late 1960s. Nevertheless, a tendency in that direction has been under way for at least a decade. Suzanne Last Stone in 1993 noted "a growing body of legal scholarship that is turning (either unabashedly or more indirectly) to the Jewish legal tradition to advance debate in contemporary legal theory."[1] Recent scholarship claims that Jewish sources might inform particular legal concerns ranging from cloning[2] to capital punishment,[3] as well as more jurisprudential matters such as the role of Jewish lawyers,[4] how the Constitution should be interpreted,[5] and the nature of constitutional amendment.[6] One law professor has even proposed a rabbinic solution to the countermajoritarian difficulty.[7] Jewish law professors also insist that the Jewish experience provides important perspectives on American constitutionalism, one that questions our national commitment to religious equality. Speaking with a different kind of Jewish voice, Stephen Feldman asserts that "from the viewpoint of an American Jew, . . . the constitutional principle of the separation of church and state . . . flows primarily from and helps reproduce the Christian domination of American society and culture."[8]

As currently conceived, critical Jewish studies is largely a spin-off of critical race and feminist studies. Many feminist scholars and scholars of color claim to speak in distinctive female, black, Latino, or Asian voices that they believe should enrich American law.[9] Jewish scholars point to a distinctive Jewish voice that they believe should similarly enrich American law. Many feminist scholars and scholars of color highlight how seemingly neutral practices are based on white male assumptions and privilege white males.[10] Feldman in *Please Don't Wish Me a Merry Christmas* claims that the first amendment's guarantee of religious neutrality similarly reflects Christian assumptions and privileges Christian believers.[11] Critical Jewish studies differs from other critical studies primarily because Jewish voices and experiences differ from other voices and experiences. The central categories that structure critical Jewish scholarship, however, have consciously or subconsciously been derived from previous forms of critical scholarship.

One unfortunate consequence of this uncritical adaptation is the tendency for contemporary forms of critical Jewish studies to privilege rhetorics commonly employed in the United States by the religious right. Important strands in the Jewish tradition might, if translatable into legal English, support more progressive interpretations of the United States Constitution. Still, claims that a distinctive Jewish voice exists may buttress claims that a distinctive religious voice exists, a claim now being used to justify a greater presence of conservative Christianity in public affairs. Critical Jewish scholars are on strong grounds when they maintain that first amendment law has always reflected Christian assumptions and privileged Christian believers. Indiscriminately labeling as "oppressive" all policies that disadvantage Jews, however, may buttress claims that any policy that inconveniences a religious minority is oppressive, a claim being made by Christian conservatives who are demanding equal state funding for their religious schools.

Critical Jewish studies will serve more progressive ends by highlighting themes that do not have clear analogies in critical race and feminist studies: the pluralism of Jewish voices and the relative success of Jews in the United States. A critical Jewish scholarship that emphasized the remarkable diversity of Jewish voices on matters of concern to American law would be truer to Jewish sources and provide an important counter to conservative calls for a public square infused with generic religious values. By demonstrating that no generic Jewish or religious voice exists, progressive Jewish scholars would help expose proposals to accommodate or advance religion in general as unconstitutional efforts to accommodate and advance particular religions. Critical Jewish scholars should also acknowledge that Jewish narratives in the United States are more often success stories than the tales told by women, persons of color, or members of most historically disadvantaged groups. The conventional claim in much critical scholarship that prejudice tends to remain fairly constant over time,[12] problematic when applied to women and persons of color, cannot without trivialization be applied to a minority whose members are disproportionately represented in virtually all desirable demographic or social categories and disproportionally unrepresented in virtually all undesirable demographic or social categories.[13] By focusing on the "trading range" of first amendment law and policy in the United States, critical Jewish scholars will better assess Jewish progress toward equality and provide other critical scholars with some intellectual tools that can help assess progress toward other elements of human flourishing.

Critical scholars lose valuable perspectives when they concentrate exclusively on the particular struggles of a particular group at a particular time. The political contests over equal rights of one era, while of great importance to participants, may seem less pressing when placed in historical context. Critical Jewish scholarship at the dawn of the twenty-first century should focus more on where battles for religious freedom are being fought and less on which side has won the latest election or Supreme Court case. Progressives cannot hope for pure religious freedom or neutrality in some global sense. "Equality," "freedom," and "religion" are essentially contested concepts.[14] Hence, struggles over religious equality and freedom are endemic to any society, whether that society be medieval France, Nazi Germany, or the contemporary United States. No neutral conceptions govern these struggles, so the dominant understandings at any given time will inevitably reflect the values and privilege the interests of dominant groups. Still, the nature of those dominant conceptions matters. Scholars steeped in the Jewish experience can provide a healthy reminder that a society debating whether a "nonsectarian" prayer may be said at a public school graduation protects more religious freedom than a society debating whether religious minorities should be expelled or exterminated.

The Voice of Jewish Law

Many critical Jewish scholars believe that greater attention to the Jewish voice will provide better grounding for progressive visions of the American legal order. The seminal piece of contemporary Jewish critical thinking,[15] Robert Cover's "Obligation: A Jewish Jurisprudence of the Social Order," suggests that "the [Jewish] rhetoric of obligation speaks more sharply . . . than that of rights," on such progressive concerns as the normative foundations "for the material guarantees of life and dignity flowing from the community to the individual."[16] Irene and Yale Rosenberg claim that "Jewish law offers a striking contrast to the Supreme Court's blossoming love affair with factual guilt as a basis for preserving the judgment of conviction."[17] Feminist legal theory is a third area where scholars assert that Jewish law might buttress progressive insights.[18]

Whether and how materials taken from Jewish law should guide a secular culture are open questions within Jewish legal circles. American law may have biblical roots,[19] but divine commandments are not authoritative sources of law in the United States, and religious laws directed at the spiritual life of an individual or community may not provide appropriate analogies for a society constitutionally committed to regulating only outward behavior.[20] Optimists nevertheless believe that "Jewish law can be used to address some important issues in contemporary American constitutional theory."[21] David Dow even asserts that "the normative ontology of the systems of Jewish and American law are so nearly identical that the Judaic resolution of certain theoretical difficulties can be wholly transplanted to the American domain."[22] Suzanne Stone is more pessimistic. In her view, the vision of Jewish law in contemporary legal theory "is often more wishful than accurate and even accurate, has limited applicability in a secular legal society."[23] Steven Friedell similarly declares that "the effort to incorporate only secular aspects of Jewish law . . . is not likely to present an accurate application of Jewish law because such incorporation will take these rules out of context." "Applying secular aspects of Jewish law in a modern legal system," he concludes, "would distort the values of both Jewish law and the modern legal system."[24]

The audience for Jewish voices presents a more significant, yet underappreciated problem for critical Jewish scholarship. Talmudic analyses of American law run great risks of preaching almost entirely to the choir. The Jewish law professors most likely to read and appreciate such essays are for the most part already considerably to the left of the political center in the United States. Law review essays pointing out that the MaHaRaL of Prague rejected law and order themes prominent in American conservative circles are, thus, more likely to increase Jewish commitments to Judaism than Jewish commitments to liberalism. Conservative Christians, by comparison, are no more likely to be converted to liberalism than to Judaism by liberal Jewish voices. Such readers are far more likely to be persuaded by an Augustine perspective on American law than a Maimonidean perspective, particularly when the two diverge.

The main impact of efforts to introduce the Jewish voice in legal scholarship, given the present constitution of the American public, will probably be to legitimate Christian-voice scholarship. To the extent the teachings of Rabbi Akiba belong in the public square, so do the teachings of Thomas Aquinas and Jerry Falwell. Moreover, the audience for Christian-voice scholarship is geometrically greater than the audience for rabbinic wisdom. Unless critical Jewish scholars have some reason for thinking that religious voices in general have the capacity to move American politics in progressive directions, the focus of Jewish-voice scholarship should be reconceived.

Critical Jewish scholars would be better off acknowledging the pluralism of authentic Jewish voices, and using that pluralism to debunk common claims made by religious conservatives. Using Talmudic insights to privilege progressive positions in American law is problematic because the Jewish tradition rarely speaks with one voice, even with respect to such basic issues as who is Jewish[25] and the legitimacy of the Jewish state. Jewish voices, past and present, can typically be found on both sides of those issues of particular concern to the contemporary American left. Professor (and Rabbi) Samuel Levine points out how important strands in Jewish thought both condemn and acknowledge a need for capital punishment.[26] Jewish organizations routinely submit legal briefs for and against legal abortion, and for and against affirmative action.[27] Few progressives want American law to be infused with values associated with the religious right in Israel, but no one could seriously argue that the ultraorthodox parties do not reflect authentic strands of Judaism. Certainly, law professors without rabbinic degrees or the equivalent should hesitate before asserting in a law review that their understanding of Judaism is somehow more authentically Jewish than the understanding of many practicing Jews and Jewish communities.[28]

Critical Jewish scholarship is more persuasive and realistic when demonstrating sociologically that religious traditions do not speak with unambiguous conservative voices on many social issues than when asserting as a theological matter that Judaism compels a progressive position on some public policy. Respect for the diversity of Jewish voices is probably as Jewish as any policy position advanced by a progressive Jewish thinker. One element of the Jewish voice, Stone suggests, is the tendency to endorse values central to both sides of disputed issues, "the tendency to think in oppositional or paradoxical interdependencies."[29] Progressive Jews can refute claims that the Bible unequivocally endorses capital punishment and condemns abortion by pointing to prominent strands in the Jewish tradition that oppose the death penalty and tolerate abortion.[30] Assertions that Jews ought to regard these strands as more authoritative than more conservative strands within the Jewish tradition should be judged by individual Jews and Jewish communities, not by federal judges or law review editors.

The diversity of Jewish voices on matters of public interest belies conservative claims that greater public accommodation of religion will provide unique, frequently neglected perspectives on important political questions. The more likely result is that participants in public debates will simply incorporate into previously existing arguments more religious references to the detriment of both politics and religion. Politics will suffer as already difficult secular issues are aggravated by sectarian divisions. Religion will suffer as law professors and political activists engage in forms of law-office Christianity, Judaism, or the like, scouring religious traditions for citations favorable to particular causes, while ignoring equally authoritative citations that support alternative policies.

The United States is not racked with debates between the religious and the secular in which the religious are being unduly gagged. The disputes most commonly presented as pitting religion against unbelief are, in fact, better characterized as pitting one set of religious adherents against another set of religious adherents. The Christian Legal Society, National Jewish Commission on Law and Public Affairs, Southern Baptist Convention Christian Life Commission, and United States Catholic Conference authorized briefs defending the constitutionality of prayers during a public school graduation ceremony. The American Jewish Congress, Baptist Joint Committee on Public Affairs, General Assembly of the Presbyterian Church, General Conference of Seventh-Day Adventists, and National Council of Churches of Christ in the U.S.A. authorized briefs declaring such practices unconstitutional.[31] Government has no business deciding on arbitrary grounds which groups are more truly religious, and Justice Scalia engaged in religious bigotry by describing school prayer cases as contests between "nonbelievers" and "a religious majority."[32] For similar reasons, government has no business selecting any Jew to present the Jewish viewpoint on any religious or secular question or, what amounts to the same thing, selecting any group of Jews to choose who will present the Jewish viewpoint.

Jewish voices have a different place than black or feminist voices in public debate because Jewish concerns and experiences are different from the concerns and experiences of women and persons of color. The call for voice scholarship in American law initially reflected the underrepresentation of women and persons of color in legal conversations about race and gender.[33] Jews, by comparison, are well represented in legal conversations on religion and on any other matter in which Jews as a group might be said to have an interest. Jewish voices will be heard on free exercise and establishment clause issues, and those voices will reflect Jewish experiences and sources, even if those voices are not self-consciously Jewish. Moreover, borrowing rhetorics aimed at promoting greater inclusion of black and female voices in the public sphere may be counterproductive for Jews, who have historically been more concerned to exclude overt Christian voices than include overt Jewish voices. Getting the Christmas tree out of the classroom has always been valued more than getting the menorah in. Critical Jewish scholarship modeled on critical race and feminist scholarship, therefore, may result in the practical abandonment of one central theme of progressive Jewish litigation.

If religious voices are to be given places of honor in public debates, Jewish voices ought to join the festivities. Nothing will be gained by unilateral disarmament, though given the limited audience for the MaHaRaL of Prague, little is likely to be lost if progressive activists refuse to speak in self-conscious Jewish voices. Still, the invitation for religious voices is more likely to increase the cacophony of public debate than provide unique perspectives on public life. Consensus will be achieved, if achieved at all, only by government actions that unconstitutionally privilege some religious values over others.[34] Rather than use Jewish sources that are obscure to the general public to reinvigorate progressive cases, critical Jewish thinkers would be better off demonstrating how religious pluralism both within and without Judaism belies more conservative understandings of the role of religion in public law. Given the powerful Jewish religious and cultural influence on the lives of Jewish academics, we can remain confident that are voices will always be authentically Jewish even if our footnotes are not.

The Voice of Jewish Experience

Stephen Feldman in 1997 introduced a second critical Jewish voice, the voice of Jewish experience. Rather than use the voice of Jewish law to illuminate hitherto unappreciated possibilities in the American law of religious freedom, *Please Don't Wish Me a Merry Christmas* details how "from the viewpoint of an American Jew" the constitutional separation of church and state is and has always been far more repressive of Jewish life than conventional commentary on the first amendment acknowledges.[35] While the "dominant story" in the United States maintains that "the separation of church and state . . . equally protects the religious liberty of all, especially religious outgroups, including Jews," Feldman maintains that "the constitutional concept of separation of church and state contribute[s] to the Christian domination of American society, including Christian cultural imperialism over religious outgroups, particularly Jews."[36] Jews in *Please Don't Wish Me a Merry Christmas* (though certainly not in Feldman's general thought) are primarily victims of Christian oppression, and not bearers of a distinct tradition that might inform the American law of religious freedom. No effort is made to set out a distinctively Jewish understanding of religious freedom, in part one suspects, because Feldman recognizes that distinctive Jewish understandings do not become law in predominately Christian America. His critical scholarship highlights those Christian understandings that necessarily structure establishment and free exercise practice in a Christian society, and does not give Jews the comfort of knowing that the law of religious freedom in a predominately Jewish society would be perceived as any less burdensome by the Christian minority.[37]

Please Don't Wish Me a Merry Christmas is probably the first self-conscious work of critical Jewish studies. Not only is the book part of a general series, Critical America, edited by two distinguished critical legal scholars, Richard Delgado and Jean Stefancic, but, more important, Feldman when analyzing the Jewish experience with religious freedom relies heavily on intellectual tools fashioned by critical race and legal scholars. Following in the footsteps of critical race scholars, critical feminist scholars, and other critical legalists, he brilliantly documents the numerous ways in which allegedly neutral policies are in fact based on majoritarian principles and privilege majoritarian practices. Feldman's analysis is weakened, however, by an uncritical borrowing from critical scholarship of rhetorical tropes that fail to distinguish meaningfully between the oppressive inequalities of the past and the insensitive inconveniences of the present. Put far too polemically, he and other critical legal scholars are more capable of discerning the subtle similarities than describing the obvious differences between a culture that celebrates holidays by accusing Jews of ritual murder and a culture that celebrates holidays by wishing Jews "a merry Christmas."

Please Don't Wish Me a Merry Christmas persuasively demonstrates that the first amendment as historically interpreted by justices and elected officials does not "equally protect[] the religious liberty of all, especially religious outgroups, including Jews."[38] Constitutional claims of religious neutrality, Feldman points out, are false in theory and false in practice. The constitutional law of religion is not neutral because that law was an historical consequence of the "New Testament prohibition against forcefully converting Jews,"[39] reflects a Christian distinction between spiritual and material life[40] that has little foundation in Judaism,[41] and is grounded in distinctively Protestant understandings of the conditions under which religion will flourish.[42] Given these Christian foundations, that first amendment law has always provided more protection for Christians than Jews or members of other religious outgroups is hardly surprising. Long after American lawyers stopped maintaining that Christianity was embodied in the common law,[43] public schools required Bible reading and judges punished as blasphemy criticisms of Christian doctrine.[44] Moreover, Feldman points out, in a society where the vast majority of persons are Protestant, the American separation of church and state legitimates substantial private discrimination, protects sustained proselytizing of Jews, and otherwise ignores the social pressures pushing Jews toward conversion or assimilation.[45] The Supreme Court, that alleged bastion of human rights, has historically been particularly insensitive to Jewish concerns, ruling that blue laws reflect a general need for a day of rest and that the military can permit personnel to wear crosses but not yarmulkes.[46] No Jew has ever won a free exercise case adjudicated by the United States Supreme Court.[47]

From the powerful points that "the separation of church and state provides far less shelter for religious outgroups than the dominant story would lead one to expect" and "imposes particular costs or disadvantages on outgroups that are not similarly borne by the Christian majority."[48] Feldman deduces the more dubious point that contemporary legal standards oppress Jews. American law, he writes, sanctions "unconscious religious oppression, and more specifically, unconscious antisemitism"; in his view, "[t]he modern democratic state" does not find the constitution a substantial obstacle when "muster[ing] the despotic power to oppress religious outgroups such as Jews."[49] "While the separation of church and state occasionally protects minority or outgroup religion," *Please Don't Wish Me a Merry Christmas* insists that "that protection often dwindles into a limited, hypothetical, or even nonexistent refuge."[50] Jewish progress in the United States is occasionally acknowledged,[51] but the more constant theme of the book is that no real change has occurred, that the United States is "an antisemitically structured society."[52] What appears to the untutored eye as progress is merely a more socially acceptable form of antisemitism replacing a less socially acceptable form of antisemitism. Thus, after noting that "[d]uring the Middle Ages, Christian rulers enacted numerous laws that forced Jews to wear badges or other signs of identification, isolated Jews in ghettos, and exiled

Jews from entire countries," Feldman observes that "[a] twentieth-century manifestation of the theme of Christian universalism is the oft-mentioned 'Judeo-Christian tradition.'" This, he claims, is "dangerous Christian dogma (at least from a Jewish perspective)," which sanctions "many public forms of Christian preaching—such as the prominently displayed signs asserting that 'Jesus is Lord,' the bumper stickers declaring that 'Jesus loves you,' and the ostentatious Christmas displays—all constantly and annoyingly rebuke the Jew for failing to convert to Christianity."[53] Feldman even suggests that Jews were better off in some sense during the fourteenth century because "the religion clauses of the first amendment may have undermined the ability of American Jews to maintain their religious identity in comparison with, for example, medieval European Jews."[54]

Something has clearly gone awry with analysis that equates medieval Europe with contemporary America. Jews in Nazi Germany did not worry about intermarriage, the major threat to the contemporary Jewish community in the United States, but no one thinks this a virtue of the Nuremberg laws. Being "bombarded by Christian . . . messages"[55] is unpleasant, but being burnt at the stake is worse. Just as not everything that is constitutional is particularly wise or noble, so not every government abridgment of the first amendment's religion clauses is a violation of fundamental human rights. The Constitution may prohibit government from taking such actions as placing a creche on the town square even though religious freedom would still exist if such behavior was permitted.[56] Similarly, not all burdens on religious practice are created equal. Orthodox Jews may not be able to participate in college football as players or spectators, but at least they can go to college. Unfortunately, too many critical legalists are led astray by rhetoric that conflates all forms of disadvantage.

Prominent progressive scholars maintain that prejudice has remained fairly constant throughout American history. According to Richard Delgado, a seemingly natural law governs race relations in the United States. "There is change from one era to another," he asserts, "but the net quantum of racism remains the exactly the same, obeying a melancholy Law of Racial Thermodynamics." "Racism," Delgado concludes, "is neither created nor destroyed."[57] Reva Siegal advances a similar claim with respect to gender. She regards most progress in gender as illusory, as at most a short interregnum until patriarchs learn how to manipulate apparently egalitarian rules to restore previous inegalitarian hierarchies. "The ways in which the legal system enforces social stratification," Siegal writes, "are various and evolve over time. Efforts to reform a status regime bring about changes in its rule structure and justificatory rhetoric—a dynamic [she] call[s] 'preservation-though-transformation.'"[58] Rogers Smith presents a more dynamic view on the influence of ascriptive theories of identity on American political practice, suggesting that we should "perceive America's initial conditions as exhibiting only a rather small, recently leveled valley of relative equality nestled amid steep mountains of hierarchy." "Though we can see forces working to erode those mountains over time, broadening the valley," he maintains that "many of the peaks also prove to be volcanic, frequently responding to seismic pressures with outbursts that harden into substantial peaks once again."[59] Smith is more willing than Delgado to acknowledge that periods exist when the forces of equality triumph. Still, his vision of American history centers on the relative constancy of conflict between inegalitarian and egalitarian forces, with little of any permanence hanging on particular battles.

The Jewish experience should cast substantial doubt on these natural laws. If "the net quantum of racism (and sexism) remains exactly the same," then "the net quantum" of antisemitism or other forms of prejudice should also not vary dramatically in the long run. Clearly, however, antisemitism has changed dramatically over the past four hundred years. Jews have historically been murdered, tortured, physically abused, exiled, barred from desirable housing or employment, forbidden to marry non-Jews, forcibly converted, barred from observing Jewish law or establishing Jewish communal institutions, denied the right to vote, hold office, or participate in the legal system, had their property confiscated, destroyed or taken through oppressive taxation, and been forced to wear degrading symbols identifying them as Jews.[60] Being excluded from private clubs, being labeled "pushy, odd, a kill-joy, or ridiculous" for objecting to public displays of Christmas, having one's children jealous of Christian classmates and being required to color Christmas decorations at school[61] are not harms of the same magnitude. Moreover, modern forms of antisemitism are not more subtle means of achieving the historic goals of antisemitism. Despite the inconveniences that Feldman catalogues at great length, Jews have enjoyed substantial success in politics, business, and the academy. Assimilation does remain a Jewish problem. Still, the vast majority of Jews live in areas that have flourishing Jewish communities. Most Jewish children have Jewish parents who do their best to bias them in favor of Judaism.[62] If Judaism does not flourish under these conditions, progressives ought to ponder whether Judaism ought to flourish.

To be fair, no critical theorist really believes that life was better for most woman, persons of color and religious minorities during the nineteenth century.[63] Rather, such rhetorical tropes as "preservation through transformation" merely highlight how significant inequalities typically remain after a particular hierarchical regime is dismantled. This claim is unobjectionable, though people may dispute the extent to which conditions have improved for particular groups. The more serious problem is that language implying that inequalities have not been remedied at all is a poor way of expressing claims that substantial strides toward equality are still necessary. Identifying the disadvantages historically disadvantaged groups must still overcome is important, but critical theorists for numerous reasons need to pay more attention to identifying those disadvantages that have been overcome.

Legal rhetoric that conflates all forms of disadvantage has profoundly conservative consequences. *Please Don't Wish Me a Merry Christmas* can easily be appropriated by right-wing Jews who believe that Jews should spend more time and effort on specifically Jewish causes than on helping other persons obtain a greater measure of equality. If Jews are at present victims of religious oppression, then the first responsibility of Jewish progressives may be to their Jewish community. Critical scholarship also provides progressives with no basis or incentive to engage in any particular cause. Progressives cannot determine which status hierarchies should be dismantled until critical scholarship provides some means for distinguishing among different forms of disadvantage. Why engage in progressive activism if success will at most merely replace one oppressive burden with an equally oppressive burden? Delgado's

Law of Racial Thermodynamics and principles of a similar nature, from this perspective, are invitations to political quiescence.

Progressives need also be aware that their indiscriminate rhetoric of oppression can be and has been appropriated by the religious right. Numerous articles published by such journals as *First Things* castigate secular liberals and their judicial allies for oppressing the religious faithful by requiring them, among other things, not to discriminate against homosexuals.[64] Many progressives find such fundamentalist claims perverse, if not unconstitutional. Nevertheless, if Jewish children are oppressed when exposed to Christmas in public schools, then Christian fundamentalist children may be oppressed when exposed to evolution and secular culture in public schools. Certainly, religious fundamentalists are disadvantaged when required to pay taxes that support schools their children do not attend. Progressives who wish to defend public schooling and antidiscrimination policies that do place more burdens on Christian fundamentalists than liberal Jews[65] need a rhetoric more capable of distinguishing disadvantage from oppression than variations on the Law of Racial Thermodynamics.

The mode of analysis used by stock market technicians provides a surprising yet promising starting place for critical theorists seeking to understand better how the status of Jews and other historically disadvantaged minorities changes over time. Particular stocks and market indices have a price and a trading range, "[t]he high and low prices between which a specific stock or some stock average has been traded or is expected to trade."[66] The high point of a trading range is generally referred to as the resistance level, the "price at which a security or the market itself will encounter considerable selling pressure" because too few investors believe the stock or stocks will continue to increase in value.[67] The low point of a trading range is generally referred to as the support level, the "price at which a security or the market will receive considerable buying pressure" because most investors believe the stock or stocks will not decrease in value.[68] Short-term investors remain concerned with daily fluctuations in their holdings. Long-term investors, by comparison, take interest only when their holdings break their resistance levels or drop below their support levels.

Persons who watch the stock market or a particular stock on random days might conclude that a version of Delgado's Law of Racial Thermodynamics also structures trading on Wall Street. By the very nature of markets, there will always be approximately the same percentage of influential brokers who think the price of a stock or stocks is too high as think the price of stock or stocks is too low. One usually finds several market gurus who maintain that a particular stock should be bought and others who think the stock should be sold immediately. From the viewpoint of an investor in the market for the long term, however, the crucial issue is not whether more experts are optimistic about their stock holdings today than they were ten years ago. The issue is whether the price of their stocks has gone up or down. Holding a share of General Electric (GE) at $90 that many experts think overpriced is better than holding a share of GE at $20 that many experts think undervalued. Similarly, persons are better off holding a share of GE at $90 than a share of IBM at $20, even if more investors have been selling GE than IBM. That the quantum of market pessimism probably remains fairly constant over time has little bearing on more vital questions concerning what the market is worth.

This notion of trading ranges may illuminate features of the American experience with religious and other equalities that much progressive scholarship obscures. Just as stock prices for periods of time may oscillate between a high and low price, so many scholars observe that politics for periods of time consists of political struggles over a fairly stable set of alternatives.[69] Borrowing from stock market technicians, critical theorists might understand the legal trading range of various forms of equality at a given time in the United States as roughly measured by the difference between the most extreme two to three Supreme Court justices on each side of various constitutional issues.[70] The political trading range of various equalities may be roughly measured by the difference between those political coalitions that could plausibly win the next election. As in the case of stocks, people involved in short-term concerns are quite interested in who won the most recent election or Supreme Court case. From the perspective of the longer term, the more important issue may be what issues are on or off the table. To make the obvious point, Jews are better off in a policy debating whether to place creches on the town green than in a polity debating when to hold the next pogrom, even if the alternative favored by most Jews usually loses in the first polity and wins in the second.

The politics and law of religious freedom in the United States have been in a relatively stable trading range for the past twenty to thirty years. The polity has drifted rightward, as the Christian coalition gains more influence on the Republican Party. Still, the range of mainstream political and legal alternatives has remained fairly constant. The legal trading range for religious freedom at the beginning of 1999 is probably the difference between the Constitution as understood by Justices Scalia and Thomas, and the Constitution as understood by Justices Stevens, Ginsburg, Breyer, and Souter. The political trading range for religious freedom at present is probably the difference between the policies that would be enacted by a Richard Gephardt administration and a Dan Quayle administration. The trading range for some specific freedom of religion issues seems to be as follows:

1. At most, the free exercise clause requires government to exempt religious groups from certain burdens when no government interest justifies a strictly neutral law. At least, the free exercise clause requires government not to discriminate intentionally against a religion.[71]
2. At most, state officials may never sponsor to any degree any prayer or religious activity. At least, government may only sponsor (but not compose) nondenominational prayers, permit students to engage in voluntary school prayer, and permit religious organizations to use public facilities that are generally open to the public.[72]
3. At most, the Constitution forbids any state funding, direct or indirect, of parochial schools and other religious institutions. At least, government cannot give funds to religious schools or institutions directly, but religious schools and institutions may obtain funds that are given to the general public.[73]

These trading ranges all reflect debates over how a secular polity should be neutral toward religion. Does neutrality require "a wall of separation between church and state" or does neutrality require government to ensure that state burdens or benefits are not distributed on the basis of religious belief? Critical theorists properly note that no conception of neutrality satisfies some absolute standard. Conceptions of neutrality consciously or subconsciously rooted in Christian doctrine and experience will differ from conceptions of neutrality consciously or subconsciously rooted in Jewish doctrine and experience. Thus, the dominant conception of government neutrality in a predominately Christian society will in practice not leave Jews as free to be Jews as Christians are free to be Christians. Still, Jewish history quite clearly demonstrates that a government trying to be neutral will protect far more religious freedom than a government that makes no pretence of neutrality.

None of the historical hazards of Jewish existence are on the political agenda in the United States at the present time. No organization or individual likely to obtain a fair degree of power in the foreseeable future regards Jews as nonentities who may be killed, exiled, or forcibly converted at will. No such organization or individual regards Jews as aliens who may be denied fundamental political rights or as second-class citizens who may be subject to explicit burdens not visited upon mainstream Christians. Most significantly, the political, legal, and social disabilities Jews in the United States experienced during the twentieth century have not prevented them from building vibrant communities that exercise substantial political, legal, and social power. Problems of assimilation and intermarriage remain, but these communities show no sign of weakening and, as Jewish institutions have historically done, are adjusting to meet these threats to Jewish existence.

The trading-range metaphor may also highlight why practices conservative Christians claim are oppressive are better understood as resulting from the weakened hegemony of Christianity over American law than any status of conservative Christians as a newly despised minority. Jews and other religious minorities expect that neutral laws and public school curricula will place them at some disadvantage with respect to mainstream Christians. Look, for example, at when the library is open at most major state universities. As society becomes more diverse and secular, conservative Christians increasingly experience some of the disadvantages that non-Christians have experienced for centuries. Religions impose costs on adherents, and no egalitarian society can promise to remove the negative consequences of religious decisions. Being forced to choose between religious values and either educational or employment opportunities may seem burdensome, but most non-Christians have experienced these burdens for ages without much support from Christian fundamentalists.

The differences between me and Professor Feldman may primarily reflect the differences between a Jew living in a Jewish enclave and a Jew living in a Jewish outpost. As recent incidents in Utah and Alabama demonstrate, Jews living in Jewish outposts still experience substantial coercive pressures that constitutional law or practice do not mitigate.[74] Jews living in Silver Spring, Maryland, however, do not worry that the public school choir will become an arm of the local church, that Jewish children will be ridiculed if they do not enthusiastically participate in fundamentalist sing-a-longs. Deborah Malamud notes in a similar context that "[h]ad there been a official religion of the New York Public Schools in [her] childhood, the New York local of the

American Federation of Teachers would have seen to it that it was Judaism."[75] Indeed, Jews in Jewish enclaves may benefit from features of American religion law that burden Jews in Jewish outposts. Fundamentalist professors are more likely to be perceived as "nutty" than are liberal Jewish academics by their liberal (Jewish or Christian) chairs and deans. Our young daughters were jealous of Christian friends during Christmas, but their Christian friends were jealous of them when every year they dressed up in frilly dresses as Queen Esther and attended a very public Purim festival full of rides, games, and candy.

The voice of Jewish experience is as diverse as the voice of Jewish law. Some liberal Jews identify more with more conservative Jews than with liberal Christians. Others believe they have more in common with liberal Christians than ultraorthodox Jews. Some Jews experience themselves as a beleaguered minority; others do not and will not even if they recognize the way present first amendment law is biased toward Christianity. *Please Don't Wish Me a Merry Christmas* offers a welcomed reminder that Jews who live in Jewish outposts experience severe coercive measures. The message gets lost in those passages that conflate the "viewpoint of an American Jew" with the viewpoint of American Jews.

Conclusion

Critical scholars should not be embarrassed to celebrate Jewish success in the United States. That members of one historically oppressed group are now well represented in the American elite gives reason for hope that other historically disadvantaged groups will one day suffer no more political, legal, and social burdens than do most Jews in the United States. Moreover, this Jewish success cannot be explained as a simple by-product of Christian self-interest. People do not come into the world with neon signs flashing both their interests and the most efficient ways of achieving those interests. Politics consists as much of struggles to define human interest as struggles to fulfill human interests. Jews are better off today in large part because Christian self-interests changed in ways that permitted greater Jewish flourishing. Progressives may, therefore, believe that majoritarian conceptions will one day change in ways that permit greater human flourishing in general.

Critical Jewish scholarship will best contribute to the greater flourishing of Jews and humankind by offering something more than mere variations on themes developed by other critical scholars, by understanding "critical" as meaning "discerning" rather than "negative." Both on questions of Jewish voice and Jewish experience, following the paths laid down by other critical scholars is likely to distort Jewish practice and privilege conservative results. Progressives recognize that women and persons of color will not necessarily succeed by imitating Jews.[76] Why should Jewish progressives think their causes will best be served by employing the rhetorics used by critical race and critical feminist scholars?

NOTES

1. Suzanne Last Stone, "In Pursuit of the Counter-Text: The Turn to the Jewish Legal Model in Contemporary American Legal Theory," 106 *Harvard Law Review* 813, 814 (1993). See Samuel J. Levine, "Jewish Legal Theory and American Constitutional Theory: Some Comparisons and Contrasts," 24 *Hastings Constitutional Law Quarterly* 441, 444 (1997) (citing numerous articles).

2. Michael Broyde, "Cloning People: A Jewish Law Analysis of the Issues," 30 *Connecticut Law Review* 503 (1998).

3. Samuel J. Levine, "Capital Punishment in Jewish Law and Its Application to the American Legal System: A Conceptual Overview," 29 *St. Mary's Law Review* 1037 (1998).

4. Michael J. Broyde, "A Jewish Law Analysis of Being a Prosecutor or Defense Attorney," 65 *Fordham Law Review* 1141 (1998); Sanford Levinson, "Identifying the Jewish Lawyer: Reflections on the Construction of Professional Identity," 14 *Cardozo Law Review* 1577 (1993).

5. Samuel J. Levine, "Unenumerated Constitutional Rights and Unenumerated Biblical Obligations: A Preliminary Study in Comparative Hermeneutics," 15 *Constitutional Commentary* 511 (1998); Levine, "Jewish Legal Theory and American Constitutional Theory."

6. Noam J. Zohar, "Midrash: Amendment Through the Molding of Meaning," *Responding to Imperfection: The Theory and Practice of Constitutional Amendment* (edited by Sanford Levinson) (Princeton University Press: Princeton, N.J., 1995).

7. David R. Dow, "Constitutional Midrash: The Rabbis' Solution to Professor Bickel's Problem," 29 *Houston Law Review* 543 (1992). Law reviews are also publishing various analyses of Jewish law that make little overt effort to inform American practice. See, e.g., Steven H. Resnicoff, "Physician Assisted Suicide Under Jewish Law," 1 *DePaul Journal of Health Care Law* 589 (1997); David M. Cobin, "Beyond the United States: A Brief Look at the Jewish Law of Manumission," 70 *Chicago-Kent Law Review* 1339 (1995); Daniel Pollack, Chaim Steimmetz, and Vicki Lens, " *Anderson v. St. Francis-St. George Hospital*: Wrongful Living from an American and Jewish Legal Perspective," 45 *Cleveland State Law Review* 621 (1997).

8. Stephen M. Feldman, *Please Don't Wish Me a Merry Christmas: A Critical History of the Separation of Church and State* (New York University Press: New York, 1997), p. 9.

9. See, e.g., Richard Delgado, "When a Story Is Just a Story: Does Voice Really Matter?" 76 *Virginia Law Review* 95, 106 (1990); Mari J. Matsuda, "Public Response to Racist Speech: Considering the Victim's Story," 87 *Michigan Law Review* 2320 (1989); Mari J. Matsuda, "Affirmative Action and Legal Knowledge: Planting Seeds in Plowed-Up Ground," 11 *Harvard Women's Law Journal* 1 (1988).

10. See, e.g., Lucinda M. Finley, "Choice and Freedom: Elusive Issues in the Search for Gender Justice," 96 *Yale Law Journal* 914, 941–43 (1987); Richard Delgado, "Rodrigo's Fourth Chronicle: Neutrality and Stasis in Antidiscrimination Law," 45 *Stanford Law Review* 1133, 1139–47 (1993).

11. Feldman, *Merry Christmas*, pp. 4–5.

12. See notes 58–60, below, and the relevant text.

13. Consider the following passages from Benjamin Ginsburg, *The Fatal Embrace: Jews and the State* 1 (University of Chicago Press: Chicago, 1993):

> Today, though barely 2% of the nation's population is Jewish, close to half of its billionaires are Jews. The chief executive officers of the three major television networks and the four largest film studios are Jews, as are the owners of the nation's largest newspaper chain and most influential single newspaper, the *New York Times*. In the late 1960s, Jews already constituted 20% of the faculty of elite universities and 40% of the professors of elite law schools; today, these percentages doubtless are higher.

Jews are elected to public office in disproportionate numbers. In 1993, ten members of the United States Senate and thirty-two members of the House of Representatives were Jewish, three to four times their percentage of the general population.

14. See, e.g., William E. Connolly, *The Terms of Political Discourse*, 3d ed. (Princeton University Press: Princeton, 1993), pp. 225–31.

15. But see Stone, "The Counter-Text," pp. 814–16 (noting earlier studies attempting to integrate Jewish and American law).

16. Robert M. Cover, "Obligation: A Jewish Jurisprudence of the Social Order," 5 *Journal of Law & Religion* 65, 73, 71 (1987).

17. Irene Merker Rosenberg and Yale L. Rosenberg, "Guilt: Henry Friendly Meets the MaHaRaL of Prague," 90 *Michigan Law Review* 604 (1991).

18. Steven F. Friedell, "The 'Different Voice,' in Jewish Law: Some Parallels to a Feminist Jurisprudence," 67 *Indiana Law Review* 915 (1992).

19. See Rosenberg and Rosenberg, "Guilt," p. 615.

20. Ibid., p. 614–15 (noting, for example, that Jewish law is less worried about "acquittal of the factually guilty" because "God will ultimately assess culpability correctly and completely and punish accordingly").

21. Levine, "Jewish Legal Theory and American Constitutional Theory," p. 444.

22. Dow, "Constitutional Midrash," p. 544. See Rosenberg and Rosenberg, "Guilt," p. 615 ("differences between Jewish and American law should not obscure their similarities").

23. Stone, "The Counter-Text," p. 814. See Levinson, "Identifying the Jewish Lawyer," p. 1607 (wondering "whether the relationship between Jewish and American law could be not only one of difference, but also of outright conflict").

24. Steven Friedell, "Aaron Kirschenbaum on Equity in Jewish Law," 1993 *BYU Law Review* 909, 910, 919 (1993). In another article, however, Friedell asserted that "a feminist jurisprudence based on Carol Gilligan's approach has much in common with Jewish law." See Friedell, "The 'Different Voice,'" p. 944. For a good summary of this debate over Jewish law, see Levine, "Jewish Legal Theory and American Constitutional Theory," p. 443.

25. See Levinson, "Identifying the Jewish Lawyer," p. 1584.

26. Levine, "Capital Punishment."

27. Ruti Teitel, "A Critique of Religion as Politics in the Public Sphere," 78 *Cornell Law Review* 748, 789–90 (1993) (analyzing the different amicus briefs Jewish groups submitted in *Webster v. Reproductive Health Services*, 492 U.S. 490 [1989]); Justin J. Finger, "Brief Amici Curiae of the Anti-Defamation League of B'nai B'rith on Behalf of Itself and the National Jewish Commission on Law and Public Affairs in Support of Petitioners," *International Association of Firefighters v. Cleveland* (1985) (opposing affirmative action); Nathan Z. Dershowitz, "Brief of the American Jewish Congress, Amicus Curiae, in Support of Respondents," *Firefighters Local Union No. 1784 v. Stotts* (1983).

28. For a discussion of the problems that result when legal scholars wander outside the law, see Mark A. Graber, "Law and Sports Officiating: A Misunderstood and Justly Neglected Relationship," 16 *Constitutional Commentary* (1999, forthcoming).

29. Stone, "Counter-Text," p. 888.

30. The Central Conference of American Rabbis has repeatedly called for the abolition of capital punishment and fought passage of various proposals to ban or regulate abortion. See, e.g., Central Conference of American Rabbis, "Capital Punishment" (Central Conference of American Rabbis, 1998); Central Conference of American Rabbis, "On Abortion and the Hyde Amendment" (Central Conference of American Rabbis, 1998).

31. See Edward McGlynn Gaffney, "Brief of Amicus Curiae of the Christian Legal Society,

National Association of Evangelics, and the Fellowship of Legislative Chaplains, Inc. in Support of Petitioners," *Lee v. Weisman* (1991); Nathan Lewsin, "Brief of Amicus Curiae of the National Jewish Commission of Law and Public Affairs ('COLPA') in Support of Petitioners," *Lee v. Weisman* (1991); Michael K. Whitehead, "Brief of the Southern Baptist Convention Christian Life Commission as Amicus Curiae in Support of Petitioners," *Lee v. Weisman* (1991); Mark E. Chopko, "Brief of the United States Catholic Conference as Amicus Curiae in Support of Petitioners," *Lee v. Weisman* (1991); Douglas Laycock, "Brief Amici Curiae of the American Jewish Congress, Baptist Joint Committee on Public Affairs, American Jewish Committee, National Council of Churches of Christ in the U.S.A., Anti-Defamation League of B'nai B'rith, General Conference of Seventh-Day Adventists, People for the American Way, National Jewish Community Relations Advisory Council, New York Committee on Public Education and Religious Liberty and James E. Andrews as Stated Clerk of the General Assembly of the Presbyterian Church (U.S.A.) In Support of Respondents," *Lee v. Weisman* (1991).

32. *Lee v. Weisman*, 505 U.S. 577, 646 (1992) (Scalia, J., dissenting).

33. Richard Delgado, "The Imperial Scholar: Reflections on a Review of Civil Rights Literature," 132 *University of Pennsylvania Law Review* 561 (1984).

34. For an excellent argument on this point, see Teitel, "Religion as Politics," pp. 815–17.

35. Feldman, *Merry Christmas*, p. 9. At times, Professor Feldman unduly homogenizes Jewish experience. His narrative rings far truer to my experiences as a Jew living in Hanover, New Hampshire, than as a Jew living in Long Island or in the Washington, D.C., community. Moreover, he is simply wrong to insist that all Jews recognize that Christmas is necessarily a Christian celebration. Feldman, *Merry Christmas*, p. 273. Much to my chagrin, my German-Jewish in-laws celebrate what they claim is a secular Christmas (and they claim that this is a German-Jewish tradition). Feldman's claim that all Christian sects "obviously have far more in common with each other than with Judaism" is also problematic. Feldman, *Merry Christmas*, p. 220. Many liberal Jews believe they have more in common with liberal Christians than with ultraorthodox Jews.

36. Feldman, *Merry Christmas*, pp. 255–56.

37. For a fascinating study of how the different religious concerns of different societies structure the law of religious freedom, see Gary Jeffrey Jacobsohn, "Three Models of Secular Constitutional Development: India, Israel, and the United States," 10 *Studies in American Political Development* 1 (1996).

38.Feldman, *Merry Christmas*, p. 255.

39. Ibid., 130. See also pp. 69, 92, 151, 156, 261.

40. Ibid., pp. 97, 229.

41. Ibid., p. 180.

42. Ibid., pp. 113–14, 117, 153–57, 173.

43. Ibid., pp. 132, 143. See also William Wetmore Story, *The Life and Letters of Joseph Story*, vol. 1 (Books for Libraries Press: Freeport, N.Y., 1971), pp. 430, 8–9.

44. Feldman, *Merry Christmas*, pp. 188, 208.

45. See ibid., pp. 18, 76, 123, 154–55, 183, 192, 200–201.

46. Ibid., pp. 187, 205. See also *Braunfeld v. Brown*, 366 U.S. 599 (1961); *Goldman v. Weinberger*, 475 U.S. 503 (1986).

47. Feldman, *Merry Christmas*, p. 246. See also ibid., p. 229; Mark Tushnet, "Of Church and State and the Supreme Court: Kurland Revisited," 1989 *Supreme Court Review* 373, 381.

48. Feldman, *Merry Christmas*, p. 8.

49. Ibid., pp. 272–73; see also pp. 6, 263, 265.

50. Ibid., p. 274.

51. Ibid., pp. 131, 163.

52. Ibid., p. 266. See also p. 164 ("For American Jews, . . . the adoption of the Constitution brought little real change").

53. Ibid., pp. 17–18. See also pp. 169, 222, 260.

54. Ibid., p. 170.

55. Ibid., p. 285.

56. See Mark A. Graber, "Book Review," 88 *American Political Science Review* 476 (1994).

57. Delgado, "When a Story Is Just a Story," p. 106.

58. Reva Siegal, "Why Equal Protection No Longer Protects: The Evolving Forms of Status-Enforcing State Action," 49 *Stanford Law Review* 1111, 1113 (1997). See also Katharine T. Bartlett and Jean O'Barr, "The Chilly Climate on College Campuses: An Expansion of the 'Hate Speech' Debate," 1990 *Duke Law Journal* 574, 581–82 (1990) ("as one behavior is recognized as sexist, racist, or heterosexist, it may be suppressed, only to take a different less recognizable form").

59. Rogers M. Smith, "Beyond Tocqueville, Myrdal, and Hartz: The Multiple Traditions in America," 87 *American Political Science Review* 549 (1993).

60. See ibid., pp. 17, 23–24, 30, 32, 37–38, 40–41, 46–48, 58, 68, 131–32, 137, 143, 154, 162, 166–67, 195–96, 209–10, 232.

61. See Feldman, *Merry Christmas*, pp. 196, 209, 260, 281–85. My major fuss is that my favorite classical music station plays one Christmas piece after another from Thanksgiving until the New Year.

62. For a provocative claim that such parenting is illiberal, see Richard S. Markovits, *Matters of Principle: Legitimate Legal Argument and Constitutional Interpretation* (New York University Press: New York, 1998), p. 320.

63. See, e.g., Siegal, "Equal Protection," pp. 1146–47.

64. The best example of conservative hysteria is "Symposium: The Judicial Usurpation of Politics," 67 *First Things* 18 (Nov. 1996).

65. The extent to which progressive principles support certain fundamentalist claims respecting public schools is a matter of serious debate in progressive circles. See Nomi Maya Stolzenberg, "'He Drew a Circle That Shut Me Out': Assimilation, Indoctrination, and the Paradox of a Liberal Education," 106 *Harvard Law Review* 581 (1993).

66. David L. Scott, *Wall Street Words: An Essential A to Z for Today's Investor*, rev. ed. (Houghton Mifflin Company: Boston, 1997), p. 392.

67. Ibid., p. 318.

68. Ibid., pp. 373–74.

69. Byron E. Shafer, *The End of Realignment: Interpreting American Electoral Eras* (University of Wisconsin Press: Madison, 1991). As the essays in that work demonstrate, vigorous debate exists over the timing, nature, and significance of various political realignments. What is important for present purposes is that the authors agree that various features of American politics do remain fairly stable for long periods of time.

70. Measuring trading ranges by the most extreme justice on the Supreme Court or on the bench anywhere seems misguided unless a real possibility exists that like-minded justices will be appointed in the near future. For a discussion of this rough rule of three, see Mark A. Graber, "The Clintonification of American Law: Abortion, Welfare and Liberal Constitutional Theory," 58 *Ohio State Law Journal* 731, 784–85 (1997).

71. See *Employment Division v. Smith*, 494 U.S. 872 (1990).

72. See *Lee v. Wiseman*, 505 U.S. 577 (1992).

73. See *Rosenberger v. University of Virginia*, 515 U.S. 819 (1995).

74. See Frank S. Ravitch, "A Crack in the Wall: Pluralism, Prayer and Pain in the Public Schools," this volume.

75. Deborah C. Malamud, "The Jew Taboo: Jewish Difference and the Affirmative Action Debate," 59 *Ohio State Law Journal* 915, 956 (1998).

76. For a particularly good essay on that theme, see Malamud, "The Jew Taboo."

Chapter 16

A Crack in the Wall

Pluralism, Prayer, and Pain in the Public Schools

Frank S. Ravitch

Recently, Mildred Rosario, a teacher in a New York City elementary school, was fired after praying with and proselytizing students in her classroom and refusing to assure school officials that she would not do so again.[1] This situation is rather unremarkable from the traditional constitutional law perspective. Her conduct was a blatant constitutional violation. Most of the controversy surrounding the situation has arisen from the fact that she was terminated from her position. Conservative politicians and religious right leaders have turned her into a martyr and rallied to her defense.[2] Separationists have treated her as a pariah who broke the law.[3] Yet lost in the morass of posturing and the response to Rosario's constitutional violation is what happened to the eleven-year-old student whose family complained about Rosario's unconstitutional behavior.

That student, a Jehovah's Witness, was harassed and threatened by other students in the class to the point of being afraid to return.[4] For example, the terrified girl was blocked by other students when she tried to run out of the classroom. A classmate told reporters, "Everybody was cursing at her. She was crying."[5]

Unfortunately, what happened to this girl is not a singular phenomenon. In actuality, it is a rather mild illustration of the discrimination facilitated by religious exercises in the public schools and reaction to those exercises. This essay will explore this discrimination directly and as a discrete issue. The social dynamics underlying the discrimination warrant this exploration, but the law, which is single-mindedly focused on the Constitution when it comes to "school prayer" issues, has all but ignored the unique characteristics of discrimination and harassment facilitated by public school religious exercises. Moreover, the media and those who frame the issues on both sides tend to ignore, or in the case of the religious right, intentionally obfuscate, the issue.

Virtually all of the discourse addressing the legal issues driving the church-state debate has focused on the Constitution. Yet the Constitution has often proven ineffective in protecting the rights of religious minorities and others who object to religious exercises in the public schools. The Constitution is not self-effectuating. Many school districts simply ignore constitutional mandates, and these mandates themselves have recently become less clear as a result of the legal tactics of school prayer advocates. This is occurring at a time when factions from the religious right are engaged in an organized campaign to influence public school policy, making great strides in influencing school boards and, in some instances, winning a majority of seats on the boards.[6] As a result, the number of religious exercises occurring at public schools nationwide is likely to increase.

In addition to the obvious constitutional concerns this turn of events may raise, there is the troubling connection between public school religious exercises and pernicious discrimination against religious minorities and those who oppose such exercises. The discrimination is not simply a matter of offense taken by those who oppose the exercises; it frequently consists of harassment, threats, and even violence directed at religious minorities and dissenters. It can become particularly attenuated when individual opponents complain or bring a lawsuit. It should hardly be surprising, then, that many people are afraid to stand up against religious practices in the public schools, even when those practices are facilitating discrimination against them.[7] In a sense, this victimizes them twice and presents them with a Hobson's choice.

Nonetheless, the law stays its course, focusing on constitutional concerns and treating the discrimination and harassment sometimes facilitated by religious exercises in the public schools more as a nasty by-product of constitutional violations than as a discrete issue. By not looking at the discrimination as a discrete issue, this approach fails to address the social dynamics that underlie it and make it predictable in certain settings. Moreover, it ignores the fact that discrimination can occur as the result of exercises that are constitutional, such as moments of silence,[8] and that constitutional doctrines in this area are in a state of flux.

The discrimination is not a fad that will extinguish itself. It has been with us since religious pluralism and public school religious exercises first clashed. United States history is replete with instances of public school religious exercises' facilitating discrimination and intolerance against religious minorities and dissenters. In some instances, the discrimination has been an unintended by-product of the exercises. In others, it has been a significant purpose behind them. Regardless, discrimination results.

From the earliest days of public school religious exercises, the exercises have called attention to difference. In particular, they have pointed out students, families, or groups who do not believe in the faith of the majority or its position on the exercises. This has led to mistreatment, discrimination, violence, and even death.

It would be wonderful if outcomes such as these were limited to the past—an interesting historical anomaly. Sadly, they occur all too often today. The modern instances and the law's basic indifference to them are the focus of this essay. In the next section, I provide some historical context for the problem that demonstrates its longevity and persistence, and I set forth some of its more current incarnations. Following that, I will discuss the failure of the law to address, or even recognize, this discrimination as an issue in its own right.

I. From Riots to Harassment: Historical and Modern Examples of Discrimination Facilitated by Public School Religious Exercises

Not long after the foundation of American public schools, more than fifty people were killed and many more injured in two riots that became known as the "Philadelphia Bible Riots of 1844."[9] The riots were part of the reaction to Catholic immigration and presence in the public schools and were fueled by a fear of increasing religious and cultural pluralism as well as by anti-immigrant zeal. In 1840, the country was in the midst of an evangelical revival, the "Second Great Awakening," and a growing nationalist fervor, which was later reflected in the anti-immigrant and reactionary Know-Nothing Party.[10] Around this time, non-Protestant religious diversity began to increase as large numbers of Catholics immigrated to North America and less-mainstream denominations such as the Mormons prospered.[11] The new religious pluralism and the immigrant status of many who gave rise to it created tensions with the Protestant majority, among whom were many who saw both a threat to their values and dominant status. The situation was aggravated by another strain of anti-immigrant sentiment, which was fueled by economic competition.[12]

The evangelical revival served to intensify Protestant animosity toward Catholics, as did nationalist sympathies, which pitted "natives" against immigrants.[13] One result was the strict enforcement of laws, school board policies, and unofficial practices throughout the country that required, or were interpreted as requiring, the reading of the King James version of the Bible, the recitation of Protestant-oriented prayers, and the singing of Protestant-oriented hymns in the recently formed public schools.[14] Such practices were not uncommon when the public schools were primarily attended by Protestants. These laws and practices were, however, sometimes created and often enforced to discriminate against Catholics, who were forbidden by canon law to read the King James version of the Bible, which was also deemed an affront because its dedicatory preface "refers to the pope as the 'man of sin.'"[15] These attempts to introduce or enforce sectarian religious exercises in the increasingly pluralistic public schools were the flashpoint for intolerance and violence. They exacerbated tensions between the religious majority and minorities, as did the use of anti-Catholic instructional materials.

During the mid-nineteenth century, Catholic children were sometimes whipped in public schools for refusing to engage in the religious exercises;[16] a priest in Maine was tarred, feathered, and ridden on a rail as the result of a dispute over Bible reading in the public schools;[17] and other incendiary incidents occurred throughout the country. However, the Philadelphia riots of 1844 brought antagonism to a new level. As the result of the riots in May and July of 1844, at least 58 people were killed; more than 140 were wounded; and property damage has been estimated at hundreds of millions of dollars.[18] The May rioting was sparked by the Bible-reading issue; the July rioting by the discovery that firearms were being stored in St. Philip's church in response to fears that it might be attacked, as other churches had been in May.[19] Regardless, the issue of Bible reading in the schools was the catalyst for the riots.[20] It exacerbated the tensions which gave rise to the riots and served as a flashpoint.[21]

In modern times, we see similar phenomena, although there are significant differences between the Second Great Awakening and the current evangelical revival. Society is becoming more pluralistic but at the same time is witnessing the immense growth and power of the Christian Coalition and other conservative religious organizations with similar agendas.[22] Much of this segment of society sees today's increasing religious and cultural pluralism as a threat to its "once-dominant" values and beliefs[23] and actively seeks to use the mechanisms of government, particularly the public schools, to reinforce its beliefs and political views.[24] Its reaction resembles the reaction of the dominant Protestant majority to the influx of Catholics in the nineteenth century.[25] Then it was often proclaimed that the United States was a "Protestant nation" founded on Protestant values.[26] Today, it is being said that the country is a "Christian nation," founded on Christian values and traditions.[27] The implication of both assertions is that those values and traditions should prevail and that people who oppose their hegemony are outsiders. This has serious ramifications in the context of public school religious exercises.

The ramifications are reflected in several recent cases that exemplify the discrimination and persecution facilitated by public school religious exercises. Despite the Supreme Court's prohibition against organized school prayer,[28] some school districts still engage in unconstitutional practices. Others try to work within the constitutional parameters the Court has laid down but still allow religious exercises, usually through moments of silence sanctioned by state legislation or under the theory that organized "voluntary, student initiated prayer" at school events is somehow constitutional.[29] When this has occurred, the result has been discrimination aimed at religious minorities and dissenters.

I am not suggesting that every time such religious exercises occur they automatically facilitate discrimination. However, as the following cases demonstrate, discrimination occurs too often to be ignored. Discrimination under these circumstances is somewhat predictable because the exercises call attention to differences, which are frequently perceived negatively and have a tendency to create an in-group and out-groups.[30] The religious orientations of those involved can also have a profound impact. Social scientists have done some interesting research on the relationship between prejudice, discriminatory attitudes, and religious motivations (for example, extrinsic versus intrinsic motivations), as well as religious orientations (for example, fundamentalist versus quest orientations). The research has noteworthy implications for the school prayer issue, but is beyond the scope of this essay. It is treated in detail in Ravitch, School Prayer and Discrimination.[31]

Significantly, many of the published cases dealing with school prayer issues do not deal with associated incidents of discrimination,[32] because, as will be discussed later, current legal doctrines in this area are not equipped to address the problem. Thus, the following cases represent only "the tip of the iceberg."[33]

In 1993, the Herdahl family moved from Wisconsin to Mississippi for work-related reasons.[34] The Herdahl children had been baptized Lutheran and attended a Pentecostal church. The area to which they moved is heavily Southern Baptist.[35] Mrs. Herdahl was alarmed when she learned that the North Pontotoc Attendance Center, the local K–12 public school in their new home, Ecru, conducted public prayer over the public address system and conducted religious Bible study thirty years after such practices had been outlawed by the Supreme Court.[36] The practices had a decidedly Southern Baptist bent.[37] The Herdahl children were ridiculed and harassed by teachers and other students because they did not share the majority faith. They were referred to as devil worshipers and atheists; and were accused of not believing in God.[38] A teacher made one Herdahl child wear headphones to avoid hearing the offending prayers, and the child was taunted as a consequence.[39] Friends of the children stopped playing with them for fear of being beaten up. One of the Herdahl children tried to avoid going to school, and another asked whether the people who were making things so hard for them were Christian. When his mother responded in the affirmative, the child volunteered that he did not want to be Christian because he did not want to be like them. Mrs. Herdahl, who is Christian, albeit of a different denomination from the persecutors, was upset.[40]

When the practices did not stop, Mrs. Herdahl filed a lawsuit, and the harassment intensified. Her family received bomb threats; she received a death threat; and the name calling and ridicule persisted.[41] Ultimately, the Herdahls won the lawsuit and an order was issued enjoining the religious exercises.[42] Mrs. Herdahl stated that others in the school district who felt as she did were afraid to say so in public.[43] This kind of self-imposed silence is common because of the harsh reactions that speaking out often brings.[44]

The Herdahl experience might seem to be an isolated one. It is not. In fact, it is not even the worst example of the willingness of a school district to facilitate discrimination and ignore constitutional requirements regarding religious exercises.

In August 1997, a lawsuit was filed against the Pike County, Alabama, School District by the Herrings, a Jewish family whose children had been subjected to severe religious discrimination in school. Many of the alleged incidents were tied to a variety of religious exercises sponsored or condoned by the schools on school property.[45]

The harassment, discrimination, and ridicule were intense.[46] Among the alleged incidents were the following. The Herring children were required to bow their heads during Christian prayers; David Herring, a seventh-grader, was physically forced to do so. A minister speaking at a school assembly told the students that those who do not accept Jesus as their savior are doomed to hell. When Sarah Herring, a sixth grader, got up to leave the assembly, she was taunted by her classmates and later had serious nightmares. Sarah endured similar treatment when the school invited the Gideons to distribute Bibles at school. Because she was Jewish, Sarah was sent to wait in the hall, whereupon the other children called her names as she left the classroom. In the hallway, a Gideon representative tried to persuade her to accept a Bible. When she explained she did not want it because of her faith, he held a cross in her face. Screaming, she ran into the classroom for help, but her teacher did nothing.[47]

The Pike County schools regularly engaged in Christian activities in classes and religious assemblies, such as "Birth of Jesus" plays and "Happy Birthday, Jesus" parties. On one occasion, a vice principal disciplined Paul Herring, an eighth grader, for a class disruption by telling him to compose an essay on the subject of "why Jesus loves me." Additionally, Paul and David Herring were prevented from participating in gym class while wearing their yarmulkes; were physically assaulted by classmates because of their religion; had swastikas drawn on their lockers, book bags, and jackets; and were regularly taunted. The verbal assaults were especially intense after religious activities at school.[48]

The Herring children were sometimes excused from the religious activities and sometimes were not. Mrs. Willis, their mother, in a sworn statement submitted to the court, addressed the ineffectiveness of allowing the children to leave to avoid the offending religious exercises: "Even when they have been given permission to leave by a teacher, however, their leaving makes them a target for name-calling, ostracism and harassment by their classmates."[49]

Like Mrs. Herdahl, Mrs. Willis was unable to effect any significant improvement by contacting school officials. In her sworn statement she declared:

> Every day that I send my children to Pike County schools, I wonder if I am sending them into a war zone. The moment one event is over, a worse one follows on its heels. Every day that I send my children to Pike County schools, I feel that the environment threatens every value that my husband and I have tried to teach them at home. I have asked school officials how they expect me to train my sons to respect other people's property when their own property is vandalized at school and no one is punished. I have asked school officials how I can teach my children to be tolerant human beings and not bigots when they are subjected to outright religious persecution and bigotry in school. The consequences of the school environment on my children's psyches are devastating. My children are growing up believing that America is a caste society and they are untouchables—except for the purpose of getting beaten up.[50]

Several of the activities described above were characterized by school officials as "student-initiated religious exercises," a concept that is being used increasingly by those who wish to return organized religious exercises to the public schools, but one that is still controversial from a legal perspective. Even in the few jurisdictions where organized, public, "student-initiated" prayer has been upheld, however, it is doubtful that the activities taking place in the Pike County Schools could survive constitutional challenge on the ground that the activities were "student-initiated."

Another example of the pain facilitated by public school involvement with religious exercises occurred in a Utah school district where, ironically, the persecutors were Mormon—a denomination that has itself been the target of a great deal of discrimination. Rachel Bauchman, a Jewish high school student, objected to overtly religious songs sung at high school graduations by the high school choir, of which she was a member.[51] The choir also performed at churches, singing the same kind of songs on numerous occasions.[52] Most of this activity was organized by the choir teacher.[53]

When Rachel protested, she was harassed and called names. The teacher commented to other students that Rachel was Jewish.[54] Rachel obtained a court order prohibiting the graduation songs, but at the urging of parents and some students, the choir performed one of the religious songs anyway, and nearly the entire audience joined in—a blatant flouting of the court order.[55] When Rachel and her mother rose to leave—Rachel in tears—parents and students jeered and spat on them.[56]

There were serious allegations that the choir teacher had engaged in such religious practices for more than twenty years, that he had suggested on an earlier occasion the choir was somehow connected to the Mormon Church, and that he had even been cautioned by school officials about such activities. Nonetheless, a panel of the Tenth Circuit Court of Appeals, over a vigorous dissent, refused to reverse a trial court's holding that the practices alleged in *Bauchman* were constitutional.[57] It is significant that the court also held that Rachel Bauchman could not obtain redress for the discrimination she suffered as a result of the negative attention called to her by her teacher, because such conduct, although insensitive, does not "rise to the level of a constitutional violation."[58]

As will be discussed later, the latter holding is consistent with current legal doctrine and is not unique. This is demonstrated by another case. From 1980 until 1982, the Little Axe Independent School District in Oklahoma was divided by a controversy revolving around religious meetings, often conducted by teachers, held before the beginning of the school day at the primary school.[59] Two families, one belonging to the Nazarene denomination and the other to the Church of Christ, complained to the superintendent of schools when their children were confronted and harassed by other students because they did not attend the meetings. The other children asserted that the children of the two families "must not believe in God."[60] On one occasion, the son of one of the families was refused early entry to the school premises to work on a class project because only those whose purpose was to attend the prayer sessions could be admitted at that time.[61]

Initially, the superintendent of schools suspended the meetings to enable the school board to make a determination. Ultimately, the board decided to allow the meetings until they were declared unlawful—the board president was said to have shouted, "Bring on the ACLU."[62] That is exactly what the two families, the Bells and McCords, did. After a lawsuit was filed, the board adopted an "equal access policy" in an attempt to enable the meetings to continue, but the court found that both this policy and the district's original policies violated the Establishment Clause.[63]

The initiation of the lawsuit brought even more persecution. The Bell and McCord children were called "devil worshipers";[64] Joanne Bell received her obituary in the mail. Her children were targeted by constant death threats.[65] Both families received numerous menacing telephone calls and letters.[66] An inverted cross was hung on one of the McCord children's school locker.[67] Joanne Bell's hair was pulled by a school employee.[68] At a school sports banquet, the only athletes not recognized were the McCords' two sons, who each played three sports.[69] There were threats that the Bells' house would be burned; and it was later burned to the ground under suspicious circumstances.[70] The persecution was so persistent and extreme that it forced both families to move out of the school district for the following school year.[71] The McCord house was subsequently vandalized.[72]

It appears that the Bells were members of the religious minority in the area and that the McCords were not. Regardless, the families' position on the issue, arising from sincere belief that it is their right to determine their own children's exposure to religious doctrine, placed both clearly in the minority.[73] In this regard, they were treated with the same disdain as the individuals belonging to religious minorities discussed elsewhere in this essay.

Mrs. Bell later said:

> The threat to burn my home was the one that I probably should have taken the most seriously. I just couldn't see in an [*sic*] civilized area—I considered that these people would not ever do that. But my home was firebombed. Unless you've ever had a fire—the devastation is something you can not ever begin to describe. To lose everything you've ever had. And with four children you really accumulate a lot of things—the trophies. . . . Everything that you saved, your baby pictures, the little things—your marriage license. You lose everything."[74]

As would happen in the *Bauchman* case, the Tenth Circuit Court of Appeals held that the school district could not be held liable for the discrimination and persecution perpetrated by the citizens in the district, despite the fact that board policy facilitated the incident.[75] The court did, however, hold that the district was liable for the harms flowing from its own violation of the Bells' and McCords' constitutional rights.[76] As will be discussed in the next section, this provides little redress for the bulk of the suffering the Bells and McCords endured.

In addition to the cases discussed above, some of the most famous Supreme Court cases dealing with religion in the public schools were accompanied by allegations of discrimination aimed at those who opposed the religious practices in question or who were in the religious minority.[77] The allegations were likely not addressed in the Supreme Court opinions because, as the *Bauchman* and *Bell* cases demonstrate, they are generally not actionable or relevant to the constitutional claims that are the focus of such cases. Much of the discrimination alleged in these cases, of course, was in response to the challenges to the offending religious exercises.

The examples cited above indicate a pattern linking public school religious exercises to discrimination and intolerance, though the pattern will not necessarily recur at every school. The types of religious exercises vary, but each is organized and public, and calls attention to religious differences. Because there is currently a highly organized and well-funded campaign aimed at bringing school prayer and other religious exercises back into the public schools, the likelihood of incidents such as those described is becoming greater. For persons subject to this discrimination, however, the law may be of little help. What follows is a brief discussion of why.

II. The Legal Response (Or Lack Thereof)

When school prayer and other religious exercises occur, the Constitution is the primary mechanism for opposing the exercises and seeking redress. Unfortunately, the Constitution is not of much help in combating the discrimination facilitated by public school religious exercises. Two obvious reasons are that what is constitutional in this area is often in a state of flux—school prayer advocates frequently come up with creative arguments to breathe new life into their cause, and constitutional exercises such as moments of silence and legal forms of ceremonial deism can facilitate discrimination. Significantly, even when the exercises in question are unconstitutional, the Constitution is not a very useful mechanism for dealing with attendant discrimination.

Conduct that may be reached and the remedies available under the Constitution are quite limited in the present context. The conduct that may be redressed under the Constitution does not include much of the discriminatory conduct facilitated by public school religious exercises and the environment they can foster. Moreover, the availability of damages for constitutional violations in the public schools is based on 42 U.S.C. § 1983, which does not reach much of the discriminatory conduct in these cases.[78]

The remedies available for constitutional violations are naturally aimed at the conduct of the government actor and the constitutional rights that government action infringes upon. In the present context, that generally does not include the actions of students, non-policy-making employees (in most circumstances), or others (such as parents and townspeople). In the school prayer context, it is frequently the conduct of these types of actors that is discriminatory, not that of policy-making school officials, even if school policies foster an environment where the discrimination is more likely to occur. More important, even if the school could somehow be charged with the discriminatory acts of these individuals, the acts are not the basis of constitutional violation. The school district's policy or practice that violates the Establishment Clause is the constitutional violation, not the discrimination by others that it fosters. The *Bauchman* and *Bell* cases are very instructive in this regard.

Bauchman and *Bell* demonstrate the futility of trying to use constitutional norms to address incidents of discrimination and harassment facilitated by religious exercises in the public schools. The Tenth Circuit Court of Appeals provides the better illustration of this point in *Bauchman*. The court spends a great deal of time explaining its reasoning as to why the alleged conduct of the choir teacher—which included selection of a number of sectarian songs, regular performances at churches, and poor treatment of Rachel Bauchman, who did not share his religious views—was not unconstitutional.[79] The court also spends a great deal of time explaining why allegations of a twenty-year pattern of religious activity during school-sponsored events by that same teacher were not useful to demonstrate that he had a religious motive in engaging in the behavior of which the Bauchmans complained.[80] Not surprisingly, there was a vigorous dissent.[81]

Aspects of the majority decision are staggering in their departure from traditional understandings of Establishment Clause jurisprudence and evidentiary rules. However, for our purposes, these are not the most significant aspects of the decision, except to the extent they show that even when existing precedent appears to mandate a decision that the Establishment Clause has been violated by religious conduct in a public school, one cannot count on that result.

It is the court's response to the discrimination alleged in *Bauchman* that is most relevant to the present discussion. That response is clear, and under existing precedent and legal norms, quite accurate:

> [W]e must next address the relevance, if any, of her [Rachel Bauchman's] remaining allegations that she was subjected to public ridicule and harassment as a result of defendants' conduct. Certainly, Ms. Bauchman's allegations [that] she was criticized and retaliated against for opposing the religious content of the choir curriculum, taken as true, evidence a lack of sensitivity, crudeness and poor judgement unbefitting of high school students, their parents, and especially, public school teachers and administrators. However, such claims do not rise to the level of a constitutional violation. Nor can they be used to breathe constitutional life into otherwise unactionable conduct. The fact that the defendants did not change their behavior in accordance with Ms. Bauchman's demands [that the religious exercises stop] and reacted negatively and/or offensively to those demands simply can not be viewed as support for her claim that the Choir's performance of religious music at religious venues furthered a religious purpose, advanced or favored religion or a particular religious belief, or otherwise entangled the public school with religion. We reject this "backdoor" attempt to substantiate an otherwise flawed constitutional claim and conclude the district court properly dismissed Ms.Bauchman's Establishment Clause claim.[82]

Essentially, the court is saying that the public ridicule and harassment that Rachel Bauchman endured was wrong but not actionable under the Constitution. If it had been based on gender or race, it might have been actionable under Title VI or IX, but since religion is not protected under those statutes, and despite the fact that the conduct of a schoolteacher facilitated the discrimination at school, Rachel Bauchman was out of luck. Unless there is some cause of action, independent of the Constitution, that directly addresses such discrimination, the number of Rachel Bauchmans without access to redress will continue to grow, and schools will be able to feel increasingly secure that they will not be liable for this kind of discrimination when it occurs. In fact, even in cases where the discrimination facilitated by school policy relating to religious exercises is far worse than in the *Bauchman* case, the result is the same.

In *Bell*, the Court of Appeals for the Tenth Circuit acknowledged that 42 U.S.C. § 1983 allowed for damages for the loss of the value of constitutional rights arising directly from the actions of the school and school officials that violated the Establishment Clause. Significantly, however, the court did not allow relief for the discrimination, harassment, and tangible destruction inflicted by others that were facilitated by the school policies and the Bells' and McCords' objection to them.[83] The court held:

> A distinction must be made between the injuries caused by others and those inflicted by the actions of defendants that violated the Establishment Clause. For the reasons set out below, we believe that plaintiffs are entitled to recover compensatory damages for the loss of the inherent value of their rights under the Establishment Clause, even if they are unable to demonstrate consequential injury.[84]

This statement goes to the heart of the problem of attempting to use constitutional norms to remedy the discrimination that can be facilitated by public school religious exercises. The Constitution and § 1983—which, as noted above provides remedial measures for constitutional violations by municipal actors such as school boards[85]—do not generally reach the conduct of nongovernmental actors. A threshold issue for determining whether a particular actor's conduct is actionable for purposes of § 1983 is whether that person was acting "under color of state law."[86] Of course, when religious exercises or environments in the public schools facilitate discrimination and harassment, the worst incidents are frequently perpetrated by nongovernment actors. Those actors may have been motivated or inspired by the attention called to the victims' religious differences or positions on the exercises as the result of a school policy or practice. But this alone is not enough to make the action government action for purposes of § 1983 or to make it part of the Establishment Clause violation that will likely be the basis for any constitutional claim.[87]

This is a significant aspect of the "one-two punch" victims of religious discrimination facilitated by public school religious exercises face when attempting to obtain redress directly for the discrimination and harassment they have suffered. As *Bell* demonstrates, much of the conduct is not attributable to the government and thus not actionable under the Constitution, and, as *Bauchman* demonstrates, even if it were, the conduct that is the basis for the harassment and discrimination is generally not part of an actionable constitutional violation. In fact, neither court paid much attention to the incidents of discrimination and harassment, focusing instead on the Establishment Clause issues arising from the alleged government action.[88] This is also true of the court in *Herdahl.*[89]

The opinions, then, make perfect sense, given the current state of the law or at least the traditional approaches taken to these types of cases. While such incidents could conceivably help to demonstrate that the environment fostered by school policies violates the Establishment Clause and, if appropriate school personnel are involved, even support an Establishment Clause claim, the discrimination itself is generally not compensable or even relevant. These courts did not err in this aspect of their holdings and analysis—such a conclusion is compelled by the nature of constitutional claims and the reach of § 1983.

Significantly, these are not the only limitations inherent in approaching the discrimination from a constitutional perspective. *Bell* raises another significant issue in this regard, namely, the nature and level of damages that are appropriate for a constitutional violation. This issue has greater ramifications than simply how much money a party might receive because the threat of significant damages may cause schools to think twice before facilitating or engaging in questionable behavior. It might also cause schools engaged in such behavior to be more sensitive to the discrimination issue. Since some schools may have their litigation costs covered by legal organizations supported by the religious right, such as the American Center for Law and Justice or the Rutherford Institute, the threat of an injunction and meager damages are not likely to induce the same reaction that the threat of significant damages and the stigma attached to them would. Thus, the remedies available against school districts for constitutional violations do not provide a great incentive for recalcitrant, or simply uninformed, school districts to comply with constitutional mandates.

To understand the limitations on the damages available to redress a constitutional violation under § 1983, it is helpful to look at two Supreme Court cases: *Carey v. Piphus*[90] and *Memphis Community School District v. Stachura.*[91] These cases have been the subject of much criticism, and have caused much confusion among courts trying to apply the standards they set forth to new situations.[92]

Carey involved the denial of procedural due process by a public high school under the Fourteenth Amendment to the Constitution. A student sued under § 1983 to recover damages for the deprivation of his due-process rights. The Supreme Court held that the student could recover compensatory damages only if he proved actual injury caused by the denial of those rights.[93] The Court wrote: "Rights, constitutional or otherwise, do not exist in a vacuum. Their purpose is to protect persons from injuries to particular interests, and their contours are shaped by the interests they protect."[94] The Court rejected the notion that damages for an unspecified injury, which is inherent in the nature of a constitutional violation, may be presumed.[95] Following the reasoning in *Carey*, if there is no provable injury resulting from a deprivation of a constitutional right, compensatory damages are inappropriate because there is nothing to compensate for. In fact, the *Carey* Court awarded nominal damages of one dollar because the student could not prove he suffered any actual injury as a result of the due-process violation.[96]

The *Carey* court held that in order to determine compensatory damages arising from a constitutional violation, we should look to analogous tort causes of action because a significant focus of § 1983 is to provide relief for injury resulting from constitutional deprivations, much as tort law is meant to provide relief for injury resulting from private wrongs.[97] This left open questions as to what rights are analogous to what tort causes of action, whether damages may be presumed for certain constitutional violations if they cannot be proven—as is true for a small number of torts—and whether there is any inherent compensatory value for the violation of a substantive constitutional right such as a First Amendment violation as opposed to a procedural due process violation. Some of these issues were clarified in *Stachura*.

In *Stachura*, the Supreme Court held that the "abstract value of a constitutional right may not form the basis for § 1983 damages."[98] The Court also held that *Carey* did not "establish a two-tiered system of constitutional rights, with substantive rights afforded greater protection than 'mere' procedural safeguards."[99] The *Stachura* Court stated that *Carey* "emphasized that, whatever the constitutional basis for § 1983 liability, such damages must always be designed to 'compensate injuries caused by the [constitutional] deprivation.'"[100] Thus, it is inappropriate under *Carey/Stachura* to allow damages based on a trier of fact's perception of the abstract value or importance of constitutional rights. As a general matter, to be compensated pursuant to § 1983 for an injury arising from a constitutional violation, one must prove that the violation caused actual injury; one cannot be compensated simply for the abstract value of the deprivation of a constitutional right. This is still a somewhat muddy area because as the concurrence in *Stachura* points out, there are some constitutional violations that may cause "injury" simply by virtue of the violation.[101] However, even then the damage award must be proportional to the "actual loss sustained."[102]

In the context of cases arising from public school violations of the Establishment Clause through the sanctioning or sponsoring of religious exercises, the problem raised by this is clear. A student who suffers discrimination as the result of such a violation cannot obtain redress under the Constitution for the harm caused by nongovernment actors, which is likely to be the basis for the greatest actual injury suffered, and can receive compensation only if a court finds that the Establishment Clause violation itself (that is, the constitutional deprivation) caused actual injury. Thus, the victims of discrimination facilitated by the exercises cannot obtain redress for the discrimination, which would likely cause the bulk of actual injury, unless it rises to the level of a constitutional violation and a government actor is directly involved.

Such victims are essentially in a crapshoot as to whether they can receive any compensation for the Establishment Clause violation itself. Even if they can, the compensation is likely to be far less than it would be if the discrimination facilitated by the religious exercises were compensable. Unlike situations in which a direct injury is inflicted by unconstitutional government action, such as an illegal search and seizure or beating of prison inmates, an Establishment Clause violation is not as easy to link to a specific injury, and proving that the violation itself caused a particular injury may be harder to achieve.

This raises an odd possibility in cases such as *Bell, Herdahl, Bauchman,* and *Herring.* A court has to decide what emotional injury is attributable to the state action depriving the victim of his or her constitutional rights and what is attributable to the actions of third parties. Thus, the existence of discrimination facilitated by the religious exercises but carried out by students, parents, and others could be used as the basis to find that the discrimination, and not the constitutional deprivation, was the cause of the bulk of injury. Ironically, in such circumstances the existence of severe and pervasive discrimination by third parties could increase the chance that little or no actual injury would be attributed to the government action giving rise to the constitutional deprivation. Of course, this is exactly what is implied by the reasoning in the *Bauchman* and *Bell* cases, which preclude redress for conduct perpetrated by third parties.[103]

Thus, while school district policies or practices may have triggered and facilitated the discrimination, and may be the most efficient place to prevent and remedy it, the school district will escape liability in most cases for the bulk of the discrimination. At least in regard to the discrimination, then, the Constitution is a weak solution. Further, it will also be very hard for the victims of such discrimination to prevail on state tort law claims against third-party discriminators.[104]

To make matters worse, over the past twenty years the Supreme Court has decided a string of cases that dramatically increase the difficulty of establishing liability and demonstrating compensable injury under § 1983. While the Constitution, as enforced through § 1983, is certainly a potential tool for obtaining redress for some of the harms discussed in this essay, its reach is limited in regard to discrimination facilitated by public school religious exercises. Of course, currently § 1983 is the only game in town because no federal law directly protects against such discrimination.[105] Therefore, unless legislation or common law rules are developed to address the discrimination that is the focus of this essay, people like the Herdahls, Herrings, Bells, McCords, and Bauchmans don't have very many options beyond § 1983.

The lack of recourse is particularly troubling because, given the harsh reaction those who oppose religious practices in the public school frequently face, many objectors may feel they risk too much by "going public."[106] Moreover, school boards and school officials may feel they have very little to lose by engaging in activity that is unconstitutional or of questionable constitutional merit. In many places, a school board that stands up for school prayer is seen as heroic and the dissenters are seen as the bad guys.[107] There have been rallies in Pontotoc, Mississippi, to raise funds to pay the school district's liability for fees and costs that were awarded in the *Herdahl* case.[108] National and local speakers have spoken on behalf of the school board, and at the rallies the school district was portrayed as the victim and the Herdahls were vilified.[109]

Conclusion

The cases discussed in this essay are but a sampling of many similar incidents tied to public school religious exercises. In the public's mind, the exercises are an extinct phenomenon, courtesy of Supreme Court decisions. But the Court's decisions are not self-executing, and many districts around the country simply ignore them. Additionally, the new evangelical "Great Awakening" that has been sweeping the country and the political activities of the religious right have fueled the tendency to ignore Supreme Court mandates or to find ways around them. Thus, the notion that organized public school religious exercises are a thing of the past is greatly mistaken.

The incidents mentioned above and many more like them demonstrate the dark underbelly of public school religious exercises—the aspects of these exercises often described in court opinions and scholarly discourse as their "divisive" nature or their tendency to violate the rights of religious minorities. But there is far more at stake than this. The fact that the exercises can be the catalyst for abuse, harassment, and discrimination, behaviors that are punishable in other contexts yet are seemingly indulged in without risk in the school context, should evoke alarm. As noted, the social dynamics underlying the behavior make it somewhat predictable. The law, however, is currently ill-equipped to address it for what it really is.

NOTES

This essay has been adapted from Frank S. Ravitch, School Prayer and Discrimination: Th Civil Rights of Religious Minorities and Dissenters (Northeastern Univ. Press 1999).

For the sake of consistency and ease of reading, I use the phrase "public schools" throughout this essay since it is commonly used today. However, in the early period of public education, these schools were sometimes called "common schools"; the common school movement was a driving force in support of public education at that time. That movement did support a nonsectarian Protestant religious foundation for state-sponsored schools, but the movement arose at a time when virtually everyone who would attend was Protestant. Lloyd P. Jorgenson, The State and the Non-Public School, 1825–1925 (Univ. of Missouri Press 1987). As Catholic immigration increased, the Protestant orientation of the movement and of the schools heightened tensions between Protestants and Catholics. *Id.* In writing about the historical incidents described herein, I use the phrase "public schools" to refer to the "common schools" as well.

1. Timothy J. Burger and Thomas DeFrank, *House Whip Flays Apple Over Booted Bx. Teacher*, N.Y. DAILY NEWS, June 26, 1998 at 5; Jacques Steinberg and Macarena Hernandez, *Teacher is Now Political Cause After Dismissal For Class Prayer*, NEW YORK TIMES, June 26, 1998 at B5.

2. *Id.*

3. They have, however, taken the time to study and report some of the discernible facts of the case. *See* Steve Benen, *When Her N.Y. Public School Students Asked About Religion, Mildred Rosario Went From Teacher To Preacher—and Unleashed A Grade-A Furor*, 51 CHURCH & STATE 175 (1998)(Americans United for Separation of Church and State report on the incident citing several news accounts reporting on the situation). Conversely, their more conservative counterparts have made arguments on behalf of Rosario that variably make comparisons between social phenomena irrelevant to the facts of her case and attacks on current interpretations of the Establishment Clause. *See* articles cited at note 1, *supra.*

4. Angela Mosconi and Susan Edelman, *Booted-Teacher's 'Snitch' Fears Classmates*, NEW YORK POST, June 18, 1998; *NYC Teacher Fired Over Prayers*, Associated Press, June 17, 1998, *available in* WESTLAW File No. 6682472.

5. Mosconi and Edelman, *Booted-Teacher's 'Snitch' Fears Classmates.*

6. Frank S. Ravitch, SCHOOL PRAYER AND DISCRIMINATION: THE CIVIL RIGHTS OF RELIGIOUS MINORITIES AND DISSENTERS (Northeastern University Press 1999) at chapter 2.

7. Steven B. Epstein, *Rethinking the Constitutionality of Ceremonial Deism*,96 COLUM. L. REV. 2083, 2169, 2171 (1996)(hereinafter *Ceremonial Deism*); Nadine Strossen, *How Much God in the Schools? A Discussion of Religion's Role in the Classroom*, 4 WM. & MARY BILL OF RIGHTS J. 607, 610, 616 (1995)(hereinafter *How Much God in the Schools?*).

8. For an excellent example of this, *see* Walter v. West Virginia Board of Education, 610 F.Supp. 1169 (D.W.VA. 1985) (moment of silence, which was held unconstitutional, was the catalyst for verbal harassment of an eleven-year-old Jewish student; case primarily focuses on constitutional issues); Gary B. Melton, *Populism, School Prayer and the Courts: Confessions of an Expert Witness*, NEW DIRECTION IN CHILD DEVELOPMENT, NUMBER 33, 63,65 (1986)(article by expert witness in the case, which also addresses the discrimination the student faced).

9. Lloyd P. Jorgenson, THE STATE AND THE NON-PUBLIC SCHOOL, 1825–1925 (Univ. of Missouri Press 1987) at 76–83 (hereinafter THE STATE AND THE NON-PUBLIC SCHOOL); Vincent J. Lannie and Bernard C. Deithorn, *For the Honor and Glory of God: The Philadelphia Bible Riots of [1844]*, 8 HIST. EDUC. QUART. 45 (1968)(the date was originally misprinted as "1840" and was corrected in a later issue).

10. Jorgenson, THE STATE AND THE NON-PUBLIC SCHOOL at 23–30, 69–110.

11. Id. at 23–28.

12. *See generally* Michael Feldberg, THE PHILADELPHIA RIOTS OF 1844: A STUDY IN ETHNIC CONFLICT (Greenwood Press 1975)(Feldberg acknowledges the role of the Bible dispute in sparking the May riots, but also places those riots within the broader ethnic and socioeconomic clashes between "natives" and "immigrants").

13. Jorgenson, THE STATE AND THE NON-PUBLIC SCHOOL at 28–30; *See also* Leo Pfeffer, GOD, CAESAR AND THE CONSTITUTION (Beacon Press 1975) at 174–75.

14. Jorgenson, THE STATE AND THE NON-PUBLIC SCHOOL at 72–83; James Hennesey, AMERICAN CATHOLICS: A HISTORY OF THE ROMAN CATHOLIC COMMUNITY IN THE UNITED STATES (Oxford Univ. Press 1981) at 122–24 (hereinafter AMERICAN CATHOLICS); Pfeffer, GOD, CAESAR AND THE CONSTITUTION at 174–76.

15. Pfeffer, God, Caesar and the Constitution at 174–78. Of course, as is the case today, there were some communities that rose above such behavior.

16. Ibid., 176–79.

17. Hennesey, American Catholics at 125. Father John Bapst, the priest involved in the incident, later became the first president of Boston College. However, the incident continued to haunt him, eventually causing him to be placed in an asylum. As a result of the incident, he "would wake up screaming that attackers were climbing through his window." Id.

18. Lannie and Deithorn, *For the Honor and Glory of God*, at 103–4; Jorgenson, The State and the Non-Public School at 82–83. Many of those killed were Protestant nativists who were shot while attacking Catholic homes and churches. Id.

19. Jorgenson, The State and the Non-Public School at 81–83; Feldberg, The Philadelphia Riots of 1844.

20. Sadly, the riots and the accompanying death and destruction were sparked by a school board resolution complying with a reasonable request by the local bishop that Catholic children not be required to read from the King James Bible. Neither the request nor the resolution took any rights away from the Protestant children within the district, since they were still allowed to read from the King James Bible. Jorgenson, The State and the Non-Public School at 76–80; Hennesey, American Catholics at 122.

21. Jorgenson, The State and the Non-Public School at 81–82.

22. *See* Ravitch, School Prayer and Discrimination at chapter 2.

23. *Id.* at chapters 2 and 4; Matthew C. Moen, *School Prayer and the Politics of Life-style Concern*, 65 Soc. Sci. Quart. 1065 (1984).

24. *See* Ravitch, School Prayer and Discrimination at chapter 2.

25. Jorgenson, The State and the Non-Public School at 28–30, 69–83. We see a similar phenomenon today in the push by the religious right to make the public schools a venue for the assertion of its values and beliefs. *See* Ravitch, School Prayer and Discrimination at chapter 2; *see also* Moen, *School Prayer and the Politics of Life-style Concern* (casting the school prayer debate as a clash between a group of traditionalists trying to reinstate prayer as an affirmation of their once-dominant values and modernists seeking affirmation of their contemporary values).

26. This was also said of the public schools. Jorgenson, The State and the Non-Public School at 78–80.

27. Pat Robertson, The Turning Tide (Word Publishing 1993). Of course, Robertson is just one prominent example of those making this claim. *See* Ravitch, School Prayer and Discrimination at chapter 2.

28. *See, e.g.*, Lee v. Weisman, 505 U.S. 577 (1992); School District of Abington Township v. Schempp, 374 U.S. 203 (1963); Engel v. Vitale, 370 U.S. 421 (1962).

29. *See* Ravitch, School Prayer and Discrimination at chapter 3 for a more detailed discussion of this.

30. *See* Ravitch, School Prayer and Discrimination at chapter 4.

31. *Id.*

32. *Compare Lee*, 505 U.S. 577 and Illinois *ex rel.* McCollum v. Board of Education, 333 U.S. 203 (1948), *with* Strossen, *How Much God in the Schools?* at 617 and Epstein, *Ceremonial Deism* at 2170–71.

33. Strossen, *How Much God in the Schools?* at 616.

34. Religious Liberty: Hearings Before the Senate Judiciary Committee, 104th Cong., 1st sess., S521–17 (Tuesday September 12, 1995)(prepared testimony of Lisa Herdahl)(hereinafter Testimony of Lisa Herdahl Before the Senate Judiciary Committee).

35. *60 Minutes, Profile: Lisa Herdahl v. Pontotoc County; Mother Sues Public School Over Prayer* (transcript of program aired Sunday, June 16, 1996); Gina Holland, *Judge Rules Out Prayer in School*, CLEVELAND PLAIN DEALER, June 4, 1996; Tom McNichol and Debbie Rossell, *A Town Divided by Prayer*, USA WEEKEND, May 21, 1995.

36. *60 Minutes, Profile: Lisa Herdahl vs. Pontotoc County; a Mother of Six Fights School Prayer in North Pontotoc County, Mississippi* (transcript of program aired Sunday, August 13, 1995).

37. *Id.; see also* TESTIMONY OF LISA HERDAHL BEFORE THE SENATE JUDICIARY COMMITTEE.

38. *Id.*

39. *Id.*

40. TESTIMONY OF LISA HERDAHL BEFORE THE SENATE JUDICIARY COMMITTEE.

41. *Id.*

42. *See* Holland, *Judge Rules Out Prayer in School.*

43. TESTIMONY OF LISA HERDAHL BEFORE THE SENATE JUDICIARY COMMITTEE.

44. Epstein, *Ceremonial Deism* at 2169–71.

45. *Complaint of Paul Michael Herring, et al.* in Paul Michael Herring v. Dr. John Key, Superintendent of Pike County Schools (filed in U.S. Dist. Ct., M.D. Ala., North. Div. on August 4, 1997); *Declaration Under Penalty of Perjury of Sue C. Willis* (filed with the complaint as Exhibit "C"); Jay Reeves, *Jewish Family Sues Public School*, ASSOC. PRESS (August 1997). As the above citation suggests, the case was filed as Paul Michael Herring v. Dr. John Key, Superintendent of Pike County Schools. The Herring childrens' mother is remarried and uses the last name Willis. The children filed suit by and through their stepfather, Wayne Willis, and their mother, Sue Willis.

46. The case has since been settled. Thus, the incidents mentioned were allegations in the case, and were decided upon by a court. However, several of the more significant allegations are corroborated by evidence such as school documents. *See Complaint of Paul Michael Herring, et al.*, Exhibit "A" (letter from Superintendent John R. Key to Sue Willis dated June 18, 1997).

47. *Complaint of Paul Michael Herring, et al.* in Paul Michael Herring v. Dr. John Key, Superintendent of Pike County Schools (filed in U.S. Dist. Ct., M.D. Ala., North. Div. on August 4, 1997).

48. *Id.*

49. *Declaration Under Penalty of Perjury of Sue C. Willis* in Paul Michael Herring v. Dr. John Key, Superintendent of Pike County Schools at 3.

50. Id. at 12.

51. Bauchman v. West High School, 906 F.Supp. 1483 (D. Utah 1995); Bauchman by and through Bauchman v. West High School, 900 F.Supp. 248 and 900 F.Supp. 255 (D. Utah 1995), *aff'd* 132 F.3d 532 (10th Cir. 1997).

52. *Id.*

53. *Id.*

54. *Id.*

55. *Id.*

56. *Id.; see also Student Pursues Case*, FORWARD, May 31, 1996, at 2.

57. Bauchman v. West High School, 132 F.3d 542 (10th Cir. 1997); *id.* at 562 (Murphy, J. dissenting).

58. *Bauchman*, 132 F.3d at 556.

59. Bell v. Little Axe Independent School Dist. No. 70, 766 F.2d 1391, 1396–98 (10th Cir. 1985); See also *America's Constitutional Heritage: Religion and Our Public Schools* at 5–7 (ACLU video transcript—transcript available via the Internet at http://www.aclu.org/issues/religion/arrf.html) (hereinafter *America's Constitutional Heritage*).

60. *Id.*
61. *America's Constitutional Heritage* at 5.
62. *Bell*, 766 F.2d at 1397; *America's Constitutional Heritage.*
63. *Bell*, 766 F.2d 1391.
64. *Bell*, 766 F.2d at 1397.
65. *America's Constitutional Heritage* at 6.
66. *Id.*; *see also Bell*, 766 F.2d at 1397.
67. *Bell*, 766 F.2d at 1397.
68. *Id.*
69. *Id.*
70. *America's Constitutional Heritage* at 6; *Bell*, 766 F.2d at 1397–99.
71. *Bell*, 766 F.2d at 1397; *America's Constitutional Heritage* at 5.
72. *Id.*
73. *America's Constitutional Heritage* at 5–6.
74. *Id.* at 6.
75. *See Bell*, 766 F.2d at 1408.
76. *See Bell*, 766 F.2d at 1408–13. The court did acknowledge that these damages should not require proof of consequential harm and may necessarily require a presumption of damages. *Id.* The issue of damages in cases brought to vindicate constitutional rights is a complex one, and the *Bell* decision is not determinative of that issue. For a discussion of this, *see* Ravitch, SCHOOL PRAYER AND DISCRIMINATION at chapter 7.
77. In response to their complaint in the famous 1948 case of Illinois *ex rel.* McCollum v. Board of Education, 333 U.S. 203 (1948), in which James Terry McCollum challenged a Christian release time program, the McCollum family was subjected to vitriolic harassment. Epstein, *Ceremonial Deism* at 2170. While the suit was pending, the family received thousands of hostile letters using phrases such as "you slimy bastard" and "[y]our filthy rotten body produced three children so that you can pilot them all safely to hell." *Id.* (citing Vashti Cromwell McCollum, ONE WOMAN'S FIGHT at 95 (Beacon Press, rev. ed. 1961)). The family's child involved in the case was regularly beaten up and called a "godless communist." *Id.*

During the pendency of the now-famous case *Lee v. Weisman*, 505 U.S. 577 (1992), the Weismans received hate mail and death threats. Strossen, *How Much God in the Public Schools?* at 617. In another well-known case, which ultimately went before the Fifth Circuit Court of Appeals, involving a challenge to a high school coach's policy requiring the team to say the Lord's Prayer, the complaining student was taunted by fellow students and spectators and was called a "little atheist" by a teacher during a lecture. Doe v. Duncanville Indep. School Dist., 994 F.2d 160, 162–164 (5th Cir. 1993).

78. Bauchman v. West High School, 132 F.3d 542, 556 (10th Cir. 1997); Bell v. Little Axe Independent School Dist. No. 70, 766 F.2d 1391, 1408–13 (10th Cir. 1985).
79. *Bauchman*, 132 F.3d at 550–58.
80. *Id.* at 558–62 (a major facet to the appeal in this case was the efficacy of an amended complaint that alleged a long pattern of religious conduct by the teacher in question to demonstrate religious motivation; for several reasons the court rejected the idea that the amended complaint could save the constitutional claims); *id.* at 562 (Murphy, C.J., dissenting) (pointing out problems with the majority decision from both constitutional and procedural standpoints and implying that the majority was straining to uphold the lower court's dismissal of Bauchman's claims).
81. *Id.* at 562 (Murphy, C.J., dissenting).
82. *Bauchman*, 132 F.3d at 556.

83. *Bell*, 766 F.2d at 1408–13.

84. *Id.* at 1408.

85. Monell v. Department of Social Services of the City of New York, 436 U.S. 658 (1978).

86. Parrat v. Taylor, 451 U.S. 527, 535 (1981); Ravitch, School Prayer and Discrimination at chapter 10.

87. *Bauchman*, 132 F.3d at 556; *Bell*, 766 F.2d at 1408.

88. *Id.*

89. Herdahl v. Pontotoc County School Dist., 887 F.Supp. 902 (N.D.Miss. 1995).

90. 435 U.S. 247 (1978).

91. 477 U.S. 299 (1986).

92. In fact, in a note, the *Stachura* Court recognizes the confusion courts had in applying *Carey*. *Stachura*, 477 U.S. at 304 n.5.

93. *Carey*, 435 U.S. at 264.

94. *Id.* at 254.

95. This does not mean that the *Carey* Court held that presumed damages can never be awarded in a § 1983 claim. Since *Carey* focuses on tort law as a model for appropriate damages under § 1983, the concept of presumed damages that exists in limited circumstances under tort law might be useful in certain situations. However, in *Stachura*, 477 U.S. at 310, the Court clarified this by explaining that presumed damages are a "substitute for ordinary compensatory damages, not a supplement for an award that fully compensates the alleged injury." Thus, *Stachura* explains that presumed damages are appropriate only when someone seeks compensation for an "injury that is likely to have occurred but difficult to establish." *Id.* at 311. The damages should approximate the harm suffered and are meant to compensate for that harm, though it may be impossible to measure. The damages are still "compensatory" in such circumstances; it is just that the harm they compensate for is hard to measure. *Id.*

96. *Carey*, 435 U.S. at 267.

97. *Id.* at 257–59.

98. *Stachura*, 477 U.S. at 308.

99. *Id.* at 309.

100. *Id.* (*citing Carey*, 435 U.S. at 265).

101. *Id.* at 314–16 (Marshall, J., concurring in the judgment). In fact, this is exactly what the court in *Bell* held. The court found that the violation of the Establishment Clause there was compensable, and to determine the most appropriate measure of damages analogized the violation to a common law action for denial of voting rights. Thus, while the Bells and McCords could not receive damages for the behavior of the third parties who caused the bulk of their actual damages, they could receive compensation for the nebulous injury flowing from the school district's Establishment Clause violation. *Bell*, 766 F.2d 1391, 1408–13.

102. *Bell*, 766 F.2d 1391, 1408–13.

103. Id. at 1408–13; *Bauchman*, 132 F.3d at 556.

104. For a brief discussion regarding state tort law claims in this context, *see* Ravitch, School Prayer and Discrimination at chapter 10.

105. *Id.*

106. Epstein, *Ceremonial Deism* at 2169–71.

107. This is the situation the Herdahls faced in regard to their case. *60 Minutes, Profile: Lisa Herdahl v. Pontotoc County; Mother Sues Public School Over Prayer* (transcript from program aired June 16, 1996); *see also* Ravitch, School Prayer and Discrimination at chapters 1 and 2.

108. *See* materials cited in notes 35–37, *supra*.

109. *Id.*

Part V

Religion and Liberal Political Theory

Chapter 17

Secular Fundamentalism, Religious Fundamentalism, and the Search for Truth in Contemporary America

Daniel O. Conkle

> I have a dream that one day every valley shall be exalted, every hill and mountain shall be made low, the rough places shall be made plain, and the crooked places shall be made straight and the glory of the Lord will be revealed and all flesh shall see it together.
>
> —Martin Luther King, Jr., *I Have a Dream*, August 28, 1963

Echoing the prophet Isaiah,[1] Dr. King dreamed of societal harmony and common understanding. Not only would "the glory of the Lord" be revealed, "all flesh" would see the truth together. In today's America, this vision seems increasingly distant; some would say increasingly fantastic. From abortion to homosexuality to affirmative action, Americans are deeply divided on fundamental issues of morality and public policy. Combatants in an ongoing culture war,[2] we disagree not only about specific issues but also about the manner in which these issues should be considered, debated, and resolved. At bottom, we are divided because we disagree about the nature of moral and political truth and about how this truth should properly be determined. Far from seeing the truth together, we see separate truths that emerge from separate ways of thinking.[3]

In the epistemic cacophony of contemporary America, perhaps our most basic dispute concerns the role of religion as a source of truth.[4] In a previous essay, I explored aspects of this question, focusing on religion's public role, that is, its role in American politics and law.[5] I argued that religion can and should play a significant public role,[6] but that some types of religion are more valuable for this purpose than others. In part, I offered epistemological distinctions, noting that different religions recognize different sources of truth and see different roles for argument and dialogue, both within and outside the community of believers.[7]

From this perspective, I was critical of religious "fundamentalism," which I defined as a type of religion that regards its sacred text (or other religious authority) as a source of truth that is absolute, plain, and unchangeable:

> This source of truth is absolute in the sense that it cannot be questioned on the basis of external evidence or arguments. It is plain in the sense that it requires little if any interpretation. It is unchangeable in the sense that it need not be adapted to contemporary circumstances.[8]

Drawing upon democratic ideals that trace their origins to the Enlightenment and to republican political theory, I contended that political decisions should be formulated on the basis of a deliberative, dialogic decision-making process, a process that at least permits the possibility that argument or discourse will lead to a change of mind. Because religious fundamentalism is not willing even to consider the possible truth of contrary positions, its contributions to America's public life, I argued, should be viewed with caution and skepticism.[9]

In a footnote to this discussion, I suggested—without elaboration—that secular thinking can take on fundamentalist characteristics and that "the public role of this 'secular fundamentalism' should also be viewed with skepticism."[10] In the current essay, I mean to elaborate on this suggestion. More generally, I intend to survey several possible meanings of secular fundamentalism and to suggest how this concept, along with the concept of religious fundamentalism, might shed light on the epistemic crisis that confounds our search for truth—not only on public issues but in private life as well. In the course of my discussion, I shall identify the basic problems that are raised by religious fundamentalism and by secular fundamentalism, and I shall explore how we might begin to move beyond them.

I. The Concept of Secular Fundamentalism

Although still uncommon, the phrase "secular fundamentalism" has begun to appear with increasing regularity. But what does this concept mean, or what might or should it mean? I shall examine four possible meanings, explaining how they might mirror the meaning of religious fundamentalism and how they might help us understand the contemporary state of American public and private life.

A. Secular Fundamentalism as Ill-Defined Pejorative

Whether applied to religious or secular thinking, the "fundamentalist" label carries a pejorative connotation. Often used loosely and without clear definition, the label can be used to mark a person, group, or institution as in some respect intolerant, militant, or otherwise dangerous.

In the religious context, the term increasingly has been linked to radical movements abroad that are perceived to be not only irrational but also violent. Professor Arthur Schlesinger Jr., for example, associates religious fundamentalism with murderous actions by people who claim to be following the will of God:

> Yigal Amir claims that God ordered him to kill Prime Minister Rabin. Nor are murderous presumptions of this sort confined to Jewish fundamentalists. So too Muslim fundamentalists receive instructions from Allah to kill Salman Rushdie and to plant dynamite in Paris subway trains. So too Hindu fundamentalists massacre Muslims and blow up their mosques. So too Christian fundamentalists in our own country feel they are serving God by murdering doctors who perform abortions.[11]

Schlesinger finds it "scary" that so many Americans (more than a third) are "fundamentalists" in the sense that they harbor "delusions" that "God speaks to them directly."[12] Schlesinger's fear undoubtedly is related to the violence that he associates with fundamentalism: "Fundamentalists are absolutists—people who believe they are appointed carriers of a sacred gospel and feel so sure they are right that they have no compunction about killing heretics or doing anything else to advance their cause."[13] "Unrebuked and unchecked," he concludes, "fundamentalists of all faiths will continue to believe that they are serving God by mayhem and murder."[14]

The label "fundamentalist," of course, had its origins in American Protestantism, where it originally was claimed as a matter of self-description.[15] But views like Schlesinger's are on the rise, especially in the popular culture. As a result, it is not surprising that American religious believers, whatever their theology, increasingly find this label insulting.[16]

Like its religious counterpart, the phrase "secular fundamentalist" often is used to characterize a person or institution as dogmatic, extreme, or fanatical. Professor Schlesinger, for example, writes that the fascists and communists of the middle half of the twentieth century were holders of "totalitarian faiths," "[s]ecular fundamentalists [who believed they were] executing the will of History."[17] In similar fashion, Professor Paul D. Carrington has referred to the violent "secular fundamentalism" of the French Revolution.[18]

With reference to contemporary America, the "secular fundamentalist" label has been extended to less extreme situations, including various types of "politically correct" ideologies or practices. Professor Carrington, for instance, has suggested that American universities sometimes act as modern-day successors to the "secular fundamentalists" of the French revolution:[19]

> Many individual members of the academic profession would punish their students or even their colleagues for utterances that they choose to deem as offensive, much as Robespierre took mortal offense at those hateful words, "Vive le roi." In many places in America, a teacher's career may be placed in grave danger if he or she is convicted, even in a kangaroo court, of holding sentiments that are characterized as racist, sexist, or homophobic, or that are deemed by sensitive auditors to be "harassment," a term that in some minds embraces all utterances implying sexual differences.[20]

In like manner, the author of a column in the New York Times has written that "schools that once believed in free speech, free love, free everything (but tuition) have turned into bastions of secular fundamentalism, equally willing to prescribe and proscribe."[21] According to Don E. Eberly, this "secular fundamentalism," in academia and elsewhere, is the work of "secular true believers."[22]

As these religious and secular examples suggest, "fundamentalism" can carry a powerful rhetorical punch. Absent further clarification, however, there is a significant danger of false association and exaggeration. As a group, religious conservatives in the United States certainly are not terrorists in the making,[23] and Robespierre is not lurking behind every campus speech code. In any event, the term "fundamentalist" does little analytical work when used as a general pejorative, and it is not particularly helpful in mapping the contours of public and private life in contemporary America.

Some would argue that "fundamentalist" has become so freighted with negative baggage and so colored with vague implications that it should not be used at all. An alternative course is to use the term more selectively and precisely, indicating the meaning that is intended and explaining the definitional or analytical work that is thereby accomplished.[24] In my previous essay, I attempted to follow this alternative course in addressing religious fundamentalism.[25] In the following sections, I shall do the same for secular fundamentalism, discussing how this concept might have meanings more helpful than that of a general pejorative.

B. Secular Fundamentalism in Textual Interpretation

As noted earlier, religious fundamentalism can be defined as a type of religion that regards its sacred text—for example, the Bible—as a source of truth that is absolute, plain, and unchanging. As such, religious fundamentalism is one among various methods of biblical interpretation. Secular documents also require interpretation and, if the documents carry normative implications, they may raise similar interpretative issues. In the American political system, for example, the United States Constitution is a normative document that embodies a type of political, or perhaps political-moral, truth. As a result, constitutional interpretation is in some respects similar to biblical interpretation.[26]

"Secular fundamentalism" can be used to describe a method of secular interpretation that mirrors the method by which religious fundamentalists interpret the Bible. With reference to the Constitution, for instance, this form of secular fundamentalism regards the constitutional text as a source of constitutional truth or meaning that is absolute, plain, and unchanging. To determine the meaning of the Constitution, one should look only to the text—not to societal, philosophical, or other values that lie outside the text. In this sense, the Constitution, like the fundamentalist's Bible, is an absolute source of truth. Likewise, one should apply the "plain meaning" of the constitutional text, which requires little if any explication, and one should adhere to that meaning as timeless, regardless of changing circumstances or changing values.

"[Constitutional] originalism is secular fundamentalism," writes Professor Morton J. Horwitz.[27] Horwitz explains:

> To the extent that Constitution worship is America's secular religion, and all religions have a tendency towards fundamentalism, originalism in constitutional discourse is the equivalent of religious fundamentalism. If you consider the Scopes trial and William Jennings Bryan's argument for the literalism of the seven day creation and then think about Justice Black's argument for the literalism of "Congress shall make no law," you can see in Justice Black's case a secularized Southern Baptist mode of argument.

> Originalists and constitutional literalists are fundamentalists. The argument about a living Constitution versus originalism is parallel to the question of modern and adaptable religion versus the old time religion.[28]

Horwitz suggests that America's attraction to what he calls "the old time religion" helps explain why "the idea of a living Constitution has had such a difficult time in American culture."[29]

Whatever the strength of Horwitz's argument, the concept of secular fundamentalism can perform a useful function in the context of textual interpretation. Indeed, if religious fundamentalism is defined as a method of interpretive inquiry, the secular analogy is very close indeed: both religious and secular fundamentalists view their normative text as a source of truth that is absolute, plain, and unchanging.[30]

Although interesting and helpful, the idea of secular fundamentalism as a form of textual interpretation is limited to its particular context, that is, the interpretation of normative secular texts, of which the Constitution is the prime example. The question that remains is whether there are other forms of secular fundamentalism in contemporary America, forms of secular fundamentalism that may have broader, more general implications for the search for truth in American public and private life.

C. Secular Fundamentalism as Political Liberalism

Religious fundamentalism is more than a method of textual interpretation. It also reflects unquestioning faith. This faith requires no reasoned explanation, and it need not be defended against challenges that proceed from contrary premises. Viewed in this way, religious fundamentalism can be seen as a method of thought that is both insulated and insular; it is insulated from competing claims of truth, and it inhabits an epistemic universe that is disconnected from other ways of thinking.

Is there a comparable type of *secular* thinking, that is, a "secular fundamentalism" that depends on faith, that shields itself from incompatible truth claims, and that effectively isolates itself as a separate system of thought? With respect to American politics and public life, at least, one could argue that there is, and that it takes the form of political liberalism (in the philosophical sense).

Needless to say, there are various theories of political liberalism. In general, however, liberalism calls for public "neutrality" toward the "private" moral choices of individuals, a neutrality that is said to require the exclusion of "personal" moralities, including religious viewpoints, from any significant role in public policy making.[31] Thus, according to liberalism, we are to "bracket our moral and religious convictions when deliberating about politics and law."[32]

Although different theories contain important variations and qualifications,[33] an essential claim of liberalism is that political decisions generally should be supported by "reason," and that religious and similar viewpoints do not qualify.[34] Professor John Rawls, for example, privileges what he calls "public reason":[35]

> What public reason asks is that citizens be able to explain their vote to one another in terms of a reasonable balance of public political values, it being understood by everyone that of course the plurality of reasonable comprehensive doctrines held by citizens

> is thought by them to provide further and often transcendent backing for those values. ["Comprehensive doctrines," for Rawls, include religious and similar belief systems.][36] . . . The only comprehensive doctrines that run afoul of public reason are those that cannot support a reasonable balance of political values.[37]

As this passage suggests, the related concepts of "public reason" and "reasonable balance" are at the core of Rawls's theory.

According to Professor Paul F. Campos, however, Rawls's explanation and defense of these concepts is seriously incomplete. Indeed, says Campos, Rawls's vision of liberalism amounts to a type of "secular fundamentalism."[38] According to Campos, "'[r]eason' and 'reasonable' fill the lexical space that in many other discourses would be filled by 'God,' or 'the scriptures,' or 'moral insight.' . . . '[R]eason' functions as the master concept that transcends the enumeration of particular reasons: *invoking* 'reason' becomes equivalent to *giving* reasons."[39] And to invoke "reason" is to exclude conceptions of truth that, according to "reason," are not "reasonable." In this way, Campos concludes, Rawls and his followers can "celebrate tolerance and pluralism while at the same time condemning any meaningful dissent . . . as not merely wrong, but contrary to the dictates of reason itself."[40]

To the extent that political liberalism—whether that of Rawls or that of other theorists—in fact embraces an exclusive and exclusionary form of "reason," it, like religious fundamentalism, is both insulated and insular. It is insulated from claims of truth that lie outside the domain of reason, and it inhabits an epistemic universe that is disconnected from these other ways of thinking. To the extent that liberalism cannot defend its embrace of reason except by adverting to reason itself, moreover, it requires a leap of faith. In this sense, it may be that liberalism is "the faith of those who have lost their faith."[41]

Secular fundamentalism, understood as the embrace of political liberalism, rejects religion as a source of truth in the public domain.[42] To the extent that religion has truth value, it is a matter of private truth, a form of truth that lacks public significance. In the public sphere, reason prevails. Modern science is one aspect of reason; it controls the resolution of empirical questions. On questions of morality and ethics, secular rationalism is controlling, and "private" moral choices are protected in the absence of tangible and demonstrable harm to others.[43]

This understanding of secular fundamentalism helps explain the public aspects of modern America's epistemic crisis. On one side are religious fundamentalists who, assuming they bring their religion to bear on public issues, regard it as the only legitimate source of truth on whatever issues it addresses. On the other are secular fundamentalists who embrace an entirely different source of truth, one that excludes religious thought as illegitimate. Each group resides in its own world of truth. These worlds are isolated from each other, and their inhabitants cannot communicate across the divide.

D. Comprehensive Secular Fundamentalism

Secular fundamentalism as political liberalism is limited to the public sphere. But some secular thinkers—let us call them "*comprehensive* secular fundamentalists"—

embrace a similar epistemology for *all* questions of truth or meaning. Thus, comprehensive secular fundamentalists resolve public *and private* questions of truth exclusively by reference to modern science and secular rationalism.[44] Other potential sources of truth, including especially religion, are excluded from consideration.

As Reinhold Niebuhr observed, secularism can lead to a type of "fanaticism" that "insinuates new and false ultimates into views of life which are ostensibly merely provisional and pragmatic."[45] Comprehensive secular fundamentalists may well adopt a provisional and pragmatic view of reason. Ironically, however, it is their very embrace of reason, as an exclusive and exclusionary source of truth, that serves as their false ultimate, that is, as opposed to the ultimate of truth itself. With reason as their ultimate value, comprehensive secular fundamentalists virtually close their minds to religious insights, and therefore to the possibility of religious truth or meaning, whether in public or in private life. Thus, like religious fundamentalists, they are absolutists in the sense that they are unwilling even to consider claims of truth that proceed from premises they do not already share.

This more comprehensive understanding of secular fundamentalism may be the one that most closely mirrors religious fundamentalism, whose claims of truth, of course, apply to matters of private as well as public concern. Otherwise, the comparison is similar to that which I have offered concerning the public domain. Thus, as applied in a comprehensive manner to private and public issues alike, religious and secular fundamentalism are systems of thought that are both insulated and insular—that is, both shielded and isolated from competing understandings of truth. Likewise, each depends on a type of faith. The faith of religious fundamentalists is the acceptance of truths without regard to competing claims of reason; the faith of comprehensive secular fundamentalists is that without reason, there is nothing.

No less than the versions of secular fundamentalism discussed previously, comprehensive secular fundamentalism is a concept that helps illuminate America's chaotic search for truth. Comprehensive secular fundamentalists follow an epistemology that separates them, on private as well as public issues, from those who regard religion as at least a potential source of truth or meaning. Religious fundamentalists are equally isolated, ignoring claims of truth that might undermine their religious understandings.

II. The Problems with Fundamentalism

In examining our epistemic struggles in public and private life, the most useful understandings of secular fundamentalism are the last two offered: secular fundamentalism as political liberalism and comprehensive secular fundamentalism. In the remainder of this essay, I shall focus on secular fundamentalism in these two senses, along with religious fundamentalism as applied to public and private issues respectively. I shall identify what I regard as the basic problems with religious and secular fundamentalism, and I shall suggest, in tentative and exploratory fashion, how we might begin to move beyond them.

A. The Problems with Religious Fundamentalism in Politics and Law

In my previous essay, I addressed the problems that arise when religious fundamentalism—reliance on a religious source of truth that is viewed as absolute, plain, and unchanging—is brought to bear on political or legal issues.[46] To summarize briefly, the American political system has intellectual roots in reason as well as religion. These roots derive from the Enlightenment, which taught that religion is not beyond the testing of reason, and from republican political theory, which emphasized the importance of deliberation in the formulation of government policies.

These themes of the Enlightenment and of republicanism continue to inform our system of governance. When religious fundamentalism enters the realm of politics and law, however, it rejects the claims of reason and relies on a source of truth that is beyond challenge or debate. This type of political involvement thus tends to undermine a basic tenet of our democratic system: that legal policies should be formulated on the basis of a dialogic decision-making process, a process requiring an openness of mind that religious fundamentalism does not allow.

It is important to emphasize that these problems are distinctive to religious *fundamentalism*; they do not extend to religion in general. Too often, this distinction is overlooked. Professor Suzanna Sherry, for example, invokes the continuing lessons of the Enlightenment and republican theory to support her argument that religious beliefs should be excluded from any meaningful role in public policymaking.[47] But Sherry reaches this conclusion only by confusing religion with religious fundamentalism, that is, by assuming that *all* religion is fundamentalist religion. Thus, she refers to religion as an "antirational" epistemology that is "likely to be impervious to persuasion."[48] "Sincerely held religious beliefs," she writes, "cannot be shaken by rational argument—that is the heart of faith."[49]

Contrary to Sherry's suggestion, religious beliefs can be the product of rational thinking no less than of faith. To be sure, faith is a critical part of religion. More to the point, this faith is typically grounded in a sacred text that serves as an important source of truth, one that may be at odds with competing secular sources. Unless they are fundamentalists, however, religious believers do not view their sacred text as a source of truth that is absolute, plain, and unchanging.[50] Thus, nonfundamentalists interpret their text not according to a perceived "plain meaning" but, rather, with an eye to competing sources of truth, including modern science and philosophy.[51] Likewise, they consider the changing condition of society for its impact on their religious understandings.

Accordingly, nonfundamentalist religious believers form and revise their beliefs, including their religious beliefs, by considering not only their religious text but also contemporary societal practices and various kinds of nonreligious thought. In so doing, they constantly strive to maintain an overall belief structure that is logical and coherent.[52] Hardly "impervious to persuasion," they are broadly open to rational dialogue, both within and outside their religious community. As a result, when nonfundamentalist religious believers bring their religious beliefs to bear in American politics and lawmaking, this practice does not conflict with the insights of the Enlightenment and republican theory. The conflict arises only if the religious believers are religious fundamentalists.

B. The Problems with Religious Fundamentalism in the Private Domain

In the private domain, the problems with religious fundamentalism are not political but theological. I am not a theologian, but these problems are basic, and they therefore are not difficult to recount. They involve the undervaluation of human reason, the sin of intellectual pride, and the lack of genuine religious faith.

Religious fundamentalism does not deny the human capacity to reason, but it strictly limits the role of reason by affirming a source of truth that is regarded as absolute, plain, and unchanging. On whatever issues this source of truth addresses, reason is thus confined within a narrowly drawn and self-contained epistemic system. As a result, religious fundamentalism severely cabins, and thereby undervalues, the human capacity for reason. Yet this capacity for reason, no less than the human capacity for faith, is a product of the Creation, and therefore should be accepted as a gift from God.

Religious fundamentalism also is theologically problematic in its claims of certitude. These claims suggest the sin of pride—in particular, the sin of intellectual pride, or pride of knowledge.[53] At the same time, they are premised on an unwillingness to confront competing evidence and arguments, an insular stance that, paradoxically, suggests a lack of genuine religious faith.

Wolfhart Pannenberg, a contemporary Christian theologian, is critical of fundamentalist religion, by which he means "religion that, in an unwarranted claim to certitude, refuses to engage the human capacity for reason."[54] He writes that authentic religion must "lay claim to reason" and at the same time "be ready to accept criticism, and to cultivate an ethos of self-criticism."[55] Pannenberg explains:

> Traditional doctrines and forms of spirituality, along with the Bible itself, are not exempt from critical inquiry. Such inquiry is required by the alliance of faith and reason. Christian confidence in the truth of God and His revelation should be vigorous enough to assume that truth will not succumb to any findings of critical inquiry. . . . [I]f we think it is necessary to protect divinely revealed truth from critical inquiry, we are in fact displaying our unbelief. Such inquiry, while it may at times pose difficulties, will finally enhance the splendor of the truth of God.[56]

Religious fundamentalists can lead lives that are rich in meaning and that are grounded in a deep sense of order as well as peace. But their religion rests on a theology that is problematic in significant respects. A more satisfying theology suggests that religion should fully accept and embrace the gift of human reason. It should engage competing claims and arguments, holding fast to a faith that such discourse will not and cannot undermine the truths of God.

C. The Problems with Secular Fundamentalism in the Form of Political Liberalism

In the public sphere, secular fundamentalism, in the form of political liberalism, is problematic for reasons that are similar to those relating to political decision making based on religious fundamentalism. Thus, like religious fundamentalist politics, liberalism—to the extent that it precludes religious involvement in politics—is inconsistent with the political foundations of our society as well as our contemporary political culture. More specifically, the historical and contemporary role of religion in American public life belies the claim of liberalism that citizens and lawmakers should "bracket" their religious convictions when deliberating about politics and law.

As noted previously, the American political system has roots in reason,[57] but it also has roots in religion. As Professors Richard Vetterli and Gary C. Bryner have explained, the Founders were overwhelmingly religious, and they did not regard religion as irrelevant to public issues:

> The Founders as a whole were deeply religious men. Religion played a vital role in most of their lives; it influenced their beliefs and activities, their ideals and hopes. The foundation of their modern republican philosophy was based on a belief in God. Whatever the concepts that blended to form this republican doctrine—the dignity of man, natural law, natural rights, the right of resistance—all were suffused with an aura of the sacred.[58]

Like many Enlightenment thinkers, the Founders—most of them, at least—regarded revelation as an important supplement to reason.[59] In their minds, religion and reason played complementary roles in the search for truth, including political truth.[60]

In the protection of religious freedom itself, for instance, religious justifications played a central role in the founding period—in the arguments "not only of ministers and religious leaders, but also of political leaders such as Madison and Jefferson."[61] In particular, Madison relied on religious arguments in his *Memorial and Remonstrance Against Religious Assessments*.[62] And Jefferson grounded his famous Virginia Act for Religious Freedom on an explicitly religious rationale. Thus, in its preamble, the act declares that "Almighty God hath created the mind free" and that compelled religion is "a departure from the plan of the Holy Author of our religion, who, being Lord both of body and mind, yet chose not to propagate it by coercions on either, as was in his Almighty power to do."[63]

The Founders' views concerning the public relevance of religion have never been abandoned. Rather, history reveals that Americans, time and again, have brought their religious convictions to bear on important questions of public policy—on issues such as slavery, temperance, civil rights, immigration, poverty, abortion, and environmental policy.[64] This is hardly surprising because the most common American religions have significant political implications. As Dean M. Kelley has noted, "[T]he formative religious traditions of the Western world—Judaism and Christianity—have for millennia embraced the conviction that their religious duty entailed active intervention in the 'body politic.'"[65] As a result, Kelley writes, "churches and synagogues can no more be silent on public issues than human beings can refrain from breathing."[66]

Liberalism's attempt to exclude religion from any role in public policy making might be plausible as a matter of abstract political philosophy, and it might even be plausible for some democratic societies. To make valid claims on the actual workings of a particular society, however, a political theory cannot dishonor that society's history, its contemporary political culture, and the fundamental beliefs of its citizens. As Professor Thomas C. Berg has written, "[R]eligion is too pervasive a factor in the lives of Americans" as well as "their concrete, historic patterns" to support a theory that proceeds "on the hope or premise that it will go away or retreat to the margins of life."[67] Berg relies on the insights of Reinhold Niebuhr:

> [S]ecularization of the public order goes hopelessly against the grain in any society, such as America, in which religion plays an important role in the lives of the people. Niebuhr's increasingly Burkean, "organic" understanding of society emphasizes that government must arise from the people, from their concrete, historic patterns. It cannot be based on imposing an abstract and ideologically consistent scheme—in this case, the rigid separation of religion from public moral reasoning—in the name of liberal philosophy.[68]

In the "incurably religious" United States,[69] at least, the claims of political liberalism ring hollow and cannot be accepted.

Republican theory does not suggest otherwise. From a historical perspective, republicanism's search for the public good certainly did not exclude religion. In the founding period, as Professors Vetterli and Bryner have argued, "[r]eligion was especially important to the development of a republican culture,"[70] with religious (including especially Christian) values and insights playing prominent and substantial roles:

> The general Judeo-Christian tradition permeated American life. There were strong sentiments of mission, a belief that this pristine land had been set apart and preserved for a chosen people, and faith that America "was not only a destined nation, but a redeeming nation." There was a general consensus that Christian values provided the basis for civil society. Religious leaders had contributed to the political discourse of the Revolution, and the Bible was the most widely read and cited text. Religion, the Founders believed, fostered republicanism and was therefore central to the life of the new nation.[71]

After the founding, moreover, religion continued to be "the major carrier of this republican tradition."[72] Thus, as Professor John A. Coleman has explained, "the strongest American voices for a compassionate just community always appealed in public to religious imagery and sentiments, from Winthrop and Sam Adams, Melville and the Lincoln of the second inaugural address, to Walter Rauschenbusch and Reinhold Niebuhr and Frederick Douglass and Martin Luther King."[73]

According to Coleman, the historical link between republicanism and American religion is hardly surprising, and it is a link with continuing relevance:

> Both the tradition of republican theory and that of biblical religion place great stress on love and sacrifice for the common good and on the need to found the health of public life on individual virtue and a morally good citizenry. Both stand in judgment of social theories which expect public virtue to arise from a healthy compromise of private vices.[74]

Professor Timothy L. Hall concurs, noting that "[r]eligious groups, in the form of voluntary associations, create a context in which individuals become sharers of a common life, and thus have occasion to acquire an other-regarding disposition."[75]

Moreover, Hall continues, religious groups "have traditionally preserved didactic resources for discourse concerning the common good. The major religions, for example, have each emphasized perspectives that temper, at least to some degree, the purely selfish impulses that war against a concept of the public good."[76] As Coleman and Hall make clear, religion has the capacity to advance, not hinder, a republican search for the common good.

From both a historical and a contemporary perspective, moreover, there is no reason to assume, a priori, that religion—at least nonfundamentalist religion—cannot use this capacity in a manner that contributes to a dialogic, deliberative truth-seeking process. As explained earlier, religious believers can be broadly open to rational discourse, not only within their religious community but also in the broader culture.[77] As a result, Professor Michael J. Perry's conclusion is sound: "[A]t its best," writes Perry, "religious discourse in public culture is not less dialogic—not less openminded, not less deliberative—than is, at its best, secular discourse in public culture."[78]

In addition to its problematic character in the public domain, political liberalism has potentially damaging spillover effects on the private sphere of life. In theory, liberalism does not deny the truth and value of religion on issues of private concern. In practice, however, to the extent that we exclude religion from public life, we suggest that religion is a second-class source of truth. As Wolfhart Pannenberg explains, "People need social support in holding that a given account of reality is plausible."[79] Pannenberg cites the work of sociologist Peter L. Berger, who has described religious believers in the modern world as a "cognitive minority," that is, "a group of people whose view of the world differs significantly from the one generally taken for granted in their society."[80] For such a group, according to Berger, "the plausibility of 'knowledge' that is not socially shared, that is challenged by our fellow men, is imperiled, not just in our dealings with others, but much more importantly in our own minds."[81]

I doubt that religious believers are a "cognitive minority" in the contemporary United States, but the devaluing of religion in public life could eventually place them in a comparable predicament. In particular, a rigidly secular public culture—a culture of the sort that liberalism might promote—would provide no social support for religious beliefs. Instead, it would tend to undermine, indirectly but inevitably, even the private faith of religious believers.[82]

D. The Problems with Comprehensive Secular Fundamentalism

Secular fundamentalism in another form, that is, comprehensive secular fundamentalism, is directly relevant to the private sphere. As discussed previously, comprehensive secular fundamentalism moves beyond political liberalism to a more complete rejection of religious ways of thinking.[83] Thus, it turns to modern science and secular rationalism for the resolution of all questions of truth, whether public or private, and regardless of whether the questions relate to matters of fact or matters of value.

From the perspective of comprehensive secular fundamentalism, science is controlling on questions of fact. Science also plays an important, albeit more subtle, role in resolving questions of value. Thus, with its emphasis on empiricism and objectivity, the scientific worldview supports the idea that moral duties do not arise in the absence of tangible, observable harm to others. It is a combination of science and secular rationalism, then, that supports the idea of personal autonomy: in the absence of tangible, demonstrable harm to others, all questions of morality—whether public or private—should be left to the autonomous decisions of individuals.

Due especially to its heavy reliance on science, comprehensive secular fundamentalism also supports the idea of naturalism. Naturalism is "the view that ultimately nothing resists explanation by the methods characteristic of the natural sciences."[84] According to naturalism, human attitudes and behavior, like other phenomena, are the product of prior causes that themselves are subject to scientific examination and explanation. Thus, "along with the rest of nature, human beings are explainable through the methods of the natural sciences. Human institutions and practices, the modes of experience of men, the goals and values of individuals and groups, are all natural, and no less so than the wheeling of galaxies and the evolution of species."[85]

Naturalism promotes the belief that what we think and do are entirely the product of naturalistic causes, that is, primarily genetics and social conditioning. Many psychologists, for instance, now claim that human happiness "seems to be largely determined by the genes, not by outside reality."[86] This kind of scientific determinism in turn promotes a sense of moral relativism. If human attitudes and values are nothing more than the product of prior, scientifically identifiable causes, how can one say that the values that some people display are morally superior to the values displayed by others? Indeed, naturalism leaves us in a universe that "has no moral character save to the extent that it contains human beings among its objects and thus contains entities that have and pursue values."[87]

Comprehensive secular fundamentalism thus supports and furthers the ideas of personal autonomy, naturalism, and moral relativism. In the end, however, these three ideas are fundamentally inconsistent. In particular, naturalism and moral relativism severely undermine the value of personal autonomy. Consider, for example, a young woman deciding the future direction of her life. She might pursue a college education and eventually a career as a doctor. Instead, she might delay college—perhaps forever—in order to wed her high school sweetheart and start a family, or in order to take a job at a local factory. Or she might become a member of a religious order, taking a vow of chastity and poverty, and devoting her life to hands-on service to the poor. Or she might pursue any of a number of other options. Needless to say, the young woman's decision is laden with moral considerations, and, according to the principle of personal autonomy, she is "free" to make this decision for herself. But just what is the point if her "choice," in reality, is nothing more than the product of naturalistic causes, and if no particular decision is any better than another? Autonomy becomes an illusion, and moral relativism sinks into the abyss of moral emptiness.

Like the problems with religious fundamentalism in the private domain, the problems with comprehensive secular fundamentalism are essentially theological. To accept the theological critique of comprehensive secular fundamentalism, however, one need not adopt any particular religious viewpoint. One need only believe that human life has ultimate meaning and purpose, that is, that human life is more than the product of naturalistic—and essentially amoral—causes.

As Professor Michael J. Perry has explained, the essence of religion—and therefore theology—is the affirmation that human life has ultimate meaning. "One polar response to the problem of meaning," writes Perry, "is to conclude that life is, finally and radically, meaningless."[88] The other polar response, he continues, "is 'religious': the trust that life is ultimately meaningful, meaningful in a way hospitable to our deepest yearnings."[89] My argument here is that anyone accepting the second response should reject the comprehensive form of secular fundamentalism.[90]

Beyond theology, moreover, comprehensive secular fundamentalism is problematic on its own terms. As I have just discussed, the three major ideas that it supports are actually in conflict. Yet there is an even more basic problem of internal inconsistency. Above all else, comprehensive secular fundamentalism purports to privilege reason. But reason requires a certain openness of mind, a willingness to confront competing evidence and arguments. Those who adhere to comprehensive secular fundamentalism, however, are absolutists in at least one respect: they are not open to the possibility of religious truth and therefore are not willing to consider arguments that depend upon religious perspectives. To this extent, then, comprehensive secular fundamentalists actually ignore the cardinal value that they claim to prefer, the value of reason itself.

III. Moving beyond Fundamentalism: Toward a Dialogic, Multilingual Search for Truth

Both in the public and in the private domain, the claim that fundamentalism is detrimental to the search for truth depends upon the belief that dialogue is beneficial. Thus, if dialogue supports the search for truth, fundamentalism—whether religious or secular—is problematic because it entails a method of thinking that categorically denies the legitimacy or value of insights that proceed from contrary premises. As such, it is not open to a dialogic search for truth, at least not outside the confines of its self-contained epistemic system.

But perhaps dialogue is not important, or at least not essential, in the pursuit of truth.[91] Whether on issues of public or of private concern, perhaps it is enough that individuals can join in common cause when their goals or interests coincide. In the public domain, for example, religious and secular environmentalists—without the need for any meaningful discourse between them—might combine to provide sufficient political support for an environmental statute that each group finds desirable, albeit for radically different reasons. Fastidious political liberals might object even to this type of religious-secular alliance. Otherwise, however, the idea of common cause would permit fundamentalists of all stripes, both religious and secular, to determine their own truth in their own way and, on public questions, to vote for the policies and the candidates that they believe their truth to require.

If dialogue in fact facilitates the search for truth, however, as I believe it does, fundamentalism—whether religious or secular—works to hinder that search. It erects a type of linguistic barrier, one that frustrates the search for truth by inhibiting communication that might lead to that end. Fundamentalists are like English speakers who adopt an "English only" rule for a society that includes people who speak not English but Spanish. Perhaps the fundamentalists, like the English speakers, will reach the truth even as they exclude the views of those who use another language, but surely the odds would be improved if everyone's arguments and insights could be considered.

For a speaker's arguments and insights to be considered, of course, his or her listeners must be able to comprehend the speaker's language. To answer this need, some have argued that, at least in the public sphere, we should prefer a common language that is secular.[92] Thus, like Spanish speakers in an English-speaking society, religious citizens should translate their religious arguments into secular terms. Professor Suzanna Sherry, for example, writes that "[p]ublic dialogue . . . is only possible where the participants speak the same language, and in political discourse, speaking the same language is analogous to Rawls's 'public reason.'"[93]

In a society as religious as ours, however, perhaps the secular speakers—at least those who embrace "public reason" as their exclusive mode of public discourse—are the ones speaking Spanish. In any event, the historical and contemporary role of religion in American public life makes it difficult to accept the argument that we should privilege secular language, and therefore secular thinking, in the manner suggested by Sherry and other liberal theorists. And in private life, there is even less reason to prefer discourse that is secular as opposed to religious.

More generally, it would be wrong—in public or private life—to adopt a single and exclusive moral language, whether secular or religious in nature. To do so would be to deny to some speakers their moral language of choice, a language that is closely linked to their sense of self, to the core of who they are as individuals. Those whose moral language is excluded would suffer affront, if not humiliation, because the exclusion would deny an essential element of their humanity. It would treat them as second-class citizens, second-class human beings. Their pain and resentment, in turn, would have adverse consequences for society at large, producing deep-seated divisions, distrust, and conflict.[94]

At the same time, limiting discourse to a single moral language would artificially confine and constrain the search for truth. A richer discourse—and a more open search for truth—would not be confined to a single moral language. Focusing especially on the need to respect religious contributions to public dialogue, Professor Stephen L. Carter explains:

> What is needed is not a requirement that the religiously devout choose a form of dialogue that liberalism accepts, but that liberalism develop a politics that accepts whatever form of dialogue a member of the public offers. Epistemic diversity, like diversity of other kinds, should be cherished, not ignored, and certainly not abolished. What is needed, then, is a willingness to *listen*, not because the speaker has *the right voice* but because the speaker has *the right to speak*. Moreover, the willingness to listen must hold out the possibility that the speaker is saying something worth listening to; to do less is to trivialize the forces that shape the moral convictions of tens of millions of Americans.[95]

Although directed to the public sphere, Carter's observations can properly be extended to support a multilingual dialogue on public and private issues alike. In such a dialogue, secular speakers could speak their language of choice, but so, too, could religious speakers.

For the multilingual discourse to be fully successful, however, participants would need to learn and understand the moral languages being used by others, and they themselves would need to communicate in moral languages other than their own. This might mean religious thinkers communicating not only in the language of their own religious traditions but also in that of others. At least in the private domain, this type of interreligious communication already occurs with some degree of frequency. Thus, as Professor Theodore Y. Blumoff has argued, "conversation is not only possible across denominations, it occurs all the time."[96] Professor Blumoff, who is Jewish, provides a personal example, explaining how he has conversed with a Mormon colleague: "I question him using the same logic and language he uses. I question him in terms of his beliefs, as he does of mine."[97] On public issues as well, there is no reason to doubt the efficacy of this sort of discourse. On the issue of capital punishment, for example, Professor Martin E. Marty, an old-line Protestant, recently has invoked the principles of more evangelical thought in an attempt to persuade Charles Colson, an evangelical Protestant, that the death penalty is immoral "in evangelical terms."[98]

In the multilingual discourse that I envision, religious thinkers might communicate not only in the language of their own and other religious traditions but also in secular language. I must concede that it can be difficult for religious believers to translate their religious arguments into secular terms,[99] and the secular translation is likely to miss important parts of the religious meaning. Even so, as Professor Blumoff argues, "religiously motivated convictions usually can be meaningfully if not always fully translated into secular language."[100] And this would not be a one-way street. Thus, in the multilingual discourse, secular thinkers might sometimes speak in religious terms, thereby communicating with religious believers in part by translating their secular arguments into language that the religious believers might find more persuasive. Indeed, as Professor Thomas C. Berg has suggested, it may be that the best form of argument, at least in many situations, appeals "to a standard that citizens on the other side of the debate accept."[101] "[B]y presenting arguments based on premises others can accept," Berg writes, "the citizen respects the limits of her own perspective and the goodness and truth in those of others."[102]

For the benefit of those who might think otherwise, it is important to emphasize the positive role that religious language—and religious insights—can play in a multilingual, dialogic exchange. As Professor John A. Coleman has written, for religious thinkers to limit themselves entirely to secular language creates a serious risk that "the specifically theological or religious vision will be undermined, betrayed or distorted."[103] Religious language, for example, can convey a communitarian impulse that is not easily captured in secular terms. The power of religious symbolism can "stir human hearts and minds to sacrifice, service, and deep love of the community."[104] The "thin" language of secularism, by contrast, tends to perpetuate "the bias toward liberty at the expense of justice in the American public-philosophy tradition and its concomitant individualistic tone."[105] Professor Michael J. Perry agrees, noting that religious insights can be meaningful even to those who stand outside the religion in question. "You certainly do not have to be Jewish to recognize that the prophetic vision of the Jewish Bible is profound and compelling," he writes, "any more than you have to be Catholic or Presbyterian or Baptist or even Christian to recognize that the Gospel vision of what it means to be human is profound and compelling."[106] As Perry suggests, religion can move us to confront the ultimate questions of private and public life. Indeed, it can move us to address the very meaning of human life, both for individuals and for the political community of which they are a part.

Although the insights of religion would be important and valuable in the multilingual discourse that I envision, no language, whether religious or secular, would receive an a priori advantage. In the public domain, the goal would be similar to that of the "ecumenical politics" that Professor Perry has advocated:

> The aim of ecumenical politics is, in words borrowed from *The Williamsburg Charter*, "neither a naked public square where all religion is excluded, nor a sacred public square with any religion established or semi-established." The aim, rather, "is a civil public square in which citizens of all religious faiths, or none, engage one another in continuing democratic discourse."[107]

Whether in public or in private, moreover, every insight, religious or secular, would be considered for the light it might shed and the wisdom it might contain.[108]

The search for truth thus would be guided not by power[109] but by persuasion. As Professor Sherry writes, "[M]oral reasoning . . . can be good or bad."[110] Although Sherry limits herself to secular moral reasoning, her analysis actually applies to religious reasoning as well. Thus, moral reasoning, whether secular or religious,

> can be good or bad. It can contain inconsistencies and failures to notice logically necessary connections. It can fit poorly with experience or with one's other beliefs, or have unpalatable implications. It can be based on faulty premises, unchallenged only because of cognitive negligence.[111]

Conversely, it might be logical. It might fit well with one's experiences. It might mesh with one's other beliefs or lead to an adjustment of those beliefs. Its implications might be attractive, and it might rest on premises that are sound.[112]

Would the language of fundamentalism, at least, be properly excluded from the multilingual discourse? Although it may seem paradoxical, the answer is no. Although I have argued that fundamentalism frustrates a dialogic search for truth, this occurs only to the extent that fundamentalists actually control the discourse or make the decisions that the discourse is designed to inform. Such control or such decision making, in my view, would indeed be problematic. In the public domain, for example, it would be problematic if fundamentalists had the strength of numbers and the political power to themselves determine our laws and policies. But fundamentalists certainly can play a "speaking" role in the search for truth. Fundamentalists, as listeners, may be unwilling to entertain nonfundamentalist positions, but that does not mean that their fundamentalist claims have no value in a discursive exchange with nonfundamentalists. To the contrary, nonfundamentalists should listen to fundamentalist claims, attempting to understand the premises on which they are based and to appreciate the truth they might contain. At the same time, at least if my arguments in this essay are sound, nonfundamentalists should urge their fundamentalist interlocutors to reconsider their fundamentalist stance. Fundamentalist minds can be changed—albeit only by conversion to nonfundamentalism.

In the world of multilingual discourse that I have imagined, humility and tolerance would be exceedingly important.[113] In America, however, these qualities could and should be supported by religious as well as Enlightenment values,[114] including, in the words of Reinhold Niebuhr, the religious "sense of humility which must result from the recognition of our common sinfulness."[115] "To subject human righteousness to the righteousness of God," writes Niebuhr, "is to realize the imperfection of all our perfections, the taint of interest in all our virtues, and the natural limitations of all our ideals."[116]

Professor Thomas C. Berg explains the significance of Niebuhrian humility in the realm of politics:

> The Niebuhrian view asks the political activist (religious or secular) not to renounce his most basic views, but to be aware of several complicating factors: his own limits, the difficulty in applying general religious truths to complex real-world problems, and the potential good and truth in the views of his opponents.[117]

Needless to say, Niebuhr's vision of humility—and the tolerance it naturally inspires—could and should extend to the private sphere as well.

Conclusion

Martin Luther King, Jr., dreamed of societal harmony and common understanding, a time when "all flesh" would see the truth together.[118] My dream is more modest: a multilingual search for truth that might be a step in that direction. In today's America, even my dream—not to mention Dr. King's—might appear to be quite unrealistic.[119] As King most powerfully showed, however, dreaming is not always a vice, and "realism" is not always a virtue. Undue "realism" can block the pursuit of dreams that are difficult but worthy. Such dreams demand our energetic support, however distant and unlikely their ultimate achievement might seem.

Dr. King not only pursued his "unrealistic" dream; he had faith that it would become a reality. "With this faith," he said, "we will be able to hew out of the mountain of despair a stone of hope. With this faith we will be able to transform the jangling discords of our nation into a beautiful symphony of brotherhood."[120]

Perhaps we cannot muster the faith of Dr. King. But if not faith, let us at least have hope.

NOTES

This essay was originally published in the Journal of Law and Religion, 12 J Law & Relig 337–70 (1995–96). (Despite the cover date, this issue of the Journal of Law and Religion was published in 1998).

1. See Isaiah 40:4–5 (King James Version).

2. See, e.g., James Davison Hunter, *Culture Wars: The Struggle to Define America* (Basic Books, 1991).

3. Indeed, we cannot even agree on precisely what we mean by "truth." See generally Michael J. Perry, *Love and Power: The Role of Religion and Morality in American Politics* 56–62 (Oxford U Press, 1991) (discussing "correspondence" and more "internalist" understandings of truth). Without entering that debate, I proceed in this essay on the assumption that truth—including moral and political truth—does or might exist in a relatively strong, relatively objective sense, and that the search for truth, so understood, is both worthwhile and important. This assumption does not presuppose the existence of a single, universal truth on every moral or political question, regardless of the cultural or historical context, but it certainly rejects the notion that truth is nothing more than "power" or "social construction." At the very least, according to my assumption, some arguments on moral and political matters are better than others and, in that sense, are closer to the truth.

4. Relatedly, there are important epistemological questions concerning the nature and significance of religious truth, including religious truth as it relates to historical events. See, e.g., Luke Timothy Johnson, *The Real Jesus: The Misguided Quest for the Historical Jesus and the Truth of the Traditional Gospels* 133–66 (HarperSanFrancisco, 1996) (arguing that the truth of Christianity, including the truth of the Resurrection, is not a matter of strictly historical inquiry); Howard Lesnick, *Religious Particularity, Religious Metaphor, and Religious Truth: Listening to Tom Shaffer*, 10 J Law & Relig 317, 328–30 (1993–94) (suggesting that religion may be true in a deep but nonhistorical sense, even for those who are not conventional "believers").

5. Daniel O. Conkle, *Different Religions, Different Politics: Evaluating the Role of Competing Religious Traditions in American Politics and Law*, 10 J Law & Relig 1 (1993–94). As Professor David Hollenbach has explained, religion can play a public role not only by direct involvement in politics but also by its influence in the broader realm of civil society and culture. See David Hollenbach, *Contexts of the Political Role of Religion: Civil Society and Culture*, 30 San Diego L Rev 877 (1993).

6. The role of religion in politics and law is constrained by the Establishment Clause of the First Amendment, but the Establishment Clause's prohibition on religiously motivated policy making is properly limited to the pursuit of *spiritual* objectives, such as attempts to sponsor prayer or other devotional activities. The Establishment Clause should not be read to preclude a religiously motivated pursuit of nonspiritual, *worldly* objectives. On the distinction between spiritual and worldly objectives, see Conkle, 10 J Law & Relig at 11–13 (cited in note 5).

7. Id. at 13–21.

8. Id. at 14. As I explain in the essay, fundamentalism actually is a matter of degree; thus, fundamentalist tendencies may be extreme or more moderate. See id at 14–15.

9. Id. at 15–16.

10. Id. at 16–17 n 55.

11. Arthur Schlesinger Jr., *The Worst Corruption*, Wall St J A10 col 3 (Nov 22, 1995).

12. Id.

13. Id.

14. Id.

15. See George M. Marsden, *Fundamentalism and American Culture: The Shaping of Twentieth-Century Evangelicalism: 1870–1925* (Oxford U Press, 1980); Ernest R. Sandeen, *The Roots of Fundamentalism: British and American Millenarianism, 1800–1930* (U Chicago Press, 1970).

16. More and more, conservative American Protestants are calling themselves "evangelicals." See Gustav Niebuhr, *Public Supports Political Voice for Churches*, NY Times A1 col 3 (June 25, 1996) (describing results of public opinion survey).

17. Schlesinger, Wall St J (cited in note 11). Referring to "the monster of Hitlerism and Stalinism," Haris Silajdzic, the former prime minister of Bosnia, has contended that in light of this history of "secular fundamentalism," Europeans are in no position to condemn religious fundamentalism as uniquely problematic. See *Premier Warns of Secular Fundamentalism in Europe*, British Broadcasting Corporation, BBC Summary of World Broadcasts (July 31, 1995) (available on LEXIS).

18.

> The French Revolution began with Mr. Jefferson's enthusiastic approval, but it lost his support when it became infected, as do so many of our causes, with excessive zeal—when the secular fundamentalists, Marat, Danton, and Robespierre, guillotined ordinary citizens and even penniless prostitutes on allegations that they had uttered the hateful words, "Vive le roi," or "Long live the King."

Paul D. Carrington, *Remembering Jefferson*, 2 Wm & Mary Bill of Rts J 455, 459 (1993).

19. Id. at 459.

20. Id. at 460. See id. ("That current academic dogma is secular in form" does not make it less problematic than religious zealotry.).

21. Allen R. Myerson, *Help Wanted: Gyration Inspectors*, NY Times sec 4 at 2 col 1 (Feb 4, 1996).

22.

> Secular true believers, much like their religious counterparts, possess a moral rectitude that is uncommon in an age of declining beliefs. Secularism's adherents hold an unshakable confidence not only in the superiority of their values, but to their right to assert them over others through the institutions of society.

Don E. Eberly, *Restoring the Good Society: A New Vision for Politics and Culture* 52 (Hourglass Books, 1994).

23. Not surprisingly, this type of false association is likely to be invoked in political attacks on religious conservatives. For example, Americans United for Separation of Church and State recently sponsored a political advertisement containing the following text: "Maybe we should let radical religious fundamentalists run this country. (After all, it's worked so well in Iran.)" The advertisement ran in the Colorado Springs Gazette Telegraph shortly before the November 1996, election; Americans United was rebuffed in its attempts to place the advertisement in another newspaper and on billboards. See Barry W. Lynn, *Billboard Battle: Who's Being Censored?*, Church & State, Dec 1996, at 21.

24. The fact that a term has a negative connotation does not necessarily mean that it should be abandoned. Perhaps the negative connotation is in some way *deserved*. But this depends on the particular meaning that the term is designed to convey.

25. Conkle, 10 J Law & Relig at 14–16, 23–24 (cited in note 5).

26. For discussions and evaluations of the analogy between biblical and constitutional interpretation, see, e.g., Sanford Levinson, *Constitutional Faith* (Princeton U Press, 1988); Thomas C. Grey, *The Constitution as Scripture*, 37 Stan L Rev 1 (1984); Michael W. McConnell, *The Role of Democratic Politics in Transforming Moral Convictions into Law*, 98 Yale LJ 1501, 1509–14 (1989); Michael J. Perry, *The Authority of Text, Tradition, and Reason: A Theory of Constitutional "Interpretation,"* 58 S Cal L Rev 551 (1984).

27. Morton J. Horwitz, *The Meaning of the Bork Nomination in American Constitutional History*, 50 U Pitt L Rev 655, 663 (1989).

28. Id. (footnote omitted). Cf. McConnell, 98 Yale LJ at 1512 (cited in note 27) ("Constitutional interpretation, performed in the manner of Orthodox Jews and Christian fundamentalists, would seek specific answers to specific questions from a particular time in the past (presumably the founding), and would enforce those answers in today's world, notwithstanding considerable pressure arising from changes in context and circumstance."). See also Gordon S. Wood, *The Fundamentalists and the Constitution*, New York Review of Books, Feb 18, 1988, at 33, 39.

29. Horwitz, 50 U Pitt L Rev at 663 (cited in note 27). For further elaboration, see Morton J. Horwitz, *The Supreme Court, 1992 Term—Foreword: The Constitution of Change: Legal Fundamentality Without Fundamentalism*, 107 Harv L Rev 30 (1993).

30. Secular fundamentalists, at least if they are judges, actually might have a more complex understanding of the text they are interpreting. In particular, judges might adopt a fundamentalist interpretive stance without rejecting the possibility that the text, in its fullest understanding, contains broader or evolving truths. In interpreting the Constitution, for example, judges might believe that the *judiciary* should do no more than enforce the Constitution's fundamentalist meaning, but they might also believe that nonjudicial decision makers, interpreting the Constitution for themselves, might properly honor other, nonfundamentalist constitutional values.

31. According to Professor Michael J. Sandel, this ideal of neutrality is one of three connected ideas that form the essence of contemporary liberal theory, the others being the priority of individual rights and the notion that individuals are "freely choosing, unencumbered selves." Together they create what Sandel describes as "the procedural republic" of modern America. Michael J. Sandel, *Democracy's Discontent: America in Search of a Public Philosophy* 28 (Belknap Press of Harv U Press, 1996).

32. Id. at 18. Some contend that political liberalism, and the privileging of secular over religious beliefs in the resolution of political issues, is constitutionally required by the Establishment Clause. For a prominent article advancing this position, see Kathleen M. Sullivan, *Religion and Liberal Democracy*, 59 U Chi L Rev 195 (1992). As noted previously, I reject this interpretation of the Establishment Clause, which, in my view, would improperly constrain the religiously motivated pursuit of nonspiritual, worldly objectives. See above, note 6.

This is not to deny that a religiously motivated law, like any other law, might violate constitutional principles—or principles of liberal democracy—that are unrelated to the law's religious motivation. See generally John H. Garvey, *A Comment on* Religious Convictions and Lawmaking, 84 Mich L Rev 1288 (1986) (arguing that liberal democracy values certain goods, including certain individual freedoms, and that religiously motivated lawmaking should not conflict with those goods); John H. Garvey, *What Are Freedoms For?* (Harvard U Press, 1996) (elaborating Garvey's theory of freedoms).

33. Professor Mark Tushnet, for example, has argued that it is permissible for lawmakers to rely on religious justifications, but only if the laws they adopt are independently justifiable on secular grounds. Mark Tushnet, *The Limits of the Involvement of Religion in the Body Politic*, in James E. Wood, Jr., & Derek Davis, eds., *The Role of Religion in the Making of Public Policy* 191–220 (Baylor U, 1991). Professor Michael J. Perry adopts a somewhat similar position in his most recent book, although he would not require secular grounding for the claim that all human beings are sacred. Michael J. Perry, *Religion in Politics: Constitutional and Moral Perspectives* (Oxford U Press, 1997).

34. Indeed, liberal theorists may define "reason" to include virtually all kinds of thinking *except* religion. According to Professor Suzanna Sherry, for example, "reason" includes thinking based on "experience, observation, logic, learned patterns, and tradition"—unless, that is,

any of these sources of judgment depend upon "[a]ppeals to a perception of reality shared only by the faithful." Suzanna Sherry, *The Sleep of Reason*, 84 Geo LJ 453, 455–56 (1996).

35. John Rawls, *Political Liberalism* (Colum U Press, 1993). Rawls limits his claim to "fundamental" political questions involving "constitutional essentials" and "questions of basic justice," id. at 214, although he adds that even with respect to other issues, "it is usually highly desirable to settle political questions by invoking the values of public reason," id. at 215.

36. See id. at 13, 175.

37. Id. at 243. Although he privileges public reason in this sense, Rawls contends that citizens who affirm his understanding of liberalism do so "on moral grounds." Id. at 147.

> All those who affirm the political conception start from within their own comprehensive view and draw on the religious, philosophical, and moral grounds it provides. The fact that people affirm the same political conception on those grounds does not make their affirming it any less religious, philosophical, or moral, as the case may be, since the grounds sincerely held determine the nature of the affirmation.

Id. at 147–48. For Rawls' most recent explication of his views, see John Rawls, *The Idea of Public Reason Revisited*, 64 U Chi. L Rev 765 (1997).

38. Paul F. Campos, *Secular Fundamentalism*, 94 Colum L Rev 1814 (1994). Cf R. Randall Rainey, S.J., *Law and Religion: Is Reconciliation Still Possible?*, 27 Loy L.A. L Rev 147, 189–90 (1993) (suggesting that "the systematic exclusion or marginalization of 'religious people' from public policy discourse and the rule of law" amounts to "'liberal fundamentalism,'" a "form of secular fundamentalism").

39. Campos, 94 Colum L Rev at 1820–21 (cited in note 38).

40. Id. at 1826.

41. Id. at 1822.

42. At least one political candidate has used the phrase "secular fundamentalism" in this way. See John Marelius, *Huffington Issues Spiritual Call to Arms*, San Diego Union-Tribune 8 (Oct 12, 1994) (quoting United States Senate candidate Michael Huffington as decrying the "secular fundamentalists" who believe that "God should . . . be kept in the closet and under wraps" and that religion should not be brought to bear on public issues).

43. On the privatization of religion and the secularization of public debate, see, for example, Stephen L. Carter, *The Culture of Disbelief: How American Law and Politics Trivialize Religious Devotion* (Basic Books, 1993); Frederick Mark Gedicks, *Some Political Implications of Religious Belief*, 4 Notre Dame J L Ethics & Pub Pol'y 419, 421–27 (1990); Frederick Mark Gedicks, *Public Life and Hostility to Religion*, 78 Va L Rev 671 (1993); Michael W. McConnell, *God Is Dead and We Have Killed Him!": Freedom of Religion in the Post-Modern Age*, 1993 BYU L Rev 163; Steven D. Smith, *The Rise and Fall of Religious Freedom in Constitutional Discourse*, 140 U Pa L Rev 149, 169–78 (1991). For a rich analysis of these developments as they relate to the issue of abortion, see Elizabeth Mensch & Alan Freeman, *The Politics of Virtue: Is Abortion Debatable?* (Duke U Press, 1993).

44. Comprehensive secular fundamentalists invariably embrace political liberalism for the resolution of public questions. Conversely, those who are secular fundamentalists in the sense of embracing political liberalism need not be comprehensive secular fundamentalists, i.e., they need not reject religion as a source of truth or meaning in the private domain.

45. Reinhold Niebuhr, 2 *The Nature and Destiny of Man: Human Destiny* 238 (Charles Scribner's Sons, 1964) (originally published 1943); see Thomas C. Berg, *Church-State Relations and the Social Ethics of Reinhold Niebuhr*, 73 N Car L Rev 1567, 1603–6 (1995).

46. See Conkle, 10 J Law & Relig at 14–16, 23–24 (cited in note 5). No less than other citizens, religious fundamentalists are entitled to the full protection of our constitutional guar-

antees of religious freedom and freedom of expression. Thus, in suggesting that religious fundamentalism can be problematic in the realm of politics, I certainly am not suggesting that it should in any way be legally restricted or legally disadvantaged.

47. See Sherry, 84 Geo LJ at 464–84 (cited in note 34).

48. Id. at 478–79.

49. Id. at 476. But cf. id. at 454 (contrasting "largely rational" religion with "religiosity of the traditional, pre-Enlightenment, antirational kind").

50. In my previous essay, I distinguished between two types of nonfundamentalist religious believers: religious "modernists," who stand at the opposite extreme from religious fundamentalists, and religious "reconcilers," who stand more in the middle. See Conkle, 10 J Law & Relig at 17–21 (cited in note 5). In the present discussion, I am treating these two types together.

51. Contrast Sherry, 84 Geo LJ at 462 (cited in note 34) ("The methods of science and rational argument are of no avail in evaluating religious beliefs.").

Writing from a very different perspective, Professor Stanley Fish challenges the coherency and persuasiveness of liberal arguments like that of Sherry's. See Stanley Fish, *Mission Impossible: Settling the Just Bonds Between Church and State,* 97 Colum L Rev (1997). But Fish, like Sherry, appears to believe that religious thinking is truly "religious" only when it amounts to religious fundamentalism: "[T]hose religions that put 'openness of mind' at the center of their faith—or rather at the center of their rejection of faith— . . . are indistinguishable from other enlightenment projects and are hardly religions at all." Id. at 2281.

52. For a wonderful description of the "continuous" epistemology of a religious believer of this type, see Larry Alexander, *Liberalism, Religion, and the Unity of Epistemology*, 30 San Diego L Rev 763, 768–70 (1993).

53. For a discussion of the sin of intellectual pride, i.e., pride of knowledge, see Reinhold Niebuhr, 1 *The Nature and Destiny of Man: Human Nature* 194–98 (Charles Scribner's Sons, 1964) (originally published 1941).

54. Wolfhart Pannenberg, *How to Think about Secularism*, First Things 27, 31 (June/July 1996).

55. Id.

56. Id. at 31–32.

57. See above, note 46 and accompanying text.

58. Richard Vetterli & Gary C. Bryner, *Religion, Public Virtue, and the Founding of the American Republic*, in Neil L. York, ed., *Toward A More Perfect Union: Six Essays on the Constitution*, at 91, 100 (Brigham Young U, 1988).

59. James Madison, for example, "arrived at a consistent, lifelong defense of Christianity on the basis both of reason and intuition, shifting gradually like many contemporaries from the first to the second." Henry F. May, *The Enlightenment in America* 96 (Oxford U Press, 1976). As such, Madison's beliefs fell at "the center of the American religious spectrum." Id.; see also id. at xiv.

60. Professor Suzanna Sherry contends otherwise, but her argument is unpersuasive. Sherry initially claims that "virtually all of the Framers—and indeed the entire founding generation—shared a common background in the epistemology of the Enlightenment," an epistemology "based on reason and empiricism, specifically rejecting faith and revelation." Sherry, 84 Geo LJ at 466 (cited in note 34). She then concedes, however, that her claim is "clouded" by the fact that "[t]he question of whether to privilege faith or reason would not have occurred to the founders for the simple reason that they did not see them as in conflict. They believed that religious belief could be (and indeed should be) supported by principles of

reason." Id. at 468. Sherry concludes that "the founding generation subscribed to the epistemology of reason," id., but the better conclusion, even by Sherry's own account, is the one that I advance in the text. In particular, the evidence suggests that the founding generation's understanding of the Enlightenment did not deny a role for religion, i.e., as long as the religion did not *conflict* with the teachings of reason.

Relying on their own historical claims, Professors Isaac Kramnick and R. Lawrence Moore have argued that the Framers created "a godless Constitution and a godless politics," and that this understanding should continue to control today. See Isaac Kramnick and R. Lawrence Moore, *The Godless Constitution: The Case Against Religious Correctness* 22 (W. W. Norton & Co., 1996). As Professor Scott C. Idleman has powerfully demonstrated, however, the authors' thesis is seriously flawed and cannot be accepted. See Scott C. Idleman, *Liberty in the Balance: Religion, Politics, and American Constitutionalism,* 71 Notre Dame L Rev 991 (1996).

61. Smith, 140 U Pa L Rev at 162 (cited in note 43); see id. at 153–66; see generally Symposium, *Religious Dimensions of American Constitutionalism*, 39 Emory LJ 1 (1990).

62. For a discussion of Madison's arguments, see Smith, 140 U Pa L Rev at 161 (cited in note 43).

63. Virginia Act for Religious Freedom, Va Code Ann § 57–1 (Michie 1996) (enacted Jan 16, 1786); see Smith, 140 U Pa L Rev at 162 (cited in note 43).

64. At the very least, this historical and continuing pattern of religious involvement suggests that "those who seek to secularize entirely the political and legal processes ought to face a presumption not in their favor." Scott C. Idleman, *The Sacred, the Profane, and the Instrumental: Valuing Religion in the Culture of Disbelief*, 142 U Pa L Rev 1313, 1339 (1994).

65. Dean M. Kelly, *The Rationale for the Involvement of Religion in the Body Politic*, in Wood & Davis, eds., *The Role of Religion in the Making of Public Policy* 159, 168 (cited in note 33).

66. Id. at 188. See also Perry, *Love and Power* at 77–82 (cited in note 3) (discussing the "essentially political" nature of religion, including especially Western religion).

67. Berg, 73 N Car L Rev at 1607 (cited in note 45).

68. Id.

69. See id. For a summary of statistics concerning the religiosity of Americans, see Conkle, 10 J Law & Relig at 3–4 (cited in note 5).

70. Vetterli & Bryner, *Religion, Public Virtue, and the Founding of the American Republic* at 92 (cited in note 58).

71. Id. (footnote omitted); see id. at 91–117; see also Richard Vetterli & Gary C. Bryner, *In Search of the Republic: Public Virtue and the Roots of American Government* (Rowman & Littlefield, 1987).

72. John A. Coleman, *An American Strategic Theology* 187 (Paulist Press, 1982).

73. Id. at 193.

74. John A. Coleman, *A Possible Role for Biblical Religion in Public Life*, 40 Theological Studies 701, 702 (1979).

75. Timothy L. Hall, *Religion and Civic Virtue: A Justification of Free Exercise*, 67 Tulane L Rev 87, 110 (1992).

76. Id. at 111.

77. See above, text accompanying note 52.

78. Perry, *Religion in Politics* at 46 (cited in note 33). Perry adds the following, parenthetical comment: "Nor, at its worst, is religious discourse more monologic—more closeminded and dogmatic—than is, at its worst, secular discourse." Id. at 46–47.

Focusing on fundamentalist religion and citing psychological and sociological factors, Professor William P. Marshall has argued that religious involvement in politics creates a special risk of intolerance. William P. Marshall, *The Other Side of Religion*, 44 Hastings LJ 843 (1993). Whatever the strength of Marshall's claim, however, it certainly cannot be extended to nonfundamentalist religion.

79. Pannenberg, First Things at 27 (cited in note 54).

80. Peter L. Berger, *A Rumor of Angels: Modern Society and the Rediscovery of the Supernatural* 6 (Anchor Books, 1990).

81. Id. at 7.

82. See Gedicks, 4 Notre Dame J L Ethics & Pub Pol'y at 432–39 (cited in note 43). But cf. Theodore Y. Blumoff, *The New Religionists' Newest Social Gospel: On the Rhetoric and Reality of Religions' "Marginalization" in Public Life*, 51 U Miami L Rev 1 (1996) (arguing that the privatization of religion does not imply its marginalization, and that, indeed, there is an overabundance of public religiosity in the United States, which actually disserves the cause of true religion).

83. See above, part I.D.

84. Simon Blackburn, *The Oxford Dictionary of Philosophy* 255 (Oxford U Press, 1994).

85. Arthur C. Danto, *Naturalism*, in Paul Edwards, ed., 5 *Encyclopedia of Philosophy* 448, 449 (Macmillan & Free Press, 1972).

86. Daniel Goleman, *Forget Money; Nothing Can Buy Happiness, Some Researchers Say*, NY Times B5 (July 16, 1996). According to Dr. David T. Lykken, any deviations from this genetic predisposition depend primarily upon "the sorrows and pleasures of the last hours, days or weeks." Id. (quoting Dr. Lykken). But "[h]owever tragic or comic life's ups and downs, people appear to return inexorably to whatever happiness level is pre-set in their constitution." Id.

According to this theory, to actively *seek* happiness, i.e., a personal "sense of well-being," is an uphill struggle at best. See id. (quoting Dr. Lykken). But according to Dr. Lykken, the cause is not entirely hopeless. He offers this advice:

> Be an experiential epicure. A steady diet of simple pleasures will keep you above your set point. Find the small things that you know give you a little high—a good meal, working in the garden, time with friends—and sprinkle your life with them. In the long run, that will leave you happier than some grand achievement that gives you a big lift for awhile.

Id. (quoting Dr. Lykken). It is difficult to imagine a thinner understanding of human fulfillment and human autonomy.

87. Danto, 5 *Encyclopedia of Philosophy* at 449 (cited in note 86). See generally Phillip E. Johnson, *Reason in the Balance: The Case Against Naturalism in Science, Law & Education* (InterVarsity Press, 1995).

88. Perry, *Love and Power* at 69 (cited in note 3).

89. Id. at 70.

90. It may be that many who regard themselves as "secularists" would accept the second response. If so, they may be more "religious" than they think.

91. As Professor Steven D. Smith has noted, the role of dialogue in the search for truth can be overstated. See Steven D. Smith, *Moral Realism, Pluralistic Community, and the Judicial Imposition of Principle: A Comment on Perry*, 88 Nw UL Rev 183, 186 (1993) ("Moral reality . . . may be best understood not through dialogue or theoretical discourse, but rather by other means or faculties such as intuition, inspiration, tradition, or revelation."); Steven D. Smith, *Skepticism, Tolerance, and Truth in the Theory of Free Expression*, 60 S Cal L Rev 649, 690 (1987) ("The suggestion that dialogue is the exclusive method of ascertaining truth does violence to the very meaning of dialogue. By its nature, dialogue is inherently parasitic upon methods other than dialogue for discovering truth.").

92. See, e.g., Robert Audi, *The Separation of Church and State and the Obligations of Citizenship*, 18 Phil & Pub Aff 259 (1989); Edward B. Foley, *Tillich and Camus, Talking Politics*, 92 Colum L Rev 954 (1992); Marshall, 44 Hastings LJ 843 (cited in note 78).

Professor Kent Greenwalt has advanced a series of sophisticated and nuanced arguments that point generally in this direction, but with significant exceptions and caveats. See, e.g., Kent Greenwalt, *Religious Convictions and Political Choice* (Oxford U Press, 1988); Kent Greenwalt, *Private Consciences and Public Reasons* (Oxford U Press, 1995).

93. Sherry, 84 Geo LJ at 471 (cited in note 34).

94. Cf. Daniel O. Conkle, *Toward a General Theory of the Establishment Clause*, 82 Nw UL Rev 1113, 1164–69 (1988) (arguing that a failure to respect religious and irreligious beliefs can cause grave injury, not only to the individuals whose fundamental beliefs are being disparaged but also to the larger community of which those individuals are a part).

95. Carter, *The Culture of Disbelief* at 230–31 (cited in note 43) (emphasis in original). Cf. Sanford Levinson, *Religious Language and the Public Square*, 105 Harv L Rev 2061, 2077 (1992) ("Why doesn't liberal democracy give everyone an equal right, without engaging in any version of epistemic abstinence, to make his or her arguments, subject, obviously, to the prerogative of listeners to reject the arguments should they be unpersuasive?").

96. Theodore Y. Blumoff, *The Holocaust and Public Discourse*, 11 J Law & Relig 591, 610 (1994–95).

97. Id.

98. Martin E. Marty, *Dear Charles Colson . . .* , Christian Century 799 (Aug 14–21, 1996).

As Professor Douglas Sturm has argued, the serious pursuit of interreligious dialogue—a dialogue that "celebrates difference" even as it affirms "connectedness"—may represent a productive response to "the political question," i.e., the question "How shall we live our lives together?" Douglas Sturm, *Crossing the Boundaries: On the Idea of Interreligious Dialogue and the Political Question*, 30 J Ecumenical Studies 1, 2, 3 (1993). Cf. Alecia Maltz, *Commentary on the Harris Superquarry Inquiry*, 11 J Law & Relig 793, 831 (1994–95) ("[E]cumenical approaches are one of the most important tools we have to integrate values into political discourse!").

99. See Richard B. Saphire, *Religious People and Public Life: Some Reflections on Greenawalt*, 23 N Ky L Rev 655, 680 (1996) (asking devout religious believers to recast their arguments in nonreligious terms can be like asking them "to recast their arguments in ancient Greek").

100. Blumoff, 11 J Law & Relig at 611 (cited in note 96). Cf. Mary Ann Glendon, *Rights Talk: The Impoverishment of Political Discourse* 181–82 (Free Press, 1991) (discussing the possibility of "translating" particular religious discourses without a loss of religious distinctiveness).

101. Berg, 73 N Car L Rev at 1622 (cited in note 45).

102. Id. Berg's points are directed to the public sphere, but they are equally valid for discourse and debate in the private realm.

103. Coleman, *An American Strategic Theology* at 195 (cited in note 72).

104. Coleman, 40 Theological Studies at 706 (cited in note 74).

105. Id. at 705.

106. Perry, *Religion in Politics* at 81 (cited in note 33). "Gandhi was not a Christian," Perry continues, "but he recognized the Gospel vision as profound and compelling." Id.

107. Perry, *Love and Power* at 45 (cited in note 3) (quoting *The Williamsburg Charter: A National Celebration and Reaffirmation of the First Amendment Religious Liberty Clauses* 19 (1988)).

108. In my previous essay, I urged religious thinkers to be "reconcilers," thinkers willing to confront and consider secular as well as religious sources of truth in an attempt to "reconcile" these sources by bringing them into harmony or agreement. Conkle, 10 J Law & Relig at 19–21 (cited in note 5). Those whose starting point is secular could likewise be reconcilers in

this sense. To be a reconciler, however, one first must be multilingual: one cannot meaningfully consider a potential source of moral truth without understanding and communicating in the moral language of that source.

109. But cf. Sherry, 84 Geo LJ at 477 (cited in note 34) ("[T]here is no way to resolve disputes between epistemologies except by recourse to power.").

110. Id. at 474.

111. Id. at 474–75 (footnotes omitted).

112. See generally Alexander, 30 San Diego L. Rev. 763 (cited in note 52) (arguing for the unity of religious and nonreligious epistemology).

At least on one theoretical understanding, the First Amendment, taken as a whole, may support my general conception of the search for truth. Thus, according to Professor William P. Marshall, the search for truth is a value that helps justify not only freedom of expression but also the Religion Clauses. William P. Marshall, *Truth and the Religion Clauses,* 43 DePaul L Rev 243 (1994). "[B]y affirming the value of religious ideas in the pursuit of truth," writes Marshall, "the search for truth value recognizes that freedom of religion and freedom of speech are complementary parts of the same enterprise." Id. at 267. For an elaboration of Marshall's views, see William P. Marshall, *In Defense of the Search for Truth as a First Amendment Justification,* 30 Ga L Rev 1 (1995).

113. This humility and tolerance would require that full consideration be given to the experiences, values, and insights of religious minorities, whose historical and contemporary experiences may lead them to be concerned, if not frightened, about an enhanced religious role in contemporary America. For powerful testimony on this concern from a Jewish perspective, see Blumoff, 11 J Law & Relig (cited in note 96).

114. See Berg, 73 N Car L Rev at 1624 (cited in note 45).

115. Harry R. Davis & Robert C. Good, eds., *Reinhold Niebuhr on Politics: His Political Philosophy and Its Application to Our Age as Expressed in His Writings* 207 (Charles Scribner's Sons, 1960).

116. Id.

117. Berg, 73 N Car L Rev at 1624 (cited in note 45). "Religious humility," according to Niebuhr, "is in perfect accord with the presuppositions of a democratic society." Reinhold Niebuhr, *The Children of Light and the Children of Darkness: A Vindication of Democracy and a Critique of Its Traditional Defense* 135 (Charles Scribner's Sons, 1944).

As Professor Jaroslav Pelikan has noted, President Abraham Lincoln exemplified the type of humility that Niebuhr later described. Jaroslav Pelikan, *Believers-in-Chief,* New Republic 30, 32 (Sept 4, 1995). Thus, Lincoln showed "a sense of reverence in the presence of a divine mystery that did not yield its ultimate secrets either to rationalism or to orthodoxy and therefore called for humility and awe on the part of all mortals." Id.

118. See above, note 1 and accompanying text.

119. And even if my proposed search for truth were in fact pursued within the United States, this might not be adequate for the increasingly global era in which we live. According to Professor Harold J. Berman, international conditions require "a transnational, cross-cultural, inter-religious" search for truth. Harold J. Berman, *Law and Logos,* 44 DePaul L Rev 143, 164 (1994). Such a search, writes Professor Berman, would draw upon

> the resources not only of Christianity, Judaism, and Islam—the traditional theistic religions—but also of various forms of Buddhism, Taoism, and other non-theistic religions, as well as on various forms of humanism that are not called religions but share with them a passionate commitment to a higher spiritual truth.

Id. at 157.

If my dream for the United States is unrealistic, all the more so is Berman's for the world. But Berman has hope even for his vision, hope he traces to the biblical account of Pentecost:

> Implicit in the story of the Tower of Babel is the story of Pentecost. . . . It tells us that at a place where a multitude of people of different nationalities had gathered to worship, certain of them received from the Holy Spirit the power to speak in "other languages," so that all the peoples of the earth could hear "the mighty works of God," "each in his own native tongue." Thus the story of Pentecost gives hope that human pride can be overcome, and that by translation from one language to another all peoples of the world may, by the power of a higher spiritual truth, share each other's experiences vicariously and become, as they were originally intended to be, united.

Id. at 165 (citing and quoting Acts 2:1–13).

120. Martin Luther King, Jr., *I Have a Dream* (August 28, 1963), *reprinted in* James Melvin Washington, ed, *A Testament of Hope: The Essential Writings of Martin Luther King, Jr.*, at 219 (HarperSanFrancisco, 1986).

Chapter 18

The Constitutional Tradition
A Perplexing Legacy

Ronald F. Thiemann

The Separation of Church and State: A Misleading Metaphor

Public religion presents a dilemma for American democracy. The reasons that some would encourage a religious voice in our public life can easily be identified. Given the pervasiveness and importance of religious convictions within the American populace, it would be odd indeed to deny such profound sentiments any role in our public life. Given the historic significance of religion in shaping our national political culture, the removal of religion from the "public square" would seem to violate our most ancient traditions.[1] If we are to gain genuine clarity on these matters, we need to look anew at the constitutional principle and the cultural metaphor that influences every discussion of the role of religion in public life: the so-called separation of church and state. If we can come to a clearer understanding of that much maligned and often misunderstood principle, we will have taken a significant first step toward resolving our current dilemma.

"Congress shall make no law respecting an establishment of religion or prohibiting the free exercise thereof." These opening words of the Bill of Rights state what one scholar has called "the most distinctive concept that the American constitutional system has contributed to the body of political ideas,"[2] a principle commonly known as *the separation of church and state*. That phrase is derived from a metaphor first used by Roger Williams in a letter to John Cotton[3] and then by Thomas Jefferson in a letter to the Baptist Association of Danbury, Connecticut,[4] but it became common constitutional parlance through a decision in *Everson v. Board of Education* written by Justice Hugo Black in 1947.[5] Despite its somewhat obscure origins and its rather recent introduction into the legal tradition, this principle has come to shape our nation's understanding of the relation between the political and religious spheres in the United States. Not only has it guided constitutional interpretation of the First Amendment, it has also molded the American public's understanding of the proper relation between government and religion.

Principles derived from metaphors have the advantage of capturing with vividness and felicity the essential elements of a complicated situation. They have the distinct disadvantage, however, of encouraging simplicity instead of precise analysis, of fostering caricature when detailed portraiture is needed. At a time when our nation is struggling to define the proper role of religion and religiously based moral convictions within public life, the phrase "the separation of church and state" and its attendant metaphor "a wall of separation between church and state" serve not to clarify but to confuse.[6] While the phrases identify one aspect of government's relation to religion, they deflect our attention from other fundamental features of the First Amendment guarantees. By focusing on religious and governmental institutions, they obscure the essential concern for individual freedom and equality that undergirds both the "no establishment" and the "free exercise" clause. By speaking of "church and state," they seduce us into thinking of these complicated and textured organizations (communities of faith and governmental agencies) in singular and monolithic terms. By defining the relation between religion and government with the simple word "separation," these phrases conceal the variety of ways in which the two entities interact, and the phrase consequently constrains our ability to imagine new possibilities for their relationship. The slogan "the separation of church and state" impedes our understanding of the proper role of religion in American public life and, I will argue in this essay, must be basically reconceived and perhaps even abandoned.[7]

"The First Amendment has erected a wall [of separation] between church and state. That wall must be kept high and impregnable. We could not approve the slightest breach."[8] On the day (February 10, 1947) on which Justice Hugo Black penned those fateful words, the United States Supreme Court was convened with the invocation "God save this honorable court." A few hundred yards across the Mall from the Supreme Court building, the two houses of Congress opened their sessions with prayers offered by chaplains supported by public funds and paid with currency inscribed with the motto "In God We Trust." Some months later President Harry S. Truman would follow the custom of nearly every president since the founding of the republic by issuing a proclamation declaring a national day of thanksgiving, and urging Americans to engage in prayers of thanks to the Creator for his manifold gifts to the nation. In light of these apparently contradictory sentiments about the role of religion in American public life, it should not surprise the reader to learn that the decision that introduced the phrase "wall of separation" into the Court's lexicon actually *sustained* a New Jersey state statute that provided public funding for transportation of children attending Roman Catholic schools. Justice Black, having affirmed that the wall of separation must not be breached, then offered the puzzling opinion that "New Jersey has not breached it here," even though the state used public tax funds to support the busing of Roman Catholic schoolchildren.

The Supreme Court's record in adjudicating cases involving the religion clauses has been spotty at best. Court decisions since *Everson v. Board of Education* have been characterized by questionable logic and contradictory opinions. Supreme Court commentators have been virtually unanimous in their censure of the justices' reasoning in cases involving the religion clauses, particularly those dealing with the "no establishment clause." Critics representing the full spectrum of political ideologies have joined voices in characterizing the Court's decision making in this area as "bizarre,"[9] "fatuous,"[10] "a hodgepodge . . . derived from Alice's Adventures in Wonderland."[11] Legal scholar Jesse Choper has argued that the current disarray in the adjudication of establishment cases "has generated ad hoc judgments which are incapable of being reconciled on any principled basis."[12] A summary of just some of the Court's decisions regarding state aid to education provides a useful illustration of the counterintuitive reasoning that seems to characterize Supreme Court opinions in matters of religion.

> [T]he Court has held that the state may reimburse parents for the costs of public bus service to take students to and from nonpublic schools, but it may not pay for buses to take students on field trips. The state may furnish textbooks, but not other educational materials such as maps or film projectors. Publicly funded remedial teaching off the school premises is allowed, but remedial teaching on the school premises is not. The state may reimburse a sectarian school for administering state-created tests, but it may not fund tests created by the school's own teachers. Finally, the state may fund a wide variety of institutions and activities indirectly through tax subsidies that it may not fund directly.[13]

Howard Ball's suggestion that the Court is involved in "judicial meandering in search of the meaning and purpose of the establishment clause"[14] surely seems correct. Moreover, the Court's lack of clarity on these issues threatens both to polarize and politicize an already complicated situation. In his unprecedented attack on the Supreme Court in July 1985, then Attorney General Edwin Meese took aim at the Court's decision making regarding the religion clauses. Characterizing the Court's doctrine of "strict neutrality between religion and non-religion" as "bizarre," Meese urged the justices to return to a "jurisprudence of original intent." He also questioned whether the Court's interpretation of the Fourteenth Amendment as mandating the application of the Bill of Rights to actions of the states could be maintained. In making these arguments, Meese relied heavily on political scientist Robert Cord's book *Separation of Church and State: Historical Fact and Current Fiction*,[15] published in 1982 with a foreword by William F. Buckley. Consequently, criticisms of the Court's use of the "wall of separation" metaphor have become associated with a conservative political agenda.[16] The tendency to align a defense of "absolute separation of church and state" with political liberalism and the critique of that position with political conservatism can only serve further to confuse and confound the current discussion.

To gain clarity on these important but controversial issues, we need a careful analytical unraveling of the many strands of judicial interpretation of the religion clauses of the First Amendment. Instead of relying upon slogans, metaphors, and political caricatures, we need to engage in a dispassionate evaluation of the various forms of reasoning that have characterized Court opinions since *Everson*. We need further to ask not simply about the *intentions* of the framers of the Constitution but about the *values* they sought to inscribe in the text. What political and cultural values are upheld by the Constitution's religion clauses? Are those values worth preserving in today's society? If so, what policies best uphold the values the founders sought to defend? How do the historical and cultural changes of the past two hundred years affect the way we apply those values to our current policy problems? By focusing on questions such as these, we might begin to gain clarity, about the proper place of religion in judicial adjudication. But before we can gain such clarity, we must plunge into the midst of the perplexing legacy that the Court has created in the confusing and contradictory aftermath of *Everson*.

The Confusion Displayed: Allegheny County v. Greater Pittsburgh ACLU (1988)

A recent Supreme Court establishment clause case illustrates the complicated and contradictory pattern of reasoning that characterizes current judicial deliberations on issues of religion in public life. In *Allegheny County v. Greater Pittsburgh ACLU*, the Court considered a case that involved the displaying of religious symbols on or near county property. The government of Allegheny County permitted the Holy Name Society, a Roman Catholic organization, to display a creche on the grand staircase of the county courthouse. The creche display, which included an angel bearing a banner with the words "Gloria in Excelsis Deo," was the sole holiday decoration within the main staircase of the courthouse. Another display, erected outside a building jointly owned by the county and the city of Pittsburgh, consisted of a 45-foot Christmas tree, an 18-foot menorah,[17] and a sign saluting liberty during the holiday season. The Greater Pittsburgh ACLU brought suit against the county, seeking to enjoin the display of both the creche and the menorah, arguing that they violated the First Amendment establishment clause. While the U.S. District Court held that neither display violated the First Amendment, the Third Circuit Court of Appeals disagreed, holding that both symbols were violations of the establishment clause. The Supreme Court, in a truly Solomonic decision, finally held that the creche was in violation of the First Amendment and the menorah was not.

The confusion reflected in *Allegheny* and other establishment cases stems in part from a more basic tension inherent in the two religion clauses themselves.[18] Former Chief Justice Burger has characterized the problem in the following terms. "The Court has struggled to find a neutral course between the two Religion Clauses, both of which are cast in absolute terms, and either of which, if expanded to a logical extreme would tend to clash with the other."[19] Since the no-establishment clause forbids any governmental assistance to religion, and the free exercise clause mandates governmental accommodation of religion, the two clauses can easily work at cross-purposes. The Court is primarily called upon to adjudicate cases that fall into the ambiguous gray area between the two clauses.[20] The tension between the two clauses produces a challenge to many.

The opinions offered by the Supreme Court justices in this case present a crazy-quilt pattern of argument, but three major positions can be discerned within their presentations: separation, neutrality, and accommodation. The majority (Justices Blackmun, O'Connor, Brennan, Stevens, and Marshall) clearly uphold a "separationist" position, though they do so on different grounds. Blackmun and O'Connor argue that the creche violates the establishment clause primarily because the display serves no clear "*secular purpose*." Justices Brennan, Stevens, and Marshall take the stronger position of "*strict neutrality*," arguing that the government is never permitted to display religious symbols of any kind; consequently these three justices argue that both the creche and the menorah are in violation of the First Amendment. Justice Kennedy, joined by Justices Rehnquist, Scalia, and White, dissent from the majority opinion and argue that neither display is a violation of the establishment clause. Their position is aptly described as one of "*symbolic accommodation*."

"*Secular purpose*." Justice Blackmun, writing for the majority, begins his opinion by confirming the principles adopted by the Court in three previous cases: *Everson v. Board of Education, Lemon v. Kurtzman,*[21] and *Wallace v. Jaffree*.[22] After quoting in full Justice Black's summary of the meaning of the establishment clause, Blackmun proceeds to reiterate the so-called *Lemon* test for determining whether a governmental practice is in violation of that clause. "Under the *Lemon* analysis, a statute or practice which touches upon religion, if it is to be permissible under the Establishment Clause, must have a secular purpose; it must neither advance nor inhibit religion in its principal or primary effect; and it must not foster an excessive entanglement with religion."[23] Finally, Blackmun invokes the notion introduced into establishment adjudication by Justice O'Connor: that government may not engage in practices that function to "endorse" religious beliefs. Thus any state action that serves to favor, prefer, or promote "one religious theory over another"[24] or "religious belief over disbelief"[25] is in violation of the no-establishment clause.

Since the Allegheny creche display proclaimed a specifically Christian message, with no secular symbols to provide a broader cultural context, Blackmun argues that this action cannot be viewed simply as the acknowledgment of a "cultural phenomenon." "[G]overnment may celebrate Christmas in some manner and form, but not in a way that endorses Christian doctrine. Here, Allegheny County has transgressed this line. It has chosen to celebrate Christmas in a way that has the effect of endorsing a patently Christian message. . . . This display of the creche in this context, therefore, must be permanently enjoined."

Despite the apparently straightforward reasoning reflected in Justice Blackmun's opening arguments, the complexity of this case emerges when he seeks to deal with the objections raised by his colleagues on the bench. Blackmun is forced to deal with the fact that the majority opinion appears to run counter to two earlier decisions rendered by the Court. In *Marsh v. Chambers* (1983)[26] the Court approved the Nebraska legislature's practice of opening each day with a prayer offered by a chaplain paid by public funds, and in *Lynch v. Donnelly* (1984)[27] the Court upheld the right of the city of Pawtucket, R.I., to erect a creche as part of its observance of the Christmas holiday season. In light of these obvious "accommodations" to religious practice, Justice Blackmun takes particular care to answer the charges of the dissenting justices that the Court's action in this case is blatantly inconsistent with two of its recent precedents. This reversal of the Court's recent practice, the dissenters argue, represents not governmental neutrality but "an unjustified hostility toward religion."[28]

In reply, Blackmun states his position that the no-establishment clause demands a "secular" government "precisely in order to avoid discriminating among citizens on the basis of their religious faiths." Legislative prayers, the national motto, and the

Pledge of Allegiance contain acceptable "non-sectarian" references to religion. Indeed, Blackmun reminds his colleagues, "the legislative prayers involved in *Marsh* did not violate this principle because the particular chaplain had 'removed all references to Christ.'" By contrast governmental actions or practices "that demonstrate the government's allegiance to a particular sect or creed" must be prohibited if the no-establishment clause is to be upheld. "The history of this Nation, it is perhaps sad to say, contains numerous examples of official acts that endorsed Christianity specifically.... Some of these examples date back to the founding of the Republic, but this heritage of official discrimination against non-Christians has no place in the jurisprudence of the Establishment Clause."

This interpretation of the First Amendment, Blackmun argues, represents not hostility to religion but "a respect for religious pluralism, a respect commanded by the Constitution." The only way religious diversity can be appropriately respected is if "government is secular in its functions and operations." By permitting a display that proclaimed the religious, as opposed to the secular, meaning of the Christmas holiday, Allegheny County was clearly discriminating against the non-Christian population. Thus the majority decision permanently enjoining the display of the creche represents not "a hostility or indifference to religion, but, instead, the respect for religious diversity that the Constitution requires." By contrast the Jewish menorah, surrounded as it was by various secular symbols, constitutes "not an endorsement of religious faith but simply a recognition of cultural diversity."

In her concurring opinion, Justice O'Connor offers some significant refinements of Blackmun's position. In particular, she seeks to show the dissimilarities between the Allegheny and Pawtucket creche displays, differences that justify the apparently contradictory decisions in *Allegheny* and *Lynch*. In *Lynch* the Court, employing the *Lemon* test, held that Pawtucket had a "secular purpose" for including a creche in the city's Christmas display, namely, "to depict the origins of that Holiday." In addition, the display did not have the "primary effect" of advancing religion, since it was formally analogous to the "literally hundreds of religious paintings in governmentally supported museums." Finally, the display did not involve "excessive entanglement" between religion and government since there was "no evidence of contact with church authorities concerning the content or design of the exhibit." The Pawtucket display continued the common governmental practice of acknowledging the role of religion in American life. Practices like legislative prayers and invocation of the divine name in the national motto "serve the secular purposes of 'solemnizing public occasions, expressing confidence in the future, and encouraging the recognition of what is worthy of appreciation in society.'" As long as a secular purpose is served, governmental acknowledgment of religion does not violate the no-establishment clause.

Governmental acknowledgment is to be distinguished, however, from governmental "endorsement," for the latter "sends a message to nonadherents that they are outsiders, not full members of the political community, and an accompanying message to adherents that they are insiders, favored members of the political community." O'Connor's endorsement test thus seeks to differentiate discriminatory and nondiscriminatory governmental action in a religiously plural democracy. Practices like legislative chaplaincies and presidential thanksgiving proclamations are acceptable because they are "nonsectarian" in nature. Thanksgiving, for example, "is now generally understood as a celebration of patriotic values rather than particular religious beliefs. . . . Such long-standing practices . . . serve a secular purpose rather than a sectarian one and have largely lost their religious significance over time." Even the Christmas tree "whatever its origins, is not regarded today as a religious symbol," but the creche, particularly as displayed in the Allegheny County Courthouse, is clearly a sectarian Christian symbol that conveys a message of marginalization to nonadherents of the Christian faith. By contrast, the broader holiday display that included the menorah conveyed a "message of pluralism . . . [and] is not a message that endorses religion over nonreligion." Thus the "combined holiday display had neither the purpose nor the effect of endorsing religion, but . . . [the] Allegheny County's creche display had such an effect."

The attempt by Blackmun and O'Connor to define the proper relationship between religion and government is plagued by a number of serious difficulties. In seeking to preserve governmental neutrality within a pluralistic democracy, they characterize the state as "essentially secular" and mandate that its actions must always have a "secular purpose." Only a genuinely secular state, they argue, can avoid preference or favoritism among competing religious groups. State secularity is the guarantor of nondiscrimination on matters religious. This position, though internally consistent, entails a number of odd consequences.

If the courts are to have the responsibility of judging whether a governmental action has a secular purpose, judges will be placed in the uncomfortable position of being both theological and social critics. They must function as theological critics in order to determine the meaning of a symbol within a religious tradition's network of doctrines and practices; they must function as social critics in order to determine whether such a symbol has been sufficiently stripped of its inherent religious meaning to function in a nondiscriminatory way in the public realm. But such governmental activities run the risk of *violating* rather than *upholding* the no-establishment clause. Members of the judicial branch appear to be particularly ill prepared to engage in even the minimal theological inquiry required to determine the meaning and function of a religious symbol within a religious community's vast network of beliefs and practices.[29] Moreover, such inquiry threatens to place the "civil magistrate" as a "judge of religious truth," a position Madison reckoned to be "an arrogant pretension."[30] In addition, the "secular purpose" requirement mandates that public officials make the formidable social assessment that the religious content of a symbol has been sufficiently muted to make it acceptable in the public realm. Such judgments will be both difficult and controversial, but the requirement itself suggests that religious symbols are publicly acceptable only insofar as they are no longer religious. Justice Blackmun's approving observation that the chaplain whose prayers were the subject of adjudication in *Marsh v. Chambers* acted appropriately because he had removed "all references to Christ" would sound abhorrent to the vast majority of Christian ministers who might be asked to serve in a similar capacity. The "secular purpose" argument as interpreted by Blackmun and O'Connor[31] would admit only the blandest symbols into the discourse of public life.[32] Not only would this requirement impoverish the already desultory rhetoric of contemporary politics, it would make religious people rightly suspicious of allowing their symbols into the public realm for fear that their meaning and significance would be lost through the homogenizing effect of our political culture.

"*Strict neutrality.*" Precisely because the middle ground Blackmun and O'Connor seek to occupy appears so unstable, their concurring colleagues devise a different justification in support of their judicial judgment regarding the *Allegheny* case. Justice Brennan, joined by Marshall and Stevens, presents a *strict neutrality* argument as the basis for their concurrence with the majority decision. In finding both the creche and the menorah in violation of the First Amendment, Brennan takes issue with the Blackmun/O'Connor appeal to pluralism as a justification for the presence of religious symbols on governmental property. In so doing, Brennan provides a different principled basis for his separationist position.

> I know of no principle under the Establishment Clause . . . that permits us to conclude that governmental promotion of religion is acceptable so long as one religion in not favored. We have, on the contrary, interpreted that Clause to require *neutrality*, not just among religions, but between religion and non-religion. (*Allegheny*, 644, italics added)

In a clever bit of theological analysis Brennan disputes the "secular purpose" requirement by showing that the argument for religious pluralism *depends* upon the continuing religious significance of the symbols displayed in front of the jointly owned city/county building. Justice O'Connor approves of that display because it "conveyed a message of pluralism and freedom of belief during the holiday season." But, Brennan points out, "the 'pluralism' to which Justice O'Connor refers is *religious* pluralism, and the 'freedom of belief' is freedom of *religious* belief. The display of the tree and the menorah will symbolize such pluralism and freedom only if more than one religion is represented. . . . Thus, the pluralistic message Justice O'Connor stressed *depends on* the tree possessing some religious significance." Consequently, the "secular purpose" and "religious pluralism" arguments work at cross-purposes with each other, and thus the Blackmun/O'Connor position cannot be consistently maintained.

Moreover, Brennan argues, by engaging in judgments about the religious significance of symbols like the menorah and the Christmas tree, the Court seeks to substitute its own judgments for that of the participants in the religious traditions. One may wonder why ministers across the nation read presidential thanksgiving proclamations from their pulpits if Thanksgiving Day has become "a celebration of patriotic values *rather than* particular religious beliefs." It may come as a surprise to millions of Christians who celebrate the Christmas season that the Christmas tree "is not regarded today as a religious symbol." So also religious Jews may be offended to learn the Court considers the menorah to be "primarily" a symbol about Jewish ethnic identity. Indeed, Brennan offers significant evidence to counter all of these judgments. The issue, however, is not which of the justices gets the best of the theological argument but whether justices are competent to engage in such disputes at all. Such theological judgments, Brennan asserts, constitute "an interference in religious matters precluded by the Establishment Clause." As Justice Stevens states in his concurring opinion, "[T]he Establishment Clause should be construed to create a strong presumption against the display of religious symbols on public property."

"*Symbolic accommodation*." The "softness" of the Blackmun/O'Connor mediating position precipitated a sharply worded and strongly argued dissent from Justices Kennedy, Rehnquist, White, and Scalia. Writing for the dissenting minority, Justice Kennedy suggests that the majority opinion "reflects an unjustified hostility toward religion, a hostility inconsistent with our history and our precedents." This ruling continues the recent pattern of judicial interpretation that would require "a relentless extirpation of all contact between government and religion," a policy clearly at odds with "our political and cultural heritage." The time has come, Kennedy suggests, to consider "substantial revision of our Establishment Clause doctrine."

Kennedy rejects the notion that government can categorically maintain a position of "no assistance" to religion.

> [A]s the modern administrative state expands to touch the lives of its citizens in such diverse ways and redirects their financial choices through programs of its own, it is difficult to maintain the fiction that requiring government to avoid all assistance to religion can in fairness be viewed as serving the goal of neutrality.

Rather, the government should adopt a policy of *passive or symbolic accommodation* toward religion. Since "a vast portion of our people believe in and worship God and . . . many of our legal, political, and personal values derive historically from religious teachings,"[33] it is proper for government to encourage the flourishing of religion as long as the government does not coerce anyone to exercise religion or provide direct benefits to religious institutions.

> Absent coercion, the risk of infringement of religious liberty by passive or symbolic accommodation is minimal. . . . Non-coercive government action within the realm of flexible accommodation or passive acknowledgment of existing symbols does not violate the Establishment Clause unless it benefits religion in a way more direct and more substantial than practices that are accepted in our national heritage.

Interpreting the establishment clause in this fashion, Kennedy argues, would be consistent with the Court's recent rulings in *Marsh* and *Lynch*. The majority's opinion, on the contrary, creates a pattern of hopeless confusion and contradiction and stands in opposition to the Court's most recent relevant precedents.

Kennedy reserves his sharpest criticisms for Justice O'Connor's "endorsement" test. "I submit that the endorsement test is flawed in its fundamentals and unworkable in practice. The uncritical adoption of this standard is every bit as troubling as the bizarre result it produces in the case before us." Kennedy zeroes in on the notion that the criterion for establishment clause violations ought to be "whether nonadherents would be made to feel like 'outsiders' by government recognition or accommodation of religion." By this standard virtually every accommodation of religion throughout our history would have to be ruled invalid: presidential thanksgiving proclamations, prayers offered at the opening of legislative sessions, the invocation of divine succor at the opening of the Supreme Court, the special prayer room in the Capitol, the national motto, the phrase "one nation under God" in the Pledge of Allegiance, and the like.

> Either the endorsement test must invalidate scores of traditional practices recognizing the place religion holds in our culture, or it must be twisted and stretched to avoid inconsistency with practices we know to have been permitted in the past. . . . In my view, the principles of the Establishment Clause and our Nation's historic traditions of diversity and pluralism allow communities to make reasonable judgments respecting the accommodation or acknowledgment of holidays with both cultural and religious aspects. No constitutional violation occurs when they do so by displaying a symbol of the holiday's religious origins.

Justice Kennedy offers some telling criticisms of the majority opinion in his carefully argued dissent. In particular, he shows how the "neutrality" and "endorsement" criteria fail to provide a consistent standard for judicial judgments regarding public religion. In addition, he raises serious questions about the adequacy of the *Lemon* test as a general framework for establishment clause adjudication. His own position regarding "passive or symbolic accommodation" fails, however, to provide a defensible alternative. Kennedy simply sidesteps the issue that both Blackmun and O'Connor suggest stands at the heart of establishment clause adjudication, the question of religious pluralism. What are the appropriate limits of governmental accommodation of *majority* religious belief and practice within a pluralistic democracy? At what point does proper accommodation of religion become improper aid or assistance to religion? When does accommodation of the majority religion become discriminatory toward religious minorities? Justice O'Connor's "objective observer" theory is undoubtedly an inadequate guide to issues of discrimination, but Justice Kennedy's refusal to address this question hardly helps us to undertake a "substantial revision of our Establishment Clause doctrine." As James Madison clearly asserted, the no-establishment clause was designed to deal with the complicated issue of the relation between majority and minority religion.[34] Any reconsideration of the interpretation of that clause that fails to address the difficult issue of religious discrimination must be judged as inadequate. Throughout his opinion Justice Kennedy equates "religion" with "Christianity," and thus his appeal to "traditional practices recognizing the place that religion holds in our culture" is in fact a covert brief for the centrality of *Christianity* within American society.[35] Until Justice Kennedy addresses the issues of religious pluralism and governmental discrimination against religious minorities, "passive or symbolic accommodation" will continue to look like improper governmental support for the symbols of America's majority religion.

Allegheny illustrates the current confusion that dominates Supreme Court deliberations regarding religion in American public life. Religion clause cases are regularly decided by bare majorities, and those in the majority often disagree about the proper judicial basis for a decision. Thus justices voting with the majority will both concur with and dissent from various aspects of the majority decision, and their concurring opinions often provide justifications that conflict with the rationale provided by the primary author. Cases like *Allegheny* and *Lynch* are decided in apparently contradictory fashion, and the justices' attempts to reconcile the antinomies appear facile and futile. Disagreements between majority and minority factions are being stated with increasing rhetorical sharpness, as justices trade charges of "Orwellian" distortion of the issues.[36] The justices rarely acknowledge the validity of opposing viewpoints, and the very terms of the discussion have become clouded and imprecise. A Court so seriously divided against itself will hardly be able to provide the leadership needed for building consensus concerning religion's proper place in a pluralistic democracy. Yet, given the decisive symbolic role played by the phrase "separation of church and state" in our national consciousness, continuing conceptual confusion within the Court could seriously damage efforts to address the broader issue. Thus clarification of the Court's confusion becomes an essential first step in resolving our broader national dilemma.

The Suspect Concepts: Separation, Accommodation, and Neutrality

As the analysis of the *Allegheny* case shows, judicial interpretation of the religion clauses is constrained by the conceptual categories traditionally employed by the Court. The three key concepts—separation, neutrality, and accommodation—are present in all of the opinions offered by members the Court, but they are used in quite different ways by individual justices. While the justices appear to be operating in the same conceptual world, they are in fact using the key terms in diverse and even contrary ways. Consequently, their arguments and criticisms often fail to engage one another directly, and the observer gets a clear sense of the justices "talking past one another."

The primary concepts employed in religion clause adjudication were introduced into the judicial lexicon through Justice Black's fateful decision in *Everson.* In order to begin the process of conceptual clarification, we must return to that decisive 1947 opinion.

> The "establishment of religion" clause of the First Amendment means at least this: Neither a state nor the Federal Government can set up a church. Neither can pass laws which aid one religion, aid all religions, or prefer one religion over another. Neither can force nor influence a person to go to or remain away from church against his will or force him to profess a belief or disbelief in any religion. No person can be punished for entertaining or professing religious beliefs or disbeliefs, for church attendance or non-attendance. No tax in any amount, large or small, can be levied to support any religious activities or institutions, whatever they may be called, or whatever form they may adopt to teach or practice religion. Neither a state nor the Federal Government can, openly or secretly, participate in the affairs of any religious organization or groups and *vice versa.* In the words of Jefferson, the clause against establishment of religion by law was intended to erect "a wall of separation between church and State."[37]

A few paragraphs later in his decision Justice Black explicitly equated the "separation of church and state" with government *neutrality* toward religion. "[T]he First Amendment," he wrote, "requires the state to be neutral in its relations with groups of religious believers and non-believers."[38] In two opinions written during the following year (*Mc Collum v. Board of Education,* 1948, and *Abington v. Schempp,* 1963) Justice Black invoked his ruling in *Everson,* once again linking the "wall of separation" metaphor to the concept of judicial neutrality. "[T]he breach of neutrality that is today a trickling stream may all too soon become a raging torrent"[39] unless the "wall between Church and State" is "kept high and impregnable."[40] This fateful joining of the language of neutrality with the Jeffersonian "wall" metaphor has had a decisive influence on the contemporary judicial process. During the past four decades the notion of "governmental neutrality" has attained doctrinal status equal to that of the separation principle itself. A sampling of the rhetoric from First Amendment decisions will illustrate how the Court has sought to interpret the notion of church/state separation through the concept of governmental neutrality.

> The Government [must] maintain strict neutrality, neither aiding nor opposing religion.[41]

> Government in our democracy, state and nation, must be neutral in matters of religious theory, doctrine and practice. . . . The First Amendment mandates governmental neutrality between religion and religion, and between religion and non-religion.[42]

> [T]he Government must pursue a course of complete neutrality toward religion.[43]

Since *Everson,* the notions of *separation* and *neutrality* have provided the conceptual baseline against which all other judicial concepts are measured. The Court has consistently asserted that "church and state" are to remain institutionally separate and that government must therefore adopt a position of neutrality with regard to religious belief and practice. Despite the apparent simplicity of this theoretical position, however, the Court has had to acknowledge that government and religion are in practice often deeply entangled with each other. Consequently, the Court has been forced to decide under what circumstances the state can appropriately "accommodate" religious belief without violating the no-establishment clause of the First Amendment. Thus a third concept, *accommodation,* has been developed in order to identify the sphere within which government and religion might properly cooperate. But the very term employed for this purpose indicates the exceptional character of such practical cooperation.

The logic of post-1947 religion clause adjudication thus proceeds as follows: The First Amendment mandates the institutional separation of church and state. Government complies with this mandate by remaining rigorously neutral toward religion, though in certain exceptional cases government is permitted to modify its normal behavior in order to accommodate some aspect of religious belief and practice. Two different problems emerge from the apparently simple logic of this position. First, while the demand for governmental neutrality has through the years remained relatively uncontroversial, the meaning of neutrality has been variously understood. Much of the conceptual confusion surrounding the interpretation of the religion clauses has resulted from the different, and often contradictory, construals of the meaning of neutrality. Second, while the Court has consistently allowed for governmental accommodation of religious belief, justices have differed decisively regarding the nature and scope of such accommodation. These problems have become especially acute in cases that require the Court to delve into the murky middle ground between the no-establishment and free exercise clauses. In the next two sections we will examine in turn the conceptual problems surrounding the notions of accommodation and neutrality.

Accommodation and Religion Clause Conflict

"Congress shall make no law respecting an establishment of religion or prohibiting the free exercise thereof."

As we saw in the *Allegheny* case, the no-establishment clause forbids any governmental assistance to religion, and the free exercise clause mandates governmental accommodation of religion, thus setting the two clauses at cross-purposes.[44] Questions such as the following arise as the Court examines the interaction between the free exercise and the no-establishment clauses. When does proper *accommodation of* religion (permitted under the free exercise clause) become illicit *assistance to* religion (forbidden by the no-establishment clause)? Under what circumstances can the government legitimately exempt individuals and institutions from responsibilities borne by the rest of the nation's citizens? How broadly or narrowly should "religion" be construed in determining whether an exemption is properly granted on the grounds of the "free exercise of religion"? In permitting institutional accommodations and individual exemptions, how does the government avoid discriminating against those not eligible for such special treatment?

One might have expected that the ambiguity created by the interaction of the two clauses would have forced the Court to seek the *common* judicial principles guiding the interpretation of *both* free exercise and establishment cases. On the contrary, the Court has responded to this situation by dealing with the two kinds of cases in isolation from each other, and in the process the Court has created two parallel and independent standards for the adjudication of cases dealing with religion.[45]

Free exercise cases provide the classic example of judicial accommodation. These cases typically arise when a religious practitioner requests exemption from facially neutral regulations on the grounds of religious belief and practice. Thus in *Sherbert v. Verner*[46] the Supreme Court permitted a Seventh-Day Adventist to receive unemployment compensation, even though she was fired for refusing to work on Saturday, her Sabbath. So also in *Wisconsin v. Yoder*[47] the Court rejected as unconstitutional the imposition of criminal penalties against Amish parents who refused to send their children to a public high school through age sixteen. In free exercise jurisdiction the Court has adopted a balancing test by which the interests of the state are weighed against the claimant's right of free exercise. Thus the conflict between governmental regulation and individual free exercise is construed primarily as a contest of *interests*. The religious interests of the individual are to be abridged only if a state interest of the "highest order" can be demonstrated. "Only those interests of the highest order and those not otherwise served can overbalance legitimate claims to the free exercise of religion."[48] The government thus accommodates its interests in order to protect the individual's right of free exercise.

Governmental accommodation on the grounds of free exercise is well established and relatively uncontroversial; however, recent court decisions[49] have broadened the range of accommodation to include so-called public sphere accommodation of religion.[50] In these cases the Court has upheld actions that not only "exempt . . . from generally applicable governmental regulation individuals whose religious beliefs and practices would otherwise thereby be infringed" but also create "an atmosphere in which voluntary religious exercise may flourish."[51] Among the various justifications offered for public sphere accommodation, the most controversial are those that stress the importance of religion among American cultural traditions[52] and the use of religion in providing shared symbols and values for the civil community.[53] These examples of accommodation occur not in the context of free exercise adjudication but under the aegis of establishment review. Despite the use of a common term, however, the Court has chosen to judge these two forms of accommodation by different standards.

Establishment jurisdiction has been decisively influenced by the principles enunciated by then Chief Justice Burger in his 1971 decision in *Lemon v. Kurtzman*. Following Justice Black's lead in *Everson*, the Court in *Lemon* adopted a three-pronged test to determine whether a governmental action violates the no-establishment clause. As noted in the *Allegheny* discussion, according to the *Lemon* test all government actions must (1) have a "secular purpose," (2) have a "primary effect" that "neither advances nor inhibits" religion, and (3) avoid "excessive governmental entanglement" with religion.[54] Decisions subsequent to *Lemon* have sought to refine and extend this standard, Justice O'Connor's "endorsement test" being the most recent attempt in this regard. All of these criteria seek to define the appropriate limits of the government's involvement in the institutional affairs of religion.

As the discussion in *Allegheny* illustrates, the *Lemon* test has come under increasing fire, from advocates both of governmental neutrality and of governmental accommodation. It is important to note that the criticisms focus precisely on that murky middle ground created by the interaction of the two religion clauses; thus the disagreements focus primarily on the question of the appropriate limits for governmental accommodation of religion. The proponents of strict neutrality find that "secular purpose" and "primary effect" inquiries have the inevitable result of involving government in just the kind of "excessive entanglement" that *Lemon* was designed to preclude. Thus they argue that government should remain strictly separate from all symbolic and institutional accommodations of religion. Proponents of "passive accommodation" are equally sharp in their criticisms of *Lemon* and its successors, but they base their objections on the conviction that the test's rigid requirements are inherently hostile to religion and to the cultural traditions of the nation. As Justice Kennedy made clear in his dissent in *Allegheny*, the accommodationists would permit a much more supportive relationship between governments and the nation's majority religion.

By dealing with free exercise and no-establishment cases in this independent fashion, the Court has avoided the complex but important inquiry into the interplay between the two clauses. It is clear, for example, that if the "secular purpose" prong of the *Lemon* test were consistently applied to free exercise cases nearly every religious accommodation would be ruled unconstitutional.[55] The Court's exemption of conscientious objectors from military service and of Amish school children from compulsory public education could not withstand scrutiny from the point of view of "secular purpose." Clearly, in granting these exemptions the state is serving an evident religious purpose, namely, the right of persons of faith to live out their convictions, even when their actions conflict with laws applicable to all citizens. Instead of addressing this implicit conflict, however, the Court has been satisfied to continue the practice of separate traditions of jurisprudence for each of the religion clauses. By adopting parallel and independent standards for interpretation, the Court has not only impeded the attempt to develop a consistent set of criteria for First Amendment cases; it has also created a heightened and artificial sense of the conflict between the clauses, thereby obscuring the unifying elements that hold them together.[56]

The entire conceptual framework within which the Court operates requires careful reconsideration and reform. The difficulties facing the Court are not *sui generis*; rather, they derive from more fundamental problems in the liberal political philosophy upon which the Court regularly draws. In particular, the notion of neutrality, a fundamental concept of liberal philosophy, bedevils every attempt of the Court to develop a consistent and coherent judicial framework for interpretation of the First Amendment religion clauses. In the next section I will analyze the use of the concept "neutrality" in the Court's adjudication.

Neutrality: A Protean Concept

Since 1947, the Court has consistently interpreted the principle of church/state separation through the doctrine of governmental neutrality. It is striking to note that for all of their pointed disputes, the justices writing in *Allegheny* are clearly agreed that state neutrality toward religion is mandated by the Constitution. While they differ decisively on the meaning and application of the concept, they, nonetheless, frame their arguments in a fashion that allows them all to remain advocates of governmental neutrality. Clearly a concept so significant and yet malleable deserves our close attention.[57]

If we were to recast the three positions identified in *Allegheny* with reference to the justices' stance on neutrality, they could be analyzed as follows: *strict neutrality* (Brennan, Marshall, Stevens), *nondiscriminatory neutrality* (Blackmun, O'Connor), and *benevolent neutrality* (Kennedy, Rehnquist, Scalia, White).

Strict neutrality[58] mandates governmental *noninvolvement* in religious matters by requiring a consistent *no aid to religion* policy. As Philip Kurland has argued, strict neutrality implies that "government cannot utilize religion as a standard for action or inaction because these clauses prohibit classification in terms of religion either to confer a benefit or to impose a burden."[59] On the basis of this doctrine Justice Brennan argued in *Allegheny* that the Constitution requires "neutrality, not just among religions, but between religion and non-religion."

Nondiscriminatory neutrality softens the doctrinal purity of the previous position by allowing some public sphere accommodation, providing the symbols or practices supported by government are nonsectarian and nondiscriminatory. This position reads the Constitution as mandating a *no aid to religion* (or *noninvolvement*) policy whenever sectarian practices are at issue, and an *equal aid to religion* (or *impartiality*) policy when the practices are generally cultural or have a discernible "secular purpose." Advocates of this position are especially alert to possible discrimination against nonadherents, particularly when the symbols and beliefs of the majority religion are under consideration. Justice O'Connor's "endorsement test" seeks to provide criteria by which the doctrine of nondiscriminatory neutrality can be applied.

Benevolent neutrality explicitly seeks to broaden the framework within which religion might be freely exercised by expanding the doctrine of accommodation to include public sphere accommodation. This position interprets the strict neutrality and the no aid to religion doctrines as implying government hostility toward religion, a policy at odds with "our political and cultural history." Benevolent neutrality proscribes only "governmentally established religion or governmental interference with religion."[60] Beyond the "two limiting principles," namely, that government may neither coerce religious belief nor provide direct benefits to religion, government is free to encourage an atmosphere in which the free exercise of religion might flourish. This position further rejects the notion that government must be neutral between religion and nonreligion. Neutrality simply implies governmental *impartiality* in its dealing with various religious groups.

While all three of these positions offer important insight into the complex relation between government and religion, each is subject to serious and perhaps debilitating criticism. The *strict neutrality* position, while logically consistent, is finally unworkable in practice. The *no aid to religion* doctrine is simply unfeasible in a democracy in which government regulation affects virtually every aspect of individual and corporate life.[61] Applied consistently, strict neutrality would render government services like fire and police protection unconstitutional. Nothing in the text of the Constitution, or in its interpretive tradition, suggests that religious institutions should be disadvantaged by being denied the benefits available to the general populace. At the same time the strict neutrality position, demanding as it does that government should be blind to religious considerations, would prohibit virtually every free exercise claim of religiously motivated litigants.[62] In order to consider exemptions from facially neutral regulations on the grounds of religious belief, the courts cannot conceivably decide such cases without carefully examining those beliefs. Inevitably, the courts will have to make value judgments, for example, concerning the sincerity with which the beliefs are held, but such judgments are unavoidable in free exercise cases. Even if the strict neutrality position worked within the confines of the no-establishment clause (and I have argued it does not), its limitations in the area of free exercise render it inoperable as a working judicial principle.

It is not clear that benevolent neutrality is really a theory of neutrality at all. This position is most notable for its criticisms, often telling, of other church/state views, but its advocates have focused more on defending the notion of benevolence than explicating the concept of neutrality. Consequently, we know more about what benevolent neutrality is not than what it is. Proponents of this view have been primarily concerned to justify public sphere accommodation and to defend religion against the unwarranted hostility they believe is implied by strict neutrality. While benevolent neutrality clearly rules out governmental coercion and direct government support, it is difficult to discern whether any other limits to public sphere accommodation would be acceptable to its supporters. In particular, defenders of this position have failed utterly to address the question of the possible discriminatory effects of a broadened view of accommodation. If the notion of neutrality is, in part, an attempt to define the conditions for governmental *fairness* in the realm of religion, then it must deal with the question of religious pluralism and the possibility of discrimination. Until the advocates of benevolent neutrality take up this challenge, their position will remain insufficient as an account of proper judicial neutrality.

Nondiscriminatory neutrality is the most inclusive of the views analyzed here, but in seeking to provide a *media via*, the position finally reveals the unresolvable ambiguity inherent in the very notion of neutrality. By seeking to embrace both the *no aid to religion* and the *equal aid to religion* policies, this view displays the irreducible tension between the concepts of "noninvolvement" and "impartiality."[63]

The basic ambiguity of the concept "neutrality" becomes clearer if we adopt an analogy from wartime behavior. A nation can be "neutral" toward two disputants either by refusing to aid any of the contending nations or by assisting all nations equally. For example, Switzerland has maintained a consistent policy of neutrality by refusing both to enter into military alliances with other nations and to send combatants into warfare during hostilities (*no aid*). It has, however, been willing to provide medical supplies and other humanitarian assistance to all parties engaged in hostilities without violating its official policy of neutrality (*equal aid*). Thus Switzerland has exemplified both the "no aid" and the "equal aid" policies associated with neutrality, but it could do so because it is a sovereign and independent nation with no antecedent ties to the nations involved in warfare.

Advocates of *nondiscriminatory neutrality* apparently assume that the relation between a government and its own citizens is analogous to the relations among sovereign nations. Consequently, a government can *seriatim* adopt a policy of no aid or equal aid, depending upon the particular circumstance involved, without losing its claim to neutrality. But clearly a government does not possess the same degree of sovereignty and independence from its own citizens that it possesses in relation to other sovereign nations. Inevitably, a government will have a complex pattern of antecedent ties with its own citizens that it need not have in relation to other nations. For this very reason the no aid policy associated with the *strict neutrality* position simply cannot work in practice, particularly in a highly regulated society like our own. At the same time the equal aid or impartiality policy appears unworkable because of the Court's limited theological expertise and the inherent dangers of "excessive entanglement" in the affairs of religious institutions. *Nondiscriminatory neutrality* thus appears to combine the worst features of the noninvolvement and impartiality policies.

Noninvolvement implies governmental isolation from matters of religion; impartiality implies governmental engagement with religion for the purpose of treating religious groups and individuals fairly and equitably. The two policies thus stand in essential tension with each other, the former supporting the ideal of separation and the latter abetting a policy of accommodation. While the two notions might be brought into coherent relation in practice, the inability of the Court to adopt a consistent standard for adjudication of the religion clauses has made the reconciliation of these two notions of neutrality virtually impossible. Consequently, the question arises whether neutrality itself is a workable judicial concept for the interpretation of the First Amendment. If every attempt to construe neutrality in a consistent fashion is unsuccessful, perhaps the time has come to jettison the concept altogether.

The Essential Tension

This extended, and somewhat agonizing, tour of judicial reasoning has, I hope, raised serious questions concerning the adequacy of the entire conceptual framework within which the Court seeks to interpret the religion clauses of the First Amendment. The conceptual contradictions inherent in the notions of separation, accommodation, and neutrality render them incapable of providing guidance for a reconsideration of the role of religion in American public life. Our investigation of the justices' arguments has not been entirely negative, however, because we have identified the essential tension that bedevils every attempt to provide a coherent interpretation of the two religion clauses.

Two independent but related patterns of reasoning have emerged in the Court's post-*Everson* adjudication. The first pattern, *strict separation*, begins from the assumption that the independent and autonomous institutions of church and state should be kept rigorously separated. The state, an essentially secular institution, preserves the freedom and equality of all citizens by maintaining *strict neutrality* in its relations with religious and nonreligious groups. Strict neutrality requires a governmental policy of *noninvolvement* in the affairs of religious institutions. Only in those exceptional cases involving the *free exercise* of religion should any *accommodation* of this policy be considered.

The second pattern, *mutual cooperation*, begins from the assumption that church and state, though independently governed, share a common history and tradition. The state should acknowledge and respect the cultural and religious heritage of its citizens by developing a policy of *benevolent neutrality* toward religious groups. Given the pervasive religious character of the American people, a stance of strict neutrality between religion and nonreligion would lead to practices that are hostile to the beliefs and practices of the majority of the nation's citizens. Therefore neutrality simply requires a policy of *impartiality* in the government's treatment of various religious groups. While the government should never coerce or proselytize, it should seek to encourage widespread *public sphere accommodation* of religious symbols and behavior.

The essential tension reflected in the Court's adjudication of the Constitution's religion clauses is a manifestation of America's basic dilemma regarding the role of religion in public life. The two patterns of reasoning identified above mirror the larger cultural tension between Christianity's legal disestablishment and its cultural and symbolic dominance. The *strict separation* position seeks to preserve the legacy of legal disestablishment, while often ignoring the patterns of cooperation between church and state created by our history of civic piety and by the expanding regulatory role of the welfare state. The *mutual cooperation* position seeks to acknowledge and encourage the historic relation between Christianity and the state, but it does so in a way that ignores the growing religious pluralism of the nation. Consequently, its effort to expand the sphere of public accommodation often appears discriminatory toward those who do not share the religious beliefs of the majority.

The inherent tension between these two patterns of reasoning has yielded such confusion in the Court's decision making because advocates of both positions use the standard constitutional concepts of separation, accommodation, and neutrality. While they employ the same words, they use these concepts for diverse and even contradictory purposes. The Court's tendency to encourage independent standards for adjudicating no-establishment and free exercise cases has so exacerbated the tension between the two patterns that the confusion begins to look like sheer chaos. Whatever commonalty may still exist between the two patterns has been masked by the Court's inability to develop a consistent framework for the adjudication of all cases dealing with religion in public life.

I believe that the time has come to reject the entire framework within which the Court has operated since *Everson*. The principle "the separation of church and state" and the associated concepts, accommodation and neutrality, have been subjected to such diverse and contradictory interpretations that they have been rendered virtually useless for the task of reconstructing a proper conception of the role of religion in public life. The knot of judicial reasoning has become so snarled that even the most dexterous attempts at clarification appear futile. Justice Kennedy's suggestion that "a substantial revision of our Establishment Clause doctrine" is needed surely seems correct, and yet that revision cannot be fruitful if the current categories are allowed to structure the Court's reconsideration of the religion clauses.

Beyond the Wall of Separation: The Role of the Courts

The time has now come to indicate the significance of my discussion of public religion and democratic values for the decision-making process in the nation's courts. Though I have sought to be an informed critic of the judiciary, I am acutely aware that I write as a theologian not as a constitutional scholar or a jurist. Nonetheless, I believe that my attempt to clarify the proper public role of religion does have consequences for the judicial branch's treatment of religion. I will highlight four issues: (1) the anachronistic categories of church and state; (2) the limited significance of the notion of "separation"; (3) the need to return to fundamental constitutional values; and (4) the necessity of developing a consistent conceptual framework within which to consider both religion clauses.

Even if the courts had not embarked upon their confusing conceptual journey in the aftermath of the *Everson* decision, the very categories of "church" and "state" would force a reconsideration of First Amendment adjudication. Given the rapid increase in religious diversity within the United States, the term "church" is simply insufficient to refer to the varieties of religious practice in our country. Moreover, by privileging the Christian term for religious community, the courts give the unfortunate impression that they define religion through the perspective of Christianity. That impression would not be so serious had the Court's actions not reinforced that view. Two recent cases raise particular concern. On June 25, 1997, the Supreme Court in a 6-3 decision (*City of Boerne v. Flores, Archbishop of San Antonio*)[64] overturned the Religious Freedom Restoration Act[65] enacted by Congress in 1993. This act (RFRA) prohibited government from "substantially burdening" a person's exercise of religion even if the burden results from a law generally applicable to the entire population. Drawing on earlier Supreme Court decisions, especially *Sherbert v. Verner*,[66] Congress declared that free exercise of religion could be constrained only on grounds of "a compelling governmental interest" and that government must use "the least restrictive means of furthering that . . . interest." The Supreme Court ruled that RFRA was unconstitutional because Congress overstepped its constitutionally mandated bounds by "altering the meaning" of the free exercise clause. The doctrine of the separation of powers grants the sole right of constitutional interpretation to the judiciary, and Congress in mandating the "compelling governmental interest" criterion engaged in improper constitutional interpretation.[67]

Justice Sandra Day O'Connor in her dissenting opinion did not disagree with the Court's interpretation of the separation of powers doctrine but pleaded that the Court reverse its earlier flawed reasoning in free exercise cases and specifically asked the Court to overturn its decision in the landmark case *Employment Division v. Smith*.[68] "I remain of the view that Smith was wrongly decided, and I would use this case to reexamine the Court's holding there. If the Court were to correct the misinterpretation of the Free Exercise Clause set forth in Smith, it would simultaneously put our First Amendment jurisprudence back on course and allay the legitimate concerns of a majority in Congress who believed that Smith improperly restricted religious liberty."[69]

I am in complete agreement with Justice O'Connor. Whatever the merits of the Court's finding regarding separation of powers, the substantive question of the meaning and application of the free exercise clause remains the primary issue. Two cases decided in the past decade demonstrate the Court's increasing tendency to restrict the free exercise of religion, particularly of minority religious traditions.

In 1986, The Supreme Court upheld a lower court decision prohibiting Captain Simcha Goldman, an Orthodox Jew, from wearing a yarmulke while on duty in a health clinic in which he served. In writing for the majority, Justice Rehnquist stated that the standard military uniform encourages "the subordination of the desires and interests of the individual to the needs of the service." In this characterization the wearing of the yarmulke is identified not as an aspect of required religious practice but of mere individual desire and interest. Consequently, the religious dimension of the case was simply sidestepped, and the Court rendered its opinion by supporting the need of the military for a uniform dress code. The irony is that the Court thus avoided altogether the religious question and refused to treat this case as one of free exercise.

Had the justices taken more seriously the wearing of the yarmulke as a matter of required Orthodox religious practice the case would undoubtedly have been decided otherwise. Had the question of religious obligation been considered, it is difficult to imagine that the Court could have sustained a judgment that the state had a compelling governmental interest. Surely, the wearing of a yarmulke is a significant religious practice and deserved the protection of the First Amendment guarantee of freedom of religion. The fact that minority religious practice received this discriminatory ruling is of particular concern.

The free exercise case that occasioned the RFRA is *Employment Division v. Smith* (1990). In this case, the Supreme Court upheld Oregon's denial of unemployment compensation sought when two employees were dismissed from their jobs for using a controlled substance, peyote, in a Native American religious ritual. By refusing to include this ritual under the protection of the free exercise clause, the Court struck at the heart of the First Amendment protections. As James Madison so often argued during the ratification debates, the First Amendment clauses are especially designed to protect the practices of minority religions from the "tyranny of the majority" whether political or ecclesiastical. The Court failed to acknowledge that religious exemptions are essential precisely for those minority faiths that the free exercise and no-establishment clauses are designed primarily to protect. The "compelling interest" criterion is crucial for the protection of the rights of minority religions, which are unlikely to fare as well in a legislative context in which majority rule holds sway. It is important to remember that when alcohol was officially a "controlled substance" during the Prohibition era, the sacramental use of wine was specifically exempted from the ordinance. Had it not been, it is inconceivable to imagine that the Court would not have acted to exempt a practice so central to the faith of the majority religion. Why should a minority religious practice not be similarly protected?

Clearly, these cases are influenced by factors more complicated than the mere use of the term "church," but that word does serve as a symbolic reminder that the notions of church and state have become dangerously outmoded. The Court must engage in much more sophisticated analysis of the relation between religious belief and practice and the long regulative arm of the government. "Church" no longer suffices to describe the religious reality of America, and "state" does not capture the complexity of the government's extensive net of welfare regulations.

The notion of separation is similarly outmoded. At best the idea of separation identifies a single aspect of the relationship between religion and government, namely, that neither institution should exercise final authority over the values, beliefs, and practices of the other. But "separation" is surely an odd word to use to make that important point. Independence of authority is necessary precisely because religion and government are deeply intertwined in so many ways. It is precisely because of the interdependence of these two complex realities that the issue of independent authority needs to be stated explicitly. Given the significant confusion that the notion of separation—and its associated concepts of neutrality and accommodation—has introduced into judicial reasoning, it is surely time to jettison it.

The courts need to engage in a fundamental reconsideration of the criteria for religion clause adjudication, focusing on the basic constitutional values of freedom, equality, and equal respect. The judicial branch needs to sit again at the feet of Madison and reassert his fundamental insight that both religion clauses are designed to defend religious freedom. Madison's presentation clearly shows that the free exercise and no-establishment clauses are both grounded in an argument regarding freedom of conscience. Both clauses are designed to defend religious freedom in its individual and corporate expressions. If both clauses are concerned with religious freedom, then the attempt by the Supreme Court to develop independent traditions of adjudication for the free exercise and no-establishment clauses is virtually doomed to failure.

More important, the Court needs to develop a conceptual framework that will take us beyond the judicial and cultural impasses created by the notion of the "separation of church and state." The religion clauses are designed to protect the freedom of religion in its individual and communal expressions and to prohibit the state from favoring any particular form of religious belief or practice. The clauses are not designed to prohibit religious individuals or communities of faith from entering into the pluralistic conversation that constitutes a liberal democracy. The Court's reasoning has been undermined by the conceptual burden imposed by the unwieldy notions of neutrality, separation, and accommodation. The Court should forgo further tinkering with the problematic "*Lemon* test"[70] and should return to the fundamental values that undergird the entire constitutional tradition and the First Amendment in particular: freedom, equality, and toleration. Four principles should guide the Court's reconsideration of religion clause adjudication. (1) Religious freedom should be protected as a fundamental right to be constrained only if there is a compelling governmental interest at stake. Religious freedom and diversity constitute no threat in a pluralistic democracy. (2) Religious traditions should be dealt with equally under the law. Government should not give preference to any one tradition, particularly the majority tradition of the nation. But this principle does not justify the "secular purpose" criterion, nor does it prohibit government from supporting initiatives that allow for the equal flourishing of diverse religious practices. (3) If religion is to play a larger role in American public life, the courts must take special care to note whether apparent "facially neutral" regulations actually create an unfair burden for religious communities. Communities of faith contribute to public life in part by offering their adherents alternative modes of meaning and interpretation to the dominant secular culture. If that unique contribution is to be maintained, then the ability of these communities to practice their faith freely becomes especially important. (4) Minority religions are particularly vulnerable to the "tyranny of the majority," and their freedoms must be guarded with especial care. This principle becomes even more important as religious diversity increases within America.

If the courts were to return to these fundamental values and principles, the disturbing trend toward restricting minority religious practice would certainly be reversed. Establishment adjudication, on the other hand, would probably not change significantly; the reasoning offered for such decisions, however, would improve dramatically. Thus prayer in public school would still be prohibited because such prayer inevitably constrains the religious freedom of some students. Moments of silence could be approved, since each individual could freely engage in some form of reflection, meditation, or even daydreaming during this uncoerced period of time. Governments should be permitted to provide parochial schools with the same type of aid offered to nonreligious private schools, as long as such aid does not directly contribute to the advancement of the religious subject matter taught in the school. Additionally, governments would be prohibited from sponsoring religious observances of any kind, though they should take no steps to constrain the ability of communities of faith to display their own symbols at times of religious holidays. If the courts refocus their attention on the basic values and principles, they may not introduce dramatic new changes in establishment law, but their decisions and opinions could be reasoned with greater clarity and could achieve broader public accessibility. If the courts dismantle the tortured legacy of post-*Everson* adjudication and embark upon a new appropriation of Madisonian reasoning, they might contribute to the clarification of religion's proper role in public life. And that would be a gift not just to communities of faith but, more importantly, to our common pluralistic democracy.

NOTES

1. This argument has been made most forcefully in Richard John Neuhaus, *The Naked Public Square: Religion and Democracy in America* (Grand Rapids: Eerdmans, 1984), and *America against Itself: Moral Vision and the Public Order* (Notre Dame: University of Notre Dame Press, 1992). See also Robert Benne, *The Paradoxical Vision: A Public Theology for the Twenty-First Century* (Minneapolis: Fortress Press, 1994), and Michael Novak, *The Catholic Ethic and the Spirit of Capitalism* (Grand Rapids: Eerdmans, 1993).

2. Robert L. Cord, *Separation of Church and State: Historical Fact and Current Fiction* (New York: Lambeth Press, 1982), 3.

3. "When they opened a gap in the hedge or wall of separation between the garden of the church and the wilderness of the world, God hath ever broke down the wall itself, removed the candlestick, and made his garden a wilderness as at this day." Roger Williams, "Mr. Cotton's Letter," *The Complete Writings of Roger Williams*, vol. 1, ed. Perry Miller (New York: Russell & Russell, 1963), 392.

4. "I contemplate with sovereign reverence that act of the whole American people which declared that their legislature should 'make no law respecting an establishment of religion or prohibiting the free exercise thereof,' thus building a wall of separation between church and State." Thomas Jefferson, "Letter to the Baptist Association of Danbury, Connecticut," *The Complete Jefferson*, ed. Saul K. Padover (New York: Duell, Sloan, and Pearce, 1943), 519.

5. "In the words of Jefferson, the clause against establishment of religion by law was intended to erect 'a wall of separation between church and state.'" *Everson v. Board of Education of the Township of Ewing et al.*, 330 U.S. 1, 15, 16 (1947).

6. Similar sentiments about the limitations of the rubric "church and state" are expressed by John T. Noonan, Jr., in his casebook *The Believers and the Powers That Are* (New York: Macmillan, 1987), xvi.

7. One of the sharpest critics of contemporary judicial interpretation of the religion clauses, Robert Cord, still believes that the phrase "separation of church and state" should be maintained as a helpful summary of the intentions of the republic's founders. "I consider the term 'separation of Church and State' to be a useful one in the extensive dialogue concerning what the Establishment of Religion Clause constitutionally precludes government from

doing. Consequently, I have no apprehension about the term itself, however, I do have a very decided quarrel with the way the term has been used." *Separation of Church and State*, 114. In contrast to Cord, I believe that the term has outlived its usefulness and should be discarded.

8. *Everson v. Board of Education*, 330 U.S. 1, 16 (1947).

9. Edwin Meese in a July 1985 address to the American Bar Association, reprinted in *The Great Debate: Interpreting Our Written Constitution* (Federalist Society, 1986).

10. Leonard Levy, *The Establishment Clause: Religion and the First Amendment* (New York: Macmillan, 1986), 84.

11. Philip B. Kurland, "The Religion Clauses and the Burger Court," *Catholic University Law Review* 34, no. 1 (Fall 1984): 10.

12. Jesse Choper, "The Religion Clauses of the First Amendment: Reconciling the Conflict," *University of Pittsburgh Law Review* 41, no. 4 (Summer 1980): 680.

13. Note, "Developments in the Law: Religion and the State," *Harvard Law Review* 100 (1987): 1677.

14. Howard Ball, "The Separation of Church and State: A Debate," *Utah Law Review* 4 (1987): 919.

15. Ibid.

16. See Ball's comments, ibid., 911.

17. The menorah was owned by a Jewish religious organization but was stored, erected, and removed by the city.

18. Among the many discussions of this issue, see especially Choper, "The Religion Clauses of the First Amendment," 673–701; Michael A. Paulsen, "Religion, Equality, and the Constitution: An Equal Protection Approach to Establishment Clause Adjudication," *Notre Dame Law Review* 61, no. 3 (1986): 311–71; and Note, "Developments in the Law," 1631–75 especially.

19. *Walz v. Tax Commission of the City of New York*, 397 U.S. 664 (1970), at 668–69.

20. As *Allegheny County v. Greater Pittsburgh ACLU* (492 U.S. 573 [1989]) illustrates, the justices face their most difficult challenges when free exercise considerations impinge upon establishment cases. On its face *Allegheny* presents a simple question, viz., does the display of Christian and Jewish religious symbols on or near government property constitute a violation of the no-establishment clause of the First Amendment? To answer that question, however, the justices were forced to consider the situation of citizens who are not adherents of the religious traditions under examination. As Madison clearly saw, establishment cases inevitably raise the question of the relation between majority and minority faiths in a religiously plural democracy. To ask whether a governmental action discriminates against nonadherents is to inquire concerning the nonadherents' right to free exercise. Justice O'Connor's strained attempt to develop an "objective observer" theory in order to adjudicate claims of discrimination would have been unnecessary if the Court had adopted a unified approach to religion clause interpretation.

21. 403 U.S. 602 (1972).

22. 105 S. Ct. 2479 (1985).

23. *Allegheny*, 592.

24. *Epperson v. Arkansas*, 89 S. Ct. 266 (1968).

25. *Accord, Texas Monthly, Inc. v. Bullock*, 109 S. Ct. 890.

26. *Marsh v. Chambers*, 103 S. Ct. 3330 (1983).

27. 465 U.S. 668 (1984).

28. *Allegheny*, 535. This charge was first introduced by former Chief Justice Burger in his dissenting opinion in *Wallace v. Jaffree*, 472 U.S. 38 (1985) at 86.

29. In his dissenting opinion, Justice Kennedy expressed similar worries. "This Court is ill-equipped to sit as a national theology board, and I question both the wisdom and the constitutionality of its doing so." *Allegheny*, 550.

30. James Madison, "To the Honorable General Assembly of the Commonwealth of Virginia: A Memorial and Remonstrance (1785)," in *James Madison on Religious Liberty*, ed. Robert S. Alley (Buffalo, N.Y.: Prometheus, 1985).

31. For a much more sophisticated account of how particular religious practices might be rightly encouraged by a genuinely neutral government, see Donald A. Giannella, "Religious Liberty, Nonestablishment, and Doctrinal Development. Part II: The Nonestablishment Principle," *Harvard Law Review*, 81, no. 3 (January 1968): 513–90.

32. For an excellent study of such homogenized civil religion, see John M. Cuddihy, *No Offense: Civil Religion and Protestant Taste* (New York: Seabury Press, 1978).

33. Quoting Justice Goldberg in *Abington School District v. Schempp*, 374 U.S. 203 (1963).

34. See Ronald F. Thiemann, *Religion in Public Life* (Washington, D.C.: Georgetown University Press, 1996), chap. 2.

35. In one of his many insightful comments, Justice Brennan notes that the holiday display outside the city/county building is hardly as "pluralistic" as Justice O'Connor had suggested. "[W]inter is '*the* holiday season' to Christians, not to Jews, and the implicit message that it, rather than autumn, is the time for pluralism sends an impermissible signal that only holidays stemming from Christianity, not those arising from other religions, favorably disposed the government towards 'pluralism'" (525, note). *A fortiori* Justice Kennedy's practice of equating religion with Christianity would be subject to similar criticisms.

36. In his dissenting opinion, Justice Kennedy accuses the majority of lending "its assistance to an Orwellian rewriting of history." *Allegheny*, 550. In response, Justice Blackmun accuses Kennedy of slipping "into a form of Orwellian newspeak when he equates the constitutional command of secular government with a prescribed orthodoxy." *Allegheny*, 506.

37. *Everson v. Board of Education*, 330 U.S. 1, 15, 16 (1947).

38. Ibid., 18.

39. *Abington School District*, 374 U.S. at 203, 225.

40. *McCollum v. Board of Education*, 333 U.S. 203, 212 (1948).

41. *Abingdon School District*, 374 U.S. at 225 (1963).

42. *Epperson v. Arkansas*, 393 U.S. 97 (1968).

43. *Wallace v. Jaffree*, 105 S. Ct. 2479, 2491 (1985).

44. As *Allegheny* illustrates, the justices face their most difficult challenges when free exercise considerations impinge upon establishment cases. On its face *Allegheny* presents a simple question, viz., does the display of Christian and Jewish religious symbols on or near government property constitute a violation of the no-establishment clause of the First Amendment? In order to answer that question, however, the justices were forced to consider the situation of those citizens who are not adherents of the religious traditions under examination. As Madison clearly saw, establishment cases inevitably raise the question of the relation between majority and minority faiths in a religiously plural democracy. To ask whether a governmental action discriminates against nonadherents is to inquire concerning the nonadherents' right to free exercise. Justice O'Connor's strained attempt to develop an "objective observer" theory in order to adjudicate claims of discrimination would have been unnecessary if the Court had adopted a unified approach to religion clause interpretation.

45. In her concurring opinion in *Wallace v. Jaffree*, 472 U.S. 38, 67–68 (1985), Justice O'Connor noted that "a distinct jurisprudence has enveloped each of these Clauses." Justice Stewart in his concurring opinion in *Sherbert v. Verner*, 374 U.S. 398, 416 (1963) noted the

conflict between establishment and free exercise standards and urged the Court to abandon "the resounding but fallacious fundamentalist rhetoric of . . . Establishment Clause opinions." In a similar vein, Justice Rehnquist issued a call for consistent religion clause jurisprudence in his dissent in *Thomas v. Review Board*, 450 U.S. 707, 726 (1981). Thus far the Court has not taken up this challenge.

46. 374 U.S. 398 (1963).

47. *Wisconsin v. Yoder*, 406 U.S. 205 (1972).

48. Ibid. at 215.

49. Especially *McDaniel v. Paty*, 435 U.S. 618 (1978), *Marsh v. Chambers*, 463 U.S. 783 (1983), and *Lynch v. Donnelly*, 465 U.S. 668 (1984).

50. See Note, "Developments in the Law," 1641–59.

51. Justice Brennan in a concurring opinion in *McDaniel*.

52. Writing for the majority in *Lynch*, Chief Justice Burger offered the following comments. "There are countless . . . illustrations of the Government's acknowledgment of our religious heritage and governmental sponsorship of graphic manifestations of that heritage. . . . Equally pervasive is the evidence of accommodation of all faiths and all forms of religious expression and hostility toward none. Through this accommodation . . . governmental action has follow[ed] the best of our traditions" and "respected[ed] the religious nature of our people." *Lynch* at 677–78.

53. In her concurring opinion in *Lynch*, Justice O'Connor offered the following observations.

> The creche is a traditional symbol of the holiday that is very commonly displayed along with purely secular symbols. . . . These features combine to make the government's display of the creche in this particular physical setting no more an endorsement of religion than such governmental "acknowledgments" of religion as legislative prayers . . . government declaration of Thanksgiving as public holiday, printing of "In God We Trust" on coins, and opening court sessions with "God save the United States and this honorable court." These governmental acknowledgments of religion serve, in the only ways reasonably possible in our culture, the legitimate secular purposes of solemnizing public occasions, expressing confidence in the future, and encouraging the recognition of what is worthy of appreciation in society.

Lynch at 692–93.

54. *Lemon v. Kurtzman*, 403 U.S. 612–613 (1971).

55. Cf. Choper, "The Religion Clauses of the First Amendment," 685.

56. "[R]eligion clause doctrine since the 1940's has exaggerated the difference between the two clauses, creating a bifurcated jurisprudence of the clauses whose operation obscures the principal values underlying them." Note, "Developments in the Law," 1639.

57. Laurence Tribe has identified four distinct aspects inherent in the principle of neutrality: strict neutrality, political neutrality, denominational neutrality, and free exercise neutrality. Although I do not employ his categories in my own analysis, I have found his discussion very useful. Laurence Tribe, *American Constitutional Law*, 2d ed. (Mineola, N.Y.: Foundation Press, 1988), 1188–1201.

58. Tribe argues that "[t]he Court has never adopted the so-called 'strict neutrality theory,' which would prohibit government from using religious classifications either to confer benefits or impose burdens." Ibid., 1167. While the Court may never have "adopted" the theory, it is clear that some of the justices regularly employ the theory's logic in arguing for or against a particular accommodation.

59. Philip Kurland, "Of Church and State and the Supreme Court," *University of Chicago Law Review* 20 (1961): 6.

60. Chief Justice Burger in *Walz v. Tax Commission of the City of New York* 397 U.S. 664 (1970).

61. The classic discussion of this issue is Donald A. Giannella, "Religious Liberty, Nonestablishment, and Doctrinal Development," *Harvard Law Review* 80 (1967): 138–143. Giannella seeks to separate the strict neutrality doctrine from the no aid to religion strategy, but I find his attempt to be unpersuasive. For the purposes of my argument, I am assuming that "strict neutrality," in the sense I am using it here, logically implies "no aid to religion."

62. "The neutrality principle produces hostility to religion by flatly prohibiting all solely religious exemptions from general regulations no matter how greatly they burden religious exercise and no matter how insubstantial the competing state interest may be. In advancing the admirable goals of government neutrality and impartiality, it downgrades the positive value that both Religious Clauses assign to religious liberty." Choper, "The Religion Clauses of the First Amendment," 688.

63. I have been assisted in my thinking about this problem by John T. Valauri's fine article "The Concept of Neutrality in Establishment Clause Doctrine," *University of Pittsburgh Law Review* 48, no. 1 (Fall 1986): 83–151. Valauri argues that the concept of neutrality, as developed by the Court, is internally inconsistent. The two principle aspects of the concept, noninvolvement and impartiality, cannot be consistently combined; therefore, the Court is doomed to a pattern of contradictory and arbitrary adjudication. Valauri shows how this problem first surfaced in Justice Black's puzzling decision in *Everson*, in which he both enunciated the principle of judicial neutrality and then ruled that the New Jersey statute allowing state funds to be used for busing children to parochial schools did not violate the establishment clause. In asserting the principle of judicial neutrality Justice Black employed a "noninvolvement" or "no aid to religion" interpretation of neutrality. In deciding the case, however, he invoked the "impartiality" or "equal aid to religion" sense of neutrality. Despite having asserted the basic principle of church/state separation, Justice Black was unwilling to apply it rigorously to the case at hand. If he had, he would have denied to these particular school children the general benefit available to other citizens of the state, thereby discriminating against them on the basis of their religion. While the principle of church/state separation appeared clear, its application became immediately problematic.

64. 177 S. Ct. 762.

65. For an insightful treatment of the significance of this act, see Angela C. Carmella, "The Religious Freedom Restoration Act: New Roles for Congress, the President, and the Supreme Court in Protecting Religion," *Religion and Values in Public Life* 3, no. 2 (Winter 1995): 1–4.

66. 374 U.S. 398 (1963).

67. As this volume goes to press Congress is preparing to pass new legislation, the Religious Liberty Protection Act (RLPA), which avoids the separation of powers problem. The RLPA, like the previous act, seeks to protect religious expression in cases in which it conflicts with other government regulations. Like RFRA, RLPA mandates that government show a "compelling reason" for interfering with religious liberty and that government use the "least restrictive manner" to infringe upon religious practices or beliefs. Backing for RLPA includes the leadership of both the House and Senate, and members of Congress from both parties and all ideological and political perspectives. Representatives of more than eighty religious organizations also support the measure.

68. 494 U.S. 890 (1990). For an explanation of this case, see p. 000.

69. 177 S. Ct. 762 (1997) at 64–65.

70.

> The trouble with *Lemon v. Kurtzman* is that it is written as though the separation of church and state is meant to protect government against religion. It ignores the point that government is the enemy. You need *Lemon v. Kurtzman* to make sure that government stays out of the religion business, and that's really all that you need. I would delete from the test the excessive entanglement clause that causes nothing but trouble, so much trouble that in my judgment it causes religious groups to be discriminated against. It brings about a situation in which the Court reads the religion clause of the Constitution as though the Founders' intention was to treat religions worse than other entities in society. That is, on its face, patently ridiculous, but that's what happens.

"A Conversation with Stephen Carter," *Religion and Values in Public Life: A Forum from Harvard Divinity School* 2 (Fall 1993): 1, 3.

Chapter 19

Toward a Normative Framework of a Love-Based Community

Anthony E. Cook

The central problem of liberalism is one consistently overlooked by its critics. The problem is that the liberal conception of community is based too much on fear and too little on love. It is fear of the "other" that generates in liberal thought the fundamental paradox of liberal theory. The liberal subject both desires and fears, needs and is threatened by community. Because community coercion is simultaneously indispensable and yet a threat to individual autonomy—itself the foundation of liberalism—theories of social justice and law are inclined toward conservative understandings of the state and are inherently suspicious of collective power. I want to suggest that we should reformulate the fundamental paradox by moving away from fear and closer to love as the basic motivation for being in community with others.

A love-based conception of community does not purport to transcend the love/fear dichotomy; it attempts only to renegotiate their relationship. A love-based conception of community incorporates but refuses to be stultified by the legitimate concerns of more prevalent fear-based conceptions of justice. The love-based conception of community is not one that is blind to the capacity for human evil, however. It does not repeat the mistakes of early progressives such as Dewey. Rather, it offers a different understanding of love that embraces both the infinite potential and finite limits of humanity, both the great capacity for good and the considerable capacity for evil. The fundamental difference between love- and fear-based conceptions of community—and this is by no means insignificant—is that the former requires a set of overlapping duties orienting us toward a constructive communion with others, and fear orients us toward a more restrictive focus on self-interest. I believe a love-based conception of community can more easily accommodate the legitimate concerns of fear than fear-based conceptions of community can accommodate the promise of love. I will discuss the particularities of this balance shortly, but first, we need to understand how liberal theory, in general, has too long depended on fear as the catalyst for community.

In early liberal theory, the social order constructed by both Hobbes and Locke is one necessitated by the fear rational subjects have of others. For Hobbes, life in the state of nature is nasty, brutish, and short. The individual is imperiled on every side by the threat of those pursuing the power needed for self preservation. For Locke, the fear of having one's property stolen by those losing out in the struggle for security necessitates a social order that, above all else, protects the natural rights of private property. Long before Darwin and long after him, Western individualism, including its more progressive variants, has presupposed the legitimacy of a survival of the fittest. A just social order was one protecting the acquisitions of the fittest. A just social order was one protecting the acquisitions of the fit from those who were basically unfit.

The most significant difference between conservative and progressive variants of this acquisitive individualism is the belief by progressives that the community has a duty to ameliorate in some way the most devastating effects of the struggle for survival. This sometimes takes the shape of providing safety nets for those who fall through the cracks, creating equal opportunity to compete, and even creating a level playing field to determine who really is the fittest and thus deserves to survive elimination.

The centerpiece of the conservative variant of this acquisitive individualism is that any interference by the government in this survival of the fittest retards the natural evolution of the species, impedes personal and social development, or fails to optimize the most efficient use of resources. To be sure, the mode of conservative expression has varied from time to time, as is the case with the progressive variant, but the underlying message is the same. A just social order should do little more than protect individuals from the threats to property and person from those within the political community and those outside that community. The rule of law and a strong police and military force are the cornerstones of such a civil order. The state is not to engage in redistributive programs that in effect rob Peter to pay Paul.

Even contemporary variants of progressive liberalism like the political philosophy of John Rawls have found it difficult to base a conception of justice on something other than the fearful self-interest of individuals. Rawls's individuals decide that a just society must protect the interests of the least advantaged in their political community, a progressive liberal commitment. Thus, legislation designed to provide the greatest benefit to the greatest number may go forward only when that legislation benefits, as well, the least advantaged members of society.

Rawls makes clear, however, that individuals will reach this consensus based not only on any feelings of altruism but, rather, on the purest of self-interest. Having located them behind a veil of ignorance where they are stripped of any knowledge of their eventual status in the community, Rawls has his participants choose a social order they would deem just. Rawls reasons that individuals will rationally fear the possibility that they will be among the most disfavored of the society with little hope of altering their status. This fear will provide sufficient incentive to establish, then, a social order protecting and promoting the interest of the least advantaged.

I am proposing that progressive liberalism move from a fear-based conception of justice toward a love-based conception of justice. Again, one can never totally transcend this binary opposition. It seems to be a permanent part of the cosmic relationship between good and evil, and the infinite and the finite. We can, however, like Martin Luther King, Jr., reorient our emphasis and, in so doing, open up possibilities that will significantly transform our understanding of the relationship between fear and love and their relationship to justice.

The conception of love-based justice I hope to use is one we have seen already in the theologies of Walter Rauschenbusch and King. I believe, however, that this conception of love is one that we can detect in every major religion, and not just Christianity. Thus I seek no primacy for Christianity but, rather, seek only to establish the legitimacy of religion as a source of values useful to the progressive liberal project. Unfortunately, the secular humanism of the modern era holds the proper province of law and social justice to be a public realm in which formally equal persons compete for the scarcities of life within fairly neutral and determinate legal boundaries regulating the behavior of each for the average benefit of all. The province of love is seen as a private realm of soft and mushy sentimentality. It is an emotion whose utility for law and justice, if it has one at all, is in ameliorating the harshness and cruelty sometimes characteristic of public life.

My understanding of the relevance of Christianity for issues of social justice rejects this separation of love from law and justice and adopts a much broader view of Christianity's supreme commandments. A love-based justice that is rooted in my understanding of the synthesis of pragmatic and prophetic strands of Christianity developed by King into a theory of the Beloved Community embodies these commandments of love. The first commandment is "Love the Lord your God with all your heart and with all your soul and with all your mind and with all your strength." The second is "Love your neighbor as yourself."

Although Nietzsche and others have read these laws as an ideology of self-denial and even self-flagellation—leading to weak and self-sacrificial personalities ill-suited for the great possibilities of modernity—I will argue that the prophetic Christianity on which the commandments of love are based is vitally concerned with the individual's self-love and empowerment, though not of a Neitzschean or Deweyan stripe. Indeed, the commandments to love one's neighbor and to love God hold promise only when the conditions of self-love and empowerment are satisfied.

What, then, are the guiding principles of a love-based conception of justice? The answer lies in an elaboration of King's Beloved Community, in his understanding of the overlapping duties owed to God, self, and others. First, to love God with all of our being requires a suitable conception of God that allows those from different traditions and with different orientations to see a common cause. Both Rauschenbusch's Social Gospel and King's Beloved Community develop an understanding of God that is compatible with democratic principles of diversity and equality. In Rauschenbusch's and King's theologies, a love for God is no longer disconnected from a love for self and humanity. A unity is achieved that sees the interconnectedness of creation, while appreciating the diversity through which that interconnectedness is expressed. To love God completely is to open one's body, heart, mind, and soul to the wonders and possibilities of this oneness through diversity. Far from being lost in a state of transcendent bliss that disconnects the faithful from the affairs of this world, one sees the world with a renewed sense of possibility and responsibility.

God, then, is love, the ideal toward which our feeble efforts incline. With all of our heart, soul, mind, and strength we seek the way of love, knowing our paths are darkened by the shadows of human frailty and sin. Yet God, whose unconditional love brightens but never fully illuminates the paths we take, is with us even to the end of time. In this lies both the comfort and the challenge of the human condition, for we walk by faith and not by sight alone. With this faith that permeates body, heart, soul, and mind, we fix the ear of our inner being to the call, faint though it sometimes may be, of God's eternal love.

Second, because we are to love our neighbor as we love ourselves, self-love is a condition for loving our neighbor, which, as I have noted, is also the only true measure of our love for God. For it is written that "anyone who does not love his brother, whom he has seen, cannot love God, whom he has not seen." That is, we must conceive and know God through our love for our fellow creatures. My contention, then, is that if self-love looks toward the higher love of other-love, and other-love toward the higher love of God-love, we can avoid the trap of narcissistic self-interest that has been the downfall of so much liberal thought. By linking each dimension of love to another, we define a set of duties and powers that provide both limits and possibilities for the individual and community. This analysis, appropriately begins, then, with an understanding of the duty of self-love.

A. The Law of Self-Love

The duty of self-love is not an explicit one in Christian theology; it is only implied by the higher duty to love one's neighbor as oneself. It is, nevertheless, a crucial duty, for we often project onto others our own self-obsession, doubt, and contempt. The reflection blinds us to the divine in others because we fail first to acknowledge it in ourselves. The great tragedy of modern Western culture is that it seeks to sever self-love from its higher purpose by exalting it as an end rather than the means it should rightly be. Taken as the end rather than the beginning of human duty, self-love often leads to self-worship and an institutionalized narcissism that rationalizes the most hideous of practices against those whom we are obligated to love.

In his *Christian Love and Self-Denial*, Stephen Post recounts an important debate within early American Protestantism over the form and meaning of Christian love, focusing on the thought of Jonathan Edwards and Samuel Hopkins. These theologians differed markedly on the question of whether all self-love is prohibited by Christian ethics. On the other hand, Post argues that through Samuel Hopkins's theory of "disinterested benevolence," American Protestantism was bequeathed a doctrine of radically self-denying love. Edwards, on the other hand, imposed limits on self-denial, thereby permitting the individual's love for God and others. Edwards believed, as do I, that when the three dimensions of love are in true communion, the excesses of self-love as well as those of self-denial are avoided.

What, then, is proper self-love? At first glance, self-love appears to require total self-denial, as Hopkins argued in his debate with Edwards above. We are compelled to love God with all our being—all of our heart, soul, mind, and strength. If total love must be given God, what is left for self? Yet, as revealed with the Social Gospel, the mystery lies rendered. If that conception is an exclusively transcendent and otherworldly Being, then love becomes transcendent and otherworldly, and an implicit denial of the particular and temporal manifestation of self and others. But, if one's conception of God keeps the transcendent and immanent, otherworldly and temporal, ideal and practical in constructive tension—denying neither and embracing both—self-love is at once given possibility as well as limit in human affairs.

Committing our heart, soul, mind, and strength to a God who measures our devotion to Him by our love for humanity—itself inspired, as we shall see, by our love for the "least of these"—means that our all-encompassing love for God is never exclusively an abstract, intellectual, or otherworldly love. Instead, it is concerned with the natural and not exclusively the supernatural other, as Dewey supposed. This focus on humanity as the window to God also suggests a more promising role for self-love, for if we are genuinely to love others as God intended, we must first prepare ourselves to love.

The duty of self-love commands that we prepare ourselves to love, that we cultivate our gifts, skills, and interests so as to serve God better by serving humanity. This general requirement of self-love carries with it three instrumental commands. The first is to satisfy our basic physical needs. The second is to protect our fundamental freedoms. The third is to affirm our self-worth. Our ability to love our neighbor and thus God through the cultivation of our gifts, skills, and interests is compromised by our failure to attend to these three basic concerns. These commands of self-love require further elaboration.

First, we are obligated to satisfy our basic physical needs for food, shelter, clothing, and all that is vital to an individual's basic physical functioning. The satisfaction of these physical needs is not without limit, for we must always ask ourselves whether the attainment of greater satisfaction is compatible with our larger purpose to love God through our love for humanity. Thus, Hobbes's account of the driving force in human beings for self-preservation captures a partial truth. God has so constituted the species to encourage its survival. We are given the natural appetites to seek sustenance, sleep, sex, and shelter. Hobbes's mistake was to see this struggle for self-preservation as an end in itself and to predicate a theory of civil society on it alone.

Second, because the satisfaction of basic needs under conditions of natural and artificial scarcity inevitably results in conflict, it follows that self-love requires us to protect the fundamental freedoms necessary to secure basic physical needs. These consist primarily of freedom from the seizure of one's possessions, and freedom of conscience and association. Again, these negative liberties, spheres of individual autonomy, do not exist as independent abstract rights to be consumed in unlimited fashion. Their purpose is to secure to the individual the space needed to fulfill a higher purpose.

Locke's emphasis on the acquisition of property and the drive to make that acquisition secure from arbitrary seizure captures a partial truth. Satisfaction of basic needs through the acquisition and security of private property is important, but it must be viewed as a means to a higher end if we are to observe vital limits. If, however, the acquisition and security of private property is elevated to the status of an end, Locke's glorification of the individual's unlimited appetite for acquiring property and power is the natural result.

Third, the duty of self-love requires that we do what is necessary to affirm self-worth. A proper sense of self-worth is a precondition for vindicating fundamental freedoms, and also a precondition for satisfying fundamental needs under conditions of scarcity. Without a proper sense of self-worth, individuals may feel that they have no rights to protect and that they must satisfy their basic needs on terms far more restrictive than those actually warranted.

The affirmation of self-worth is of critical importance in a culture that elevates the self-worth of some at the expense of others. The Social Gospel's conception of sin indicated how some individuals exploit collective power to perpetuate the subordination of others on the basis of class, race, and other forms of identity. Self-love may require the individual to develop rhetorical, discursive, and counterhegemonic practices to challenge the systematic evisceration of self-worth perpetuated by these systems.

The duty of self-love commands, then, that we prepare ourselves to love, that we cultivate our gifts, skills, and interests so as to serve God better by serving humanity. The quality of this self-cultivation will depend largely on our ability to satisfy basic physical needs, protect fundamental freedoms, and affirm self-worth. This understanding of individualism unleashes the great possibilities of creative intelligence and imagination but does so within limits that protect us from ourselves. Love, properly understood, provides humanity with both possibility and limit, giving us simultaneously something to strive for and boundaries to strive within.

B. The Law of Love for Others

If love commands that we love others as we love ourselves, it stands to reason that we should desire for others what self-love requires of us. That is, we should strive to satisfy the basic needs, protect the fundamental freedoms, and affirm the self-worth of others. As with ourselves, this permits others to cultivate their gifts, skills, and interests to serve God better through service to humanity.

A proper love for others provides a normative vision for majoritarian democracy. Although its underlying maxim, do unto others as you would have others do unto you, resonates with a political philosophy of enlightened self-interests, it goes far beyond this. We are to act not with reference to how others actually treat us but with reference to how we would have them treat us.

This aspirational, and some would say utopian, dimension of love gives it prophetic and transformative power. That is, our present endeavors must always be filled with the hope born of faith in the possibilities of love. Sobered, to be sure, by a sense of human finiteness and frailty, we must transform the present by our hope for the future, teasing out of existing structures and processes an unknown potential. The projection of present values into a world not yet experienced is what I call the aspirational pull of God, the lure of the divine. With each act of love, we testify to its present reality and power.

To be sure, this love is to be cultivated by all for all, but with special attention to the "least of these"–that is, to those whom we despise or socially marginalize—a focus that reminds us of the indelible worth of all humanity. In one of his parables of the final judgment, Jesus told his disciples that the son of man would return to judge the nations, dividing them into the sheep on his right and the goats on his left. To those on his left he will say, "Depart from me," for when I was hungry you fed me not, when I was thirsty, you gave me nothing to drink. When I needed shelter and clothes, you gave me neither, and when sick and in prison, you visited me not. Those on the left will then ask, when did we fail to do these things, and the King will answer, inasmuch as you did it to one of the least of these, you did it to Me.

Few will question Jesus' commitment to the poorest and most marginalized segments of the community. He set his priorities when announcing the commencement of his ministry: "The Spirit of the Lord is upon Me. He has anointed Me to preach the gospel to the poor; He has sent Me to heal the brokenhearted, to proclaim liberty to the captives . . . to set at liberty those who are oppressed." "Blessed are the poor in spirit," he later preached, "for theirs is the kingdom of heaven." What does this normative commitment to the "least of these" mean for the restoration of a progressive liberal vision in America? A commitment to the "least of these," as King understood, has spiritual, social, and strategic implications.

Spiritually, this normative commitment challenges us to see in others a reflection of ourselves. When we see some remnant of ourselves in those we deem "the least of these, " that is, those we perceive as most unlike ourselves, we build bridges to each other's world and lay claim to a wonderful gift of spirit—the gift of unconditional love. No longer would one say of even the most wretched of the earth, "But for the grace of God, there go I." Rather, one would say, simply but profoundly, "There am I." Inasmuch as I think, say, and do to the "least of these," I think, say, and do unto God and myself.

The beauty of this gift is that by transforming our orientation toward "the least," it transforms our orientation toward all. That is, our acceptance of this gift liberates us from the sickness that weakens all relationships—the need to judge, control, and manipulate. When we find in our own hearts an acceptance of those we find most reprehensible and unworthy of our love, our relationship to all of humanity is transformed. Suddenly, quite miraculously perhaps, the great divide between I and thou, and us and them is bridged. We see for the brief moment in which spirit speaks to spirit a oneness our finiteness cannot long sustain.

We learn to love others more fully because in learning to love "the least," love of others is made easier. When once we reckon "the least" to be part of us and see ourselves as part of them, what demons can overcome our quest to love others whom we deem more like us than the least. Furthermore, through our practice of loving the least, we learn better to love ourselves, for we cannot truly love unless we ourselves feel loved. This is why Jesus said you shall know them by the fruits that they bear. Our ability to love the least is a measure of our own self-love and spiritual growth, for that which we see in the lives of the least that makes them undeserving of our love is often a reflection of what we see in ourselves. Do we not most see hope when we ourselves are hopeful? Are we not more inclined to see despair when our lives are consumed by despair? Conversely, does not love cover a multitude of faults, frailty, and failure? What sorrow cannot be transfigured by the joy that stirs a soul to rapture?

When we have conditioned ourselves to see in those we deem most unlike ourselves—the despised, downtrodden, and degraded—something worthy of love, it can be only because we now know and feel our own worth and love. To feel our own worth and love, that is, to feel it unconditionally, is to surrender the judgment, condescension, and pride that blinds us to human interdependency.

When our eyes are opened to this fundamental truth, the command of other-love, discussed above, seems not so onerous. We can desire for others what we desire for ourselves, for we know that, given our interdependency, we cannot be free unless all are free. We know that , as King put it, we all are woven into a single garment of destiny.

It is important, I believe, to talk about this spiritual dimension of love at the individual level, for we have little hope of institutionalizing the value of love and the normative commitment to the "least of these" at the social level if we do not simultaneously cultivate a temperament of love at the individual level. Just as Dewey came to see that democratic institutions were no substitute for loving individuals.

"Soul work" that no laws or institutions can do must be initiated and diligently pursued by the individual. My hope, however, is that soul work done by the individual who is in the process of becoming more love- rather than fear-centered will shape social institutions that come to reflect the same, and that social institutions in the process of institutionalizing love will simultaneously shape the individuals who compose those institutions. In this way, individuals and institutions will simultaneously undergo the spiritual and social conversion necessary to move toward a Beloved Community here on earth.

What, then, are the social implications of this normative commitment? Socially, a commitment to the "least of these" means that we must institutionalize our love for the least. We must desire for others, as we desire for ourselves, a fulfillment of their gifts, talents, and skills in preparation for service to others. As developed above, this requires that we satisfy their basic physical needs, protect their fundamental freedoms, and affirm their self-worth. But who constitutes "the least of these" for purposes of our social and institutionalized love?

Those who constitute the least of these will differ depending on the society, culture, and setting. Various criteria are employed to relegate various groups to the lowest rung of the community in question. The social commitment requires that we become cognizant of the overt and subtle ways communities construct their "least of these." It also requires that we attempt to transform those institutions and practices to reflect the spiritual understanding of love and interdependency discussed above. As I said, who constitutes the least will depend on the context in which one is operating. It could easily shift from African Americans to women, gays and lesbians, Indians, immigrants, foreigners, or some combination of these and others, depending on the particular community and context in question.

I am particularly interested, however, in the ways economic subordination interplays with these other forms of oppression. Because I believe the American context has largely been one where the pursuit of material wealth has necessitated the construction of inferior identities deserving of oppression and exclusion from the bounty of America's meteoric rise to economic supremacy, I will use economic stratification as a preliminary measure of who constitutes the least in terms of the distribution of American income and wealth.

When one cross-references information about the general distribution of income and wealth in America against the disproportionality of income and wealth among certain groups relative to their numbers in the population, it becomes clear that some groups are impacted more than others in terms of relative economic marginality. When one cross-references this information against the severity and longevity of American legal and extralegal modes of excluding groups from the economic bounty of America, the picture becomes even clearer.

Under my two-pronged approach, economic stratification is the first indicator of who constitutes the least in the American context. As King envisioned, then, certain interventions are needed to address the problems of the poor. I follow this broad categorization with further inquiries into which groups are disproportionately represented among the poor, and which have been subjected to the most intense histories of legal and extralegal exclusion. Knowledge gathered from this inquiry would require that the social intervention be designed to respond adequately to this history of disproportionality, its causes and cures.

For instance, while African Americans constitute only 12 percent of the national population, they constitute more than 30 percent of those in poverty. Institutionalizing a normative commitment to the least of these, then, means simultaneously alleviating poverty among all races and groups, and responding to the historic racism that has disproportionately located some groups, such as African Americans, among the poor.

One can safely assume that it is racism that accounts for this disproportionate representation of African Americans among the poor for two reasons. First, African Americans are the only group in American society forced to directly bear the cultural, political, and economic legacy of racism in such magnitude. This racism and its legacy have legitimated more than two hundred years of slavery and more than fifty years of Jim Crow segregation, and are currently subverting a scant thirty years of post-1965 freedom.

Second, there can be little doubt that racism continues to be a pervasive force in American culture, even after a "second" civil rights movement purporting to give equal rights to African Americans. The most comprehensive national opinion poll on racial attitudes administered in twenty-five years was taken in 1990. It revealed that a majority of whites surveyed still believed African Americans were lazier, less patriotic, more violent, and less intelligent than whites. Charles Murray's recent book, entitled *The Bell Curve*, is only one link in a chain of works dating back to the eighteenth century that purport to produce "scientific proof" of the intellectual inferiority of African Americans.

In other words, along the mixed spectrum of poor whites, Indians, Hispanics, Asians, women, and children who make up the "American least," African Americans constitute the extreme case, with poor African Americans occupying the most vulnerable position.

Finally, there are strategic implications for the commitment to the least of these that must be considered. As we can see from the outline of its social dimensions, such a commitment entails an appreciation of the particularity of cultural identity, the specific ways in which rhetoric, ideologies, and practices have constructed particular groups as "the least."

As King understood so well, however, if an appreciation of our interdependency is the spiritual goal, our rhetoric, ideologies, practices, and the strategies we adopt to realize our spiritual and social aspirations should reflect this goal as well. We cannot divorce means from ends in our struggle for a Beloved Community. In other words, strategically, a commitment to the least of these should bring us all into a greater understanding of our interconnection with and mutual dependence on others. This normative commitment should aspire to make all of us more loving and just individuals. Our relationships to all and not just to "the least" should be transfigured by this normative commitment.

What this means specifically for an interrogation of the impact of race and class on the status of African Americans is that we should try to shape our interventions to respond both to the particularity of the African-American experience and to the experiences of those sharing a common destiny. That is, strategies should shun an insularity and particularism that further fragment and divide humanity. We should always preserve the possibilities of broad-based alliances that reflect the goals of true interdependency. Grasping what we share in common through an understanding and appreciation of our particular experiences is to be preferred over an abstract embrace of what we share in common that is blind to particular histories and realities.

In conclusion, this is the normative role that a commitment to the least of these can play in the revival of a progressive liberal vision in American politics. Its spiritual, social, and strategic dimensions respond to serious problems faced by progressive liberals today. As I stated at the outset, the first problem is the need to develop a religiospiritual basis for the progressive liberal agenda, one that speaks to the profound spiritual need of individuals to live meaningful existences. The second is the need to engage directly the ways racism, particularly against African Americans, is deployed to limit the progressive agenda of the years following World War II.

Chapter 20

Mission Impossible

Settling the Just Bounds between Church and State

Stanley Fish

Introduction

The thesis of this essay can be simply put. All of liberalism's efforts to accommodate or tame illiberal forces fail, either by underestimating and trivializing what they oppose or by mirroring it. Michael Walzer provides a concise example at the beginning of his book *On Toleration*. "I won't have much to say," he says, "about the arrangements that get ruled out entirely—the monolithic religious or totalitarian regimes."[1] That is, he won't have much to say about those forms of thought indifferent or hostile to the tolerance that is his subject. But tolerance as a political strategy and a moral stance must stand or fall by its ability to deal with hard cases. If the case for and analysis of tolerance is made with respect only to regimes and discourses already predisposed to it, what is the point? As Thomas Nagel observes, "[L]iberalism should provide the devout with a reason for tolerance."[2] That is, it is the devout—those who feel compelled by their religious faith to acts of judgment and exclusion—who put liberal tolerance to the challenge, and it is my contention that it is a challenge liberal tolerance cannot meet. Nevertheless, despite the repeated demonstration of the incoherence of tolerance as a workable ideal, its appeal remains strong. In what follows I shall attempt to show how that appeal survives every assault on it (this will give many heart) and even survives in the writing of those who set out to debunk it.

In the body of the essay I take up the arguments of three kinds of theorists, (1) those who urge fairness and deliberative rationality as ways of securing political order against disruptive energies, especially the energies of fundamentalist religions, (2) those who believe that fairness and deliberative rationality are stalking horses for a political agenda that will not announce itself, and (3) those (actually one) who offer as an antidote to disorder more of the same. These theorists contend mightily and discover in one another no end of confusions, but in my argument they are all in the same line of work, and it is empty.

I should warn the reader that I use two key words in ways that might seem strange. The first is "theory" and the second is "principle." By "theory" I mean, largely, liberal theory, theory that seeks to establish a space of judgment and order to the side of any substantive moral vision. I am aware that "theory" is often used in a broader sense to cover large generalizations, heuristic questions (what if we rewrite history from the point of view of women?), policy recommendations, and "big" beliefs (as in "I believe in God" or "I don't"). I do not refer to any of these as theory because they all proceed from a strong angle of conviction, whereas it is theory's project—at least in the writings of those I critique—to proceed from no angle, or from an angle so wide that it takes in everyone, no matter what his or her religion, political affiliation, ethnic identification, and so on.

I am particularly anxious not to conflate theory and belief. As I have put it elsewhere:

> A theory is a special achievement of consciousness; a belief is a prerequisite for being conscious at all. Beliefs are not what you think *about*, but what you think *within*. . . . Theories are something you can have . . . beliefs have you, in the sense that there can be no distance between them and the acts they enable.[3]

The distinction between theory and belief is especially important in the context of liberal discourse where, typically, beliefs are what theory—in the form of fairness or impartiality or mutual respect—is supposed to bypass or blunt.

My use of "principle" tracks the same argument. When I say that there are no principles, I mean that there are no principles not tied to some moral or political agenda. I know that "principled" is often thought of as a synonym for "moral," but in the discourse of liberalism principle names the effort to stand to the side of competing moralities, and it is that kind of principle whose existence I deny. If someone wants to insist that moral conviction is principled, he or she will get no disagreement from me. I'm all for moral principles (which certainly don't need my endorsement) and it is in their defense that I finally write.[4]

I. Every Church Is Orthodox to Itself

Although analyses of the relationship between church and state continue to appear faster than they can be read, the discussion of this vexed issue has not advanced one millimeter beyond the terms established by John Locke in *A Letter Concerning Toleration* (1689). Locke's statement of purpose could, with only slight stylistic alterations, be incorporated into the first paragraph of almost any essay or book written today:

> I esteem it above all things necessary to distinguish exactly the business of civil government from that of religion, and to settle the just bounds that lie between the one and the other.[5]

More than three hundred years later we are still at it and no closer to achieving the exact distinctions or settling the just boundaries than Locke was when he identified the condition that made his project at once so urgent and so difficult:

> For every church is orthodox to itself; to others, erroneous or heretical. Whatsoever any church believes it believes to be true; and the contrary thereupon it pronounces to be error. So that the controversy between these churches about the truth of their doctrines, and the purity of their worship, is on both sides equal, nor is there any judge, ei-

> ther at Constantinople, or elsewhere upon earth, by whose sentence it can be determined. The decision of that question belongs only to the Supreme Judge of all men.[6]

The first point is the most important and is one modern theorists try in every way possible to avoid: if you believe something you believe it to be true, and, perforce, you regard those who believe contrary things to be in error. Moreover, persons grasped by opposing beliefs will be equally equipped ("on both sides equal") with what are, for them, knock-down arguments, unimpeachable authorities, primary, even sacred, texts, and conclusive bodies of evidence. And since anyone who would presume to arbitrate disputes between believers will himself be a believer for whom some arguments, authorities, and bodies of evidence will seem "naturally" weighty, no one's judgment will display the breadth and impartiality that would recommend it to all parties. (The question "But who is to judge?" asked with the knowledge that there could be no answer, serves to support a "hands-off" policy in both the free speech cases and the religion clause cases.) It follows, then, that the only sensible course of action, if we wish to avoid "all the bustles and wars, that have been . . . upon account of religion,"[7] is to remove religious issues from the table of public discussion, leaving their ultimate resolution to the "Supreme Judge" (or, as we would say today, to the marketplace of ideas) and adopting an official policy of toleration toward all professions of belief.

In urging toleration, Locke does not intend, as do some who invoke him, to devalue religion. Rather, he wishes to identify, and protect from state interference, the essence of true religion, which is, he says, the war everyone must wage "upon his own lusts and vices."[8] His own, not anyone else's. The field of battle is internal to the soul that struggles to prepare itself for "the world to come."[9] That struggle is obligatory, but it is also private and no one can wage it for another or be the judge of another's progress. Therefore every man should be left free to work out his own salvation as his conscience dictates, and the civil authority should not infringe upon that freedom by setting itself up as an arbiter of what is orthodox and what is not. Nor should any church attach itself to the civil power with the design of using that power to impose its particular doctrines on those who do not adhere to them. Any such design, no matter what pieties it is wrapped in, would be a departure from the gospel creed of "charity"[10]—"no man can be a Christian without charity"[11]—and would indicate a base desire "to carry on persecution, and to become masters."[12] Not only is this desire base, it would, Locke insists, be unrealizable because doctrines cannot be imposed; they are not that sort of thing. One might impose their outward profession—making it a law that your prayers must have a prescribed form and content—but no such prescription could compel belief:

> All the life and power of true religion consists in the inward and full persuasion of the mind; and faith is not faith without believing. Whatever profession we make, to whatever outward worship we conform, if we are not fully satisfied in our own mind that the one is true, and the other well-pleasing unto God, such profession and such practice, far from being any furtherance, are indeed great obstacles to our salvation.[13]

This account of belief as something that cannot be coerced is not restricted to doctrinal matters but extends to all the operations of the understanding: "[S]uch is the nature of the understanding that it cannot be compelled to the belief *of anything* by outward forces."[14] External authorities may attempt to command belief, but belief will be secured only by the internal force of "reason"[15] and the "light and evidence" that accompanies it. Even if the threat of penalties were to cause a change in a man's opinions, that change, insofar as it were superficial and forced—superficial *because* forced—would not be a "help at all to the salvation" of that man's soul. Once this point is fully accepted, Locke's two basic theses follow inescapably, first that "[t]he care of the salvation of men's souls cannot belong to the magistrate,"[16] and second, that "toleration [is] the chief characteristical mark of the true church"[17] because the true church will respect the sanctity of the soul's inward journey and refrain from coercing its direction.

It would seem that with these arguments in place, Locke can fairly claim to have achieved his goal of settling the just bounds between the business of civil government and that of religion. The key is the identification of the "religious interest" with the salvational aspirations of the individual soul. With these aspirations the civil magistrate has nothing to do, first, because he lacks the authority and wisdom to distinguish the false from the true and, second, because even if he were to declare an official doctrine and compel its profession, that profession would neither produce nor alter the *inward* persuasion that is the mark of true faith. What remains to the magistrate and is appropriate to his office are the care and protection of "outward things, such as money, land, houses, furniture, and the like," and it is his duty "by the impartial execution of equal laws, to secure unto all people in general, and to everyone of his subjects in particular, the just possession of these things belonging to this life."[18] Subjects, in short, are to be treated equally no matter what opinions they believe and profess, and they should neither be deprived of worldly advantage nor given a greater share of it because they hold those opinions rather than others. If this sounds familiar, it is because what we have here, already fully articulated in 1689, is the basic structure of liberal political theory: a firm distinction between the public and the private realms (underwritten by a distinction between body and soul/mind) and a determination to patrol the boundaries between them so that secular authorities will not penalize citizens for the thoughts they have (no thought control) or the opinions they express (no censorship), and religious authorities will not meddle in the worldly affairs of their parishioners (no theocracy).

But as coherent as all this seems at first glance, it is not without its problems, some of which Locke sees clearly. The chief problem is that the strongest point of the argument is also the point of its greatest vulnerability. If toleration is the mark of the true church and the obligation of the civil magistrate, will we not have a religion without content (any doctrine is O.K. so long as someone believes it) and a civil authority prevented from dealing with behavior it thinks wrong if those who engage in it say that they are moved to it by faith? There are two questions here: (1) Can religion, supposedly a matter of belief, possibly require none and still remain religion? and (2) How far should the freedom of religion from state scrutiny extend, given that it is the function of the state to secure good order and stability? How can tolerance be practiced as a general policy without undermining the basis for, and justification of, the judgments both church and state must make in order to be what they are? This question haunts church-state jurisprudence to this day, and Locke's answer to it has not been improved on. Tolerate as much as you can so long as the basic shape of the enterprise, whether spiritual or civil, is not compromised; identify a baseline level of obligation that leaves believers free to live out their faiths within limits and provides the magistrate with a measure for determining when those limits are breached and a justification for enforcing them.

It is to this end that Locke invokes a set of related distinctions: first, between what the "Holy Spirit has in the holy Scriptures declared, in express words, to be necessary to salvation"[19] and what is left either unexpressed or a matter of indifference; second, between the "truly fundamental part of religion"[20] and "what is but a circumstance" ("the time and place of worship, the habit and posture of him that worships");[21] and third, between the inward performance of faith and "outward show."[22] In each of these binaries, the first pole sets the limits of tolerance—anything goes so long as it respects the fundamentals—and the second pole identifies the areas of indifference—the particular forms one's faith might take—areas in which the believer is free to choose and the magistrate free to regulate (because his regulation will not harm the integrity of a faith whose field of exercise is internal).

Although the problem posed by toleration in its strong form (it leaves no basis for distinguishing between true and false or lawful from unlawful) is thus solved by establishing limits to its scope, that solution creates its own problem: how to justify the stigmatizing of those doctrines and actions that violate the limits as drawn. It is my thesis that there can be no justification (apart from the act of power performed by those who determine the boundaries) and that therefore any regime of tolerance will be founded by an intolerant gesture of exclusion. Those who institute such a regime will do everything they can to avoid confronting the violence that inaugurates it and will devise ways of disguising it, even from themselves. The favored way is to redescribe the exclusionary gesture so that it appears not to have been performed by anyone but to follow from the nature of things; and this is what Locke does when, quite late in the tract and long after he has put on toleration's mantle, he identifies those views no society, however generous, can tolerate:

> But to come to particulars. I say, first, no opinions contrary to human society or to those moral rules which are necessary to the preservation of civil society are to be tolerated by the magistrate. But of those indeed examples in any church are rare. For no sect can easily arrive to such a degree of madness, as that it should think fit to teach, for doctrines of religion, such things as manifestly undermine the foundations of society, and are therefore condemned by the judgment of all mankind.[23]

There are (at least) two moves here and together they forecast the next three hundred years. Locke first rules out of court views so subversive that no society could allow them to flourish, but then he immediately declares that, since no sane person wold urge such views, they are condemned in advance of their unlikely appearance by the judgment of all mankind. Everything happens so quickly here that the reader may not pause to raise the question that emerges as soon as one stops to reflect. How can there be something called "the judgment of all mankind" if the entire project of toleration is a response to the *bottom line* fact of plural judgments issuing from plural orthodoxies? How can you get to the judgment of all mankind, to what we now call "common ground," if you begin by declaring that differences are intractable because every church is orthodox to itself?

These are questions no one has been able to answer to this day, although answers are forthcoming all the time. Usually the answers take one of four forms: (1) Common ground is sometimes found in a very high level of generality ("be good," "don't be cruel") that floats above the situations that provoke disagreements. The problem with this answer is that the generalities are so general that no line can be drawn from them to the particulars they supposedly order. (2) Others find common ground in a (claimed) universal distaste for certain views which, once identified,[24] allow one to arrive at more widely acceptable views by a process of subtraction. The problem with this answer is that the views supposedly rejected by everyone will always have supporters who must then be eliminated or declared insane so that the common ground will appear to be really common. (3) Still others find common ground in a set of procedural rules, akin to traffic lights or the rule of driving on the right side of the road, with no substantive content whatever, while substantive matters are left to be debated in the spaces provided by the private associations of home, church, social club, and so on. The problem with this answer is that procedural rules always have content and that specifying them will always be a matter of substantive judgment, even when—especially when—substantive interests are being disclaimed. (4) And finally, common ground is often identified with whatever distribution of goods and powers a majority has ratified (or at least not rebelled against). The problem with this answer is that it is political rather than theoretical, and because it is political, the common ground it delivers will only be as firm as the contingencies of history.

These routes to the marking out of common ground are not exclusive of one another, and are often in play together, although the third develops somewhat later with the emergence of what Michael Sandel has termed "the procedural republic."[25] Each represents an effort to find a way between the Charybdis of intractable difference, with its disheartening vista of a Hobbesian war of all against all, and the Scylla of pure toleration, with its unacceptable vision of a world where anything goes and no one can say of something that it is wrong; and each achieves its apparent success only by performing a conceptual sleight of hand in which a distinction that is either debatable or permeable is passed off as perspicuous to everyone, usually by defining "everyone" in a way that excludes (or marginalizes) those who would be likely to dispute either the fact or the shape of the distinction. This sleight of hand, in turn, has the virtue of covering up (by rushing past) an embarrassment that would be fatal to the whole project if it were noticed: the strategy of finding common ground assumes a capacity that has already been denied by the framing of the problem. Indeed, if that capacity were available to you or to me or to anyone there would be no problem and the lawful configurations of the state would arrange themselves. If general truths were perspicuous and easily applicable to specific situations, or if there were agreement about which policies and practices are beyond the pale, or if procedural rules that respect no persons and are fair to all were easily identifiable, tolerance's limits would be self-establishing and no coercion would be required since everyone would readily agree *to* what they already agreed *about*.

To see that this is not (nor ever could be) the case, one need only look to Locke's more specific list of proscribed opinions: "For example . . . any sect that teaches expressly and openly that men are not obliged to keep their promises; that princes may be dethroned by those that differ from them in religion. . . . Lastly those are not to be tolerated who deny the being of God."[26] This is not a hypothetical list; its items name some of the positions championed by those who supported Cromwell's commonwealth and who perhaps even in 1689 were lamenting the demise of what John Milton (a defender of Charles I's execution on very much the same grounds Locke here dismisses) called the "good old cause." The list, in short, consists of opinions held by the *losers* in a recent struggle, and one can imagine that if the outcome had been reversed and it was Milton or someone of his party writing a letter on toleration, there would still be a list of intolerable views but its items would be different. (Milton's of course would have begun with Catholic doctrine.)

My point is that if the absence of common ground (because every church is orthodox to itself) initiates a search for a form of government that will accommodate diversity, and you begin (and end) the search by identifying a common ground, what you will have done is elevated some or other orthodoxy to the status of "common sense" and stigmatized as dangerous to the very "foundations of society" those orthodoxies whose common sense is contrary to the preferred one. This is not simply a description of Locke but a description of anyone who would invoke some common ground as the solution to the problem of what Hobbes called "multiplying glasses,"[27] the lens of "Passions and Self-love" through which all men see truth and their duty. Common ground is what emerges when you assume the normative status of your own judgment and fix the label "unreasonable" or "inhuman" or "monstrous" to the judgment of your opponents. (John Rawls's out-basket category of "unreasonable comprehensive doctrines" is only the latest and most elaborate version of the strategy.) The irony—not a paradox because it is inevitable—is that while adhering to "common ground" is proclaimed as the way to sidestep politics and avoid its endless conflicts, the specifying of common ground is itself a supremely political move.

II. Higher Order Impartiality

The irony is something liberals are notoriously unwilling to admit, except perhaps for Hobbes, who does not have clear title to the label. Hobbes begins, as all liberals do, with the insight that values and desires are plural and therefore the source of conflict. Where Locke says that every church is orthodox to itself, Hobbes declares that "all men are by nature provided of notable multiplying glasses (that is their Passions and Self-love)."[28] Both reason that since "some mens' thoughts run one way, some another,"[29] and no man is a god, no one is authorized by nature to judge his fellows. Here, however, is where the agreement ends. Locke, and those who follow him (nearly everyone in the liberal tradition) conclude from the fact of equality that the best government is the least government, a structure of minimal constraint that leaves equal men equally free to pursue their equally authorized or unauthorized visions. Hobbes concludes exactly the reverse: because equality of right and ability breeds "equality of hope in the attaining of our ends" and because each man's ends are naturally to be preferred to his rival's, the two will inevitably "become enemies," and in the absence of a neutral arbiter they will "endeavor to destroy, or subdue one another."[30] Equality, rather than a condition that argues for our freedom, is the condition that argues for its curtailment. If society is to endure and perpetual conflict kept at bay, a cure must be found for this disease of equality and freedom, and that cure can only be "a common power to keep them all in awe."[31]

"The only way to erect such a Common Power," says Hobbes,

> is, to conferre all . . . power and strength upon one man, or upon one assembly of men, that may reduce all their Wills, by plurality of voices, unto one Will; which is as much to say, to appoint one man, or Assembly of men, to beare their Person; and ever one to owne, and acknowledge himselfe to be Author of whatsoever he that so beareth their Person, shall Act or cause to be Acted . . . and therein to submit their Wills, every one to his Will, and their Judgments to his judgment.[32]

Because the "plurality of voices," if left to itself, will generate cacophony and because there is no mechanism in nature to harmonize it, an *artificial* mechanism must be put in place and rigorously adhered to. Men who are equal in power and desire are now equal in subjection; each surrenders a large part of his freedom and liberty on the condition that his fellows do the same, and in this way peace and security are established for everyone.

It is an elegant solution to the problem of "multiplying glasses," and it certainly provides an answer to the question of what independent value could be invoked such that committed and passionate men would be persuaded to abate their natural desire to have the world's order reflect their visions of the good. Just remember, says Hobbes, "*The Fundamental Law of Nature, That every man, ought to endeavor Peace.*"[33] If peace cannot flourish so long as "masterlesse men are allowed a full and absolute Libertie," liberty must be curtailed so that all will be free from the fear of "perpetuall war."[34] So long as every man is encouraged to "do any thing he liketh," "so long are all men in the condition of Warre," but if every man surrenders that right and does not reserve to himself what he would deny to others, peace will be assured. This, says Hobbes, "is the Law of the Gospel: *Whatsoever you require that others should do to you, that do ye to them.*"[35] Notice what has happened here to the golden rule. Rather than commanding that you honor the inherent worth of your fellow men (who are to be treated as ends not means), it invites you, in Hobbes's version, to join with your fellow men in a defensive compact based on mutual distrust. Rather than calling you to the higher perfection of charity and universal love, it teaches the universality of self-love, a condition impossible to leave behind, but one that can be managed and contained if an authoritarian structure is firmly enough in place.

It is not difficult to understand why Alan Ryan declares that "it would be absurd to call Hobbes a liberal."[36] What disqualifies Hobbes in Ryan's eyes, and in the eyes of many, is his refusal to derive from the doctrine of equality the *positive* values—autonomy, free choice, free association, individual self-realization—that inform the modern liberal state. For Locke, Kant, Mill, and Rawls (in their different ways), the equality of men and of the values they variably espouse points to the rejection of any form of absolutism: if no one's view can be demonstrated to be absolutely right, no one should occupy the position of absolute authority. For Hobbes, the same insight into the plurality of values and the unavailability of a mechanism for sorting them out implies exactly the reverse: *because* no one's view can be demonstrated to be absolutely right (and also because everyone prefers his own view and believes it to be true), someone *must* occupy the position of absolute authority.

There can be no question as to which of these ways of reasoning won the liberal day, but it might be said that Hobbes's is the more consistent with the twin premise from which both begin, the premise that, first, every church is orthodox to itself, and, second, that there is no principled way of adjudicating disputes between opposing orthodoxies. Both Hobbes and his liberal detractors declare this to be our situation, but where Hobbes asks, "How can we make it work for us?" Locke, Kant, Mill, and Rawls ask, "How can we work our way our of it?" Surely, however, this is the wrong question if the initial premise is taken seriously. If we really do live in a world of plural orthodoxies and lack an independent measure for assessing them, we can't work our way into a better world unless we reinvent the transcendental point of reference declared unavailable when we began. That is, we can't first remove certainty and a unified viewpoint from the human landscape and then propose to get them back through a program of social engineering.

Still, it is easy to see why anti-Hobbesians are tempted by a transcendence their liberalism has already rejected. The alternative, as Hobbes poses it, seems so sordid, so illiberal. His Golden Rule is "do this and ye shall be safe." Liberals in the tradition of Mill and Kant prefer a version of the old one, "do this and ye shall be better." They don't want to answer the question "How would you persuade the true believer to abandon his efforts to write his beliefs into the law?" to be "by scaring him with the spectre of perpetual conflict." They want to answer by holding out a promise—of a better life, a better community, a better self—that will make the believer happy to forgo his present zeal for the sake of a brighter and even glorious future. In short, they want an answer that is not merely prudential but moral.

Little wonder that Hobbes falls short, since his answer, as Thomas Nagel explains, is "premoral"; its starting point is a mere fact of brute nature, the concern "each individual has . . . for his own survival and security" and its ending point is any arrangement that will accommodate that concern.[37] All that Hobbes requires of the arrangement is that it be acceptable to those who will live under it, and that acceptance, Nagel observes, will be entirely contingent, since it could easily fall out that "our personal motives . . . fail to point us toward a common goal."[38] Our private agendas may converge on some political scheme, but then again they may not.

In place of what he calls a mere "Hobbesian convergence," Nagel offers a theory in which "reasonable agreement is . . . sought by each person as an end and not merely as a means necessary for social stability."[39] The person who is party to this kind of agreement will not be acquiescing in a *modus vivendi*, a way of just getting along; he will be affirming something he believes in and believes in as *good*. What might that something be? What could be so compelling that to believe in it is sufficient reason to soft pedal your deepest convictions? Nagel's answer to that question is "the fundamental moral idea . . . that we should not impose arrangements, institutions, or requirements on other people on grounds they could reasonably reject."[40] Where Hobbes's test is "would you want someone to do it to you?" Nagel's test is "wouldn't it be *wrong* to do it to someone else, even if you could?" Although we may believe a course of action to be true and good, we should not pursue it if others with different conceptions of the true and good reject it on the basis of arguments we understand, even if we are not persuaded by them. If we hew to this "fundamental moral idea," says Nagel, we will subordinate the beliefs we happen to hold to "a higher order impartiality,"[41] that is, to an impartiality higher than any our beliefs could deliver, and we will thus institute a decorum of constraint more principled than the merely prudential decorum urged by Hobbes.

Nagel's is the authentic voice of the liberal theorist. He is a liberal because he recognizes that each of us is embedded in some structure of belief and value. He is a theorist because he thinks that we are capable of distancing ourselves from our embeddedness (if only for purposes of public decision making) if we submit our beliefs to the discipline of the higher-order impartiality. The question is, Why should we? And prior to that question is another: What is the status of this higher-order impartiality? In his argument, Nagel opposes it to "appeals to the truth,"[42] on the reasoning that since truth claims issue from particular perspectives, putting them forward will not resolve disputes but fuel them. Rather than appealing to the truth, appeal instead, Nagel advises, to a higher-order impartiality that honors everyone's truth without endorsing or rejecting any. But that can't be right. If you are not appealing to the truth of the higher-order impartiality, if you are not identifying it as something more worthy of your allegiance than the truths it trumps, what claim does it have on you? Why should you prefer it to the truths it asks you to discount? There are only two answers to these questions, either the Hobbesian answer (rejected by Nagel) that has you acting out of a fear of civil chaos (and what of those true believers whose zeal for their souls and yours overrides or cancels any such fear?) or an answer that ties the idea of a higher-order impartiality to a profound moral principle (that is, a Kantian respect for the autonomy of free agents). If, however, you give the second answer (as the would-be normative liberal always does) you will be recommending the higher-order impartiality because you think it is true; it is precisely to its truth that you will be appealing. How could it be otherwise? It makes no sense to set aside some of your beliefs unless in doing so you are affirming another of your beliefs as higher.[43] Deferring to a higher-order impartiality is not to constrain or bracket "your own beliefs"[44] but to enact them; it is to testify to the truth, as you see it. The so-called higher-order impartiality is anything but impartial; for those (like Nagel) committed to it, it is not "a standpoint that is independent of who we are"[45] but a declaration of who we are or would be. It is our notion of the good, as contestable as any other, although Nagel does everything he can to palm it off as something lesser and therefore as something less controversial.

Of course Nagel does not think of himself as doing that, but his prose betrays him when he simultaneously acknowledges a paradox and fudges his way past it.

> It may seem paradoxical that a general condition of impartiality should claim greater authority than more special conceptions which one believes to be, simply, true—and

that it should lead us to defer to conceptions we believe to be false—but that is the position.[46]

The trick here (one that fools Nagel himself) is to hide the truly tendentious assertion inside the assertion that is acknowledged to be paradoxical. The tendentious assertion is that the impartiality Nagel urges is "general" while the conceptions that bow to its authority are "special." Once these adjectives are slipped in, what Nagel calls the "position" seems self-evidently right. After all the special always defers to the general, and so the argument is won the instant the labels are applied and accepted. What one doesn't notice is that if you stop to think about it—something the prose does not encourage—there is no reason to accept them, no reason to believe that the higher-order impartiality is really higher and not just one more special conception of the good in competition with other conceptions. It is one thing to say that respect for the views of others even when you reject them is the highest morality, and quite another to say that respect for the views of others even when you reject them is a position above (or to the side of) any morality, including your own. Nagel is saying the first thing and thus opening himself up to a debate (about what is and is not the highest morality) that he forecloses by claiming to be saying the second.

He performs the same sleight of hand in a smaller compass with the word "reasonably." "We should not impose arrangements . . . on other people on grounds they could reasonably reject." "Reasonably" is offered as a standard or measure that everyone knows and can recognize: it is offered, that is, as a *general* standard. But its generality is belied by its function in the syntax where it acts to put a limit on the tolerance ("we shouldn't impose") the sentence announces: arrangements should not be imposed on those who reject them on reasonable grounds; they can, however, be imposed on those who reject them on *un*reasonable grounds. The question, as always, is, who gets to decide what is and is not an unreasonable ground? It can't be those who are to suffer the imposition, since by their lights the grounds of their action are perfectly reasonable. It must be someone—like Nagel perhaps—whose notion of the reasonable differs from theirs, which means that not only will they have "arrangements" imposed on them, they will have imposed on them someone else's idea of what is and is not reasonable. A "special" definition of reason is passing itself off as general, and is being used to perform an act of exclusion that pronounces itself to be impartial.

The usual objection to Hobbes is that he is willing to sacrifice the autonomy of free agents to an arbitrarily imposed power for the sake of political stability, but in the end this is no less true of Nagel, who asks free agents to subordinate their autonomy to a principle of "epistemological constraint."[47] The difference—and it is all to Hobbes's credit—is that in one scheme the operation of power is acknowledged and agreed to by all parties, each of whom can then be said to have authorized, in an original act of contract, "all the Soveraigne doth";[48] in the other the operation of power—of the imposition on those who reject it of a political morality *this* moralist happens to favor—is performed under cover of a few fine-sounding abstractions like impartiality and reasonableness. In one scheme those who will be constrained are given a choice, perpetual war or a limitation on your desires; in the other they are given no choice (and not even a hearing) and told that if they do not assent, they will be ruled anyway because they will be in conflict with "a highest order framework of moral reasoning,"[49] where "highest order" is nothing more than the instant transmutation of a contestable point of view into the view from nowhere.

It is nicely done and Nagel is so good at it that he can do it in a blink of the eye. He begins a sentence from another essay by declaring that "there is no higher-order value . . . abstractly conceived which is capable of commanding the acceptance by reasonable persons of constraints on the pursuit of their most central aims of self-realization," but then ends the same sentence by saying "except for the need to respect this same limit in others."[50] Here the equivocation occurs with the word "need." Is the need dictated by a normative moral vision, in which case it identifies just the kind of higher-order value whose existence has just been denied; or is it a need in relation to a lower-order morality (we had better respect others if we want them to be respectful in return), in which case Nagel is urging the kind of "convergence theory" or prudentialism he disdains.

Nothing I have said should be taken as a criticism of Nagel's substantive vision, only of his claim that it is not substantive. There is more than a little plausibility to the argument that everyone wins if each of us agrees to forgo winning; it is just not the kind of argument Nagel thinks it is, one that outflanks belief; rather, it is a form of belief, the belief that one's "central aims of self-realization" will be best achieved privately and in spaces separated from the ordinary business of daily socioeconomic life. Those who believe something else, and especially those who believe that separating the realm of self-realization from the public sphere means a public sphere empty of value and inimical to its flourishing, will find no scope for *their* self-realization in Nagel's republic, where they will be labeled "unreasonable" or worse. Nor is this result one Nagel could avoid, for as Locke made clear (although he would not have put it this way), acts of exclusion and stigmatization are inevitable in any liberal regime that really wants to be a regime and not an endless philosophy seminar; and it is inevitable too, given liberalism's vaunted opposition to coercion, that such acts will want to be known by other names, names like "reasonable," "neutral," and "impartial."

The options, after all, are limited. If you begin by acknowledging the inevitability of difference, and the desirability of preventing the conflicts that will erupt if proponents of opposing religious and moral viewpoints are left free to vie for control of the state and its coercing mechanisms, you have only three alternatives:

1. Institute a regime of tolerance and face the difficulty of a system of government (hardly government at all) without the power to constrain and punish what it thinks wrong.
2. Institute a regime of power and recommend it as an alternative to the chaos everyone fears.
3. Institute a regime of power but don't identify it as such; instead claim for it the status of an impersonal law tied to the interests of no one but capable of safeguarding the interests of everyone.

Pretty much all liberals save Hobbes (and remember, Ryan excludes him from the category) go for the third option, with the result that almost every interesting question has been answered (or evaded) in advance and all that is left are in-house debates about just who or what to exclude and how best to package the exclusions so that they will appear to have been dictated by universal principles. That, as they used to say at the beginning of *Mission Impossible*, is your assignment. But unlike the complicated political tasks given to the television heroes, this assignment *is* impossible, although that fact seems not to have put the smallest dent in the confidence of those who accept it and cheerfully announce that they have finally done the job. In reality, what they have done is what Nagel does and what Locke did before him, perform some version of a basic double move: first announce that there exists no mechanism capable of adjudicating between competing systems of belief, and then install in a position of privilege just such a mechanism; declare something to be unavailable, and then, almost in the next breath, discover it.

III. Mutual Respect as a Device of Exclusion

A spectacular example of this third form of argument, and of the ways by which its springs are hidden even from those who make it, is provided by an essay much cited by Thiemann, Amy Gutmann and Dennis Thompson's "Moral Conflict and Political Consensus."[51] The piece begins by observing, "Religious controversy has traditionally been regarded as the paradigm of moral conflict that does not belong on the political agenda" (because it is intractable), and fairly quickly turns into a discussion of how to exclude from that agenda policies favoring racial discrimination. The authors think of themselves of going against the grain of Nagel-like appeals to higher-order principle, but in the end (and predictably) they make just such an appeal themselves in the name of "mutual respect."

In the old debate between those who think of liberalism as a device for managing and minimizing conflict, and those who think of liberalism as a device for producing a better society populated by better persons, Gutmann and Thompson are clearly on the side of the latter, and that is why they are uneasy with a liberalism that requires of the state only that it be tolerant, neutral, and inactive. The trouble with these principles, they say, is that although they might succeed in keeping divisive issues off the political agenda, they do so in a blanket way that does not allow for the discriminations a state concerned with its own health and the health of its citizens should be making. If the state adopts a posture of live and let live, refrains from either favoring or disfavoring any moral position, and limits itself to presiding over the fray without trying to influence it in any direction, all controversial positions will be regarded in the same way, either as distractions we would be better off without (let the clergy and the philosophers worry about these questions) or as matters so difficult of adjudication (there is simply no truth to be discovered at the bottom of such disputes) that they are best left to the marketplace of ideas. As a result, peace, if we achieve it, will have to be bought at the price of future edification, for the citizenry will have been prevented by a strict hands-off policy from engaging in debates that might have led to its moral and political improvement.

Not that Gutmann and Thompson are recommending unrestricted public debate on controversial positions; rather, they wish to limit debate to those positions that speak to a genuine moral question in ways that have the potential, at least, of advancing the conversation. What is required is a means of distinguishing between these bona fide positions and positions whose ascendency would have the effect of subverting morality altogether. Blanket toleration and neutrality will not be these means, for they set the bar either too high or too low. The bar is set too high by someone like Nagel, who would exclude from public forums beliefs that cannot be justified from "a standpoint that is independent of who we are." By this standard, Gutmann and Thompson complain, "[T]he liberal's belief in human equality" (which Nagel would embrace and want the state to enforce) would fall into the same category as a belief that "sanctions racial discrimination."[52] Neither is independent of "who we are" and so would be excluded, but surely, say Gutmann and Thompson, "they are not equally acceptable (or unacceptable) starting points for public deliberation."[53]

The situation is no better when the bar is set too low and positions, rather than being excluded because they are controversial, are let in because they are controversial. Indiscriminate lumping in either direction brings its dangers; in the case of a policy favoring racial discrimination the danger is that if the policy becomes a serious contender for state action, it might prevail and we would be headed back in the direction of slavery; whereas if the state washes its hands of the question (because it has been and continues to be disputed) and leaves it to each individual's conscience, citizens will then be "free to discriminate or not according to their religions."[54]

The dilemma is clear (and classic). How does the liberal state deal with doctrines—like racial discrimination or religious intolerance—inimical to it and threatening to its survival? If such doctrines are welcomed into the conversation, they may shut it down; if the door is closed to them, liberalism will seem to be exercising the peremptory authority it routinely condemns. Long ago Oliver Wendell Holmes declared himself willing to grasp the first handle of this dilemma and take his (or our) chances: "If in the long run the beliefs expressed in proletarian dictatorship are destined to be accepted by the dominant forces of the community, the only meaning of free speech is that they should be given their chance and have their way."[55] Gutmann and Thompson, however, are less libertarian in their sentiments and less willing to trust the matter to fate. They want the state to act positively in the "right" direction, and yet they want also to be true to the liberal principle of giving as much scope as possible to moral and intellectual debate.

They get what they want by cutting the Gordion knot and declaring "that the defense of racial discrimination is not a moral position at all,"[56] and because it is not a moral position, keeping it off the political agenda violates no principle of tolerance. This is an amazing statement, but it is no more or less than an up-to-date version of Locke's invocation of the "judgment of all mankind" in justification of his preferred intolerances, and it is no accident that Gutmann and Thompson find their own justification in Locke. They note, correctly, that Locke does not urge "neutrality among all religions . . . only among those religions that accept the voluntary nature of faith."[57] If faith is voluntary, something one can come to only on one's own, it will be both wrong and futile for the state to command it "by the force of its laws because faith cannot by its nature be commanded." This must mean,

Gutmann and Thompson conclude, that faith "follows rational persuasion."[58] Of course what Locke means by rational persuasion—or as he puts it, "light and evidence"—may not be what Gutmann and Thompson mean. He means the expostulation and remonstration of Christian conversation among brethren. They mean the rule-governed give-and-take of a philosophy seminar. Between these two is a space of equivocation they eagerly enter, and in a flash they declare that the "secular analogue" to Locke's insistence on the voluntary nature of faith is the requirement that "moral judgments by society must be a matter of deliberation,"[59] with deliberation being understood as the formal interplay of assertion, challenge, and the marshaling of evidence. It follows then that a position that cannot be deliberated in this way (because it fails to respond to challenges or is buttressed by no evidence) is not a moral position, and, therefore, "racial discrimination is not a moral position," for "no one can claim that . . . it is a position about which reasonable people might morally disagree."[60]

But wait a minute: there are certainly people, even today, who would make that claim and back it up with reasons. Yes, that's true, say Gutmann and Thompson, but their reasons "fail . . . to qualify as moral reasons."[61] Why? Because they "can be shown to be rationalizations," that is, proxies for motives (a desire to oppress, a lust for power) that those who give them would be unwilling to acknowledge. And how do you know that? Because, while they offer "evidence," they either refuse to consider "accepted methods of challenging" it or the evidence they offer comes from a source rational beings cannot take seriously, as when they "claim that God speaking literally from the Bible or the laws of nature forbids the mixing of races."[62] Notice that what looks like an argument is really a succession of dismissive gestures designed to deflect objections to a position the authors are unwilling to relinquish or even examine. (Ironically, they are the best example of the closed-mindedness they inveigh against.) Anyone who favors racial discrimination is just sick and has no reason except hate and prejudice; if he has reasons, they are unaccompanied by evidence; if he has evidence, it is the wrong kind; if he has the right kind, it is not as good as the evidence we have. You know that they could go on forever in this vein because all they are doing is negotiating a very small circle that begins and ends with their own prior conviction and a vocabulary made in its image. The key word in that vocabulary is "reasonable," but all that is meant by the word is what my friends and I take to be so. After all, we are reasonable persons; *we* know that no argument for racial discrimination could have any moral or rational basis; therefore anyone who makes such an argument is unreasonable.

To be sure, there are repeated attempts to present this in-house parochialism as if it were the expression of an impersonal and general rule, as when they describe their position as issuing from "a disinterested perspective that could be adopted by any member of society" and distinguish it from the "implausible beliefs"[63] of those who cite the Bible or the laws of nature. But aren't those for whom the Bible is authoritative members of the society and isn't the fact that these believer/citizens refuse the authors' perspective evidence that it is not disinterested at all (unless believers of a fundamentalist type are regarded as second-class citizens whose views don't count, which is just how they are regarded here)? And isn't "disinterested" one more word—

like "impartial" and "reasonable"—that claims the high ground of neutrality while performing exclusionary work?

In Gutmann and Thompson's argument it is the notion of "mutual respect" (their version of "higher-order impartiality") that does the work of exclusion in the name, supposedly, of generosity. Mutual respect, they say,

> manifests a distinctively democratic kind of character—the character of individuals who are morally committed, self-reflective about their commitments, discerning of the difference between respectable and merely tolerable differences of opinion, and open to the possibility of changing their minds or modifying their positions at some time in the future if they confront unanswerable objections to their present point of view.[64]

The idea is simple enough and as usual it seems unexceptionable: regard those with whom you disagree not as enemies to the death but as partners in the search for truth, and hold yourself ready to change or modify your point of view if you are unable to refute a reasoned challenge to what you believe. But the imperative will begin to seem less "reasonable" and commonsensical if you ask a simple two-part question: Where do the challenges to your belief come from, and when should you be distressed if you cannot meet them? If the challenges come from within the structure of your belief (since you have already acknowledged that all men are created equal, how can you support a policy of racial discrimination?), then the standard to which you are being held is one that you have already acknowledged, and what is being asked of you is, simply, that you be consistent with yourself. If, however, the challenge comes in terms not recognized by the structure of your belief, why should you be the least bit concerned with it since it rests on notions of evidence and argument to which you are in no way committed?[65] If you tell a serious Christian that no one can walk on water or rise from the dead or feed five thousand with two fishes and five loaves, he or she will tell you that the impossibility of those actions for mere men is what makes their performance so powerful a sign of divinity. For one party, the reasoning is "No man can do it and therefore Christ didn't do it"; for the other, the reasoning is "Since no man could do it, he who did it is more than man." For one party, falsification follows from the absence of a plausibly empirical account of how the purported phenomena could have occurred; for the other, the absence of a plausibly empirical account is just the point, one that does not challenge the faith but confirms it.

What Gutmann and Thompson will say is that the second party is not really reasoning. This is what they mean when they distinguish between "respectable and merely tolerable differences of opinion." A difference of opinion you respect is an opinion held by someone who argues from the same premises and with the same tools you do; an opinion you merely tolerate—although we won't imprison you for holding it, neither will we take any account of it in the process of formulating policy—is an opinion held by someone who argues from premises and with tools you and your friends find provincial at best and dangerous (because fanatical) at worst. It is at this point that you dismiss those premises (that is, biblical inerrancy) as ones no rational person could subscribe to, whereas in fact what you have done is define "rational" so as to make it congruent with the ways of thinking you and those who agree with you customarily deploy. "Mutual respect" should be renamed "mutual self-congratulation" since it will not be extended beyond the circle of those who already feel comfortable with one another.

But, someone might reasonably object, this is hardly helpful. Suppose that you believe (as I in fact do) that policies favoring racial discrimination have no place on the political agenda and believe too that if a state or the nation should turn in the direction of theocracy, it would be a bad thing. What do you do if, by my arguments at least, there is no principled way—no way not tied to a particular agenda—of lobbying for the exclusion from public deliberations of points of view you consider dangerous? Do you simply allow such points of view to flourish and hope for the best? Or do you do what the theorists discussed here do (although they would no doubt dispute this description), cast about for an abstract formula under whose cover you can exclude things left and right while all the while claiming clean (neutral, impartial, mutually respectful) hands? Is there no alternative?

Gutmann and Thompson actually have an answer to that question, but for reasons that are finally not surprising, they don't see it even though they provide evidence for it in an observation they rush right past:

> A policy favoring racial discrimination, it is now generally agreed, deserves no place on the political agenda. Such a policy is not an option that legislatures or citizens would seriously consider, and if it were to [become] so, we should expect courts to prevent its adoption.[66]

Although more than fifteen pages of the essay remain to be written, one wonders why the authors didn't stop here since it would seem that what they seek—a way of keeping policies favoring racial discrimination off the agenda—has already been found. What's the problem? The problem (they never say this, but it is implied by the fact that the essay continues) is that the solution has been the accomplishment of politics rather than theory. The agreement on which they report has been reached in the course of a history that includes the civil rights struggles of the 50's and 60's, the election in 1964 of a president from the South, two speeches by Martin Luther King, the televising of official violence against freedom riders, a Republican president who not only went to China but put in place mandatory programs of affirmative action, the Civil Rights Act of 1964, the Voting Rights Act of 1965, the immense popularity of Alex Haley's *Roots*, and the breaking of the color line in professional sports. No one of these was either decisive or inevitable, but as a result of their entirely contingent occurrence in an equally contingent sequence, saying certain things—you must keep those people in their place, America belongs to the Americans, you wouldn't want one to marry your sister—became at the least unfashionable and at the most socially and economically disadvantageous, while saying certain other things—people should be judged on the content of their character, not the color of their skins, diversity is a good that should be reflected in the classroom and the workplace, this country is committed to the eradication of racism—became de rigueur and a ticket of entry into public life. This does not mean that the old sentiments were erased from the hearts of those who had previously expressed them or that minds once confused had now been cleared of mistaken notions; rather, it means that one vocabulary fell into favor and disuse while another stepped into the place it had formerly occupied, and that this new vocabulary was at once a response to shifts in the political wind and an event in those shifts.

The problem is that the political winds may shift again. That is why Gutmann and Thompson are not satisfied with timely and prudential "reasons for rejecting racial discrimination" and require reasons of a "different, stronger kind,"[67] reasons whose force does not vary and/or diminish with circumstances. After all, if policies favoring racial discrimination have been only politically discredited—discredited by contingent events and the ascendency of one rhetoric over another—the same policies could be politically rehabilitated, perhaps by generating "scientific evidence" that gives them new justificatory life (witness *The Bell Curve*) or by quantifying their effects and discovering that they promote efficiency and wealth maximization. To be sure, any such rehabilitation seems unlikely, but the fact that it is even possible is enough to make the point that politics can go backward. It is because politics cannot be freeze-framed at the moment its wheel of fortune delivers an outcome you favor that Gutmann and Thompson want to bypass the political process and turn to reasons of "a stronger kind," to principled reasons. These better reasons would hover above the political process and intervene whenever it was about to take a wrong turn. In this way, the "hope of liberal theory," the hope that citizens can "agree on principles"[68] that will once and for all circumscribe the political agenda, will have been realized.

But where will these reasons of a stronger kind have come from? Who will have thought them up? The answer is that they will have come from one or another of the viewpoints contending in the political arena. After all, the desire to remove policies favoring racial discrimination from the agenda is not universal; if it were, there would be no problem and the agenda would circumscribe itself. Whatever "principle" one might offer as a device for managing the political process will itself be politically informed, and any agreement it secures will be the result of efforts by one party first to fill the vocabulary of principle with meanings reflecting its agenda and then to present that vocabulary, fashioned as an adjunct to a political program, as the principled, apolitical, source of that same program.

I do not mean this as a description of anyone's intention. There are no cynics in my scenario, only persons whose strongly held beliefs and commitments lead them to understand, and understand sincerely, notions like "equality," "fairness," and "neutrality" in one way rather than another. It is when someone's understanding of these resonant words (which do not interpret themselves) is regnant in the public space that something like an "agreement" has been secured. Once that agreement is in place, some policies will be (at least publicly) unthinkable and everyone will regularly say of them "no one would seriously urge . . ."; but in time the unthinkable will be reintroduced in a new guise and the agreement that once seemed so solid will fall apart preliminary to the fashioning of a new one, no less political, no less precarious.

IV. The Dream of Managing Politics

What this means is that there are no different or stronger reasons than policy reasons and that the announcement of a formula (higher-order impartiality, mutual respect, the judgment of all mankind) that supposedly outflanks politics or limits its sphere by establishing a space free from its incursions will be nothing more or less than politics—here understood not as a pejorative but as the name of the activity by which you publicly urge what you think to be good and true—by another name. Bonnie Honig makes the general point when she observes that "most political theorists are hostile to the disruptions of politics" and "assume that the task of political theory is . . . to get politics . . . over and done with."[69] The goal is to replace large-P Politics—the clash between fundamentally incompatible vision and agendas—with small-p politics—the adjustment through procedural rules of small differences within a field from which the larger substantive differences have been banished. The problem is that the distinction between what is procedural and what is substantive is itself a substantive one, and therefore in whatever form it is enacted, it will engender the very conflicts it was designed to mitigate as those who would have enacted it differently or not enacted it at all cry foul, or error, or blasphemy. When this happens (as it always will), the would-be engineers of peace and stability always respond in the same way, by calling the malcontents unreasonable, or fanatical, or insufficiently respectful of difference, or some other name that dismisses their concerns by placing them beyond a pale whose boundaries, they continue to claim, have been drawn by nature. Honig calls those stigmatized others "the remainders,"[70] those who have been exiled to the margins in the name of a policy of inclusion that can only call itself such with a straight face by labeling them monsters.

Although it is Honig's intention to give these remainders their due as an inescapable component of any political situation, in the end she surrenders to the very form of liberal theorizing she critiques. She divides the world into two kinds of theorists, "virtue theorists," each of whom "believes, mistakenly, that his own theory soothes or resolves the dissonances other theories cause" and "*virtú* theorists," who argue that "every politics has its remainders, that resistances are engendered by every settlement, even those that are relatively enabling or empowering."[71] The fact that those in this second camp (in which she places herself) are called "theorists" too is a tipoff to what happens in a few pages when *virtú* theory turns out to have a *program*: "to treat rights and laws as a part of political contest rather than as the instruments of their closure."[72] Such a program, however, gives the *virtú* theorist more power than her own insight authorizes. What matters is not the way you think about the relationship between rights and laws and political contest but what the relationship, in fact, *is*; and if, as Honig herself asserts, the relationship is one of inescapable entanglement, then that is the way it will continue to be no matter how you decide to "treat" it.

Indeed, the very idea that you could "treat" it one way or another makes sense only if you have once again imagined a space outside or to the side of the politics whose ubiquity you have just affirmed. What Honig calls "the remainders"—the resistances and unforeseen consequences produced by an effort of control, no matter how sophisticated—cannot properly be the objects of a new strategy, if only because they are not objects but ever-present possibilities whose shape is contingent and unpredictable. If the "spaces of politics, power, and resistance" are always, as she says, opening up, and opening up where you least expect them, you can hardly resolve that "they should be preserved, even aggravated, for the sake of the remainders of politics."[73] They can no more be preserved than they can be closed, and to think that you could preserve them (and therefore exercise that much control over them) is only the other side of thinking that you can close them. The "remainders of politics" will frustrate containment all by themselves—that is what being a remainder means—and when you forget that you have turned into a "virtue theorist," as Honig does when she comes out for "those sets of arrangements that resist the temptation to ontologize [identify the permanent location of] the conditions of resistance."[74] But if resistance, in the form of ever-proliferating remainders, is already defeating efforts at ontologization, no set of arrangements is needed to provide resistance nor could any set of arrangements close it down. The temptation to ontologize, to institutionalize the uncontainable, is surrendered to here when the theorist imagines resistance as something she and her colleagues can stage manage.

In the same year that saw the appearance of Honig's book, Chantal Mouffe made essentially the same argument and fell into the same error. Like Honig, Mouffe critiques standard liberal theory for "evacuating the dimension of the political and conceiving the well-ordered society as one exempt from politics."[75] Noting the reliance of theorists like Rawls on supposedly "self-evident" norms of neutrality and fairness, she observes that the easy invocation of these values, "far from being a benign statement of fact . . . is the result of a *decision* which already excludes from the dialogue those who believe that different values should be the organizing ones of the political order."[76] (You will recognize this as the argument of the present essay.) The arbitrariness of this exclusion is denied by these same theorists who hide it from themselves by calling "those who disagree with them . . . either unreasonable or irrational."[77] Mouffe urges that we substitute for this "current brand of liberalism" a view of democracy "that would not present it as the rational, universal solution to the problem of political order" nor "attempt to deny its ultimately ungrounded status by making it appear as the outcome of a rational choice."[78] "It is very important," she declares, "to recognize . . . forms of exclusion for what they are and the violence that they signify, instead of concealing them under the veil of rationality."[79]

But you could recognize forms of exclusion and violence for what they are only if "what they are" could be uncontroversially identified. No one thinks of himself as unfairly excluding anyone, and acts of violence always come accompanied by the adjective "justified," indicating the agent's conviction that what he does he does in the name of a deity or a supreme value or a higher-order impartiality. The idea of recognizing something for what it is rather than for what it appears to be presupposes the apolitical space whose availability Mouffe denies. If what was and was not violent and/or excluding could be identified apart from anyone's interests, politics would be immediately tamed and reduced (as liberalism always wants to reduce it) to low-level debates about the particular realization of agreed-upon ends.

Taming politics is finally what Mouffe has in mind, despite her pronouncements to the contrary. The process of taming unfolds in two (impossible) steps, first the step of recognizing "domination and violence" for what they really are—a recognition you perform from a distance; whatever they are, they are not you—and, second the step of "the establishment of a set of institutions through which they can be limited and tested."[80] That step is taken the moment you imagine it, for if you assume that domination and violence can be isolated long enough to become the objects of institutional manipulation, they have already been limited, if only in your mind. When Mouffe ends her book by naming as our task the creation of "the conditions under which . . . aggressive forces can be defused and . . . a pluralist democratic order made possible,"[81] she has joined the ranks of those who, in her own accusing words, seek to "negate the political" and "make it disappear." If Rawls and Nagel conceive "the well-ordered society as one exempt from politics,"[82] she conceives the well-ordered society as one that keeps politics in check. The difference between thinking that politics can be eliminated and thinking it can be managed is certainly real, but it is a family difference and those on either side of it are united in their determination to avoid the lesson Mouffe wants to be teaching: that politics is an inescapable condition and one that is present in every effort to contain its effects, whether that effort is attached to the high hopes of the liberal rationalists or to the more modest hopes of someone who has come to "accept the consequences of the irreducible plurality of values."[83]

Mouffe thinks that because she does accept those consequences, she has a purchase on them denied her less-self-aware fellow theorists. She thinks that by recognizing "the dimension of conflict and antagonism within the political" she has "come to terms"[84] with it. She thinks that by acknowledging contingency, she has fashioned (or is on the way to fashioning) a "political philosophy that makes room for contingency."[85] But contingency is precisely what you can't make room for; contingency is what befalls the best-laid plans of mice and men, and that includes plans to take it into account or guard against its eruption. And by the same reasoning "the dimension of conflict . . . within the political" is not something you can come to terms with. You can come to terms only with something that stays put and remains at a distance from you, but if the political is, as Mouffe acknowledges, the realm in which we live and move and have our beings, conflict—the clash of opposing points of view—is not simply a dimension of it but the whole of it, and structures everything we do, including any (vain) attempt we might make to come to terms with it. "Accepting" the plurality of values is another such attempt. It is to be sure a possible mental action, but not one that could alter your relationship to the condition it affirms. If the plurality of values is really "irreducible," accepting it will not insulate you from its effects and denying it will not magnify them. To think otherwise—to think, as Mouffe seems to, that by accepting plurality you can outflank or surround it or be in a better position than those who deny it—is to reduce the "irreducible" even as you are supposedly affirming it. All of Mouffe's efforts to escape her own insight—whether they go by the name of "accepting" or "coming to terms with" or "making room for"—are efforts to establish an outside position in relation to an inside that is, as she herself says, everywhere.

Mouffe, Smith, and Honig all make the same mistake. They begin by declaring that politics cannot be contained, and they end by claiming to have contained it. (The "return to the political" doesn't get very far before it is put back into the box.) William Corlett makes an even more rarified mistake. Not only does he think that politics cannot be contained; he thinks that its disruptions should be celebrated and maximized. Corlett stands at the far end of the spectrum this essay examines. If rationalists like Nagel, Gutmann, and Thompson want to eliminate disorder or at least confine it to the margins, and Mouffe and Honig (for different reasons) want to have a better purchase on disorder so that it can be managed, Corlett wants to promote disorder even to the point of courting madness. Where others ask, how can we fashion a community that will accommodate and contain the energies of human difference? Corlett asks, how can we derail the operations of community so that the energies of human difference can be released? The answer, he says, is to "use in the least orderly way possible the forms which political theories provide in the name of order" and to "reject the reassurance political theory offers" in favor of a militant provisionality—he calls it a "politics of extravagance"—that refuses "to permit any form to become entrenched."[86] Corlett would not be misunderstood. He is not recommending that we *choose* extravagance or chaos over order; rather, he is insisting, with Derrida, that extravagance or chaos "is a constitutive element of order,"[87] and that therefore "irrationality" can never be "exiled," that is, thought of as being somewhere *else*. "Wherever one finds a structure one finds an excess,"[88] something excluded, but whose exclusion constitutes the inside supposedly free of it. "Reason is already unreasonable."[89] One occupies a "reasonable" moment only by forgetting the borders (and monsters) that mark it out and make it what it is and is not. "All reason and order requires an 'other'" and therefore the "possibility of purity . . . is out of the question."[90]

What this amounts to is the formulation in a somewhat more dramatic vocabulary of the point I have been making throughout: if you begin by assuming the intractability of difference (because every church is orthodox to itself), any line you then draw between the reasonable and the unreasonable or the normative and the obviously eccentric will be drawn from an unreasonable (not everyone would assent to its perspicuity) and eccentric (marginal to an unavailable center) perspective. And, moreover, any attempt to compensate for eccentricity will only produce more of it; however you define and demarcate the normative, its space will always be parochial. The difference is that where I make the point as a matter of (nonculpable) fact—that's the way it always is and must be, positions have to be taken and every position borrows its intelligibility from that from which it would be distinct—Corlett makes it as a matter of blame—those who fail to see the provisionality and impurity of every "unitary form"[91] allow the "metaphysical pretense of the hour"[92] to work its inevitable exclusions. What I take as a situation that cannot be avoided and need not be remedied—exclusion is inevitable but it's nothing to apologize for since it comes along with any effort to put the beliefs you hold into practice—Corlett takes as a situation that remedies (or at least mitigates) itself if only we are sufficiently aware of it.

In short, he makes the critical-self-consciousness mistake in the direction of extravagance rather than stability, and thus provides himself with a political payoff; if we *know* that no arrangement of things is natural or coextensive with the boundaries of reason, we will be less inclined to defend to the death (usually someone else's) the arrangements that we favor:

> If all order is in principle provisional . . . it may well become increasingly difficult to defend let alone to justify, hegemonic dominance in political life.[93]

> [I]f the relation between political thinking and its forms is never presumed to be fixed, then one is less inclined to fight flux with reasonable, orderly strategies. If everything is boundless without limit, it is difficult to detect an enemy.[94]

For all the radical talk, what we have here is liberalism all over again. The assertion that forms of order and stability are always provisional is equivalent to the assertion that values are plural and nonadjudicable. Both are offered as reasons for withdrawing from conflict: if the clash of values is irremediable and if the forms of order (and thus the configuration of "us" against "them") is continually shifting, it is best not to insist too strongly on the values you happen to favor or the forms of order you prefer. If everything is up for grabs, why grab anything with the intent of hanging on to it?

Everything, however, is not up for grabs, at least not in the temporally demarcated spaces in which we live our lives and make our choices. And neither is everything boundless and without limits, except from a perspective above the bounds and limits that make experience intelligible from beings not God. And enemies are difficult to detect only if you reserve the label "enemy" for someone who fills the role unambiguously and forever. The absence of such a permanent and stable enemy cannot be a reason for withdrawing from the fray unless you demand of the fray that it take the form of a mythopoeic drama—absolute good versus absolute evil—and that is exactly the drama Corlett has been busy deconstructing. In a world where nothing is fixed or permanent and the relationship between present urgencies and ultimate ends is continually changing, one must take one's constructs not "less seriously,"[95] as Corlett advises, but more seriously, for if we wait for constructs that are in touch with eternity, we will fail to act in moments when action is possible for limited creatures. One may know, as Corlett does, that "the clearing within which" one does one's work "is already infested with chance, accident, chaos,"[96] but that knowledge, if it is a reason for anything, is a reason for doing the work with all the energy possible and with every intention of doing it successfully, which means, when there is a battle brewing, with every intention of winning. That, finally, is the only lesson to take away from the insight (shared by Smith, Honig, Mouffe, and Corlett) that politics is pervasive and inside all-out attempts to avoid it: play it (the lesson is superfluous; what else could you do?) and play it to win.

Winning is a dirty word in liberal theory; it is what is supposed never to happen, unless it is imagined as the impersonal outcome of some agentless mechanism like the marketplace of ideas or universal reason. That is why it is so easy and seems so natural for liberal theorists to reject the strong claims of religion, claims that can be realized only if the adherents of religion succeed in institutionalizing their views and thus marginalizing or even suppressing the views of their adversaries. In the endless (and intended to be so) debates about the relationship between church and state, one rarely hears this acknowledged, and it is a moment of unusual candor that finds David Smolin, a law professor *and* a fundamentalist Christian, declaring aloud that as a "traditional theist" what he wants is a chance to win out over the "modernist liberals" with their "gospel" of autonomous individualism and radical egalitarianism."[97] Smolin feels that he is unlikely to get that chance because the field of battle is configured by the very modernist assumptions he would defeat, specifically by the assumptions of fallibilism (there are no incontrovertible truths) and pluralism (the more points of view in play the better), which, by giving winning a bad name, mandate that liberalism wins.

But why, Smolin asks, "should those who view pluralism and fallibilism as vices accept them as norms of civic virtue?"[98] and thus ratify their own exclusion from public debate? This is the right question, asked this time not of the devout but by the devout, and its answer is obvious. Those for whom pluralism and fallibilism mark the path of error should not accept this imposed disadvantage but should resist it, as Smolin claims to be doing here. And yet the terms of his resistance are such that in the end he too is complicit with the ideology that oppresses him. The trouble begins with the vocabulary of his complaint. The exclusion from public life he and his coreligionists suffer is, he says, "unfair."[99] But fairness is a—no, *the*—liberal virtue; its invocation always signals the subordination of truth to the process of debating it; fairness is the virtue that militates against winning, and by invoking it, Smolin works against the interests of his own party, as he has defined them. He joins the ranks of his enemies again when he calls for a "*full* political dialogue."[100] One understands the logic: right now the dialogue is skewed because "one side's victory"[101] has been written into its rules with the result that the other side is forced to leave its best arguments at the door. The game is rigged. But calling for a nonrigged game in the name of "a truly 'open society'"[102] is to call for exactly what modernist liberalism most cherishes, the enfranchisement of all points of view independently of their moral status. What Smolin should want is not a fair and full game but victory.

To be sure it is victory he seeks, and he is even willing to acknowledge that if he gains it, the losers will *not* be treated fairly but will "live in a society that is hostile to the continuance of their ways of life"[103] (a great moment and unique in the literature). In the end, however, he wants something more—actually something less—than victory; he wants to win the victory fairly, and late in the essay he declares himself in search of "a concept of fairness to which persons of differing allegiances and presuppositions can agree."[104] That is as good a statement of the liberal project as one might hope for; it is a statement Nagel, Gutmann, Thompson, Greenawalt—the entire crew—could all sign on to, and when Smolin signs on to it, he reveals himself to be just one more modernist liberal for all his talk about winning and giving the losers a choice of marginalization in the society or "migration."[105] This sounds tough (get with it or get going); it sounds as if someone is finally going to embrace exclusion rather than push it away or disguise it as tolerance, but Smolin, like everyone else who comes to this brink, draws back from it and ends by calling upon the relevant authorities, and especially the judiciary, to take action "in the interests of all."[106] This is where we came in, with Locke's invocation of the "judgment of all mankind" (of which "the interests of all" is simply a version) only a few paragraphs after he has declared that there is no such thing; and this is where we exit, with Smolin (illiberalism's best hope) repeating Locke's double gesture and recapitulating the entire history of liberal thought, first affirming that every church is orthodox to itself and then contriving in every way possible to forget it.

Conclusion

There can be no conclusion if one means by that a recommendation of a policy or recipe for action superior to those I have critiqued. The whole point of the essay has been that there is no such policy or recipe and therefore no conclusion. The end of the argument is implicit in its beginning. Liberalism's attempt to come to terms with illiberal energies—especially, but not exclusively, religious ones—will always fail because it cannot succeed without enacting the illiberalism it opposes. This is true whether the effort is made by rationalists who put their faith (a word carefully chosen) in forms of fairness, impartiality, and mutual respect, or by clear-eyed realists who know that disruptive energies, like the poor, will always be with us and tell us to get used to it, or by the celebrator of extravagance who invites us to be wild and crazy guys.

Each of these makes the mistake (albeit in different ways) of thinking of conflict either as a "problem" or as an opportunity. No, conflict is the name of our condition, and moreover, naming it does nothing to ameliorate it or make it easier to negotiate. The negotiations have to be done one at a time in the context of the urgencies and choices life continually throws in our way. If I have any recommendation, it is, by my own argument, entirely superfluous. Figure out what you think is right and then look around for ways to be true to it. (Here I am, the new Polonius.) Not very helpful, I admit, but it has the (perhaps not so small) advantage of promising nothing and sending you on your moral way.

This may seem a strange thing to say at the end of an essay that has been preaching the gospel of politics. Politics, after all, is what is usually opposed to morality, especially in the texts of liberal theorists. Politics, interest, partisan conviction, mere belief—these are the forces that must be kept at bay. What I have attempted here is a reversal of this judgment. Politics, interest, partisan conviction, and belief are the locations of morality. It is in and through them that one's sense of justice and the good lives and is put into action. Immorality resides in the mantras of liberal theory—fairness, impartiality, and mutual respect—all devices for painting the world various shades of gray.

NOTES

This is a condensed version of a much longer essay in which I consider the arguments of Jeremy Waldron, Daniel Conkle, Franklin Gamwell, Ronald Thiemann, Kent Greenawalt, Larry Alexander, Colin Bird, Mark Geddicks, Michael McConnell, and Steven Smith. The full essay was published in the *Columbia Law Review* 97, no. 8 (Winter 1997).

I am grateful for the comments and suggestions for revision offered by an embarrassingly large number of friends and colleagues: Larry Alexander, James Boyle, Paul Campos, Peter Goodrich, Marci Hamilton, Stanley Hauerwas, Howard Horwitz, Sandy Levinson, Kirstie McClure, Judd Owen, Jed Rubenfeld, Nomi Stolzenberg, and Laura Underkuffler.

1. Michael Walzer, *On Toleration*, New Haven, Conn., 1997, 6.

2. Thomas Nagel, "Moral Conflict and Political Legitimacy," *Philosophy and Public Affairs* 16, no. 3 (1987): 229.

3. Stanley Fish, *Doing What Comes Naturally: Change, Rhetoric, and the Practice of Theory in Literary and Legal Studies*, Durham and London, 1989, 326.

4. One more preliminary gloss. I shall several times deny the availability of any mechanism or calculus for determining the truth about a matter. This does not mean that I believe there to be no such truth, only that I believe there to be no way of flushing it out so that everyone, however situated, will assent to it. My skepticism (if that is the word, and it probably isn't) is epistemological, not ontological. These of course are issues that have provoked volumes of debate, and my bald declarations hardly do justice to them.

5. John Locke, *John Locke: A Letter Concerning Toleration in Focus*, ed. John Horton and Susan Mendus, London, 1991, 17.

6. *Id.*, at 24.

7. *Id.*, at 52.

8. *Id.*, at 14.

9. *Id.*, at 19.

10. The theological virtue of love for others as fellow creatures created by and sustained by a benevolent deity.

11. *John Locke: A Letter Concerning Toleration in Focus*, 14.

12. *Id.*, at 25.

13. *Id.*, at 18.

14. *Id.*, emphasis added.

15. *Id.*

16. *Id.*, at 19.

17. *Id.*, at 14.

18. *Id.*, at 17.

19. *Id.*, at 21.

20. *Id.*, at 29.

21. *Id.*, at 35–36.

22. *Id.*, at 32.

23. *Id.*, at 45.

24. Kent Greenawalt offers as one such view, "unrestricted governance by sadists is undesirable," an observation that is as safe as it is unhelpful. See *Private Consciences and Public Reasons*, New York and Oxford, 1995, 27.

25. Michael Sandel, *Democracy's Discontent: America in Search of a Public Philosophy*, Cambridge, Mass., 1996, 28.

26. *John Locke: A Letter Concerning Toleration in Focus*, 45–46.

27. Thomas Hobbes, *Leviathan*, ed. C. B. Macpherson, New York and Hammondsworth, 1968, 239.

28. *Id.*

29. *Id.*, at 135.

30. *Id.*, at 184.

31. *Id.*, at 185.

32. *Id.*, at 227.

33. *Id.*, at 190.

34. *Id.*, at 266.

35. *Id.*, at 190.

36. Alan Ryan, "Liberalism," in *A Companion to Contemporary Political Philosophy*, ed. Robert E. Goodin and Philip Pettit, Oxford, 1995, 298.
37. Thomas Nagel, "Moral Conflict and Political Legitimacy," *Philosophy and Public Affairs* 6, no. 3 (Summer 1987): 219.
38. *Id.*, at 219.
39. *Id.*, at 220.
40. *Id.*, at 221.
41. *Id.*, at 227.
42. *Id.*
43. On this and related points, see Joseph Raz, "Facing Diversity: The Case of Epistemic Abstinence," *Philosophy and Public Affairs* 19, no. 1 (Winter 1990): 3–46.
44. Nagel, "Moral Conflict and Political Legitimacy," 232.
45. *Id.*, at 229.
46. *Id.*, at 228.
47. *Id.*, at 229.
48. Hobbes, *Leviathan*, 232.
49. Nagel, "Moral Conflict and Political Legitimacy," 228.
50. Thomas Nagel, *Equality and Partiality*, Oxford and New York, 1991, 164.
51. Amy Gutmann and Dennis Thompson, "Moral Conflict and Political Consensus," *Ethics* 101 (October 1990).
52. *Id.*, at 67.
53. *Id.*, at 68.
54. *Id.*, at 69.
55. *Gitlow v. People of New York*, 1925, 268 U.S. 652, 45 S.Ct. 625 L.Ed. 1138.
56. Gutmann and Thompson, "Moral Conflict and Political Consensus," 69.
57. *Id.*
58. *Id.*, at 68.
59. *Id.*
60. *Id.*, at 69–70.
61. *Id.*, at 70.
62. *Id.*
63. *Id.*, at 71.
64. *Id.*, at 76.
65. This doesn't mean that you cannot slip out of the bonds you have fashioned, only that you will have to do some work. Whereas if alien bonds are put on you, you won't even feel them.
66. Gutmann and Thompson, "Moral Conflict and Political Consensus," 69.
67. *Id.*
68. *Id.*, at 64.
69. Bonnie Honig, *Political Theory and the Displacement of Politics*, Ithaca, N.Y., 1993, 2.
70. *Id.*, at 4.
71. *Id.*, at 3.
72. *Id.*, at 15.
73. *Id.*, at 146.
74. *Id.*, at 159.
75. Chantal Mouffe, *The Return of the Political*, London, 1993, 139.
76. *Id.*, at 143.
77. *Id.*
78. *Id.*, at 145.

79. *Id.*
80. *Id.*, at 146.
81. *Id.*, at 153.
82. *Id.*, at 139.
83. *Id.*, at 152.
84. *Id.*
85. *Id.*, at 145.
86. William Corlett, *Community Without Unity: A Politics of Derridean Extravagance*, Durham and London, 1989, 12.
87. *Id.*, at 15.
88. *Id.*, at 88.
89. *Id.*, at 147.
90. *Id.*, at 156.
91. *Id.*, at 88.
92. *Id.*, at 83.
93. *Id.*, at 89.
94. *Id.*, at 139.
95. *Id.*, at 102.
96. *Id.*, at 13.
97. David Smolin, "Regulating Religious and Cultural Conflict in a Postmodern America: A Response to Professor Perry," *Iowa Law Journal* 76, no. 5 (July 1991): 1094.
98. *Id.*, at 1079.
99. *Id.*
100. *Id.*, at 1085.
101. *Id.*, at 1087.
102. *Id.*, at 1090.
103. *Id.*, at 1097.
104. *Id.*, at 1094.
105. *Id.*, at 1104.
106. *Id.*, at 1094.

Chapter 21

Liberal Thought and Religion in Custody and Visitation Cases

Linda J. Lacey

Religious differences were at the heart of Barbara and Jeffrey Kendall's bitter divorce.[1] At the time they married, the differences did not seem insurmountable—he was a lapsed Catholic who didn't appear to take religion all that seriously, and she was a Reform Jew. They mutually agreed the children would be raised as Jews. Ariel, Moriah, and Rebekah were given Jewish names, enrolled in a Jewish school and brought up with a strong sense of identity as Jews.[2] However, as the marriage went on, Jeffrey's religious views underwent a dramatic change—he became a fundamentalist Christian. Barbara Kendall had also changed her religious views somewhat—she had become a strictly observant Orthodox Jew. It is not surprising that this marriage was doomed to failure and sadly predictable that one of the biggest bones of contention was the children's religious upbringing.[3]

Barbara was granted custody of the children and continued to raise them as observant Jews. But Jeffrey was now a man with a mission: to save his children's souls. He testified that he believes that unless his children become Christians, they are doomed to go to hell. As a result, he "will never stop trying to save his children."[4] Saving the children took an especially harsh form with the oldest child, Ari, who was forced to cut off his sidecurls and violate the Jewish Sabbath. All the children were taken to Jeffrey's church, where they were told about the perils of hell awaiting "unsaved" people.

Concerned about her children, Barbara Kendall went to court to attempt to restrain Jeffrey's practices. The trial court agreed with her contention that the children could be seriously harmed by their father's actions and ordered Jeffrey to cease from engaging in activity that "promotes rejection rather than acceptance of their mother or their own Jewish self-identity."[5]

The decision, which represents a minority viewpoint in terms of case law, was condemned by commentators on both the left and right.[6] The conservative criticism was predictable. Conservative columnist Joe Fitzgerald characterized the opinion as "hostility toward evangelical Christianity."[7] This reaction is consistent with the attempts by fundamentalist Christians to portray themselves as victims of a liberal culture.[8] Conservative commentators contend that the judiciary, like other powerful institutions is controlled by a liberal elite that is hostile to their brand of Christianity.

Fitzgerald was clearly upset because it was *his* kind of religion being suppressed, not just any religion.

If the conservative perception that liberals are generally opposed to fundamentalism is accurate (as it undoubtedly is), then one would expect the decision to be greeted with acclaim by liberals. That was not the case. Instead, liberal columnist Ellen McNamara wrote that the decision transmits a "message that ideas in and of themselves are dangerous to children" and stands for the proposition that "intolerance of religious beliefs is compatible with American law."[9]

McNamara is wrong of course. The decision stands for nothing more than the entirely sensible proposition that children should not be used as pawns in their parents' religious wars. As trial judge Cristina Harris wrote, "If the children continue to be caught in the cross-fire of their parents' religious difference, they are very likely to be harmed."[10] Since the children identified themselves as Jews, constantly being told their religion is wrong and evil would diminish their sense of self-worth. This is especially true when the person telling them they are doomed to eternal hellfire is their father. Columnist Jeff Jacoby's argument is convincing: "If children raised as strict vegetarians were being hectored by their noncustodial father to eat meat—and threatened with dire results if they didn't—who wouldn't be appalled? If on such relatively minor issues as these we would spare our children emotional turmoil, how much more so on a matter as grave and fundamental as their relationship with God."[11]

These fairly obvious statements are unthinkable from a liberal perspective. The failure of liberal thought to recognize the perspective of the Kendall children is inevitable. To admit that exposure to their father's religion might harm Ari, Moriah, and Rebekah would be tantamount to admitting that the fundamental principles liberalism claims to apply to religious issues—tolerance, equality, and neutrality—are in fact impossible to achieve. As Stanley Fish puts it: "All of liberalism's efforts to accommodate or tame illiberal forces fail, either by underestimating or trivializing the illiberal impulse, or by mirroring it."[12]

In this essay, after I have discussed the classic liberal approach to religious dilemmas in custody and visitation cases, I will expand on Fish's thesis and argue that liberal methodology in the context of custody and visitation decisions is deeply flawed and inherently unworkable.

I. Religion and Visitation

The result in Kendall v. Kendall, which I believe is the right result, does not represent the majority viewpoint.[13] A Pennsylvania case, Zummo v. Zummo,[14] is more typical of the way courts resolve conflicts between a custodial parent and a noncustodial parent over their children's religious upbringing.[15] As in the Kendall case, Zummo involved a dispute between a Jewish mother and a Christian father.[16] Before they married, both parents agreed that their children would be raised as Jews. At the time of the divorce, Adam, the oldest child, was about to begin preparation for his bar mitzvah. After the divorce, the father attempted to take the children to Catholic services and refused to take them to Jewish Sunday school. The mother objected to this behavior, contending that the premarriage agreement should be enforced and that exposing the children to a second religion would "confuse and disorient them."[17]

The trial court entered an order prohibiting the father from taking his children to "religious services contrary to the Jewish faith."[18] On appeal, the Superior Court of Pennsylvania removed the restrictions on the father and emphatically rejected the mother's attempt to preserve the childrens' Jewish identity.[19] In a classic display of liberalism, the appellate court disagreed with the trial court's statement that "the practice of Judaism and that of Roman Catholicism cannot be squared. . . . To accept and adhere to the teachings of one necessarily requires a rejection of the other."[20]

The trial court's opinion appears fairly obvious—there is a profound difference between a religion that believes that Jesus was the son of God and one that does not. Judge Kelly, writing for the majority, blithely ignores this fundamental difference and, in a burst of the type of rhetoric we hear on officially designated interfaith days, proclaimed,

> Nevertheless an active dialogue has developed this generation between Christians and Jews and particularly Catholics and Jews which has focused on the similarities between the religions as well as the differences. As a result of the dialogue, much of the formal and informal religious education of Jews about Christianity and of Christians about Judaism has become more respectful and less critical.[21]

This statement completely ignores the difference between knowledge about religion and belief in a religion. Knowledge of the incompatible is possible, belief in the incompatible is not. It is possible for someone to intellectually appreciate the differences and similarities between Judaism and Catholicism, but no one can be both a believing Catholic and a believing Jew.

Judge Kelly continued by saying that we shouldn't even be talking about differences between Catholicism and Judaism:

> It would be impermissible for us to determine orthodoxy in either religion, let alone turn and compare orthodox beliefs in one of these to the other to make a judicial determination of the reconcilability of Judaism and Christianity or any other religions. . . . Consideration of the presumed irreconcilability of Judaism and Christianity in this case was constitutionally impermissible and an abuse of discretion.[22]

Therefore, the father could continue to force his children to attend Catholic services unless the practice "actually presents a substantial threat of present or future emotional harm to the particular child or children involved."[23]

Most courts follow Zummo's approach of requiring substantial harm to children before they will interfere with a noncustodial parent's "right" to raise his children in his religious beliefs.[24] Commentators generally applaud the principle that both parents must have an equal opportunity to raise their children in their own religious beliefs,[25] absent a very difficult to prove showing of harm to the child.[26] In Munoz v. Munoz, a court specially rejected the idea "that duality of religious beliefs, per se, creates a conflict upon young minds."[27] This is the standard liberal approach to these cases—a complete denial of the conflicts that children may feel being raised in two incompatible religions.

Not only does the liberal approach harm children in many instances, it also cannot achieve its goal of giving each parent "equal" rights to raise the child in his or her religious beliefs. The liberal mind-set is clear: if one religion is good, then two are even better. Just as exposure to more speech is always the liberal's answer to free speech issues, exposure to more religion is the answer to any religious conflict. This approach reflects a deeply ingrained failure of liberal thought to recognize the difference between exclusive training in one religion and training in two conflicting religions. To a true liberal, no religion can ever be "right" or "wrong" because religion cannot be measured by "objective standards." Therefore, there is nothing to be gained by raising the children exclusively in the "right" religion. The problem with this theory is that most Western religions believe they are right and others are wrong, that theirs is the only true religion. Instilling a belief in the uniqueness and truth of their religion is critically important to many religious people. The difference between being raised exclusively in one religion, with a consistent indoctrination about of the infallibility of that particular religion, and being raised with constant exposure to conflicting religious beliefs, cannot be ignored. Raising a child exclusively in one religion will generally create a deeper and more absolute belief in that religion's tenets than exposing her to a smorgasbord of religions. I was raised as a Unitarian, the ultimate liberal religion, and I cannot even imagine having an absolute faith in an afterlife or an unshakable belief that a given course of action is prescribed by God. My lack of unwavering certainty about my religious beliefs is not necessarily "bad"; on the whole I think it is probably "good," but it is certainly critically different from the perspective of believers in the inerrancy of the Bible, and it is this difference that liberal thought fails to acknowledge.

As Nomi Stolzenberg has illustrated in discussing cases involving required readings in public schools, liberal thought simply cannot comprehend why exclusive exposure to one religion is so important to some parents.[28] This is because liberals cannot understand why the "objectivity" they hold so dear is threatening to members of some religions. As Stolzenberg explains,

> [T]he objective mode of exposure and critical discourse, characteristic of the liberal marketplace of ideas, claims to stand outside particular traditions, mediating among them. In the process, however, it also asserts a kind of authority over them. The glare of critical judgment does not just bring the affective, ritualistic processes of traditional cultural transmission into light. In illuminating traditional mechanisms of cultural reproduction, it also threatens to defeat them.[29]

Because some religions are more relativist and less dependent on exclusive training, giving each parent equal time to expose the child to his or her religion will almost always confer an advantage on the parent whose religion is more compatible with a relativist approach.

"Equality" for the custodial and noncustodial parent is also problematic when one parent is Christian and the other is not. True "equal time" for each religion is not possible—Christianity has an ingrained advantage in a culture where children are exposed to a daily barrage of Christian messages, especially at Christmastime.[30] Jane Praeger, who is Jewish and married to a Christian, poignantly describes her experience:

> So that night, after the kids were asleep, I tried, and not for the first time, to make my husband understand—truly understand—my reaction to the tree that nearly reached the ceiling of our living room. I reminded him again of why Jews still perceive themselves as a threatened minority. . . . I told him I could not look at our tree, at its twinkling lights, its whimsical wooden pigs and clay reindeer and tin drums, without seeing 2,000 years of persecution and genocide, of horror and sorrow. And that having a Christmas tree in my home, inside my refuge from the world, stirs in me nothing less than a fear of total utter annihilation.[31]

As Ms. Praeger's words indicate, to a member of a minority religion the concept of "equal" rights to raise a child in her religious tradition in a culture dominated by Christianity is a hollow one.

II. Religion and Custody

In visitation cases the courts are forced to deal with religious issues whether they like it or not, but in custody cases the standard approach is to completely avoid any mention of religion. In fact, the general rule is that the religion of parents competing for custody cannot be considered at all, unless there is some sort of harm to the child caused by the religious beliefs.[32] One of the leading cases that illustrate how far judges are willing to go to maintain this posture of "religion blindness" is Quiner v. Quiner.[33] The case involved a custody battle for a five-year-old boy. The mother was a member of the "Exclusive Brethren," a religious sect that advocated extreme principles of separation. Members of the group, including children, could not affiliate with any outside organization, engage in any extracurricular school activities, or eat meals with anyone except members of the group. They could not listen to the radio, watch television, play any types of games, or have pets. Reading of any written material except the Bible was discouraged or banned. The child was be told by his mother and grandparents that his father was sinful and that he could not "break bread" with him.[34] Taking all of these factors into account, the trial court awarded custody of the boy to the father, finding among other things that "[i]n the socially and intellectually impoverished environment available to the child in the defendants custody, he could not achieve or approach his potential mental development."[35]

On appeal, the California Court of Appeals reversed, stating that "it is clear from the record that the trial judge predicated his findings and conclusions in respect of what is the best mental welfare of the child entirely upon the appellant's zealous belief and espousal of the principle of separation, inculcated by the religion to which she is devoted."[36] This was impermissible. The court announced:

> Precisely because a court cannot know one way or another, with any degree of certainty, the proper or sure road to personal security and happiness or to religious salvation, which latter to untold millions is their primary and ultimate best interest, evaluation of religious teaching and training and its projected as distinguished from immediate effects (psychologists and psychiatrists to the contrary notwithstanding) upon the physical, mental and emotional well-being of a child, must be forcibly kept from judicial determinations.[37]

Only if there was evidence of actual impairment to the child's physical, emotional, and mental well-being could the mother's practices be considered.[38]

In a similar analysis, in Petersen v. Rogers,[39] an appellate court faced a complex situation involving adoptive parents and a birth mother. Pamela Rogers, who had become a member of a group called The Way, decided while pregnant to relinquish her child for adoption. Members of The Way arranged for a couple to adopt the child. Later, the birth mother watched a television show that portrayed The Way as a dangerous cult, stating that members of The Way were "trained to bear arms and deal in mind control."[40] Alarmed, the birth mother and the child's birth father filed a motion for relief from the interlocutory order allowing the adoption by the Petersens. During the trial, an expert from the Cult Awareness Network testified on the religious practices of members of The Way. The trial court ordered that the child be returned to his biological parents. On appeal, the North Carolina Court of Appeals reversed, on the grounds that the trial court violated the Petersens' religious freedom rights by allowing evidence regarding the religious practices of The Way.[41] It stated: "To allow Ms. Kisser to speculate that the general practices and beliefs of the members might be detrimental to children is to condemn the entire membership of The Way as unsuitable parents."[42] This argument ignores the possibility that a decision maker will hear conflicting expert opinions in any custody suit and will weigh each opinion according to its credibility.

The rule that *nothing* about a parent's religious beliefs can be considered in custody decisions unless there is demonstrated harm to the child is another example of how liberal thought is oblivious to the actual context of custody hearings. Under the extremely broad "best interests of the child" standard that family law courts use in custody cases, it is clear that the environment in which the child will be raised is an important consideration. The decision in custody cases often hinges on factors such as which parent will send the child to an academically superior school and expose the child to activities commonly felt to help a child's emotional and intellectual development.[43] Thus testimony about ways in which a religious practice might inhibit a child's development is clearly relevant in determining the best interests of the child.

I can hear the counterargument forming in some of your minds. "Who is to say that being a member of the drama club or the chess club is more conducive to a child's growth than being a member of the Exclusive Brethren? Can we allow courts to substitute their own value judgments about which environment is better?" The answer to those questions, which may shock readers unfamiliar with family law, is that the best-interests standard not only allows but intrinsically requires judges to use their own value system in deciding which parent should have custody. When neither parent is unfit, judges must look at a variety of factors to make the difficult decision regarding custody, and it is inevitable and generally acknowledged that their personal beliefs influence this decision. Sometimes this leads to "good" results,[44] sometimes to "bad" ones.[45] My argument is not necessarily that custody of the child in Quiner should have been awarded to the father, although based on my own value system that does seem to be the right result, but that the court should have been allowed to consider the effect the mother's religious belief and practices would have on the child. In essence, the Quiner court was saying that a family law judge may consider any imaginable factor except religion. If a parent is deeply religious, so that religion permeates most of his life, this result means that virtually nothing about the way the religious parent plans to raise the child is relevant. On the other hand, every detail about the nonreligious parent's lifestyle may be considered. This "neutrality" clearly favors the religious parent and arguably is even a violation of the establishment clause.[46]

III. The Concept of "Harm" in Custody and Visitation Cases

Custody and visitation cases have one major factor in common: the emphasis on "harm" to the child as a factor that must be proven before the alleged religious rights of the parent can be infringed.[47] This standard of harm varies from the most stringent and difficult to prove standard of "actual" present harm[48] to the more flexible concept of a likelihood of future harm.[49] Both standards as applied are used very narrowly. It is extremely rare for a court to find that religious beliefs harm a child in custody cases or that conflicts between religious beliefs harm children in visitation cases.

The only type of harm caused by religious beliefs that courts will consistently recognize is physical and potentially life threatening. For example, most courts would recognize that handling snakes is harmful to children, regardless of the sincerity of their parents' religious beliefs.[50] A religious belief in the necessity of snake handling might therefore disadvantage a parent in a custody case or restrict a noncustodial parent's rights to expose his children to his religion.

Because of the concern about life-threatening practices, courts in noncustody cases often order medical treatment for children against their parents' wishes.[51] It is worth noting that these decisions, far from being neutral and objective, involve an unspoken assumption—that life is preferable to death. This seems obvious to most people, but not to those who believe with absolute certainty in an afterlife and who are equally certain that their beliefs are the only path to this afterlife.[52]

Although courts recognize life-threatening behavior as "harm," a decision not as objective as it seems, they are extremely reluctant to consider any type of emotional or psychological problems as harm. In Zummo, for example, the appellate court expressly rejected the trial court's determination that "to expose the children to a competing religion after so assiduously grounding them in the tenets of Judaism would unfairly confuse and disorient them and quite possibly vitiate the benefits flowing from either religion."[53] Instead, it proclaimed:

> We also emphasize that while the harm involved may be present or future harm, the speculative possibility of mere disquietude, disorientation, or confusion, arising from exposure to "contradictory religions" would be a patently insufficient "emotional" harm to justify encroachment by the government upon constitutional parental and religious rights of parents, even in the context of divorce . . . stress is not always harmful, nor is it always to be avoided or protected against. The key is not whether the child experiences stress, but whether the stress experienced is unproductively severe.[54]

The failure to consider stress as harm to a child is inexplicable. It is well documented that stress can cause or contribute to life-threatening conditions, such as cancer or heart problems. Yet courts blithely dismiss this concern. Carl Schneider's analysis is typical: "No doubt the psychologists and courts are right in saying that the children in these cases are or soon might be in some pain. But pain is inherent in being a person, in being a child, and in growing up."[55]

Courts require physical manifestations of emotional or psychological harm, and even this is often not enough. Instead of tracing the physical problems to the child's concern about being raised in two competing religions, courts commonly blame the divorce and the parents.[56] It is undoubtedly difficult to determine the exact causes of manifestations of stress in a divorce situation, but if any stress can be attributable to religious conflicts, it should be taken into account in determining the best interests of the child.

The failure of family law courts to recognize that religious conflicts can harm a child contrasts with the Supreme Court's decisions regarding compulsory religion in schools. If it is true, as the Court has recognized, that being required to read a passage of the Bible or say a prayer that conflicts with your religious beliefs is harmful to children, then surely being forced to participate in Holy Communion or listen to a minister tell you that all members of your faith will go to hell is even more harmful. It is true that the coercion in the Supreme Court cases comes from the state, but in terms of harm, the damage to the child is likely to be even greater when the coercion comes from a beloved parent.

This is not to suggest that children cannot be successfully raised within two conflicting religions. Many interfaith families have positive results with a dual religion upbringing, but the decision is most successful when a child is raised from birth in an interfaith marriage, not when a child who has been raised all his life in one religion is suddenly required to have constant exposure to a conflicting religion.

The liberal failure to recognize intangible harm from coerced exposure to conflicting religions especially disadvantages members of historically persecuted religions. For example, through much of their existence, Jews have been forcibly required to attend Christian services. American Indian children were kidnapped and sent to boarding schools, in an attempt to "civilize" them by turning them into Christians.[57] A child raised in a minority religion with this history of persecution will feel especially harmed by being forced against her will to engage in acts contrary to her religious beliefs.

IV. Liberalism and Religion

Three basic principles animate liberal thought in the area of religion:

1. Formal equality. No one religion is better than another or should be preferred to another. Therefore, if one religion is good, then two are better. This is the controlling principle in cases involving rights of noncustodial parents.

2. Neutrality. Courts can never examine a religious belief, other than within a few narrow boundaries, to decide whether it might be harmful. To do so would be to decide that a religion is right or wrong, which would impermissibly violate the First Amendment. This is the controlling principle in the cases involving an initial custody decision.
3. Tolerance. The concept of tolerance toward religion permeates decisions in all aspects of family law.

These principles sound fine on the surface, but as actually applied in child custody and visitation cases, they are fraught with hypocrisy and a denial of common sense. Ultimately, liberal analysis fails to achieve the goals it holds most dear. When courts fail to consider any behavior or lifestyle choices with religious elements as a factor in a custody decision, they privilege the religious parent over the nonreligious parent, thus violating formal equality and neutrality principles. In visitation cases, when courts permit both the noncustodial and custodial parents to have equal authority over their children's religious upbringing, they are actually choosing the relativist "all religions are good" approach over the approach of raising children exclusively in one religion. This choice privileges the parent whose religion is more conducive to relativist thinking and disadvantages the parent whose religion requires an exclusive upbringing in the tenets of that religion. In visitation cases, liberalism is confronted with an insolvable dilemma—it cannot tell either parent his or her religious belief is wrong. But if each parent belongs to a religion that requires a training permeated with a sense of the infallibility of that religion, it is impossible to give each parent "equal" rights with respect to their children's religions upbringing. If a court is to uphold a custodial mother's "right" to raise her children as Jews, it must deny the noncustodial father's "right" to raise them as Catholics. But this result appears to favor one religion over another, which of course liberal thought cannot permit. So the solution is inevitable: the children must be raised as both Catholics and Jews.

The underlying problem, as Nomi Stolzenberg and Stanley Fish have recognized, is that liberal thought by its very nature is incompatible with religious beliefs. Liberals *want* to believe they are tolerant of every religion, but as Stanley Fish explains:

> "Tolerance" may be what liberalism claims for itself in contradistinction to other, supposedly more authoritarian, views; but liberalism is tolerant only within the space demarcated by the operations of reason; any one who steps outside that space will not be tolerated, will not be regarded as a fully enfranchised participant in the marketplace (of ideas) over which reason presides. In this liberalism does not differ from fundamentalism or any other system of thought; for any ideology—and an ideology is what liberalism is—must be founded on some basic conception of what the world is like (it is the creation of God; it is a collection of atoms), and while the conception may admit of differences within its boundaries (and thus be, relatively, tolerant) it cannot legitimize differences that would blur its boundaries, for that would be to delegitimize itself. A liberalism that did not "insist on reason as the only legitimate path to knowledge about the world" would not be liberalism: the principle of a rationality that is above the partisan fray (and therefore can assure its "fairness") is not incidental to liberal thought; it is

> liberal thought, and if it is softened by denying reason its priority and rendering it just one among many legitimate paths, liberalism would have no content.[58]

The unwillingness of liberals to confront this hard reality results in cases like Quiner, where the welfare of an actual child is sacrificed so that a judge may appear tolerant.

There is no answer to the tension between liberalism and religion. Fish is right: "Liberalism's attempt to come to terms with illiberal enterprises—especially, but not exclusively religious ones—will always fail because it cannot succeed without enacting the illiberalism it opposes."[59] I am certainly not suggesting that our legal system should be restructured to privilege the fundamentalist view of the world over the liberal one. History is fraught with evils when one absolutist religion gains complete control. On the whole, liberal beliefs about religion are more compatible with my worldview. But it should be recognized that the goals to which they aspire are unobtainable ideals. In trying to achieve the unachievable, family law courts have too often done violence to the concept that should remain at the heart of all cases involving children—the best interests of the child.

V. Toward a More Realistic Approach to Religious Issues in Custody and Visitation Cases

I know that most postmodernists scorn prescriptive writing, and perhaps rightly so.[60] But I can't help myself. The urge to tell courts what to do is too deeply ingrained. Here's how I think family courts should approach religious issues in custody and visitation cases.

1. In cases involving the initial determination of custody, courts should not shy away from examining whether one parent has religious beliefs that may prove detrimental to the child. The way the parents' beliefs may affect their children's upbringing should be considered relevant, as is everything else about a parent's lifestyle.[61]
2. After the divorce, the children's religious upbringing should remain the same as before the divorce. This means if children have been brought up exclusively as Catholics, a noncustodial parent cannot be allowed to brandish his newly discovered "right" to have them raised as Baptists. This approach will provide the sense of continuity children need after a divorce.[62]

Although I suggest these general guidelines, I do not want to argue that they should be absolutes. Instead of liberal rhetoric about religion, which is so dominant in the current cases, courts should undertake a more contextual undertaking of what is involved. "Harm" to a child cannot be categorized as either "actual" or "speculative"—no child is exactly like another and generalizations about what is or is not harmful are doomed to fail. It should be openly acknowledged that there is no abstract solution that can solve the problems caused by divorce and religious differences. We don't know, we will never know with absolute certainty, what is best for a child. All we can do is try our best, unfettered by abstract principles that ignore reality and common sense.

NOTES

1. Kendall v. Kendall, 426 Mass. 238, 687 N.E. 2d 1228 (1997); cert. denied 118 S.Ct. 2369 (1998).

2. Kendall v. Kendall, 426 Mass. at 240 (1997).

3. Id.

4. Id. See Jeff Jacoby, "True to the God of Their Mother," TULSA WORLD, Friday, December 19, 1997, A-25.

5. Kendall v. Kendall, 426 Mass. at 241 (1997).

6. Jacoby, supra note 4.

7. Id.

8. See generally David M. Smolin, Regulating Religious and Cultural Conflict in a Postmodern America: A Response to Professor Perry, 76 IOWA L. REV. 1067 (1991) (book review).

9. Jacoby, supra note 4

10. Kendall v. Kendall, 426 Mass. 238, 687 N.E. 2d 1228.

11. Jacoby, supra note 4.

12. Stanley Fish, Mission Impossible: Settling the Just Bounds Between Church and State, 97 COLUM. L. REV. 2255 (1997).

13. For a comprehensive overview of decisions in religion and custody cases, see Jennifer Ann Drobac, For the Sake of the Children: Court Consideration of Religion in Child Custody Cases, 50 STAN. L. REV. 1609 (1998). See also Kevin S. Smith, Religious Visitation Constraints on the Noncustodial Parent: The Need for National Application of a Uniform Compelling Interest Test, 71 IND. L.J. 815 (1996); R. Collin Mangrum, Religious Constraints During Visitation: Under What Circumstances Are They Constitutional?, 24 CREIGHTON L. REV. 445 (1991).

14. 394 Pa. Super. 30, 574 A2d 1130 (1990).

15. Most commentators approve of the result in Zummo; see, e.g., Iru Lupu, The Separation of Powers and the Protection of Children, 61 U. CHI. L. REV. 1317, 1350 (1994). But see Rebecca Korzec, A Tale of Two Religions: A Contractual Approach to Religion as a Factor in Child Custody and Visitation Disputes, 25 NEW ENG. L. REV.1121 (1991).

16. 394 Pa. Super. 30, 574 A2d 1130 (1990). The court described the mother as actively practicing "her faith since childhood" and the father as having been raised a Catholic but attending Catholic services "only sporadically."

17. Zummo v. Zummo, 121 Mont. Co. L. Rptr. at 255 n.1.

18. Zummo v. Zummo, 394 Pa. Super. at 37 (1990).

19. Id. The court did affirm the part of the order requiring the father to take the children to Jewish Sunday school.

20. Zummo v. Zummo, 121 Mont. Co. L. Rptr. at 255 n.1.

21. Zummo v. Zummo, 394 Pa. Super. at 75–76 (1990). For a less rosy view of the relationship between Christianity and Judaism, see STEPHEN FELDMAN, PLEASE DON'T WISH ME A MERRY CHRISTMAS: A CRITICAL HISTORY OF THE SEPARATION OF CHURCH AND STATE (1997).

22. Zummo v. Zummo, 394 Pa. Super. at 77 (1990).

23. Id. at 78.

24. Generally, the cases and most of the commentators focus on the competing rights of the parents rather than any rights the children might have. It is well established that parents do have a constitutional right to control their children's religious upbringing, but the major Supreme Court decisions concern children in an intact family, not divorce situations. See e.g. Prince v. Massachusetts, 321 U.S. 158 (1944); Wisconsin v. Yoder, 406 U.S. 205 (1972). The issue of whether and at what age children have independent rights to their own religious

beliefs is still an unresolved issue that deserves more discussion than it usually gets. See Wisconsin v. Yoder, 406 U.S. 205 at 231–32 (1972).

25. An alternative way of explaining these cases is to look at the gender issues involved. Custodial parents are usually mothers; noncustodial parents are usually fathers. The cases can also be viewed as reaffirming the patriarchal notion that a man's children are his property.

26. See, e.g., Carolyn Wah, Religion in Child Custody and Visitation Cases: Presenting the Advantages of Religious Participation, 28 FAM. L.Q. 269 (1994); Note, "Religious Visitation Constraints on the Noncustodial Parent: The Need for National Application of a Uniform Compelling Interest Test, 71 IND. L.J. 815, 818 (1996); Smith, supra note 13; Mangrum, supra note 13.

There is one major exception to the deference courts generally give to the noncustodial parent's right to take the children to his church. If the noncustodial parent is gay, many courts forbid him to take the child to a gay church. In J.L.P. (H) v. D.J.P., 643 S.W. 2d 865 (1982) a court upheld an order prohibiting a gay father from taking his son to a "church at which a large proportion of the congregation are homosexuals." Id. In sharp contrast to the concern about first amendment rights manifested in cases where the noncustodial parent is not gay, the court claimed, "[T]here is no attempt by the trial court to dictate to the father with respect to any facet of his lifestyle, attendance at church, or rights of speech." Id.

27. Munoz v. Munoz, 489 P.2d 1133 (Wash. 1971) at 1136.

28. Nomi Maya Stolzenberg, "He Drew a Circle That Shut Me Out": Assimilation, Indoctrination, and the Paradox of a Liberal Education," 106 HARV. L. REV. 581 (1993).

29. Id. at 634. Stolzenberg elaborates on this theme: "The fundamentalists' argument against exposure is truly difficult for one raised in the liberal tradition to grasp, because it relies on a dizzying subversion of the contrast between the objective and inculcative methods of education."

30. See FELDMAN, supra note 21.

31. Jane Praeger, "When Is a Tree Not a Tree," NEWSWEEK, December 21, 1998, 12.

32. See Note: The Establishment Clause and Religion in Child Custody Disputes: Factoring Religion in the Best Interest Equation, 82 Mich. L. Rev. 1702 (1984); Donald L. Beschle, God Bless the Child? The Use of Religion as a Factor in Child Custody and Adoption Proceedings, 58 FORDHAM L. REV. 383 (1989). The question of what type of harm is sufficient to permit consideration of religion is the basic point of difference among family law jurisdictions. See Drobac, supra note 13. Drobac does identify a few cases where harm of some sort is not required, id. at 1639–1640. Drobac herself takes the traditional liberal position: she argues that any consideration of religion in a custody cases is unconstitutional.

33. Quiner v. Quiner, 59 Cal. Rptr. 503 (1967).

34. Id.

35. Id.

36. Id.

37. Id.

38. Id. An alternative standard is the one articulated in In re Marriage of Hadeen, 27 Wash. App. 566, 619 P.2d 374 (1980): "We hold that the requirement of a reasonable and substantial likelihood of immediate or future impairment best accommodates the general welfare of the child and the free exercise of religion by the parents." 619 P.2d at 382.

39. 111 N.C. App. 712, 433 S.E. 2d 770 (1993); rev'd on other grounds, 337 N.C. 397, 445 S.E. 2d 901 (1994). See Gary M. Miller, Balancing the Welfare of Children with the Rights of Parents: Petersen v. Rogers and the Role of Religion in Custody Disputes, 73 N.C. L. REV. 1271, 1273 (1995).

40. Petersen, 111 N.C. App. at 699.

41. Id. at 714.The case was ultimately reversed by the North Carolina Supreme Court on other grounds. Petersen v. Rogers, 3777 N.C. 397 (1994).

42. Petersen, 111 N.C. App. at 722.

43. See, e.g., Birnbaum,v. Birnbaum, 211 Cal. App. 3d 1508, 260 Cal. Rptr. 210, 1989. The court noted with approval the fact that the father, to whom it awarded physical custody, wanted to send his children to a school "blessed with adequate resources to provide extensive extracurricular and honor course and music lessons...." Id.

44. E.g., In Re Marriage of Carney, 24 Cal. 3d 725 (1979).

45. See, e.g., Garska v. McCoy, 167 W.Va. 59 (1981) in which a trial judge awarded custody of a child to his father, despite the fact that the child had been raised exclusively by his mother, because the father was "better able to provide financial support and maintenance than the natural mother" and "has a somewhat better command of the English language than the natural mother." My characterization of the trial judge's reasoning as "bad" of course reflects my own subjective bias.

46. The tension between the free exercise clause and the establishment clause has been recognized by religion scholars. Whenever courts give someone a free exercise right, as courts do in custody and visitation cases, they are arguably conferring a benefit and thus favoring one religion, in violation of the establishment clause.

47. See, e.g., Deborah Marks, Religious Freedom v. Parental Responsibility Determinations, 1998 FLORIDA BAR JOURNAL July/August 1998; Beschle, supra note 32 at 401; Drobac, supra note 13.

48. This was the standard utilized in Quiner v. Quiner.

49. See Drobac, supra note 13. Drobac actually identifies three categories of harm, but most case law recognizes only two categories.

50. See "For God's Snakes," TULSA WORLD, Sunday, December 6, 1998 at A-2. The article describes a custody battle between two sets of grandparents. Both the children's parents died of snakebites. At a preliminary hearing, the judge told the children's paternal grandparents, who continue to handle poisonous snakes, that he needed to determine whether their snake handling would harm the children. Temporary custody was given to the maternal grandparents, who testified that the children woke up in cold sweats from nightmares about snakes.

51. See, e.g., State v. Perricone, 37 N.J. 463, 181 A2d 751 (1962), cert. denied 371 U.S. 890 (1962).

52. This belief is often manifested in ways many people would find incredible. The following quotation describes the death of a snake-handling minister:

> Brown doesn't even flinch when the rattler sinks one fang into the base of his left middle finger. If he is scared, it doesn't show."God don't ever change," he says, his voice ever so slightly less forceful than before. "God don't ever fail and He never will."... Brown starts to fail. His head is down and he swallows hard. Brown raises both hands in the air. His friends hold him for a few seconds, then lower him to the floor.... Someone asks Brown if he wants a doctor. He shakes his head and points to the sky.

"For God's Snakes," supra note 50.

53. Zummo v. Zummo, 394 Pa. Super. 30, 574 A2d 1130.

54. Id. at 30 (1990).

55. Carl Schneider, Religion and Child Custody, 25 U. MICH. J.L. REFORM 879, 902–3 (1992).

56. Smith, supra note 13 at 821.

57. See Linda J. Lacey, The White Man's Law and the American Indian Family in the Assimilation Era, 40 ARK. L. REV. 327, 356–364 (1987).

58. STANLEY FISH, THERE'S NO SUCH THING AS FREE SPEECH, AND IT'S A GOOD THING, TOO 137 (1994).

59. Fish, Mission Impossible, supra note 12 at 2332.

60. See, e.g., PIERRE SCHLAG, LAYING DOWN THE LAW: MYSTICISM, FETISHISM AND THE AMERICAN LEGAL MIND 17–41 (1996). As Schlag puts it, "Normative legal thought . . . cannot wait to reduce worldviews, attitudes, demonstrations, provocations, and thought itself to norms. In short, it cannot wait to tell *you* (or somebody else) what to do." Id. at 28.

61. The obvious objection to this recommendation is that courts cannot consider religion as a factor in family law cases without violating the First Amendment. However, as almost every commentator has recognized, the current Supreme Court's jurisprudence in the area of law and religion is hopelessly confused and contradictory. Almost any result is possible in a given case, provided the acceptable arguments are made. The argument that must be made in family law cases is that the welfare of children is a compelling state interest. Courts have consistently required medical treatment for children whose parents' religious beliefs forbid this treatment. This action is a clear infringement on the parents' right to practice their religious beliefs, but the courts have been willing to do it to protect the children.

62. This approach is taken from Elizabeth Scott's sensible proposal that custody arrangements after divorce should replicate as much as possible parenting patterns in the predivorce family. Elizabeth S. Scott, Pluralism, Parental Preference, and Child Custody, 80 CAL. L. REV. 615 (1992).

Chapter 22

There Can Be Only One

Law, Religion, Grammar, and Social Organization in the United States

Larry Catá Backer

I begin with a mantra of modern America:

> *Law and "religion" can peacefully coexist as equals in American society. American society can support the rule of law, and simultaneously "religion" can prosper, as long as each is placed in its respective and independent realms. In this way, "law" and "religion" can "accommodate" each other. The only item up for discussion is the manner in which this mutual equal accommodation is to be implemented.*

This pablum reeks of a mindless sentimentality reminiscent of the worst excesses of Victorian hypocrisy. Such is the sort of delusional fantasy that seeks reality through the repetition of mantras of falsehoods. This sort of exercise serves only to distort and ultimately destroy the basis on which this Republic is sustained.

Reality paints a very different picture. Every society is ordered through systems of norms. These norms can be supplied by law, Religion, or grammar—but not all three, or for that matter, any two.

Law and Religion

- cannot coexist peacefully *as equals* within the American Republic;
- cannot accommodate each other with equal dignity;
- do not occupy independent realms;
- *must* occupy the same space, one subordinate to the other.

Religion, as a social ordering system, once stood as the foundation of the cultural structuring of American society; law serves that role today. Today Religion, no longer a social ordering system, is limited by and can be understood only through the social structuring or ordering that law imposes.

> The *R*eligion of which I speak here is to be distinguished from *r*eligion. *R*eligion connotes *communities of faith* bound by fully formed formal integrated belief systems. Such systems may include more or less fully formed codes of everyday conduct derived from the tenets of the community's beliefs. This is what we normally think of when we hear the words Catholic, Methodist, Muslim, or Jew. The other—*r*eligion—is the more amorphous; it implies systems of religious sentiment which can be personal

> or collective, free floating or coercive, open or exclusive. The former is a subset of the latter. All Religion can be deemed to be expressions of personal religious sensibilities. But amorphous religious sensibilities do not necessarily constitute Religion.
>
> The basic building blocks of social ordering—law, Religion, and grammar—all share the singular property of creating basic rules that can operate as a social common sense, that is, that can function on the social body as the autonomic nervous system functions in the human body. Though all three exist in every society, each society must choose one of them as the basis for its social ordering. In the United States that ordering is now the function of law, with Religion and grammar accorded subordinate dignity.

The three exist in every society, though only one provides core social structure. The relationships among them are both circular and hierarchic. These relationships exclude and tolerate. These relationships expose the chameleon nature of those objects upon which society builds its structures. More precisely, what is exposed is the tenuousness of the labels Religion, law, and grammar, for each of them is precisely the others. And at any point in time, in any particular place, there can be just one.

> The Federal Constitution creates the grammar in which law "rules" as a formal matter over a system whose underlying structure is founded on Religion.

Neither the rule of law nor the relegation of Religion to the status of object and servant to the law is accidental nor superficial; this we imposed on ourselves at a time when the meaning of the separation was more benign to Religion and served the religious foundation of the nation.

> Religion and Law are Incompatible as Joint Social Structuring Forces. Though each can be accorded great dignity, only one of them can serve as the source of social order.

Religion and law may not jointly form the rock on which to build our society. The choice of one requires the denaturing of the other. At the time of the founding of the Republic, the choice made in the United States was to denature law, which was to support the norms derived from our foundation in Religion. Since the middle of this century, we have chosen to denature Religion, reducing it to a collection of sentiments that can act (in sheep's clothing) to advise law and otherwise neutralizing its effect on norm making by relegating it to its own separate (and subordinate) space.

> Religion IS Different; it can never be merely another basis for grounding law because it has been and remains a primary basis for ordering society. In the West, Religion is imprisoned in its own history and by the consequences of the society it constructed.

The project of American religionists is a counterrevolutionary exercise shot through with, and requiring for its success, a substantial amount of cultural amnesia; yet the amnesia is ineffective against old nonconformists, and the underlying pain of the failure of the older foundationalist construction of Western society is not erased.

> Overthrowing the "rule" of law would transform the substructure of American society.

The adoption of Religion as the American social foundation would fundamentally alter us in ways we have rejected. Its success would depend on the reinvention of Religion and the rejection of the primacy of law as an independent ordering principle.

> Law triumphs only in places of religious diversity; Religion remains foundational in places where one law and one religion are dominant or where one Religion is dominant in a space subject to overlapping systems of law; grammar triumphs only where multiple systems of law and Religion coexist.

The struggle among law, religion, and grammar for primacy as the ordering language of the social order has become increasingly complex. Even as law has assumed formal and actual dominance in the West, the web of linkages among and between systems of law has multiplied into a world network of layered systems of law. Religion has multiplied as well, attempting through ecumenism to create its own web of layered relations. What will emerge in any geographic space shared by these multiple laws and Religions can range from the merger of Iran, to the triumph of law in the American Republic, to the reemergence of feudal relationships, to the emergence of grammar as an ordering principle of social organization. The last describes the current international world order.

Theory

A. A Context for the Problem: Choosing Religion, Law, and Grammar as the Basis for Social Ordering

"In the beginning was the Word, and the Word was with God, and the Word was God" (John 1:1). From this Logos proceeded law, Religion, and grammar—*fiat lex, fiat ecclesia, fiat gramatica . . . fiat mundi!*

My examination of the Logos trinity as sociopolitical foundation will take some ironic inspiration from the perspective of midcentury Protestant biblical scholarship:

> The Bible is a "historical" literature in which God is proclaimed as the chief actor in history who alone gives history its meaning. To study the Bible in such a way as to make abstractions of its spiritual or moral teachings, divorced from the real context of their setting in time, is to turn the Bible into a book of aphorisms, full of nice sayings which the devil himself could believe and never find himself particularly handicapped either by the knowledge of them or by their repetition. (Wright and Fuller 1960 at xi)

Some Protestant commentators have tied the Stoic notion of Logos to the Book of Wisdom as well. They note that "the Stoic concept of the Logos (literally, "word"; here "reason") . . . is at once the divine reason within man, enabling him to acquire knowledge of the physical constitution of the world and its ways (Wisdom 7:15 ff.) and guiding him in his moral life (9:9b–13), and at the same time the principle of coherence immanent in the material universe (1:7; 7:24–27)" (Wright & Fuller 1960 at 248). Philosophers, of course, have been intimately involved in various attempts to map, to picture for us, this unifying Logos. For some, Logos has been transformed into Goethe's *Urphenomänen*, universal, unifying principles with or without the intervention of a Divinity (Curran 1998 at 72–73). "It is to the great and fundamental principles of society and civilization—to the common usage universally consented to, and mutually and reciprocally maintained—to the unceasing circulation of interest, which passing through its million channels, invigorates the whole mass of civilized man—it is to these things, . . . that the safety and prosperity of the individual and of the whole depends" (Paine [1792] 1945 at 193–94). For many in this modern age of identity and ethnicity, *Urphenomänen* is strictly of a community, universal within its own boundaries but bounded by other communities similarly founded. These notions nicely capture the idea of Logos, of social foundation that I explore here.

Religion, law, and grammar each represent the basis for an exclusive ordering of social reality within each discrete community, that is, for ordering the universe from which a community constructs its reality, its "common sense" of how "things" ought to be. All share critical basic characteristics. Each gives rise to systems of social organization. Each is normative. Each bounds the reality of a community, that is, each sets up the framework within which social problems can be conceived, solutions can be identified, and choices made. While each basis for social ordering can create significantly different normative structures and normative horizons for social behavior, each operates in a very similar fashion in relation to the community for which it supplies a social reality.

Law, Religion, and grammar are thus the three faces through which we construct our culture. Through law, Religion, and grammar we communicate, we apply, we define, we *enclose* our collective (conscious and unconscious) view of how each of us, and groups of us, must live in the world.

Religion: a system of belief, worship, or conduct derived from the word or command of an absolute authority (God) existing outside and superior to the community and the core principles that are imposed through formalized canons.

Law: a system of principles and rules based on a community's sense of itself and containing within it the norms of governance established and enforced by those able to enforce them on the community that has submitted to them.

Grammar: a system of rules of conduct for communication based on the study of its word structure and arrangement, which conforms to evolving usage or which determines such evolution.

Law, Religion, and grammar are mutually self-reinforcing and self-referencing. They create a complete closed system within which each unique culture achieves form and life. Law, Religion, and grammar are each, in this sense, the sort of autopoietic systems that produce and reproduce their own elements by the interaction of their elements (Teubner 1988 at 3). These systems operate as organisms in which the self-consciousness of each is possible only in relation to itself (Luhmann 1988–89 at 139). Consider, again, in this light, the beginning of the Gospel of John: "In the beginning was the Word, and the Word was with God, and the Word was God. He was in the beginning with God; all things were made through him, and without him was not anything made that was made" (John 1:1–3).

That law, Religion, and grammar provide an exclusive means of social ordering does not mean that in the presence of one, the others do not exist within a community. No society exists without law, Religion, and grammar. However, the choosing of one as the ordering principle creates hierarchy, with one serving as a social "prime" and the others accorded a subordinate dignity. This ordering "prime" functions as the social grammar of a community, leaving the other two as objects of its regulation. Tom Paine captures this idea, and its consequences, nicely with respect to systems in which Religion has pride of place:

> The adulterous connection of church and state, wherever it has taken place, whether Jewish, Christian or Turkish, had so effectively prohibited, by pains and penalties, every discussion upon established creeds, and upon first principles of religion, that until the system of government should be changed, those subjects could not be brought fairly and openly before the world, but that whenever this should be done, a revolution in the system of religion would follow. (Paine [1793] 1945 at 286)

As embodiments of order based on shared subterranean cultural assumptions, each serves as a mirror of the others. Each is the active force within its own foundation. But each distorts the others even as each captures the reflections of the others. Each converts, that is, digests the others within its own sphere. As such, law, Religion, and grammar also exist as an object of regulation and as a vehicle for the implementation of the norms extracted by a particular community from the particular regime of communication that that community has imposed on itself. Consequently, the label that we give the ordering of reality a community chooses for itself determines the direction of the foundation constructed with each. This is precisely the point of departure for this essay—direction is everything.

Law foundationalism arose after 1500 and "marked a shift from classical to rational natural law by separating law from theological speculations and then placing law upon a foundation of utilitarianism based upon human wants" (S. Herman 1984 at 602). The rule of law provides the prime animating force. It constructs the limits of Religion and grammar to intrude on the regulation of the body politic. Systems founded on the rule of law, Religion, and grammar are the subordinate principles through which the primacy of law is reinforced. That is, Religion and grammar are bent to serve the primary foundational ordering principle—law. The bending of Religion to law is accomplished by regulation, and by what we in the United States refer to as "disestablishment." Disestablishment serves to legitimate the rule of law by posing as a manifestation of the democratic principle at the core of rule of law systems in the West. The bending of grammar is

> not only to provide a medium of expression for the world view and mental habits proper to the devotees of Ingsoc [the dominant ideology], but also to make all other modes of thought impossible. It was intended that when Newspeak [the official language of Oceania] had been adopted once and for all and Oldspeak [Standard English] forgotten, a heretical thought—that is, a thought diverging from the principles of Ingsoc—should be literally unthinkable, at least so far as thought is dependent on words. (Orwell [1949] 1992 at 312)

The separation of law from theological speculations permits law, as the source of normative rules, to treat Religion and grammar (the means of communicating rule-of-law norms) as objects upon which the normative enterprise of law works. Religion is confined within the social space created and supported by law. Religion is free only within this space, the borders of which are not within its control. Grammar is bounded by the construction of the basic law of the land (our federal Constitution) or the central animating idea on which the social order is constructed (for example, the supremacy of the *volk* or the dictatorship of the proletariat). In a sense, we come close to understanding the status of grammar in rule-of-law societies when we are heard to say we are speaking like lawyers. This special language, this language of law, provides an ordering function on a secondary level. Grammar preserves the normative project of law and provides law its language. The federal Constitution is our primer. This configuration is the essence of the American Republic. To some extent, the rule-of-law principle forms the basis of systems of international human rights norms such as the European Convention for the Protection of Human Rights and Fundamental Freedoms (November 4, 1950, 213 U.N.T.S. 222). Yet this configuration is also the essence of totalitarian states—Stalin's USSR, for example, in which law held pride of place.

For communities in which Religion is the basis for social ordering, law and grammar are the objects through which religion is communicated. Law and grammar are the principal means through which religion is regulated and expressed. In ecclesiastical usage, all divine commandments are law. Each is formulated and regulated through the filter of Religion. Religion provides the rules for the grammar of communication and the basis for the imposition of rule structures. This configuration is the essence of geographies such as the Iranian state after 1979. The state proceeds from and expresses a belief (or faith) in some power that controls or directs or has a plan for human destiny. Law and grammar are bent to the religious enterprise. Law (Shari'a) is both the object of religion and the means of its expression. Grammar proceeds from religion (the word of God as expressed in the Holy Books) and absorbs all expression within its confines. In a variant of this model, the state is viewed as the "secular" arm of the administrative organizations of the Religion, the function of which is defense, the protection of property, and use of its legislative and police powers to implement the norms of Religion. Religious norms are usually transcendent, absolute, and eternal. Flexibility is directly related to the possibility that either the priestly caste or some other authoritative segment of the social order has reserved for itself the power to interpret the "Word of God." The greater the power of interpretation, the more flexibly applied the divine norms.

For systems based on grammar, law and Religion provide the exemplars of the workings of the grammatical project. We understand law and Religion only within the confines of our ability to communicate through the constrictors of signs. Animated by an idea, or group of ideas (the Word), the language of the state (law) and religion are contorted to the service of this idea, even as they become the subject of regulation in the service of the Word. The structure of communication drives law and "religion" understood here in its broadest sense. Word meaning becomes contextual and subject to manipulation. This is a malleable language of the sort contorted by rival factions during the Corcyrean Revolution (Thucydides [411 B.C.] 1951) at 189–91), or reinvented as "newspeak" in Orwell's classic 1984 (Orwell [1949] 1992). Yet grammar as a primal ordering principle provides a weak foundation indeed. It is the recourse of communities that cannot or will not be torn apart but in which no other foundation can claim a decisive supremacy. The international community provides the best example of a regime of grammar. The United Nations provides a fifty-year example of the project of the construction of a common language on which to build norm structures such as "human rights." The extreme reluctance of many communities to subscribe to the tentative international attempts at a common language of things such as the treatment of women in society, attest to the fragility of grammar to mediate between foundations. But emerging multicultural states also provide an example of growing importance in this era of permeable borders. States constructed as metacommunities of multicultural groups also evidence the fragility of grammar as foundation. The implosion of Yugoslavia into its foundationally different component parts—Catholic Croatia, Orthodox Serbia, heterodox Bosnia (with its rule of law), and (the attempted separation of) Muslim Kosovo—serves as a parable and warning.

Law, Religion, and grammar, as I have suggested, are the key ingredients in creating the foundation of any world, or at least the way people "know" or "understand" the world. But this understanding varies from foundation to foundation, from community to community. Moreover, choices, even foundational choices, are dynamic. Such choices are even more dynamic in the face of the *possibility of choice.* Stability is a function of ignorance. A community questions the basis of its choice of political ordering only when alternatives, *successful alternatives,* stand before it. Communities existing in isolation have the most stable foundations. There have been many examples of communities, especially both traditional (Imperial China, Imperial Japan, Iran) and revolutionary (Cambodia, Soviet Union, Maoist China) communities, that have sought to isolate themselves to protect themselves from the impurities of the outside. The socialist phobia with the corruption of Western bourgeois culture, the Saudi fear of contamination, the recent attempts by Zambian society to rid itself of the corrupting influences of the West by reintroducing traditional notions with respect to the status of women and the regulation of sexual conduct—all suggest this protective mechanism. As communication increases, as a common grammar is fashioned, foundations can be compared, foundations can be questioned, challenged—and overturned. For those, in every society, who fear change, this can be a very destabilizing prospect indeed.

Consequently, to understand the relationship between law, Religion, and grammar, to understand how *those* relationships are directly dependent on the choice every society makes as to which among them is to serve as the principal basis of its social ordering, is to unlock the mysteries of social understanding. To grasp the ways in which each forms a facet of the others is to encounter the limitations built into the weaving together of our society's law, Religion, and grammar. This is not to suggest that non-European or other systems of law, Religion, and grammar do not enjoy the same sorts of relationships. Clearly they do—Mao's China, the mullahs' Iran, and Castro's Cuba provide spectacular examples of such constructions and their effects.

The dynamics of objectification and subordination are similar irrespective of the foundation society chooses. The major differences are the identity of the animating social force and the particularities of the way in which the others are regulated as objects and bent to the purposes of the principal animating force. The existence of the foundation, however, is not to be avoided.

B. Foundation in the United States

We in the West, and in the United States in particular, have sought to have our cake and eat it too. We chose as our social foundation the nominal, the fictive, framework of law. Yet this foundation of law we permeated with and made beholden to an even deeper foundational choice. We held as beyond dispute the primacy of the Christian religious foundation of that legal foundation. Secular law was to be the official basis of the ordering of our world; religion its object and handmaid, living in her own chamber and presiding over her own adherents in the space made available to her (Locke [1689] 1937). The understanding, however, was that only schismatic theology was to be relegated to the world of the subordinate. *Practice* of the Christian religions was to be subordinate to the generality of law, but Christian teaching was to be supreme; law was to remain subordinate to the fundamental belief structures of the Christian religions. We were to remain a nation constructed on the rock of Christian biblical foundationalism with respect to which there was unquestioned agreement of its naturalness (Backer 1997b). "The vast majority of Americans assumed that theirs was a Christian, i.e. Protestant country, and they automatically expected that government would uphold the commonly agreed on Protestant ethos and morality" (Curry 1986 at 219). We said one thing and meant another at a time when the meaning *and limits* of our foundational nation-building subterfuge was clear and well understood.

But we have truly reaped the whirlwind. For the rock of biblical foundationalism has been shattered by the staff of it servant, law. We now have inherited our structural choice in full measure. The nominal structure created, the pseudofoundation of law overlaying the true foundation of (the Christian) Religions, has become our foundation *in fact*. Like so much dross within the crucible of our sociocultural migration, Religion has fallen away as the undercoating of our fictive legal foundationalism. It is victim not only to the antipode—law—but to the theological struggles over the true source of belief as non-Christian Religions vie with the old monopoly religious group for the right to serve as the "true source" of religious sociocultural foundation in the United States.

Now *here* have Religions become truly the object of law and law's subordinate. Law is now the normative foundation of our society. Law is the filter through which we see and understand our culture. Law is the sieve through which we express our religion and our grammar. Law is the way in which we have chosen to order our political society. Traditionalists howl at the betrayal this represents.

So is joined here in the United States the battle of law, grammar, and Religion. The contest is foundational: On which rock shall our society be built? Consequently, the impulse to reduce the relationship of law, grammar, and Religion to the discourse of rights, or to debates on the repercussions of grammar (original intent and statutory construction), and constitutional niceties divorced from the context in which sociopolitical norms are made and maintained is to turn the relationship into a parody of itself, of use only to scholastics completely oblivious to the realities of American life.

Yet the true battlefield is a distorting plain. Religion comes onto a field occupied by law. It must use the grammar of law to wage its campaign. Thus have we seen the rise of the canticle of religion within our law. We plead for religious convictions within political and legal choices (Greenawalt 1988). We speak of "love and power" (Perry 1991). We argue that law does not exist except as a foundation, that it merely provides an expression of religion through the grammar of law (*cf.* Dworkin 1986 at 90), a sophistry pointing to the world of the mullahs. Yet, the tools of law that Religion must use evidence its subordination and its objectification in the social structure built on the rock of law.

The struggle between law and Religion to occupy the place of *ordering principle* of reality in the United States is being fought on the rock of our legal edifice. The battles reveal the objectification and subordination of Religion and grammar within a regimen of the foundationalist legal order in the United States. The battles illuminate the stakes involved. Should the rock of law be shattered, the boulders of our new (old) civilization await a rebuilding, for a foundation we shall have.

> If the community of I (and I and I) know not that I have chosen the rock upon which to build the world,
>
> If I believe that this rock must be, that there is nothing more basic or sturdy upon which to build, the world in which I order my life would be "natural," I would have no reason to recognize, much less question, that fundamental choice.
>
> Yet, when I can be brought to question this basis, the rock upon which I build my world is irremediably shaken.
>
> Now must I defend the basis of my essence as a person, or a clan, or a community, or a nation.
>
> Now may those who question, who are discomfited by the essence of my community, seek sanctuary in another way.
>
> They would undo all our community builds; they would break the rock on which stands our community; they would substitute their own foundation for mine and that of mine.
>
> How much more is this true when I seek to establish a community from out of another! For I have, in my time shattered the rock on which stood the house of my parent, and built my own foundation which I labeled—"Eternal."
>
> Now must I meet my enemies on the rock of my foundation.

Application: Shifting the Basis of Social Ordering in the United States

The disestablishment of Religion in the basic law of the United States provides a concrete site where the battle over foundation and influence has been fought in this country. An examination of the foundational place of law and Religion in the United States will help to illustrate the relationships described in the prior section. What emerges is an understanding of the fact of foundation shifting in this country, and that the *institutional forms* of social ordering need not change in order to effect great changes in the social foundation. To look at the institutional structure of the United States since 1789 is to see an institutional framework that, on its surface, has remained substantially stable. To look underneath the surface, however, is to encounter the "struggles beneath tranquil surface waters" (Greenawalt 1998 at 1905) and huge shifts in the source of our normative social base.

A. Religion as an Object of the Structuring Project of Law in the Federal Constitution

It is a commonplace notion that Religion has been disestablished as a formal matter in the United States. Ours is, as we enjoy telling ourselves and any who will listen elsewhere, a society founded under and bounded by rule of *law*. Formal disestablishment was enacted as a constitutional limitation on the federal government through the First Amendment. This disestablishment was extended to the states, according to the courts at least, through the Fourteenth Amendment.

We also understand that our legal culture has extended the reach of this formal disestablishment well beyond that minimally required under the Constitution. The result is a deep and enduring deprivileging of Religion as a normative basis for decision making. Religion is relegated to *object*. As *res*, it is inconceivable to think of Religion as part of the *grammar* that is bent to the construction of a norm structure we label "law." Indeed, the only (though significant) privileging of Religion in our public culture is possible precisely because it is identified and regulated as a special sort of *res* (Howe 1965). Still, the substantial deprivileging of Religion as authoritative has troubled academics, especially in this generation. "If an unspoken and irregular but nonetheless powerful prohibition excluding religion from public and especially legal discourse has been in effect for some time, then those of us who are interested in "law and religion' need to pay attention to that phenomenon" (Smith 1998b at 227).

This is a standard discursive stance, popular, even mandatory, among legal academics. This aesthetic convolution veils—no, it distorts—the essential nature and interrelationships of law, Religion, and grammar.

The American approach to Religion is not haphazard or serendipitous. Neither is the approach accidental. Rather, de facto disestablishment reflects a basic normative choice made at the time of the founding of our Republic. The discursive quality of the Establishment Clause itself serves to compel treatment of Religion primarily as an *object of law*. That we understand that religion is something that is acted on can be readily seen in the recent attempts to constitutionalize institutionalized prayer in public places. I refer here, of course, to the constitutional amendment concerning public prayer, a recent example of which provides: "To secure the people's right to acknowledge God: The right to pray or acknowledge religious belief, heritage or tradition on public property, including public schools, shall not be infringed. The Government shall not compel joining in prayer, initiate or compose school prayers, discriminate against or deny a benefit on account of religion" (Seelye 1997).

The hornbook of our grammar, the modern foundationalist grammar of law, is set forth in our basic law—the federal and state constitutions. The poetics, the construction and aesthetics, of our basic law imposes its grammar on religion and on grammar itself. Both become objects, subject to the will, to the needs, postulates, and outlook, of law.

> Even when it does not dictate the result in particular cases, legal doctrine has the power to orient and direct the kind of discourse in which those cases are debated and decided. . . . [I]t can powerfully influence the way the debate is framed. (Smith 1994 at 525)

The Constitution itself serves this discursive purpose. It has a strong discourse-orienting power that has crafted the framework within which Americans have bound ourselves to think about Religion. With respect to Religion, the Federal Constitution has oriented Religion as a *noun* within the grammar of the law.

This orientating power is especially apparent in the Religion Clauses of the First Amendment: "Congress shall make no law respecting an establishment of religion or prohibiting the free exercise thereof." The Religion Clauses orient Religion as an *object* of law. Those provisions gather up Religion as a bundle of issues involving worship by or through the state, and treats this bundle as a tangible *res.* I would argue tangible, at least as to its manifestations. But it is with respect to the regulation of those manifestations with which the law is concerned.

Religion, as a body corporate, is separable and distinct from law. Indeed, as Justice O'Connor and Justice Scalia clearly illustrate in their dueling opinions in *City of Boerne* (City of Boerne v. Flores, 117 S. Ct. 2157 [1997]), our American colonial lawmakers, as well as the Founders, were concerned with Religion (as a formally constituted *res*) only as an object upon which law might act (*see id.*, at 2172–76 [Scalia, J., concurring] and 2176–85 [O'Connor, J., dissenting]). Even in an age of great deference to Religion in all aspects of life, the American approach appeared to be "that the appropriate response to conflicts between the civil law and religious scruples was, where possible, accommodation of religious conduct" (*id.*, at 2183 [O'Connor, J., dissenting]). Accommodation is a curious word—one that does not suggest the incorporation of Religion in the process of everyday lawmaking. Rather, it suggests a political largesse, whether or not ensconced in our Constitution, that permitted a superior or foundational force upon a lesser one. Indeed, as Justice Scalia noted, "Religious exercise shall be permitted so long as it does not violate general laws governing conduct" (*id.*, at 2173 [Scalia, J., concurring]).

Indeed, this discursive quality of the Religion Clauses themselves follows the pattern laid down by our English progenitors as they struggled to effect religious peace in the realm after almost two centuries of strife. In a society in which Christian principles as the moral philosophical substructure of law was unquestioned, Religion became noteworthy only in the guise of *practices.* One need look little further than John Locke for an understanding of the basis on which our constitutional discourse is framed (that is, bounded, and thus bounded, limited) (Locke [1689] 1937). The freedom to exercise Religion was understood as the right "to do only what was not lawfully prohibited" (West 1990 at 624).

Yet, understand that Religion was treated as *res* not because of a desire to disestablish "religious principles." Rather, the reason implied quite the opposite rationale. Religion could be treated as *res* in a society in which Christian principles were firmly and unconsciously entrenched in the interstices of everyday lawmaking. Religious disestablishment of the kind described by Professor Smith becomes noteworthy only because civil decision making has strayed from the traditional religious principles that underlay lawmaking through the end of the Second World War. Only in an America in which the normative substructure of systems of civil law have strayed from those of the juridico-moral systems of the old dominant religious discourse could disestablishment at the level of mundane lawmaking become *visible*. "Consensual pluralism at mid-century had been marked by a simply envisioned matrix of religious groups. Succeeding and replacing this was a more complex but still informal polity, one that did not focus on religious groups" (Marty 1997 at 101).

For Religion to form an independent part of the discursive paradigm of law while at the same time existing as the object of that paradigm would appear inconsistent with the discourse of our basic law. "[G]overnment's ability to enforce generally applicable prohibitions of socially harmful conduct . . . cannot depend on measuring the effects of a governmental action on a religious objector's spiritual development" (Employment Div., Dept. of Human Resources of Oregon v. Smith, 110 S. Ct. 1595, 1603 [1990]). In a society in which multiple Religions vie for the allegiance of the population, the singular law that unites them all cannot be placed in a situation where law is applied only as and to the extent that no Religion objects. In a system in which Religion forms an object of law, however, such a situation is extremely subversive, and on that basis ultimately intolerable. To permit individuals to ignore laws of general applicability where such a laws conflicted with practices central to such individuals' Religions is therefore to be resisted. It "is not within the judicial ken to question the centrality of particular beliefs or practices to a faith, or the validity of particular litigants' interpretations of those creeds" (*id.*, at 1604).

City of Boerne also well demonstrates the power of our discursive model, in which Religion is relegated to the subordinate role of object of regulation. In a case in which the extent of the enforcement power of the Fourteenth Amendment was ostensibly the issue, Religion was treated as the object of the regulatory power of the legislature. Thus, the central questions of that case revolved around the powers of the legislature incidentally to burden "religion," or to permit the legislature to allow "Religion" the power to "burden" law within the federal system and all of its component parts (City of Boerne v. Flores, 117 S. Ct. 2157 [1997]). The Religious Freedom Restoration Act of 1993 ("RFRA," 107 Stat. 1488, 42 U.S.C. §§ 2000bb et seq.), the statute at issue, appeared to mandate the use of Religion in the grammar of law in a limited range of legislative activity—when legislation might burden an individual's "exercise" of "Religion." A majority of the Supreme Court substantially agreed that the intrusion of Religion into the grammar of law, even in this area of most direct affect on and concern to Religion, was beyond the power given the Congress under the federal Constitution, even as amended by Section 5 of the Fourteenth Amendment. Indeed, Justice Stevens was concerned that the RFRA amounted to a preference for "Religion" over "irreligion" and, as such, established Religion in violation of the First Amendment (*City of Boerne*, at 2172 [Stevens, J., concurring]). For Justice Scalia, concurring in part, and Justice O'Connor, dissenting, the issue was the extent of state power to burden affirmatively or incidentally the "right to participate in religious practices and conduct . . . even when such conduct conflicts with a neutral, generally applicable law" (*id.*, at 2176 [O'Connor, J., dissenting]). For Justice O'Connor, Religion would prevail as the foundation of law's limits. For the majority, and especially for Justice Scalia, law triumphs to regulate its subordinate object—that matrix of practices and beliefs we understand as Religion.

If this discursive power emanates from our basic law, then it follows that the antiestablishment of Religion within a foundation in which legal discourse is paramount should seem unproblematical. Indeed, some commentators have demonstrated the strength of this necessary objectification of Religion as it has affected the curricular structure of legal education almost from its inception. "But the important point is that even when religion *is* considered, it typically appears more as a specialty item or a distinctive type of problem, *not* as a valuable way of thinking about law and legal issues generally" (Smith 1998b at 212). Thus understood, we did not blunder into antiestablishmentarianism. To have Religion work as a *verb* within the grammar of law would require a sharp departure from our discursive orientation of constitutional theory, which may, at some point subvert the framework within which we interpret our basic law.

This is perhaps the intuitive understanding of writers such as Scott Idleman (Idleman 1993 at 434) and judges like Raul Gonzalez (Gonzalez 1996 at 1148). Each considers the use of "religion" as something important for the process of lawmaking. But each reserves this active use of "religion" to shape lawmaking for the exceptional case. In a sense, they seem to suggest that Religion remains an object unless a matter directly impacts on an area of direct concern to the ability of Religion to conduct its "internal affairs."

To fail to recognize the discursive quality of our Constitution, and the limits this quality suggests, especially in the guise of the Religion Clauses, may lead one to overstate the importance or nature of the lack of Religion as a discursive element of lawmaking. We accepted the necessary repercussions of characterizing Religion as object with the crafting of the federal Constitution. Such a characterization was no accident; neither is the resulting disestablishment at the level of the prosaic. Any change of this state of affairs may well require deliberate and constitutional remaking. Lawmaking based on a Judeo-Christian normative substructure (and Religion as formal object may be treated as *res* for law) can no longer be taken for granted. This cultural transformation of (ir)religious normativity may impact on the way those with religious sensibilities must approach lawmaking. What makes this difficult is that it requires us to abandon ways of thinking about law that were commonplace and deeply held since the time of the European colonization of North America.

B. The Incompatibility of Religion and Law as Joint Social Structuring Forces

Much of the effort of late-twentieth-century American commentators has been to move away from a conceptualization of Religion as an object of law. In its place, we seek to substitute Religion as the foundation of the *grammar of our law*. However, when we seek to stretch the utility of Religion, that is, when we attempt to make Religion serve as the foundation of the grammar of our law while retaining law as the primary foundation of our social order, *we must cheat*. We do this by pretending that we do not speak of traditional Religion at all, and therefore do not intend to imperil the standing of law as the bedrock of our social order. Instead, we hide Religion behind the cloak of religion, that is, of any one of an infinite number of amorphous personal belief systems. Yet, to engage in that enterprise is to belittle the normative significance of Religion as *independent imperial systems of law*.

I have suggested that when we attempt to treat Religion within law as something other than as an object of regulation, we "go against the grain" of the discursive scheme of the federal Constitution. In this section, I submit that when we seek to stretch the utility of Religion, that is, when we attempt to make Religion serve as part of the grammar of law, we must invariably fail . . . *unless we cheat*. To cheat is to equate private subjective religious sensibilities with Religion, and to confer on the comprehensive and exclusive systems of Religion the same benign indulgence that we would accord these private subjective sensibilities. The result is an intolerable state of affairs where incompatible systems battle, using as "fronts" the personal subjective "religious" and "civil" sensibilities of individual proxies. Our civil law began as an aping of religious law; it incorporated the basic postulates of religious law. To the extent that we have begun to reject that model (as we have begun to reject the dominance of Christian moral philosophy as the root of law in this century), religious sensibilities may of necessity offer not merely a different approach to lawmaking but an incompatible one.

Religion, after all, comprises wholly developed systems of laws, as comprehensive as anything devised by the secular state. Systems of Canon Law, of Talmudic Law, of Shari'a have from time to time, and to this day, functioned as separate, independent bases on which life and society are regulated. Law, in these systems, is the form of expression, existing as the means of communicating norms that proceed from the grammar emanating from the Word as received by His servants on Earth. Religion as legal codex and jurisprudence demands an exclusive allegiance every bit as jealous as that traditionally required by the state in civil matters. To merge such systems requires the disappearance of one in favor of the other. This is not mere theory. The American academic legal community has finally begun to taste the ramifications of this reality with the attempt by the Catholic Church to secure for itself greater control of the content of legal education in the United States (On Catholic Universities: Ex Corde Ecclesiae 1990). While academic freedom is preserved for law, religion is to be recaptured for the Catholic Church. It is possible, though, to define most law as substantially a component of religion, that is, flowing out of and directly related to the theological norm boundaries of central concern to the Catholic Church. On that basis, of course, almost all law is reduced to the servant of Religion. Indeed, A[t]he commitment of the religiously affiliated university, and with it, the religiously affiliated law school, to foundational values beyond open inquiry, sometimes places it at odds with the concept of the university underlying the AAUP's [American Association of University Professors] notion of academic freedom" (Wagner & Ryan 1995 at 516).

Despite the incompatibility of systems of law and Religion, Americans especially have developed a taste for the conflation of the incompatible. We have become quite adept at substituting a notion of religious sensibilities, and politically expedient religious moral philosophy, for what used to pass for Religion. We have the temerity to do this in the name of Religion. Yet to do this is to pretend that *R*eligion does not exist, at least in the sense commonly understood at the beginning of the Republic. Americans know that this complete system of law—Religion—does exist. We persist, however, in this strange enterprise. Increasingly, we have chosen to substitute *r*eligion for Religion when describing the relationship of "Religion" to civil "legal culture."

But such recasting ignores the traditional normative significance of Religion in its own right as independent, fully formed systems of *law*. Such Religion does not blend into our law, it tends to supplant or retreat. And the problem is not ameliorated because the "results" under each may be similar. Religion has become "object" in our system in order to avoid such "conflict of laws" problems. We early on in our history chose to avoid having to engage in the political battles implied by any necessity of "compar[ing] secular contract, tort and property law with Catholic, Protestant, Mormon, Jewish and Muslim versions of the same subject" (Smith 1998b at 218) and choosing a "winner" from inconsistent approaches. Consequently, treating "Religion" as "religion" in order to provide a place for it within the grammar of law merely finesses the problem without confronting it. Such can do little but create another site for potentially irresolvable conflict.

Yet the late twentieth century has seen the attempt to conflate religion and belief. Worse, this century has seen the attempt to loosen grace away from submission and obedience. "What we call religion typically amounts to a comprehensive way of perceiving and understanding life and the world; it affects everything." (Smith 1998b at 216; *cf.* Locke [1689] 1937 [on the separation of Christian culture from Christian doctrine]).

The notion of "religion" indeed has been deconstructed by academics in recent years. Some have intimated that any comprehensive system of belief may well be a "religion" under any inclusive legal definition of Religion. "A generous functional definition would seem to classify any deep rooted philosophy as religion, Marxism as well as Methodism" (Tribe 1988 at § 14-6, 182–83). Judge Adams has noted that "moral or patriotic views are not by themselves "religious,' but if they are pressed as divine law or a part of a comprehensive belief system that presents them as "truth,' they might well rise to the religious level" (Malnak v. Yogi, 592 F.2d 197, 209 [3d Cir. 1979] [Adams, J., concurring]; *but see* Choper 1982).

Traditionalists have attempted the same conflation, arguing that "secular humanism" is as much a religion as traditional monotheistic faiths (Lacey 1993 at 6–7;

Whitehead and Conlan 1978). These claims have made their way to the courts (Smith v. Board of Comm'rs, 827 F.2d 684 [11th Cir. 1987] [claim that textbooks promoted religion of "secular humanism"]). This is an ironic concession that traditional Religion no longer provides our social foundation—"something else" is doing so. If one's conceptual universe admits only Religion as an ordering principle of society, then it follows that whatever is the basis for societal ordering must be "religious"—and as such, a competitor within the realm of Religion. It is always hard to escape the conceptual boxes one builds for oneself!

A central problem has centered on the indeterminacy of the concept of religion. We cannot seem to agree on a formula for "knowing religion when we see it." The problem has been described as originating from the necessity of creating a definition useful in a world in which religious diaspora exist everywhere and where the old Religious definitions of "religion" have ceased to be definitive. The two basic methods of defining Religion take very different approaches. The *objective* approach looks to group norms to "find" religion. Religion is encountered as a community. Evidence of Religion centers on community—written doctrine or oral tradition, systems of rules or codes of behavior, mechanisms for policing conformity to community norms, and the like. The object is to make a determination that a requisite level of shared norms and beliefs exist so that, as an "objective" matter, it would be possible to say that a multigenerational community of believers exists. The *subjective* approach concentrates on the individual. Religion is not equated with community; religion is a function of evidence of the existence of some threshold set of coherent personal spiritual beliefs (Fallers Sullivan 1998).

Religion becomes a benign, individualized, subjective spiritualism. This modern view has become increasingly accepted in the West. Indeed, acceptance of the notion of the indeterminacy of religion is one of long standing in legal academia. Even the act of defining religion might, it has been said, violate the First Amendment (Weiss 1964 at 604; *cf.* Choper 1982, advocating definition of religion specific enough to help courts draw reasonable lines between religion and nonreligious belief systems). Winnifred Fallers Sullivan might have us pay more attention to the idea of religion as a sort of varied and shifting phenomenon (Fallers Sullivan 1998 at 454–58). We must, we are now told, discard the tendency to objective classification and adopt a subjective view of belief. Wrapped in the veil of subjectivity, we can more palatably embrace individual belief as spiritualism and spiritualism as Religion. The argument follows by persuading us that my personal belief ought to be accorded the same dignity and likened to the equivalent of, say, Islam, Catholicism, or Judaism. My moral philosophy ought to be accorded the same weight as the Shari'a, the Canon Law, or the Talmud. And all of this I ought to bring to my construction of the civil law; especially with respect to how the civil law embraces you. These notions are a basis of the defense of the teaching restrictions or bent of religiously affiliated schools, especially against the charge that such restrictions violate academic freedom. "Religiously sponsored law schools do not, as a rule, teach, but rather apply, the tenets of religion" (Wagner & Ryan 1995 at 516).

This notion of subjectivity as the basis of acknowledging "religious" belief is fundamentally right, as a matter of anthropology. It is certainly right as a matter of faith, that is, of faith understood (and this understanding should be absorbed in its fully ironic splendor) as the Calvinists would have us understand the concept, as grounded in "full and fixed certainty" (Calvin [1559] 1960). As a matter of the historical experience of America, however, such a definition may prove more dangerous than useful. It will serve as a cloaking device—to raise personal belief to a dizzying dignity while hiding the way in which the "personal" religious "sensibilities" of adherents of Religions with powerful and well-developed traditions of "law" actually exalt assimilation of the norms of the more influential of these communities. Think of it at the level of the mundane. When you speak as an individual, do I hear the collective voices of the group of which you are a member? I suspect that most of us will hear you as an individual and then weigh the value of your sentiments by the strength of the conformity of that view to those officially professed by the Religion to which you belong. In this context, for your audience, there may be no such thing as individual voices. Ironically, when you speak as an individual member of a minority Religion, the opposite may be true. A Muslim or Buddhist speaking in Idaho may well be vested with authority to speak officially for the entire Muslim or Buddhist community. This creates its own distortions.

Ironically, what this new "subjective" theoretics of the sociology of religion calls to mind is not so much late-twentieth-century pluralism as third-century Imperial Roman spiritual *anomie.*

> We can never be certain what was happening. But we can often guess what contemporaries thought was happening. We can see that the material troubles of their day had sharpened, without creating, their sense of unease both with the classical and the Christian explanations of man's function in society. Some contended that Antiquity was passing away; others that it was not; some that Christianity and classical culture were good bedfellows; others, including some Christians, that they were not. The history of the times is the fact rather than the outcome of this deep dispute. (Wallace-Hadrill 1962 at 20)

We now seethe with official subjective spiritualisms standing in the place of Religion; rather, subjective spirituality is now treated like Religion. We are attempting to change the traditional conceptions of Religion, yet we have not begun the hard process of reconfiguring the political superstructure that we built on the basis of the traditional definitions.

The stresses of this dislocation constantly show up in the litter of our Religion Clause cases. The traditionalism of Justice Scalia is a model of political disestablishment coupled with a fear of subjective spiritualisms:

> Values that are protected against government interference through enshrinement in the Bill of Rights are not thereby banished from the political process. . . . But to say that a non-discriminatory religious practice exemption is permitted, or even that it is desirable, is not to say that it is constitutionally required, and that the appropriate occasions for its creation can be discerned by the courts. It may fairly be said that leaving accommodation to the political process will place at a relative disadvantage those religious practices that are not widely engaged in; but that unavoidable consequence of democratic government must be preferred to a system in which each conscience is a law unto itself or in which judges weigh the social importance of all laws against the centrality of

all religious beliefs. (Employment Div., Dept. of Human Resources of Oregon v. Smith, 494 U.S. 872, 890 [1990])

Perversely, this form of political disestablishment would seemingly approve the use of subjective moral/religious "sensibilities" to disenfranchise discrete groups of voters. "Morality" was one of the core bases for the attempted exclusion of gay men and lesbians from the political processes of the state of Colorado (Romer v. Evans, 116 S. Ct. 1620 [1996]; Backer 1997b at 384–85). On the other hand, Justice O'Connor would have us believe that such subjective spiritualisms, in the form of religious practices, are entitled to an "affirmative guarantee of the right to participate in religious activities without impermissible governmental interference, even where a believer's conduct is in tension with a law of general applicability" (City of Boerne v. Flores, 117 S. Ct. 2157, 2177 [1997] [O'Connor, J., dissenting]). Justice O'Connor "would return to a rule that requires government to justify any substantial burden on religiously motivated conduct by a compelling state interest" (*id.*, at 2178) without regard to the origin of such religious expression. But even for Justice O'Connor, such guarantees as these are limited by the constraints imposed through the foundational hegemony of Religion. Justice O'Connor herself (unconsciously) argues this point (against herself) by noting that even the accommodation of Religion could "be overridden only when necessary to secure important governmental purpose" (*id.*, at 2181). This accommodationist guarantee, therefore, might not prevent the government from regulating "licentiousness"; thus the New York Constitution of 1777 stated that it could not be "construed to excuse acts of licentiousness" (*id., see also* at 2180). *Yet here is the great irony*: the notion of licentiousness is itself a concept deeply rooted in the moral paradigms of the old Christian legal discourse hegemony. That term also suggests an exceeding of the limits of law (*id.*, at 2174 & n.1 [Scalia, J., concurring]). Even those inclined to open our discourse to spiritualisms find themselves trapped within the boxes constructed from out of traditional Religious systems.

Disestablishment underlies the Pandora's box that was the now invalidated Religious Freedom Restoration Act (*see supra*, "Religion as an Object of the Structuring Project of Law in the Federal Constitution"). Iranian clerics understood the power of religious structure well, engaging in the project of bending law to the foundational grammar of Religion. There is a thin line between the use of religious sensibilities in forming political decision making and democratic theocracy based on absolutist obedience to the interpretive powers of religious leaders. We ought not to pretend that religious sensibilities of individuals can mask the potentially incompatible systems of Religion for which they are meant to substitute when we think of "religion" informing "politics." Nor can we fail to remember that, until quite recently, Religion, or at least the Christian Protestant Religion, WAS different in this country. It is to an appreciation of the notion of the special place of Religion in our traditional civil society that I turn next.

C. Religion IS Different

Religion IS different. Religion, and the Protestant version of this Religion, has had a critical place in the development of American civil society. To assume otherwise requires us to *forget*. Even assuming that society is inclined to permit the elevation of Religion as the foundation of the grammar of our law (its process), we must be willing to *sanitize* Religion of both its context and its history. That is, we must strip Religion of its foundation and reinvent it as an iteration of our law. To accomplish this task will require that we induce a national cultural amnesia. Yet it seems to me most odd in this day of cultural and historical reawakening that we engage in a project of official "forgetting." Those who bear the effects of history and context find it harder to forget. Those whose Religion is built on such history and context, especially in relation to other Religions, cannot but continue to behave in accordance with those dictates, even under the guise of "individual subjective belief."

We have fought wars over Religion. That is, we have fought wars to determine which system and practice of Religion will serve as the foundational source of social ordering. Indeed, the hegemony Anglo-American notions of "civil society" have enjoyed is both of fairly recent origin and hardly free from challenge. Civil society, even in the advanced British realms, was slow in coming. The example of Scotland is telling, where civil society developed in the eighteenth century only after a long period of civil and religious war (Becker 1997 at 469–71). But the force of Becker's Scottish example is equally relevant in the United States (Noonan 1998). The foundational enterprise of Religion is not abandoned merely because Religion shares political space with law.

Indeed, civil society could emerge in the West only after the 1648 Treaty of Westphalia ended the Thirty Years War. "A second dimension of sovereignty became evident when the Treaty of Westphalia ushered in a new European order based on the understanding that the former world of Latin Christendom—a world once unified, however tenuously or even nominally, under the authority of the papacy—could never be repaired. In this new order, there was no authority to replace the papacy as a potential mediator of secular strife. In theory, each of the emerging nation states was equally sovereign within its own borders and in its relation to other sovereigns. Nations might vary in power, of course, but as legal entities, they claimed an equal sovereign status" (Rakove 1998 at 36–37). Here is marked the point where the *unity* of Religion as a foundational force was formally abandoned, to be replaced by a number of variants on the old Religion now amenable to subordination to the state (Cao 1997 at 246–47; Zacher 1992 at 59). Each of these was thereafter forced to vie with the other for the status of foundational force.

We still engage in warfare over the primacy and effect of particular religions even within ostensibly "civil" societies. Consider in Europe, the religious disharmony underlying the wars between Irish Protestants and Catholics. Or, for that matter, between Catholic Croatia, Muslim Bosnia, and Orthodox Serbia. Indeed, some have argued that current religious violence evidences a decline of the intellectual hegemony of the Enlightenment notion of civil society, spawning attempts to reimpose some version or other of society based on modern renditions of traditional religious norms (Juergensmeyer 1993; Horowitz 1993). This remains a worldwide problem, consuming such far-flung places as Nagorno-Karabakh, Chechnya, the regions of the former Yugoslavia, Northern Ireland, East Timor, and Tibet.

We still worry about the "status" of Religion—whether, indeed, it ought to be treated as a belief system or nation/state. The status of the Vatican is a case in point (Abdullah 1996). The internationalization of Jerusalem provides another (Baron 1998; Ferrari 1996 [Catholic position on the status of Jerusalem]). The conflation of the religion/nation binary has plagued the People of Israel since the time of the Prophets. Christians were once fond of reminding their Jewish elder brothers (when the conversion of the Jews loomed as a larger issue in European Christian consciousness) that the punishment for disobedience, for abandonment of the absolutist belief system Religion, was severe indeed—loss of status as a nation and the passing of the mantle of sole keeper of the Word of God.

> O city that sheddest blood in the midst of thee. . . . thou hast caused thy days to draw near . . . therefore have I made thee a reproach unto the nations and a mocking to all the countries! Those that are near and those that are far from thee, shall mock thee, thou defiled of name and full of tumult. . . . And I will scatter thee among the nations, and disperse thee through the countries; and I will consume thy filthiness out of thee. (Ezekiel 22:3–4, 15)

In these endeavors we are truly the inheritors of Gentile Rome. Consider in this light the contrast between the condition of the Jews and early Christians in Rome:

> The difference between them is simple and obvious, but, according to the sentiments of antiquity, it was of the highest importance. The Jews were a *nation*, the Christians were a *sect*: and if it was natural for every community to respect the sacred institutions of their neighbors, it was incumbent on them to persevere in those of their ancestors. (Gibbon [1737] 1960 at 448)

We have inherited an old tradition indeed.

We have used Religion as an identifier on the basis of which we segregate groups within our nation. Sometimes groups have embraced this choice, segregating themselves into their own communities of faith (Board of Education of Kiryas Joel Village School District v. Grumet, 512 U.S. 687 [1994]). Sometimes segregation is imposed on nonconformists by bending the language of law to the foundational will of Religion (Noonan 1998). Our early history as colonials includes exile for Christian nonconformists. "During the colonial era, Puritan Massachusetts banished Quakers from the state on pain of death" (Underkuffler-Freund 1995 at 883). The founding of Rhode Island colony provides another case in point, as well as a point of origin for what became the American solution to the multiple-sects dilemma—formal disestablishment retaining the foundational position of Religion (Franck 1997 at 597). "But Jews could not vote, even in tolerant Rhode Island, despite the fact that Parliament enacted a statute in 1740 conferring the rights of British citizens on Jews and Quakers living in the American colonies" (Dargo 1996 at 354; Curry 1986 at 19–26). There have been times recently when Religion was used as a marker for social or unofficial segregation. Justice Ruth Bader Ginsberg recounts the difficulty of getting a job as a young lawyer in a New York City in which it was assumed that Jews should work "with their own" (Ayer 1994 at 33).

We have used Religion to establish social and political hierarchy. Official state religions persisted well into the nineteenth century. Vermont disestablished in 1807,

Connecticut in 1818, New Hampshire in 1819. Massachusetts was the last to disestablish in 1833 (Adams and Emmerich 1990 at 20). This use of Religion to impose hierarchy is currently most evident in the case of homosexuals. Homosexuals and Jews have been inextricably bound together by a common core of religious sentiments that have been used to subordinate the one and then the other. Indeed, as Didi Herman has shown us, Religion, or at least the religious sentiments of certain groups of self-professed Christians, has used the old language of separation and hierarchy, developed over the centuries to maintain the reduced status of Jews, in the battle to maintain the social and legal disabilities of gay men and lesbians (Herman 1997).

We have racialized Religion. The Spanish were early practitioners of this art; their subjects were the People of Israel. Consider that the first set of Jim Crow–type laws were developed in Spain in the sixteenth century and were aimed at excluding newly converted Jews from the economic and gene pools of the "old" Christians (Dominguez Ortiz 1992). The Germans were the most ferocious practitioners of this sort of sensibility in the twentieth century (Goldhagen 1996 at 65–69). Jews did not escape as the object of myths of racialized difference within the Anglo American tradition (Feldman 1997; Between Race and Culture 1996).

Each new wave of immigrants has brought to these shores the baggage of their traditional view of and adherence to Religion and the use of Religion to define (and regulate) the world from which they came (*cf.* Pollis 1996 [Greek Orthodox view of church-state relationship]; Amede Obiora 1997 [African female circumcision]). That history—Religious culture—does not disappear merely by the expedient of entry into the United States. Yet a bloodless discussion of individualized religious sensibilities would pretend that such things neither exist nor influence such individual expressions of such "religious sensibilities."

We still compete fiercely for religious loyalty—and are not above using the instrumentalities of the state to advance the interests of Religion. This is a worldwide phenomenon. Consider the recent efforts of the Russian Duma to limit the influx of charismatic Christian sects (Gunn 1998), or the efforts of the Catholic hierarchy in Spanish-speaking America against Protestant and Mormon missionaries (Sigmund 1996 at 178–79), or that of Muslim Indonesia to pacify Catholic East Timor (Kelly 1999 at 267–68). Indeed, sectarian rivalries reflect more than a struggle for the souls of men; as so often manifested over the past several thousand years, such rivalries also seem to reflect a contest for the control of the mechanisms of political power. Our marketplace of ideas is meant to accommodate this foundational proselytizing as well, with the hope that, as Marx suggested in the secular version of this vision, in the end there shall be just one.

Our Constitution was written at a time when the ferocious use of Religion for this or that political aim was fresh in the minds of the American postcolonial populace (Noonan 1987). As a consequence, we formalized our fears about the use of Religion for oppressive purposes by regulating and limiting the use of Religion for making political and economic decisions about people. Thus, for example, we have prohibited the making of (most) economic or political decisions based on the religious beliefs of the object of their decision. Justice Scalia's dissent in Romer v. Evans provides a nice summary of these notions (Romer v. Evans, 116 S. Ct. 1620, 1629 [1996]

[Scalia, J., dissenting]). However, in the style of John Locke, we still permit making private social decisions on the basis of religious beliefs. We also permit individual Religions to discriminate against certain forms of social intercourse (for example, marriage outside the faith and so on) in the enforcement of its own norms, as long as enforcement is limited (Locke [1689] 1937).

And yet, the Founding Fathers meant to be only formally successful. The price (gladly paid) for formal dissociation between Religion and the state was the retention of the value systems of the dominant (Christian) Religion(s) as the basis for the ordering of that very same civil society. Noonan's analysis of James Madison's views of religious liberty is instructive. In Madison we encounter a principal Enlightenment rationalist Founding Father expressing the strong belief in divine conscience under a governing God guiding the lawmaking hand of the state (Noonan 1998). None of this can be easily brushed aside by the simple expedient of converting Religion into the sort of individualized set of spirituality we understand as religion. That we would look to individual expression rather than to the underlying formal web of conformity and obedience that constitutes systems of Religion when we speak about "religion" and its "use" in arriving at political decisions does nothing to change the historical character of Religion.

Consider that, until recently, such notions of "individualized subjective spiritualism" could exist only within the umbrella of Christianity. It existed because the basic acceptable tenets of such spirituality were firmly grounded in Christian cosmology and moral philosophy. There was no major rift between basic religious notions, so understood, and the civil state. "Unsurprisingly, of course, even in the American colonies, inhabited by people of religious persuasions, religious conscience and civil law rarely conflicted. Most seventeenth and eighteenth century Americans belonged to denominations of Protestant Christianity whose religious practices were generally harmonious with colonial law" (City of Boerne v. Flores, 117 S. Ct. 2157, 2182 [1997] [O'Connor, J., dissenting]). We never spoke of it, but why should we have? "Notions fundamental to the dominant world view and operation of a society, precisely because they are taken for granted, often are not expressed in a manner commensurate with their prominence and significance or, when uttered, seen as worthy by others to be noted and recorded" (Goldhagen 1996 at 32). From our perspective, at the end of the twentieth century, we cannot see Religion and civil society intimately intertwining. But we live in an age of competing Religions. In a prior age, the conversation about Religion and civil society was hardly heard. At the level of cultural, normative, and political life, Religion (understood as the Protestant Religion) had completely penetrated law.

Evidence of this union, of this "knowing" in the biblical sense, is available at the margins. Consider the regulation of "sodomy."

> The early cases speak substantially in religious terms. The conduct proscribed represents the type of "moral filthiness and iniquity" which ought to be controlled through the criminal law. This was a crime committed against the very foundation of the Christian, and therefore, social, order, and of so vile a magnitude as to be unidentifiable by Christians—"*Peccatum illud horrible inter christianos non nominandum.*" The crime was considered "one of the most revolting known to the law" [LeFavour v. State, 142

> P.2d 132, 137 (Okla. Crim. App. 1943)]. It was simple as that. . . . In this sense, the scope of the legal proscription reflected the moral condemnation of the community. This was thought a sound basis of criminalization, especially where the moral order was unquestioned. (Backer 1993 at 77)

> Prior to the First World War, then, a consensus appeared to have been reached by American courts. . . . This consensus was based in large part on acceptance of the Christian paradigm of sex and sexual conduct. There were two kinds of sex, only one of which was, within the confines of marriage, licit. All other forms of sexual conduct were illicit—and an unthinkable violation of the absolute commandment of God. The "goodness" or "badness" of particular conduct was judged from the perspective of Christian sexual taboos—the closer the conduct resembled "good" sex the less offensive the conduct. The less the conduct proscribed resembled the only form of licit conduct the more vile the conduct became. (*Id.*, at 79)

> To courts of an earlier age, there was perhaps only a difference of degree between the vileness of fellatio and that of, say, murder. Both amply demonstrated the election of the perpetrator to ignore as a matter of indifference the moral and ethical rules of a society based on the marriage relationship imposed on humankind by God. In a society which unthinkingly accepts these fundamental norms of social ordering, any activity in derogation of the family, especially non-marital sexual activities, is not merely immoral, and sinful, but also threatens the secular order of society, and is therefore a matter of state regulation. This notion has been reflected from the time of American independence. Thus, in the guidebook published for Virginia justices of the peace in 1795, the form to be used for indictments for buggery declared that the acts giving rise to the crime resulted from a lack of fear of God, the order of nature, and the result of the instigation of the devil, which greatly displeased Almighty God, and against the peace and dignity of the state. Good public order, therefore, requires the containment of activity which might pose a threat to the state as well as to the divine order. (*Id.*, at 80–81)

"When a conversation is monolithic or close to monolithic on certain points—and this includes the unstated, underlying cognitive models—then a society's members automatically incorporate its features into the organization of their minds, into the fundamental axioms that they use (consciously or unconsciously) in perceiving, understanding, analyzing, and responding to all social phenomena" (Goldhagen 1996 at 33–34). It was not so long ago, and consistent with the values we imputed to the First Amendment, that states could criminalize blasphemy against the Christian sacred. For example, consider the existing (though legally obsolete) provisions in states like Oklahoma. "Blasphemy consists in wantonly uttering or publishing words, casting contumelious reproach or profane ridicule upon God, Jesus Christ, the Holy Ghost, the Holy Scriptures or the Christian or any other religion" (Okla. Stat. Ann. § 901; § 903 (["Blasphemy is a misdemeanor"]).

We still appear to share the same religiously based revulsion about polygamy (Reynolds v. United States, 98 U.S. 145 [1879]; Davis v. Beason, 133 U.S. 333 [1890]). In Church of Lukumi Babalu Aye v. Hialeah (508 U.S. 520, 569 [1993]), Justice Souter made the suggestion that polygamy could be suppressed as a "substantial threat to public safety, peace and order" under existing Supreme Court doctrine (citing Sherbert v. Verner, 374 U.S. 398, 403 [1963]). However, as traditionalists have pointed out, we have begun (passively and perhaps blindly) to dismantle legal objections to the practice. "If homosexuality may not be discouraged by state constitutions, it is difficult to see how the provisions of various state constitutions banning polygamy can stand. They can't as a logical proposition, but the Court (like modern liberal culture) is not as solicitous of polygamy as it is of homosexuality" (Bork 1996 at 113–14) [commenting on the decision in *Romer*]).

When we speak of the use of "religious" values in civil debate, we forget, at our peril, that to many ears, what is heard is a traditionalist call, not so much to spirituality and morality as to the restoration of Christian moral values hegemony in the civil state. Or, because of the political exigencies of the time, of the return to an orthodox hegemony, in which debate remains in the thrall of the most conservative elements of Christianity (Protestant, Catholic, and Orthodox), Judaism, and Islam. That, certainly, has been the pattern in the Muslim world and appears to be emerging in Russia as well. Indeed, in certain Religious revivalist nations, the law again is bent to the service of the Religious foundation, regulating membership in the community of believers and sanctioning heresy and apostasy (Arzt 1996 [Islam]; Lerner 1998 [Russia]).

The baggage of Religion as the fundamental ordering principle of society is hard to overcome. "For good or ill, Biblical foundationalism has shaped our social ordering in ways in which the merely political or economic cannot fundamentally change" (Backer 1997a at 372). Religion creates community. The *Christian* moral order once created the uncontested basis for lawmaking (and its limits) in this society. Christianity provided what Professor Fish might describe as the foundationalist basis for lawmaking within the American interpretive community (Fish 1980). Consequently, I do not believe one can divorce Religion from the context in which it has existed in the world. Religion is not merely a series of conduct codes and precepts. Religion is not merely a moral philosophy, nor a naked spirituality. It is a worldview, which necessarily incorporates judgments about others, and particularly other religions, as well as a sense of its relationships with those not of that particular religious community.

Understand that the sanitizing that I describe is not limited to Western European religious history and context. Islam provides its own sets of oppressions, no less nasty than anything coming out of Europe. Consider the situation of the Coptic Christians in Egypt (Wakin 1963), who are now subject to charges of well poisoning reminiscent of the Christian practice against the Jews (Rosenthal 1997). "The persecution of the Bahais in Iran is well known; less well known, however, are the widespread instances of mistreatment of non-Muslim Africans in the Sudan and the Ahmadiyas in Pakistan. Non-Muslims cannot play any meaningful political role in a Muslim state that follows traditional Shari'a" (Nanda 1993 at 329). Asia provides its own context with, for example, the recent efforts of the People's Republic of China to suppress Christianity (Turack 1995). One could go on and on. But this suffices to make the point. Even if we are prepared to concede that religion can exist as a collection of subjective spirituality, it is hard to apply Religion as the grammar of law shorn of the history and context of the religious values thus infusing the debate. Yet, to reinvest American religion with its histories is to substitute the law and grammar of religion for the religion and grammar of law.

D. If Religion Assumes the Role of Primary Social Organizer, Do We Abandon Assimilation as a Force in American Life?

Last, if we *must* insist on reincorporating Religion into the grammar of law, if we mean to replace law as the primary basis of social ordering, we must be prepared for the consequences. Religion will objectify law and bend it to religion's grammatical project if it is raised to the status of primary means of social ordering. I will speak here briefly to what I consider the most important negative ramification of such a course. We must be prepared for the possibility that such an enterprise will endanger other great cultural projects of this nation—the project of assimilation.

This project of assimilation is less appreciated today than in earlier times.

> Indeed, in recent years it has been taken for granted that assimilation—as an expectation of how different ethnic and racial groups would respond to their common presence in one society, or as an ideal of how the society should evolve, or as the expected result of a sober social, scientific analysis of the ultimate consequence of the meeting of people and races—is to be rejected. (Glazer 1997 at 96)

The dislike of assimilation is, I would argue, I matter of aesthetics, an affectation that hides the reality behind the dislike. That reality is one in which control of the machinery of assimilation is contested among several groups. The use of the language of dislike shrouds this battle and is meant to prevent any of the contestants from usurping the machinery completely prior to the end of the contest (Backer 1996a at 34–46).

However, the project of assimilation now defines our character as a nation. It is an integral part of the mythology of the rule of law. Assimilation speaks to the grammar of legal foundationalism in the United States. This is not to say that Religion will be the cause of the demise of assimilation. Rather, it forms part of that assault on the assimilative model that had dominated American thinking through the end of the Second World War. Leading that assault, of course, has been what has been described as "multiculturalism." In its guise as political diversity, it has sought quite openly to force the abandonment of all assimilative notions and substitute any one of a number of other bases for union within one nation-state (Glazer 1997 at 1–21, 57–78; Salins 1997 at 95–99; *cf.* Delgado & Stefancic 1991).

Incorporation of Religion into the grammar of law might at first blush be seen as an effort, on the part of traditionalists, to counter this antiassimilationist thrust. It is sometimes marketed under that banner (Bork 1996). However, it is better understood as a traditionalist version of antiassimilation by reinstitutionalizing, as political, those cultural bases of governance and norm setting that predated the loss of hegemony by Protestants in this nation, at least among the political elites. The only way to conceive of the traditionalist project as assimilationist is to admit that the only assimilation required under their foundationalist view is into their view of absolutist truth. Some traditionalists have been more explicit about this ultimately antiassimilationist project (Smolin 1988; Whitehead 1991). Any "theoretical defense of public religion will be of little effect unless religious communities reform their views on faith's contribution to a pluralistic society" (Thiemann 1996 at 160).

Religion, therefore, can be dangerous as a source of the grammar of a law-based system, especially as another moral/ethical component of legal decision making. Again, this is not to imply that other normative structures are any less dangerous. Marxism, for example, may be as dangerous as Religion when it serves as a basis for law's grammar. I do not speak to the value of religious community or to the utility of fostering such communities of believers. However, when applied as the grammar of the law of the *American* community, Religion threatens the great American project of *assimilation.* The danger does not arise because Religion is illogical or "bad" in itself. Instead, the danger lies in the power of Religion to *exclude.* Were this merely a theoretical danger, perhaps it would not be so great. However, Religion, unsanitized of its history and context, provides a powerful site for exclusion, racialization, and antipluralism. Religion comes with too much baggage, it is imperialist and uncompromising, *it is conversation ending.*

The Word of God cannot not be the subject of democratic debate. The Kingdom of God is not a Republic. The Word of God was not memorialized in an eighteenth-century constitution representing a covenant between the governed and their government, subject to the will of the governed. The Word of God is the covenant at Sinai between God and humankind, subject to the will of the former. It is a *community of faith* emanating from outside the body of humankind. "[W]e hold faith to be a knowledge of God's will toward us, perceived from his Word" (Calvin [1559] 1960 at 549). "For, as faith is not content with a doubtful and changeable opinion, so it is not content with an obscure and confused conception; but requires full and fixed certainty, such as men are wont to have from things experienced and proved" (*id.*, at 560). "Here, indeed, is the chief hinge on which faith turns: That we do not regard the promises of mercy that God offers as true only outside ourselves, but not at all in us; rather that we make them ours by inwardly embracing them" (*id.*, at 561).

In a society that makes the basic decision to accept as binding the fundamental norms animating a Religion, such a Religion is unproblematic. In such a society, Religion serves its natural role as supplier of the foundation of politics, society, and culture—as providing the language of discussion and the limits of thought. Disagreement, in such a society occurs at the margin and involves small questions of hermeneutics within a well-defined moral-political world. But the core, absolute (and absolutely true) Word of God, on which the social system is constructed, is beyond question (though not beyond interpretation). Toleration is permitted for social and religious characteristics that are not too dissimilar from the fundamental Religion. "[T]oleration need not be an infinitely elastic principle and tends to cluster around a norm. The norm itself assumes critical importance as the referent for determining whether and to what extent a given form of expression is to be suppressed" (Backer 1993a at 77). That, indeed, might well have characterized the basic agreement of this nation prior to the Second World War (Marty 1986, *but see* Kramnick and Moore 1996).

Sometime thereafter, our elites decided with the acquiescence of some, but by no means all, of the rest of us, that in a pluralist society, these characteristics are potentially dangerous to a free people. Formally divorcing official Religion from law permits the development of a unifying language of law and social discourse shorn of the divisive effects of differences in dogma in an America in which differences in religious dogma and religious dogma's effects on fundamental approaches to lawmaking have been magnified. Yet, in contesting the traditional binding of civil norm to Religious value, we have chosen to *substitute* a different sort of faith for that we seemingly abandon. Thus, for example, in *The Godless Constitution*, not only do the authors attempt to refute the current conservative Christian arguments that the Founding Fathers intended to establish some sort of Christian nation but they make the further argument that a secular nation, free of religious sensibilities was what they intended (Kramnick and Moore 1996). This was a natural progression from Religious foundationalism. The notion of societies based on covenants, in imitation of the covenant between God and humankind, and the existence of hierarchies of such covenants, is deeply embedded in European Christian thought (Elazar 1964 at xxxvi–xl).

Ironically, then, the irresistible force of faith in the foundational imperatives of law sustains the drive to this modern form of assimilation of and conformity by the not yet *saved*. "If you believe you are saved, you can easily come to believe that you can do no wrong. Because you believe in God, you will believe you are God, or at least that you're in tight with Him" (Delgado 1996 at 78). And yet, Professor Delgado would limit the application of its principles to dominant group culture—no others suffer this infection. I am not convinced this is so, especially given the (for example) vibrant separatist traditions of African Americans in this country. The critical change, however, lies in the fact that Religion no longer occupies an exclusive position as the source of social ordering. It now concedes this role to the competing system of law, which now provides the basis of assimilation within the polity.

McGowen v. Maryland (366 U.S. 420 [1961]) provides the classic example of this substitution syndrome. It stands as stark evidence of the foundationalist torch passing from Religion to Law. In *McGowan*, the Court expressed the view that the "Establishment Clause does not ban federal or state regulation of conduct whose reason or effect merely happens to coincide or harmonize with the tenets of some or all religions" (*id.*, at 442; see also Noonan 1988). As long as we are able to supply rationales not explicitly "religious," then even the "religious" can pass muster under our basic law.

This arguably sophistic but critically important transformation is quite explicit in the American approach to "welfare reform."

> Our species of late twentieth century welfare foundationalism is little more than a secularized Christian aesthetics of the care and maintenance of a proper world order. . . . [T]he fundamental substructure animating poor relief has not changed since the Fourth Century. The basic framework of our thinking about poverty is as old as the dominant religion of our Anglo-European culture. It was first shaped by the early Fathers of the Roman Catholic Church and adopted by their Protestant heirs. Its basis is the direct, immutable and unavoidable command of God. Religious teaching mirrors the civil notion of the social maladjustment of the destitute. What emerges is a reminder that God has not lifted the command to be self-sufficient, first delivered at the time of the expulsion from the Garden of Eden. Sloth is still sin; the taking of alms when one can work is theft (from the giver as well as from the deserving who would

> now have to make do without) and therefore a double sin. Children born out of wedlock are *illegitimate*, and that illegitimacy *means something* quite real and concrete. Poverty is a sign of sin, to be remedied by greater devotion to religious teaching and greater application to work. . . . [T]he modern manifestations of these teachings are as religiously neutered as our own public culture, they have found their way into the core of our economic conception of the ideal society, peopled by the self-sufficient. Our notion of a pauper's place in our social order has become enshrined in our social sciences as well. (Backer 1996a at 34–35)

Yet, this substitution has had a significant effect on the way we order our society. Today, we speak the unifying language of fairness in lawmaking in the late twentieth century. This is the age of *due process*. The language of fairness provides the unifying glue to our lawmaking, formerly exercised by Religion, irrespective of the similarity of result to that which might have been determined through the application of traditional religious value. To the extent that explicit resort to religious sensibilities may fit within this structure, there may well be a subordinate place for it within the new assimilative model that we have adopted.

This is a perverse, or rather, a "modern" view of assimilation and its relationship to religion. Until fairly recently, the great imperatives of assimilation and that of the Christian Religion were for all practical purposes little more than two ways of describing the same thing. As John Winthrop explained, in justifying the exclusion of heretics (including Catholics) from the Massachusetts Commonwealth: "The rule of the Apostle (John 2:10) is that such as come and bring not the true doctrine with them should not be received to house, and by the same reason not into the commonweal" (Winthrop [1638] 1943 at 422–26, 423). Understand that I use the phrase "Christian Religion" deliberately and ambiguously. In the West, the Christian religion might at times have been understood to exclude either Catholics or Protestants, depending on the perspective of the speaker. When used in relationship to non-Christian religions, the term might unite Catholic and Protestant (though not necessarily always). Also in the West, Eastern Christians have almost automatically been excluded, either on the grounds of heresy or exoticness, since the eleventh century of our common era. My sense is that it has been used more frequently in its widest meaning as the number of Catholics in the United States has grown in this century.

The decision to treat Religion primarily as an object of law, as law's subordinate, is thus a critical change in our assimilative discipline. Indeed, *e pluribus unum* assumes a role of civil antipode to the assimilative potential of majoritarian Religion. The mix becomes murkier when one throws into this stew the historical reality that until very recently, it was a subconscious commonplace to speak the language of mainline Protestant religious sensibilities in lawmaking, and thus treat Religion, in its formal manifestations, as *object*. But we have crossed the Rubicon—we have distanced our lawmaking from its religiously based normative roots. The reintroduction of those ancient roots suggests an overturning of the postwar liberal consensus of lawmaking. Or it suggests the imposition of some newer version of religious orthodoxy in an age of more militantly clashing orthodoxies.

The fine line between using Religion as a tool for legal discourse and reconverting legal into Religious discourse, advocated by some (Smith 1998a; McConnell 1992), is thus a distinction without a difference. Or rather, it is the means by which Religion will bend law to its purpose again. This line was invisible to our Founding Fathers because they were all parties to the old Religious foundation, the general consensus of Christian values guiding lawmaking in the first two centuries of our independent existence. With the loss of that consensus, the disestablishment of religious discourse even at the level of mundane lawmaking becomes plainly obvious. Its reintroduction becomes painfully more dangerous as well as we struggle for a new basis of consensus on which the peoples of America choose to join (*cf.* Marty 1997; Glazer 1997).

> What remains is a kind of dialogue based on mutual non-recognition. This is a dialogue which breeds subordination as groups apply the normative principles of conformity and assimilation to as large a group of people as possible. Social cohesion, the discipline of the group in the face of mutual incompatibility, requires choice. From the perspective of the dominant group, subordination means reducing contrary cultural norms to a silence in the public (though not the private) space. Polyculturalism can exist in theory—in reality it describes a transitional period between the dominance of one set of socio-cultural norms and another. A set of norms must govern, and yet all norms are subordinating of those who are defined as outsiders—and every group has its outsiders. (Backer 1996b at 439)

What we have left, then, is an assimilation imperative shorn of its roots in Religion, but in which Religion(s), along with a host of other voices, vie for norm-setting *influence*, subject to the constraints of the rule of law yet always attempting to (re)attain dominance. Each community of norm setters, within the context of the current language of *fairness* as a foundational postulate of the rule of law, hears all others as the strident attempts by another group to impose its norms on the others—norms that will subordinate and exclude in ways different from that of the current norms, but exclude and subordinate in any case. For traditionalists, the late twentieth century clearly uncovers the truly tragic—explicitly religious sentiments have been transformed from the ever-present subconscious arbiter of legal normativity to just another voice vying to be heard among the cacophony of systems seeking norm-setting dominance in our nation.

E. Primacy in a Diverse World

For all the whining, for all the theory emerging as a counterpoint to the triumph of law as the ordering basis of American society, Religion is relegated to primary ordering principle only within the area permitted it by law. This has been largely limited to expressions of belief and core religious practice (Church of Lukumi Babalu-Aye, Inc. v. Hialeah, 508 U.S. 520 [1993] (in which facially neutral regulations were voided because they were enacted primarily to suppress religious practice rather than as a general regulation)). However, especially in connection with non-Christian Religions, and even more especially with respect to Religion originating or practiced by non-Europeans, the regime of law provides a grammar for significantly limiting the breadth of this area (Employment Div., Dept. of Human Resources of Oregon v. Smith, 494 U.S. 872 [1990] [regulation of peyote as a drug does not offend the basic principles of American constitutional law even if it interferes with religious practice]). "The dominant recent trend in free-exercise law has been to withdraw special constitutional protection for religious claimants in favor of a view that people with religious reasons to violate laws should be treated like other violators *unless* a legislature grants them an exemption" (Greenawalt 1998 at 1906). In one of the greatest ironies perpetuated in this twentieth century of irony, law has now inherited the place given it in name only at the founding of the Republic. Law now reigns supreme.

I have explored some of the reasons for the supremacy of law at the turn of this century. I have suggested the odd arrangement, arising consciously or unconsciously, with the founding of the Republic and the forging of the American basic law. Yet, the explanations are incomplete and simplistic. They assume a flatness to social relationships absent in the world we occupy. The reality is more complex. I here suggest some of the complexity, and the relationships they imply in the creation of the substructure of American governance as well as the emerging attempts at world governance.

The relationship between law and Religion in the West, especially, cannot be understood as a simple binary. Europe has not seen a unified Religion of any strength since the eleventh century and the Great Schism. Western Europe has seen even greater fracture since Martin Luther posted his protest letter in the early part of the sixteenth century and launched the Protestant Reformation. As a result, we cannot speak of Christianity in the singular at all. It is, instead, a plural set of intimately related, yet diverse and quarrelsome Religions.

In a world in which multiple Religions exist in a geography bound by a unified law, law can exist as the paramount regulator of the sociocultural order. Law, in this context, assumes two roles. The first is as sociocultural substructure. The second is as the regulator of the relations between the Religions themselves. Law is the "neutral" third party that can arbitrate between the competing claims of Religions within a nation or other political or ethnic unit. This was the situation in the United States, with the government given the task of rising above religious difference and given the task of protecting against religious "establishment" (U.S. Constitution, Amend. 1). Where one Religion among many secures a place of preeminence in this situation, it can force a reversal of roles. Religion will then dominate law and use it to suppress Religious difference. The machinations of the Catholic and Protestant elites in the France of the later half of the sixteenth century provide a vivid example; the St. Bartholomew's Day Massacre of Protestants by Catholics in France provides a cautionary tale.

Ironically, as Religion fractured after the fourteenth century, law began to recover from a long period of fracture. The medieval period of European history, and feudalism in particular, saw a social organization in which Religion was strong and essentially monolithic, at least as a matter of sociocultural "common sense," while law was largely splintered, based on layered relationships of loyalty and trust (Bloch 1961) at 123–285). In a world of this sort of fracture, Religion could be dominant as both divine and political basis for social organization. This is a regime in which the state served as the secular arm of divine law. This was an era in which the highest prelate of the Catholic Church could declare that all monarchs received their crown from, and subject to compliance with, the ecclesiastical *dictates* of the church. This was a time in which an emperor of the Holy Roman Empire could be forced to wait on the pleasure of the pontiff at Canossa to seek absolution and retain his authority within the empire (Tellenbach 1940). The irony of course, was not that the investiture contest pitted the state against Religion but, rather, that it pitted emperor against pope for control of the levers of Religion (and therefore of society).

The dynamics of the changing basis of Western sociocultural organization that have molded us for the last thousand or so years leads me to assert several hypotheses about the relationship between law and Religion; the secular and the spiritual; reason and faith; God and humanity. Each simple binary, when painted one atop the other, creates an exquisitely subtle and complex web of interlocking forces.

The interaction of foundationalist communities affect, to a great extent, the manner of social organization *across* communities as well as within them. I offer here a brief and quite preliminary delving into the relationship between foundationalism and the nature of nation-states and communities of nation-states. Consider what follows a brief statement of the postulates describing the ways in which "interpretive" communities determine the basis of their social organization within and among themselves and the basis of the stability of such choices.

Regimes of nation-states and empire. Nation-states become possible in what I will call *merger, rule-of-law,* or *divine-dominance* systems. Each permits the creation of specific boundaries. These boundaries can be geographic or psychic (and in that sense commonly understood as "cultural"). Self-identification comes from the singularity—law or Religion—that forms the basis, the substructure, the foundation, of social organization. Thus arises what we in the West commonly understand as domestic law—law applicable by the community to the *individuals* who claim membership (or on whom membership is imposed), on the basis of shared common understandings based on law, religion, or their merger. These communities can coexist in contiguous space (either physical or psychic) and can seek to expand or look inward. Self-identification also suggests homogeneity on some level—either one law or one Religion or a singular merger of both. Courts have suggested at times that nations cannot exist in the absence of some foundational homogeneity (*cf.* Weiler 1995 at 223–24).

Merger systems are characterized by the regime: One Law, One Religion. Merger systems include Shari'a states as well as Islam in Persia. The Russian Orthodox state was a merger system (one state, one religion, one emperor). The form of the Imperial Russian state was mimicked by the recently defunct Soviet state. Ironically, the Soviet state can also be conceived of as a rule-of-law system in the way the United States was one until the twentieth century. The form of governance was law based, but the understanding was that Religion of a sort (Soviet Marxism) was the true foundation of the social order. Fusion is the primary characteristic of merger systems. Law does not exist independent of Religion; Religion functions as law. Grammar, the norms of communication, serve to buttress norm policing. Language is focused on serving as the very justification of the norms that proceed from Religion. This foundation is simple, easy, and powerful, if only because of the cultural inertia built into such systems. It is difficult to achieve escape in a system in which there are few splits. However, any split tends to bring the system down.

Rule-of-law systems are usually found in communities in which there exist One Law, Many Religions. Rule-of-law systems are characterized by what we in the West have come to call the regulatory state. In this regime, Religions are bent to the will of the state through law. The classic examples remain the Roman Republic and its descendant, the American Republic. Perversely, as a formal matter, rule-of-law states include the old Soviet Union and the Cambodia of Pol Pot as well. The reality of the broadness of systems that can be rule-of-law systems is usually hard for Americans to accept. The difficulty comes, of course, from Americans' strong need to believe that one's foundation cannot be put to uses other than "good" ones. We have been trained to believe in the uniqueness of our version of "rule of law." Ours is the standard by which "good" systems need be judged, and only the law of good systems can be acknowledged supreme over other foundational models. Other systems based on "law" that are not "good" could not be rule-of-law systems. Yet there is no reason rule-of-law systems ought to behave differently in this regard from divine-dominance or merger systems, which can order their respective societies in a number of different ways. Under regimes of rule of law, layered political spaces, including what we have come to understand as federalism, is possible. Federalism merely layers systems of laws implementing the same set of core legal norms derived from the supreme basic law of the land. While sovereignty can be as diffuse as in the European Union or as controlled as in the United States, the basic principles governing lawmaking apply to all.

In communities characterized by many laws, one religion, social foundations are generally Religiously based. These are divine-dominance-system communities. This is pre-Reformation Christendom(s), as well as the classical political Islam of the Ommayid and Abbasid Caliphates. The United States of the Founding Fathers was to a large extent a "many laws, one religion" community; the nature of Protestant Christianity, however, permitted a Religious organization less structured and formally hierarchical than permissible in other forms of Christianity. The feudal relationship provides the divine-dominance system counterpart to the federalism of the rule-of-law systems. Law is bent to the service of the unity whose geography is defined by the community of believers. Ultimate norm-sovereignty is preserved in the Word; its implementation, however, can be left to differ as local conditions might warrant so long as the superior norm objects are satisfied. Religion-based federalism is thus possible; all laws conform to the same set of core religious norms. Communities of faith, which are the essence of divine-dominance systems, draw sharp distinctions between the community of the faithful and others. These distinctions create borders every bit as effective as the geographic borders separating nation-states. The dhimmies of Islam, reserving second-class status to communities of faith other than Islamic, living within Islam provide a case in point (Arzt 1996 at 378–84 [under classical Islam], 410–18 [on the modern treatment of non-Muslims in Muslim countries]).

The development of the classic nation-state, the maintenance of empire, especially empire governing otherwise dissimilar communities, is possible only within foundational systems of merger, rule of law, or divine dominance. Irony rules in any comparison of these systems. For example, there may be little outward difference in system structure between rule-of-law and divine-dominance systems. Their sources are vastly different; the former deriving core norms from the "community itself," and the latter deriving such norms from the Divine Authority. Yet there may be little difference in the way either develops. One of the reasons the transition from Divine Authority to rule of law was possible within the United States was the compatibility of both to the lived existence of the populace. The significant difference, of course, is in the relative status of the foundational elements themselves. In merger systems, on the other hand, law and religion are fused. There is no distinction made between them. Law is Religion or Religion is law, each an inextricable part of the other. This sense is best conveyed by the prophetic writings of the Hebrew Testament.

Regimes of international association. In the absence of the unifying singularity of law or religion, neither the nation-state or empire nor traditional societies can be utilized as the basis for sociopolitical organization. As a result, social organization at this level is absent, and individuals who do not share a community are deemed outside (as we commonly understand, though in an attenuated way today, the ancient notions of infidel or outlaw). This provides the boundary of human organization; this is the biblical Babel (Genesis 11:1–9) from which Religion in the West reminds us that only the Absolute can bring unity through its organizational norms. Alternatively, organizational "Babel" can be overcome (or at least mediated) through grammar that provides a basis for social organization of a tenuous kind. The social organization possible under a rule of grammar arises at the level of community and as a means of mediating between *communities* based on law or religion. Thus arises what we in the West call international law, or the law among nations. As grammar—the singularity, the unifier among communities—becomes practice, and practice becomes coercive, law or religion (whichever provides the source or basis of practice and the rules of coercion) can become foundational.

Where a community is characterized by the regime many laws, many religions, we enter the archetypical Babel. The foundation and hierarchy of neither Religion nor law is possible. Yet order we must have—even anarchy has its foundation, that is, its rules of ordering. Within communities such as these, grammar itself supplies the foundation for ordering within the community. This is a foundation of limited ambition. Grammar's goal is to provide a basis for common communication. Grammar, in this sense, provides a metafoundation in a community in which subordinate groups possess an allegiance to law- or Religion-based foundations of their own but must coexist within a greater community of conflicting foundations.

Grammar systems encompass at their core a rule of mediation between communities of belief. This is the system for ordering communities that have already found a basis for order in law or Religion, yet which must simultaneously find points of commonality with other communities. Law and Religion serve as the tangible means of communication within this limited regime of grammar. Resort to law and Religion is inevitable in a community in which either forms the basis for the understanding of the world. Norms are communicated as rules (law) that are based on imperatives outside the rules themselves (Religion) and can thus be understood within the communities of law and Religion.

Grammar provides the foundation of much of that which is emerging as pluralist discourse. So-called multicultural states are essentially multifoundational communities in which intrafoundational communication becomes paramount for survival of the community. Multicultural unions have existed. Most have failed after a short and tense existence. The kingdom-empire of Austria-Hungary is a case in point. Yugoslavia provides a modern example of a state that worked throughout the twentieth century, only to crack beneath the strain of the absence of a state party autocrat (first in the form of the Yugoslav monarchy and then in the form of the Communist Party) and the allure of the politics of hyperidentity (Anderson 1993 at 399–409). These examples provide unhappy harbingers of the future in many of today's nation-states, for the multicultural states may be the state of things to come, as large groups of people, foundational communities, migrate more and more frequently and in larger numbers from one geographic space to another. Yet multicultural states historically have had a very short shelf life.

Multicultural states can be seen as reflections of the world at large. The earth itself is a polyglot of communities of distinctive foundations. The communities of the earth seethe with conflicting and overlapping realities that can be compromised only by betraying their fundamental distinctiveness. The development of international law has been the response to the consciousness and acknowledgment of multiple foundations. The "new world order" and other such terms have been created to foster communication. The United Nations, regional trade associations, and even highly integrated multinational military alliances are built on foundations of grammar. These organizations attest to both the need for and the weakness of grammar as a foundation of social organization. Without grammar as an organizing principle, there is anarchy, and communities are impelled to a regime of communal conquest or isolation, that is, hegemony or withdrawal. But the strategy of withdrawal from intercommunity intercourse is extremely difficult; the recent histories of both the Chinese and Japanese empires attests to the difficulty. In the case of China, the withdrawn empire was overrun; in the case of Japan, the empire abandoned the policy of withdrawal and embraced the foreign to the extent compatible with its own foundational notions. Yet such organizations are necessarily weak because they must be built across mutually incompatible foundations. Lowest-common denominator communication is the order of the day; compulsion is difficult.

Indeed, international law serves first and foremost as a universal translator. Translation is the first step to communication between foreign (and alien) bodies. Translation itself forms the basis of communication; its rules become the grammar through which communication is possible. We communicate—through ambassadors—and provide for their protection. We communicate on a more sophisticated level by developing an impersonal grammar of conduct—through standards incorporated as international "norms." Communication as metafoundation then serves as a means of regularizing the contests among foundational states (war, peace, trade, and other relationships). From this system of universal grammar can (but need not) emerge a recognition of the commonalities (such as they may be) of worldwide competing foundations. Indeed, the maturation of grammar itself suggests the possibility of harmonization through translation. The communication of certain types of communal conduct (for example, peace rather than war) may become the source of foundational norms for system building. The work of the United Nations, though clothed in the language of law (that is, after all, the "language" most nations "understand," though the understanding may be different for each), expresses the normative possibilities of the communication itself.

Taking Stock

Religion has certainly been deprivileged. Indeed, Religion has been displaced by the language of law. Disestablishment exists now in the very heart of places once almost exclusively reserved to Religion in the construction and maintenance of the social order. But we are stuck on the horns of a dilemma of our own creation. We conceived of the separation of church and state, of the treatment of formal Religion and its values as *res* at a time when religious consensus made these religious sentiments an unconscious and almost inextricable part of the legal dialogue. We have entered an age when this unconscious acceptance of underlying religious Christian norms is contested. Indeed, courts since McGowen v. Maryland have adapted the language of the law to reflect the new primacy of law.

Yet, the old unconscious "deal"—the nominal primacy of law as the basis of our social structuring overlaying the deep fundamental agreement that Religion, fundamentally Christian norms, were to serve as the actual basis for lawmaking—remains powerful in this society. This layered understanding is contested in ways unheard of fifty years ago, and eroded in some areas of lawmaking. It remains to be seen, however, whether dialogue over lawmaking must now make room for what had once been the dominant norm-setting voice. This enterprise, I have suggested, is doomed to failure. Religion cannot serve as yet another and perhaps important voice in lawmaking, even at the level of the mundane. For those who would preserve the place of law as social norm setter, even the suggestion of making space for Religion is threatening. "As long as the "myth of absoluteness' dominates the self understanding of religious communities, they cannot be confident participants in a pluralistic society" (Thiemann 1996 at 161). Religion cannot be an *equal participant* in a society constructed on the foundational basis of law.

REFERENCES

Yasmin Abdullah, Note: *The Holy See at the United Nations Conferences: State or Church?* 96 Colum. L. Rev. 1835 (1996).

Arlan M. Adams & Charles J. Emmerich, A Nation Dedicated to Religious Liberty: The Constitutional Heritage of the Religion Clauses 20 (1990).

Leslye Amede Obiora, *Bridges and Barricades: Rethinking Polemics and Intransigence in the Campaign Against Female Circumcision*, 47 Case W. Res. L. Rev. 275 (1997).

Kenneth Anderson, *Illiberal Toleration: An Essay on the Fall of Yugoslavia and the Rise of Multiculturalism in the United States*, 33 VA. J. INT'L L. 385 (1993).

Donna E. Arzt, *Heroes or Heretics: Religious Dissidents under Islamic Law*, 14 WIS. INT'L L.J. 349 (1996).

ELEANOR H. AYER, RUTH BADER GINSBERG: FIRE AND STEEL ON THE SUPREME COURT (1994).

Larry Catá Backer, *Raping Sodomy and Sodomizing Rape: A Morality Tale about the Transformation of Modern Sodomy Jurisprudence*, 21 AM. J. CRIM. L. 37 (1993).

Larry Catá Backer, *Exposing the Perversions of Toleration: The Decriminalization of Private Sexual Conduct, the Model Penal Code, and the Oxymoron of Liberal Toleration*, 45 FLA. L. REV. 755 (1993a).

Larry Catá Backer, *Essay: Poor Relief, Welfare Paralysis, and Assimilation*, 1996a UTAH L. REV. 1.

Larry Catá Backer, *By Hook or by Crook: Conformity, Assimilation, and Liberal and Conservative Poor Relief Theory*, 7 HASTINGS WOMEN'S L.J. 391 (1996b).

Larry Catá Backer, *The Many Faces of Hegemony: Patriarchy and Welfare as a Women's Issue* (reviewing MIMI ABRAMOVITZ, UNDER ATTACK, FIGHTING BACK: WOMEN AND WELFARE IN THE UNITED STATES (1996)), 72 NW. U. L. REV. 327 (1997a).

Larry Catá Backer, *Reading Entrails: Romer, VMI, and the Art of Divining Equal Protection*, 32 TULSA L.J. 361 (1997b).

Charles Bryan Baron, *The International Legal Status of Jerusalem*, 8 TOURO INT'L L. REV. 1 (1998).

Marvin Becker, *An Essay on the Vicissitudes of Civil Society with Special Reference to Scotland in the Eighteenth Century*, 72 IND. L.J. 463 (1997).

BETWEEN RACE AND CULTURE: REPRESENTATIONS OF "THE JEW" IN ENGLISH AND AMERICAN LITERATURE (Bryan Cheyette, ed., 1996).

Wendell R. Bird, *Freedom from Establishment and Unneutrality in Public School Instruction and Religious School Regulation*, 2 HARV. J. L. & PUB. POL'Y 125 (1979).

MARC BLOCH, 1 FEUDAL SOCIETY: THE GROWTH OF TIES OF DEPENDENCE (L. A. Manyon, trans., 1961).

ROBERT H. BORK, SLOUCHING TOWARDS GOMORRAH: MODERN LIBERALISM AND THE AMERICAN DECLINE (1996).

JOHN CALVIN, CALVIN: INSTITUTES OF THE CHRISTIAN RELIGION, Bk. III, ch. II [1559], *reprinted in* 20 THE LIBRARY OF CHRISTIAN CLASSICS at 542 et seq. (John T. McNeill, ed., Ford Lewis Battles, trans., 1960).

Lan Cao, *Toward a New Sensibility for International Economic Development*, 32 TEX. INT'L L.J. 209 (1997).

Jesse Choper, *Defining "Religion" in the First Amendment*, 1982 U. ILL. L. REV. 579.

Vivian Groswald Curran, *Cultural Immersion, Difference, and Categories in U.S. Comparative Law*, 46 AM. J. COMP. L. 43 (1998).

THOMAS J. CURRY, THE FIRST FREEDOMS: CHURCH AND STATE IN AMERICA TO THE PASSAGE OF THE FIRST AMENDMENT (1986).

George Dargo, *Religious Toleration and Its Limits in Early America*, 16 N. ILL. U. L. REV. 341 (1996).

Richard Delgado, *Rodrigo's Eleventh Chronicle: Empathy and False Empathy*, 84 CALIF. L. REV. 61 (1996).

Richard Delgado & Jean Stefancic, *Norms and Narratives: Can Judges Avoid Serious Moral Error?* 69 TEXAS L. REV. 1929 (1991).

ANTONIO DOMINGUEZ ORTIZ, LOS JUDEOCONVERSOS EN LA ESPANA MODERNA (1992).

RONALD A. DWORKIN, LAW'S EMPIRE (1986).

Daniel A. Elazar, *Althusius' Grand Design for a Federal Commonwealth, in* JOHANNES ALTHUSIUS, POLITICA: POLITICS METHODICALLY SET FORTH AND ILLUSTRATED WITH SACRED AND PROFANE EXAMPLES (Frederick S. Carney, trans. & ed., 1964).

Winnifred Fallers Sullivan, *Judging Religion*, 81 MARQUETTE L. REV. 441 (1998).

STEPHEN FELDMAN, PLEASE DON'T WISH ME A MERRY CHRISTMAS: A CRITICAL HISTORY OF THE SEPARATION OF CHURCH AND STATE (1997).

Silvio Ferrari, *The Religious Significance of Jerusalem in the Middle East Peace Process: Some Legal Implications,* 45 CATH. U. L. REV. 733 (1996).

Stanley Fish, *Is There a Text in This Class? in* IS THERE A TEXT IN THIS CLASS? 303–4 (1980).

Thomas M. Franck, *Is Personal Freedom a Western Value?* 91 AM. J. INT'L L. 593 (1997).

EDWARD GIBBON, 1 THE DECLINE AND FALL OF THE ROMAN EMPIRE 448 ([1737] 1960).

NATHAN GLAZER, WE ARE ALL MULTICULTURALISTS NOW (1997).

DANIEL J. GOLDHAGEN, HITLER'S WILLING EXECUTIONERS: ORDINARY GERMANS AND THE HOLOCAUST (1996).

Raul A. Gonzalez, *Climbing the Ladder of Success—My Spiritual Journey*, 27 TEX. TECH. L. REV. 1139 (1996).

KENT GREENAWALT, RELIGIOUS CONVICTIONS AND POLITICAL CHOICE (1988).

Kent Greenawalt, *Hands Off! Civil Court Involvement in Conflicts over Religious Property*, 98 COLUM. L. REV. 1843 (1998).

T. Jeremy Gunn, *Caesar's Sword: The 1997 Law of the Russian Federation on the Freedom of Conscience and Religious Association,* 12 EMORY INT'L L. REV. 43 (1998).

DIDI HERMAN, THE ANTI-GAY AGENDA: ORTHODOX VISION AND THE CHRISTIAN RIGHT (1997).

Shael Herman, *From Philosophers to Legislators, and Legislators to Gods: The French Civil Code as Secular Scripture,* 1984 U. ILL. L. REV. 597.

David Horowitz, *The Challenge of Ethnic Conflict in Divided Societies*, 4 (4) J. DEMOCRACY 18 (1993).

MARK DEWOLFE HOWE, THE GARDEN AND THE WILDERNESS (1965).

Scott C. Idleman, *The Role of Religious Values in Judicial Decision Making,* 68 IND. L.J. 433 (1993).

MARK JUERGENSMEYER, THE NEW COLD WAR? RELIGIOUS NATIONALISM CONFRONTS THE SECULAR STATE (1993).

Michael J. Kelly, *Political Downsizing: The Re-emergence of Self-Determination, and the Movement toward Smaller, Ethnically Homogenous States,* 47 DRAKE L. REV. 209 (1999).

ISAAC KRAMNICK & LAWRENCE MOORE, THE GODLESS CONSTITUTION (1996).

Linda J. Lacey, *Mimicking the Words, but Missing the Message: The Misuse of Cultural Feminist Themes in Religion and Family Law Jurisprudence,* 35 B.C. L. REV. 1 (1993).

Natan Lerner, *Proselytism, Change of Religion, and International Human Rights,* 12 EMORY INT'L L. REV. 477 (1998).

John Locke, *A Letter Concerning Toleration, in* 35 GREAT BOOKS OF THE WESTERN WORLD 1 ([1689] Charles L. Sherman, ed., 1937).

Niklas Luhmann, *Law as a Social System,* 83 NW. U. L. REV. 136 (1988–89).

MARTIN E. MARTY, PROTESTANTISM IN THE UNITED STATES: RIGHTEOUS EMPIRE (2d ed. 1986).

MARTIN E. MARTY, THE ONE AND THE MANY: AMERICA'S STRUGGLE FOR THE COMMON GOOD (1997).

Michael W. McConnell, *Accommodation in Religion: An Update and a Response to the Critics,* 60 GEO. WASH. L. REV. 685 (1992).

Ved P. Nanda, *Islam and International Human Rights Law: Selected Aspects,* 87 AM. SOC'Y INT'L L. PROC. 321 (1993).

JOHN T. NOONAN, THE LUSTRE OF OUR COUNTRY: THE AMERICAN EXPERIENCE OF RELIGIOUS FREEDOM (1998).

JOHN T. NOONAN, JR., THE BELIEVER AND THE POWERS THAT ARE: CASES, HISTORY, AND OTHER DATA BEARING ON THE RELATION OF RELIGION AND GOVERNMENT (1987).

John T. Noonan, Jr., *The Constitution's Protection of Individual Rights: The Real Role of the Religion Clauses,* 49 U. PITT. L. REV. 717 (1988).

ON CATHOLIC UNIVERSITIES: EX CORDE ECCLESIAE, Apostolic Constitution, August 15, 1990, Washington, D.C., U.S. Catholic Conference.

GEORGE ORWELL, 1984 ([1949] 1992).

Tom Paine, *Rights of Man, in* THE SELECTED WORKS OF TOM PAINE 96 ([1792] 1945).

Tom Paine, *The Age of Reason, in* THE SELECTED WORKS OF TOM PAINE 285 ([1793] 1945).

MICHAEL J. PERRY, LOVE AND POWER: THE ROLE OF RELIGION AND MORALITY IN AMERICAN POLITICS (1991).

Adamantia Pollis, *Cultural Relativism Revisited: Through a State Prism,* 18 HUM. RTS. Q. 316 (1996).

Jack N. Rakove, *Making a Hash of Sovereignty, Part I,* 2 GREEN BAG2D 35 (1998).

A. M. Rosenthal, *On My Mind: The Well Poisoners,* NEW YORK TIMES, April 29, 1997, sec. A, p. 23, col. 5.

PETER D. SALINS, ASSIMILATION, AMERICAN STYLE (1997).

Katharine Seelye, *Lawmaker Proposes New Prayer Amendment,* NEW YORK TIMES, March 25, 1997, sec. A, p. 20, col. 4.

Paul E. Sigmund, *Religious Human Rights in Latin America,* 10 EMORY INT'L L. REV. 173 (1996).

Steven D. Smith, *Free Exercise Doctrine and the Discourse of Disrespect,* 65 U. COLO. L. REV. 519 (1994).

Steven D. Smith, *Is a Coherent Theory of Religious Freedom Possible?* 15 CONST. COMMENTARY 73 (1998a).

Steven D. Smith, *Legal Discourse and* de facto *Disestablishment,* 81 MARQUETTE L. REV. 203, 227 (1998b).

David M. Smolin, *The Judeo-Christian Tradition and Self-Censorship in Legal Discourse,* 13 U. DAYTON L. REV. 345 (1988).

G. TELLENBACH, CHURCH, STATE, AND CHRISTIAN SOCIETY AT THE TIME OF THE INVESTITURE CONTEST (Oxford, 1940)

Gunther Teubner, *Introduction to Autopoietic Law, in* AUTOPOIETIC LAW: A NEW APPROACH TO LAW AND SOCIETY 1, (Gunther Teubner, ed., 1988).

RONALD F. THIEMANN, RELIGION IN PUBLIC LIFE: A DILEMMA FOR DEMOCRACY (1996).

THUCYDIDES, THE PELOPONNESIAN WAR ([411 B.C.], Crowley, trans., 1951).

LAWRENCE TRIBE, AMERICAN CONSTITUTIONAL LAW (2d ed., 1988).

Daniel C. Turack, *The Clinton Administration's Response to China's Human Rights Record: At the Half-way Point,* 3 Tulsa J. Comp. & Int'l L. 1 (1995).

Laura Underkuffler-Freund, *The Separation of the Religious and the Secular: A Foundational Challenge to First Amendment Theory,* 36 WM. & MARY L. REV. 837 (1995).

William J. Wagner & Denise M. Ryan, *Symposium on Religiously Affiliated Law Schools: The Catholic Sponsorship of Legal Education: A Bibliography,* 78 MARQ. L. REV. 507 (1995).

EDWARD WAKIN, A LONELY MINORITY: THE MODERN STORY OF EGYPT'S COPTS (1963).

J. M. WALLACE-HADRILL, THE BARBARIAN WEST, A.D. 400–1000: THE EARLY MIDDLE AGES (rev. ed., 1962).

J. H. H. Weiler, *Does Europe Need a Constitution? Reflections on Demos, Telos, and the German Maastricht Decision*, 1 EUR. L.J. 219 (1995).

Jonathon Weiss, *Privilege, Posture, and Protection: "Religion" in the Law*, 73 YALE L.J. 593 (1964).

Ellis West, *The Case Against a Right to Religion-Based Exemptions*, 4 NOTRE DAME J. L., ETHICS & PUB. POL'Y 591 (1990).

John W. Whitehead, *Civil Disobedience and Operation Rescue: A Historical and Theoretical Analysis*, 48 WASH. & LEE L. REV. 77 (1991).

John Whitehead and John Conlan, *The Establishment of the Religion of Secular Humanism and Its First Amendment Implications*, 10 TEX. TECH. L. REV. 1 (1978).

JOHN WINTHROP, 3 WINTHROP PAPERS 422–26 ([1638] 1943).

G. ERNEST WRIGHT & REGINALD H. FULLER, THE BOOK OF THE ACTS OF GOD: CONTEMPORARY SCHOLARSHIP INTERPRETS THE BIBLE (1960).

MARK W. ZACHER, *The Decaying Pillars of the Westphalian Temple: Implications for International Order and Governance*, in GOVERNANCE WITHOUT GOVERNMENT: ORDER AND CHANGE IN WORLD POLITICS (James N. Rosenau & Ernst-Otto Czempiel, eds., 1992).

Contributors

Robert Audi works in the fields of ethics, theoretical and applied, epistemology, including moral and religious epistemology, and the areas of philosophy of mind and action related to both, especially the theory of rational action. His books include *Practical Reasoning* (Routledge, 1989), *Action, Intention, and Reason* (Cornell University Press, 1993), *The Structure of Justification* (Cambridge University Press, 1993), *Moral Knowledge and Ethical Character* (Oxford University Press, 1997), and (jointly with Nicholas Wolterstorff) *Religion in the Public Square: The Place of Religious Convictions in Political Debate* (Rowman and Littlefield, 1997). He is currently Charles J. Mach Distinguished Professor of Philosophy at the University of Nebraska, Lincoln and (for the winter of 1999) Distinguished Professor of the College of Arts and Sciences at Santa Clara University.

Larry Catá Backer is Professor of Law and Executive Director, Comparative and International Law Center, University of Tulsa College of Law.

Daniel O. Conkle is the Robert H. McKinney Professor of Law and a Nelson Poynter Senior Scholar at Indiana University-Bloomington. He is the author of numerous articles on constitutional law and theory, religious liberty, and the role of religion in American law, politics, and public life.

Anthony E. Cook is a Professor at the Georgetown Law Center. He has appeared on CNN, C-Span, Donahue, NBC, and many other broadcasts as a nationally recognized authority on civil rights and race relations. He has written on diverse topics but has a special interest in African-American studies, law and religion. His first book was published in 1997 by Routledge and is entitled *The Least of These: Race, Law, and Religion in American Culture.* He is currently at work on his second book, entitled *Race Against Time: A Spiritual Approach to Racism in the 21st Century.*

Christopher L. Eisgruber is Professor of Law at the New York University School of Law. He is the author of numerous articles in the fields of constitutional law, religious liberty, and jurisprudence. He is co-convener (along with Lawrence G. Sager) of NYU's Colloquium in Constitutional Theory.

Stephen M. Feldman is Professor of Law and Associate Member of Political Science at the University of Tulsa. He has written *Please Don't Wish Me a Merry Christmas: A Critical History of the Separation of Church and State* (New York University Press, 1997) and *American Legal Thought from Premodernism to Postmodernism: An Intellectual Voyage* (Oxford University Press, 2000), a history of American jurisprudence that was supported by a National Endowment for the Humanities Research Fellowship. Professor Feldman also has authored numerous articles on jurisprudence and constitutional law.

Stanley Fish is Dean of the College of Liberal Arts and Sciences at the University of Illinois at Chicago and is author of two forthcoming books: *The Trouble with Principle* and *How Milton Works.*

John H. Garvey is a Professor at the Notre Dame Law School. He is the author of *What Are Freedoms For?* (Harvard University Press, 1996) and other books about constitutional law, freedom of speech, and religious freedom.

Mark A. Graber is an Associate Professor of Government at the University of Maryland. He is the author of *Rethinking Abortion* (Princeton 1996), *Transforming Free Speech* (California 1991), and numerous articles on constitutional history, politics, and theory.

Abner S. Greene is a Professor at the Fordham University School of Law. He has written articles on religion and the Constitution, free speech, and separation of powers.

Marci A. Hamilton is Professor of Law and Director of the Intellectual Property Law Program at the Benjamin N. Cardozo School of Law, Yeshiva University, where she specializes in constitutional law, the First Amendment, and copyright law. During 1997–1998, she was a visiting scholar at the Princeton Theological Seminary and a fellow at the Center of Theological Inquiry. She was the Distinguished Visiting Professor of Law at Emory University School of Law during the fall of 1999. Professor Hamilton has written and lectured frequently on the topics of constitutional and copyright law. She is currently writing a book about the historical and theological origins of the Copyright Clause and another book on the influence of Calvinism on the choice of a representative form of government.

Scott C. Idleman is an Assistant Professor at the Marquette University Law School. He has written articles on various aspects of law and religion, on federal jurisdiction, and on the judicial process. His current research focuses on the civil adjudication of religious questions.

Linda J. Lacey is a Professor of Law at the University of Tulsa College of Law. She received her bachelor of science degree from the University of Wisconsin, Madison, and her juris doctor from the UCLA College of Law. Her publications include *"O Wind Remind Him That I Have No Child": Infertility and Feminist Jurisprudence*, Michigan Journal of Law & Gender; *As American as Parenthood and Apple Pie: Neutered Mothers, Breadwinning Fathers, and Welfare Rhetoric*, Cornell Law Review; *We Have Nothing to Fear but Gender Stereotypes: Of Katie and Amy and Babe Feminism*, Cornell Law Review; and *Of Bread and Roses and Copyrights*, Duke Law Journal.

William P. Marshall is Visiting Professor, Northwestern University School of Law; Galen J. Roush Professor of Law, Case Western Reserve University; B.A. 1972, University of Pennsylvania; J.D. 1977, University of Chicago Law School.

Martin E. Marty is the Fairfax M. Cone Distinguished Service Professor Emeritus at The University of Chicago, where he directs the Public Religion Project. He has written numerous books on American religious history, including the National Book Award–winning *Righteous Empire* and the three-volume *Modern American Religion*.

Father Richard John Neuhaus is acclaimed as one of the foremost authorities on the role of religion in the contemporary world and is President of the Institute on Religion and Public Life, a nonpartisan interreligious research and education institute in New York City. He is editor in chief of the institute's publication, *First Things: A Monthly Journal of Religion and Public Life.* Among his best-known books are *Freedom for Ministry; The Naked Public Square: Religion and Democracy in America; The Catholic Moment: The Paradox of the Church in the Postmodern World*; and, with Rabbi Leon Klenicki, *Believing Today: Jew and Christian in Conversation*. Appearing in 1992 were *America against Itself* (Notre Dame Press) and *Doing Well and Doing Good: The Moral Challenge of the Free Economy* (Doubleday). In 1995, he edited, with Charles Colson, *Evangelicals and Catholics Together: Toward a Common Mission* (Word). *The End of Democracy?* (Spence) appeared in 1997 and *Appointment in Rome: The Church in America Awakening* (Crossroad) in 1998.

Michael J. Perry holds the University Distinguished Chair in Law at Wake Forest University. From 1982 to 1997, Perry taught at Northwestern University, where he held the Howard J. Trienens Chair in Law. He has lectured at several universities in the United States and around the world, including the University of Tokyo and Trinity College (Dublin). Perry's books include *The Constitution, the Courts, and Human Rights* (Yale, 1982); *Morality, Politics, and Law* (Oxford, 1998); *Love and Power* (Oxford, 1991); *The Constitution in the Courts* (Oxford, 1994); *Religion in Politics* (Oxford, 1997); *The Idea of Human Rights* (Oxford, 1998); and *We the People, the Fourteenth Amendment, and the Supreme Court* (Oxford, 1999).

Frank S. Ravitch is an Assistant Professor of Law at Barry University of Orlando School of Law. He is the author of *School Prayer and Discrimination: The Civil Rights of Religious Minorities and Dissenters* (Northeastern University Press, 1999) and *Employment Discrimination Law* (Prentice Hall, expected 2000). He has written a number of articles dealing with civil rights issues such as affirmative action, workplace harassment, and disability discrimination. His current projects include an examination of the religious right's attempts to claim victim status by using the rhetoric of victimization.

Lawrence G. Sager is the Robert B. McKay Professor of Law at the New York University School of Law. He is the author of numerous articles in the fields of constitutional law, religious liberty, and jurisprudence. He is co-convener (along with Christopher L. Eisgruber) of NYU's Colloquium in Constitutional Theory.

Steven D. Smith is the Robert and Marian Short Professor at Notre Dame Law School. A graduate of Brigham Young University and Yale Law School, he has written extensively in the areas of law and religion, constitutional law, and jurisprudence. Recent works include *The Constitution and the Pride of Reason* (Oxford, 1998) and *Foreordained Failure: The Quest for a Constitutional Principle of Religious Freedom* (Oxford, 1995).

Winnifred Fallers Sullivan is Assistant Professor of Religion at Washington & Lee University and a member of the Illinois bar. Her research focuses on the comparative study of religion and law. She is the author of *Paying the Words Extra: Religious Discourse in the Supreme Court of the United States* (1994).

Ronald F. Thiemann is Dean and John Lord O'Brian Professor of Divinity at Harvard Divinity School. He recently coedited *Why Are We Here? Everyday Questions and the Christian Life* (1998). He is the author of *Religion in Public Life: A Dilemma for Democracy; Constructing a Public Theology: The Church in a Pluralistic Culture*; and *Revelation and Theology: The Gospel as Narrated Promise.*

Mark V. Tushnet is Carmack Waterhouse Professor of Constitutional Law at Georgetown University Law Center. He is the author of several books on constitutional law and theory, most recently *Taking the Constitution Away from the Courts* (Princeton University Press, 1999).

Index